D0715560

MODERN BRITISH HISTORY

Mark Garnett is the co-author of *Whatever Happened to the Tories* (1997), *Keith Joseph: A Life* (2001), and *Splendid! Splendid! The Authorized Biography of Willie Whitelaw* (2002).

Richard Weight is a cultural and social historian, currently teaching at the University of London. A regular broadcaster and Fellow of the Royal Society of Arts, his previous books include *Patriots: National Identity in Britain 1940–2000* (2002).

MODERN BRITISH HISTORY

The Essential A–Z Guide

MARK GARNETT
and
RICHARD WEIGHT

PIMLICO

Published by Pimlico 2004

2 4 6 8 10 9 7 5 3

First published in Great Britain by Jonathan Cape 2003

Pimlico edition 2004

Pimlico
Random House, 20 Vauxhall Bridge Road,
London SW1V 2SA

www.rbooks.co.uk

Addresses for companies within
The Random House Group Limited can be found at:
www.randomhouse.co.uk/offices.htm

Random House UK Limited Reg. No. 954009

A CIP catalogue record for this book is available from the British Library

ISBN 9781844131044

The Random House Group Limited supports The Forest Stewardship Council (FSC), the leading international forest certification organisation. All our titles that are printed on Greenpeace approved FSC certified paper carry the FSC logo. Our paper procurement policy can be found at:
www.rbooks.co.uk/environment

Printed and bound in Great Britain by
CPI Antony Rowe, Chippenham, Wiltshire

For Peter Hennessy

When I was a lad I served a term
As office boy to an Attorney's firm
I cleaned the windows and I swept the floor
And I polished up the handle of the big front door
I polished up the handle so carefully
That now I am the ruler of the Queen's Navy!

W.S. Gilbert, *H.M.S. Pinafore*, 1879

Meet the new boss,
Same as the old boss.

The Who, 'Won't Get Fooled Again', 1971

CONTENTS

∎

Acknowledgements   ix

Introduction   1

Modern British History: The Essential A–Z Guide   6

Supplementary Index   515

∎

ACKNOWLEDGEMENTS

■

The idea for 'a reference book with attitude' was first broached by Will Sulkin and we are extremely grateful for his good-humoured perseverance. Jörg Hensgen has been an exemplary editor: an attentive, supportive presence and a constant source of useful information, practical advice and intellectual stimulation.

Mark Garnett would like to record his thanks to Dili Satha, his family and the many friends who have been essential to him while this book was being written. Richard Weight extends his love and thanks to Angela Weight, Steve Ball, Jim Hicks, Tom Crawford, David Whiteman, Kathy Schïcker, Doug Stewart, Terri Barker, Ed Davie, Nick Black, J-C Nowers, Andrew McIlroy, Dave Martin, Peter Hennessy and any other friends who know what 'Waterloo Sunset' means to him.

We are grateful to those people who have commented on individual entries, in particular to Larry Elliot, Rob Garner, David Gilmour, Nick Lamb and Francis Wheen. We would like to stress that even when our views have been re-shaped by their advice, any remaining errors of fact or interpretation are entirely our own.

ACKNOWLEDGMENTS

INTRODUCTION

■

'History,' wrote the great A.J.P. Taylor in 1965, 'gets thicker as it approaches recent times'. There are several respects in which that is thought to be true, not least the one that Taylor originally had in mind: 'more people, more events, and more books written about them. More evidence is preserved, though by no means all is yet available'. This book aims to make sense of that density for the student and the general reader alike.

Judging from television schedules, history is highly fashionable in Britain today. Along with chefs, gardeners, DIY experts and motoring correspondents, able and eloquent scholars have become members of a burgeoning cult of celebrity. While Taylor had to rely on his mastery of the language to bring the past to life when he first gave televised lectures in the 1950s, his successors hold forth on location, or provide running commentaries as actors re-create memorable scenes. At its best, such work is a judicious blend of information and entertainment and it should be a permanent fixture on television screens.

However, the new television history suffers from a self-imposed limitation. Those who want to learn about the wives of Henry VIII have their cups running over, and there are no uncharted aspects of the Third Reich. But anyone who is interested in social and political developments in Britain since 1900 will be hard pressed to find much in the TV schedules, apart from the occasional documentary claiming to expose the 'secret' lives of significant individuals, or ones that chart the history of interior design in order to provide lovers of 'makeover TV' with more ideas for home furnishings.

As keen students of the recent past we find this regrettable. Britain is changing faster than at any previous time, and the generation that was plunged into world conflict in 1914 seems as alien to us as the court of Henry VIII. Yet the suspicion remains that documentary subjects are being selected because of a presumption that the potential audience will want to use history as a means of escape, rather than learning anything of relevance to their daily lives. But even if we think of history simply as another form of entertainment, there is no reason to think that the last few decades have anything less to offer in this respect than the 1530s.

Perhaps, ironically, commissioning editors take their cue from academic historians, most of whom persist in disdaining anyone who studies events which they have experienced at first hand. The opponents of contemporary history rarely make their objections explicit – they don't have to, so strong is the prejudice within the profession. But their outlook seems to rest on an assumption that when someone writes about a time that they have lived through, they are bound to betray a bias of some kind. Our own view is that human beings are predisposed to take a position on events that interest them, and if the price of 'objectivity' is to write about subjects that bore us, it hardly seems worth the effort. If those who are interested in a subject are certain to let the mask of detachment slip despite every precaution, being biased about the recent past seems as worthwhile as betraying a sneaking admiration for the Cavaliers or the Roundheads while re-rehearsing the issues of the 'English' Civil War.

If pressed, historians would probably accuse people who write about the recent past of indulging in 'journalism'. Given the standards that govern what usually pass as newspapers in the UK, this would seem to be a heavy indictment. Yet our serious journalists are as stylish and enlightening as they have ever been. Far from being irretrievably biased, the best contributors to the Op-Ed pages show that they are aware of alternative arguments. Instead of trying to distance themselves from journalists as much as possible, historians should try to emulate their better qualities.

Our main purpose in writing this book was to provide information and argument for those with an interest in the recent past. We have deliberately expressed our opinions, in the expectation of provoking disagreement but more importantly in the hope that we will generate constructive thinking. We have focused on those individuals, events and trends that seem to us to have played a significant role in making Britain the place it is today. Any book of this kind is bound to be selective – partly because of the restrictions of space and partly because the process of selecting subjects is as subjective as how one writes about them. However, within our selections we have tried to cover all the subjects that are discussed in more orthodox books of this kind. Inevitably, readers will still disagree with some of our inclusions and omissions, but if this leads to a debate about the proper subject matter for historians, so much the better.

The book can be read as a reference work, to be dipped into by those in search of specific subjects. But we prefer to see it as a road map for one continuous journey which is clearly signposted. It lacks an entry for every letter of the alphabet, unlike the familiar 'A–Z' maps of Britain's major cities. But it resembles the A–Z in that it can be used to plot a variety of shorter trips, with the busiest intersections reflecting the richly interwoven nature of social, cultural, political or economic developments. We hope that whatever the purpose and length of your journey, there will be moments when you are intrigued enough to take unplanned detours.

We have tried throughout to give equal scope to information and to argument. In most of the entries, we have used the essay form to present a particular case, while providing the reader with enough data to construct different interpretations. We should add that neither of us is committed to any overarching theory of history, or any 'party line'. We merely think that people who love history of all kinds tend to be committed one way or another, and that the recent past should be presented in a way that encourages such commitment.

Although our own investigations have uncovered no single key to understanding the recent changes in Britain, several themes stand out. No one can overlook the vast improvement in living standards since 1900. Partly this has resulted from deliberate policy decisions by government, and the experience of total war that led to the found-ation and elaboration of the network of institutions known as the 'welfare state'. Technological innovation has been another vital ingre-dient, first developing labour-saving devices and then bringing their costs within reach for the vast majority of the British public. In this case, too, the ingenuity encouraged by war has turned out to be an engine of more positive changes.

A second, and closely related theme is the transformation in the position of most women. Virtually excluded from public life in 1900, a hundred years later they were only a few steps away from equality with men. The availability of consumer goods and services, like washing machines and foreign travel, was a vital supplement to more formal equalities like the right to vote and the legal obligation of employers to pay women the same wages as men of the same seniority. So too was the greater control that women acquired over their bodies as a result of better contraception and of the financial, moral and legal ability to terminate unsatisfactory relationships. These develop-ments, and many others, made the twentieth century an unparalleled period of opportunity for most Britons. By 2000 there were even signs that after several hundred years of racial discrimination black and Asian citizens could look forward to the same opportunities. But this is not to say that we have just emerged from an unqualified 'century of progress'.

Indeed, the twentieth century discredited the very idea of progress, although the potential is still there to turn our opportunities into concrete realities. We are currently wrestling with a 'paradox of progress', in which increasing material prosperity has allowed Britons (like others in the West) to look around them and realise that there are

3

no easy answers to the human condition. Surveys suggest that unhappiness has increased since the 1950s, when the mundane tasks which made a drudgery of so many lives had already been eased by technological innovations. For example, the incidence of clinical depression in young adults born in 1970 was double that of the generation born in 1958 (14 per cent compared to 7 per cent). A separate survey in 2002 found that 4 per cent of British adults had seriously contemplated suicide over the previous 12 months. People were more solitary than ever before; in 1981 nearly two-thirds of households were occupied by married couples; twenty years later this figure had fallen to less than a half. Meanwhile, for all the talk of an open, meritocratic Britain, the proportion of people who thought that a class struggle was taking place rose from 56 per cent in 1956 to 81 per cent in 1995. At one time democratic politics might have provided a useful outlet for these feelings. Yet in 2001 Britain recorded its lowest ever turnout in a fully democratic general election.

The suffragettes who endured imprisonment and force-feeding in the struggle to win the right to vote would have been astonished and dismayed that so many of their fellow Britons refused to cast a ballot less than a century later. The usual explanation was that orthodox politicians had slipped 'out of touch' with the lives of ordinary people. Yet this presupposes a time when politicians were recognisable as normal human beings, and that is pretty doubtful: compared to Gladstone and Disraeli people like Margaret Thatcher and Tony Blair were meritocratic paragons. Even in their amply-reported failings, contemporary politicians are more representative of the average person, at a time of soaring divorce rates and ubiquitous material greed. A more serious problem was that the traditional model of two-party competition no longer fitted with a highly complex society. As a result, people were channelling their energy into new forms of activism, notably pressure groups associated with environmental issues.

Westminster also mattered less than it had done in the first half of the twentieth century. Partly, this was because in foreign affairs Britain became a prisoner of American global domination, and because co-operation with Continental European states became more important, however unpopular each process was with large sections of the British people. Partly, too, Westminster mattered less because Scottish and Welsh dissatisfaction with the constitutional status quo led to devolution which, however flawed, made the 'mother of parliaments' more of a sibling than a parent for the people of Scotland and Wales. However, another reason for the growing political apathy of the British people as a whole was a decline in deference towards authority figures of all kinds. In principle, a decline in deference towards the 'Establishment' is a welcome development. Yet it cannot be fully embraced when it is fostered by institutions and organs of the mass media, many of which have no positive values of their own to offer.

Another word is required in explanation of our title. Our subject is 'Britain', and like most historians writing about this state we have found ourselves making generalisations that apply more to England than to Wales, Scotland and Northern Ireland. In itself, the tendency even of careful scholars to confuse 'England' with 'Britain' is a leading theme of the recent past, and the struggle to define a British identity is partly the product of the failure of schools and universities to pay it sufficient attention. We have tried to point out the contrasting conditions in each country where the differences are particularly striking. But authorial intrusions to remind the reader that the general conclusions are always subject to qualification would be frequent enough to fill up an additional volume.

Calling the book a guide to modern British history might also upset some academic purists. They will probably think that we should have chosen 'contemporary history'. Postmodernists will also take exception to our inclusion of very recent events, on the grounds that the 'modern' world is dead and gone. We have no intention of making a statement with our title, and certainly do not wish to tweak the noses of postmodernists, who have said much that is of value about our present condition. Rather, in plumping for the word 'modern' from the list of available options we are following what we take to be common usage. Our time-line in tracing our themes roughly begins in 1900, but this is not deliberate either. We have tried to compile a volume that will provide an adequate explanation of who we are and how we got here. The legacy of the Victorians is far more potent than most people appreciate, and to some extent we are still standing on their shoulders. Yet it is pretty clear that we no longer exist within the framework of thought which kept them steady, whether we regard that development as the regrettable loss of an essential prop, or a liberation from a stultifying strait-jacket.

A final word is in order from one of our intellectual sponsors, the critic and lexicographer Samuel Johnson. Johnson's unashamedly polemical dictionary, published in 1755, eschewed the pretence both of objectivity and completeness. Writing to a friend in 1784, he said, 'Dictionaries are like watches, the worst is better than none, and the best cannot be expected to go quite true.' We hope that even if readers feel that our book does not 'go quite true', the sound of its ticking will at least echo in the mind.

■ Agriculture

Farming has survived due largely to subsidies from UK governments
▸ and, more recently, from the **European Union**. Indeed, it is one of the
▸ few areas of British life apart from the **National Health Service** where
▸ the **Labour, Conservative** and **Liberal** parties agree that the influence
of market forces should be kept to a minimum in order to ensure that
basic foodstuffs remain cheap. This earned them little gratitude from
farmers, either because they continued to struggle financially or
because they were congenitally suspicious of the state. Farm subsidies
earned governments even less gratitude from the urban electorate,
who regarded the countryside as a picturesque playground and/or as
a larder, in the workings of which they took little interest.

From 1870 to 1940, there was a prolonged agricultural depression
▸ caused by cheap **food** imports, especially from the Americas. There
was a brief boom after the First World War when **aristocratic**
landowners were hit by rising taxation and forced to sell land, while
low interest rates enabled enterprising farmers (many of whom were
former tenants) to buy it, resulting in a rise of owner-occupation from
16 per cent in 1914 to 36 per cent in 1927. In the decade after 1918, a
quarter of English land changed hands. However, the continued
unwillingness of governments to prevent cheap imports through
▸ **tariff reform** kept prices low and forced thousands to sell up. Small
farmers with no capital to fall back on suffered the most. This helped
to ensure that Britain's total land mass remained in the hands of
approximately 5 per cent of the population, a figure that represented
little advance on that of the Victorian era. The agricultural depression
also kept British farms bigger than those on the Continent as they
were amalgamated in order to survive. But as a result, they did become
more efficient and better able to invest in new equipment. For
example, between 1925 and 1939, the number of tractors rose from
5,000 to 55,000. By 1955, the 650,000 farm horses still in use at the
outbreak of the war had virtually all gone.

During the Second World War agriculture, like heavy industry,
underwent a revival: 5.75 million acres were reclaimed as Britain,
starved of imports, struggled to grow enough food to feed itself.
Although farming was a protected occupation, many farmers joined
▸ the **armed forces**. The 87,000 recruits to the Women's Land Army,
most of them from urban areas, made up the shortfall. Of more significance was the elaborate system of state subsidies to farmers that was
established in order to keep food coming. Limited forms of subsidy
had been dispensed before, for example with the setting up of the Milk
Marketing Board in 1933. But, as in other areas of British life, it was
the war that truly rolled forward the frontiers of the state. In 1939, the

UK was still only 33 per cent self-sufficient in food, compared to Germany's 86 per cent. By 1944, the amount of imported food had halved, from 22 million tonnes to 11. By 1983 Britain was virtually self-sufficient in temperate foodstuffs.

In the Agriculture Act of 1947 the Attlee government codified the wartime system. It worked like this: the taxpayer gave farmers a guaranteed income, via the Ministry of Agriculture, to produce food; in return, the farmer promised to sell what he produced at a fixed and reasonable price. In theory, farmers kept their livelihoods and everyone else got 'cheap' food. In essence, it was tariff reform through the back door but with less pain caused all round. When the UK joined the European Community in 1973, the deal which the taxpayer struck with farmers in 1947 turned as sour as a pail of milk left in the sun. The Common Agricultural Policy (CAP), which formed the basis of the Community's budget, was a similar system of subsidies to that in Britain. But because Europe's farms were smaller, more numerous and less efficient than Britain's they required a greater amount of money to keep them going. The annual cost of the CAP to UK consumers was £6.5 billion net of gains to farmers. This was the main reason why membership of the EU cost Britons £10 billion each year, 1.5 per cent of the nation's GDP. Furthermore, the CAP led to overproduction, creating massive food mountains while half the world starved. The solution to this scandal was another one: 'set-aside', in which people were paid *not* to produce food on parts of their land.

Farmers may have benefited but the workers they employed did not. Mechanisation, coupled with a huge rise in the number of chemical fertilisers used on animals and crops, meant that the industry became less labour-intensive. Between 1950 and 2000, 80 per cent of the UK's 550,000 agricultural workers lost their jobs. Almost half of those left in work rented 'tied cottages' from their employers on a semi-feudal basis. Many other country people were priced out of local housing by an influx of urban middle-class families. State investment ◄ in rural infrastructure plus mass car ownership added to the picturesque allure of the countryside by making it easier to commute between country and town.

The British did not become concerned about agriculture until it made some of them terminally ill. During the 1980s, environmentalists made the public more aware that intensive farming methods meant cruelty to animals and carcinogens in the food chain. But it was not until those same methods led to the BSE ('Mad Cow Disease') scandal that the nation really took notice. When it was revealed in 1996 that animals could pass on to humans a disease that was caused by poor agricultural practices, blame stuck to the UK's farmers. They lost public sympathy, and by the time of the foot-and-mouth

A

epidemic in 2001, farmers were seen as one of the last bastions of corporatist Britain: greedy, slipshod workers who had yet to feel the bracing wind of the free market on their ruddy cheeks; and worse still, willing collaborators with a corrupt and dictatorial European Union. Mass demonstrations by farmers organised by the Countryside Alliance in 1998 (180,000 marchers) and 2002 (400,000) did not change that outlook.

■ Americanisation

'Anti-Americanism is a dangerous and quite useless state of mind,' wrote Harold Nicolson in 1953, 'but gradually they are ousting us out of all world authority. I mind this as I feel it is humiliating and insidious . . . they are decent folk in every way but they tread on tradition in a way that hurts.' Hostility towards Americanisation was directly related to the growing political and economic power of the United States and it reached a peak in the 1950s when the US established itself, at Britain's expense, as the superpower of the West. Fear of Americanisation cut across party political divisions and it was voiced at one time or another by people from all social backgrounds. But it

▶ was primarily a concern of the left-wing middle classes.

▶   During the Edwardian era, a number of British aristocrats married American heiresses, providing the women with titles and themselves with money in order to make up for the financial losses incurred by Liberal governments' taxation of their wealth. Despite the resentment this caused among British debutantes, the United States was still widely admired as the vibrant, inventive nation behind the creation of the telegraph and the mass production of cars. In addition, liberals and socialists continued to admire the anti-colonial, democratic and polyglot foundation of the United States. It was not until after the First World War, when America began to have an impact on mass society, that hostility towards it became febrile.

Hollywood and Tin Pan Alley caused the most concern. By the mid-
▶ 1920s, American cinema had established itself as the most popular in Britain. Its more overt sexuality and violence, the less deferential society it illustrated, together with the glamorous off-screen lives of the stars, appealed to a newly enfranchised and more aspirational working class. So too did American popular music like jazz and swing, the former introduced in 1919 during a UK tour by the Original Dixieland Jazz Band. These cultural formations were buttressed by American-style magazines for women that showcased the lifestyles of film and music stars; by pulp fiction (so called because they were printed on rough paper made of cheap wood pulp) for men offering adventure stories that glamorised cowboys and gangsters; and by

comics for children that replaced stuffy imperial gentleman heroes with more exciting 'super' heroes like Superman, created by Jerry Siegel and Joe Schuster in 1938.

Dismayed that the benefits of state education were being squandered on such trivial pursuits, critics argued that people were being seduced by a powerful narcotic that threatened to vulgarise and, ultimately, destroy the British way of life. There was an element of racism to this critique. Hollywood, it was noticed, was run largely by Jews, ◄ while popular music was mostly black in origin, criticisms which later attended the rise of television and rock 'n' roll. In 1934, for example, J.B. Priestley condemned the 'weary negroid ditties' of jazz which, he ◄ lamented, were undermining the popularity of the British music hall. ◄ Racist or not, opponents of Americanisation knew that Britain was especially vulnerable to it because it had no language barrier with ◄ which to defend itself, a fact highlighted by the widespread adoption of American idioms. The most common of all – the substitution of 'OK' for the term 'all right' – was not peculiar to the UK, but for many it symbolised the assent of a generation to foreign takeover.

The arrival of American troops during the Second World War brought Britons into closer contact with Americans than ever before (by June 1944 there were 1.75 million in the UK). The mythical glamour that accrued to ordinary GIs was augmented by their higher pay and better uniforms, and the romances they had with British women caused a resentment among men similar to that felt during the dowry boom at the turn of the century. Yet this ill-feeling soon passed and it did not prevent David O. Selznick's film *Gone With the Wind* (1939) and Glenn Miller's melody 'Chattanooga Choo Choo' (1940) filling cinemas and dance halls (the latter was the first million-selling single in popular music). 'I always talk to myself in an American accent, and often think that way too,' an 18-year-old girl told a survey of British filmgoers in 1945.

Few in Whitehall shared her habits and outlook. Anti-Americanism increased among the governing classes after 1945. Because the UK could not have won the war without help from the US, and because post-war reconstruction depended initially on Marshall Aid, Britain's ◄ leaders saw the necessity of the 'special relationship'. But they did not ◄ want the culture that came with it, a view summed up by Chancellor of the Exchequer Hugh Dalton when he remarked, 'We want bacon but not Bogart from the Americans.' Although cultural protectionism was never as pronounced as it was in France, the British state tried to legislate America away. Quotas for the number of Hollywood films that could be shown in the UK, introduced in 1927, were increased by Dalton in 1947. The Television Act of 1954 placed advertising restrictions on commercial TV companies which were expressly designed to

A

limit American influence. And panic about the corrupting influence of US comics resulted in the 1955 Children and Young Persons (Harmful Publications) Act. None of this contained the popularity of Americana, a fact demonstrated by the hysteria that greeted Bill Haley and the Comets during their tour of Britain in 1957.

▸   By demonstrating that the **British Empire** had been superseded by
▸ an American one, the 1956 **Suez crisis** fuelled right-wing resentment about American power. During the same period, affluence and the
▸ **consumerism** it produced inflamed left-wing hostility to the US. Mass production techniques, introduced to Britain in 1911 when Henry Ford (1863–1947) set up his first UK factory in Manchester, were not only, it seemed, destroying British craftsmanship. More worryingly, they were also producing a new kind of self-interested 'affluent worker' who was
▸ no longer automatically voting **Labour** but for whichever party promised to line his or her pockets. Some American influences were welcomed: the work of 'Beat' writers like Jack Kerouac invigorated the English novel; abstract expressionist painters like Jackson Pollock did the same for art; and jazz belatedly won left-wing approval as an antidote to rock 'n' roll. But these were minority interests.

The more Britons earned, the more they consumed goods and trends of American origin that were seen to be malignant fripperies:
▸ the barbecue, Coca-Cola, **DIY**, denim jeans, supermarkets and **soap operas** were the most famous things imported during the 1950s. But American material culture also brought things of undeniable value, in that they made everyday life easier: the washing machine, hairdryer, zip fastener, tampon, Sellotape, sliced bread, razors, pop-up toaster, Formica, frozen food, teabags, Elastoplast, paper tissues, the Polaroid camera, cooking foil, emulsion paint, the microwave oven and superglue to name but a few. The British list is much shorter, consisting primarily of the rubber glove, roll-on deodorant and the 'catseye' road stud.

Leftist concerns about consumerism were intensified by America's nakedly imperial foreign policy in Korea and then Vietnam. By the time anti-Vietnam demonstrators gathered outside the US embassy in Grosvenor Square on 17 March 1968, the American advance had been slowed down. Not only did Harold Wilson refuse to send British troops to South-East Asia when asked to do so by Lyndon B. Johnson; he also championed a transformation in the lives of the young Britons he had
▸ spared. The revolution in pop music, **fashion**, photography and television led by working- and lower-middle-class cultural entrepreneurs,
▸ epitomised by the **Beatles**, revived native popular culture so successfully that for a time it was even exported back to the US in what was dubbed 'the British invasion'. America's popularity with the British working classes had rested primarily on their admiration for its less

snobbish, class-bound society. As the UK itself became a land of fewer prejudices and greater opportunity, that admiration was tempered. Sport had always divided Britain and the US. When **football** became ◄ the UK's most popular game during the 1960s, Americans' relative lack of interest in it distanced them from the British.

Despite these checks the United States continued to penetrate. Hollywood still dominated British cinema screens, accounting for 70 per cent of the films shown. American popular music (especially black dance genres like Hip Hop) held sway in teenage bedrooms, either in the work of American artists or in that of the British ones who imitated them as supinely as Cliff Richard had once imitated Elvis Presley. US retail practices continued to shape the British high street. In some places they destroyed it altogether. The supermarket concept was extended to shopping malls/centres (the first, Birmingham's 'Bull Ring', opened in 1965) and to pointedly-named 'shopping villages', comprising large, impersonal warehouse stores that could only be reached by car, situated on the outskirts of towns. The volume of ◄ American **food** making its fetid passage through the British digestive system also increased. Wimpy opened the first British hamburger outlet in 1962, followed by Kentucky Fried Chicken in 1965, Pizza Hut in 1973 and McDonald's in 1974. Those who could not get enough of American culture second hand were increasingly able to experience it at first hand thanks to cheaper long-haul flights. By 1981 the US had become the fourth most popular **holiday** destination after Spain, ◄ France and Greece, the majority of visitors choosing Florida, home of Disney World.

Scepticism about the European Union, in both its xenophobic and pragmatic forms, helped to maintain a popular belief that the Atlantic was a narrower stretch of water than the Channel. For the duration of the **Cold War** (1947–89) US governments approved of Western Euro- ◄ pean union as a buffer against Eastern European Communism. The British tended to see the US as a buffer against both. Whether it was using the island as an airbase to attack its enemies or whether it was bypassing the island altogether (as in the invasion of Grenada, a Commonwealth member, in 1983), America's disregard for the UK was somehow seen as proof of its respect for British freedom. At the same time, the evident concern of Continental countries to work in partner-ship with the UK was taken as proof of an authoritarian conspiracy to extinguish a 'British way of life' – one that was becoming more Americanised with every passing generation.

Americanisation may have been as extensive as its detractors claimed. But it was not as malevolent. Much of the American culture that Britons adopted, whether high or lowbrow, made a valuable contribution to their way of life, and in any case a lot of it

A

was naturalised once it crossed the Atlantic, merging with British culture to take on a wholly new form. However, if the two nations had a 'special relationship', ultimately it amounted to this: a shared history and the lack of a language barrier, together with a fear of Continental power, led the British people to exaggerate American regard for the UK and to be complacent about the extent to which they became a cipher and a servant of American global power. By the twenty-first century, for the British to be against Americanisation was to be against a substantial part of themselves.

■ Animals

The British are more sentimental about animals than any other nation except America. It was not always so. Until the nineteenth century they had little conception of them as domestic pets, nor did they believe that farm animals ought to be treated with the same compassion as human beings. Animals primarily existed to serve the practical needs of man: providing food, clothing and other resources like glue, or as aids to hunting and **agriculture**. Any emotional comfort derived from their company was incidental. When animals were sources of entertainment, they were usually unwilling participants in a bloody spectacle of cruelty, such as that enjoyed by devotees of bear-baiting and cock-fighting.

Attitudes were changed by the Industrial Revolution. As nature began to be tamed by mechanisation, the upper and middle classes began to keep cats, dogs, birds and fish for their amusement and comfort. Out of necessity, pets kept by the working classes still had to earn their keep – for example, by catching rats or by earning cash in sporting competitions like greyhound and pigeon racing, both of which became popular in the Edwardian era. The story of Noah's ark was reconfigured from a gathering of creation to aid the survival of man, to a compassionate rescue of animals faced with drowning. The gradual acceptance of Darwin's theory of evolution added to the British fascination for animals, as they came to be seen as central to human history and therefore worthy of greater respect. The Natural History Museum, which opened to the public in 1881, was designed to educate people about their ancestors. So too were zoos. The first public one was founded in London by the Zoological Society in 1828, but they did not proliferate until the second half of the nineteenth century. Municipal zoos were augmented by privately-owned safari parks, the first of which was opened by the Marquess of Bath on his estate in Longleat in 1964.

The growth of pet ownership was reflected in a proliferation of breeding clubs and competitive shows designed to find the most

A

perfect specimen of each animal. The most famous, Cruft's dog show, was founded in 1886 by Charles Cruft (1852–1939), General Manager of the dog-biscuit manufacturers, Spratt's. By the 1930s, a pet food and accessories industry had been established, with pet shops to be found in virtually every town and village. Pet ownership was also responsible for the expansion of the Royal Society for the Prevention of Cruelty to Animals. The RSPCA was originally concerned with working animals. Founded in 1824 by the Revd Arthur Broome to enforce the Cattle Cruelty Act (1822), it pre-dated the police by five years and can, therefore, claim to be Britain's first modern law-enforcement agency. Queen Victoria gave the society patronage, and its royal style, in 1840. By the First World War, it was dealing with more domestic cases than industrial ones. By 2000, its minuscule force of 328 uniformed inspectors and 146 collection officers were annually carrying out over 14,000 inspections and 13,000 rescues, removing over 180,000 animals from abuse and danger, and securing the conviction of 2,473 people.

The Second World War highlighted these changes. Whereas on the Continent domestic animals often starved or augmented rations by ending up on dinner plates, in the UK people fed their rations to their pets at the expense of their own health. When the government complained, the public response was that animals provided vital companionship for people enduring the stresses of war. When London Zoo began the world's first animal adoption scheme in 1942, people of every social class contributed money in return for having their names on the creature's cage.

Pet ownership shot up after the war, from a quarter of the population in 1950 to half by 1970. Dogs continued to be the most popular. The nineteenth-century Scottish legend of Greyfriars Bobby (a little dog who kept a vigil on its master's grave until its own death) was given a new lease of life by the eponymous Walt Disney film of 1961. Cats were the second most popular pet, their character celebrated in a host of books, among them T.S. Eliot's *Old Possum's Book of Practical Cats* (1947). The keeping of caged birds (like zoos and circuses) came to be seen as an incarceration of nature. Bird watching, however, became a national hobby. In 1959, 14,000 people descended on a remote Scottish loch just to see a pair of ospreys nesting. Even rats and other rodents, once the scourge of human habitation, were now welcomed into it, fed, bedded and groomed. Rats were among the pets which appeared on popular TV shows like *Animal Magic* (BBC, 1962–83) and *Animal* ◀ *Hospital* (BBC, 1994–). By 2003 it was estimated that Britons were spending more than £7 billion on their pampered friends.

Three factors were responsible for the growing number of pets. First, **housing** conditions improved and home ownership increased, ◀ providing the space and freedom to keep them (many landlords

A

prohibit pet-keeping in their properties). Second, greater affluence made it easier to feed and care for domestic animals. Third, more people were living on their own than ever before thanks to higher incomes, higher divorce rates and less moral opprobrium towards them doing so. As a result, the need for some form of domestic companionship increased, and with it a greater tendency to see
▶ animals as miniature human beings. **George Orwell**'s satire of Communism, *Animal Farm* (1945), was, among other things, a testament to British anthropomorphism. So too was the nation's response to the Soviet Union's launch of the space rocket Sputnik 2 in 1957. In
▶ America, it caused **Cold War** panic; in Britain, the Canine Defence League held a demonstration outside the Soviet embassy on behalf of Laika, the little dog which the Russians had placed in the capsule for the purpose of scientific experiment.

Ironically, animal experimentation increased in the post-war
▶ period for the same reason that pet ownership did: **consumerism**. A plethora of new chemically-based products, particularly cosmetics, had to be tested to ensure they were safe for humans to use and the tests were often carried out on species that were popular as pets. This led to the creation of militant groups like the Animal Liberation Front, formed in 1970, whose members went to prison for releasing animals and for violently attacking laboratories and the people who staffed them. Public awareness of the suffering caused in order to satisfy human vanity did not lessen consumption. Indeed, the quality of life that people enjoyed as a result of mass affluence made it easy for scientists to argue that rabbits' agony was a price worth paying for medical advances which increased human life expectancy. There was more public support for campaigns against fox-hunts which by the 1970s were being regularly sabotaged. Since a smaller number of animals were killed by what Oscar Wilde called 'the unspeakable in pursuit of the uneatable' than were ever killed in laboratories, it
▶ seems clear that **class** hatred of the landed gentry was the main motive for such protests.

Other religious cultures regard certain animals as sacred. Their devotees are among the people who see the more secular British attitude to animals at best as eccentric and at worst as unhygienic. The British, on the other hand, see it as an example of their superior compassion and sensibility. In 1837, Darwin wrote, 'Animals, whom we have made our slaves, we do not like to consider our equals.' Whether lying on loving laps or grazing in green fields, animals in the UK were still slaves to human need. A lot of hypocrisy also attended the sentimentalising of them. The mortuary is still a place the British would rather visit than an abattoir or animal laboratory. Nevertheless, if pets could think and speak as we do (as many of their owners wish they could) they would probably agree that Britain has become a better place to be born a cat, a dog or a rabbit than most other countries in the world.

■ Apathy

At the beginning of the twenty-first century the prevalence of apathy was almost the only political topic which roused any interest in Britain. Even stories of political 'sleaze', which had helped to produce the apathetic mood in recent years, were no longer certain to sell newspapers.

Things had looked very different after the general election of April 1992, when the turnout was nearly 78 per cent – not far short of the record (84 per cent, in 1950). As a result, in 1992 the victorious **Conservative Party** received the highest-ever number of votes. Yet in 1997 there was a slump in the turnout, which at 71 per cent was the lowest since 1936. Although elections to the European Parliament had never attracted much interest, the 1999 turnout of 24 per cent was the worst figure ever recorded in any nationwide poll. When the 2001 general election brought out less than 60 per cent of the voters – a proportion last seen in the unusual circumstances of 1918 – even senior politicians had to give some consideration to the problem. The **'New' Labour** government tested the appeal of voting via the internet, and it was suggested that general elections should be held on a Sunday, instead of the traditional Thursday.

Falling turn-outs were a general feature of Western states. The US Presidential election of 2000, for example, attracted only half of the potential voters. But its appearance was particularly disturbing in a country still widely acclaimed as 'the Mother of **Parliaments**'. The previous century had seen the last great battle over voting rights – the fight for women's **suffrage** – and after 1969 almost all British citizens over 18 were on the electoral rolls. Just thirty years later there was talk of following the successful Australian example, and making voting compulsory in Britain.

What made people feel disinclined to vote in 2001? **Public opinion polls** suggested that there had been no decline of interest in politics; almost a third of voters said that they were either 'quite' or 'very' interested, which was the same proportion as in 1981. But while people still felt a commitment to political questions, they no longer had much faith in the solutions offered by politicians. This was not just because of the 'sleaze' scandals, which had mainly concerned the sexual antics of some Conservative ministers and obscure backbenchers. It was also because when the minds of politicians reverted back to the problems facing the country, they tended to come up with similar, uninspiring

A

ideas. A survey after the 2001 general election found that 44 per cent of voters thought there was hardly any difference between the policies on offer from the Conservatives and 'New' Labour. It seemed like a ▶ return to the era of **consensus** – the period between the end of the Second World War and the mid-1970s, when the major parties generally agreed on the main policy issues. But during those years the lowest turnout had been 72 per cent (in 1970), suggesting that even if the main parties thought alike in that period the voters had generally agreed with them.

The 2001 election differed from that of 1970 because the opinion polls had been relatively stable throughout the parliament, suggesting that the national result was a foregone conclusion. This was sure to reduce turnout, particularly since the media focused on the overall picture to the virtual exclusion of local contests. But even if the circumstances of the 2001 election were particularly unpromising, there were good reasons for thinking that the trend towards low turnout would persist. Between 1974 and 1996 the proportion of Britons who expected the government to put the national interest ahead of other considerations fell from 39 per cent to just over a fifth. If a third of voters were still interested in politics, the remainder were more hostile than ever before. Another survey, conducted in 2002, found that two-thirds of the electorate thought television gave too much coverage to politics. This attitude was particularly common among young people. Among 18 to 24-year-olds the 2001 turnout was only 39 per cent. It had been 68 per cent as recently as 1992. Many were not just indifferent towards politicians; they regarded the nation's elected leaders as uniformly corrupt and 'out of touch'.

The disaffection of the young is particularly worrying for anyone hoping to reverse the tide of apathy. Those who turned 18 after the 1997 general election, and were first-time abstainers in 2001, were unlikely to develop the voting habit in the future. Since their lack of enthusiasm for politics was matched by their obsession with conspicuous consumption, these people formed the main target audience for the media and the advertising industry. Under pressure to attract the right kind of viewer, even broadcasters with a mission to inform the public were tempted to reflect the prevailing mood in their coverage of politics. But the most likely result of 'dumbing down' would be that even those with an interest in the subject would stop watching.

Some optimists found comfort in an upsurge in pressure-group activity, reflected (for example) in the million-strong London demonstration of February 2003 against war on Iraq. Yet it can hardly be healthy in a representative democracy when people feel it necessary to express discontent between elections, while refusing to participate through the ballot box. In part, though, the new activism reflected a realisation that power had moved away from Westminster. Euro-sceptics bemoaned the loss of British **sovereignty** entailed by membership of the **European Union** (EU). But others were increasingly aware that political institutions of all kinds were losing their relevance in the West, as giant multi-national companies pulled the strings. These organisations could only be made to feel 'accountable' by direct action, by demonstrating in the streets or boycotting goods in the shops. This, rather than voting, seems to be the most appropriate political activity for a **consumerist** society, in which the real choice lies between an apathetic enjoyment of material comfort and a sense of outrage against the system which produces it.

■ Appeasement

On 15 November 1938 the Tory MP Henry 'Chips' Channon recorded his reaction to news of anti-semitic terror in Germany. 'I must say Hitler never helps, and always makes Chamberlain's task more difficult,' he wrote. The comment provides an excellent insight into the mind-set of 'appeasement'. The self-appointed task of Neville Chamberlain, Prime Minister since 1937, was to prevent another general war in Europe by accommodating **German** territorial demands. While there was nothing shameful about the original aim in itself, Chamberlain made appeasement into a synonym for cowardice by misreading Hitler's intentions, and failing to realise his mistake until it was far too late. He (and the French, who fully agreed with his strategy) tacitly accepted that the Versailles Treaty which brought the First World War to an end had been unfair to Germany, and that Hitler's initial demands were reasonable. Once Hitler had detected that his enemies suffered from a guilt complex, he knew that they would try to compromise even when the demands he made became utterly *un*reasonable.

Appeasement pre-dated Chamberlain. **Stanley Baldwin** was Prime Minister when Hitler defied the Versailles Treaty by invading the Rhineland in March 1936. In fact, the British government was already quietly rearming in case no peaceful solution could be found, having abandoned as early as 1932 its ludicrous assumption that there would be no major war for ten years. The Rhineland crisis was the best opportunity for an effective demonstration against Hitler. But Britain would not act without the French, the French would not act without the British, and the chance was missed. The British Foreign Secretary at the time, Anthony Eden, was later awarded an undeserved reputation as an anti-appeaser. In fact, Eden was happy to use the dreaded word to characterise his policy, and his resignation in February 1938 was

A

more the product of personal grievances against Chamberlain than substantive differences.

Although the pitiful pattern of the next few years was already established when he took over from Baldwin, Chamberlain fully deserved his dire post-war reputation. In domestic matters, he had proved an imaginative minister throughout his career. But he had a high opinion of his diplomatic skills – encouraged in this delusion by *The Times* newspaper – and it was under his leadership that appeasers like Channon openly exulted in their spurious self-righteousness. Whatever their original motivations, they ended up praying for the success of appeasement as a means of dishing their internal critics,

▶ notably **Winston Churchill**, rather than a way of stopping Hitler. The peoples absorbed into the Third Reich meant nothing to them; Chamberlain's protest against the idea of shedding British blood on behalf of 'people of whom we know nothing' was a neat summation of their moral outlook.

Chamberlain was temporarily mortified by Hitler's next breach of the peace settlement, the union of Germany and Austria in the month after Eden's departure. But British protests were brushed aside, and when Hitler turned his attention to the Sudetenland area of Czechoslovakia the scene was set for the 'Munich crisis' of September 1938. Chamberlain (who had never experienced aviation before) flew to Germany three times during the Czech crisis, only to be duped by the dictator. After the last trip, to Munich, Chamberlain was acclaimed as a hero by German crowds – an understandable reaction, since he had tried to concede everything to them without the unpleasant necessity of a war. On his return to Hendon aerodrome he spoke of having secured 'peace with honour'. Whether 'honourable' or not, it was merely an appetiser; the rest of Czechoslovakia was gobbled up by Germany in March 1939.

At this point Chamberlain complained to a meeting of Tory backbenchers that he had been 'betrayed by Hitler'. He was loudly cheered, and his announcement on the following day of an Anglo-French guarantee of Poland's territorial integrity was also well received. But even 'Chips' had his doubts about this policy, which might give the Poles the misleading impression that Britain and France actually intended to lift a finger on their behalf. Not only was Poland less accessible to French (or British) armies, but its own forces

▶ were far weaker than those of Czechoslovakia had been. **David Lloyd George** was nearer the mark when he called the guarantee 'demented'. At the end of April Channon grumbled at the failure of the British press to respond warmly to a conciliatory speech by the German leader. But two months later even he finally conceded that 'Hitler is a bandit'.

A

When Germany attacked Poland at the beginning of September 1939 Chamberlain invited the nation to offer its sympathy after the failure of what he described as 'my long struggle for peace'. Even after Hitler ignored his futile guarantee to the doomed Poles, he had been reluctant to issue an ultimatum to Germany. Receiving no reply, he was forced to declare war on 3 September. Towards the end of the twentieth century some historians tried to rehabilitate him, arguing that his tactics provided a breathing space for British rearmament, and that his policy closely reflected the public mood. Some have even suggested that appeasement did not go far enough: Britain should have come to a final agreement with Hitler, allowing him a free hand against the real enemy of civilisation – the Soviet Union.

So far as it affects Chamberlain himself, the issue is very simple: whatever his purpose, his policy failed because he was not equipped to carry it through. The public mood is largely irrelevant. In these matters most people were bound to take their cue from the government, so to a considerable extent opinion merely echoed back the message of appeasement. Finally, leaving aside the moral argument for resisting German aggression, those who imagine that Britain might have preserved its world status, and maybe even its **Empire**, if it ◄ had cut a cynical deal with Hitler, can only do so by ignoring the extent to which appeasement was inspired by steady national decline since the late nineteenth century.

In the short term, memories of appeasement contributed to the **Conservative** election defeat of 1945 (although until the mid-1930s ◄ **Labour** had been even worse, acting like a moralistic pressure group ◄ rather than a serious opposition party). Within the Conservative Party itself resentment against the appeasers slowly died away. Alec Douglas-Home, who had been Chamberlain's PPS, was made Prime Minister in 1963; one of his rivals at that time, 'Rab' Butler, had also supported appeasement, and another, Quintin Hogg, had defeated an 'anti-Munich' candidate in a fiercely contested 1938 by-election. In 1956 Anthony Eden imagined that Egypt's President Nasser was a rein-carnation of his old enemies and launched the notorious **Suez** adven- ◄ ture. Even after this unfortunate experience anyone who opposed war (or hoped for a peaceful solution to the **'Troubles'** in Northern Ireland) ◄ tended to be labelled as an 'appeaser'; and in the last decades of the twentieth century Britain did involve itself in several squabbles between 'people of whom we know nothing', notably in the Balkans which Bismarck had thought unworthy of the sacrifice of a single soldier. In February 2003 the British Foreign Secretary, Jack Straw, played on memories of appeasement when appealing for support in the impending war against Saddam Hussein's Iraq. But it was unlikely that these considerations played much part in determining British

A

policy. As a general rule, now the country merely seconded American decisions; it was no longer important enough to appease on its own initiative.

■ Architecture

In the twentieth century, British architects attempted to become public servants and instead became public enemies. Between the 1940s and the 1980s, they were blamed not only for importing an alien modernist style into the UK but also for dislocating society with ugly, impractical and dangerous buildings which incubated anger, despair and crime. Mistakes were certainly made, for which the working classes mostly paid. But, on the whole, the architectural profession was made a scapegoat for the arrogance of town planners, the greed of property speculators, and the failure of politicians properly to address the social problems which the worst mistakes of modern architecture merely exacerbated.

The story of modern architecture in the UK also illustrates the country's tendency to deny its cultural links with Continental Europe. By the time the French architect Le Corbusier published the modernist bible *Vers une Architecture* (1923), which argued that houses should be 'machines for living in', Britain's built environment already reflected the emergence of a new age of mass production. Although the Ritz Hotel in London's Piccadilly (1903–6) is associated with old-world glamour, it was actually the first large building to be constructed in Britain using concrete and steel. Many others followed in the years leading up to the First World War, among them the Liver Building, Pier Head in Liverpool (1908–11). But whereas in America and Continental Europe such structures often proclaimed their modernity, in Britain they were disguised with traditional materials and historicist styles.

The two most popular were neo-baroque and neoclassical, both products of an Edwardian Francophilia that was given impetus by the Entente Cordiale signed between Britain and France in 1904 in an effort to contain the growing might of Wilhelmine Germany. France was the model used to modernise architectural training in Britain, transforming it from an informal apprenticeship system into one based on organised higher education (the first university professorship in architecture was established in Liverpool in 1894). But in the stone-clad domes and marble and wood interiors of the buildings themselves, a flight from the twentieth century was apparent.

The finest examples of neo-baroque are Lanchester and Rickard's Cardiff City Hall; Brumwell Thomas's Belfast City Hall (both 1897–1906) and E.W. Mountford's Central Criminal Courts, Old Bailey,

London (1900–6). Examples of neoclassicism include the previously-mentioned Ritz, by the Anglo-French partners Mewes and Davis, and their Royal Automobile Club in Pall Mall, London (1908–11). That a building devoted to such a symbol of modernity as the car should be designed in such a way was especially telling. It provoked the critic Clive Bell (1881–1964) to write: 'we shall have no more architecture until architects understand that all these tawdry excrescences have got to be simplified away, till they make up their minds to express themselves in the materials of the age – steel, concrete and glass – and to create in these admirable media vast, simple and significant forms'.

Although the last country house to be built in the UK was Castle Drogo in Devon (1910) by Edwin Lutyens (1869–1944), architecture continued to reflect the rural romanticism that was so prevalent in British culture between the 1890s and 1930s. Its finest expression came in the work of Lutyens, who fused the decorative Arts and Crafts style of William Morris with austere neoclassicism to produce a unique vernacular. Munstead Wood, Surrey (1893–7), which he designed for the landscape gardener Gertrude Jekyll, and Hampstead Garden Suburb, Barnet (1908–10) express the former; while the Cenotaph memorial in Whitehall, London (1919) and the Viceroy's House, New Delhi (1912–31) express the latter. Other architects influenced by the Victorians, like Charles Voysey (1857–1941) and Charles Rennie Mackintosh (1868–1928) combined the lush Gothic revivalism of Augustus Pugin with the even lusher Art Nouveau of the Continent, adding muscularity with a touch of minimalism from the work of America's Frank Lloyd Wright (1867–1959). Although the Gothic revival is commonly associated with the English Anglo-Catholic movement, Scottish Calvinism had given it a welcome too, producing a darker more brooding style north of the border which added to its influence on the Glaswegian-born Mackintosh. His finest work, and one of the great buildings of modern Britain, is the Glasgow School of Art (1896–9; 1907–9). Like Morris and Pugin before him, Mackintosh designed everything from door handles to furniture. The School of Art contains one of his few interiors to have survived intact, but the Mackintosh style reached out to a wide and admiring public through commercial replication and mimicry after his death.

British architecture was therefore a melange of styles long before postmodernism turned eclecticism into an ideology. And it was a melange, moreover, that was admired by the more humane pioneers of Continental modernism. Still, they had a more radical outlook than most of their British counterparts and they brought it with them to the UK in the 1930s. The key figures responsible were all immigrants escaping totalitarian persecution: two Russians – Serge Chermayeff (1900–96) and Bertholdt Lubetkin (1901–90) – and three

Germans – Erich Mendelsohn (1887–1953), Marcel Breuer (1902–81) and the founder of the Bauhaus movement, Walter Gropius (1883–1969). Combining the principles of the Bauhaus, begun in Germany in 1919, with those of Art Deco, started in France in 1925, their work became known as the International Style. Their British disciples, with whom they worked closely, included Maxwell Fry (b. 1899). Their achievements included Chermayeff and Mendelsohn's De La Warr Pavilion, Bexhill-on-Sea, Sussex (1935–6) – an early civic leisure centre commissioned by the local Labour council with the aim of promoting working-class vitality by combining facilities for exercise and entertainment.

Most of the émigrés' designs were built in southern England and in particular around coastal resorts like Bexhill. Although the popular image of the seaside is rooted in Victorian culture, coastal resorts, rather than inner cities, are the birthplace of British modernism. The clean, horizontal lines of their buildings suited the horizontal lines of seascapes and, more importantly, the flat roofs and white concrete were better suited to a region that enjoyed more sunshine and less rain.

Just as Art Nouveau had gained wider attention through its use in
▶ **pub** architecture of the 1890s, so the International Style won public acceptance in the 1930s through Harry Wheedon's (1887–1970) use of
▶ it in the Odeon **cinemas** like that at Colwyn Bay (1935); in the
▶ **suburban** extensions to the London Underground by Charles Holden (1875–1960), like the Arnos Grove station (1932–3); and in the design of light industry factories, notably the Hoover building by Wallis, Gilbert and Partners in the London suburb of Perivale (1932). Purists despised these beautiful buildings because of their commercial purpose and because they retained a strong decorative element (colourful Egyptian motifs were a special favourite). However, the white knuckles that angrily gripped *Vers une Architecture* were not given the opportunity to implement their own vision until Luftwaffe planes appeared overhead in 1940.

The Second World War had a twofold impact on British architecture. First, bombs dropped by the regime which had forced German architects into exile cleared a path for them in the UK by destroying ancient city centres, from which their work had been largely excluded before the war. Second, the consensus for state planning which emerged during the 1940s provided the political will, money and patronage for modernists to shape post-war reconstruction (by the 1960s, 60 per cent of UK architects were engaged on new projects, compared to only 14 per cent in the United States). The destruction of old buildings did not start in this period. The Victorians thought nothing of removing whatever stood in the way of financial gain and self-aggrandisement. The Town and Country Planning Act 1947 was designed to protect citizens from unscrupulous private developers and it began the system of 'listing' by which local authorities are able to enforce the preservation of buildings deemed to be of historical significance. Unfortunately, the Act also gave sweeping development powers to local authorities, and in exercising those powers, many proved to be as contemptuous of public needs as the worst property speculators.

What became known as New Brutalism made its first appearance in the Erith Oil Works (1916), built on the Thames marshes to process the vegetable oil needed to make margarine. The temporary structures erected under the direction of Hugh Casson at the 1951 Festival of Britain and Basil Spence's Coventry Cathedral (1951–62) – poignantly sited next to the bombed ruins of the city's fourteenth-century Gothic cathedral – warned the British of what was to come. So too did Peter and Alison Smithson's Hunstanton Secondary School, Norfolk (1950–3), which echoed the austere functionalism of Mies van der Rohe (1886–1969), the most influential purist after Le Corbusier.

New Brutalism got into its stride in the 1960s and 70s. Thousands of Tudor, Jacobean, Georgian and Victorian buildings which had survived the Blitz were bulldozed to make way for utopian visions. Opposition from groups like **John Betjeman**'s Victorian Society proved ◀ hopeless (in 1963 they failed even to prevent the demolition of a London landmark, the Euston Arch, which made way for a new railway station). Prime examples of what was inflicted on the British people are Ernö Goldfinger's Trellick Tower flats (1968–72) and Richard Seifert's Centrepoint offices (1971), both in London. What must have looked impressive in architectural models turned into a nightmare for families trapped in concrete tower blocks with broken lifts and no external space of their own except, if they were lucky, a balcony from which to view the urban wastelands below. Whereas Gothic spires had reached for the sky to proclaim the glory of God, tower blocks proclaimed the arrogance of man. Some of these machines for living in compounded their aesthetic failure by simply breaking down. The collapse of jerry-built flats at Ronan Point in 1968 forced governments and planners to take notice of what had been done in the name of progress.

However, we should not lose sight of the modern movement's achievements. Denys Lasdun (1914–2001) used the Corbusian style on a human scale in buildings like the National Theatre (1967–76) and the University of East Anglia (1962–8). Universities were prominent patrons of the movement and the History Faculty Library at Cambridge (1964–9) by James Stirling (1926–92) is one other building that justified their belief in it. Modernism made mammon beautiful in many stunning glass towers; Richard Rogers's design for the insurance brokers Lloyds

A

of London (1979–85) and Norman Foster's ITN headquarters (1988–90) were two of the best. Even the state's architectural departments had the odd success. The 600-foot cylindrical Post Office Tower by Eric Bedford of the Ministry of Works (1956–62) became a more popular landmark than the Euston Arch ever had been.

The so-called postmodern movement, which emerged in the 1980s to challenge Brutalism, often descended into an historicist pastiche that had more in common with Walt Disney than Walter Gropius. Nonetheless, postmodernism's more sensitive mixture of traditional and contemporary materials and styles restored the reputation of the architectural profession, thanks partly to the public support which it got from the Prince of Wales during his desperate search for a role in public life. Local authorities no longer waited for tower blocks to collapse, regularly blowing them up in front of grateful crowds and replacing them with low-level, brick-based housing similar to that which they had destroyed only a generation before. Perhaps the postmodern movement's greatest triumph was the MI6 Headquarters (1993–5) by Terry Farrell (b. 1938), which made the secret services seem almost approachable. Such was the change in architects' fortunes that Richard Rogers (b. 1933) and Norman Foster (b. 1935) – defiant modernists responsible for some of the worst as well as some of the best buildings of the post-war era – were knighted and seen as exemplars of British creative talent.

Like most aspects of its culture, Britain's architecture was shaped and usually enriched by the influence of Continental Europe. Modern architects were not as zealous as their critics claim nor as misanthropic as their excesses suggest. For a brief period, due to extraordinary circumstances, they were given an unprecedented degree of influence over the everyday lives of the British people. Some certainly abused that influence. But most used it to improve the nation's built environment and in doing so they helped to prove that the UK was not a backward offshore province of the Continent but an avatar of European modernity.

■ Aristocracy

For casual observers of British society and politics, the failure to dispense with its aristocracy proved that even at the end of the twentieth century it was still stumbling at the threshold of the modern
▶ world. 'New' Labour's attempts to reform the House of Lords were motivated by an impatience with any potential sources of opposition, combined with a desire to camouflage a lack of radicalism in other areas. The reform process drew attention to hundreds of obscure and often elderly peers (759 in all), who by accident of birth were entitled

to interfere in the legislative process. Those members of the House who voted on a regular basis could be portrayed as reactionaries; the 'backwoodsmen', who preferred to lurk on their estates rather than draw their attendance allowance and were only activated by the prospect of voting down some progressive idea, were obviously parasites. The fact that the Commons had been wholly impotent during the Thatcherite heyday of the 1980s, while the Lords at least managed ◄ a whimper of protest from time to time, made no impression on British 'progressives'; and it made no difference that while the award of new hereditary titles had virtually stopped in 1970, the Life Peerages Act (1958) meant that the Lords had become a refuge for the best-respected politicians of the post-war period. The impression that a hereditary title effectively disqualified one from a worthwhile role in public life was reinforced by a new Act of 1963, which allowed heirs to renounce their titles if they wanted to retain some vestige of utility.

Yet if acknowledging the 'modern world' entails an acceptance of the dominance of wealth without too much investigation of its origins, the British aristocracy has always been ahead of the game. Unlike many of its counterparts on the European mainland, its representatives were never too proud to marry into money if the occasion required. By the beginning of the twentieth century rich tradesmen no longer needed to sell their children in order to ennoble their families. Between 1886 and 1914 more than 200 new families were elevated to the peerage, bringing bankers, brewers, shop-owners and newspapermen into the den of reaction at Westminster. Between 1916 ◄ and 1922 David Lloyd George created 90 new hereditary peers – a twentieth-century record – and some of these titles could be bought, starting at around £50,000.

In 1900 the 3rd Marquess of Salisbury was Prime Minister, and more than half of his Cabinet were aristocrats. The lower levels of government were adorned by some prize feudal relics, including the 15th Duke of Norfolk who served as Postmaster-General. But Salisbury himself, for all his lofty disdain of democracy, knew which way the wind was blowing. It became a gale in 1909–11, when the crisis triggered by Lloyd George's 'People's Budget' ended with the power of the Lords constrained, and its occupants saddled with new financial liabilities. Higher death duties (first introduced in 1894), and a new super tax, seemed to their Lordships like a declaration of class war. The impact of these measures was accentuated by the First World War, when the heedless courage of many heirs meant that their families were prematurely lumbered with the death duties. Quite often the grief of bereavement helped their fathers to their graves, doubling the expense at a stroke. Then to mop up any remaining resistance the level of death duties was raised again, to 40 per cent after the war.

A

Landed property was the essence of aristocratic society, but after 1919 a large estate was a financial liability rather than a lucrative status symbol. Fierce resistance against the 'confiscatory' policies of the state were rather ironic, since many aristocratic fortunes had been based on Henry VIII's theft of the monasteries. As it was, the estates were relinquished with a sigh. In the first three years after the war up to 8 million acres were sold, mainly to tenant farmers but also to industrial magnates. Rents from **agricultural** land had already been declining, and between the wars cheap **food** imports reduced them further. Domestic servants, by contrast, were more expensive. Many of the great London houses were closed down and sold or even demolished. Assets in other towns were often handed over to municipal authorities, and turned into museums.

During the Second World War many of the great country houses were requisitioned to accommodate evacuees or troops. In these circumstances Evelyn Waugh's *Brideshead Revisited* (1945), with its picture of decadence born of something like despair, threatened to become the only viable model for young members of aristocratic families. The aristocracy would provide several well-publicised Sebastian Flytes (minus the charm) before the end of the century. But there was another option: to work within the emerging system and hold on to anything that could be saved from the wreckage. The National Trust was soon fully occupied, and the Treasury struck deals which allowed landed proprietors to live in part of their stately homes, while paying customers poked around in the other rooms. If belts needed to be tightened, the family art collection could always be pruned; the paintings were expensive to insure anyway, and often they could be bequeathed to the state in lieu of death duties.

Meanwhile, estates were run more professionally, and aristocrats became entrepreneurs. Even if they had no business acumen, their names looked impressive on company letter-heads. The results of this association were not always satisfactory. For example, the 12th Duke of Manchester (1938–2002) resided in an American prison for more than two years after adding the lustre of his name to fraudulent business practices. Although the family had once owned nearly 50,000 acres, Manchester had inherited little besides his historic title. His previous attempts to revive the family fortunes had included spells as a water-skiing instructor, a trouser salesman and a crocodile wrestler.

At the beginning of the twenty-first century the Duke of Westminster, whose family had clung on to most of its ex-monastic London properties, was still one of the richest men in Britain. The Duke of Devonshire continued to preside over more than 25,000 acres at Chatsworth in Derbyshire; the Duke of Buccleuch had over a quarter of a million, mainly in Scotland. Even when property was of limited

A

agricultural value, it could be let to foolish businessmen who hoped to acquire an aristocratic air by slaughtering grouse. The real victims of the century, though, had not been the largest landowners but the 'lesser' aristocracy and gentry. For many of these, it was tempting to sell up and move abroad. They were the ones who were lured by the prospect of easy profits, and many families which had survived the depredations of Lloyd George now succumbed with Lloyds of London.

Thus like the **monarchy** the British aristocracy survived into the ◄ new millennium by transforming itself. But whether the change has brought tangible benefit for society as a whole is open to question. Aristocracy stood out like a swollen thumb amid the prevailing antipathy towards 'undeserved' status. But there was still a conspicuous mismatch between the distribution of wealth and 'merit' (as people generally understood the latter term). Most people resented the inflated rewards of businessmen (and, increasingly, those of the best-paid entertainers); yet such luminaries could not be attacked within the prevailing ideology of the free market, which asserted that everyone had their price and some were just more valuable than others.

The fact that aristocratic children were allegedly guaranteed a life of riches by the mere chance of being born in the right bed might be abhorrent; but it was difficult to say that it was any worse than the golden opportunities awaiting the offspring of, say, a mediocre singer or a flashy **footballer**. The difference, if any, was that once the aristo- ◄ crats began to feel vulnerable to 'meritocratic' arguments the best of them decided that they should compensate for their good luck by devoting much of their time to public service, thus turning their advantages to constructive use. Ironically, this ethos found perhaps its greatest exemplar in **Winston Churchill**, who for five years was heir to ◄ the Duchy of Marlborough but held high office during most of the years in which his own order was undone.

■ Armed forces

At the end of the twentieth century Britain's armed forces were widely admired, with approval ratings over 80 per cent. Numbers had declined – in total the army, navy and air force employed 215,000 people in 1997, down from 503,000 in 1960 (when **conscription** was ◄ still in force). But personnel were regularly praised for their motivation and efficiency, which ensured that despite a century of relative decline Britain could at least 'punch above its weight' in world affairs. Although most people accepted that British security ultimately lay in its membership of NATO (from its formation in 1949), victory in the **Falklands War** was taken as proof of adaptability and courage which ◄

A

were equal to any challenge short of an encounter with the Soviet Union, China or (in some implausible scenario) the USA. Particular units, such as the Special Air Service (SAS), had achieved legendary status; several former officers turned their experiences into best-
► selling books, and at the 1995 **Conservative Party** conference the Defence Secretary, Michael Portillo, tried to enthuse the octogenarians in his audience by comparing them to that rugged fighting force.

But the days before 1914, when the public demanded increased naval expenditure, were long gone. Two years after Portillo's speech the Conservatives left office with spending on defence just over £22 billion – slightly below the level in 1990, allowing for inflation. The fall was more significant if one considers the cost of keeping equip-ment up to date at a time of rapid technological change. Although it had been regarded as a vote-winning issue for the Conservatives in the
► 1980s, this was mainly because of **Labour's** opposition to nuclear weapons. In reality, rather than rhetoric, defence cuts had been a significant contributory factor to the war with Argentina (which had been encouraged to invade the Falklands by a British plan to withdraw the single protection vessel from the South Atlantic) and the Ministry of Defence was planning further economies throughout the Thatcher period. The 'Options for Change' study, commissioned in 1990, envis-aged sweeping cuts across the board, taking advantage of the end of
► the **Cold War** to reduce Britain's commitments, particularly to the newly-reunited Germany.

More than ever, Britain depended on its nuclear arsenal. This had been authorised by the Attlee government (with minimal consulta-tion) back in 1946. While nuclear technology was soon mastered, Britain's difficulty lay with delivery systems. The Polaris missile, to be launched from submarines, had to be acquired from the US. In 1980 the Thatcher government decided on the Trident missile as a long-term replacement for Polaris. The cost was to be more than £7 billion, spread over fifteen years. While the government argued that its nuclear deterrent was a guarantee of security against the Soviet threat, others thought that Britain's possession of these weapons was itself the most likely reason for an attack, and when American cruise missiles arrived at British bases at the end of 1983 there was an
► upsurge in support for the **Campaign for Nuclear Disarmament** (CND).

The presence of British troops in Northern Ireland after 1969 was another source of contention. While some imagined that the mission
► reflected a hankering after the days of **Empire** – or even a desire to train up a force which would suppress a revolution on the mainland – others took the view that the cause was not worth the sacrifice of a single British soldier. At its peak in 1972 the contingent included more

than 16,000 troops (more than a hundred were killed – the worst year of the 'Troubles'). The 1998 Good Friday Agreement offered the possibility that the troops could be withdrawn completely before very long, giving Britain a 'peace dividend' in the form of further defence cuts.

In the last years of the twentieth century Britain played a part in operations which would once have carried a serious risk of over-stretching, but which now, thanks to technological change, could be treated as short-term trouble-shooting actions. The Gulf War of 1990–1 represented the most significant commitment, but losses were slight and, thanks to contributions from allies in the area, Britain spent virtually nothing. In 1993 and 1999 British troops were deployed in the former Yugoslavia. Again, losses were minimal. Even the new conflict with Iraq in 2003 could be combined with international peacekeeping missions and commitments at home.

These operations proved the value of well-equipped, mobile and highly skilled forces. But they also carried an obvious risk. While **appeasement** had been influenced by the notion that war of all kinds might destroy British civilisation, it was now possible to conceive of 'policing' missions from which all the boys (and girls) really would return before Christmas. Yet Britain increasingly followed America's lead, and after the Cold War it was no longer so easy to claim that the two powers shared common interests. There was every chance that one day Britain would be asked to help out in a far more ambitious (and, from the British viewpoint, highly dubious) undertaking. In this context, it was not surprising that at the end of the century the US seemed to be cooling towards the idea of European defence co-operation – even before the 2003 war against Saddam Hussein exposed the underlying transatlantic divisions. At least in Britain arguments about the creation of a 'Reaction Force' with its Continental neighbours no longer revolved around the much-contested notion of '**sovereignty**' – or if they did, the opponents of European co-operation would have to admit that their concern was not for sovereignty, but for the contamination that would arise if British troops were ever placed under the regular command of European officers, rather than their American 'cousins'.

In the winter of 2002/3 the armed forces proved their value once again, coping admirably with outdated equipment and unfamiliar duties during a firefighters' strike. Yet no one in Britain could be entirely immune from scandal, and conditions at an army camp were under investigation after a series of suspicious deaths and allegations of bullying. Recruitment was proving difficult, and new recruits were leaving in significant numbers. Demands were growing to increase the ethnic minority contingent from a paltry 1.5 per cent. It was understandable that service chiefs should fret at these trends, but politicians could afford to be more relaxed. High-tech weapons and public squeamishness at the thought of high casualty figures already ► made the full-scale encounters of two world wars seem anachronistic. With the emergence of a worldwide terrorist threat, the most appropriate role for an army seemed to be 'homeland defence', while the enemy was sought by small groups of specialised troops. It looked as if international emergencies of the future would be tackled by budding James Bonds, leaving the mundane tasks to people who would need little more training than Dad's Army. Idealists of the past had dreamed of a world without war; now optimistic politicians could fantasise about wars without armies.

■ Art

Until the 1960s it was received opinion that the British had produced fewer artists of international calibre than France, Italy or the United States. Two explanations have been advanced for why this was thought to be so. First, a lingering Protestant belief that images are less important than the Word; and second, a conservatism born of the country's failure to undergo a secular revolution. In the 1955 Reith Lectures, published as *The Englishness of English Art*, the German-born critic Nikolaus Pevsner declared that the nation's dislike of revolution 'is a forte in political development but a weakness in art . . . what English character gained of tolerance and fair play, she lost of that fanaticism or at least that intensity which alone can bring forth great art'.

Edwardian artists left behind the moral didacticism and sentimentality of the Victorians while remaining figurative enough for that departure to be aesthetically accepted. The fluid brushwork of Velásquez, evident in the painting of the American-born James MacNeill Whistler (1834–1903), continued in the work of the Glasgow School, led by John Lavery (1856–1941), and in that of the Englishmen William Nicolson (1872–1949) and Augustus John (1878–1961). But it was another American émigré, John Singer Sargent (1856–1925), who dominated British art in the run-up to the First World War. His suave yet sensitive portraits of the Edwardian aristocracy captured both its opulence and its fragility, much as Van Dyck had captured those elements in his studies of the doomed court of Charles I during the 1630s. As well as to Velásquez, Sargent's style owed much to his knowledge of French Impressionist painting acquired during his years in Paris in the 1880s.

Despite the Impressionists' evident debt to the English landscape artist J.M.W. Turner, their work was rejected by the educated public when it was brought to their attention in 1905 at an exhibition staged in London by the dealer Durand-Ruel. But it did not deter the Impressionists' many British followers, led by Walter Sickert (1860–1942).

'Taste is the death of a painter,' Sickert declared. 'The plastic arts are gross arts, dealing joyously with gross material facts . . . and while they will flourish in the scullery, or on the dunghill, they fade at a breath from the drawing room.' To that end, he returned from France in 1905 and settled in Camden, north London, where he painted its dingy world of bedsits, inhabited by railway workers, prostitutes and enter-tainers. Sickert's studies of **music halls**, notably *Noctes Ambrosianae* ◄ (1906), are typical of the Camden Town Group which he set up in 1911 with eight like-minded artists. The group included two women later expelled because they were thought to be a distraction.

However, by the time the Group was active, another revolution had taken place. The Post-Impressionist exhibition staged in 1910 by the critic Roger Fry (1866–1934) at the Grafton Galleries in London is the event from which modern art in Britain is commonly dated. It intro-duced Britons to the works of Van Gogh and Cezanne, while the Second Post-Impressionist exhibition of 1912 introduced them to the more radical Picasso and Matisse. As elsewhere in Europe, the disinte-gration of traditional form was directly linked in the public mind to the horrors of the First World War and the social unrest it helped to provoke. The revolt against naturalist art was led by Wyndham Lewis (1882–1957) who founded the Rebel Art Centre (1914) and attacked the smug complacency of British culture in the pages of *Blast*, a short-lived journal that he edited. Out of this came Britain's first truly avant-garde movement, Vorticism. Other members of the movement included David Bomberg (1890–1957), a scion of **Jewish** immigrants to ◄ London, C.R.W. Nevinson (1889–1946) and the American-born sculptor Jacob Epstein (1880–1959). On 2 July 1914, Lewis issued 'The Vorticist Manifesto'. Just as British architects were being urged by Clive Bell to embrace the machine age with concrete and steel, so Lewis urged artists to embrace it with the jagged, anarchic shapes of Cubism. Lewis was supported by modernists in other fields, notably the poet Ezra Pound and the philosopher T.E. Hulme.

For all their love of the machine age, they shared a detestation of the working people who made it tick: the conservative-minded managers, clerks and factory hands who still liked a picture to be easily discernible and, if possible, to tell a story. An exhibition of Sur-realist art in 1936 also had little immediate impact on taste, despite the presence of Salvador Dalí and the support of the anarchist critic Herbert Read (1893–1968) who wrote, 'It is defiant – the desperate act of men too profoundly convinced of the rottenness of our civilisation to want to save a shred of its respectability.' The Surrealists' celebra-tion of the subconscious did not appeal to a nation that was suspicious of and embarrassed by the **Freudian** obsession with sex and the ◄ confessional demands that psychotherapy made on the individual.

Moreover, followers of the Post-Impressionists within the artistic world were not convinced of the rottenness of their civilisation. The figurative and decorative work of the Bloomsbury Group, primarily that of Duncan Grant (1885–1978) and Vanessa Bell (1879–1961), rejected the full force of Continental modernism and won public approval for doing so. So, to a lesser extent, did the neo-Romantic movement that dominated the 1940s. Its main exponents were John Minton (1917–57), Graham Sutherland (1903–80) and John Piper (1903–92). In 1944 Piper wrote, 'as a race we have always been conscious of the changeable climate of our sea-washed country . . . The atmosphere has sunk into our souls. It has affected our art as it has affected our life.'

▶ A close friend of **John Betjeman**, Piper was one of several neo-
▶ Romantic artists who turned from agnosticism to the **Church of England**. His dark, brooding pictures of English churches captured the decay of Christian faith in Britain that he was powerless to halt. But the artist most influenced by Anglicanism, Stanley Spencer (1891–1959), belonged to no coterie or movement. An eccentric figure, he spent most of his life in Cookham, the Berkshire village where he was born. Spencer's best paintings, like *The Resurrection* (1922–7), figuratively depicted the Second Coming taking place in Cookham and springing the latent, sensual communality of its people into life. This was a form of surrealism to which the British responded. The modernist sculptor Henry Moore (1898–1986) was virtually the only British artist with an international reputation in the early post-war period, but his work never attracted the adoration of ordinary people in that way that Spencer's still does. However, neither could compete with the popularity of L. S. Lowry (1887–1976), whose simple paintings of industrial Lancashire and its people demand little from the viewer.

State patronage of the arts took longer to develop than on the Continent because Britain's rulers were more sceptical about state interference in civil life. The Tate Gallery, Britain's first museum of modern art, was founded in 1897 by the sugar magnate Henry Tate after parliament had refused to give money to house the collection of British art he gave the nation. Most provincial galleries and museums were established between the 1880s and 1920s, through acts of civic philanthropy. World war galvanised the British to act. A War Artists
▶ scheme was set up in 1916 by **Lord Beaverbrook**, commissioning artists to depict the home front and the battlefield. The scheme was revived with greater purpose in 1939 under the direction of Sir Kenneth Clark (1903–83) who used it to patronise the work of neo-Romantics at the expense of modernists, although Henry Moore's
▶ sketches of civilians sheltering from the **Blitz** in London Underground stations are the most famous of Clark's commissions. Clark

also helped to found the Arts Council of Great Britain (1946), a semi-independent, Treasury-funded body. With his co-founders, John Maynard Keynes and R.A. Butler, he convinced the political establishment that the arts had an educative, civilising purpose in society that justified the spending of taxpayers' money. The Council became an important national institution. But it was a far from popular one, and ongoing suspicion of the art world meant that Britain did not get its first Minister of Arts until Harold Wilson appointed the widow of Nye Bevan, Jennie Lee (1904–88), to the post.

Lee's expressed wish was to make Britain 'a gayer and more cultivated place'. As far as making it a more cultivated place, her problem was that her tenure (1964–70) coincided with the reign of abstraction and the beginnings of conceptual art, little of which the public understood or liked. The first exhibition of abstract art in Britain had taken place in 1935, but its leaders Ben Nicolson (1894–1982) and his wife the sculptor Barbara Hepworth (1903–75) had to wait until the 1950s for their work to be properly recognised. In a rather British way, they had incubated their vision in the Cornish fishing village of St Ives where they drew others inspired by its dramatic seascapes, like Patrick Heron (1920–99) and Terry Frost (b. 1915).

Back in London, others flourished in a new atmosphere of experimentation that vindicated the pioneering work of pre-war modernists. The distorted, serpentine figures of Francis Bacon (1909–92), starting with his *Three Figures at the Base of a Crucifixion* (1945), were a disturbing counterpoint to the humanistic religious vision of Spencer, (though that did not stop the Vatican purchasing Bacon's work). The brightly-painted metal sculpture of Anthony Caro (b. 1924) displayed the fact that he had once been a student of engineering as well as the American Minimalist Kenneth Nolan. Conceptual and performance artists poked even more fun at traditional canons, notably Tony Cragg's (b. 1949) use of household rubbish, and Bruce Maclean's (b. 1944) 'float-away' sculptures on the Thames. The School of London – a term coined by the American ex-patriate R.B. Kitaj (b. 1932) in 1976 – encompassed painters as stylistically diverse as Kitaj himself, Bacon, Frank Auerbach (b. 1931), Leon Kossoff (b. 1926) and Lucien Freud (b. 1922). What they shared was a belief that abstraction need not be the basis of modern art.

American Pop Art reached a wider audience however. Its British followers included Eduardo Paolozzi (b. 1924), Richard Hamilton (b. 1922), Peter Blake (b. 1932) and David Hockney (b. 1937). Their work was an ironic scrutiny and a celebratory expression of the democratic potential of mass consumer culture. They were determined not only to affront accepted taste but also to break down barriers between 'high' and 'low' art. Examples of their work include Hamilton's *What is it that*

makes today's homes so different, so appealing? (1956), Hockney's *The Sunbather* (1965), Peter Blake's *Children Reading Comics* (1954) and his
▶ cover for the **Beatles'** *Sgt Pepper* (1967). Hamilton was a member of the Independent Group, which included the modernist architects Peter and Alyson Smithson. In 1957 he told them that Pop Art should be 'Popular (designed for a mass audience), Transient (short-term solution), Expendable (easily forgotten), Low cost, Mass produced, Young (aimed at youth), Witty, Sexy, Gimmicky, Glamorous, Big Business'. Op Art was a contemporaneous movement whose most famous British exponent was Bridget Riley (b. 1931). Riley's early black-and-white paint-
▶ ings influenced British **fashion** in the 1960s but her reputation survived the association and her colourful optical abstractions are now classic museum pieces.

Like all successful art movements, Pop Art became big business and turned out to be neither transient nor expendable. Its influence stretched into the twenty-first century, although as consumption failed to deliver the degree of democracy once expected of it, the Pop Art style was used in a more ambiguous way. The flat colour fields of Patrick Caulfield's (b. 1936) studies of domestic interiors and their objects conveyed the emptiness of possession. The 'photo pieces' of Gilbert and George (Gilbert Proesch, b. 1943, and George Passmore, b. 1944) used graffiti to cast a critical eye at urban deprivation, for example in *Are You Angry or Are You Boring?* (1977).

The Tate Gallery did not display Continental art until 1926. The Tate's creation of the Turner Prize, in 1984, demonstrated how much the British had opened themselves up to foreign influences and how much, as a consequence, they were producing world-renowned talent like the Anglo-Indian sculptor Anish Kapoor (b. 1954; winner 1991). But the prize came to be associated with what the public saw as the absurdity, cynicism and meaninglessness of modern art. In fact few artists lost their belief in the necessity of making art as accessible as possible. Pop and Conceptual art came together in the Young British Artsts (YBAs) movement of the 1990s, sponsored by the advertising guru Charles Saatchi and brought to a wider public in the Royal Academy's 1997 'Sensation' exhibition. Its leading exponents were the Turner Prize-winner Damien Hirst (b. 1965), Tracey Emin (b. 1963) and Sarah Lucas (b. 1962).

Unlike Britain's architects, relatively few of its artists fully embraced Continental or American modernism. This did not stop British art being derided by the public; nor did it stop state subsidies being condemned as a waste of taxpayers' money. However, the notoriety of modern art, both domestic and foreign, did make the public more aware of it than they were of contemporaneous literature and 'classical' music. Ironically, too, the YBAs brief leadership of Western art was the source of some national pride, even if few people would have swapped their ceramic flying ducks for the carcass of a dead shark. The American sculptor Carl Andre once declared, 'Art is what we do. Culture is what is done to us.' Most Britons felt exactly the opposite. Yet by the twenty-first century, British art had come to be internationally renowned. Foreign artists came to London to study, live and work. British artists were represented by dealers in New York, Paris and Milan and, ironically, more contemporary British art was purchased by foreign collectors and museums than by domestic ones. For all their pride, insularity and xenophobia, sometimes, it seemed, the British did not value themselves enough.

■ Baldwin, Stanley (1867–1947)

Stanley Baldwin was Prime Minister three times (1923–4, 1924–9 and
▶ 1935–7). In his heyday he symbolised the **Conservative Party**, and even
England itself. Although he suffered badly from nerves he managed to
project an image of avuncular reassurance. He had a gift for language
▶ shared (and sometimes assisted) by his cousin **Rudyard Kipling**. His
speeches often evoked a nostalgic image of the rural shires, but he
could also communicate with both sides of industry. In his last years
his record was heavily criticised; but in the domestic sphere, at least,
he is still an inspiration to many Conservatives – the living embodiment of the 'One Nation' ideal.

Baldwin was the only son of a prosperous Worcestershire iron-
master. Discovered in possession of some self-penned pornographic
material at Harrow, he left the school early but proceeded to Trinity
College, Cambridge. His father – a Methodist who later converted to
High Church Anglicanism – was MP for Baldwin's birthplace, Bewdley.
After working for twenty years within the family firm Stanley
succeeded him in the seat in 1908.

At 41 Baldwin was a relatively late political starter, and he did not
take a ministerial post until 1917, when he became joint Financial
Secretary to the Treasury. But after that his rise was dramatic. He was
a key figure in the decision of his relative, the Conservative Party
▶ leader Andrew Bonar Law, to break the **Lloyd George** coalition in
October 1922. Bonar Law made him Chancellor of the Exchequer –
some better-known candidates having refused to join the government
out of loyalty to Lloyd George – and when the Prime Minister was
forced to retire through ill health in May 1923 senior party figures
advised George V to name Baldwin as the successor. Before the end of
the year the new Prime Minister had called a general election, on the
▶ issue of **tariff reform**. Baldwin had been persuaded that British industries needed to be protected against overseas competition, and felt
that since this policy contradicted earlier Conservative assertions he
should seek a new mandate from the electorate. But the election cost
his party its overall parliamentary majority, and Baldwin had to resign
in January 1924.

The setback of November 1923 showed that Baldwin was capable of
placing principle ahead of his party. But it made little difference to his
ultimate strategic aims. Baldwin's greatest achievement was to help
make the Conservative Party the obvious choice for voters who feared
▶ **Labour**. Divisions within the **Liberal Party** played into his hands, and
helped to ensure that it won only 40 seats in the general election of
October 1924, which saw Baldwin's return as Prime Minister with an
overwhelming majority. If the Conservatives had been led by a more

'reactionary' character British politics might have been polarised in the late 1920s and the 1930s. While regarding capitalism as an essential means to prosperity, Baldwin's outlook was indicated by his dislike of 'hard-faced men' who had done well out of the war; by contrast, he himself had started a campaign to induce the rich to convert War Loan into outright gifts to the government. He was sanguine when Labour formed its first two minority governments (1924, 1929–31), merely allowing the Liberals to expose themselves to claims that a vote for them was really a vote for 'socialism'. The same confidence in the unrevolutionary nature of the British left ensured that during the **General Strike** Baldwin restrained the wilder spirits within his ◄ government, such as **Winston Churchill**, who might have deepened ◄ existing class divisions.

After losing power in the 1929 general election (fought under the uninspiring slogan 'Safety First'), Baldwin had to fight to retain the leadership of his party, which was challenged in a campaign orchestrated by the 'press barons', Rothermere and **Beaverbrook**. He had ◄ only just fought off his critics by the time that the second Labour government fell over expenditure cuts (24 August 1931). Baldwin was suspicious of coalition governments, but George V appealed to his patriotism, and he committed his party to a National Government. Until June 1935 he acted as Lord President of the Council, succeeding **Ramsay MacDonald** as Prime Minister only when the latter's health ◄ was broken. MacDonald's party had been smashed in 1931, so that the Conservatives were able to win 432 seats at the general election of November 1935.

Yet the last two years of Baldwin's public career were overshadowed, by the marital affairs of **Edward VIII** and the martial antics of ◄ Hitler. Baldwin handled the abdication crisis with great skill (unlike Churchill). But his touch was far less certain in foreign policy. When in November 1936 Churchill accused him of making inadequate preparations for a possible war with Germany, Baldwin had to admit (with what he himself described as 'appalling frankness') that he should have begun to warn the country of the looming danger as long ago as 1933. Baldwin was aware of the strong anti-war sentiment in the country, and he feared that a new conflict dominated by air power could lead to intolerable civilian casualties. But although opinion will always be divided about Baldwin's own culpability in the failure to act against Hitler, his government did take at least the first steps towards British rearmament.

Baldwin resigned on 28 May 1937, just after the coronation of George VI. He retired to the Lords, but played no further part in public affairs in the ten years before his death. By that time he was widely regarded as the father of **appeasement**. In 1942 some ornamental ◄

gates at his home in Astley were requistioned by the government as scrap metal, although they were almost useless for that purpose and were clearly of artistic value. Lord Beaverbrook, who was Minister of Supply at the time that the decision was taken, seems to have been personally responsible for this act of petty vindictiveness. Perhaps wisely, Baldwin never wrote a memoir to vindicate himself; but he was unfortunate in his choice of the embittered G.M. Young as his official biographer. Towards the end of the century his posthumous reputation was beginning to improve, possibly because of the contrast
▶ between his conciliatory style of government and that of **Margaret Thatcher**. The latter's successor John Major tried to strike a Baldwinesque pose as Prime Minister. His failure to convince as a social and political conciliator underlines Baldwin's own skill, although Major was dogged by a news media which made even Rothermere and Beaverbrook seem public-spirited.

■ Balfour Declaration

On 2 April 1917 Arthur James Balfour, the languid, philosophical Foreign Secretary in the British wartime coalition government and formerly Prime Minister (1902–5), released the text of a letter he had written to Lord Rothschild. Balfour had declared that 'His Majesty's Government views with favour the establishment in Palestine of a national home for the Jewish people'. The government would 'use its best endeavours to facilitate this object', but the civil rights of the existing population of more than 600,000 Arabs would be safeguarded.

Balfour was personally committed to a Jewish homeland – in short, he was a Zionist – but his words were authorised by the whole War Cabinet. It was a cynical manoeuvre, which could only be justified as a means of affecting opinion in other countries, notably America, Germany and Russia. This it failed to do; indeed, it could only have been of real significance if the later Nazi *canard*, that the war was the result of an international Zionist conspiracy, had been true.

For Britain in the long term, the Declaration was far from being a harmless tactical ploy. At the end of the war Balfour was faced with having to take responsibility for his own words. He tried to pass a League of Nations mandate to govern Palestine on to other countries, including the US, but by 1920 he had to admit defeat. The principles behind the Declaration were incorporated within the mandate. Unfortunately, as Balfour and his colleagues should have known, the principles had no chance of being peacefully implemented. The only possible compromise was a partition of Palestine between the Arabs
▶ and the **Jews**, but the territory was tiny and neither statelet would have been viable. Britain thus found itself morally committed to a

policy which offered the alternatives of repression or a war of extermination between peoples who had previously lived in relative harmony. Before his death the statesman who had been dubbed 'Bloody Balfour' because of his policy towards Ireland found the epithet bestowed upon him within the Foreign Office for other reasons. Unwittingly, Balfour had set a precedent. Just a few months after issuing his Declaration he objected to a draft Cabinet statement on self-government for India, protesting that 'we shall be promising something which . . . we neither can nor ought to give'. Although the published text was watered down it still succeeded in fuelling nationalistic feelings on the Asian sub-continent.

The issues raised by Balfour's Declaration were allowed to drift until the renewal of world war, while the British contradicted the spirit of the policy by trying to prevent European Jewish refugees from entering Palestine in the face of Arab protests that Jews would soon become a majority. During the Second World War the Jewish residents in Palestine remained fairly quiet, since they had no desire to distract Britain from the war with Germany. But once the allied victory looked certain a terrorist campaign began, and more than 300 British soldiers were killed.

Even without the Balfour Declaration, there would have been much public sympathy for Zionism because of revelations of German atrocities during the war. But the British government was now painfully aware of the rights of the Arabs in Palestine, which Balfour had ignored. Its inactivity in the face of a cruel moral dilemma provoked tension with the US, which was now taking an interest in this vital strategic area. A UN plan was devised, under which the Jews would be given 55 per cent of Palestine. The British could not accept this, and decided that the only remaining course was to play the part of Pontius Pilate. In September 1947 the Cabinet declared the surrender of its mandate, and prepared to evacuate its troops as fast as possible. Apparently it calculated that there was bound to be a war, which the Arabs were equally certain to win given their powerful allies in the Middle East. Against expectations, between May 1948 and January 1949 the Jews seized almost the whole of the 'mandated' territory, leaving the Palestinian Arabs essentially stateless and creating a problem which, at the beginning of the twentieth-first century, was no nearer a satisfactory solution than it had been when Balfour scribbled his fateful note.

■ **Battle of Britain**

The defining struggle of the Second World War. Following France's capitulation, on 18 June 1940, **Churchill** declared: 'the Battle of France ◄

B

▶ is over; I expect that the Battle of Britain is about to begin.' Hitler, reluctantly convinced that Churchill would not negotiate a settlement giving him control of Europe, ordered invasion plans to be drawn up on 2 July, codenamed 'Operation Sealion'. Given the superiority of the Royal Navy, air supremacy was necessary for an invasion of the UK to stand a chance. On 10 July, the Luftwaffe began bombing shipping in the Channel; on 13 August they switched to airfields and aircraft factories in the south-east of England. The battle lasted until 15 September at the cost of 915 British aircraft and 1,733 German ones.

Without Hugh Dowding (1882–1970), Commander-in-Chief of Fighter Command, Germany might have won the war. In May 1940, the political and military leaders of Britain and France demanded that the whole RAF should be flung across the Channel, but Dowding persuaded Churchill to hold back seven squadrons. When Germany attacked two months later, the RAF was heavily outnumbered but stood a chance. Dowding's pilots were helped by four things aside from their bravery: the development of the Spitfire, which matched
▶ the Messerschmitt 109 for speed; Lord Beaverbrook's ability as Minister of Production to cut enough red tape and keep them coming to the airfields; the chain of radar stations and observers who reported incoming enemy planes to sector headquarters, who then scrambled RAF squadrons in time; and, lastly, the tactical ineptitude of Hitler.

By the first week of September 1940, losses were almost equal and Fighter Command was near breaking point. Then, on 7 September, the
▶ Germans switched to bombing London. The RAF had begun night raids on Germany on 25 August and Hitler's pride was stung,
▶ provoking him to overrule Air Marshal Goering and start the Blitz. The diversion gave Fighter Command time to regroup and by 15 September Luftwaffe losses outweighed those of the British by nearly three to one. Concluding that air supremacy had not been won, on 17 September Hitler postponed the invasion of Britain and abandoned it on 12 October. The victory persuaded Roosevelt to assist Britain in continuing the war and when Germany attacked the Soviet Union in
▶ 1941, it did so with its western flank exposed. The military Establishment never forgave Dowding for proving them wrong and he was forced out in November 1940, then sank into obscurity. His men, on the other hand, were glorified as knights of the air. On 20 August 1940 Churchill paid tribute to the 3,000 RAF pilots of Fighter Command, of whom 507 were killed: 'Never in the field of human conflict was so much owed by so many to so few.'

Thanks to another phrase of Churchill's, the period incorporating the Battle of Britain and the Blitz became known as 'the Finest Hour'.
▶ In fact, Britain never stood alone from 1940 to 1941. It had an Empire at its disposal which meant that an extra 5 million people fought

under the Union Jack between 1940 and 1945; and most were volunteers, not conscripts like their counterparts in the UK. Still, the conceit was perpetuated for another 40 years in books, comics and, above all, in film, from *The Way to the Stars* (1944) to *The Battle of Britain* (1969). At its most self-congratulatory, the legend of the Finest Hour contributed to Euro-scepticism. The idea that Britain was the only combatant European nation to remain undefiled by invasion led the British to claim the moral leadership of Europe while at the same time reserving the right to remain distant from it.

■ The Beatles

The most successful pop group of all time, who transformed Western popular music and in doing so made Britain the epicentre of youth culture during the 1960s. The group was made up of four working-class Liverpudlian men: George Harrison (1943–2001), John Lennon (1940–80), Paul McCartney (b. 1942) and Richard Starkey (b. 1940), known as Ringo Starr.

The song-writing core of the group, Lennon and McCartney, first joined forces at a church fête on 6 July 1957 where they played together in a skiffle group, the Quarrymen. A year later, Harrison joined, together with Stuart Sutcliffe (1940–62), a friend of Lennon's from art school. After a spell as Johnny and the Moondogs, in 1960 they were renamed the Beatles and a drummer, Pete Best (b. 1941) was added. That summer they secured a residency at the Indra Club in Hamburg where, over several drug- and sex-fuelled months, they honed their repertoire of rhythm and blues and rock 'n' roll classics. Thanks to Sutcliffe's **German** photographer girlfriend, Astrid ◄ Kirchherr, they also acquired a new image, shedding their rockers' quiffs for low-fringed, pudding-bowl haircuts which earned them the nickname 'Moptops'. Sutcliffe left the group to pursue his painting and died of a brain haemorrhage soon after.

Following their return to Liverpool, the Beatles secured a residency at the Cavern Club, and quickly became exemplars of the so-called 'Merseybeat' sound, pioneered by a loose conglomeration of groups from north-west England, which included Gerry and the Pacemakers and the Tremeloes, all of whom added fast, guitar-driven, melodic close harmony to American pop, utterly transforming it in the process. In November 1961 the Beatles acquired a new manager: Brian Epstein, a local middle-class, **homosexual** Jewish record dealer, who replaced ◄ their black leather outfits with sharp suits and ties and got them an audition with Decca on New Year's Day 1962. Decca's Dick Rowe rejected them on the grounds that guitar groups were going out of fashion and in May 1962 they joined EMI. There they were assigned to

B

a producer with classical training, George Martin (b. 1926), whose technical knowledge and disciplined imagination became crucial to their work. Dissatisfied with Pete Best's drumming, in August 1962 Lennon and McCartney replaced him with Ringo Starr, shortly after releasing their first single, 'Love Me Do'. It was a success but the cultural phenomenon of Beatlemania effectively began when they performed their second single, and first major hit, 'Please Please Me'

▶ on the ITV show *Thank Your Lucky Stars* on 13 February 1963, watched by 6 million Britons. On 23 August they released 'She Loves You', which went to the top of the charts, and its raucous chorus of 'Yeah! Yeah! Yeah!' became an emblem of the national frenzy that the group set in motion.

That frenzy – wittily captured in the films *A Hard Day's Night* (1964) and *Help* (1965) – was generated by the Beatles' good looks, dynamism and infectious harmonies. But their long-term cultural influence rested on three other factors. First, the Beatles overturned the American dominance of popular music which had prevailed since the 1930s – from jazz and swing through to rock 'n' roll. All these genres had been slavishly imitated by British artists – notably Henry Hall's impersonation of Glenn Miller and Cliff Richard's of Elvis Presley. Unlike the Kinks and the Small Faces, the Beatles sang in American accents, but

▶ they did utilise native genres, notably Edwardian **music-hall** song. Most important of all, they sang explicitly and affectionately about British life – a tendency which had effectively died out after the Second World War with the demise of the Lancastrian comedy singer George Formby. The group continued to pay tribute to American influences, both historical – Lennon once said 'before Elvis there was nothing' – and contemporary – the album *Sgt Pepper* was partly inspired by the Beach Boys' *Pet Sounds* (1966). Ultimately, however, these influences were absorbed into the distinctive idiom they fashioned.

By re-creating an overtly British music and then seducing America with it, the Beatles earned respect not only from the millions of young Britons who screamed themselves hoarse at concerts but also from

▶ members of the **Establishment**, from *The Times* music critic to the
▶ leader of the **Labour Party**. Profit, as always, accompanied patriotism. The Beatles were the first British pop group to top the American charts, with 'I Wanna Hold Your Hand', which they performed live on the *Ed Sullivan Show* on 9 February 1964, the moment at which Beatlemania became an international phenomenon. By April, their songs occupied the top five places in the US *Billboard* chart and, thanks to the lead they gave, by 1968, 72 per cent of records in the UK charts were British – double the average before 1963. The Beatles were also the first pop group to follow Elvis Presley in becoming a brand, selling

a multi-million-dollar cornucopia of merchandise, from wigs to pencil cases. The only British entertainer of any kind who had comparable transatlantic success was Charlie Chaplin, and that rested on a persona that Chaplin developed in and through Hollywood. The Beatles were a true, home-grown export and it was for export that they received MBEs from the Queen at Buckingham Palace on 26 October 1965.

Second, the Beatles spearheaded a working-class assault on British culture which transformed the way it was defined, produced and experienced, making the wall erected by the Victorians between elite and popular forms more permeable. This assault – generated by the expansion of mass education following the 1944 Butler **Education Act**, was manifest in the number of pop stars who began their careers at **art** school, among them Lennon and McCartney, Mick Jagger, Pete Townshend and Ray Davies. Their cheeky, irreverent humour – always on display at press conferences – was seen as evidence of a less deferential society, without threatening the established order. When, at a Royal Command Performance in 1963, Lennon invited people in the cheap seats to clap and those in the expensive ones to 'rattle your jewellery' (he promised to say 'rattle your *fucking* jewellery' in the dressing room before Epstein intervened), he was satirising not only Britain's social barriers but the cultural ones that sprang from them. And it was with this in mind that the group commissioned the Pop artist Peter Blake to design the cover of their album *Sgt Pepper*, replete with icons as diverse as Diana Dors and T.S. Eliot.

Third, they reformed the music industry. By writing most of their own songs, the group returned some power to performing artists from the 'Tin Pan Alley' of music publishers and distributors who, since the birth of commercial popular music in the 1900s, had dominated the industry and exploited most of its young charges. The Beatles actively encouraged other groups to do likewise, notably the Rolling Stones – promoted as demonic, more sexualised rivals, but in fact lifelong friends with whom they co-operated professionally. The Beatles' influence was such that, for a brief time, Liverpool was the focus of pop in Britain. After the band moved to London, in 1968 they set up their own company, Apple Corp., with the intention of helping any aspiring artist with a bright idea. Part record label and part artistic utopia, its Savile Row offices thronged with people taking **drugs** and requesting money for everything from studio time to the purchase of a Fijian island where, a Californian couple reassured them, they would create an alternative universe. The Beatles tolerated this mayhem for two years until they grew tired of losing money and closed the company down. Apple symbolised their strength and fragility. Few groups had the means to set up such an independent enterprise; yet, for all their wealth and clout, the Beatles were no match for the corporate power of the music industry, while those who were less talented continued to remain at the mercy of it. The group's challenge to America ended ironically in 1985, with Paul McCartney failing to wrest ownership of their early songs from Michael Jackson.

Their musical achievement transcended these failures. The Beatles' imagination and willingness to experiment produced a unique body of work which extended the parameters of popular music and influenced successive generations of artists and producers. Exhausted by touring and disillusioned with live performances in which the screams of hysterical fans made it impossible to hear themselves play (their last official performance was at Candlestick Park, San Francisco, on 29 August 1966) the Beatles began to concentrate on composing and recording. The highlights of this phase of their career were the albums *Rubber Soul* (1965), *Revolver* (1966), *Sgt Pepper's Lonely Hearts Club Band* (1967) and *Abbey Road* (1969). The LSD-drenched *Sgt Pepper* – generally seen as the best of these – was hailed by the critic Kenneth Tynan as 'a decisive moment in the history of Western civilisation'. Reality matched hyperbole. When, on 25 June 1967, an estimated worldwide audience of 400 million people watched the Beatles sing 'All You Need Is Love' live on the BBC, the group proved that commercial pop music need not be ephemeral or artistically worthless but could, in fact, enrich and transform lives, bringing people of disparate cultures closer together.

However, the Beatles themselves were beginning to fall apart. Brian Epstein's suicide on 27 August 1967 removed a stabilising influence on four young men living a surreal life of superstardom for which they were ill-prepared. When Lennon and McCartney fell in love respectively with Yoko Ono, a Japanese performance artist, and Linda Eastman, an American heiress, they found a measure of personal happiness. But their relationship with each other – always testy thanks to Lennon's more radical nature – disintegrated, as Yoko Ono began to demand a say in the group's affairs. These tensions were compounded by a bitter dispute between Lennon and McCartney over who should sort out the group's chaotic finances, and by the creative dissatisfaction of George Harrison whose song-writing talents Lennon and McCartney never allowed to flourish. The Beatles last-ever performance was an impromptu live concert on the roof of the Apple offices on 30 January 1969, in which they sang the plaintive 'Get Back', from their last album, *Let It Be*, released shortly after McCartney announced that the Beatles had spilt up, on 10 April 1970.

Like so many other pop groups who split up, their subsequent careers proved that even if they could no longer bear to be in the same room together, their individual talents could not be fully realised

B

apart from each other. Only Harrison's *All Things Must Pass* (1970) and Lennon's *Imagine* (1971) came close to recapturing the glory of the Beatles. Lennon grew more politically radical in the 1970s and by the time he was assassinated in New York on 10 December 1980 by a deranged American Christian, he had acquired a reputation as the spokesman for Western youth. Had the public been aware that he secretly donated a small proportion of his vast personal fortune to the IRA and the Black Panthers, they would have been less sympathetic than they were when he returned his MBE in protest at the Vietnam war. As it was, Lennon's canonisation, and with it that of the Beatles, was assured by an early death.

■ Beaverbrook, Lord (1879–1964)

Born William Aitken, Lord Beaverbrook made his fortune in Canada from a variety of business ventures before moving to England in 1910. Inspired by dreams of imperial unity, he recommended himself as a **Conservative** candidate to his friend (and fellow Canadian) Andrew Bonar Law. In December 1910 he narrowly won the seat of Ashton-under-Lyne, near Manchester. Within six months he had been knighted, although his services to his newly-adopted country at that early stage were obscure. Perhaps it was something to do with a public-spirited loan of £25,000 to the *Daily Express*, a staunch supporter of the Conservative Party and of Bonar Law in particular. By 1916 Beaverbrook had acquired a controlling interest in the newspaper.

Aitken had a happy knack of adding to his collection of influential friends. By 1916 he was on intimate terms with both **Lloyd George** and **Churchill**, as well as **Rudyard Kipling**. After encouraging Lloyd George to supplant Asquith as Prime Minister of the coalition government in December 1916, Aitken was rewarded with his peerage. But his friend would not give him the government post he craved. Only in February 1918 did he become Minister of Information; he resigned due to frustration and ill-health in the same October.

Beaverbrook's newspaper interests continued to expand: he started the *Sunday Express* in 1918 and bought the London *Evening Standard* in 1923. But he had too much energy, too many contacts, and too much love of intrigue to keep out of politics. Having helped to create the Lloyd George coalition he assisted in its downfall, advising Bonar Law to ditch the 'goat' in 1922. Even so, Lloyd George and Beaverbrook remained on cordial terms. But when Bonar Law resigned in May 1923 his successor was **Stanley Baldwin**, who never fell for the Beaverbrook magic. Indeed by the end of the decade the two were mortal enemies; Beaverbrook joined Lord Rothermere in launching the **Empire** Free

Trade Crusade, which won a by-election at South Paddington in November 1930. But before the next contest, at St George's, Westminster, Baldwin hit back, claiming (with literary assistance from Kipling) that the newspapers were trying to exercise 'power without responsibility – the prerogative of the harlot through the ages'. A crushing victory for the official Conservative candidate at St George's halted Beaverbrook's Crusade.

The 1930s brought several setbacks for Beaverbrook. Although the *Express* surpassed the circulation of the *Daily Mail*, its bitter rival, the ▶ proprietor threw his weight behind two losing causes – **Edward VIII** ▶ and **appeasement**. Even after Germany invaded Poland it was said that Beaverbrook wanted to use the *Sunday Express* to press for peace. All this should have caused lasting damage to his relationship with Churchill; but in May 1940 the latter made him Minister of Aircraft Production. After a year in that post he became Minister of Supply, which brought him into the War Cabinet. In February 1942 his duties were redefined under the new title of Minister of War Production, but he left this post after less than a fortnight.

Although as always personal reactions to the mercurial minister had been mixed, Beaverbrook had certainly justified Churchill's confidence with his energetic conduct of vital business. After an interval in which he used his newspapers to press for a closer understanding with the Soviet Union, Beaverbrook rejoined the Cabinet, as Lord Privy Seal. This time he stayed until the end of the war. His continuing personal influence over Churchill was deplored in some quarters, and rebounded badly on both when the *Express* tried unsuc- ▶ cessfully to whip up a 'red scare' against **Labour** before the 1945 general election. But the friendship was enduring and Beaverbrook remained a power behind the throne when the Conservatives returned to office in 1951.

With his ministerial career now over, Beaverbrook was free to exercise his dictatorial whims in the running of his newspapers. For him interference with the editorial line was a matter of course; after all, a man should have full control of his property. But at the same time he was prepared to give a free rein to people whose judgement he respected, even when they seemed poles apart politically. Although at one time Michael Foot accused his old boss of megalomania, after Beaverbrook's death he wrote that 'I loved him, not merely as a friend ▶ but as a second father'; A.J.P. **Taylor's** admiration extended to a massive, flattering biography. Unlike most other domineering 'press barons' of the twentieth century, Beaverbrook at least had the excuse of being a gifted journalist; and unlike some of his successors who shared his populist instincts, his errors invariably arose from an excess of patriotic spirit.

■ Best, George (b. 1946)

The most naturally gifted British **footballer** ever, whose hedonistic ◄
lifestyle and subsequent disintegration into alcoholism, bankruptcy,
prison and organ transplantation came to symbolise the perils of fame
and excess. Born to a working-class Protestant family in Belfast, he was
the best-known Northern Irishman of modern times and rather more
popular than the Revd **Ian Paisley** or Gerry Adams. ◄

Best was brought to the British mainland in 1961 by Matt Busby,
who was rebuilding the Manchester United team in the wake of the
1958 Munich air crash that had killed fourteen players. Best turned
professional in 1963 and made his debut that autumn against West
Bromwich Albion at Old Trafford. The 17-year-old forward made an
immediate impression, combining to an unusual degree the traditional skill of dribbling the ball with the more modern one of passing
and running. Years later the West Brom full back, Graham Williams,
said to him, 'Will you stand still for a minute so I can look at your
face?' 'Why?' asked Best. 'Because all I've ever seen of you,' explained
Williams, 'is your arse disappearing down the touchline.'

His career reached a peak in 1968 when he was voted European
Player of the Year and helped Manchester United to win the European
Cup. In the final, against Portugal's Benfica, he scored two of the goals
in a 4–1 victory. Best also won the League Championship with United
in 1965 and 1967, and scored 115 goals in 290 games during his six
years with the club. Pele judged him to be his favourite player but
because Best was loyal to his native Northern Ireland, he never played
in the World Cup finals. His dark, ruggedly boyish looks, his charm
and charisma, together with his evident delight in women and nightclubs, helped to make him the first footballer with the celebrity status
of film and pop stars. At one point, he received 1,000 fan letters a week
and was dubbed 'the fifth **Beatle**' by the press. ◄

He soon began to disintegrate. Matt Busby retired at the end of the
1968–9 season, and his successor Frank O'Farrell was unable to control
an already wayward talent. Best's mother was an alcoholic; but any
genetic predisposition to self-destruction was intensified by his
inability to handle the fame and fantasies thrust upon him. He could
still occasionally turn on the magic, as when he scored six goals in
United's 8–2 defeat of Northampton in an FA Cup fifth round tie
during the 1969–70 season. But he missed training sessions and then
began to miss matches, sometimes disappearing without trace for
days on end. On 1 September 1970, aged 24 and burnt out, he moved
to Stockport County and began a descent that took him to clubs as
varied as Dunstable Town and the San Jose Earthquakes. After twelve
clubs, three marriages and many more drying-out clinics, he ended his

B

career in 1978, playing his last competitive match for the Brisbane Lions.

'Tell me, Mr Best, where did it all go wrong?' a hotel porter is once supposed to have asked him. There was £20,000 in cash scattered on a bed which also contained the current Miss Universe. The story captures the enduring appeal of George Best. The British like their heroes to be tragic ones: possessed of enough glamour and talent for stardom to be lived vicariously through them; yet flawed and vulnerable enough for the public not to be threatened by their success. Best fulfilled that role perfectly, not least by appearing regularly on chat shows after his retirement from the game. In 2002, he had a liver transplant. A few argued that because his ill health was self-inflicted, Best did not deserve the operation. But medical ethics and the public were on his side, glad that their fragile legend had survived for a while longer.

■ **Betjeman, Sir John** (1906–84)

The most popular British poet of the twentieth century, whose verse celebrated middle-class English life, yet spoke humanely of universal experience in an accessible style and so transcended its subject matter. Betjeman was born in Highgate, north London, the son of Ernest Betjemann, a manufacturer of furniture and decorative objects for the rich. The family were Dutch in origin, having settled in Britain in the 1830s; an extra 'n' was added during the 1860s when **German** culture was briefly made fashionable by the cult of Prince Albert; it was removed by the poet's mother, Mabel, during the First World War when Germanophobia became central to the British outlook.

Mabel's intervention did not stop her son being tormented at Highgate Junior School by bullies singing 'Betjemann's a German spy/ Shoot him down and let him die'. As his verse autobiography *Summoned By Bells* (1960) recalls, he also suffered acutely from the snobbery of classmates and their parents, being described on one occasion as 'that common little boy' on the grounds that his father was in trade rather than in finance, land or the professions. This early experience of xenophobia and snobbery produced the twin themes of his life and work. First was a desire to be accepted by the British ruling **classes**. Though he never posed as an **aristocrat** like Evelyn Waugh, his insecurities led him into an unhappy marriage in 1933 to Penelope Chetwode, daughter of Field Marshal Lord Chetwode, Commander-in-Chief in India. The second and more productive result of Betjeman's rejection was an affinity with ordinary people and a desire to reach and enrich them through his work. This culminated in his appointment as Poet Laureate in 1972.

Betjeman was educated at Marlborough, which he hated, and at Magdalen College, Oxford (1925–8), which he loved, flinging himself into the group of hedonistic aesthetes who gathered around Harold Acton, and whom he called 'the Gorgeoisie'. On leaving Oxford, he took a post as master at a preparatory school, before being appointed assistant editor of the *Architectural Review* in 1930. There, he championed Victorian **architecture**, an unfashionable cause ◄ during a period in which Art Deco and other modernisms were all the rage. In 1932, he co-founded the Victorian Society and spent his life campaigning against the destruction of Britain's nineteenth-century buildings, vividly expressing his concerns in *Ghastly Good Taste* (1933). Betjeman's love of the Gothic Revival was largely fuelled by his High **Church of England** faith. His ability to communicate ◄ that faith to a wide audience made him the most prominent British Christian intellectual of his age next to the Northern Irish theologian, C.S. Lewis (1898–1963).

Betjeman's most famous poem, 'Slough' (1937), in which he implored 'friendly bombs' to destroy the Thames Valley dormitory town, its petit bourgeois inhabitants and their culture based around the radio, the car and 'bogus Tudor bars' compounded his reputation in radical quarters as a crusty reactionary. In fact, Betjeman loved most aspects of modern Britain; what he detested was the secular nature of mass democracy. He had a fascination for **suburbia**, cele- ◄ brating its peculiar mixture of individualism and communality in 'Metroland' (1972). He loved the **cinema**, becoming film critic of the ◄ London *Evening Standard* in 1933 and working in the Films Division of the Ministry of Information (1939–41), before becoming press attaché at the British Embassy in Dublin (1941–3) and then at the Admiralty (1943–5).

And it was through the most powerful medium of the century that Betjeman became famous after the Second World War. His television documentaries on British life, made for the **BBC** and **ITV**, were char- ◄ acterised by a sensitive, often melancholy patriotism. The screen persona he perfected – of a kindly but impish and slightly dotty uncle – made him an adored figure and laid the foundation for the phenomenal success of his *Collected Poems* (1958, 1962, 1970, 1979). The best-selling British poetry book of all time (over a million copies) sparked jealous condemnation from the literary **Establishment**, with ◄ one critic comparing his verse to 'the jingles on Christmas cards' and this probably delayed his elevation to the laureateship. His admirers (who included W.H. Auden) compared him to **Kipling**. But, Kipling's ◄ bombast and prejudices were absent from Betjeman's work and a more accurate comparison is with a prose writer, Dickens, with whom he shared a belief that literature could reach the common man

B

without surrendering either its aesthetic or critical imperative.

Such was Betjeman's influence that by the time of his death he had become a cultural paradigm, in direct opposition to T.S. Eliot, whose insistence that poetry had to be 'difficult' in order to have merit made
▶ him a byword for **cultural elitism**. It is sublimely ironic that Betjeman was taught English at Highgate Junior School by Eliot, and after one lesson in 1916 he presented the American with a collection of his boyhood poems which he called *The Best of Betjeman*. Eliot never commented on them nor ever referred to the incident in later life as his former charge was showered with honours: the Queen's Medal for Poetry and a CBE (1960); knighthood (1969); honorary fellowship of Magdalen College (1975) and honorary degrees from seven British
▶ **universities**. Betjeman claimed that the greatest honour of his career was to appear on the popular TV programme *Jim'll Fix It* in 1974, in order to present a medal to a young boy for his first attempts at poetry. Betjeman may have forgiven Eliot's silence but he never forgot it.

■ Bevan, Aneurin ('Nye') (1897–1960)

Nye Bevan was born in Tredegar, on the South Wales coalfield. His father was a miner, a lover of poetry and music. Nye was a stammering schoolboy who showed little promise, and became a miner himself on his thirteenth birthday. It was a time of militancy in the coal industry, and Bevan quickly developed his self-confidence, taking on the management on behalf of himself and others at the slightest opportunity; he gave another defiant performance in his successful battle to
▶ evade **conscription** in 1917. At the same time he was educating himself, and in 1919 he went to London to study at the Central Labour College, Earls Court. In two years he absorbed Marxist doctrine, adding theoretical weapons to his well-developed sensitivity to social injustice.

Bevan returned to a South Wales which was suffering badly in the post-war depression. He lost his own job, but this experience provided him with additional impetus. Eventually he became a miners' agent, and in that capacity was deeply involved in the organisation of the
▶ **General Strike**. He began to win a national reputation; locally, he was elected to Monmouth County Council in 1928, after having served as a District Councillor.
▶   In 1929 Bevan was selected by **Labour** to fight the safe seat of Ebbw Vale, in place of the sitting MP who was seen as too moderate. In parliament he met his future wife, Jenny Lee, the young MP for North Lanark. But although he quickly attracted notice for his eloquence –
▶ more than matching his countryman **Lloyd George** in one debate – it was a difficult period for Bevan. Disillusionment with the Labour

government of **Ramsay MacDonald** set in well before it fell; he flirted ◄
for a time with **Oswald Mosley**, although he decided not to join the ◄
latter's New Party. Instead, he was briefly expelled by Labour in March
1939, when he joined calls for a 'Popular Front' of anti-**Conservatives**. ◄
Through his columns in the *Tribune* newspaper, Bevan opposed both
fascism and rearmament, his case being that the Tory-dominated
National Government could not be trusted to resist Hitler. This
dilemma was resolved for Bevan when Hitler's invasion brought the
Soviet Union into alliance with Britain. But he continued to criticise
the conduct of the war. He frequently clashed with **Churchill** who ◄
thought of him as a 'squalid nuisance'.

If Britain had to bear Conservative leadership during the war, Bevan
was determined that Labour should win the peace. To this end he
wrote the fierce polemic, *Why not trust the Tories?* in 1944. After his
party's landslide victory, Clement Attlee made Bevan Minister of
Health. This was a surprise, not least to Bevan himself – although he
had been elected to Labour's National Executive Committee (NEC). But
it turned out to be one of the most inspired gambles in British political history. With responsibility for both health and **housing**, Bevan ◄
had far too much to do. But the inexperienced minister proved to be
an able administrator and a flexible negotiator. His creation of the
National Health Service (NHS) by 1948 was a remarkable personal ◄
achievement – even though the Conservatives would have designed a
similar institution had they held on to power. He was forced to make
concessions to the British Medical Association (BMA) and his organisation has always been criticised for being over-centralised. But Bevan
needed the co-operation of the doctors; and his aim was to produce (so
far as possible) a free service for all, with uniform standards of treatment across the country.

Bevan's record in housing was less impressive. He was shackled by
a complex bureaucracy, Britain's economic weakness, a sudden surge
in the number of young families waiting to be housed, and his own
desire (commendable in itself but unrealistic at the time) to build
genuine 'homes for heroes' rather than the second-rate structures of
the inter-war years. He was moved by romantic visions of a Britain in
which professional people lived alongside manual labourers,
providing (as he put it) 'the living tapestry of a mixed community'.
Even with these exacting (if not anachronistic) standards, more than a
million new houses were built between 1945 and 1951.

Although he had occasionally proved a volatile ministerial
colleague, Bevan had every reason to expect promotion (even to the
Treasury) after the second Labour victory of 1950. Instead, he had to
wait until January 1951 for his promotion into the Cabinet, as
Minister for Labour. Three months later he resigned in protest at the

51

imposition of charges for dental treatment and spectacles. It was a principled resignation, provoked not just by the 'betrayal' of the founding principles of the NHS, but also by the reason for the charges – the need to pay for Britain's participation in the Korean War.

In 1952 Bevan published *In Place of Fear*, a statement of his socialist beliefs. This looked very dated by the end of the twentieth century, because unlike Labour's middle-class fellow-travellers Bevan really *was* a socialist, with a wholehearted belief in **nationalisation**. In 1955 these ideas suffered a decisive setback, when Bevan was crushed by the 'revisionist' Hugh Gaitskell in the election to succeed Attlee as leader. Bevan detested Gaitskell, describing him as a 'dessicated calculating machine'. It was an inappropriate jibe, because both men were criticised for enjoying the good things in life (Bevan himself had been described as a 'Bollinger Bolshevik' by Churchill's friend Brendan Bracken). Before the election, Bevan's differences with Attlee over a range of issues (including nuclear weapons) had led to a furious row and the temporary withdrawal of the party whip. Gaitskell's allies believed that Bevan was leading a 'party within a party', based around the *Tribune*. Such fears were largely imaginary – though predictable enough among a group which was itself set on hijacking the 'workers' party'. Bevan might not be a good team player, but the same headstrong individualism made him a very unlikely plotter.

Even so, after Gaitskell's victory Labour looked in danger of splitting, and the re-elected Conservative government might be handed a permanent lease on power. Bevan duly established some sort of accord with Gaitskell. After distinguishing himself in debates during the **Suez crisis** Bevan returned to the front bench as Shadow Foreign Secretary, then Deputy Leader of the party. At the Brighton conference of 1957 he made one of the greatest political speeches of the twentieth century, accusing nuclear disarmers of basing their views on an 'emotional spasm', and claiming that the absence of an 'independent' deterrent would send a British Foreign Secretary 'naked into the conference chamber'. It was magnificent oratory, but somewhat contradictory of Bevan's own earlier thoughts on the issue. Ironically, he was now vulnerable to the charge he had repeatedly levelled against Churchill – relying on his gift for words which signified little or nothing.

In 1960 Bevan died of stomach cancer. Since Gaitskell himself perished before the 1964 election which returned Labour to office, the fiery Welshman might have inherited the leadership after all, had he lived. Instead, his mantle passed to Harold Wilson, who had resigned with him back in 1951. On Wilson it proved to be an ill-fitting garment. The ensuing travails of Labour in government and in opposition made Bevan a greater hero than ever before, particularly to close personal friends like Michael Foot (who succeeded him at Ebbw Vale).

Rightly, the NHS continued to be recognised as Labour's greatest monument; but it was convenient for the leadership of 'New' Labour to overlook the idealism which had created it.

B

■ Beveridge, William (1879–1963); the Beveridge Report

William Beveridge was born at Rangpur, like many great twentieth-century Britons the child of an official in the Indian civil service. He was brought to England by his mother in 1890; his father joined them later. After Charterhouse and Oxford William started his career as a social worker in London, before joining the British civil service and reaching Permanent Secretary level (in the Ministry of Food) by 1919. Between the wars he was Director of the London School of Economics, then (from 1937 to 1945) Master of University College, Oxford. Although he was renowned for his abrasive arrogance – a more familiar trait for a minister than a civil servant – his capacity for creative ideas was legendary within Whitehall. As early as 1909 he had influenced the introduction of Labour Exchanges through his book *Unemployment*. His new academic commitments did not exclude a bit of freelance governmental activity, particularly since this provided a stream of gifted researchers to satisfy his lust for statistics. In 1934 he was appointed to head an official committee on social insurance, and two years later he was asked to draw up a scheme of rationing, based on his experience in the First World War.

Among his other gifts, Beveridge had a great talent for self-publicity. In 1941, when he was made chairman of a new committee on social insurance, it was widely felt that he should have been entrusted with more important work. In fact, the Minister of Labour, Ernest Bevin, had wanted to keep his infernal energies occupied well away from his own territory. Yet when the *Report on Social Insurance and Allied Services* was published on 1 December 1942, it created an immediate sensation. In providing an idealistic blueprint for the future, Beveridge's timing was extremely fortunate. Less than a month earlier Britain had celebrated its first major success of the war, at the battle of El Alamein. Thoughts could now turn towards post-war reconstruction. Together with a cheaper summary of its contents, the unwieldy Report sold more than 600,000 copies.

Although Beveridge claimed that the Report was 'revolutionary', it drew heavily on pre-war principles. It might best be seen as the logical culmination of the process begun under the Asquith government before the First World War (Beveridge himself was a Liberal). National insurance already existed, even if its coverage was grossly inadequate. Now Beveridge proposed that it should embrace every worker, and contributions from the individual, the employer and the state should

B

all increase. The result would be an assured standard of living for all
▶ in the event of **unemployment**, sickness or retirement. But Beveridge
assumed that everyone fit for work would be willing to take available
jobs: he named 'Idleness' among the 'Five Giants' (along with Want,
Disease, Ignorance and Squalor) that had to be overthrown. The
'national minimum' would be adequate, but Beveridge hoped that he
was leaving plenty of incentive for the thrifty individual to take out
private insurance to guarantee a life of real comfort.

The Report was generally popular because it promised that it would
only be part of an overarching welfare structure, in which the state
would take care of the citizen 'from the cradle to the grave' (as
▶ **Churchill** put it). The Report itself proposed that wives who stayed at
▶ home to look after **children** would be covered by their husbands'
contribution, and there would also be child allowances; there was
▶ even help for women if their **marriages** broke down. But although his
▶ own remit was relatively narrow Beveridge argued for a free **National
Health Service** (NHS); other 'Giants' would be slain through educational reform and, crucially, 'full' employment (at this time Beveridge
himself thought that the government should aim for a jobless rate of
around 8 per cent; later he revised this to 3 per cent). Before the end
of the war there was general agreement on the principles behind all
▶ of these measures, although this **'consensus'** did not extend to the
details. When the Report was debated in the Commons the coalition
government gave a lukewarm response; apart from the understandable feeling that Beveridge had tried to force its hand, there were also
genuine misgivings on the grounds of cost. But more than a hundred
backbenchers rebelled against the government's line, including **Lloyd**
▶ **George** who was casting his last vote in the Commons.

For understandable reasons 'The People's William' was not invited
by the government to produce further plans for reconstruction. But he
plunged almost immediately into a new private inquiry, published as
Full Employment in a Free Society in 1944. This envisaged the full-scale
manipulation of the market to ensure the demise of the 'Giant' of Idleness. Although Beveridge himself had no doubts that the 'free society'
would be protected rather than endangered by such measures, the
book might be regarded as the point at which his thinking left even
▶ the confines of 'new' liberalism. J.M. **Keynes** had encouraged the
Report, but hinted that he found some of the thinking 'Utopian'; in
▶ particular, Beveridge envisaged a level of **economic planning** by the
state which could not be squared easily with any variety of liberal
ideology. Even so, Beveridge was elected as Liberal MP for Berwick in
1944. Yet although he made many speeches before the 1945 general
election, he gave too little attention to his own constituency and was
▶ defeated by the **Conservatives**.

A few months later Beveridge was elevated to the House of Lords. Until 1951 he was still included by the government among the 'Great and the Good' who were asked to serve on committees. But his next report, on broadcasting, could not be implemented before the Conservatives returned to power. There was no chance that Churchill's new administration would pass any further interesting work in Beveridge's direction. But he continued to write and think: he attacked apartheid, campaigned for more 'mixed' marriages, and criticised plans to link pensions with final earnings on the grounds that they would encourage inflationary wage demands. He was writing and broadcasting until shortly before his death in Oxford.

■ Blair, Tony (b. 1953)

Anthony Charles Lynton Blair was born in Edinburgh. His father Leo had been adopted; Tony Blair's biological grandparents were in the acting profession. Leo was a Communist in his youth, but soon put away such childish notions. By 1953 he was an academic lawyer who seemed destined to sit as a **Conservative** MP, on the right wing of that party.

Tony Blair attended the prestigious Durham Choristers' School, then the private Fettes in Edinburgh, which had produced the Conservative Chancellors, Selwyn Lloyd and Iain Macleod. But when the boy was only 10 years old his father had suffered a major stroke, and the family's comfortable lifestyle was undermined. The place at Fettes was only secured because young Blair won a scholarship. He was a mildly rebellious schoolboy, and at Oxford was lead singer in a band called Ugly Rumours. He was not active in student politics, but he did develop what he considered to be an adequate philosophical foundation for a political career. In fact, the vague ideas he absorbed through reading and conversations with friends were liberal rather than distinctively socialist, and in these formative years he seems to have been interested in unequivocal examples of political injustice, like South African apartheid, rather than the class struggle at home. Nevertheless, after leaving university with a law degree (and before enrolling as a pupil for the Bar) he joined the **Labour Party** in London.

During his legal training, under Derry Irvine, QC, Blair met his future wife, Cherie Booth, who had been an outstanding undergraduate. Booth's father was an actor, like Blair's paternal grandparents; she shared Blair's interest in religion (although unlike him she was a **Roman Catholic**); and her Labour loyalties inspired her to stand for **parliament** in an unwinnable seat. Blair himself made his debut in an equally hopeless fight, a by-election at Beaconsfield in May 1982.

During the campaign he endorsed most of the policies which his allies later denounced as electoral liabilities, including unilateral nuclear
▶ disarmament and withdrawal from 'Europe'. The contest was held
▶ during the Falklands War, at a time when normal partisan conflict was overshadowed by the mood of national unity. Blair duly lost his deposit.

After a tough campaign which demanded some imaginative tactics by his allies, Blair was selected as the candidate for the safe Labour seat of Sedgefield just before the 1983 general election. By this time he had refined his views, moving from the 'soft left' to the centre-right of his party. It was a timely switch, as the 'extreme' policies of 1983 were held responsible for Labour's humiliating defeat in the election (Blair himself won a comfortable majority in Sedgefield). He voted for the moderate left-wing candidate, Neil Kinnock, in the contest to succeed Michael Foot as leader after the election. He made an early impression in the Commons. His well-prepared speeches and parliamentary questions marked him as a rising star, and he was unusual in combining obvious professionalism with a boyish charm. Only a few months after Blair became an MP Kinnock recruited him to the shadow Treasury team. After the 1987 election he moved on to shadow Energy (where he denounced the Thatcher government's privatisation of electricity),
▶ then to Employment. In this post he convinced trade union leaders that they would have to accept many of the government's industrial relations reforms. This was one of the key moves in Kinnock's drive to make the Labour Party 'electable' again by convincing the public that it was no longer in the pocket of the unions.

By the end of the 1980s Blair's potential was unmistakable even to senior Conservatives. Within the Labour Party, the only obvious rival of his generation was his close friend Gordon Brown, who was Blair's intellectual superior but lacked his easy manners and smart repartee
▶ in debate. Another important ally was Kinnock's 'spin doctor', Peter Mandelson, who was awarded much of the credit for Labour's softened image. Blair was also friendly with the Shadow Chancellor, John Smith. Before the 1992 general election Smith and Kinnock quarrelled over taxation policy; although Blair agreed with Kinnock, he failed to speak up for him.

In the circumstances it was another stroke of luck for Blair that Labour lost badly again in 1992, and Kinnock resigned immediately. His successor was John Smith. Although another ambitious Scot, Robin Cook, had been Smith's titular campaign manager, Mandelson's briefings to the press suggested that Blair and Brown had brought life to a lacklustre team. After Smith's comfortable victory Brown became the Shadow Chancellor, while Blair took on Home Affairs.

This was yet another fortunate development for Blair, and he took full advantage of the opening. Law and order were seen as traditional Tory issues, but even for Conservatives the Home Office was a political graveyard, since the incumbent had to appease both the raucous demands of party activists and the relatively liberal views of those who really knew about the subject. As a result Blair had everything to gain and nothing to lose if he put forward some distinctive ideas of his own, particularly after the unpopular Michael Howard became Home Secretary in May 1993. Blair could do no wrong after encapsulating his own approach in a winning soundbite – 'Tough on crime, tough on the causes of crime'. Predictably, when the time came to put the slogan into action Labour ministers found it easier to crack down on the symptoms than to root out the disease, but this made no difference to Blair's compassionate image.

Although John Smith shared little of the 'modernisers'' drive to reform the Labour Party's constitution, important progress had been made in breaking the influence of the unions before the new leader died suddenly in May 1994. Blair had considered running for the Deputy Leadership in 1992. This time he was determined to stand for the top post, despite the fact that Brown would have been the obvious successor in the days before the media ran British politics. While the party was supposed to be in mourning for Smith, Brown came under pressure to delay (if not completely to abandon) his dream of leading the party. For some reason, the press became very interested in Brown's private life at this time. Peter Mandelson's public statements also made it clear that he favoured Blair. At the end of May Brown bowed to the inevitable, ensuring a comfortable victory for Blair.

The Conservative government was already in terminal decline before Blair took the leadership of what he quickly dubbed 'New' Labour. But activists were desperate for power after four consecutive general election defeats, and offered no resistance when their new leaders told them that they were still unelectable. Thus Blair was able to push through changes in the party's policy stance and constitution which Kinnock could never dream of. Labour would have won easily under John Smith in 1997, but the scale of its 179-seat landslide election victory in that year probably owed something to Blair's personal appeal, which ensured that the party won even in 'safe' Tory territory. The transition from despair to triumphalism on 1 May 1997 was so abrupt that die-hard Labour supporters could be forgiven for their disorientation, at least in the short term. Later, when they woke up to what had really happened to their party, their protests were futile; if Blair had taken them for granted, he could do so without risk because they had no other political home.

Yet the Prime Minister remained an ambiguous figure even after nearly a decade of intense media scrutiny. When asked about his

B

personal tastes, he seemed anxious to choose books or records which would cause minimum offence; he named *Ivanhoe* as his favourite book, even though it was the most backward-looking production of a reactionary Tory. He seemed to be confused about some aspects of his past; certainly he had forgotten the policy commitments to which he had happily subscribed back in 1982. By 2003 there had been no decisive break with the Conservative policies which had changed Britain so radically since 1979. Most importantly, while a stated commitment to 'community' had been the philosophical prin-
▶ ciple which most clearly distinguished Blair from **Margaret Thatcher**, there was no evidence at all that the acquisitive individualism which disfigured eighteen years of Tory rule had been tempered. Blair seemed unduly impressed by successful businessmen, even if the methods which had brought them prosperity would not bear close inspection from the man who prided himself on his personal sense of morality. He even invited Thatcher to Downing Street, despite the fact that her eviction from that address in 1990 had been almost the only thing to cheer Labour supporters between 1979 and 1997.

Superficiality seemed to be enthroned in Number 10. The millennium celebrations, which had Blair's personal sanction, bore the aspect of a grandiose attempt to spin away the social divisions which Labour had been elected to reduce. Briefly, there was an idea that the election had transformed a tired old country into 'Cool Britannia' – merely because more gifted musicians than Blair had been invited to the Prime Minister's house. While few of these celebrities stayed within the charmed circle for very long, Blair was fiercely loyal to other friends. Mandelson, for example, returned to the Cabinet less than a year after an enforced departure from Trade in December 1998. This second stint, at Northern Ireland, was cut short by new evidence of the minister's poor judgement; but even then it seemed that Blair was only waiting for a new opportunity to bring him back. Mandelson was only the most celebrated of 'Tony's Cronies'; he found posts for other personal friends in a government which suffered from personality clashes to compensate for the absence of any debate over principle.

Very soon, commentators on the Blair premiership seized on the idea that Britain now had a presidential government. Blair rarely attended the Commons, and seemed to prefer direct addresses to the nation. Cabinet meetings were brief, and nothing of importance was decided in that forum. Whenever trouble was encountered in a specific policy area, the spin doctors would let it be known that Blair would be taking personal charge of it (although he always seemed to escape the blame if matters subsequently failed to improve). He relished the role of an international statesman, apparently believing in the 'special relationship' with the US and irritating European ◄ leaders with lectures on the superiority of British capitalism. On the European single currency Blair paid a backhanded compliment to his predecessor John Major by adopting exactly the same 'wait and see' policy. The government's initial commitment to an 'ethical foreign policy' should have suited his religious streak, but more familiar priorities soon re-asserted themselves and Cook, the then Foreign Secretary, was lumbered with the blame. The only constructive domestic policy achievements came from Brown, who enjoyed a free hand at the Treasury. This underlined the fact that in 1994 Labour's kingmakers had chosen style over substance.

In the general election of May 2001 it was still possible for the government to attribute every problem to the legacy of the previous administration; and in any case, for reinsurance Blair had promised very little before the 1997 contest. Initial approval ratings for the government had exceeded 75 per cent, but on the eve of the millennium they were down to just over 50 per cent. Even so, this was a remarkable achievement and 'New' Labour's second general election victory was a foregone conclusion. Re-elected with a parliamentary majority of 167, the government could have slipped into a more radical gear to satisfy its moderate left-wing supporters. Yet Blair was still anxious to retain the affection of disillusioned Conservatives. Neutralising the Tories had become an end in itself, even at the cost of neutralising Labour.

In the spring of 2003 Blair's career took a new turn. Previously, he had been accused of enslaving himself to the opinion polls, despite one spectacular miscalculation over fuel taxes in September 2000. Now his determination to stay on good terms with the occupant of the White House – even an extreme right-wing Republican – led him to gamble his career on a war on Iraq which he had previously described as unnecessary. Initially, the polls reflected deep hostility to the conflict, and more than a million people from across the political spectrum marched through London to register their feelings. In the Commons, there was a record rebellion among Labour backbenchers, and Cook resigned from the Cabinet. For the first time there was serious speculation about a replacement for Blair as Prime Minister and Labour leader.

Blair seemed to be aged physically by the experience, but it did not wither his rhetorical powers. Although he was merely playing Dixon of Dock Green to George W. Bush's Judge Dredd, he defended his stance with a passion which he now rarely displayed on domestic matters. When the polls moved in his favour after the outbreak of war he seemed to be vindicated. Yet a third of voters still refused to accept

B

his moral advocacy of war. These dissidents were predominantly 'progressives' – the very body of opinion which had continued to hope that things would get better under Blair. With the loss of this constituency, Blair was left with something very similar to Mrs Thatcher's Falklands coalition: those who gloried in the exercise of Britain's residual power – even in someone else's quarrel – and others who shared Blair's evident belief that Saddam Hussein was the reincarnation of Adolf Hitler, and that he presented a tangible threat to British security.

At the time of writing, Blair's status on the world stage has been greatly enhanced. It remains to be seen whether he can persuade his US allies that the fall of Saddam should be used to reshape the Middle East according to his own moral imperatives. If he succeeds, he will be forgiven by most of the people who marched against him. But even this might not be enough for Blair and his party. In the eyes of his critics, his greatest legacy has been to complete the process of political dealignment in Britain, which gathered pace under Thatcher. Few voters now love their parties, and fewer still love a Prime Minister whose adamantine moral certitudes distance him from the vast majority of Britons. For all of his preaching, Blair is the product of an era of pocket-book politics. In a serious economic downturn, the man who put himself at the head of Bush's 'coalition of the willing' may find himself the helpless captive of a coalition of the greedy.

■ The Blitz

A colloquial term for German air attacks on British cities, derived from *Blitzkrieg*, or 'lightning war'. The term is actually inappropriate, because it describes the speed of the German invasion of Poland and France using fast-moving tank-led armies. This, on the other hand, was a war of attrition. It began with a raid on London on 7 September 1940 and ended with one on Birmingham on 16 May 1941. It was also an improvised strategy. The bombing was concentrated on the capital from 7 September to 2 November, then switched to centres of heavy industry like Coventry and Manchester, then to ports like Glasgow and Plymouth. So-called 'Baedeker Raids' on picturesque cities like York took place in 1942, and rocket attacks hit London in 1944. But once Hitler invaded the Soviet Union in the summer of 1941, the full force of the Luftwaffe was felt elsewhere.

▶ The **Germans'** broad aim was to destroy the morale of the civilian population as well as strategic economic and military targets. They failed on all counts. A lot of destruction was caused, especially when the Luftwaffe switched from blast to incendiary bombs, creating huge firestorms. Approximately 42,000 people were killed and 50,000 seriously wounded, more than the number of British combatants killed in 1940–1. Over 3.5 million houses were damaged or destroyed; for every civilian killed, thirty-five were made homeless. The House of Commons was badly hit, forcing MPs to debate in the House of Lords for the rest of the war. In Coventry, the city's fourteenth-century Gothic cathedral was blown to pieces, along with the entire city centre, in one raid on 14 November 1940 that killed 600 people.

However, factories were quickly returned to production and civilian morale was not destroyed. The idea that 'Britain can take it' soon became widespread and generated one of the enduring legends of the Second World War. The Blitz was the patriotic counterpoint to the **Battle of Britain**: while the 'the Few' were warrior-heroes idolised by ◄ civilians, the Blitz conjured up a spirit of *mass* resistance. The survival of St Paul's Cathedral, thanks to round-the-clock efforts of firemen, clergy and local volunteers, symbolised that resistance. In 1941, J.B. ◄ **Priestley** wrote, 'Britain is being bombed, blasted and burnt into democracy.' The extent to which the Blitz fostered the idea of a 'People's War' and led to the creation of social democracy after 1945 has been exaggerated. Six out of ten Londoners slept at home during the bombing and many who ventured into communal shelters often took their **class** prejudices with them when they left the next ◄ morning.

But once the sentiment is stripped away, it remains true that the Blitz created a potent sense of national unity at a crucial juncture in the war. It also provided the moral foundation for the RAF's area, or 'carpet', bombing of German cities. Arthur Harris (1892–1984), Commander-in-Chief of Bomber Command, promised that Germany had 'sown the wind' and would 'reap the whirlwind', a policy that culminated in the destruction of Dresden on 14 February 1945. Bishop George Bell (1883–1958) led opposition to the policy; after the war, peaceniks condemned it as immoral and branded Harris a war criminal. British bombing did not destroy German morale. But by being sustained it did damage the Third Reich's infrastructure; and it allowed the British to feel that they were hitting back. 'I would not regard the whole of the remaining cities of Germany as worth the bones of one British grenadier,' Harris said. Fuelled by hatred of the Germans, most Britons agreed.

■ Bond, James

Created by Ian Fleming (1908–64), Britain's best-known film character combined the patriotic derring-do of the pre-war imperial spy thriller with the sex and travel allure of the post-war colour supplement.

Fleming was educated at Eton and Sandhurst, before becoming a journalist and City stockbroker. He spent the Second World War as personal assistant to the director of naval intelligence, during which time the idea for Bond came to him. The series began with *Casino Royale* (1953) and ended fourteen best-selling novels later with *The Man With the Golden Gun* (1965).

Albert 'Cubby' Broccoli's film adaptations of the books, starting with *Dr No* (1962), turned James Bond from a stalwart of pulp fiction into a British legend. Of the five actors to portray the character, Sean Connery (1962–71; 1983) was the most popular. Born in Edinburgh in 1930, Connery was a former bricklayer, a Scottish entrant in the Mr

▶ Universe contest and a lifelong supporter of the **Scottish National Party**. Yet he captured better than anyone the freewheeling lifestyle and irreverent patriotism of Fleming's suave English gentleman hero.

The Bond films allowed the British to fantasise that they were still a world power. They constructed an imaginary world where Britain is

▶ leading the defence of Western civilisation during the **Cold War**. American CIA agents play second fiddle to '007' as he dispatches an assortment of Asiatic, Oriental and Slavic villains like Ernst Blofeld with wit and ingenuity, aided by the technical gadgetry invented by MI5's stiff-upper-lipped Quartermaster, 'Q'. It is a world in which you only have to scratch a foreigner to find a villain; but more importantly,

▶ it is a world where Burgess and Maclean never defected and the **Suez crisis** never happened. However, the immense appeal of James Bond in Britain rested, as it did internationally, not on imperial nostalgia but on the contemporary world of mass consumption. Bond's jet-setting adventures portrayed a world of sports cars, casinos, exotic beaches and luxury hotels which appealed to audiences in an era when foreign

▶ **holidays** were just becoming affordable to them.

The success of 007 was also due to the more sexually open nature of British society in the second half of the twentieth century; Bond was rarely without a beautiful woman for the night and this appealed to people enjoying or fantasising about the new opportunities for sexual fulfilment. The American crime novelist, Raymond Chandler, observed that 'Bond is what every man would like to be and what every woman would like to have between the sheets'. The stories contain elements of sado-masochism, which reflected Fleming's own desire to dominate his lovers. 'Honey, get into the bath before I spank you' (*Dr No*) was a typical Bond command. However, the 'Bond Girls' were always intelligent, independent women, well versed in the martial arts and a match for any man, whether working for Britain, like Pussy Galore, or for its enemies, like Rosa Kleb. This, as much as Bond's tuxedoed machismo, explains the popularity of the films

▶ among **women**.

After *The Living Daylights* (1987), producers ran out of Fleming works to adapt and the films became more contrived. But in 2002, the books won a new lease of life, and literary respectability, when they were re-issued as 'Penguin Modern Classics'. Penguin explained their decision to place Fleming's work alongside authors like Kafka and Camus in terms that would have pleased Bond's creator: 'It sets out a sense of very English style which, for good or ill, defines what Englishness is for most people in the world.'

■ **Botham, Ian** (b. 1955)

The summer of 1981 saw the marriage of the Prince of Wales and Lady **Diana** Spencer. But while the memory of that excuse for national cele- ◀ bration was tarnished by subsequent events, the victory of the English **cricket** team in the 'Ashes' Test series still ranks highly among the ◀ finest British sporting achievements of the twentieth century. In the third Test match at Headingley Australia looked certain to win; England were forced to follow on, and at one stage odds of 500–1 were offered against them winning. But a scintillating unbeaten innings of 149 by Ian Botham transformed the match; set 130 to win, the Australians capitulated in the face of brilliant bowling from Botham and Bob Willis.

'Beefy' Botham (known in India as 'Iron Bottom') was one of England's greatest cricketers, a ferocious striker of the ball and a medium-pace bowler who somehow managed to take wickets even with generous half-volleys. His Test record was highly impressive – 383 wickets and more than 5,000 runs – but arguably his greatest contri-bution to the team was his inspiring presence. There was a sense that when Botham was in the England side the unpredictable was inevitable. In 1980 these qualities were recognised when he took over the captaincy, but his form dipped when the formal duties were added to the natural leadership role which he always adopted. A liberated Botham starred throughout the 1981 Ashes series; in another of the matches he recorded a bowling analysis of 5 wickets for 11 runs. England won 3–1.

But while Botham seemed indispensable to the England team, he always attracted controversy and was regarded as an outsider by most members of the cricketing **Establishment**, whether at national or at ◀ county level. He left his first county side, Somerset, in solidarity with the brilliant West Indian players Vivian Richards and Joel Garner, who had been sacked in a bitter factional dispute. In the same year, 1986, rumours about his personal life came to a head. He admitted smoking cannabis, and was banned from first-class cricket for two months. Typically, after his return to the Test team he took a wicket with the

B

first ball he bowled (a particularly poor delivery). But in the last years of his career Botham was handicapped by back injuries. He played the last of 102 Test matches in 1992, and retired in the following year, becoming a television pundit, an indefatigable charity campaigner and an occasional pantomine performer (at one time a Hollywood career was mooted).

Botham was always a heroic figure to most Britons, despite the disapproval from Lord's. His competitive nature, and his obvious zest for the game, made him seem like a character from a schoolboy's comic. At the beginning of the twenty-first century England seemed no closer to finding his successor as match-winning all-rounder. In one sense, at least, Botham would probably never be replaced. His conflicts
▶ with officialdom reflected his working-class roots, contrasting with the comfortable origins of his home-bred contemporaries in the
▶ England side. **Football** provides a more obvious outlet for the talents of young men of Botham's stamp (typically, the latter was gifted enough to make several appearances for Scunthorpe United). Even in football an off-the-field lifestyle which includes more than a nodding acquaintance with intoxicating substances is now held to be incompatible with sporting excellence, even if it never seemed to affect the performances of Ian Terence Botham.

■ **Brady, Ian** (b. 1938) **and Hindley, Myra** (1942–2002)

'God save Myra Hindley / God save Ian Brady / even though he's 'orrible / and she ain't what you call a lady.' So sang the Sex Pistols in their 1978 song 'No One Is Innocent'. The rest of the country believed that these notorious murderers were beyond saving. Most of the dozen or so people that Brady and Hindley randomly killed in their four years together were aged between 16 and 55. But it was their killing of three children in the period 1963–4 that made them folk devils, their crimes underpinning an exaggerated belief that Britain had become a more
▶ violent and perverted country as a result of the '**permissive society**'.

Brady was the dominant partner. The illegitimate son of a Scottish waitress, he was raised by foster-parents in the Gorbals, Glasgow's toughest slum. As a child, he had a reputation for sadism, torturing other children and animals for fun. He graduated to teenage alcoholism and burglary and in 1954 a juvenile court sent him to live with his father in Manchester, where he took his father's name, developed
▶ an interest in the Third Reich and continued a life of petty **crime** that earned him a two-year prison sentence in 1956. On his release, Brady returned to the Gorbals where he got a job as an invoice clerk at a chemical supply company. It was there in January 1961 that he met Myra Hindley.

B

Hindley had been brought up by her grandmother and when she arrived to take up her post as a typist she was a shy, impressionable woman who was soon swept off her feet by Brady's morose intellectuality (he read *Mein Kampf* in his lunch break). Brady nicknamed her 'Myra Hess' and on their first date he took her to a film about the Nuremberg war crimes tribunal, after which they returned to her grandmother's house where he introduced her to sex. The two were soon inseparable and there was nothing Hindley would not do for her lover. She dyed her hair blonde, dressed in Nazi-style uniforms and posed for erotic photos – complete with whips and a dog – which Brady tried unsuccessfully to sell. When he suggested they rob a bank instead, she took shooting and driving lessons. But neither had the courage to go through with the plan and instead they turned their attention to Brady's lifelong obsession with child molestation and murder.

Their first victim was a 16-year-old girl, Pauline Reade, who vanished from her home in Manchester on 12 July 1963. John Kilbride (12), Keith Bennett (12) and Lesley Anne Downey (10) followed over the next 18 months. Police were baffled by these seemingly unrelated disappearances until Hindley's brother-in-law, David Smith, told them he had witnessed the couple commit murder. On 6 October 1965, they had kidnapped a 17-year-old homosexual called Edward Evans and, in the hope of recruiting Smith, invited him round to their flat to watch Evans being killed. When the police responded to Smith's horrified phone call the next day, they arrived at Brady and Hindley's flat to find the couple carrying the corpse out of their bedroom.

At the trial that followed, the depth of their sadism was revealed in the tapes they had made of Lesley Anne Downey's last minutes, in which the 10-year-old was heard pleading for her life while being tortured. Brady's bland description of the tapes as 'unusual' added to the jury's shock and the couple were sentenced to life imprisonment on 6 May 1966, for the murders of Evans, Downey and Kilbride. The pair had buried most of their victims on Saddleworth Moor, north-east of Manchester, a fact which led them to be dubbed 'the Moors Murderers'. Only two bodies were recovered in 1966; a third followed in 1987 after Brady and Hindley helped the police search Saddleworth. The others were never found.

Brady and Hindley spent the rest of their lives in prison. A lone campaign by the maverick Catholic peer Lord Longford for their release provoked public outrage. So too did any attempt to depict or discuss them un-hysterically, like The Smiths' song 'Suffer Little Children' (1984), Marcus Harvey's painting of Hindley, exhibited at the Royal Academy's 'Sensation' exhibition (1997), and Beatrix Campbell's play *And All the Children Cried* (2002). In a rather Calvinistic way, the pair were seen as proof that human beings were innately good or evil; that environment played little part in a person's actions and that redemption for some was impossible. Like Charles Manson in America, Brady and Hindley also came to represent the dark side of the sexual revolution for those who were opposed to it on principle. The pair provided a convenient moral warning of where permissiveness had led and a cipher of collective guilt for it.

Although Brady had initiated the murders, it was Hindley who received the worst vitriol, on the ultimately sexist grounds that there can be no mitigating circumstances when a woman kills a child. Sexual crime reported to the police rose dramatically in the post-war era. For example, recorded rape cases increased by 460 per cent in England and Wales between 1957 and 1987, from 480 a year to 2,228. By 2001, 47,000 sexual crimes were committed annually in the UK. But most of that rise was the result of a greater willingness on the part of victims to come forward thanks to a more sexually open society and a more sophisticated judicial system. Moreover, around 70 per cent of sex crimes continued to be perpetrated within the family unit. However disturbed Brady and Hindley were, their demonisation rested on the British public's refusal to accept that the family home and not the stranger's bedsit was the prime locus of child abuse.

■ British Broadcasting Corporation (BBC)

The most important cultural institution in Britain and, arguably, the entire world. Structurally, it was a compromise between the morally policed but unregulated commercial broadcasting network of the United States, and the overtly authoritarian state control of public monopoly that operated in the Soviet Union. On 18 October 1922, the government licensed the UK's six radio manufacturers to form the British Broadcasting Company, with an initial staff of four and financed by a Post Office licence fee of ten shillings, payable by anyone owning a receiver. Despite many attempts to commercialise the BBC, this remained its prime source of funding. The first broadcast was made on 14 November 1922 from Alexandra Palace in north London.

The political power of the medium became apparent during the
▶ General Strike of 1926. **Stanley Baldwin** forbade **Ramsay MacDonald** the right to reply to his broadcast calling for a halt to strike action; and he stopped the Archbishop of Canterbury, Randall Davidson, making a conciliatory speech to both sides. Fearing the revolutionary potential of radio, the government took control of it soon after the strike ended. The Company was dissolved, shareholders were compensated and on 1 January 1927 a royal charter granted to a new British

Broadcasting Corporation. This arm's-length **nationalisation** worked ◄ thanks to two things: firstly, the conservatism of the Board of Governors (twelve public figures appointed by the Crown on advice from government ministers); and, secondly, Sir John Reith (1889–1971), BBC General Manager (1922–6) and Director-General (1926–38), who shared the late Victorian outlook of the British **Establishment** and ◄ ruthlessly imposed it on the BBC.

Reith was a devout member of the **Church of Scotland** who ◄ believed that the BBC had a mission to raise public taste and create a common culture around it. The Corporation became a patron of the arts. Among other things, it began sponsoring the Henry Wood Proms, set up the BBC Symphony Orchestra (1930) and commissioned works from British composers, notably the uncompleted Third Symphony of **Sir Edward Elgar**. In 1926 Reith set up a Committee on Spoken English ◄ in order to police the accents and diction of announcers and performers. Protestantism was upheld by a Central Religious Advisory Committee. Set up in 1928 and consisting of church leaders from the main denominations, until 1947 CRAC imposed strict limits on the airtime given to atheists and other faiths, especially **Roman Catholics**. ◄ When Reith retired, Sir Cecil Graves was vetoed as his successor on the grounds that he was a Catholic, and the post was given instead to an inept but Protestant Oxford don, Sir William Ogilvie (1938–41).

For all its bigotry and snobbery, Reith's BBC became genuinely popular and did more than any other institution to foster a sense of nationhood in the first age of mass democracy. Between 1922 and 1939, the number of 'wireless' licences rose from 1 million to 9 million; the readership of the *Radio Times*, which started publication in 1923, rose to 2.6 million in 1939 and reached 8.8 million in 1955. Music, comedy and sport were the Corporation's staples. The most popular programmes were Henry Hall's BBC Dance Orchestra, Arthur Askey's *Bandwagon* and football coverage. The first running commentary for a sporting event was the **rugby** match between England and ◄ Wales in 1927; Wimbledon, the Boat Race, the Grand National and the FA Cup Final soon followed. In 1932, the **Empire** Service was set up, ◄ transmitting news and talks to British territories, the most popular of which was the King's Christmas message. In 1938, it was renamed the World Service and began broadcasting in foreign languages around the world, with 153 million devoted listeners by 2003.

During the Second World War the BBC reached its zenith, acquiring a reputation as the voice of democracy which it never entirely lost. News coverage was increased (previously, it had been limited to placate press barons worried about the effect radio would have on newspaper circulation) and reporting was relatively truthful except where it had to be censored in order to protect battle plans. The news thus acquired an almost liturgical appeal, especially to those under Axis occupation who often risked their lives to listen to the World Service. The Corporation's features output became the fountainhead of British wartime propaganda. **Churchill** had a lifelong dislike of the BBC, believing that it was 'honeycombed with socialists' and once described it as 'the enemy within the gates'. He threatened to take over the Corporation unless it proved itself capable of maintaining national morale, which it did. The Prime Minister's rousing speeches formed a tiny fraction of the 80,000 words a day directed at the British people from 1940 to 1945 through talks, drama, comedy and discussion shows which celebrated the nation's way of life.

Reith was suspicious of the invention of television by fellow Scot John Logie Baird (1888–1946), believing it to be 'an awful snare' that would encourage more populist broadcasting. Though less dictatorial than Reith, William Haley had a similar view of the BBC's role, and as Director-General (1942–53) he took the policy of 'compulsory uplift' a stage further in 1946 by adding a station devoted entirely to the arts, the Third Programme, which failed to attract listeners. Executives' dislike of television was nearly the Corporation's undoing. The BBC is usually credited with the first TV broadcast. In fact it was made by the Third Reich, when the German Post Office transmitted pictures of the Berlin Olympics in 1936. On 2 November 1936, the first regular TV pictures were broadcast from Alexandra Palace in London (Japan followed in 1940, the US in 1945 and France in 1947). However, the service was limited, sets were expensive and by 1939 there were only 20,000 licence-holders, most in the London area. The service was closed on the outbreak of war. Haley only reluctantly re-introduced it in 1946 to cover the Victory Parade that year, and starved it of investment. **William Beveridge**'s 1949 Report on Broadcasting upheld the BBC's monopoly on the grounds that its *raison d'être* was educative.

But when Churchill returned to power two years later, he approved the introduction of commercial television, outlined in a 1952 White Paper. The successful televising of the Coronation of Elizabeth II, watched by 56.6 per cent of the population (compared to 32 per cent who listened on radio) boosted the BBC's reputation, but did not prevent the passing of the Television Act on 31 July 1954. During the Bill's passage through the House of Lords, Reith accused its supporters of 'doing moral hurt to Britain'. In fact, they began a media revolution which, over the next half-century, transformed British life, mostly for the better.

At first, the BBC was trounced by the commercial network, which began broadcasting on 22 September 1955. Within two years, **ITV** had won 76 per cent of audience share, a situation made worse by the fact that many of the BBC's best producers, technicians and performers defected to the competition. ITV's popularity was partly the result of its populist approach of 'giving the people what they want', by offering more variety shows and crime drama, and by adapting American formats like the **situation comedy** and quiz show (*Double Your Money* [1955–68], based on the US show *The $64,000 Question* was an example of the latter). The Pilkington Inquiry of 1962 condemned the output of the commercial network as 'trivial' and praised the BBC for maintaining broadcasting standards.

However, the fierce competition which the BBC continued to endure forced it to modernise. In 1958, the money it spent on TV outstripped that spent on radio for the first time; in 1960 a new Television Centre was opened in Shepherd's Bush, west London; and in the same year, Hugh Greene became Director-General. Greene (1910–87) was the first holder of the post to take popular culture seriously and he relaxed the Corporation's guidelines on nudity and swearing which had previously shaped its policy of 'compulsory uplift'. The result was that the BBC began to produce quality programmes with mass appeal, some of which became defining points of British life: situation comedy like *Dad's Army* (1968–77), **crime** shows like *Z Cars* (1964–74), science fiction like *Doctor Who* (1963–89), sport like *Match of the Day* (1964–) and drama like *The Wednesday Play* (1965–70). Greene also sponsored the so-called 'satire boom' which gave birth to a more anarchic and politicised form of British comedy, in the programmes *That Was The Week That Was* (1962–3) and **Monty Python's Flying Circus** (1967–75). The renaissance of British pop music, and of youth culture in general, were celebrated in the TV show *Top of the Pops* (1964–) and with the launch of Radio One in 1967 (the old Light, Third and Home stations became Radios Two, Three and Four). The creation of Radio One followed the Labour government's closure of offshore, 'pirate' radio stations in 1967, and it was not until the Broadcasting Act of 1972 that commercial radio was licensed in the UK (the first, London's Capital Radio, launched in 1973).

A second TV channel, BBC2, was introduced in 1964, devoted largely to the arts but with a more open-minded approach to educative broadcasting than that which had discredited the Third Programme. From 1972, when broadcasting time limits were lifted, BBC2 screened lectures for the Open **University**, helping to give millions of adults a second chance to gain a university degree. Colour transmissions began in 1967. The BBC Complaints Commission was started in 1971 (replaced by the government's Broadcasting Complaints Commission in 1981) in an effort to show that it was listening to the public, although most of the complaints it received were from conservatives unhappy about the Corporation's abandonment of Reithian moral values. In 1977, the **Morecambe and Wise** *Christmas Special* was

▶ watched by half the UK population and in 1985, the Corporation
finally launched a **soap opera**, *EastEnders*, to match ITV's *Coronation
Street* in popularity. All of this helped to push up the number of TV
licence holders from 4.5 million in 1955 to 23.7 million in 2002.

Although politicians of left and right were perennially convinced of
the BBC's political bias, it remained a neutral institution. This was
reflected in the fact that most Britons still turned to the BBC in
▶ moments of national crisis like the **Falklands** conflict and the 9/11
attacks on America (on which day 35 million Britons watched BBC
news). That tendency, coupled with the developments described
above, meant that the BBC was in good health when faced with the
biggest challenge of its life: the satellite broadcasting revolution.

The video revolution of the early 1980s gave viewers the choice of
when to watch the programmes they liked (by the end of the decade
over 64 per cent of the population had a video recorder). Satellite
broadcasting, which began in 1989 with the launch of Sky TV, and
digital broadcasting, which followed in 1998, gave people a greater
choice of *what* to watch. The BBC, led by a new breed of Director-
Generals who had made their reputations in commercial TV – John
Birt (1991–9) and Greg Dyke (2000–4) – responded in two ways. First,
the internal market known as 'producer choice' was introduced.
Although some argued that it stifled creativity with too many
bureaucrats and accountants, it did make the production process
more variegated because the Corporation now had a statutory obligation that 25 per cent of its commissioned output would be made by
independent producers. Second, the BBC launched new channels
from 1994 onwards which raised its annual TV output to over 30,000
hours. These included BBC World, a TV version of the World Service
designed to rival America's CNN, and UK Gold, a repeats channel
designed to help the BBC exploit its archives, in which task it was
assisted by a new BBC merchandising company, BBC Worldwide Ltd.
The corporation's website, launched in 1997, is the most popular in
Britain, attracting 6.4 million regular users, a third of the country's
internet population.

Like their predecessors in the 1950s, liberal critics of the new BBC
argued that commerce and culture were not compatible. In fact, it had
remained one of the great British institutions by adapting to a
changing world in order to show that public service broadcasting had
a crucial role to play in it. 'We are not Britain. We are the BBC,' said a
news editor rebutting claims of political bias during the Falklands
war. The corporation's achievement was to convince the world that
the two were not entirely dissimilar.

■ British Empire

The British Empire, wrote the imperial apologist J.R. Seeley in 1883, was acquired 'in a fit of absence of mind'. There was never a master plan for world domination sitting in Whitehall and Threadneedle Street. But, like most European empires, the British one was driven by the desire of the nation's ruling **classes** to enrich and aggrandise themselves, and it was primarily justified by a view of other nations and races as inferior. The British Empire made global pursuits of capitalism, Protestantism, parliamentary democracy, the English **language**, railway travel and **football**. That was no mean or malevolent achievement. But in the process, millions of people were enslaved and exploited. Even at its most benign, the main economic beneficiaries were the British, and later the Americans, who built their own empire on the rubble of Europe's. As **George Orwell**, once a police officer in Burma, observed in *Not Counting Niggers* (1939), 'It is quite common for an Indian coolie's leg to be thinner than the average Englishman's arm.'

In its first three hundred years, the British Empire was a loose conglomeration of trading posts run by chartered monopoly companies. A proto-English Empire was established in Scotland, Wales, Ireland and France in the twelfth and thirteenth centuries, but it was not until Tudor times that colonisation began in earnest with the settlement of Virginia in 1585. The first Indian colony followed in 1610 and the first Caribbean one in 1623. Once the Scots had put aside their differences with the English in the Union of 1707, they proved to be a rapacious imperial partner, providing proportionately more investors, engineers, troops and governors than the English and Welsh. Indeed, Empire was the foundation of the modern British state, welding together the island's three nations in a common cause like no other. Neither the loss of America in 1776 nor the abolition of slavery in 1809 halted the Britannic advance. The Antipodes began to be colonised in 1788 and Africa in 1882. The Empire reached its zenith in 1918. Victory in the First World War enabled the British to grab former **German** and Ottoman territories, mostly in the Middle East. By the time that the British people won the right to vote in 1928, they ruled a fifth of the world's population, covering a quarter of the planet – some 500 million people.

The majority of those subjects were people of colour and few had the right to vote themselves. By the 1880s, the Empire had become a more formal political one: run by **civil servants** as much as merchants; kept in check by armed force; and justified, both at home and abroad, by the ideology of *imperialism*. This was partly based on a belief in white supremacy that was 'scientifically' grounded in the

▶ **social Darwinism** of the British eugenics movement. But it competed with a more liberal ideology which saw the British imperial mission as a benign one. Variously described as 'the white man's burden'

▶ (**Rudyard Kipling**) or 'the greatest secular agency for good that the world has ever seen' (Lord Rosebery) the Empire was designed not to

▶ exploit people but to liberate them from **poverty**, ignorance and superstition. Or so claimed a ruling class which, by the turn of the twentieth century, was worried by the growth of mass democracy and socialism in Britain, and by the spread of militant discontent in the colonies. Imperialism offered a way of uniting otherwise antagonistic classes and races around the Union Jack, and for a time it succeeded.

In schoolrooms from Hackney to Harare, children were taught the benefits of *Pax Britannica*. Outside school, imperialism was fostered in

▶ a variety of ways: through Test-match **cricket** (1878); at the track and field events of the Commonwealth Games (an alternative to the Olympics, started in 1930); at royal ceremonials like the Jubilees of 1897 and 1935, and George V's coronation as Emperor of India at Delhi

▶ in 1911; through **BBC** broadcasts like the King's Christmas Empire

▶ message (1932); at **great exhibitions** and massed rallies like that at Wembley (1924–5); in comics like the *Boy's Own Paper* (1879–1967); films like Alexander Korda's *Sanders of the River* (1935) and, above all, through

▶ the **Scouting** movement of Baden-Powell. In 1916, the Empire Day Movement, led by a Scottish aristocrat, Lord Meath, persuaded the government to make Queen Victoria's birthday (24 May) 'Empire Day'. This remained the focal point of imperial festivities around the world until the 1940s (it was abolished in 1962).

Propaganda was underpinned by pragmatism. Even at its height, the Empire consisted of different states with varying degrees of autonomy: Dominions (e.g. Canada), Protectorates (e.g. Egypt), Colonies (e.g. Nigeria) and Mandates (e.g. Palestine). Partly this reflected the haphazard way that Britain's sprawling Empire had developed, through conquest, settlement and the exigencies of war and diplomacy with other colonial powers. But from the 1840s onwards it was also the result of a deliberate strategy to rule, where possible, by proxy. Like the Romans, on whom the British liked to model themselves, Britain's Empire was maintained by allowing others to take the strain. When Canada, Australia and New Zealand became self-governing Dominions in the mid-nineteenth century, white settlers were empowered to control indigenous populations. They did so as much by playing off different tribes, religions and races against each other as by brute force. In countries like India which remained under direct rule, 'native' cultures were allowed to flourish and their upper classes, or castes, helped the British to rule. Collaborative Asians were also enlisted to govern African and Caribbean colonies, sometimes going there especially for that purpose, as in Kenya and Trinidad. The second Anglo-Boer War (1899–1902) proved that this policy was fallible. Although Britain was victorious, the Union of South Africa which emerged in 1910 was bitterly divided between English colonists who favoured a degree of racial integration and Dutch settlers who favoured what they called *apartheid* or separate development.

Partly as a result of the Boer War, and partly because of imperial competition from Germany, Japan and the United States, attempts to make the Empire a more cohesive unit gained a new urgency in the first half of the twentieth century. The **Tariff Reform** League (1903–6) ◄ led by Joseph Chamberlain sought to create a unified trading block that gave preferment to imperial goods. Eventually, the Ottowa Conference of 1932 established a limited system of imperial preference, elements of which remained in place until the UK joined the EEC in 1973. The Round Table Movement (1909–39) argued that the Empire should become a federation of equal states, united by an imperial parliament at Westminster. This met with less success, although in the 1930s its leading activists, like Lord Lothian (1882–1940), transferred their interest in federalism to the idea of a United States of **Europe** ◄ and influenced the French founders of the European Union. Meanwhile, the preferred policy of British governments remained **devolu-** ◄ **tion**, based on the idea of a new 'Commonwealth of Nations', a phrase coined in 1884 by the liberal imperialist Lord Rosebery (1847–1929). Although devolution was fiercely resisted within the United Kingdom, notably over Irish Home Rule, the granting of more autonomy to the imperial periphery accelerated between 1918 and 1939 as the threat from nationalist movements grew (plans to make India a Dominion were drawn up in 1935).

The Second World War began the end of Empire. Approximately 5 million people from 50 different nationalities fought in the British armed services during the war. Three and a half million were people of colour, most of whom defied nationalist pressure to revolt against the British and chose instead to fight fascism. But the rapid conquest of Far Eastern colonies by the Japanese in 1941–3 dispelled the myth of British invincibility and so made independence movements more plausible, popular and ferocious. In 1942, the Viceroy of India, who had declared war against Germany without consulting Indian leaders, put down the biggest uprising in the sub-continent since the Indian Mutiny of 1857, killing 2,000 people and imprisoning 60,000. As Chancellor of the Exchequer Hugh Dalton (1887–1962) said of Palestine, 'You cannot have a secure base on top of a wasps' nest.' After 1945, the huge financial cost of defeating Germany, coupled with the burden of **Cold War** against the Soviet Union, also made it harder for the British ◄

B

to maintain their Empire at full stretch. As a result of these pressures, India was partitioned and, together with the new state of Pakistan, granted independence in 1947. Palestine was handed over to the United Nations in the same year.

However, British governments continued to believe that the vestiges of Empire could be maintained by managing its transition to a Commonwealth. Between 1947 and 1957 the number of recruits to the colonial service rose by 50 per cent. Only four colonies – Ceylon (1948), Sudan (1956), the Gold Coast and Malaya (1957) – became independent in that period. And in 1949 parliament passed the Colonial Development Act, a Keynesian measure which injected state funds into the poorest colonies in an attempt to offset discontent by raising black living standards, as well as to maintain corporate profits. When the Soviet Union began funding colonial rebels during the Cold War, the fear of Communism among the black and Asian middle classes helped to shore up the appeal of British rule. Attempts were also made to federate the worst trouble spots like Rhodesia and Nyasaland (1953). Most importantly of all, in 1948, Westminster passed the British Nationality Act. This granted full British citizenship to every inhabitant of the Empire, in theory making ruler and ruled equal. However, all this failed to stem demands for independence and the UK became embroiled in several nasty colonial wars, including Cyprus (1954–9) and Kenya (1952–60).

▶ Britain's failure to complete the invasion of Egypt during the **Suez crisis** showed that Empire could no longer be maintained by force without American support. The Americans had long been critical of British imperialism, though more out of jealousy than principle. Still, the US now had the economic muscle to make its ally act. The British government's decision to secure an alternative power base by applying for membership of the European Community led Prime Minister Harold Macmillan to herald 'a wind of change' in a speech to the parliament of South Africa on 1 March 1960. The scuttling of Empire got under way soon after. Of the sixty-four nations that ceased to be ruled by the British between the independence of India in 1947 and the ceding of Hong Kong to China in 1997, thirty-seven were given up between 1960 and 1973. Fifty-one remained Commonwealth members, including twenty-nine which became republics. Far-right groups like A.K. Chesterton's League of Empire Loyalists and die-hards within the

▶ **Conservative Party** opposed decolonisation, and many more Britons regretted the loss of national prestige.

But the majority broadly supported decolonisation. Popular imperialism had been in decline since the 1930s, and by the 1950s indifference reigned – a fact demonstrated by the government's failure to revive Empire Day observance in a new 'Commonwealth

Week' between 1958 and 1962. Opposition to Common Market membership was partly motivated by a sentimental attachment to the Commonwealth. But this was mainly a racist attachment to white Dominions rather than support for the Commonwealth as a viable post-imperial polity. Ultimately, the British cared more about keeping their country white than they did about being members of a multi-racial 'family of nations'.

This was proved by the massive public support for the 1962 Commonwealth Immigrants Act, which limited black immigration to the UK, and began to close the door which had been thrown open by the 1948 Nationality Act. The public also supported the 1981 Nation-ality Act which repealed that of 1948 and so ended the illusion that all Commonwealth citizens were equal under the law. Few people cared how much these measures offended black and Asian Commonwealth states. And few were vexed when South Africa declared itself a republic and left the Commonwealth in 1961 in order to secure the apartheid system. Anti-apartheid campaigns between then and majority rule in 1994 excited left-wing activists and church leaders, but among the rest of the population only cricket fans, angry at the boycott of the South African team, cared about the issue. The Falklands War of 1982 briefly revived imperial sentiment among ◄ right-wing Conservatives. But to the nation at large, the conflict was primarily about standing up to dictators and so echoed the patriotism of the Second World War. And the emotion generated by the episode had dissipated within a generation.

The British Empire was never as benign as its apologists claimed, nor as oppressive as its critics said. The wealth that it generated mostly benefited the inhabitants of the UK and the patriotism it inspired until the 1940s underpinned the union of Scotland, England and Wales rather than the imperial 'family' that romantic imperialists liked to dream of. The end of Empire also mainly affected Britain by undermining the *raison d'être* of the United Kingdom and so helping to foster Scottish and Welsh nationalism. British rule rarely matched the systematic barbarity of, say, the Belgian Congo or the Americans in Vietnam. Moreover, the corruption and violence that continued to blight countries like Nigeria and Zimbabwe after independence showed that not all the problems of the Third World could be blamed on British rule. But the final analysis must rest with the people of former colonies. Few of the millions who died resisting, or enduring, British rule, nor even those who died resisting post-colonial dictators would wish to see the Union Jack raised again outside the compound of a British Embassy.

■ British Legion

B

Umbrella organisation for war veterans in the UK, formally known as the Royal British Legion. Founded in 1921 by the amalgamation of four ex-servicemen's organisations, it was a product of the First World War and the combination of altruism towards, and fear of, the working class which the war intensified. The social dislocation caused by veterans' mental and physical trauma, coupled with industrial unrest and disillusionment with war as an instrument of foreign policy, made the need to bring officers and men together in one body seem more pressing than hitherto. Like the **Women's Institute**, the Legion was established and run by the upper classes and like the WI it became a genuinely popular and useful organisation.

In 1921, the Legion introduced Poppy Day, selling artificial poppies (symbolising the fields of Flanders) to raise money for veterans in distress from disability, sickness and unemployment. It became the best-known charity appeal in the UK. The Legion also campaigned successfully to improve war pensions. A Royal Charter was granted in 1925, and with it came valuable royal patronage. During the Second World War, its members played a significant part in civil defence, staffing the ARP and Home Guard. The organisation grew in size after 1945. Its ranks were swelled not only by those who had fought Continental fascism, but also by former national service **conscripts** who fought against colonial independence movements, for example in Korea (1950–3) and in Kenya (1952–60). Professional veterans of the civil war in Northern Ireland (1969–) added to its numbers.

The British Legion's welfare work served veterans of all conflicts. But the organisation was best known for the part it played in memorialising the two world wars against Germany. Each year, veterans laid wreaths on memorials around the UK on Remembrance Sunday, established in 1919; at the annual Cenotaph service in London, the central feature was a march-past by legionnaires. The public's relative indifference to the veterans of other conflicts lay not just in the smaller losses incurred during those conflicts, but also in the fact that the motives for and outcomes of them were less glorious.

Conscious of the need to involve younger Britons in the act of Remembrance, the Legion enlisted a pop group, the Spice Girls, to help **Vera Lynn** launch the Poppy Appeal in 1994. It also campaigned for a two-minute silence to be observed on 11 November each year, a custom established in the 1920s but which had died out after the Second World War. A slight revival took place but observance remained sporadic. The Legion recognised the limits of Remembrance. It decided that the 50th anniversary celebrations of VE Day, in 1995, should be the last of their kind and it criticised the **Conservative** government for trying to make political capital out of the event. By the 1970s, membership of the British Legion was beginning to dwindle, down from over 3 million in 1950 to half a million in 2003. This was a testament to the relative peace that legionnaires, and those who never lived to become one, had helped to win. But growing public indifference towards the Legion indicated that world war had become a distant memory for most Britons. And, perhaps, it demonstrated that the first casualty of peace is sometimes the vigilance of generations who enjoy its benefits.

B

C

■ Campaign for Nuclear Disarmament (CND)

In May 1957 Britain successfully tested a hydrogen bomb for the first time. It was committed to an independent 'deterrent', to be delivered by bombers or a missile which was under development. Actually, its first atomic test had occurred back in October 1952, on an island off the north-west coast of Australia. But the advent of the H-bomb marked a decisive step into the shadow of the mushroom cloud. To signal the changed emphasis in defence strategy, a White Paper
▶ published at this time proposed the phasing out of **conscription**.

Later in that year, those who opposed Britain's membership of the
▶ world's 'nuclear club' were dismayed by the decision of the **Labour Party** conference to reject the case for unilateral disarmament. In fact, Britain had first committed itself to atomic weapons under a Labour government, in January 1947. On that occasion the issue had been decided by just six ministers. At the 1957 conference the procedure was equally dubious from the democratic point of view, but the tally of 5.8 million votes to 781,000 at least sounded more conclusive and
▶ **Nye Bevan**, who might have been a standard-bearer for disarmers, had
▶ delivered a crushing speech against their position. The **Liberal Party** was anti-nuclear, but it had no chance of forming a government. The only way forward for opponents of the bomb seemed to be the application of extra-parliamentary pressure. A group dominated by intel-
▶ lectuals and politicians, such as **J.B. Priestley, Bertrand Russell** and Michael Foot, formed the Campaign for Nuclear Disarmament on 17 February 1958. This left-wing line-up was in itself significant. Since the Soviet Union possessed nuclear weapons, there was no good reason
▶ why independent-minded **Conservative** supporters should not join the movement to rid the whole world of this menace. As it was, from the outset CND was seen as a movement exclusively for fellow-travellers and their dupes, even though it was formed at a time of general left-wing disillusionment with Moscow. This ideological profile made
▶ it much easier to discredit in the **Cold War** context.

That Easter, CND organised the first march from central London to the weapons research facility at Aldermaston in Berkshire. The four-day walk was completed by around 4,000 people. The 1960 renewal, taking the reverse route and ending with a rally in Trafalgar Square, attracted up to 75,000. At that year's Labour conference the party finally adopted an anti-nuclear resolution. However, at the 1961 conference Hugh Gaitskell persuaded delegates to drop the policy, despite the fact that the attendance at the Trafalgar Square rally had swollen to almost 100,000. The decline of the movement in the wake of the Cuban missile crisis of October 1962 (and Britain's new reliance on US delivery systems) was surprising. But there had been internal disputes over civil disobedience, leading to the formation of a splinter group, the inaptly-named 'Committee of 100', which attracted disproportionate publicity because of the adherence of rebellious celebrities like Russell and **John Osborne**. The year 1963 saw the release of ◄ Stanley Kubrick's savage comedy *Dr Strangelove*, which won Oscar nominations despite its unflattering portrait of US foreign policymaking. But the Aldermaston march attracted a much smaller body of pacifist pedestrians this time, and led to several arrests. It was decided not to hold it again.

In 1980 CND revived, in response to the US decision to site cruise missiles at British bases. In June a demonstration in London attracted over 50,000, including Foot who became leader of his party before the end of the year. In August 1981 a march of **women** to Greenham ◄ Common, one of the offending bases, led to the establishment of a permanent peace camp. At that time opinion polls suggested that CND's objectives were shared by around a third of the public, and at its 1981 conference Labour re-adopted the policy of unilateral disarmament. Local councils and student unions declared themselves 'nuclear free zones'. However, within two years public support had more than halved, and at the 1983 general election Labour's unilateralist stance was used against it by the Conservatives. It had already helped to persuade dissidents like David Owen to form the breakaway **Social Democratic Party** (SDP), although, ironically, this much-hyped ◄ body never attracted as many members as did CND in its heyday (in 1986 the latter claimed more than 100,000 members, and around double that figure if one included local-based groups).

Certainly, unilateralism was never a vote-winner for Labour, and the policy was ditched after the 1987 general election. The 1986 accident at Chernobyl in the Soviet Union had brought a new spasm of fear against all things nuclear. But improved East–West relations were undermining the movement. It seemed foolish for Britain to renounce nuclear weapons at a time when they could be used as a bargaining counter in a more general disarmament. After the fall of Communism, and the removal of cruise missiles even from Greenham, it was widely believed that the argument in favour of the British 'deterrent' had paid off after all.

Observers of the early CND marches were struck by the tendency of supporters to be young and middle-class. Of course, this was the social group with the most to lose from the destruction of life on earth. But this eventuality might also be inconvenient for older, working-class people, and their scanty representation in the duffel-coated ranks was significant. It suggested that the argument for nuclear weapons at its most basic – that they were unpleasant things in themselves, but that if others had them Britain had better stay in the 'club' – was good enough for people who were preoccupied with 'bread and butter' issues, even at times of heightened international tension.

This line of argument was reasonable enough when club membership was restricted to great powers, who in any case had a reasonable chance of wiping each other out by conventional means. But the logic assumed that unwelcome states could be blackballed if they tried to develop their own infernal devices. After the end of the Cold War, while Western leaders were still congratulating them-selves for having triumphed by standing up against the threat of Soviet aggression, the real nightmare began as the weapons spread to the sub-continent of Asia. And having lectured former Commu-nist countries about the moral superiority of the free-market system, capitalist leaders could hardly complain if their pupils prof-ited by selling weapons-grade material to 'rogue' states, or even to terrorist organisations which regarded the prospect of 'mutually assured destruction' with equanimity.

Yet there was no chance of a belated victory for the ideals of CND. Once it had been released, it was impossible to talk (or march) the nuclear genie back into the bottle.

■ Carry On films

A series of 31 low-budget comedy films produced by Peter Rogers between 1958 and 1992 which epitomised the British love of slapstick farce, bawdy, toilet humour and camp posturing. The first, *Carry On Sergeant*, set in an army base, was not overtly sexual; although by sending up the British class system, it did establish another theme of the series. The second, *Carry On Nurse* (1959), displayed the hallmarks that made the *Carry Ons* so popular and it contained many of the actors who became stalwarts of the series: Kenneth Williams (prudish); Sid James (lecherous); Barbara Windsor (vacuous); Charles Hawtrey (wet); Hattie Jacques (pompous); Kenneth Connor (weak); Bernard Bresslaw (gormless); Joan Sims (coy) and Jim Dale (gauche). Their dialogue was based on the *double entendre*. The plots involved men pursuing women for sex and being thwarted by domineering wives and disapproving bosses. The settings ranged from the Wild West to ancient Egypt. But most of the films were based in Britain and, in particular, NHS hospitals which offered ample scope for jokes about bodily functions, together with curvaceous, tightly-uniformed nurses, a common object of sexual fantasy for British men.

The majority – nineteen – were made in the decade 1963–73 and at their best the *Carry Ons* were reminiscent of Joe Orton's (1933–67) plays, in which anarchic sexual transgression was used to subvert authority. Coincidentally, Kenneth Williams (1926–88) was a close

friend of Orton and both were working-class **homosexuals**. 'I do not ◀
object to jiggery, but I do take exception to pokery,' says Charles
Hawtrey in *Carry On Doctor* (1967). Together with *Carry On Camping*
(1968) and *Carry On Up the Khyber* (1969), this formed the high-point of
the series. At their worst, the films were formulaic emblems of a
furtive, predatory sexual culture in which women were either ugly
matrons or half-witted sex objects. As such, *Carry Ons* belonged, with
Confessions of a Window Cleaner (1975), in a tatty British genre – the sex
comedy – that attracted few cinemagoers outside the UK. By the time
Carry on Dick (1974) was released (the last to include Sid James and
Barbara Windsor) the films had begun to lose their appeal to the
British as well. In a new age of sexual frankness and explicitness, the
double entendre was less amusing and the sight of a woman in bra and
knickers was less exciting. Only five more were made before the last,
Carry On Columbus (1992).

Carry Ons marked a halfway point in British culture between the
prurient, late Victorian world of the saucy seaside postcard and the
erotic, carnivalesque world of promiscuity and **pornography** which ◀
emerged in the 1960s. The films pushed forward the boundaries of
slap-and-tickle humour but remained trapped within it. Their continuing popularity among older Britons was based on two things:
nostalgia for what some imagined was a more innocent era; and a
humorous reaction to contemporary political correctness that was
certainly necessary but which the *Carry Ons* were ill-equipped to serve.
Just before killing himself with an overdose of barbiturates in 1988,
Kenneth Williams wrote in his diary, 'Oh – what's the bloody point?'
It might stand as an epitaph to the films in which he threw away a
promising career in the Shakespearian theatre.

■ Children

Sentimentality towards children was a marked feature of Britain in
the second half of the nineteenth century. For evangelical philanthropists, it seemed far more sensible to save tender young souls from a life
of sin than to waste precious time on their corrupted elders (later, this
assumption gave anti-abortion campaigners their cue to prioritise the
rights of the unborn child over those of the mother). Hence, for
example, Dr Barnardo opened his first home for orphans in 1870.
Where private charity led, the state was sure to follow. Also in
1870, Forster's Education Act brought universal literacy within reach,
and the Factory Act of 1874 increased the minimum age for half-time
work (five hours per day) from 8 to 10.

Yet children needed to survive their first few months in order to
enjoy these new privileges, and infant mortality scarcely improved

during the nineteenth century. In this sense children in the fiction of
▶ **Thomas Hardy** generally fared even worse than Little Nell and other
doomed Dickensians. In 1900, 142 infants under the age of one died
for every 1,000 live births: they accounted for a quarter of the annual
death rate. Afterwards the improvement was dramatic. In the first
decade of the twentieth century standards of midwifery were enforced
by law, and advice for pregnant women and new mothers was more
readily available. Under the Children Act (1908) parents were held
legally responsible if they neglected their children; and the youngsters
who had proved less than angelic were winnowed out from adult
offenders in the legal and penal systems. By 1910 the mortality rate
was down to 110 per 1,000; in 1950 it was 31; and by the end of the
twentieth century it was less than 6. Death before a baby's first
birthday was now so rare (about 1 per cent of the annual toll) that
sinister explanations were often sought when it happened.

Although the evangelical heart was still beating, the new paternalism arose from a more pragmatic spirit. The most effective way to
refresh a sickly and ill-educated population was to look after the rising
generation. The state could compensate for the shortcomings of poor
parents with free school meals and regular medical inspections. At the
same time, the new realisation that a child was for life had a marked
effect on parental attitudes. For middle-class couples, at least, it now
made sense to map out the future for their children. This tendency has
entered the realm of the surreal in recent years, since proud parents
are allowed to discover the sex of the child in advance even in the
absence of any medical need to know. Some hospitals, though, decided
not to offer this service because they fully expected to be dragged
through the courts if they gave out the wrong information.

In his brilliant book *The Rise of the Meritocracy* (1958), Michael Young
had predicted that a decline in class loyalty would displace parental
aspirations onto their children. 'The cult of the child', he thought,
would become 'the drug of the people'. The prophecy was uncannily
accurate. Children became proxy warriors in the battle to keep up
with (or preferably beat) the Joneses; conversations over the garden
fence, complete with unpardonable exaggerations, would focus on
how well little Johnny and Jane were 'getting on' at school. But Johnny
and Jane were unlikely to have many siblings. The near-certainty of
infant survival meant that parents could plan the size of their families
without having their calculations disrupted by bereavements; and
they could also anticipate (with increasing dismay) the costs incurred
on each happy event. The birth rate declined steeply between 1900 (28
per 1,000 population) and 1930 (16.8). It then stabilised, partly because
of the introduction of tax incentives (a cunning ruse which encour-
▶ aged only the tax-paying classes to breed). But in the **'permissive'** era

decline set in again, and by the end of the century it was barely more than 10 per 1,000 – well below the level required to sustain existing population levels without large-scale immigration.

It was no part of the new rational approach to family life that the little cherubs should develop into hooligans, but after the Second World War middle-class adults began to wonder if they had been nurturing cuckoos in their suburban nests. The rising statistics for **crime** among young people led to a proliferation of anguished books ◄ on the subject and, in 1956, the establishment of a Home Office committee. Policy-makers were increasingly interested in the problem of boredom among the young, which seemed to be at the root of 'teenage delinquency'. Crime was only the most troubling manifestation of a growing gap between attitudes across the generations. The real cause of the problem was the increasing affluence which politicians were hell-bent on perpetuating, and the technological developments which accompanied it. But the most common reaction was the attempt to bribe children into obedience (or even love) with higher pocket-money. In 2002 research suggested that even in relatively poor households children aged between 11 and 14 received an average of over £6 per week. Naturally, this only accentuated the original difficulty. A third of children admitted that they 'spent their cash without thinking', with the trend becoming more marked as they grew older. In a nice snapshot of modern **morality** in a **consumerist** society, one ◄ market analyst happily noted the 'positive consequences for products and services' directed at children.

One way of rationalising the generation gap was to concede that children were now growing up more rapidly. Evidence of 'maturity' typically depends on the viewpoint of the beholder; at best, it could be said that post-war children grew up differently. But the obvious gulf in sensibilities seemed to demand some sort of recognition by the state. The 1969 Family Law Reform Act reduced the official age of majority from 21 to 18. In part, this was merely a reflection of existing trends – that young people were wanting to set up their own households long before the old rite of passage which granted them 'the key of the door'. At the same time, it implied a concession of defeat – and possibly even a sense that the early departure of a troublesome teenager would be more liberating for the parents than the children. For two years the 'child' could have been bringing home a partner for sex; twelve months later the family car would no longer be forbidden territory.

The rationale behind these contrasting legal landmarks was obscure. But compared to general attitudes towards children the politicians were models of lucidity. The feeling that children were becoming more unruly was matched by a movement for the abolition of corporal punishment in schools, and restrictions on the disciplinary rights of

C

parents. In the abstract these were welcome moves; but social policy is never made without a context, and it seemed that middle-aged people who never really deserved the punishments meted out to them in their youth were displacing their feelings on to a new generation which really might have benefited from a collective clip round the ear.

Unfortunately, where children were concerned the liberal conscience was now rampaging out of control. Worries about teenage promiscuity and under-age pregnancies coincided with – and often were used as a justification for – the teaching of sex education by visibly embarrassed staff, to pupils who knew everything already. In most cases their practical work had gone well beyond the furtive explorations celebrated by Laurie Lee in *Cider with Rosie* (1959) as 'a
► hornless charging of calves'. **Housing** policy gave priority to parents; and whether there was much truth in the common story or not, if teenage girls really did put a home of their own above every other consideration, they had a clear incentive to forget all their lessons in birth control. The rate of births to unmarried women under 20 doubled over the decade after 1975. Only recently has the general public begun to register the true extent to which practical sex education began in the home (although people tried to cling to the belief that most paedophiles were not blood relatives). Among better publicised tales of horror which partially lifted a veil from practices that previous generations had tacitly condoned, it was revealed in 2002 that one 16-year-old girl had been made pregnant 10 times by an abuser since she was 12. The outcry over child abuse was led by tabloid newspapers, some of which regularly featured partially-clad teenage girls as their main attraction to 'readers'.

The British, in short, had no idea what to do about their children, providing an ironical backdrop to liberal boasts about a new enlightened approach to the subject. In hindsight the cynical inter-war drive
► to stock the **Empire** with 'the right breed' at least had a consistent theme, which could be accepted or denounced as a whole. The subject had now been invaded by social engineers with polarised views, ignorant armies clashing by night. Child abusers and murderers were treated with particular abhorrence, and for good reason. But the violent propensities of children themselves were well known long before William Golding's *Lord of the Flies* (1954), and the brutal murder of a toddler, James Bulger, by two children in 1993 was a vivid real-life illustration of the point. In 2001 legislation allowed the police and local authorities to impose curfews on children aged between 10 and 15; the Blair government also reduced the age of criminal responsibility to 10.

Yet now there was a new motive for the British obsession with children. Increasingly disillusioned with their own lives, couples looked to the arrival of the stork as a rebirth of themselves. In the Victorian age children were symbols of innocence; now they were bundles of academic and (ultimately) wealth-creating potential. At the same time, parents were too busy to actualise this potential themselves. So the buck was passed to teachers. Instead of being condemned for driving children towards nervous breakdowns (or worse) through constant academic testing, governments were pressurised to force them over more and more academic hurdles. Teachers won little support when they pointed out that the 'league tables' of achievement were in fact pretty meaningless. They could hardly expect a rational debate; when middle-class parents claimed that education had been failing Britain for many decades, they presumably did not notice that they were undermining their own intellectual credibility (and that of their beloved *Daily Mail*).

The best illustration of the British attitude to children was the 'family Christmas'. Tears and tantrums were now as traditional as turkey during this festival. But most people with children used it as an opportunity to worship their brood. The fact that Jesus was a baby was now far more pertinent than his relationship to the Christian God. By 2002 average expenditure had soared to more than £120 for each child between 7 and 10; one toy-making firm estimated that the tribute from starry-eyed grandparents was as much as £1 billion overall. Apart from the long-established desire to buy affection there was now an additional spur, since a child who lacked fashionable merchandise (electronic gadgets, footwear, memorabilia of films and pop stars, etc.) would be teased or bullied by the other classroom terrorists. By the end of the twentieth century figures suggested that around 4 million children were being 'brought up in **poverty**'. If hard-pressed parents were unable to hand out the mobile phones and other fashion accessories dressed up as necessities, the child could always provide for itself. This helped to account for a new outbreak of delinquency, inspiring protests against the lenient treatment of children by the courts. In some cases, young people were literally being killed by what passed as kindness.

> *'Bliss was it in that dawn to be alive,*
> *But to be young was very Heaven!'*

■ Church of England

The established national Church of England, popularly known as 'the C of E' and still the largest Protestant body in the world, with 70 million adherents in 38 provinces and 450 dioceses spread across 161 countries (compared to only 72 dioceses at the end of the nineteenth century). Christianity existed *in* England from the second century, but the Church *of* England (*Ecclesia Anglicana*) was founded by parliament in 1534 as a result of Henry VIII's assertion of royal supremacy over papal authority, in order for the King to obtain a divorce from Catherine of Aragon. Three centuries of conflict with the Catholic Church, and with other Protestant denominations, left the authority of Anglicanism unshaken. What undermined it was the secularisation of British society during the twentieth century. In 1900, its active membership stood at 8 million, 20 per cent of the population. By 2000, this had fallen to 1.7 million, 2.4 per cent of the population.

The effect of secularisation on membership was compounded by the Church's uncritical support for the First World War, its active role in recruiting conscripts and in glorifying their deaths as a blood sacrifice for the nation. As a direct consequence of the war, the muscular, nationalistic Anglicanism of the Victorian era fell out of favour. The church's response was to begin a process of theological and structural reform which, by the end of the century, had made Anglicanism one of the most liberal faiths in the world.

A succession of reforming primates, starting with Randall Davidson (1848–1930; 1903–28) were catalysts for change. But the foundation of it was an unofficial separation of church and state, made possible by parliament's declining interest in religion and a consequent willingness to let the church decide its own affairs. In 1919, a National Assembly of the Church of England was set up by Act of Parliament. Divided into three houses – Bishops, Clergy and Laity – it allowed active churchgoers a say in formulating Anglican policy submitted to parliament for consideration. This was superseded in 1965 by the General Synod, a body with the power to decide all policy independently except that which had a bearing on constitutional matters.

Disestablishment of the Church of Wales was one such issue. To the annoyance of the Nonconformist Welsh majority, Anglicanism enjoyed constitutional privileges despite having been the minority faith in the Principality since the mid-nineteenth century. Davidson was personally against disestablishment but accepted it for pragmatic reasons, and after forty years of nationalist discontent, parliament allowed the Welsh to go their own way in 1920 (the Episcopalian structure was renamed the Church *in* Wales). An attempt to reform Anglican liturgy met with less success. Church leaders were keen to make services more accessible by modernising the language of the 1662 Book of Common Prayer. But parliament (concerned at the speed of change) threw out the Prayer Book Reform Act in 1928, a blow that hastened Davidson's resignation and his replacement by the more conservative Cosmo Gordon Lang (1864–1945; 1928–42). Davidson's reforms were eventually passed in 1960 and a wholly new Alternative

Service Book (ASB) was introduced in 1980, but it remained unpopular, most congregations preferring the more arcane but poetic sixteenth-century language of the church's founder and first Archbishop of Canterbury, Thomas Cranmer (1489–1556).

During the interwar era, the Church of England became committed to **appeasement** and Anglican theologians justified war as a terrible ◄ trial to be endured rather than a thrilling opportunity to make a blood sacrifice for God, King and Country. The church's detachment from the declining cult of St George was one manifestation of that change. Another was its support for the left/liberal Industrial Christian Fellowship (ICF). The ICF was founded in 1921 by one of the more popular vicars of the trenches, A.E. Studdart-Kennedy, known as 'Woodbine Willie' because of his tendency to distribute cigarettes rather than prayer cards to the troops. Through a combination of open-air evangelism and practical social work the ICF shored up religious belief in urban areas of England. The abolition of tithes replicated that success in the countryside, where a traditional reluctance to pay the church was aggravated by the **agricultural** depression of the time. The Tithe ◄ Riots of 1934-6, in which churches were violently attacked (with the support of **Oswald Mosley**'s Fascists), forced a historic re-think in 1937. ◄

The Second World War slowed the decline of Anglicanism because it offered spiritual solace amid the traumas of war. Vicars also augmented the state's provision of food, shelter and entertainment for the bereaved and homeless during the **Blitz**, and did so in urban ◄ areas where church attendance had declined the most. Although church leaders continued to distance themselves from the militarism of the previous war, they did support the morally contentious carpet bombing of German cities, and Bishop George Bell of Chichester was censured for criticising the RAF. A sign of the importance of Anglicanism to the English was the fact that the survival of St Paul's Cathedral during the Blitz became the symbol of the whole nation's survival. The primacy of the first socialist Archbishop of Canterbury, **William Temple** (1881–1944; 1942–4), lasted only two years but in that ◄ time Temple increased the popularity of the church by supporting the creation of a **welfare state**, which earned him the sobriquet 'the ◄ People's Archbishop'. He also won international respect by being the first religious leader in the world to condemn Hitler's treatment of the **Jews**. ◄

Although Temple's successor, Geoffrey Fisher (1887–1972; 1945–60), was politically more conservative, he too presided over a late flowering of Anglicanism. During the 1950s, there was a 24 per cent rise in active membership; the circulation of the *Church Times* reached its highest level since the 1900s; two major new cathedrals were consecrated, in Guildford (1961) and Coventry (1962); and the New English Bible (1961) became a best-seller (its success showed that while most people preferred traditional liturgy, they welcomed a fresh translation of Bible stories). Anglicanism was promoted by a new generation of lay

▶ intellectuals with mass appeal – notably C.S. Lewis and **John Betjeman**. During this period the Church of England secured its position as the world's largest Protestant body. Davidson was the first Archbishop to visit foreign dioceses (Canada and the USA, 1904), but it was Geoffrey Fisher's extensive foreign tours during the 1950s which established a quasi-papal role for the Archbishop of Canterbury. That, together with his leadership of the Lambeth Conference (held every decade since 1888, to bring together Anglican leaders from around the world), and a more vocal opposition to racism by clergy like Bishop Trevor Huddleston (1913–98), enabled the church to transform itself

▶ from the missionary agency of the British **Empire** into a modern multi-racial, international fellowship.

Domestically, the revival was short-lived. Church membership fell back by 20 per cent in the 1960s to 4 million, 10 per cent of the population. Participation in religious rites of passage also declined: the

▶ number of baptisms, confirmations and **marriages** all fell by half to less than a third of the population (between 1962 and 1978, the number of church weddings fell from 68 per cent of the total to 43).

▶ Although the 1944 Butler **Education Act** made religious instruction compulsory in state schools for the first time, it came at a time when the teaching profession was becoming more left-wing and less willing to promote religion of any kind. Furthermore, by reducing the funding of church schools, the Act forced many to close. The number of Anglican schools was halved, so that by the end of the century, only 5 per cent of secondary school pupils were receiving an Anglican education, compared to 40 per cent in 1900.

Traditionalists blamed the liberalisation of the church, a process that gathered pace during the primacy of Michael Ramsey (1904–88; 1961–74). His acceptance of liberal theology, such as that elucidated by John Robinson, Bishop of Woolwich (1919–83) in the best-selling *Honest to God* (1963) was criticised. So too was the support Ramsey gave to the liberal social legislation of the time, especially the reform of divorce law in 1969, an issue that previous Archbishops had refused to countenance, despite the fact that the Church of England owed its existence to a divorce. The ecumenical movement developed to the point where it became almost an article of Anglican faith to seek the dissolution of the Church of England. In 1960, Fisher made the first visit to the Vatican by an Archbishop of Canterbury since the Reformation and Ramsey followed in 1966, although it was not until 1982 that a Pope, John Paul II, was invited to visit the UK.

After the unspectacular primacy of Donald Coggan (1909–2000;

C

1974–80), Robert Runcie (1921–2001; 1980–91) continued the process of reform. The report of the Archbishop's Commission on Urban Priority Areas, *Faith in the City* (1985), criticised the social effects of the Thatcher governments' monetarist policies, and earned the wrath of ◄ Conservatives for doing so. The Church Commissioners' own faith in the City was severely shaken in 1992 when they lost £800 million speculating on shares. More significant was the introduction of **women** ◄ priests. The General Synod approved them in principle in 1975; women were admitted to the deaconate in 1984 and to the clergy in 1993. A handful of clergy and congregations converted to Catholicism, and the Anglo-Catholic wing of the ecumenical movement was damaged. But predictions that the Church of England would be split from top to toe were unfounded. Although the number of practising Catholics in England outstripped the number of Anglicans in 1980, by 2000 the situation was again reversed.

Ultimately, the decline of Anglicanism had more to do with social change than it did with anything that took place at Lambeth Palace. As elsewhere in the West, religious worship declined as rising standards of living and increased leisure time, coupled with better access to education and healthcare, made life more enjoyable and the fear of death less acute. Furthermore, the decline of Anglicanism was not as severe as the Jeremiahs made out. Around 70 per cent of the English people still believed in God – the vast majority of those were latent Anglicans. That is to say: whatever their threshold of belief, if the English went to church at Christmas and Easter, participated in religious rites of passage like weddings, or simply enjoyed the musical and architectural heritage of the church, they generally did so as Anglicans. If anything, evidence suggests that a century of sweeping reform made the Church of England more popular than it would otherwise have been because it was better able to reach out to the increasingly sceptical nation it faced after the nineteenth century.

■ Church of Scotland

One of three Scottish institutions, along with law and education, that retained their independence following the Treaty of Union of 1707. Although considered by many English people to be a branch office of the **Church of England**, it is in fact Calvinist, not Lutheran, in ◄ theology and Presbyterian, not Espicopalian, in organisation. As a Protestant body, established under the Crown and so sharing the same titular head as the Church of England, it continues to form a cultural bridge with its southern neighbour. However, from the 1960s, it became a focal point for champions of **devolution** and independence, ◄ lending symbolic and practical support to their campaigns.

C

Popularly known as 'the Kirk', the Church of Scotland was founded in 1560 when its governing body, the General Assembly, first met. Battle continued between Episcopalians and Presbyterians, led by John Knox, for control of the Scottish Reformation until the former faction won out during the Glorious Revolution of 1688. From then until the twentieth century, the Kirk was riven with disputes over whether ministers should be elected by their congregations or by patronage. Patronage was finally abolished in 1874, though this did not prevent the creation of the United Free Church in 1900. In the face of creeping secularisation, the Scottish churches put aside most of their differences. In 1921, parliament passed the Church of Scotland Act which guaranteed the Kirk's spiritual independence while maintaining its constitutional subservience to the Crown in parliament. This paved the way for reunion with the United Free Church in 1929. A rump of the latter – known as 'the Wee Frees' – resisted, but their support was confined to remote highland areas and foreign missions.

During the 1950s, discussions took place with the Church of England about the possibility of unification. The bodies agreed that the members of each could worship and take the sacrament in the other. However, the Anglican insistence that the Kirk should become Episcopalian – enshrined in the Bishops' Report of 1957 – provoked accusations of English imperialism and the plan collapsed. Amicable relations were restored during the 1960 celebrations of the 400th anniversary of the Scottish Reformation, at which Elizabeth Windsor became the first British monarch to address the General Assembly. But the question of unification was not raised again, and by the 1970s the Kirk was closely involved in the devolution movement.

Church attendance in Scotland is the highest on mainland Britain (30.1 per cent of the population in 1990, compared to 16.5 in Wales and 11.1 in England). That figure was made up partly of Catholics, who had a large presence in the industrial west of Scotland as a result of Irish immigration during the nineteenth century. But most churchgoers – around 600,000 – were Church of Scotland members. The Kirk also remained more democratic than its southern counterpart. The Moderator of the General Assembly is not the head of the Kirk but the Assembly's spokesperson, and a different Moderator is elected each year by its 850 members, who are themselves elected by Scotland's 1,400 presbyteries (congregations). Women were allowed to become elders (lay preachers) in 1966 and ministers in 1968, over 20 years before Anglicans accepted them.

■ Churchill, Winston Leonard Spencer (1874–1965)

Winston Churchill was born prematurely at Blenheim Palace, after his

American mother Jennie had tumbled from her horse. His father, Lord Randolph, was a younger son of the 7th Duke of Marlborough, the owner of Blenheim. As Winston grew up he witnessed the rapidly changing fortunes of his gifted, erratic father, who became Chancellor of the Exchequer at the age of 37 but resigned shortly afterwards. This proved to be a tactical error, and was followed by a lingering death from syphilis; it was even claimed that Randolph had contracted the illness from a housemaid before Winston's birth. In his two-volume hagiography of his father (1906), Winston tactfully attributed the 'rare and ghastly disease' to the effects of overwork.

Contrary to legend Churchill was not a backward schoolboy. But the prospect of a military career meant that he went to Sandhurst rather than an Oxbridge college after his time at Harrow School. He served in the Sudan, taking part in a cavalry charge at the battle of Omdurman (1898). But his ambitions already extended beyond soldiering. He became a national figure after a daring escape from captivity in the early stages of the Boer War (1899–1902), to which he had been assigned as a journalist. Defeated as **Conservative** candidate ◄ for Oldham at an 1899 by-election, he returned in time to win the seat in the following year.

Churchill quickly reinforced his fame with some combative parliamentary speeches, mostly aimed at his own front bench. A convinced free trader, in 1904 he 'crossed the floor' and joined the **Liberal Party** ◄ in reaction against Joseph Chamberlain's emerging policy of **tariff** ◄ **reform**. It was a well-timed departure; when the Liberals won the 1906 election Churchill was given office, and he joined the Cabinet as President of the Board of Trade two years later. In this post he worked with **Lloyd George** to lay the foundations of the **welfare state**. But his ◄ progressive reputation was damaged after he became Home Secretary in February 1910. He intervened to quell a violent outbreak at Tonypandy, South Wales, where striking miners had been clashing with the local police. Churchill was accused of using strong-arm tactics when in reality he had tried to avoid any violence. He was already finding that fame could be awkward; the absurd myth of Tonypandy haunted him for the rest of his career.

In 1911 Churchill was moved to the Admiralty, where he quickly discarded his earlier opposition to high naval expenditure. Before the outbreak of war he wisely mobilised the fleet, but his thirst for action led him to suggest dramatic initiatives such as the calamitous Gallipoli campaign (1915). The fact that he could be portrayed as a danger to shipping (as well as other sections of the **armed forces**) gave ◄ a plausible cloak of principle to his personal enemies. When the Conservatives joined the government in May 1915 they secured Churchill's removal from the Admiralty. He remained within the

Cabinet, as Chancellor of the Duchy of Lancaster. But this provided limited scope for his energies, and he resigned after six months to act as a battalion commander on the Western Front.

Churchill's political fortunes suddenly revived when his friend Lloyd George replaced Asquith as Prime Minister. In July 1917 he was recalled – much to the chagrin of the Conservatives – as Minister for Munitions. In January 1919 he became Secretary of State for War and Air, and in February 1921 he was appointed Secretary of State for the Colonies. But since the 1918 general election the Conservatives had dominated the Commons, and the Lloyd George coalition was dissolved in October 1922. In the ensuing general election Churchill lost his seat.

With the Liberals badly divided, Churchill began to shuffle back towards the Conservative Party. Although opportunism undoubtedly helped to inspire this change of loyalties, he was a furious opponent of 'Bolshevism' and rightly saw his old party as the best rallying point
▶ against **Labour**. By 1924 he was back in the Commons, having fought Epping as a 'Constitutionalist' (but with strong Conservative backing). His peregrinations were over; after this he stuck to his party, and he continued to sit for Epping (despite periodic threats of deselection) until 1964.

▶ The Prime Minister **Stanley Baldwin** immediately made Churchill Chancellor of the Exchequer. This might have looked like a master-stroke of psychological insight on Baldwin's part, since the emulation of his revered father might have been expected to satisfy the ambitions of the wayward minister. Indeed, he remained in the post until the government fell in 1929. But the main flaw in the theory was that Churchill had no claim to economic expertise. Britain's return to the Gold Standard in 1925 was the financial equivalent of Gallipoli,
▶ helping to deepen Britain's economic plight during the **Great Depression**. Baldwin might also have guessed that his Chancellor would look for action outside the parameters of the Treasury, and during the
▶ **General Strike** he caused lasting resentment through his conduct of the scurrilous *British Gazette*. True to his lifelong belief that victors should always be magnanimous, Churchill argued for compromise once the strike was over – thus displeasing right-wingers without mollifying any of his critics on the left.

The 1929 Conservative defeat marked the beginning of Churchill's 'wilderness years'. Naturally he continued to attract headlines, and the books he produced were invariably successful. But he was constantly at odds with his leaders, and showed an amazing propensity to back the wrong horses. Before the formation of the National Government in 1931 he had resigned from the Shadow Cabinet over Indian self-government, and continued to harry his colleagues on this

issue. In 1936 his fervent support for **Edward VIII** during the abdica- ◄
tion crisis seemed to be a fatal misjudgement. Churchill was younger
than Baldwin's heir apparent, Neville Chamberlain. But at 62 his years
of promise had been used up.

Yet Churchill was still a fearless (and much feared) orator when he
stumbled on the right cause; and his frequent warnings about Nazi
Germany found a response, not least in the press where he still
enjoyed important friendships (in particular with **Lord Beaverbrook**). ◄
At the outbreak of war Chamberlain was compelled to bring Churchill
back to the Admiralty. Although he bore much responsibility for some
of the early misfortunes of British forces, it was clear that only
Churchill could provide the dauntless leadership required for a
protracted struggle. After Chamberlain's resignation in May 1940 he
achieved his lifelong dream, but only because his main rival, Halifax,
was in baulk as a member of the House of Lords.

Churchill's belief in himself as a 'man of destiny' had previously
made him many enemies. Now it seemed to be a modest evaluation of
his qualities. He performed no overnight miracles, and despite his
marvellous oratory during the darkest days of the war his position was
by no means secure in the absence of good news. The final outcome
should not obscure the fact that his military judgement was still open
to serious question; and although his personal diplomacy was effective, it did not bring the Americans into the war. However, as the
symbol of British defiance he was incomparable, and he fully deserved
his legendary post-war status.

Despite his uneven record as a party man, Churchill had accepted
the Conservative leadership when Chamberlain died in October 1940.
Nevertheless, the result of the 1945 election might have been closer if
the electorate had not been confused about the Prime Minister's party
allegiance. But Churchill's own performances during the campaign, in
which he reverted to type and portrayed his erstwhile coalition
colleagues as dangerous extremists, was another contributory factor
to Labour's landslide victory. In opposition Churchill proved to be far
less dangerous to his own side, partly because he made his most
important speeches on international affairs and spent much of his
time abroad. In 1951 he returned to office, and even a serious stroke in
July 1953, combined with increasing deafness, could not prise him out
of Downing Street. In part his reluctance reflected well-founded fears
about his deputy, Anthony Eden; but in any case it would have been
difficult for him to face the fact that his great adventure was over.

At home, Churchill's second administration was a relatively
peaceful period which could almost seem like a golden age to
nostalgic Conservatives today. But despite all the honours showered on
Churchill – he refused a peerage, but was made a Knight of the Garter

▶ in 1953 – by the end of his life he had many reasons to feel that his career had been a failure. The **Empire** had unravelled, and Britain seemed unable to forge a new role in world affairs. Nazism was dead,
▶ but the continent of **Europe** was still threatened by a totalitarian power. In 1964 the Labour Party had ended the long period of Conservative domination which began in 1951. Churchill was a unique individual, so that there had never been any chance of a successor to fill his shoes adequately. But even so his passing seemed to symbolise the close of a political era. It was not an epitaph that he would have
▶ relished, and his victory in a 2002 **BBC** poll to decide the greatest-ever Briton would have been inadequate compensation, even for such an ebullient egoist.

■ Cinema

'To put it bluntly,' the French director François Truffaut once remarked, 'isn't there a certain incompatibility between the terms "cinema" and "Britain"?' Truffaut's Gallic hauteur was unwarranted. Certainly, the influence of Hollywood on British cinema has been
▶ greater than anywhere else in the world due to the lack of a **language** barrier, the reluctance of British financiers to invest in film and political hostility towards state funding. But despite these handicaps, the UK did create a distinctive national cinema in the twentieth century,
▶ one that reflected the British obsession with **class** and sex, their worship of stoicism and their ironic sense of humour. Technically, too, the British did much to develop the medium. Their inventors and entrepreneurs helped to pioneer cinematography and although the US soon overtook the UK, as it did with the computer and the jet engine, British technicians remained the most sought-after in the world.

The nation's love of amateurs led the penniless inventor William Friese-Greene (1855–1921) to be credited for many years with developing movies, but credit should go to Robert Paul (1869–1943). After the creation of celluloid in 1889, the Lumière brothers won the race to build a projector and staged the first commercial, public film show in Paris in 1895. Paul staged one at Olympia in 1896, and in the same year produced the world's first feature film, *The Soldier's Courtship*. It caused a sensation; shops, music halls and meeting rooms were rapidly converted into viewing arenas known as 'Penny Gaffs'; and several French entrepreneurs crossed the Channel to get involved. The two most notable were Léon Gaumont (1864–1946), who by 1900 was producing and distributing 100 films a year and showing them at his chain of auditoria, Gaumont cinemas; and secondly, Charles Pathé (1863–1957), whose eponymous company dominated newsreels until TV news took over.

The first purpose-built picture house was opened in 1905 but most were drab, uncomfortable places until the Cinematograph Act of 1909 established a licensing system. Like the Beer Acts of the late nineteenth century which forced pubs to become more respectable, the Cinematograph Act made the picture house a salubrious, even luxurious, place by imposing strict criteria of comfort, hygiene and safety which had to be met in order to obtain a licence from local authorities. A building boom took place as a result, with 3,500 picture houses erected between 1909 and the outbreak of the First World War. The advent of talkies in 1927 was the catalyst for another boom, with 715 being built from then until 1932. The advent of the **Great Depression** ◄ made cinemas more lavish, as they offered working people a respite from daily hardship. Known as 'Dream Palaces', they either mimicked the Rococo style of **music halls** and theatres or adopted the more fash- ◄ ionable Art Deco style. The Deco cinemas, notably Oscar Deutsch's Odeon chain, helped to make modern **architecture** and design ◄ acceptable to the British public. Deutsch (1893–1948), the son of Hungarian **Jewish** émigrés who settled in Birmingham, opened 258 ◄ cinemas between 1931 and 1941. The name 'odeon' was borrowed from the Greek word for auditorium, though the company liked to claim that it stood for 'Oscar Deutsch Entertains Our Nation'.

Building beautiful cinemas was one thing; getting people to watch British films was quite another. From the 1920s onwards, the influence of Hollywood on national culture vexed all European governments, forming the basis of concern about **Americanisation**. Before ◄ 1918, only 15 per cent of films shown in the UK were British-made and by 1926, the figure had fallen to 5 per cent, as Hollywood's greater financial power began to tell, with moviegoers flocking to the more lavish and risqué films produced in California. The British Board of Film Censors was set up in 1912 and at evidence it gave to an inquiry set up by the National Council for Public Morals in 1916, it listed 43 ◄ grounds for deletion. Among them were cruelty to **animals**, 'the *modus* ◄ *operandi* of criminals', 'relations of capital and labour', the disparage- ment of Britain's **monarchy, Empire** or its allies, the 'realistic depic- ◄ tion of warfare', **drug** use, the 'visualisation of Christ' and, above all, ◄ 'impropriety in conduct and dress', which prevented any overt display of sexuality. Liberalisation did not take place until the tenure of John Trevelyan in the 1960s.

Meanwhile, the Cinematograph Act of 1927 imposed quotas on the number of Hollywood productions that could be shown in the UK. More stringent limits were imposed in 1947, and though they were relaxed two years later after US pressure, quotas formed the basis of government film policy until they were completely abolished in 1970. This was augmented by the creation of two semi-autonomous organisations: one to promote native film, the British Film Institute (1933); and one to dispense production grants, the National Film Finance Corporation (1949). These moves bore fruit in Carol Reed's *The Third Man* (1949) but little else.

To make matters worse, British talent regularly defected to the US in search of the greater opportunity and riches on offer there. Charlie Chaplin (1889–1977) was discovered by Mack Sennett in 1912 while on a musical hall tour of the US and he remained there until the Americans decided he was a Communist in 1952. The best British director of the age (and the only one Truffaut admired) moved to Hollywood in 1939. Alfred Hitchcock (1899–1980) began his directorial career in 1925 on an Anglo-German production *The Pleasure Garden* (in the 1920s, the studios of Britain and Weimar Germany often joined forces in an effort to combat the US). He made the first British talkie, *Blackmail* (1929), but it was in Hollywood that he won the accolade 'Master of Suspense'. Hitchcock used imaginative camerawork and editing to suggest rather than display danger, and so perfected the modern thriller in works like *Rear Window* (1954), *North By Northwest* (1959) and *Psycho* (1960). He did not return to Britain to direct until *Frenzy* (1972). Meanwhile, realising the growing importance of television, he also produced a series of TV shows like *Alfred Hitchcock Presents* (1955–62). Still, the advent of TV hit the cinema hard, especially in the UK where it was a more fragile industry. Annual cinema admissions fell from 1,396 million in 1950 to 193 million in 1970, while the number of cinemas fell from 4,584 to 1,529. Video also had a serious effect for a time with attendances dropping again to 67 million in 1987 before picking up to 112 million in 1996.

There were, however, several periods and genres in which British film flourished. The left-wing documentary movement had a world-wide influence. Founded in 1929 by a Scotsman, John Grierson (1898–1972), with the aim of accurately portraying working-class life, it reached a creative apogee in Basil Wright's *Night Mail* (1936), with music and words by Benjamin Britten and W.H. Auden. But despite being employed to great effect during the Second World War – notably in Humphrey Jennings' (1907–50) rousingly patriotic *Heart of Britain* (1941) – documentary films did not have a mass following. The Hungarian émigré Alexander Korda (1893–1956) established London Films and directed the first British movie to achieve international commercial success, *The Private Life of Henry VIII* (1933). The UK's reputation for historical costume drama was cemented by Gainsborough Studios in the 1940s with films like *The Wicked Lady* (1945). At the same time, Ealing Studios, whose boss Michael Balcon gave Hitchcock his first break, established a reputation for whimsical comedy mixed with social comment. This was amplified in the 1950s by the films of the

Boulting brothers, John (1913–85) and Roy (1913–2001) for the British Lion company. Their best work satirised the British class system as it manifested itself in the army, *Private's Progress* (1956); universities, *Lucky Jim* (1957, based on the eponymous novel by Kingsley Amis); industry, *I'm All Right Jack* (1959); and the church, *Heaven's Above!* (1963).

A bleaker, more hard-hitting approach to class was developed by the New Wave of social realist or 'kitchen-sink' cinema dominated by the producer and director Tony Richardson (1928–1991) and his Woodfall Films. These pictures were mostly based on the work of working-class novelists and playwrights like Shelagh Delaney, *A Taste of Honey* (1961), Alan Sillitoe, *Saturday Night and Sunday Morning* (1960), and **John ◄ Osborne**, *Look Back In Anger* (1959). Like the literary works from which they sprang, New Wave films also dealt more frankly with sex, and with a maturity lacking in **Carry On** films. The cultural revolution of ◄ the 1960s briefly invigorated British cinema and it produced an international star, Michael Caine (b. 1933), who came to personify the less deferential, more meritocratic society which emerged in that period. 'Swinging London' was portrayed cheekily in the Caine vehicle *The Italian Job* (1967), enigmatically in Michelangelo Antonioni's *Blow Up* (1968), and darkly in Donald Cammell and Nicolas Roeg's *Performance* (1970). However, **war** films remained the most popular genre ◄ throughout the 1950s and 60s. Over a hundred were produced between 1955 and 1965. Their stiff upper-lipped action heroes peddled the fantasy that the British had beaten Hitler single-handedly, while also maintaining public hostility towards the **Germans** by showing ◄ them to be irretrievably militaristic. Moreover, the cinematic revival of the 1960s relied heavily on American financing, and when 'Swinging London' ran its course, the money left with it.

Thereafter, a British film revival was regularly heralded but never fully materialised. David Puttnam's *Chariots of Fire* (1981), Richard Attenborough's *Gandhi* (1982), Richard Curtis's *Four Weddings and a Funeral* (1994) and Peter Cattaneo's *The Full Monty* (1997) all won international awards. Indeed, British films won on average a third of the Oscars despite the paltry output of UK studios. But they had no consistent international reach, despite the benefit of being made in the lingua franca. The only exceptions to this were Cubby Broccoli's glossy, high-tech **James Bond** films which gave audiences the high quota of sex and ◄ violence that they required. British directors like Alan Parker (b. 1944) and Ridley Scott (b. 1937) trod Hitchcock's path to Hollywood, combining its resources and their talents to make mainstream movies, notably Scott's brilliant postmodern dystopia *Blade Runner* (1982). Subject matter was as much a problem as financing. The British tendency to make thoughtful, small-scale films that were usually about social class, whether in a period or contemporary setting, like those of

Ken Loach (b. 1936), limited them to a domestic audience, and an educated one at that.

The perennial obsession about competing with the US and the inevitable sense of unfulfilled potential that accompanied it, did as much damage as poor financing and parochialism. It reflected a continuing failure to accept that Britain was no longer top dog in the world. Perhaps, like Continental Europeans, the British should accept that a limited, quality output, reflecting their national culture but with fewer international pretensions, is the way to prove Truffaut wrong.

■ Civil service

From 1870, entry into the British civil service was decided on the basis of competitive examination, completing the programme of reform suggested by the Northcote-Trevellyan Report (1854). The business of the state was becoming more complex, and there was a growing
▶ Empire to govern. Over the following century the newly profession-alised bureaucracy surmounted several serious challenges. During the two world wars it was supplemented by outside experts; but the ethos of a body of 'gifted amateurs', offering impartial advice to ministers regardless of their party, survived the shock. If anyone thought about this unglamorous subject at all, they regarded the civil service as a source of pride.

The post-war increase in state responsibilities led to a steep rise in the number of civil servants. In 1938 there were around 375,000 non-industrial civil servants; a decade later the ranks had swollen by 200,000. These were halcyon days for 'the man in Whitehall'; while post-war prosperity and full employment lasted, the civil service was generally regarded as a smooth-running machine, and hostility towards 'bureaucrats' was confined to those groups, like the self-employed, who preferred to be left unmolested (for obvious reasons).

For the civil service, as for the public as a whole, the good times came to an abrupt end in the mid-1970s. The economic crisis which followed the oil shock of 1973-4 brought the whole central apparatus
▶ into discredit. Under **Margaret Thatcher** (the daughter of a self-
▶ employed businessman), the **Conservatives** drew up radical plans to reduce numbers. This might not have been a significant vote-winner, but the civil service could now be stigmatised as both inefficient and
▶ inept. For extreme **Thatcherites** the service was a symptom of all that had gone wrong with Britain. If the bureaucrats were really so clever they should be out in the 'real world', setting up their own businesses. The hostile climate was fostered by the appearance of Leslie Chapman's hard-hitting critique *Your Disobedient Servant* (1978), and the

successful comedy shows *Yes, Minister* and its sequel, *Yes, Prime Minister* (1981–7). In fact, the latter programmes conveyed an ambiguous message; the scheming Sir Humphrey Appleby really *was* far better equipped to run the country than his political boss. But the public was hardly likely to draw the most plausible moral – that if the democratic process lumbered Whitehall with hapless masters like Jim Hacker, perhaps it had better be abolished.

After 1979 the civil service was subjected to three complementary attacks. Numbers were reduced, though not as rapidly in the non-industrial sector as the hard-liners would have liked. Around a million at its peak, the overall figure had been cut by more than half before the end of the twentieth century. Those who remained were increasingly demoralised as targets were introduced, ostensibly to re-create some of the working practices of the private sector. Later, John Major's 'Citizen's Charter' obliged many government servants to wear name-badges, as if they were official tour guides. Additional responsibilities were not matched by better pay and conditions.

The second attack was the 'Next Steps' reform programme, based on a 1988 report. The reforms broke the old departments into numerous semi-autonomous agencies – some of which were 'hived off' with a view to their eventual **privatisation**. One of the effects of this change was to undermine the civil service **trade unions**, which were increasingly restive in the 1970s and called a damaging strike in 1980. But it also pointed towards a more narrowly specialised bureaucracy, threatening the old idea of the 'gifted amateur'.

The third wave of attack began under Mrs Thatcher, but gathered pace under **Tony Blair**. After 1979 it was often claimed that the civil service was being 'politicised'. This could take various forms, but the most damaging accusation was that ministers were now instructing their supposedly neutral staff to provide critical analyses of opposition proposals in advance of general elections. Under Blair, the number of 'outsiders' drafted into the service was greatly increased. In the circumstances of 1939–45, these temporary civil servants had for the most part slotted in and out without too much trouble. But now, with the old bureaucratic ethos in rapid decline, it seemed more likely that the interlopers would set the tone themselves. Britain looked to be on the verge of restoring the system which had proved so inefficient before Northcote-Trevellyan – a civil service based on patronage.

As in so many aspects of British life, the fortunes of the civil service since 1870 have largely been shaped by the likelihood, or actual experience, of major **wars**. In Britain's hours of need the professional civil service was ready to organise the country's war effort. For a few decades after 1945 a large bureaucracy still seemed essential, as the state took on extra functions to provide a secure future for its war-

C

weary subjects. But the diminishing prospect of total war allowed critics to question the necessity of a large bureaucratic machine – and to challenge the policies which it administered. By the year 2000 the civil service was bowed down (if not exactly on its knees); and it was most unlikely to recover its old prestige.

■ Class

▶ 'England,' **George Orwell** famously wrote, 'is the most class-ridden country under the sun.' In fact, there are many societies, especially in Asia, where social hierarchies are more rigid and the penalties for breaking out of them are more severe. But the English, along with the Scots and Welsh, compare themselves most often to America and as a consequence they find themselves wanting. In the United States, class is defined to a greater extent on income levels rather than social
▶ origins because it is a nation created by revolution and **immigration**. Britain has experienced revolution and immigration too but the former has been less successful and the latter less pronounced.

The Industrial Revolution made the British class system more flexible as commercial success came to count for almost as much as land and titles. But the *ancien régime* was mimicked and permeated more than it was overthrown by the upwardly mobile. The fear of revolution never entirely disappeared and that, leavened with compassion, prompted the gradual creation of a universal franchise and the
▶ amelioration of **poverty** through the development of **education** and welfare. This was augmented by patriotism, a natural emotion, but one that was manipulated to convince the classes that their interests
▶ were the same, particularly at the zenith of the **British Empire** between 1870 and 1920. However, all the polling booths, schools and Union Jacks in the world could not disguise the huge income disparities that continued to exist in Great Britain. Moreover, a common interest is one thing; a common culture is quite another, for it requires a higher degree of social engagement. The continuing fear of and, equally, the desire *for* radical change helped to maintain social divisions, as people defined themselves according to a strict range of
▶ attributes and activities. In some cases, like the use of **language**, divisions became more not less entrenched.

Consequently, for all the changes wrought by the nineteenth century, in 1900 the British class structure functioned in much the same way as it had a hundred years earlier. At times of acute tension it was reduced to a polarisation of 'us and them'; but it was generally triadic, the three categories being: the upper classes, characterised in the public mind by bowler hats, stately homes, land-ownership and
▶ fox-hunting; the middle classes: professional, **suburban**, trilby-

wearing home-owners, **gardeners** and **rugby**/tennis enthusiasts; and ◄
the working classes: urban-dwelling, council tenants and cloth-capped
denizens of the **pub** and the **football** terrace. Reviled and romanti- ◄
cised in equal measure, the working classes remained the largest of
these groups with, on average, 60 per cent of the population consistently describing themselves thus, compared to 30 per cent middle
class and 10 per cent upper.

There were, of course, many nuances to this structure. The
country–suburb–town divide never precisely corresponded to that of
upper, middle and working class. To begin with, the farm labourers of
rural Britain were every bit as poor (and in many cases, poorer) than a
factory worker or shipbuilder in the great industrial conurbations like
Manchester and Glasgow, even if their culture was more localised,
seasonal and less commercial than that which existed in town.
Furthermore, the wealth of the upper classes was not only based on
their readiness to profit from rural poverty. Despite the reputation of
the aristocracy and landed gentry as idle *rentiers*, they were heavily
involved in commerce, industry and government.

Their political power declined in the first half of the twentieth
century as a result of the 1911 Parliament Act, and their wealth as a
result of inheritance tax. They compensated for these losses by
assuming gubernatorial control of many cultural institutions like the
National Gallery, and by turning their estates into Britain's first theme
parks. The **aristocracy** was never a closed circle, and it became more ◄
accessible as the sale of titles became more common (over 200 peers
were created between 1886 and 1914); and then by the more subtle
form of patronage encouraged by the creation of Life Peers in 1958.
However, despite aristocrats' efforts to present themselves as an impartial check on party politicians and as benign custodians of the nation's
heritage, the British people continued to associate the upper classes –
titled or untitled – with inherited privilege.

The middle classes were not as suburban as their image suggested.
Most continued to work in Britain's towns and cities, where they
dominated commercial and professional life. That dominance was
entrenched by the growing number of professional bodies like the Law
Society (England 1825; Scotland 1949) and the British Medical Association (1856). These were partly designed to codify good working practices and to promote their members' welfare, both of which they
succeeded in doing. But like the more working-class **trade union** move- ◄
ment, they also became quasi-Masonic organisations motivated more
by self-interest than the common good, a fact demonstrated by the
BMA's opposition to the setting up of the **National Health Service**. ◄
The middle classes' dominance of urban society was also maintained
through their control of town halls, especially following the 1888

C

▶ **Local Government** Act. Indeed, their power grew as towns continued to sprawl and the remit of the British state expanded. Government policy continued to be framed at Westminster, but the actual provision of education, health, leisure, welfare and transport was largely managed by local authorities.

'I assert with some confidence,' wrote the Christian socialist thinker R.H. Tawney in 1912, 'that there has rarely been a period when the existing social order was regarded with so much dissatisfaction by so many intelligent and respectable citizens as it is today.' The First
▶ World War and the **Great Depression** increased class tensions. The
▶ 'epauletted egoism' of the officer classes that **Lloyd George** condemned in wartime was replaced by double-breasted egoism in
▶ peacetime, as their ruthless response to the **General Strike** demonstrated. Still, the consensual politics of the National Government were
▶ supported by a majority and calls to revolution by the **Communist Party** and the British Union of Fascists were mostly ignored. And,
▶ despite new diversions like radio and **cinema**, the working-class culture which had solidified in the late Victorian period around the
▶ pub, **gambling, music hall**, football (rugby in Wales) and seaside **holidays** remained intact.

Yet the inter-war period also brought a degree of social mobility, especially in the Midlands and south of England that continued to prosper. The expansion of light industry, the service sector of the British economy and of public-sector administration increased the size of the lower-middle class. Many skilled manual workers and clerical staff were able to afford homes and gardens in the suburbs, and the car that was usually necessary to commute to and from town. Class barriers softened further between 1940 and 1945. Because the Second World War was a patently just one, people shared a common cause; and, because the Home Front was a battleground for the first time, the war required a higher degree of social unity for it to be effectively prosecuted. 'There is no change more marked in our country,' Winston Churchill told the boys of Harrow School in 1940, 'than the continual and rapid effacement of class differences. The advantages and privileges which have hitherto been enjoyed by the few shall be far more widely shared by the many.'

The camaraderie that the war generated did not long survive
▶ victory and the creation of the **welfare state**. Some blamed affluence for its dissipation. Yet the consumption of a vast range of goods and services, from cars and washing machines to eating out and going on holiday, not only improved the quality of people's lives; it also gave them a self-esteem and a status denied to their forebears. So too did the increased career choices provided by a flawed but nonetheless free secondary and higher education system. And those choices extended

beyond the worlds of pop music, **fashion** and football about which the ◄ press got so excited. By 1972, 16 per cent of middle-class British men claimed to have working-class origins. By 1984, the figure was 29 per cent. 'Ancient universities welcome the upstart sons of hobnailed workmen,' wrote the TV presenter David Frost in 1967, optimistically concluding that, 'The archaic pyramid, upper-middle-lower, an unholy trinity of jealousy, malevolence and frustration, cracks and crumbles and those at the top no longer signify. The three great classes melt and mingle. And a new Britain is born.'

Sociologists doubted the extent of mobility or what they called *embourgeoisement*. Michael Young, who authored the 1945 **Labour Party** ◄ manifesto heralding the welfare state, and founded the Consumers Association (1960) to enhance consumer rights, also wrote *The Rise of the Meritocracy* (1958), in which he argued that consumption, based extensively on hire purchase, was creating not a classless society but an indebted one. John Goldthorpe's *The Affluent Worker* (1968) found that affluence was merely enabling people to find different, more enjoyable, ways of being working-class. Workers were not adopting middle-class pastimes like the dinner party, just because they could walk through the doors of a car showroom or an estate agent with their heads held high. Nor were they joining golf clubs in great numbers or, for that matter, political parties.

But attitudes to class changed even if its fundamental structure did not. The decline of deference, which found a focus in the concept of the **Establishment**, was not only manifest in an eagerness to read ◄ about disgraced politicians, clergy and royals in the tabloid press, but also in the continuing desire of people to better their lives. When that desire met with the failure of Britain's rulers to create a society based on equal opportunity, the result was anger, primarily manifested in the violent industrial disputes of the period 1968–85. The number of Britons who believed that class struggle was a feature of British life rose from 60 per cent in the 1960s to 80 per cent in the 1990s, a fact that seems to support the view of the Labour politician Anthony Crosland (1918–77): 'Never have class divisions been so acute and anguished as since they were theoretically abolished.'

Margaret Thatcher was one of those who tried to abolish them. ◄ Class struggle was, she said, 'an outmoded Marxist doctrine', although in truth she favoured the lower-middle-class shopkeeping background into which she had been born. 'The interests of the middle class of a country' were those, she declared, on which its 'future prosperity largely depends'. In 1990 her successor, John Major, professed a desire to create 'a classless society'. Both invited aspirational Britons to realise their ambitions through entrepreneurial zeal instead of strike action. Those who most zealously accepted the invi-

tation were known as Yuppies (Young Upwardly-mobile Urban Profes-
▶ sionals), an acronym invented in America in the early 1980s. 'Thatcherism' never transformed Britain into a 'share-owning democracy',
but it did encourage many people to set up their own businesses. The
self-employed increased by nearly a third during the 1980s, to 3.3
million.

The aspirational working and lower-middle class, whom Disraeli
once approvingly described as 'Angels in Marble', were always the
object of snobbish disdain. As the middle and upper classes struggled
to keep one step ahead by basing status on the extent to which one
consumed things like the arts and property or how one dressed and
spoke, their need to codify social attributes became more intense. One
example of the phenomenon was Nancy Mitford's categorisation of 'U
and Non-U' language and behaviour in *Noblesse Oblige* (1956). A later
example is the term 'Essex Man', coined in a *Sunday Telegraph* article in
1990 and comedically fleshed out by the Harry Enfield character
'Loadsamoney', on the TV satire show *Saturday Live* (later *Friday Night
Live*, Channel 4, 1985–8). Both Essex Man and Loadsamoney were
composite portraits of a ruthlessly self-interested, philistine, Godless
and bigoted boor, whose extreme manifestation was the football
hooligan. On the left, snobbery was intensified by the fact that the
lower-middle class (or *petit-bourgeoisie* as they were pejoratively known)
were conservative-minded and crucial to the continued electoral
success of the Tory Party after the granting of universal suffrage.

Unlike the monster of Mary Shelley's gothic novel, that created by
the Frankenstein of affluence was not entirely a figment of the imag-
▶ ination. Even when **consumerism** was accompanied by social mobility
and not simply greed, it often fostered unsavoury anti-social attitudes
that made Britain a less, not more, open society. 'Middle England', a
term coined in the 1990s to describe John Major's apparently consensual vision of classlessness was, the Marxist commentator Martin
Jacques observed, loaded with prejudice. 'Middle England is a
metaphor for respectability, the nuclear family, heterosexuality,
conservatism, whiteness, middle-age and the status quo.' And dissatisfaction with the status quo was increasingly expressed by political
▶ apathy rather than political action.

However, the story of class in Britain is one of progress and not
decline. More than in most Western countries, class continued to be
defined in cultural rather than economic terms – sometimes through
a well-meaning desire to set standards of life for people to reach, but
just as often in order to redraw boundaries in order to keep them in
their place. Ultimately, any class system must be judged according to
the material standard of living that it makes possible, for that is the
basis of further progress. In 1967, the socialist thinker and politician

Richard Crossman (1907–74) pondered why his country home and its 200 acres meant so much to him and his wife. 'It's not merely that I'm more detached than my colleagues, able to judge things more dispassionately and to look forward to retirement, it's also more crudely that I'm comfortably off now and have no worries about money. I can eat, drink, and buy what I like . . . Anne and I have the facility of freedom and amplitude of life here which cuts us off from the vast mass of people.' In the twenty-first century, the vast mass could still only dream of such freedom. But more and more were getting closer to it, thanks to their pursuit of what Crossman described as the more crude aspects of human existence.

■ Cold War

Britain was hostile to the Communist Soviet Union from the beginning of its existence, in 1917. Only in part was this a product of Lenin's negotiated peace with Germany, which meant that Britain's enemy only had to fight on one front. There was also an ideological element, which led to British intervention to assist the 'Whites' against the 'Reds' in the civil war of 1918–20. In response, **trade unionists** in ◄ London's docks refused to load supplies which, they suspected, were destined for anti-Communist fighters in Poland.

This episode was a significant breach from nineteenth-century British foreign policy, which had been driven by pragmatic interests since the fall of Napoleon in 1815. But after 1914–18 it was clear that the world had entered the era of war between peoples, and when an enemy could not be personified (as in the case of the Kaiser) it was convenient to conjure up fears of a faceless foe. 'Bolshevism' fitted the bill perfectly, and the 'red scare' stories between the wars worked only too well. The first inconvenient result was the Second World War, which would have been avoided if the British had taken seriously the logical gambit of an anti-German alliance with Moscow.

Thankfully for Britain, Hitler made up for the mistake by invading the Soviet Union in 1942, with disastrous results for himself. While the country was allied to 'Uncle Joe' Stalin, some **national newspapers** ◄ (particularly the *Express* controlled by **Lord Beaverbrook**) campaigned ◄ for a 'second front' to relieve German pressure on the Soviet Union. But policy-makers had secretly hoped from the outset that the Nazi war machine would be concentrated against the red menace, and old habits of thinking died hard. Again there was an inconvenient result for Britain; it was Soviet resistance at Stalingrad that broke the German spirit, and the success of Stalin's armies helped to ensure that Eastern Europe was left under the control of a hostile power – the very outcome that Britain had fought to avoid. Despite the apparent amity of the

▶ meetings between Roosevelt, Stalin and **Churchill**, the true lesson of
▶ pre-war British **appeasement** was not lost on the Soviet dictator.

While it is customary to date the 'Cold War' from Churchill's 'Iron Curtain' speech at Fulton, Missouri, in March 1946, British hostility had been almost continuous since 1917 and nothing really changed until the mid-1980s. The only new feature during the period of the Cold War was that Britain's attitude was now backed by the USA – or, rather, that British leaders battled for the right to hold the coats of successive American presidents while the remaining superpowers traded verbal blows. In hindsight, the most dangerous period came during the Berlin blockade of 1948–9, when American and British planes supplied the divided city. At the height of the crisis, US nuclear bombers arrived at British bases without a formal agreement, thus
▶ revealing the reality of the so-called '**special relationship**'.

For the British, the Cold War only turned hot between 1950 and 1953, when their forces were engaged against Communists in Korea. On this occasion, and in the later Cuban missile crisis of October 1962, British leaders reverted to their old pragmatic roles, seeking to restrain their American paymasters. No longer hoping to pose as a significant world power, Britain was able to stay out of the Vietnam War (1965–73). Neither did Britain suffer from the totalitarian atmosphere which afflicted the US during the 'McCarthyite' 1950s. The country's leaders had accepted Communism as an unpleasant fact of life, and their anxiety to build a nuclear 'deterrent' with a tenuous claim to be independent marked a desire to distance themselves from both sides of the ideological quarrel. Only the overwhelming power of the US military forced them to choose sides; but the developing move-
▶ ment for **European** unity offered a potential 'third way' which Edward Heath was glad to pursue as soon as he became Prime Minister in 1970.

At the time, the Americans looked on the prospect of European unity with favour, as an anti-Soviet bulwark. Whatever else might be happening in the world, the Iron Curtain had begun to look like a stabilising factor in Europe. On the Western side of the Berlin Wall (erected in 1961) Communism had limited appeal – except for a
▶ minority of **university** students. The realities of Stalin's regime were now notorious, and despite Soviet achievements during the 'space race' the Americans had outpaced them by putting men on the moon.
▶ But under **Margaret Thatcher** after 1979, Britons had reason to fear that peaceful coexistence might come to an end. Her anti-Soviet rhetoric, which in opposition had earned her the sobriquet of 'the Iron Lady', marked a return to Churchill's posture of 1946 as if nothing had happened since those early post-war days. When she was paired with an equally ideological US President in Ronald Reagan (1980–8) the
▶ moribund **Campaign for Nuclear Disarmament** revived, and for good

reason. From the end of 1983 Britain was used as a potential launching pad for US cruise missiles, and only knee-jerk adherents of the 'special relationship' could dismiss the argument that the presence of these weapons actually made war in Europe more likely.

Lady Thatcher's admirers will always argue that she took a firm line in full knowledge that the Soviet economic system was beginning to crack, but equally her detractors will continue to think that she was putting her nation at risk without giving thought to the possible consequences. Fortunately, even such a violent anti-Communist as herself proved capable of putting aside her armour in government. When Mikhail Gorbachev became General Secretary of the Soviet Communist Party in March 1985 he had already made a favourable impression at Downing Street. With the passage of years it is possible to cut through the **Thatcherite** rhetoric and to recognise that the end ◄ of the Cold War was Gorbachev's achievement, and no one else's. Even if the Soviet Union was losing the economic battle, the recent example of North Korea showed that under unscrupulous leadership an embattled regime with access to nuclear weapons can hold the whole world to ransom. Disdaining the idea of blackmail, Gorbachev threw away the only card in his hand and his fall from office in 1991 was unsurprising.

In January 1991 President George Bush felt confident enough to declare that the Cold War was over; the Berlin Wall had been breached in 1989. But almost as soon as the bi-polar world was consigned to history, far-sighted strategists began to want it back. This feeling was particularly acute in Britain. Basing foreign policy on ideological differences had been alien to its diplomatic tradition. But the same pragmatic outlook could appreciate the advantage of being on the stronger side in a dispute which carved up the world into two spheres of influence. Ordinary Britons who met Russians during the Gorbachev years could suddenly appreciate that the hostility had been entirely manufactured by politicians. Whereas antipathy towards the **Germans** persisted long after the political causes had gone, the people ◄ of Britain and Russia had always liked each other very much. The thought that natural allies might have obliterated each other if their leaders had followed their rhetoric might have been unsettling; but it remained the case that the Russian people must have been the most congenial enemies in the whole of British history.

The end of the Cold War just made everything more complicated; it did not even clarify relations with the former Soviet Union, which rapidly became a battleground between the 'forces of reaction' who wanted to cling to some vestiges of the Communist state, and 'entre-preneurs' who were often difficult to distinguish from the Mafia. After almost half a century when Britons braced themselves for a violent

C

death in a war to defend capitalist 'freedom' against 'totalitarian' Communism, it was now difficult to say which of the rival Russian forces was right or wrong. Meanwhile, to justify their defence expenditure Western leaders sought new enemies among former allies (given that China was now too powerful to confront). They did not have to look for long.

■ Communist Party of Great Britain (CPGB)

The CPGB was founded in London in 1920 by members of the British
▶ Socialist Party, a left-wing group affiliated to the **Labour Party** but disillusioned with its support for the First World War and inspired by the Bolshevik Revolution of 1917. The party's first leader was Harry Pollitt (1887–1965), a boilermaker in London's docks, who said of the Revolution, 'The workers have done it at last . . . lads like me have whacked the bosses and landlords and taken their factories, their lands and their banks.' Sadly for Pollitt and his followers, Britain's
▶ working classes showed a marked reluctance to follow suit over the next eighty years.

In 1920, and again in 1925, the CPGB applied for affiliation to the Labour Party, a tactical ploy that was rejected by the Labour leadership who, for the rest of the century, struggled to keep Communists out of
▶ the party and **trade unions**. The CPGB's fortunes were further damaged in 1924 by the Zinoviev Letter. Supposedly written by Grigori Zinoviev, leader of the Communist International, it called on British Communists to sow subversion among the armed services. Although it was forged by MI6, it accurately reflected the desire of the party to take over the British state. Pollitt relentlessly pursued a Stalinist line, both because the party's Moscow paymasters demanded it and because he genuinely believed in the goodness of the Russian dictator.

Despite this, British Communists enjoyed modest success during the interwar period. In 1922, they won two seats in parliament and another in 1935 when Willie Gallacher, a leader of the 'Red Clyde' strikes of 1917–22, took West Fife. The CPGB's support came mostly from the coal-mining areas of South Wales and the Central Belt of Scotland, with a smattering in the East End of London. The party was
▶ heavily involved in organising the **General Strike**. Over 1,000 of the 2,500 arrests made during it were CPGB members. As a result, membership doubled from 5,000 to 10,000 in September 1926 and reached a peak of 45,000 in 1945. The party also helped to organise the Hunger Marches that took place between 1927 and 1936 in protest at
▶ **unemployment** caused by the **Great Depression**. In 1930, the CPGB launched a newspaper, the *Daily Worker*. Despite the refusal of many newsagents to stock it, daily circulation averaged 40,000. Communists

were also at the forefront of anti-fascist activity. In the 'Battle of Cable Street', fought on 4 October 1936, they countered attempts by **Oswald Mosley**'s blackshirts to march through **Jewish** parts of East London; and in the same year Communists made up around half of the 1,500 volunteers who joined the British Battalion of the International Brigade that went to Spain in an attempt to save the republic from defeat by General Franco.

However, when the international struggle against fascism got fully under way, it inflicted serious damage on British Communism. From the signing of the Nazi–Soviet Pact in August 1939 until Germany invaded the Soviet Union in June 1941, the CPGB parroted Moscow's line that the conflict was 'an out and out imperialist war to which the working class in no country could give any support'. In January 1941, it organised a 'People's Convention' to agitate for a negotiated peace. **Churchill**'s Cabinet considered banning the party but contented itself with closing the *Daily Worker* for 15 months, rightly surmising that Communists were digging their own grave by opposing Britain's stand against Hitler. When Hitler attacked Russia, the CPGB finally declared the war to be a just one. Government-sponsored pro-Soviet propaganda between 1941 and the start of the **Cold War** in 1947 made the British people more sympathetic to 'Uncle Joe' Stalin; but it did not turn them into Communists.

At the general election of 1945, the CPGB returned two MPs: Willie Gallacher, again successful in West Fife, and Phil Piratin for Mile End in east London. But in 1950 the seats were lost, along with 97 deposits, and they never won another. The party tried to distance itself from the Soviet Union by manipulating nationalism (much as Stalin had done in Russia), a policy that culminated in the manifesto *The British Road to Socialism* (1951). But simultaneous attacks on the **Americanisation** of British culture only appealed to a clutch of intellectual fellow-travellers and not the millions that experienced the benefit of **Marshall Aid** and the pleasure of Hollywood blockbusters. Moreover, the CPGB's support for the Soviet invasion of Hungary in 1956 revealed where its loyalties still lay. Hungary undermined the sincerity of Pollitt's long-standing attack on British imperialism; and it lost the party what little support it still had among left-leaning intellectuals. In 1945, **George Orwell** had found it difficult to find a publisher for his anti-Stalinist allegory *Animal Farm*. A decade later it was one of the most popular books written in the English language.

The academic world was the last redoubt of British communism. A succession of Marxist theories, now imported from France and Germany rather than Russia, sought to explain away the British reluctance to storm the Houses of Parliament. The thought of people like Herbert Marcuse and Jürgen Habermas excited middle-class students

but it had little impact outside the nation's campuses and was skil-
▶ fully satirised by the **Beatles** song 'Revolution' (1968). The CPGB did
make some inroads into the trade union movement between the 1950s
and the 1980s, which increased shop-floor militancy and contributed
▶ to civil disruption like that of the 1979 '**Winter of Discontent**'. But it
further soured the public's view of Communism. Party membership
declined steadily, as did the readership of the *Daily Worker*, despite
being renamed the *Morning Star* in 1966. In the 1980s a more liberal
ideology – 'Eurocommunism' – emerged through the journal *Marxism
Today*. However, this only split the movement into still more splinter
groups, each claiming to be the authentic voice of proletarian revolution. In the general election of 1991, all CPGB candidates lost their
deposits, polling an average of 150 votes each. In 1995, the party finally
gave up the struggle to 'whack the bosses' and disbanded.

■ Comprehensive schools

The core of the system in operation since the 1960s by which all state-
▶ educated **children** receive the same education regardless of ability or
aptitude. The two-tier system of grammar schools and secondary
▶ moderns established by the Butler **Education Act** of 1944 was initially
▶ approved of by the middle **classes** because grammars gave a return on
their taxes by offering their offspring the chance of a free education in
a sound academic environment modelled on that of the public
schools. Although they were not guaranteed a place as they were in the
▶ single-tiered **National Health Service**, the middle classes' greater
ability to coach their children through the eleven-plus entrance exam
enabled them to have a disproportionately high presence in grammars.
This fuelled left-wing criticism that the system was socially divisive.

The first purpose-built comprehensive school, Kidbrooke in
London, opened in 1954. But the system did not become a nationwide
phenomenon until the Labour Minister for Education, Anthony
Crosland (1918–77), promised to 'destroy every fucking grammar
school in England, Wales and Northern Ireland'. Crosland, who had
been educated at Highgate independent school, began doing so in
1965. The eleven-plus examination was abolished and local authorities were pressured into setting up comprehensives. Grammars that
didn't wish to admit less able pupils usually began to charge fees. By
2002, this left only 5 per cent of children in grammar schools, 3 per
cent in secondary moderns and 86 per cent in comprehensives,
compared to 19, 33 and 37 per cent respectively in 1970. Grant-maintained church schools of various denominations (which numbered
around 4,000 in 1970, serving 25 per cent of children) joined the long
comprehensive march.

The end of formal selection at the school gates was accompanied by the decline of selection in the classroom, with the introduction of mixed-ability teaching up to school-leaving age (raised to 16 in 1970). The basis for this was the 1967 Plowden Report, *Children and their Primary Schools*. The author, Bridget Horatia Plowden (1910–2000), was the daughter of an admiral, had been educated by governesses in England and Ceylon and sent her two sons to Eton. Plowden argued that in mixed-ability classes, brighter children would lift the performance of the less able. She also argued that pedagogical teaching techniques should be replaced by 'child-centred learning', in which knowledge was acquired through a process of playful self-discovery rather than through instruction and examination – ironically, a system which, like the eleven-plus, benefited children who had recourse to parental instruction in the home.

The results of this well-meant revolution were apparent by the late 1970s: some of the lowest literacy and numeracy rates in the **European ◄ Union**; a decline in the proportion of working-class children progressing to university; and endemic indiscipline in Britain's schools. The so-called 'Black Papers' (1973) edited by Professor Brian Cox of Manchester University caused a furore by attacking the system but failed to dent its egalitarian ethos. By the mid-1970s, both the **Conservative** and **Labour** parties had recognised the problem. But ◄ they were handicapped by the fact that the British teaching profession had more power than its Continental counterparts, being run by local teacher training colleges, education authorities and examining boards, over which the state had comparatively little executive control.

The Education Act of 1988 tried to remedy the situation. As Education Secretary from 1970 to 1974, the grammar-school-educated **Margaret Thatcher** had accelerated the introduction of comprehen- ◄ sives. As Prime Minister she tried to atone by personally taking charge of what she regarded as the flagship legislation of her third term. First, power was transferred from LEAs to schools' boards of governors, who were allowed to opt out of local authority control altogether and be grant-maintained by the Ministry of Education. This enabled them to control admissions policy and so re-introduce selection by merit.

Second, a national curriculum was introduced in order to promote 'the spiritual, moral, cultural, mental and physical development of pupils' and so prepare them for the 'opportunities, responsibilities and experiences of adult life'. The National Curriculum codified what children learned and made the study of maths and English compulsory (previously only religious instruction had been). A renewed emphasis was placed on British history, a move that provoked accusations of nationalism. A new General Certificate of Secondary Education, divided up into four 'key stages', replaced the old GCE or 'O' level and the simpler CSE, which had been designed to allow less able children to pass exams (the National Curriculum did not apply in Scotland where the curriculum had been effectively codified since 1977).

Third, testing of children was introduced at 7, 11 and 14 and league tables of schools' performance were published to make teachers more accountable to parents. Fourth, Her Majesty's Inspectors of Schools, a central government body, was placed in the hands of independent inspectors, chosen by a tendering system. Finally, a new sort of state school, City Technical Colleges, were established and, in 1995, a new exam, the General National Vocational Qualification. Partly funded by sponsorship from industry, the colleges were designed to provide a fast track into industry for less academic pupils.

The counter-revolution failed. The teaching profession fought a rearguard action on school governing boards and by 1996, only 2,000 out of 24,300 schools in England and Wales had opted out; in Scotland only 2 out of 3,700 chose to. The staff of examination boards helped by making exams easier in order to maintain pass rates. Also, business proved more reluctant to invest in secondary education than in higher education, both because research offered a faster return than teaching and because **universities** were still devoted to the pursuit of excellence and therefore provided a more solid foundation for corporate investment than blighted inner-city schools.

The consistently best exam results in the state sector came from the 12,000 schools of the most socially segregated country in the United Kingdom: Northern Ireland. There, the eleven-plus and streaming remained in operation until the year 2000 when it was abolished after pressure from Sinn Féin/**IRA**. Schools were either directly run by central government in Belfast and London (these were mainly Protestant) or they were semi-independent grant-maintained church ones (mainly Roman Catholic). However, only 32 of the province's schools were integrated, serving 2 per cent of the population (directly run by London). The sectarian nature of Northern Irish society negated a system which, in theory, gave Protestant and Catholic pupils alike the kind of life chances once available to the rest of the UK.

Teachers were right to argue that more funding was necessary for the state sector. Salaries declined in real terms by about a third between 1979 and 1990, which made it difficult to attract the best people; classrooms were overcrowded; buildings were run-down and facilities poor. Unfortunately, the millions of middle-class parents who opted out of the failing state sector were unwilling to pay higher taxes to improve comprehensives on top of the school fees they were now paying. Meanwhile, those who kept their children in the state sector tended to colonise the best schools, mainly through their ability to buy a home in the appropriate catchment area, just as they had once colonised grammar schools by coaching their children through the eleven-plus.

The real inequality in British education was always that between the state and private sectors. Had Labour governments found the courage to reform **public schools** when advised to do so by Education ◄ Commissions in 1946 and 1968, the social apartheid they fostered might have been ameliorated. Instead, a long and bitter battle was fought *within* the state sector, most of it over teaching methods, which in the long run only benefited the privileged. **Nationalised** industries ◄ bore the brunt of attacks on the **welfare state** because their failure to ◄ make a profit and their drain on taxpayers' money could be more easily tabulated; and because industrial **trade unions** exercised their ◄ power more blatantly than the National Union of Teachers exercised theirs. Yet what took place in classrooms had a more damaging long-term effect on Britain than what took place on shop floors. State-school teachers played their part in the failure to create a meritocratic society based on equal opportunity. However, by the time that a 'New' ◄ **Labour** spokesman condemned the 'bog standard' nature of comprehensives in 2002, teachers had long since become the scapegoats of a political class that itself lacked the will to do so.

■ Conscription; conscientious objectors

On 5 January 1916 the **Liberal** Prime Minister Herbert Asquith intro- ◄ duced a Military Service Bill. By this time the First World War had cost the British almost half a million men (dead or wounded), and voluntary recruitment was no longer producing adequate replacements. The terms of the Bill fell a long way short of universal conscription, applying only to single men and to childless widowers between the ages of 18 and 41. But even this was too much for the tender consciences of around 50 Liberals, who voted against the measure, although only one minister (Sir John Simon, the Attorney-General) left the government as a result of this grievous breach of liberal doctrine. A second, comprehensive Bill was introduced in May 1916, partly in response to the threat of further trouble in Ireland after the **Easter Rising**. Prudently, ◄ conscription was never applied to that turbulent territory.

Conscription brought to light young men who, for one reason or another, were not prepared to fight. Summoned to a tribunal, the author Lytton Strachey tried to argue that he had no principled objection to war in general, but merely disagreed with the present one. Fortunately for him, various medical ailments provided a more convincing reason for exemption. Facing the tribunals was a far more unpleasant experience for those who lacked Strachey's upper-class ◄ insouciance, and his connections in high places. The panels contained military representatives who made it their business to humiliate the applicants. Three thousand conscientious objectors were sent to labour camps; a further 7,000 agreed to serve as non-combatants. Strachey's painful haemorrhoids meant that he was excused even from these duties, and he spent the remainder of the war free from the contaminating proximity of the working class.

Conscription lasted until 1919. Although conscientious objectors had not scuppered Britain's war effort, the emergence of a No Conscription Fellowship and a National Council against Conscription – the partial pacifist Strachey joined both organisations – caused

▶ concern, and in a remarkable act of vindictiveness **parliament** removed the right to vote from objectors for five years after the war.

In April 1939, after Hitler had broken the Munich agreement by marching into Prague and the British government had promised to defend Poland, Neville Chamberlain introduced a limited revival of conscription. Men aged 20 and 21 would be called up for 6 months of military training. Presumably the main intention was to concentrate Hitler's mind; but like most of Chamberlain's gambits during the

▶ period of **appeasement**, it failed. As before, there was opposition from
▶ the Liberals and **Labour**; but when the call-up was extended to all men between 18 and 41 after the outbreak of war, there were no ministerial
▶ resignations. This time conscription was extended to **women** (in December 1941).

Nearly 60,000 people resisted conscription on conscientious grounds during the Second World War. Chamberlain had promised that their views would be respected, presumably because the Peace Pledge Union claimed more than 100,000 supporters. The authorities had no need to persecute objectors, because after the outbreak of war social pressures could be relied upon to soften up all but the most determined pacifists (such as the composers Benjamin Britten and Michael Tippett). The number who served in non-combative capacities was almost the same as in the First World War. But of the remainder only about a thousand were jailed.

The atomic attacks on Hiroshima and Nagasaki suggested that the era of conscription was over. Yet the National Service Act of 1947 extended it into peacetime. At first the period of compulsory service was limited to one year; subsequently, though, it was extended to eighteen months (1948) and two years (1950). At least in part, this measure represented a concession by the Attlee government to the

▶ demands of service chiefs, particularly **Montgomery**. The new realities of warfare only seemed to register in 1957, by which time Britain was a fully-fledged member of the nuclear club. The Defence White Paper of that year envisaged a phasing out of National Service; conscription was to cease in 1960.

But although National Service was now utterly irrelevant to Britain's military requirements, it was still widely perceived to be useful. Whenever large numbers of young men behaved in an undisciplined fashion, the call to 'Bring back National Service' went up. The end of conscription seemed to mark a dividing line in the British story – after National Service came the deluge of the 1960s. Even a level-headed politician like William Whitelaw (Home Secretary from 1979 to 1983) seemed to think that young offenders would benefit from a 'short, sharp shock' in military-style camps – despite the warnings of others that a strict regime would merely groom a new generation of super-fit criminals. The moral fabric of the nation had survived despite the absence of conscription between 1919 and 1939. But presumably the advocates of National Service had forgotten this awkward fact.

■ 'Consensus'

It is often argued that a governing 'consensus' prevailed in Britain from the end of the Second World War until the election of the **Conservative** government of **Margaret Thatcher** in 1979. On this view, ◄ all the major parties agreed on the broad outlines of policy: they accepted the **welfare state** and the **nationalisation** of key utilities like ◄ the railways, tried to ensure 'full' employment, and managed the economy in accordance with what were held to be **Keynesian** theories ◄ of demand management. Although there were differences of emphasis between the parties on secondary issues, these points of agreement were fundamental and dissident politicians found it difficult to win a hearing for their views.

Towards the end of the 1980s it seemed that although the old consensus had broken down in the wake of the oil crisis of the mid-1970s, the parties were still in broad agreement. The alleged new consensus marked the general acceptance of 'Thatcherism'. Thus the ◄ state should try to ensure low **inflation** rather than full employment, ◄ it should control spending on welfare, and it should no longer interfere in the detailed workings of the economy. Whereas the earlier consensus had largely been shaped by the Attlee government, this new one meant that the parties were all contesting office on natural Conservative territory.

Like most broad explanatory theories, the idea of consensus can be attacked in detail. But it still provides a useful tool for understanding the post-war period. It can even be extended backwards into a period when the ruling ideas were different, to explain why (for example) the **Labour** government of **Ramsay MacDonald** rejected the radical policy ◄ ideas put forward by **Oswald Mosley**. When Labour proved incapable of ◄

▶ resolving the economic dilemmas presented by the **Great Depression**, the party entered a coalition with the Conservatives who represented the traditional 'class enemy'.

▶ One key point sometimes overlooked is that despite the mediocre electoral record of the **Liberal Party**, liberalism as an ideology was in the ascendant throughout the twentieth century. The first recognised 'consensus' was heavily influenced by two Liberal Party members,

▶ Keynes and **William Beveridge**; and despite Labour's ventures into the public ownership of industry, the underlying principles behind the

▶ welfare state had been established by Liberals such as **David Lloyd George** before the First World War. The liberalism of the welfare state was based on the assumption that no one can be 'free' unless they are guaranteed at least a basic level of prosperity. The change after 1979 can be exaggerated – the welfare state was not dismantled, for example – but there was a definite shift to a different, *laissez-faire* variant of liberalism, which claims that the individual is *unfree* if he or she is dependent on the state. This idea outlived the end of Conservative government in 1979, but might come under increasing pressure if the world economy continues to stagnate.

■ Conservative Party

On 1 January 1900 the British Prime Minister was a Conservative, the 3rd Marquess of Salisbury. When Salisbury's party won the 1992 general election – an unprecedented fourth successive victory – it looked as if the century would end with another Conservative government, this time led by the son of a garden gnome manufacturer. John Major, indeed, had once failed in an application to become a London bus conductor. Although his government was ejected from office in the 1997 election, it still seemed fair to say that it had been a 'Conservative Century'. The party (still sometimes known as the Tory Party, reflecting its seventeenth-century origins) had been in office, either on its own or in coalition, for more than two-thirds of the previous hundred years.

During the second part of the nineteenth century the Conservatives had shown remarkable adaptability. Originally dominated by members of the 'landed interest' – like Salisbury himself – the party seemed to emulate the British social elite by absorbing talented outsiders (like Benjamin Disraeli) without changing its essential character. Yet the twentieth century, which saw a significant expansion of

▶ the electoral franchise, the loss of the **British Empire**, and the erosion

▶ of national **sovereignty** through membership of the North Atlantic

▶ Treaty Organisation (NATO) and the **European** Economic Community (EEC), confronted the Conservative Party with an even sterner test.

There were times when its survival seemed in doubt. Their furious opposition to Home Rule for Ireland laid some Conservatives open to the charge of inciting armed rebellion before the First World War. This was no grass-roots agitation; the party's leader, Andrew Bonar Law, fully supported the resistance movement in Ulster. For most of the period up to the Second World War the Conservatives were divided over the issue of **tariff reform**. Beginning with the **Suez** misadventure ◄ of 1956–7, the party has also suffered grave internal dissent over Britain's reduced status in the world. At the end of the century, the main source of division was the European Union. This provoked John Major's unprecedented decision to resign as leader (though not as Prime Minister) in 1995. Although he defeated his critics in the ensuing contest the issue continued to dog the party into the new millennium.

From 1900, the party's leaders have been Salisbury (1881–1902), Arthur Balfour (1902–11), Bonar Law (1911–21), Austen Chamberlain (1921–2), Bonar Law again (1922–3), **Stanley Baldwin** (1923–37), ◄ Neville Chamberlain (1937–40), **Winston Churchill** (1940–55), ◄ Anthony Eden (1955–7), Harold Macmillan (1957–63), Alec Douglas-Home (1963–5), Edward Heath (1965–75), **Margaret Thatcher** ◄ (1975–90), John Major (1990–97), William Hague (1997–2001), Iain Duncan Smith (2001–3), and Michael Howard (since 2003). The party's longest period out of office was between 1906 and 1915, when it was invited to join H.H. Asquith's wartime coalition.

One important reason for the party's success in the twentieth century was its ability to pose as the custodian of the national interest (while **Labour** was portrayed as a class-based party). Although it was ◄ the natural home for the affluent, in the democratic age it depended crucially on working-class votes and it proved remarkably successful in attracting support even from **trade unionists**. In 1987, for example, ◄ around 30 per cent of union members voted Conservative, only 12 per cent less than Labour achieved. At that time, just over two-thirds of Conservative MPs had been educated at public school – a higher proportion than the figure at the start of the century. If the Conservative appeal crossed class boundaries, it also extended throughout the UK for most of the century. In 1935 it won 43 out of 71 Scottish seats; in the same election, it carried 11 of the 35 Welsh constituencies. Until 1974, it could also count on the support of the Ulster Unionists who dominated the politics of Northern Ireland.

By 2000, though, the party had lost all of its MPs outside England. In 1992 it had attracted the highest vote for any British political party – more than 14 million. But the figure in 1997 was less than 10 million – its worst numerical performance since 1929. At 30.7 per cent, its share of the vote was the lowest in the twentieth century. It

had already been revealed that membership had slumped to around 300,000; at its peak in 1953 a figure approaching 3 million had been claimed. The dwindling band of the faithful was also ageing, to underline the impression that the party was 'out of touch' with the average voter. Since the Second World War the business community had funded a series of effective advertising campaigns. But unex-
▶ pected competition from **'New' Labour** for these resources meant that the Conservatives were almost bankrupted by their attempt to cling on to power in 1997. In the following election of 2001 the scale of defeat was almost identical.

Was this stunning transformation a temporary setback, or the symptom of a deeper-seated decline? Broadly speaking, the record of Conservative governments up to the 1980s can be interpreted as a series of attempts to manage unavoidable change. Thus, after Labour's landslide victory of 1945 the party accepted the general principles of post-war reconstruction, merely promising to dismantle unnecessary
▶ regulations and opposing any further **nationalisation** of industry. But after its two defeats of 1974 the party leadership turned against this policy framework, arguing that excessive state intervention had only
▶ created **inflation**, without tackling the roots of Britain's economic decline. While this approach was highly controversial – not least within the party itself – Margaret Thatcher's early policies only differed from the previous attitude to change because for once the Conservatives had *anticipated* a worldwide trend, instead of reacting to it.

However, after the party's victory in the 1983 general election (which might not have been secured without the recapture of the
▶ **Falkland** Islands in the previous year) there was an unmistakable change of gear. Radical reforms affected almost every British institution; only the Lords and the Commons, with their comfortable Conservative majorities, emerged virtually unscathed. Previously, the party had profited from deference towards people and institutions – unsurprisingly, since so many of its senior figures held high offices in the shires and in voluntary organisations. But under Thatcher nothing seemed sacred – as the Prime Minister discovered herself when she was deposed in 1990. The name of the party had always been slightly misleading – it certainly had not existed to 'conserve' at all costs – but many of Thatcher's supporters were radical ideologues who confused
▶ public disillusionment with some aspects of the post-war **'consensus'** with a conscious desire to reshape the whole country on free-market principles. John Major's early speeches suggested a desire to restore Stanley Baldwin's conciliatory style of leadership; he clearly hoped to heal domestic divisions and seemed realistic about Britain's international standing. Yet the party membership had become addicted to

Thatcher's iconoclasm, and since he lacked the authority to oppose this mood Major was compelled to appease it.

The Conservatives could still continue to win elections by appealing to the 'contented' majority. But this depended on the retention of their reputation for economic competence, which could be destroyed by a sudden crisis. There were, in fact, two serious recessions between 1979 and 1992. The second of these, in particular, undermined the party in its heartlands; so that when the Major government was forced out of the Exchange Rate Mechanism (ERM) of the European Monetary System soon after the 1992 election, there was no longer anything to sustain it. Not even a divided opposition, which had proved crucial during the Thatcher years, could keep the party in office.

Thus at the end of the 'Conservative Century' the party's future prospects looked bleaker than ever before. Its only distinctive policy was an attachment to the 'nation', but William Hague's attempt to exploit this by campaigning to 'save the pound' never seemed promising, when so many of Britain's traditional institutions were decaying. The Conservative Party itself was being reformed, in an attempt to emulate the success of 'New' Labour's 'modernisers'. Arthur Balfour once said that he would sooner take advice from his valet than from the activists at a Conservative Party conference. Hague had a judo partner (Sebastian Coe) rather than a valet; and whatever he thought of party members he could no longer treat them with open disdain. Until Edward Heath was elected by his fellow Conservative MPs in 1965, the leader had 'emerged' after informal consultations. This change was a direct result of the controversial elevation of Douglas-Home – the last aristocrat to lead the party – in 1963. Since then the various leaders have been subjected to constant criticism, even when in power, and the party's divisions have been impossible to conceal. This was a sharp contrast to the pre-war position, when the party's ability to unite at crucial moments had arguably ensured that it, rather than the Liberals, had survived as the main electoral rival to Labour. By the end of the century the party had travelled even further along the path of internal democracy, allowing its constituency members the final choice in the leadership selection process.

It would be reckless to write off the Conservative Party – the chameleon of the democratic world. The two depressing defeats of 1997 and 2001 might have been unprecedented in scale, but the party had bounced back after 1966, when Labour was re-elected with an overall majority of 98. Nevertheless, there were good reasons for thinking that while previous defeats had merely resulted from the normal swing of the electoral pendulum, in 1997 the clock finally stopped for the Conservative Party.

■ Consumerism

In 1921 the socialist academic R.H. Tawney wrote *The Acquisitive Society*, a passionate attack on the pursuit of individual self-interest. For Tawney, the purpose of **manufacturing** industry was to provide 'things which are necessary, useful, and beautiful, and thus to bring life to body or spirit'. But in Britain, as Tawney pointed out, a high proportion of industry was devoted to objects of conspicuous consumption for rich people who felt the 'need' to flaunt their wealth.

Tawney's book was widely read, and his message was politely ignored. When he wrote, there were 300,000 private motor cars. By the outbreak of the Second World War this figure had risen to 2 million. There were 1 million telephones in 1922, and three times as many in 1938.

Between 1922 and 1939, Britain was transformed from an 'affluent' society, where only a privileged minority could indulge themselves with 'luxuries', to a consumerist society in which new-fangled devices like radios and vacuum cleaners were affordable for most people in work. Partly this phenomenon reflected the general rise in living standards between the wars, but demand and supply fuelled each other as 'Fordist' techniques of mass production allowed manufacturers to keep prices low, and one invention triggered off another. The process came to a head in the **house**-building boom of the 1930s, as young couples took advantage of low interest rates to set up their own homes and equip them with the new labour-saving devices, such as refrigerators and gas or electric fires.

Social commentators of all persuasions were unsettled by this development, but it was particularly disturbing to the left. Writers like **J.B. Priestley** and **George Orwell** emphasised the growing divergence between the haves and the have-nots, reflected in a widening **North–South divide** between the prosperous suburbs of the South in particular and the declining Northern industrial cities. The problem of wealth distribution seemed more acute than ever, and the persistence of real **poverty** amid so much material comfort was, if anything, an even greater moral outrage. But at least part of the left-wing concern was an echo of the old puritanical distaste for enjoyment of any kind. Even more important was an anxiety about the prospects for socialism. In the early nineteenth century Shelley had written revolutionary poems in the hope that even overworked proletarians would read them and absorb the message. Now the workers had more leisure time. But instead of rising like lions after slumber in unvanquishable number they were trooping off to the **cinema**. When they saw glamorous Hollywood stars on the screen, enjoying even more sophisticated household comforts, their envious thoughts were directed across the Atlantic rather than to their brethren in the Soviet Union.

The Second World War was a decisive period in British social history. For some, the impact of rationing reinforced existing attitudes, so that even when the restrictions were lifted they continued to exercise the old Victorian values of thrift and self-denial. But they were the minority, and as their ranks thinned out in the post-war years there was nobody to replace them. Even the 1945–51 **Labour** ◄ government could not overlook the popular demand for a return to the consumerist outlook which had taken a stranglehold before the outbreak of war. Exposure to the American GIs in the latter stages of the conflict undoubtedly helped to reinforce this mood. But it was there already.

In the 1950s rates of **economic growth** in Britain lagged behind its ◄ **European** competitors, but living standards continued to improve. ◄ The new focus of demand was the television set. In 1947 the numbers were negligible; ten years later the sets occupied a place of honour in almost half of all households. When the **Conservative** Prime Minister ◄ Harold Macmillan remarked in 1957 that 'most of our people have never had it so good', it was quickly forgotten that he had used the phrase in the course of a warning that continued prosperity could not be guaranteed. As a One Nation Tory, Macmillan had been anxious to qualify his statement; times were good for 'most', but not 'all'. This vital clause was dropped whenever people misquoted Macmillan in the future. The poor no longer counted as part of 'our people'.

In the post-war period British society made the next transition, beyond consumerism to decadence. One difficulty for the interwar critics was that almost all of the new consumer goods really were useful, in that they spared people (usually housewives) from monotonous, time-consuming tasks. The war did not put a stop to new inventions of this kind. But consumers moved on, to equip themselves with items which 'saved' fractions of minutes. Of all the surreal examples, the television remote control stands supreme. Although it was first produced in the mid-1950s, it did not really take off in Britain for thirty years, for obvious reasons. It merely saved the consumer from the labour of having to move towards the set to press a switch. Instead of saving time, the remote control actually resulted in many wasted minutes as the consumers scrambled to locate the accursed object. At least this meant that an increasingly overweight population received the benefit of a little exercise; but the accompanying debates to establish who had mislaid the device did little to improve blood pressure.

The motor car was another telling symbol of a real change in the post-war period. Of course, the British were not alone in regarding this ▶ individualistic means of **transport** as either a toy, a temple or a murder weapon (as early as 1938 the annual slaughter on Britian's roads was around 7,000; the toll has diminished since its peak in the 1960s largely because there are fewer cyclists to destroy). In 1951 only 14 per cent of households had a private car. By 1996 a quarter of households had two cars, or even more. The absence of a car was by now regarded as an inexpressible deprivation, but fortunately only 30 per cent of households suffered from it. It was also essential to purchase the kind of car which said something about one's personality. What it usually said was that the owner was incapable of expressing personal attributes in the old ways, such as conversation.

Like most other things, the obsession with the car was largely produced by advertising. Cars were usually depicted gliding smoothly over deserted roads in exotic locations, although the grim reality for motorists was that during their lifetimes they would spend months in traffic queues. Other advertisements played on the superior speed of the car in question, despite the existence of legal limits which almost every car could exceed comfortably.

So it would be a mistake to say (as most people did) that the ▶ consumer was king. Or rather, he or she was a **monarch** much like the British Queen, surrounded by status symbols but almost entirely lacking in power. The other resemblance was the fact that the consumer was living on the productive efforts of other people. By 2003, unsecured personal debt (excluding mortgages) had soared to £140 billion; the average household owned £12,000. But the 'health' of the economy was said to depend on consumer spending, and spending more than one could afford had become a patriotic duty.

There were few signs that consumers were unhappy under the despotism of the advertising industry and the peddlers of 'essential' equipment which was built to be obsolete within a few years. But towards the end of the twentieth century some were beginning to ▶ notice that the production of these items had damaged the **environment** – indeed, that the process of manufacturing, and the pollution produced by the burning of fossil fuels, had already caused irreversible changes to the climate. Earnest programmes about the endangered planet began to jostle in the TV schedules with advice on the ▶ most prestigious cars, and **DIY** guidance for new home-owners hoping to impress the neighbours with their shining appliances. Thanks to the remote control, consumers could flick between the channels without rising from their seats, or thinking.

■ Cookson, Catherine (1906–98)

The best-selling British author of the century, her 90 novels were translated into 20 languages, and by the year 2000 had sold almost 100 million copies. She was born Catherine McMullen, illegitimately, in Tyne Dock, County Durham, to a poverty-stricken family of Irish stock. For most of her childhood she was brought up by an aunt; she never knew her father and until her teens was led to believe that her mother, a violent alcoholic, was her sister.

Despite the minimal education available to a woman of her background, she was determined to become a writer, and at the age of 11 she submitted her first story, 'The Wild Irish Girl', to the *South Shields Gazette*. She left school two years later and worked as a maid in the houses of Tyneside's rich and powerful, where she gained further insight into Britain's class divide. From 1924 to 1929 she worked in a ◄ laundry and saved enough money to establish a small lodging house in Hastings. One of the tenants was Tom Cookson, a schoolteacher, whom she married in 1940 and remained with for the rest of her life. After several miscarriages, she became acutely depressed and began writing again in order to recover, joining a local writers' group for encouragement and enlisting her husband to help with grammar and spelling.

Her first book, *Kate Hannigan* (1950), tells the story of a working-class girl who becomes pregnant by a middle-class man; the child is brought up by Kate's parents and believes Kate to be her sister. Most of Cookson's novels, though not as heavily autobiographical as her first, had as their central theme a heroine who uses education to overcome poverty and win love and prosperity. Most had as their background the mines and shipyards of north-east England and were set in the nineteenth and early twentieth centuries, although occasionally they had a contemporary setting, notably *Colour Blind* (1953) which addressed the issue of **miscegenation**. Cookson never had any children and ◄ remained tediously obsessed with her own childhood, publishing three volumes of autobiography, *Our Kate* (1969), *Let Me Make Myself Plain* (1988) and *Plainer Still* (1995), to augment her many fictionalised accounts of it. Cookson's novels appealed to **women** struggling to rise ◄ above their mundane lives, fantasising about doing so in a post-war world where escape from drudgery was finally becoming a possibility for all. Because the books had marriage and money as their objects, and because they were written in a romantic style, they were dismissed by feminist critics. It didn't bother her. She received an honorary degree from the University of Newcastle in 1970, the freedom of the Borough of South Shields in 1977 and was made a Dame in 1983.

Cookson was a proud and ambitious woman who loved fame, though she never had serious literary pretensions. 'I am merely a teller of tales,' she once said. Yet hers was a formidable achievement. By the time of her death, her books were still best-sellers and nine of them were on the list of the ten most borrowed books in British libraries. Her cultural significance lies in the fact that her popularity was singled out by critics as *the* barometer of the failure of working people
▸ to make use of the literacy that state **education** had given them.

■ Cricket

Cricket is a ball game, with rules and terminology which are allegedly
▸ incomprehensible to anyone born outside the old **British Empire**. Certainly Field-Marshal Rommel would have been bemused to hear
▸ General **Montgomery** inviting the Eighth Army to knock the Germans 'for six' on the eve of battle at El Alamein; and any stranger who
▸ witnessed Sir Geoffrey Howe complaining that **Margaret Thatcher** was like a captain who had broken the bats of her own players might have wondered why this odd simile had helped to bring her premiership to an end in November 1990.

Despite its later associations with the Empire and the upper
▸ classes, cricket seems to have originated back in the sixteenth century, when Britain clung to the periphery of European power-politics. In itself it was not socially exclusive; in the nineteenth century many factories and churches organised their own teams. Nevertheless, there was something about cricket which appealed to the self-image of society's leaders in the Victorian period. There was the opportunity for
▸ exercise, without the sustained excitement of **football** or **rugby**; captains could affect the course of games through tactical changes born of quiet reflection in the field or the pavilion; and players could demonstrate their sense of fair play by giving themselves 'out' before learning the umpire's judgement, or cheerfully confessing when they had failed to achieve a clean catch.

▸ It was, in short, the perfect game for **public schools** hoping to groom a generation of gentlemen. Whether they continued to play or not, affluent old boys were happy to patronise a sport which inculcated such agreeable habits – all the more so because they could
▸ **gamble** on the results. County sides were often subsidised by the local aristocracy. The annual 'Gentlemen versus Players' match, first contested in 1806, was a highlight of the season into the second half of the twentieth century. The social distinction only ended in 1963 – just before the ultimate 'Gentleman', Alec Douglas-Home, was supplanted as Prime Minister by the unsporting Harold Wilson. Coming three years before the England football team won the World

Cup, the reorganisation was much too late to allow cricket to compete for national affection. A similar global tournament was only organised for cricket in 1975, but to date England has not managed to win – unlike the tiny, tea-growing former colony of Sri Lanka.

At the end of the century it seemed that the class bias would become more firmly entrenched, despite the all-pervasive rhetoric of 'meritocracy' off the field and the success of interlopers like Ian ◄ **Botham**. State schools were having to sell off their sports facilities. And in any case the basic equipment of cricket is more expensive than that of alternative outdoor activities for the young. Amateur 'village green' cricket continued to thrive in some areas, presenting urban office workers with an opportunity for fresh air and exercise during their weekends at their second homes. But only around 1 per cent of the adult population now played the game, compared to 20 per cent who slogged around muddy football pitches.

Public attention focused on the ever-increasing number of 'Test' matches, held over five days between national teams. The first of these was Australia versus England, held at Melbourne in 1877. Five years later the visiting Australians beat England by seven runs, and a writer in the *Sporting Times* was moved to claim that English cricket had 'died at the Oval on 29 August 1882 . . . The body will be cremated and the Ashes taken to Australia.' The author could not know it – partly because the run of success for the mother country was quickly resumed – but he had created the prototype for late twentieth-century sporting journalism in Britain. Even when British teams performed well there was a general impression of a plucky but declining nation, persistently outplayed by others in games of their own invention. The 'Ashes' themselves – the sacred remains of either a ball or a bail – continued to reside at Lord's, the 'headquarters of cricket' in north London. By the end of the century, when England was stuck in what seemed an endless run of defeats in the Ashes matches, the retention of the sacred urn was beginning to look rather dubious.

Cricket was a natural export for energetic imperialists. In almost every outpost the **weather** was better, and at that time the English ◄ had not developed the habit of praying for the intervention of rain to stave off another defeat. The contagion spread to the indigenous populations, and occasionally the English would sneak a particularly gifted overseas player into their own side. In 1926 three other teams (New Zealand, India and the West Indies) were given official Test status (South Africa having joined the fray in 1888). Pakistan (1952), Sri Lanka (1981), Zimbabwe (1992) and Bangladesh (2000) were later arrivals. Scotland, Wales and Northern Ireland had no such aspirations, though occasionally representative teams took part (as did the Netherlands, for obscure reasons). Really gifted players from these

countries could play for 'England' without anyone taking much notice; indeed Wales and Scotland both supplied 'English' captains (Tony Lewis and Mike Denness) in the early 1970s – a time of growing
► support for **devolution**.

In theory sporting links should bring nations together, full-blooded rivalry on the field leading to lasting amity between players and peoples alike. Something in the nature of Test-match cricket makes the practice somewhat different. If the national team is struggling, there is a prospect of a five-day humiliation (as opposed to ninety minutes of footballing agony). If the sides are closely matched, the nerves are subjected to prolonged strain. But the cricketing nations have found many other reasons to fall out. The tactics used by English bowlers to thwart the prolific Australian Donald (later Sir Donald) Bradman during the 'Bodyline' tour of Australia in 1932–3 caused political tension between the two countries. Games between India and Pakistan were always fraught, for obvious reasons. By the late 1960s the status of apartheid South Africa was an additional cause for concern. The English tour of 1968–9 was cancelled because the racist government could not stomach the inclusion in the visiting party of the 'Cape Coloured', Basil D'Oliveira. Even so, the English authorities were anxious that the South African team should tour in 1970; the matches were only called off under pressure from protestors. South Africa only rejoined the cricketing fold in 1991.

To the average English cricketing enthusiast, the row over South Africa was an egregious intrusion of political correctness into a beautiful game. To the members of cricket's governing body up to 1969, the Marylebone Cricket Club (MCC, based at Lord's), the racial composition of teams was at best a secondary consideration. They believed that talented cricketers should not be barred from top-class competition because their countries were governed by racists. To other observers, though, the MCC itself was a highly political organisation, riddled
► with class prejudice and misogyny like most of the British **Establishment**. Just as the alleged 'old farts' who ran Rugby Union were coming under scrutiny, the denizens of Lord's seemed hopelessly anachronistic, in social terms but also in relation to the game itself, which was becoming increasingly one for full-time 'Players' rather than the retired 'Gentlemen' who persisted in thinking that they could domineer from their armchairs.

Until the mid-1970s, English cricket was still sticking to the old ways as far as possible in a changing environment. Fittingly, the conclusive stroke came from the old Dominions. In 1977 the Australian media magnate Kerry Packer launched a cricketing 'circus', offering irresistible financial inducements for professionals of all nations to perform for his TV channel. The English 'mercenaries' who seized Packer's dollars became social and sporting outcasts (they included the captain, Tony Greig, a South African by birth). But the damage had been done.

It was not that cricket was incapable of drawing large crowds. In 1947, when spectator sports of all kinds were still buoyed up by what remained of the wartime spirit of community, attendances at first-class matches approached 3 million. The average crowd on the first day of a county match was 15,000 in 1890. But by 2003 anything over a thousand was regarded as respectable. In response to this decline, radical changes had been initiated. Limited-overs cricket had been introduced to entice the paying public, to disapproving tutting from the 'Gentlemen' assembled in the pavilion. After more than a century of serene, single-league complacency, counties could even be relegated from the first division, to inject a greater spirit of competition. Purists did have a point, though, when teams were decked out in coloured outfits which resembled pyjamas and bashed a white ball around a floodlit field. In 2003, a new variant of the one-day game invited batsmen to slog for a derisory 20 overs per side.

Meanwhile, standards of behaviour on the field declined, with players questioning umpiring decisions and trying to break each other's concentration with juvenile insults. The phrase 'it's just not cricket', to denote unfairness, was now rarely heard. It was assumed that winning by any means was preferable to defeat within the letter and spirit of the rules. The public assumed that, just as in its dealings with **Europe**, the nation suffered because its rivals were far better at ◄ cheating. Yet the English had invented cricketing 'gamesmanship' back in 1932. No one seemed to realise that consistent success for the English team would undermine the nation's favourite pastime – whingeing.

■ Crime

The overall crime figures for Britain in the twentieth century paint a startling picture. In 1900 the total of all 'notified' offences for England, Wales and Scotland was just over 110,000. By 1990 it had exceeded 5.5 million. Some of the detailed statistics were even more dramatic. In England and Wales there were only 256 crimes classed as 'robberies' in 1900; in 1997 the figure was 63,100. That was almost the exact number of 'thefts' in 1900; the corresponding tally in 1997 was 2,165,000. Respect for persons had fared no better than the sanctity of private property. There were more reported rapes in 1997 (6,600) than there had been burglaries in 1910, and there was more than a tenfold increase in woundings between 1960 and the end of the century. At least these assaults rarely led to death. Although the figure doubled over the century, there were still less than two cases of murder, manslaughter, etc. per day in 1997. Northern Ireland was exceptional, with a peak of 349 deaths through terrorist activity in 1972. Residents of the province would find scant consolation in its resistance to other criminal trends within the UK. For example, while recorded incidents of criminal damage soared from 387,000 to 930,000 in England and Wales between 1981 and 1994, in Northern Ireland they actually fell from 5,000 to 3,000.

Recorded levels of crimes notified to the police have often been questioned, and some prefer to use the British Crime Survey (BCS) which draws on the experiences of a representative sample of the population. Sometimes an increase in the official figures will actually reflect an improvement in reporting. Thus the general change in the attitude to sex crimes probably accounts for some of the rise in recorded rapes (even though the figure was probably still grossly under-reported); and wider insurance cover probably affects the level of reported property crime. Even so, the overall trend is unmistakable, and with the exception of Portugal, Britain now has the largest propor-
► tion of prisoners in the EU. The upward surge was not consistent. Crime fell between 1945 and 1950, following a 60 per cent rise (contrary to popular wisdom) during the war. But while many people look back on the 1950s as something like a golden age for British society, the figures began to climb again. For example, even in a quiet north-western market town, Kendal, in separate incidents within a few months in the mid-1950s two men were kicked to death outside pubs.

The steepest increase, though, took place in the early 1960s, when the overall figure for England and Wales exceeded 1 million for the
► first time. The 1960 report of the Committee on **Children** and Young Persons underlined the most worrying trend – a marked increase among offenders between the ages of 8 and 21. The committee suggested a link between boredom and crime; but policy-makers seemed short of answers. Later saloon-bar criminologists bemoaned
► the phasing out of **conscription**; but the rise of unruly youth (symbol-ised in particular by the 'Teddy Boys' of the mid to late 1950s) pre-dated this. By 1994 over 40 per cent of offenders in England and Wales were 21 or younger.

The 1960s seems to have been a decade of adjustment to a high-crime society; or, perhaps, it was simply unusual because there were so many high-profile cases. The Great Train Robbery, the murders by
► **Brady and Hindley** and the activities of the **Kray** twins made indi-vidual criminals into regular fixtures on the front pages. But the days of the gentleman thief – or the gentleman gangster – were apparently over (the female murderer had always been a hate-figure, particularly when children were involved). When the Great Train Robber and

prison escapee Ronnie Biggs returned to Britain just before the end of the century, after many years of exile in Brazil, it was not just his age and frailty which made him seem a grotesquely anachronistic figure.

For the adult population, at least, very little glamour was attached to criminals any more; the problem, once again, was with the young, who seemed to think that criminal activities were honourable rites of passage. And, as social conservatives constantly emphasised, the courts seemed powerless against them. Even when they were detained, they seemed to be released as quickly as possible, often through the intervention of the European Court of Human Rights. The killers of the toddler James Bulger in 1993 aroused a storm of protest when they were let out after only 8 years, equipped with new identities. Public outrage (fuelled by the tabloid press and cheerfully abetted by the electronic media) tended to focus on short-lived scares rather than individuals. Thus in the 1990s 'road rage', the problem of 'travellers' and paedophilia all had their spells under the spotlight. But then the bandwagon would roll on and attention move elsewhere, as if the problem had vanished and Bishop Berkeley was a Chief Crime Correspondent. Public fears of falling victim to criminal activity rarely reflected the real situation. But at least people were justified in being much more frightened in 2000 than they had been twenty years earlier.

The rise in crime was highly complex, and **Tony Blair's** soundbite of ◀ the early 1990s – 'Tough on crime, tough on the causes of crime' – was question-begging even by his standards. There was one obvious 'cause' which he had no intention of being 'tough' about. The most gaudy badges of affluence, such as flashy cars and expensive wristwatches, were provocations for theft. The cliché, 'If you've got it, flaunt it', could be met with the reply, 'If you flaunt it, I'll steal it.' But many other desirable consumer goods were easily affordable – and, in the case of items like video machines, easily transportable. By the end of the century the mobile phone had emerged as a convenient and quick way of reporting crimes; the drawback was that it was itself an irresistible target for thieves, particularly when brandished by a child. In 2002 it was estimated that the theft of mobile phones accounted for a third of all London's street robberies.

The ubiquity of consumer goods, and the fact that every self-respecting householder was under an obligation to procure the latest gadgets, meant that burglars no longer had to 'case the joint'; they could calculate their gains with reasonable accuracy merely by checking their victim's postcode before they set off. The fact that many of these consumer luxuries-turned-necessities soon became obsolete – indeed, commercial priorities meant that they were usually intended to do so – fostered a casual attitude to goods which would have been cherished before the war. For those with full insurance it was often a case of 'easy come, easy go'; it was common to hear victims saying that they were appalled by the intrusions into their homes, rather than their temporary material losses. This attitude was more understandable because people who suffered one burglary were likely to be targeted on a regular basis, as the criminals just needed to wait for them to replace their electronic devices before striking again. In 2002 more than 40 per cent of burglaries were committed in less than 1 per cent of households, and the majority of these crimes took place in deprived areas. It might have been better if the feeling of resignation had been universal. But elderly people, who had retained some of the old outlook, were stricken by the whole experience. In some cases they did not survive, although their 'natural' deaths from shock or other emotional traumas did not register in the manslaughter tally as they ought to have done.

An obsessive desire to possess, coupled with a lack of real attachment to the possessions, must surely breed criminals (and provide them with their opportunities). As well as wanting to steal, those who were excluded from the circle of **consumerist** comfort were also more tempted to destroy. Between 1987 and 2002 cases of arson rose from an annual rate of 31,600 to 111,000. In so far as they worshipped the market economy – which they almost invariably did – social conservatives were debarred from peering too closely into the real underlying causes of these trends. Instead, they railed against a general decline in respect for authority. What this really meant was a lack of respect for society's *deterrents*, arising from allegedly soft sentences. That was a plausible argument, but it tended to weaken when the remedy was suggested. Normally this turned out to be longer stretches in more unsavoury cells – as if the person who eventually emerged would be transformed by the experience into a pillar of society. The notion that the prospect of this variety of 'toughness' would make a would-be thief think again as he passed a sports car with an open window was based on the assumption that most thieves undergo the same process of rational decision-making as the law-abiding citizen. Somewhere lurking behind the argument was the suggestion that everyone would commit a crime if they could be sure of getting away with it.

The most worrying implication of these common assumptions was that far from failing to internalise society's norms, the criminals accurately reflected what most people were thinking. They were only different because they acted on their thoughts. The stock saloon-bar comment, that parents were failing to bring up their children properly, only pushed the indictment back one generation. If parental example is so crucial, what went wrong with those who brought up the parents of the criminals? In short, as elsewhere the social conservatives had a case, but they did not follow its logic far enough – for understandable reasons, because the trail of guilt extended to earlier generations, who were supposed to have lived blameless lives and everyone left their back doors open. Presumably they would resist any attempt to map the graph of criminality on to the statistical chart of consumerism; but if so they would almost certainly be missing the real point.

■ Cult of celebrity

Human beings have always felt the urge to worship something bigger than themselves, and usually the object of veneration has either displayed some human attributes, or actually taken human form. But the popular icons of the twentieth century were often very ordinary people, who found it impossible to hide their feet of clay. Indeed, human frailties had become an essential part of the celebrity package. The mixture of the sacred and the profane, the worship and the debunking, was neatly illustrated in a song about the **footballer** ◄ **George Best**, set to the tune of 'Jesus Christ, Superstar'. Those who ◄ disliked Best's team, Manchester United, could add the second line 'Walks like a woman and he wears a bra'. Earlier, the **Beatle** John ◄ Lennon had felt it necessary to apologise after claiming that his group was 'more popular than Jesus'. But at least the Beatles did produce works of genius, and when they sought spiritual enlightenment in India they showed an awareness that the attractions of public acclaim had their limits.

The distinction between (lasting) fame and (transient) celebrity is easier to talk about in theory than to draw with precision in practice. Long before the twentieth century it was possible to win a permanent place in the history books without doing anything of significance. Britain's **monarchy**, for example, has rarely risen above the mediocre. ◄ Some people of obscure birth, like the poet Thomas Chatterton (1752–70), even managed to become famous because of what might have been, rather than any concrete achievements. But at a time when showbusiness commentators are unable to do more than distinguish an elite of 'A-list' celebrities from the ranks of the ephemeral, the concept of fame deserves to be revisited.

Conveniently, it can be argued that the boundaries between fame and celebrity blurred in the early years of the twentieth century. The life of Oscar Wilde (1854–1900) illustrates this transition. Wilde can be regarded as the first famous person to seek a celebrity lifestyle, and like many pioneers he was hounded to death for his pains. His quip that 'there is only one thing worse than being talked about, and that is not being talked about' should be framed above every celebrity's mantelpiece. The period since the Second World War has been marked by the development of an unambiguous celebrity culture, in which a fifteen-minute television appearance could win someone more public attention than a lifetime's endeavour in the arts or the sciences.

C

On the face of it, this was a surprising development. With the decline of orthodox Christian ideas, it might have been expected that the drive for substantial achievement would have increased. If the soul perished with the body the ambition to leave behind a name that might live for ever would have remained as the only spur for noble minds. Probably this feeling is still present. But it was adulterated into a lust for celebrity when combined with the technological revolution, which has induced the fantasy that a fleeting visit to a television studio can ensure a kind of immortality for anyone. Despite the efforts

▶ of Sir John Reith at the BBC, the medium has proved to be a catalyst for the triumph of transience. 'Reality' television has featured there as well as on the channels which depend upon advertising revenue (the most lamentable of these shows, *Big Brother* [2000–] was a Channel 4 innovation). On other programmes, obscure people battled to reveal their most embarrassing secrets in front of a 'live' audience, in search of catharsis, fame, or both. Viewers so minded could tune in to daytime TV to console themselves for their own misery by witnessing someone else's toe-curling anecdotes.

The other vital ingredient, though, has been the Anglo-Saxon capitalist model. Today's celebrities are disposable people for a throwaway society. They act as convenient tailor's dummies, advertising a range

▶ of **consumer** goods which sometimes (but by no means always) have a distant connection to the cause of their celebrity. The acceptance of such work was a reliable clue to a person's real status; celebrities who had no reason to expect long-term demand for their services were far more eager to cash in than people who were confident of sustained achievement. With the emergence of the rival magazines *Hello!* (1988) and *OK!* (1993), the trend entered the realms of the surreal. Instead of being used to sell goods and services, in these publications the celebrities themselves were the 'product'. They were highly rewarded for allowing photographers to intrude into their homes, or to witness

▶ rites of passage, especially their **marriages**. In an interesting sidelight
▶ on the role of **women** in contemporary life, it seemed that while well-known men could still marry people who were determined to maintain their privacy, it was compulsory for a female celebrity to pair off with someone who had at least an equal claim to the limelight. So whenever a female celebrity tied the temporary knot, the celebrity magazines got two people for the price of one. When celebrities remarried it was often a victory for material greed rather than optimism.

The motives of those who bought such magazines were unclear.

But undoubtedly envy was a potent force behind the purchases. Since celebrities had little to distinguish them from anyone else, it was possible to fantasise about changing places with them, leaving behind relative **poverty** for a life of glamour. Envy is an advanced ◄ staging post to hatred, and there was widespread public exultation whenever the frailties of a 'much-loved' celebrity were reported in the press. For the celebrities themselves, prolonged public exposure to a ravenous media meant the end of privacy, excessive stress and, in some cases, a premature death, as in the case of **Diana, Princess of** ◄ **Wales** who made the fatal mistake of hankering after celebrity instead of contenting herself with membership of the world's most famous family. Being cut off in one's prime was the best way of keeping up an appearance on thousands of t-shirts and posters, at least until the next tragic figure bit the dust. But many celebrities (including Diana) were stalked by their fans, and the television presenter Jill Dando was shot by one outside her London home in 1999. Other celebrity-worshippers took the more passive option of destroying themselves on hearing that their favourites had died.

When a trend becomes so absurd as to be a satire on itself, there is reason to hope that it is about to decline. In 2002, this expectation seemed to be confirmed in a survey which found that two-thirds of the British public believed there was too much coverage of celebrities in the media. Significantly, while **Tony Blair** had courted celebrities early ◄ in his premiership, he and his advisers lost interest in this cheap form of image-building as quickly as the celebrities themselves decided not to play along. Yet the priorities of the media showed no sign of switching, and even the supposedly serious **national newspapers** paid ◄ tribute to attention-seeking celebrities. In 2003 an academic study identified the footballer David Beckham as the most influential person in Britain.

All this was the more depressing since a more hopeful development of the mid-1980s had apparently lost momentum. The Irish pop singer Bob Geldof had used his celebrity to build from nothing a coalition of 'stars' who made a record and performed at a concert to raise funds for the starving in Africa. 'Band Aid' and 'Live Aid' were wildly successful, and Geldof himself deservedly moved into the ranks of the 'famous' (one ironic result was that his singing career which had been in the doldrums before he started his movement went into free-fall afterwards). But Geldof had always tried to convey a serious message as a musician who had owed his popularity to the temporary vogue of 'New Wave' music (or **Punk** rock). Once this was over, dull frivolity ◄ held sway over popular culture. Celebrities did continue to back good causes – for example, some 'supermodels', perhaps the most spurious celebrity group of all, appeared in advertisements to attack the trade

C

in animal furs. Yet there was a feeling that when they betrayed a sense of social responsibility celebrities were breaking their part of a tacit bargain with the public. Their role was to be photographed at parties, to appear on television game shows, and when they had been drained of any conceivable interest even to readers of *Hello!*, to bow out in a final blaze of indignity.

■ Cultural elitism

In November 1956 the eminent scientist, civil servant, broadcaster and novelist C.P. Snow contributed an article on 'The Two Cultures' to the *New Statesman*. With his varied interests, Snow had a better right than most to pronounce on what he saw as a large and growing gulf between science and the arts. Later, he developed his argument into a book, *The Two Cultures and the Scientific Revolution* (1959).

Hostility towards science in post-war Britain had three main strands. The first was entrenched in the education system. The
▶ curriculum of nineteenth-century **public schools** had been designed to turn the sons of tradesmen into 'gentlemen'. The process demanded a smattering of Greek and Latin rather than any knowledge of science or technology – even though these provided the essential bedrock of Britain's prosperity. This cultural bias carried over into the
▶ state sector, thwarting the good intentions of R.A Butler's **1944 Education Act**, which established a tripartite system of secondary schools. Few of the proposed technical institutions ever appeared, and the route to scholarly recognition still lay through aptitude for the arts, despite Britain's highly respectable record in producing Nobel laureates in many scientific subjects.

The second strand was a feature of Britain's literary tradition. Romantic poets, notably Wordsworth, Coleridge and Southey, and
▶ many great novelists, including Dickens and **Thomas Hardy**, had shown their distaste for industry. In the twentieth century, futuristic
▶ visions produced by H.G. Wells, **George Orwell** and Aldous Huxley painted a dismal prospect, with the soul of mankind ground down by the relentless machine of scientific 'progress'. The implication of such work was that the scientists themselves were at best amoral, and invariably hostile to the 'sweetness and light' generated by artistic excellence.

While the first two lines of attack against science were long established, the final strand was a post-war development. Fears about the likelihood of nuclear war were growing when Snow wrote his article,
▶ and before his book was published the **Campaign for Nuclear Disarmament** (CND) had been established to protest that science was threatening the existence of mankind, as well as endangering its

C

spirit. Although CND had little impact on political decisions, there was a lasting effect on attitudes towards the scientific community in general. Towards the end of the twentieth century these misgivings increased further, particularly in the wake of experimentation into genetic engineering of crops and animals.

Since science in itself was (supposedly) unconcerned with value-judgements, there was clearly a case for a dialogue between scientists, artists and philosophers as nature's veils were progressively ripped away. Yet Snow's argument was interpreted more as a disparagement of the arts than a valuable appeal for literary types to take a deeper interest in scientific developments, and vice versa. As such, it was repulsed by the literary scholar F.R. Leavis in another Cambridge lecture delivered in 1962.

The lack of a constructive conversation between the arts and the sciences was scarcely surprising, because the artistic community was hardly on speaking terms with itself. Snow's initial premise had been mistaken. There were not 'two cultures', but many. What used to be designated by the word 'culture' was now the preserve of an embattled, embittered and shrinking minority.

Leavis himself symbolised the dilemma, and his influence was to make it worse. He was a spiky, dogmatic critic, who argued that certain works of literature were worth reading, while others should be spurned with horror. His personal likes and dislikes were laid down like the testamentary tablets – only if works passed the Leavis test could they become part of the 'canon', worthy of study in the university literature departments which began to appear at the start of the twentieth century. But the more Leavis insisted that literary criticism was the highest form of intellectual endeavour, the more obvious it became to a public growing accustomed to **moral** and cultural relativism that his ◄ tastes were utterly subjective. In fact, they could hardly have been more erratic. For example, he had no time for Milton or Shelley, and he preferred D.H. Lawrence to Hardy. One suspects, in fact, that Lawrence was only smuggled on to the approved list to bring it up to date.

Thus the champion of the arts against science turned out to be not only a cultural elitist, but one who combined vehement rhetoric with indefensible views on his own subject. Predictably, the debate with Snow generated a lot of heat but precious little light. The contest continued in newspaper correspondence columns, but then died away without a satisfactory outcome. In the year after Leavis's speech, the new **Labour Party** leader Harold Wilson spoke of the 'white heat' of a ◄ 'scientific age' in which **economic planning** would restore the ◄ nation's fortunes. British students continued to specialise too early in either arts or science subjects, in marked contrast to other **Europeans** ◄ like the French. Whatever their specialism, students continued to

C

resemble each other in forgetting most of their lessons as soon as they
▶ had left school or **university**. After the rise to power of **Margaret
Thatcher**, an unapologetic philistine who had trained as a chemist,
governments encouraged the expansion of 'vocational' courses at all
levels of the system. This only aggravated the problem, making the
arts community feel even more defensive and raising fears that Britain
would become ever more addicted to materialism without wondering
(as Matthew Arnold had once put it) that the light it pursued might
actually be darkness.

The focus on vocational study was merely a new instalment of a
long-running problem for the remaining cultural elitists, who were
faced with the challenge of explaining how their beloved subjects
could be made to seem 'useful' in an age when spiritual development
was perceived to be a handicap rather than an asset. Their reaction
was schizophrenic. They turned inward, distancing themselves from
▶ the 'lowbrow' majority and pouring scorn on mass, **consumerist**
culture. But at the same time, they developed a penchant for the most
'difficult' works of art, as if they possessed the kind of specialist
knowledge associated with science. The first symptom of this response
was the cry of 'art for art's sake' raised as long ago as the 1890s, largely
in response to technological developments. Faced with competition
from photographers, the other visual arts turned increasingly towards
abstraction. While James MacNeil Whistler's imaginative techniques
had led John Ruskin to accuse him of 'flinging a pot of paint in the
public's face', his successors made even ruder gestures towards the
man on the Clapham Omnibus. In a delicious touch of postmodern
irony, by the end of the twentieth century the judges of the annual
▶ Turner Prize for art had noticed that the general public rather enjoyed
being offended, and winners of the 'prestigious' award appeared to be
selected accordingly.

The fate of literature was an even sadder story. The emergence of
the periodical press in the nineteenth century had actually been beneficial to many literary people, who found a new and lucrative outlet
for their work – and, incidentally, a forum in which developments in
the arts and the sciences could be explained to the educated layman.
▶ **National newspapers**, though, were a different matter. Even if their
content had been meritorious, their demands for instant copy would
have unsettled writers who liked to mull over their work in tranquillity
prior to publication. In the 1890s the growth of the 'popular press',
deliberately appealing to the lowest common denominator in taste
and logical argument, created a howl of outrage from the elite which
has been ridiculed in John Carey's entertaining polemic, *The Intellec-*
▶ *tuals and the Masses* (1992). The development of **cinema** was even more
ominous. While great literature depends upon the exercise of imagi-

nation in the audience, spoon-feeding from the big screen was sure to undermine the habit. Television and home videos have driven this 'dumbing down' even further, since even intelligent viewers can take the easy option of switching on a machine instead of using their minds when they get home from work. The printed counterpart of the ratings-grabbing TV show, 'airport fiction', caters for this market when the television set is unavailable. But the ubiquity of in-flight movies and of satellite television channels, accessible all over the world, might put paid even to this genre.

Before the arrival of near-universal literacy after the education reforms of 1870 and 1902, artists (and political theorists) had feared the likely consequences, on the assumption that 'a little learning is a dangerous thing'. This argument deserves more serious inspection than the enemies of cultural elitists would like their readers to think. True, some artists of the late nineteenth century scoffed at writers like Anthony Trollope, whose prodigious ability to churn out accessible prose for intelligent readers would have exhausted most newspaper correspondents. But earlier in the nineteenth century Walter Scott had been equally prolific, and at the time he had been almost universally admired.

Yet twentieth-century artists have done themselves few favours. The trend known as 'modernism', reflected in atonal music and abstract art, was an attempt to put high culture back on its pedestal. The danger was that instead of restoring public esteem for the artistic community, the new vogue for obscurity would make art seem irrelevant to the average person (or, in the case of Hanns Johst, make the would-be consumer reach for his revolver). In literature, the movement is usually identified with the work of the American-born T.S. Eliot (1888–1965), whose poem *The Waste Land* (1922) became famous overnight because it enjoyed the support of cultural elitists. In particular, it won the patronage of the 'Bloomsbury Group' of intellectuals, which included the biographer Lytton Strachey and the novelist and critic Virginia Woolf. Eliot's poem was supposed to sum up the postwar mood of disillusionment, but perhaps it should be read as an attempt by elitists to reclaim cultural territory from poets like Wilfred Owen and the much-abhorred **Kipling**, who tried to convey the same ◄ feelings in comprehensible verse. By contrast, Eliot included explanatory notes for *The Waste Land*, although they failed to illuminate lines such as 'Twit twit twit / Jug jug jug jug jug'. Residual piety towards elite culture ensured that Eliot pocketed an Order of Merit along with a Nobel Prize in 1948, and at one point he was invited to recite his 'masterpiece' to the (baffled) royal family. His work continued to be inflicted on students of English Literature who were taught to look down on anything accessible to the 'common reader'.

Attitudes towards the cultural elite are conveniently summarised in the varying responses to the establishment of a permanent, government-funded Arts Council in 1946. Like the **BBC**'s 'Third Programme' which purveyed improving works to an audience that rarely rose above a quarter of a million, the Council was often attacked as an attempt to enforce 'high' culture against the clear preferences of the people. The fact that the driving force behind the Arts Council was the economist **J.M. Keynes**, a representative of 'Bloomsbury' elitism, is advanced as proof of malign intentions. Others might agree with Keynes in thinking that immediate sensual gratification is not the only form of pleasure, and that people of all classes should at least be given the opportunity to explore 'the best which has been thought and said in the world' before opting for the charms of mass-produced mediocrity. The continued existence of such dissident voices at the beginning of the twenty-first century ensured that there were still more than 'two cultures' in Britain. But a global free market, operating on condescending assumptions about standards of public taste, represented a growing threat. Those who supported the pursuit of excellence in any non-sporting activity were now collectively lumbered with the sneering label of 'the chattering classes', by people who were well aware that the capacity for independent thought is the last remaining enemy of the profit motive.

■ Death

'No pleasure is worth giving up for the sake of two more years in a geriatric home in Weston-super-Mare,' the novelist Kingsley Amis (1922–95) remarked towards the end of his life. The comment not only expressed a bon viveur's refusal to temper his habits in the face of ill-health. It also illustrates the fact that although the British lived longer thanks to rising living standards and medical advances, they continued to view decrepitude and death as distasteful and frightening prospects.

Death was more of a taboo in the UK than in most countries because of a suspicion of public displays of private emotion, inherited from the Victorians. Obituary columns in broadsheet newspapers were avidly read and some celebrity deaths, notably that of **Diana,** ◀ **Princess of Wales**, prompted lachrymose communal grief. The growing level of violence on **cinema** and TV screens showed that the ◀ British did at least relish the dramatisation of death. Yet, despite these trends, the stiff upper lip remained a coping strategy and a benchmark of nobility for individuals experiencing grief for someone they knew personally or when facing their own mortality.

What changed as a result of the decline of religious belief was that the rituals of death became more secular. The popularity of cremation is a prime example. The Romano-British practice of burning the dead was replaced by burial in the third century AD and only became common again in the second half of the twentieth century. Cremation was legalised in 1885 but it remained unpopular, except among Britain's small Hindu population, mainly because the Christian churches saw it as a heathen practice and actively discouraged it. Consequently by 1939, only 4 per cent of the deceased were being cremated.

Thereafter, practicality led piety. Cremation increased during the Second World War when the high civilian death rate, coupled with the destruction of urban spaces, made it a more efficient and hygienic way of dispatching the dead than burial. The **Church of England** offi- ◀ cially sanctioned the practice in 1944, and in 1952 the Cremation Act made it easier to build crematoria. Desperate for land in order to pursue urban reconstruction, local authorities invested heavily in them. By 1967, 50 per cent of the population were choosing to be cremated and by 1998 the figure had risen to 78 per cent.

Although funeral services were still conducted by the clergy, the surroundings in which they took place were less religious because most crematoria were run by local authorities and were denominationally neutral. The change in practice also reflected the fact that Britain had become a more mobile, less communal society. Crematoria had wide catchment areas, sometimes encompassing hundreds of thousands of people who were linked to the local hospital rather than to the local church. On the positive side, this allowed more imaginative ceremonies to take place. Pop music that actually meant something to the deceased and their loved ones began to replace the hymnal dirge that churches had once forced on parishioners. The scattering of ashes created more choice too. For example, many people preferred the prospect of being absorbed by the turf of a **football** pitch on which their sporting heroes had played than rotting in a casket next to a neighbour they had despised.

However, tombs and gravestones, once a showcase for the stonemason and poet's art, became less common, making it harder for family and friends to memorialise a loved one. Also, the once common practice of having a coffin lying, usually open, in a front parlour used only for special occasions, had become a rarity by the 1970s. This was partly a reflection of the fact that domestic living space had become less divided between the formal and informal, and the prospect of spending a week eating dinner with the body of a relative in the middle of the room was not an appetising one. It also reflected the fact that the British had become more hygiene-conscious, even though cadavers presented less of a health hazard than the average fast-**food** takeaway outlet.

The sanitisation of death was also a result of the fact that it was a less common experience. People had smaller longer-lived families, so a person under 40 was more likely to experience the loss of a pet than a relative. The shock of death, and the inability to come to terms with it, is greater in a society that expects longevity as a right, however much priests and psychiatrists counsel differently. This was especially apparent in people's attitude to the elderly.

The expectation that quality of life should not decline significantly with old age meant that families viewed the prospect of an aged relative decaying mentally and physically in their sitting room with as much grace as the prospect of one lying dead in it. Fortunately, the **welfare state** was prepared to pay for their removal to a 'care home'. For all the oppressive restrictions that Asian mores placed on **women**, Asians maintained a tradition of geriatric support within the family that other ethnic cultures in Britain lost. Despite reports that physical abuse was as common in old people's homes as it was in children's homes, the number of English senior citizens in professional hands rose from 25,000 in 1900 to 341,000 in 2001. By that time only 14 per cent of those who cared for incapacitated relatives in the home looked after the elderly. Those who were left to live alone did not fare much better, despite the creation of the 'home help' system in 1950. It was estimated, for example, that in Greater

London up to a thousand elderly people were found decomposing in their homes every month.

Youth was no guarantee of happiness, even in an age of affluence and permissiveness from which the young appeared to benefit the most. The overall suicide rate fell slightly, from 12.9 per 100,000 in 1938 to 9.1 in 1996, thanks to better psychiatric care and anti-depressant drugs. It reached an all-time low of 8.9 during the Second World War when, despite immense hardship, Britons felt that they were working together for a common cause. The number of suicides shot up during the 1980s when the cults of competition and consumption were at their peak. Young men were the most vulnerable, the rate among the 25–44 age group rising to 24 per 100,000 by 2001, more than double the average and four times higher than that of women.

The absurd law prohibiting suicide was repealed by the **Conservative** government of Harold Macmillan in 1961 but helping someone to kill themselves was not. The formation of the Voluntary Euthanasia Society (now known as EXIT) by a group of doctors in 1935 led calls for euthanasia to be legalised. Their campaign was motivated by a humanitarian belief in the right of the individual to choose the manner and timing of their death and by the bravery of those prepared to do so. But fear that euthanasia may sometimes have baser motives prevented any change in the law.

The British continued to witness death on a regular basis. But they generally did so by watching TV, **cinema** and game screens. The popularity of gritty hospital dramas like *Casualty* (BBC1, 1986–) and *ER* (Warner Brothers/Channel 4, 1995–) testified to the sexual allure of doctors and nurses. But it also highlighted an eternal fascination with calamity. Life in the West was inflicting it on individuals less frequently and with less devastating effect; and even when it did so – notably with the rising **crime** rate – the emotional pain caused was not being ministered to as effectively. The artificial depiction of suffering and the comforting resolution of it that drama usually provided therefore filled a psychic hole left by secularisation.

Claims that the entertainment media actually contributed to the rise in violent crime are unproven, although it seems clear that the British became desensitised to violence. The infrequency of **war** in Europe after 1945 was a factor in that process. But it was mainly due to the belief – shared by politicians, media moguls and public alike – that the display of an erection was more obscene than that of a shooting.

Despite a continuing faith in God, few Britons still believed in the Devil, and Hell was now seen as a rhetorical device rather than a site of eternal physical torment. However, as their quality of life improved, the British realised they had more to gain by clinging on to that life, and so became more, not less, afraid of death. Health consciousness, whether it took the form of giving up smoking, having a more sensible diet or of going to the gym was a positive result of that anxiety. But the fear of death also resulted in a vain pretence that the quality of life could be prolonged by spending money on plastic surgery and treatments like Botox injections. Human longevity is a form of progress. But the peace and prosperity on which it was based sometimes caused people to forget that when the Grim Reaper sharpens his scythe in a shopping centre the result is as final as it is on a battlefield or in a slum.

■ Denning, Alfred Thompson, Baron (1899–1999)

The longest-serving and most controversial British judge of the century, whose contradictory views, and the judgements that sprang from them, helped to foster a growing belief that the judicial system of England and Wales was at best a lottery and at worst corrupt. The son of a draper, Denning came from a lower-middle-class background in rural Hampshire, two things of which he was immensely proud and which throughout his life he cited as evidence of an independent mind (unlike other humbly-born ambitious people of his time he didn't refine his accent in order to progress). He was called to the bar in 1923, became a King's Counsel (1933), High Court judge (1944) and Lord Justice of Appeal (1948). In 1957, he joined the House of Lords in Ordinary, but found that he was unable directly to influence the development of the law. So, when offered the post of Master of the Rolls in 1962, he jumped at the chance to return to the Court of Appeal, where he remained until 1982.

During those twenty years, Denning established himself as a champion of the individual, notably in cases involving the victims of unfair contracts and the rights of wives. Where the latter were concerned, his rulings – like that on 'deserted wife's equity' – pre-empted the 1970 Matrimonial Property Act, which established that a wife's work, either as wage-earner or housewife, was equal to that of a man, thereby entitling her to half an estate in the event of divorce. Denning had less sympathy for the rights of unmarried **women**, regarding those who were sexually active as Jezebels who were a hazard to the smooth working of a world that was justly dominated by the male of the species. He was a devout Protestant who kept his Bible to hand when writing judgments. This invaluable legal primer helped him to decide that the wearing of make-up and a short skirt was a calculated invitation to sexual congress. Feminists were not the only people who Denning enraged.

In 1963 he chaired the judicial inquiry into the **Profumo Affair**, in

142

which the Secretary of State for War, John Profumo, was discovered to have been sharing a mistress, Christine Keeler, with a Russian naval attaché. The Denning Report became a best-seller and made him a household name, but for all the wrong reasons. On the one hand, he scorned conservative claims that there had been a lowering of moral standards since the war, pointing out that the media had simply become more powerful and, like the public, less deferential. However, he regarded the sexual aspects of the affair as 'vile and revolting'. More importantly, he quashed evidence that much of the British **Establishment** was involved in it all, and he regarded Keeler as a ◄ whore and Stephen Ward (who introduced her to Profumo) as a pimp, serving a small group of society deviants. Although consumed by the public with salacious gusto, the Denning Report was seen as a whitewash, further proof that there was still one law for the rich and one for the poor. It begged the question, 'How meritocratic is Britain?' While Denning's rise from country boy to Master of the Rolls suggested that there was room at the top, his Report showed that remaining there depended on one's willingness to keep silent about the hypocrisies of ruling-class life, in which sense little had changed since Henry VIII appointed a butcher's son, Thomas Wolsey, to be Lord Chancellor in 1515.

Denning remained popular with morally conservative Britons who were dismayed at the post-war rise in **crime** and who, like him, ◄ believed that the duties of the individual were being forgotten in the clamour for rights. Despite his Christian faith, he had a more punitive than redemptive view of criminal justice, as a result of which he was a vocal supporter of corporal and capital punishment. This made him unpopular with the more liberal members of the legal profession and with people working in the social services, the numbers of whom expanded during the 1960s and 70s as the criminal justice system became more attuned to the sociological causes of crime. At the same time, Denning's frequent rejection of precedence in favour of immediate justice also made him unpopular with traditionalists in his profession.

However, his admirers' claims that he was an anti-Establishment maverick do not hold water. He was a fierce patriot who liked to remind defendants that they were lucky, as Englishmen and women, to be tried by the best courts of law in the world. Unfortunately, this did not seem to apply if you were Irish. Following the conviction of the 'Guildford Four' for the **IRA** pub bombings which killed five people in ◄ Guildford in 1974, Denning turned down their appeal, despite evidence that the forensic reports were tenuous and that the defendants' confessions had been obtained under extreme duress. In the short term, public anger towards the IRA was such that few people

D

cared whether or not the four men were guilty. But by the time they were eventually released by the Court of Appeal in 1991, tempers had cooled and, more importantly, attitudes towards the police and the criminal justice system had become more critical. Consequently, there was outrage when the 92-year-old Denning opined that the Guildford Four were 'probably guilty' and should have been hanged. Changing attitudes in another sphere had already triggered his departure from office. In 1982, commenting on a trial arising out of the inner-city riots the previous year, he claimed that black defendants had packed a jury with 'as many coloured people as possible', who in any case were 'not fit to serve in that capacity'. It was an indiscretion too far
▶ even for the government of **Margaret Thatcher**, and after the jurors threatened to sue him for libel, he was forced to resign.

▶ After Dennings's death, **Tony Blair** said 'he was prepared to use the law for its true purpose in the interests of fairness and justice. He had a tremendous feel for ordinary people'. The fact that even liberal lawyers paid tribute to Denning in this way testifies to the reactionary nature of their profession.

■ Devolution

Term given to the transfer of power from central to regional government, deriving from the medieval Latin *devolutio*, meaning to roll down. In twentieth-century Britain it became associated with the granting of more autonomy to the smaller nations of the United Kingdom – in principle to offset the greater power and wealth of England but in practice to curtail the development of Scottish, Welsh and Irish nationalism.

During the Irish Home Rule debates of the period 1880 to 1920, the
▶ **Liberal Party** developed the idea of 'Home Rule All Round'. The creation of an Irish Free State within the British Commonwealth would be accompanied by the creation of separate parliaments for England, Scotland and Wales, all bearing allegiance to the Crown and overseen by a federal parliament at Westminster. Following the creation of a southern republic outside the Commonwealth in 1949, the Northern Irish parliament became the vestige of a lost dream until the abuse of its powers by the Protestant Ascendancy of Ulster became public knowledge and discredited it. Meanwhile, Home Rule All Round lived on in the Liberal Party and, like many Liberal policies, it
▶ was adopted by **Labour** in 1918. Although the idea had its champions
▶ among **Conservatives** who wanted to unify the **Empire** through im-
▶ perial federation, most of the British **Establishment** was against devolution on the grounds that it would weaken the Union and foster rather than foil Celtic nationalism. The preferred solution for dealing

with Scottish and Welsh discontent was limited political devolution within the existing constitution, backed up by a greater degree of cultural devolution.

A landmark of cultural devolution was the 1920 disestablishment of the Church of Wales, which had been unpopular since the 1870s when Nonconformist Protestantism became the main religious faith of the principality. Other landmarks were the establishment of a Welsh National Library in 1905 and a Scottish one in 1925. A Welsh national museum and gallery was established in Cardiff in 1907 (Scotland had had its own since 1859). Meanwhile, England remained content with the British Library (1757), the British Museum (1759) and the National Gallery of Great Britain (1838). The Arts Council of Great Britain (1946) was split into separate organisations for Scotland, Wales *and* England in 1967. The British Film Institute (1933) was augmented by the Scottish Film Council (1935). The **BBC** established semi-autonomous units in Scotland (1923), Northern Ireland (1924) and Wales (1965) and Broadcasting Councils were set up for each country in 1952 to monitor the development of programmes that reflected their cultural distinctiveness. State-sponsored festivals also grew in number. The Welsh National Eisteddfod had showcased Welsh music, poetry and drama since it was founded in the twelfth century. Scotland got its own event when the Arts Council set up the Edinburgh Festival in 1947. It was more international in outlook but also, according to Scottish nationalists, more elitist – criticism that led to the creation of the Edinburgh Fringe Festival in 1952.

Political devolution began in 1885 when a Scottish Office was set up by the Conservative government of Lord Salisbury, with the Duke of Richmond as the first Scottish Secretary. The post was given Cabinet status in 1892 by Gladstone, but its incumbents had no exclusive remit over any area of government and depended on their personal relationship with the Prime Minister for what little influence they had. Even educational autonomy, which the Scots had retained under the Act of Union of 1707, was managed by a separate agency, the Scottish Board of Education, based in Edinburgh. Although a branch of the Scottish Office was also opened there in 1909, the Secretary and his senior officials remained at Dover House in Whitehall, their purpose being to ensure that Scottish interests were served in the evolution of British government policy rather than to actually govern.

The relative decline of the Scottish and Welsh economies after the First World War began a new phase of devolution, as economic hardship acted upon cultural nationalism to produce demands for greater political autonomy. Nationalist parties – **Plaid Cymru** and the **Scottish National Party** (SNP) – were formed in 1928 and 1934 respectively. During the interwar period they never attained more than 5 per cent

145

▶ of the vote at general elections. But the additional economic problems caused by the **Great Depression** led to the creation of the Scottish National Development Council in 1930, a nationalist initiative that won grudging government support and provided a model for future ventures designed to ameliorate economic decline in north and west Britain. Meanwhile, the implementation of the Gilmour Report on Scottish Administration in 1939 marked the start of effective devolution. It created a 'Home Department' within the Scottish Office, with responsibility for implementing policy across a range of areas from

▶ **agriculture** to **housing**. And, symbolically, most of its work was carried out at a new, purpose-built headquarters in Edinburgh, St Andrew's House. Between 1937 and 1992 the number of Scottish Office civil servants rose from 2,400 to 13,500.

Scotland and Wales had a good Second World War. Mass mobilisa-
▶ tion revived their economies, and in doing so it reduced **unemployment** in each country to virtually nothing, while also slowing migration to the affluent south and midlands of England. This, coupled with the national unity generated by the need to defeat Hitler (mani-
▶ fested most clearly in a near total support for **conscription**) slowed the development of nationalism. In 1941, the wartime Scottish Secretary, Tom Johnston (1882–1965) – a Labour MP and Home Ruler known to
▶ **Churchill** as 'the King of Scotland' – set up a quasi-Cabinet body in Edinburgh made up of assorted worthies, called the Council of State for Scotland. But it was poorly attended and last met in 1945. Similarly, the creation in 1944 of an annual 'Welsh Day' at Westminster to discuss legislation that affected the principality failed to excite the Welsh.

However, to the surprise and irritation of the English political Establishment, calls for devolution increased immediately after the war. The greater role of the state in British life led to more adminis-
▶ trative centralisation (the **nationalised** industries were mostly run from London). Furthermore, it soon became apparent that the downward spiral of the Scottish and Welsh economies had only temporarily been halted by the war. Decolonisation made matters worse by reducing British markets and by removing the political allure of partnership with England. All of this seemed to be a poor reward for the sacrifices made by the Scots and Welsh to defend Britain. A cross-party petition demanding a Welsh Office was delivered to Downing Street in 1946 and the Scots followed a year later with one demanding a parliament. In 1949, the Scottish Covenant Association was formed by the Duke of Montrose and John McCormick, a former SNP leader, collecting signatures from two-thirds of the Scottish electorate in support of Home Rule. A Parliament For Wales Campaign, begun in
▶ 1950 and led by **Lloyd George**'s daughter, Megan, won support from a fifth of the Welsh electorate.

The repatriation of the Stone of Scone (on which Scottish kings had reputedly once been crowned) from Westminster Abbey by Covenanters on Christmas Day in 1950 brought Celtic nationalism to the attention of the English public for the first time, but it did not alter their contemptuous attitude to the issue. Over the next twenty years, scraps were periodically thrown from the Westminster table in an effort to appease discontent. Two powerless talking shops were established: a Scottish Economic Conference in 1948 and a Council for Wales in 1949. Separate financial estimates were published for Scotland from 1952 onwards, and for Wales from 1967. Cardiff was designated a capital city in 1955; and in 1960 the Welsh flag was officially recognised by the British state (permission to fly it had previously had to be sought from the monarch). In 1964, the government of Harold Wilson finally created a Welsh Office, and a Secretary of State in Cabinet, the first of whom was James Griffiths (1890–1975).

A severe downturn in the Scottish and Welsh economies from 1960 onwards led to a doubling of unemployment in both countries and a renewed strategy of state intervention through treasury subsidy for key industries and amenities, together with the setting up of new corporatist development agencies. This process culminated in the Barnett Formula of 1978 (devised by the Chief Secretary to the Treasury, Joel Barnett) which codified and entrenched the subsidy system for England's poorer neighbours. The system ameliorated hardship and contained support for independence from England. But it did not halt the rise of nationalism. This was especially true of Scotland. Traditional pride in having retained autonomous institutions like the **Church of Scotland** was intensified by the discovery of North Sea oil ◄ in 1971. Many Scots became convinced that if the vast revenues from it could be appropriated from the British Treasury, Scotland would be a viable independent nation.

In 1954, a Royal Commission on Scottish Affairs, chaired by the Earl of Balfour, pointed out that the 'emotional dissatisfaction' of the Scots was partly due to the 'thoughtlessness, lack of tact and disregard of sentiment' shown by the English towards their partners. In 1973, a Royal Commission on the Constitution, under the chairmanship of the Scottish Liberal peer Lord Kilbrandon, reached a similar conclusion and recommended 'Home Rule All Round' to 'the historic nationalities of Britain'.

The electoral success of the nationalist parties between 1966 and 1974 prompted the Labour Party to accept the broad conclusions of the Kilbrandon Report and in 1977 it put before parliament proposals for Scottish and Welsh Assemblies with no tax-raising powers. The Devolution Bills finally received royal assent in 1978, but only after the adoption of the Cunningham Amendment (so-called after the Labour

MP George Cunningham) which stipulated that 40 per cent of the Scottish and Welsh electorate would have to vote yes in the referenda that followed on 1 March 1979. On a turnout of 63.63 per cent in Scotland, only 32.85 were for devolution, while in Wales, on a turnout of 58.3 per cent, only 11.8 per cent were in favour. Nearly a century of debate and campaigning seemed to have run into the ground until the
▶ arrival, two months after the referenda, of **Margaret Thatcher**.

▶ Thatcher's **monetarist** policies removed much of the protection given to the Scottish and Welsh economies since the Second World War. In addition, the four Conservative election victories between 1979 and 1992 were all achieved as a result of the Tory vote in England, as a consequence of which the Scots and Welsh once more lost faith in the constitutional status quo and came to blame their plight on what they perceived to be English nationalism. At the general election of 1997, for the first time in their history, neither country returned a single
▶ Conservative MP. On its return to office under **Tony Blair**, the Labour Party resumed its attempt to secure devolution, and this time with more success. Referenda held on 31 August 1997 resulted in 74.3 per cent of the Scottish electorate voting yes for a parliament with tax-raising powers, on a turnout of 60.4 per cent. In Wales, the offer of an assembly without such powers was accepted by 50.3 per cent on a turnout of 51.3 per cent. In the elections of May 1999 the SNP and
▶ **Plaid Cymru** came second to Labour in their respective countries, but were excluded from the resulting coalition governments.

From the nineteenth century to the twenty-first, devolution was essentially a pragmatic exercise, carried out reluctantly, in order to contain discontent with the economic, political and cultural imbalances caused by England being much the largest nation in the British Isles. It made less concrete difference to Scottish and Welsh standards of living than the subsidies given to each country by the Treasury, and it did little to reduce the widespread Anglophobia in each country. But devolution in its various forms did help to restore the self-respect of the Scots and Welsh and their faith in the United Kingdom as a viable and perhaps necessary multi-national state. The fresh imbalances caused by the pragmatic nature of devolution have yet to provoke a majority demand for an English parliament. Politically, English nationalism remains at the embryonic stage that its Scottish and Welsh counterparts were at in the 1930s.

■ Diana, Princess of Wales (1961–97)

Lady Diana Spencer was born at Park House on the royal family's
▶ Sandringham Estate on 1 July 1961. Her parents were both **aristocratic**; her mother Frances was a daughter of the 4th Lord Fermoy, and

her father, Johnnie, Viscount Althorp, was the heir to Earl Spencer. The Spencer family could claim kinship with a remarkable roster of great historical figures, but its original fortune was founded in the sixteenth century, on the ruins of the **Roman Catholic** church. ◄

Probably the central event of Diana's life was the break-up of her parents' marriage, which was finalised by a divorce in 1969. The couple had been unhappy for some time, and Diana's mother had abruptly packed up and left in 1967. Critics later found it easy to scoff at Diana's lack of academic qualifications, and she would never have sat for an All Souls fellowship even if her childhood had been blissful. But this miserable background can hardly have helped her school-work.

Whether or not she might have excelled in other spheres given a fair chance, Diana was good with young children and seemed ideal for a career as a nursery assistant. However, before she took up a suitable job in Pimlico her name had been linked romantically to the Prince of Wales. Her sister Sarah had already been mooted as a possible bride, but during a skiing holiday with the illustrious personage she had flattened the rumours with unnecessary brusqueness. Diana, though, seemed genuinely to be in love with the Prince. Some thought that even at this early stage she was using the media to get what she wanted; but when reporters followed up the stories they presented the world with a natural star. Tall, blonde and bashful, when Diana was pictured among her young charges in Pimlico most Britons made the obvious connection between the visual images. Diana was obviously the perfect match for the wayward heir to the throne.

The longed-for marriage – the first between an heir and a fellow Briton – took place in July 1981. The bride had just celebrated her 20th birthday; Charles was 32. The country needed some consolation: July 1981 was a month of widespread inner-city rioting. Charles looked businesslike, at best, during the ceremony. Neither had he exhibited the usual symptoms of romantic intoxication in a televised pre-match interview, characteristically musing on the nature of love rather than satisfying himself with a fervent declaration. But at the time much more attention was paid to the new 'fairy-tale' Princess, in a gown which would grace any wedding cake. The worldwide audience for the ceremony at St Paul's Cathedral was 750 million. The streets of London were said to have been lined with 1 million people (suspiciously, this was the official estimate for the attendance at almost every royal occasion, as opposed to radical demonstrations where the **police** were ◄ more creative in their calculations).

Fairy-tale unions between handsome princes and dazzling (if not dazed) princesses usually end with the words 'happy ever after'; the precise details of their domestic bliss can be left to the reader's imagination. But to the public, at least, the enchanting story seemed to be playing out splendidly when a son was born just before the couple's first anniversary. A second followed in September 1984. But subsequent revelations showed that all was far from well. Then all of the factors which had made the couple seem so complementary – the differences in age, character and interests – could be reinterpreted as compelling evidence that the marriage was doomed from the start.

▸ Diana adored pop music and **fashion**; Charles was interested in
▸ **architecture**, and **agriculture**.

Here were the necessary ingredients for national polarisation. The Charles camp thought that Diana was frivolous, media-obsessed and neurotic; to Diana's fans, the Prince of Wales was, at best, other-
▸ worldly. Although Prince Charles had grown up during the '**permis-sive**' era – and, by all accounts, had entered into the spirit rather vigorously in certain respects – he seemed hopelessly out of tune with modern life. While his opponents thought that he should keep his crotchety views to himself, he actually spoke for a significant body of opinion without committing the constitutional *faux pas* of criticising the government. So those who thought that he was right also upheld his right to speak out. By contrast, they saw Diana as a 'loose cannon' – an embarrassment waiting to happen – and they disliked her all the more because her interests reflected everything that they deplored about contemporary trends. To add further piquancy to the public debate, the behaviour of each principal could be attributed to their respective upbringings; each camp could portray them as victims, absolved from personal responsibility.

By 1992, after the publication of a biography of Diana which had obviously been inspired by 'sources close to the Princess', the problems in the marriage were impossible to conceal. The Prime Minister, John Major, announced a separation in the House of Commons in November 1993. After much wrangling the divorce was finalised in 1996. The news was sadly received, and thousands of once-cherished wedding souvenirs found their way into car-boot sales and charity shops. The House of Windsor was falling into line with the rest of the population, at least in the matter of divorces. In fact, they were soon outstripping their subjects. Princess Anne and Captain Mark 'Foggy' Phillips had divorced earlier in 1992, following Princess Margaret's precedent of 1978; Prince Andrew and the 'fun-loving' Sarah Ferguson followed the same course in 1996. Yet the split between Diana and Charles involved more than a financial settlement and the division of the joint musical collection (which in their case must have been relatively straightforward). If and when Charles became king, would Diana be crowned alongside him? What would her title be? Historians were wheeled out to discuss the inauspicious royal record on this matter. Leaving aside

Henry VIII's patchy performance, George I had imprisoned his wife, and George IV's consort Caroline had been left banging on the doors of Westminster Abbey when 'Prinny' was elevated to the throne.

Princess Caroline had been adept at using the early nineteenth-century media; radicals like William Cobbett had championed her cause, in the hope that this would damage the **monarchy**. In the late twentieth century, republican newspaper proprietors nursed the same objective. Diana also enjoyed the considerable advantage of the electronic media. It was alleged that she was coached in advance of a famous **BBC** interview; but even if it was all an act she showed remarkable gifts in this area. Compared to the unfortunate Caroline, at any rate, she was a considerable beauty. While her appearance on the front cover of *Vogue* magazine in December 1991 could not be attributed entirely to her looks, at least she was unmistakably female unlike most of the 'supermodels' of the day. Her emotional 1996 television appearance, in which she confessed to adultery and laid claim to the role of 'Queen of Hearts', was more than a match for anything Buckingham Palace could muster. In fact, Charles had put his retaliation in early, alluding to his own extra-marital interests in a halting performance which was oddly reminiscent of his inarticulate interview before the marriage. By contrast, for Diana talking about love was almost as easy as falling into it.

After the divorce it looked as if the royal family would be lumbered with the 'Diana problem' indefinitely. She spoke of cutting down her charitable commitments, but this only drew attention to her significant contribution in that sphere. The royal family themselves generally prided themselves on doing good by stealth; Diana inevitably attracted the cameras, especially in her campaigns to raise funds for AIDS treatment and to rid the world of anti-personnel mines. Even worse, her search for unquestioning devotion from a partner led her into liaisons which would have raised eyebrows even if she had never married the heir to the throne. When she took up with Dodi Fayed, the son of a man who had been connected to the 'sleaze' scandals of the Major years, even she seemed to have gone too far.

Diana's quiet retirement to some remote hermitage would have been very welcome to the royal family. But she had intimated that she would not 'go quietly', and so it proved. It was difficult to say whether her death in a Paris motor accident in August 1997 was more to be deplored for its timing or its manner. Lurid conspiracy theories were inevitable anyway, but in the atmosphere of hysterical grief it seemed almost compulsory to express the view that 'they' had tipped the 'loose cannon' off the deck. Those who indulged in such theories missed the essential point. Even if there had been a grain of truth in them, the success of the 'plot' would have depended on the crazed media obsession which provoked the fatal car chase. Thus on any scenario the sinister perpetrators were the public themselves.

In the days before Diana's funeral Britain embarked on an orgy of lamentation, as befitted a materialistic nation which had replaced ▶ religious figures with a **cult of celebrity**. All this culminated in the Queen's enforced broadcast to the nation, and her equally reluctant decision to break precedent by flying the flag over Buckingham Palace at half-mast. It was the closest Britain had ever come to reproducing the humiliation of the French monarchy during the Revolution. More than two centuries after the British radical Dr Richard Price had exulted that 'I have lived to see thirty millions of people, indignant and resolute . . . their king led in triumph, and an arbitrary monarch surrendering himself to his subjects', the same scene was enacted in London. The key difference, though, was that Price could delude himself into thinking that the Parisian mob would usher in a glorious 'Age of Reason'. By contrast, London in the days leading up to the funeral on 6 September was seething with irrationality. The Prime ▶ Minister, **Tony Blair**, glided into the role of Robespierre, hailing Diana as 'the People's Princess'. This intervention was so widely acclaimed that his office subsequently allowed his name to be associated with a ▶ campaign to force the scriptwriters of the **soap opera** *Coronation Street* to 'liberate' the victim of a fictional miscarriage of justice. The other hero of the hour was Diana's brother Charles, whose passionate speech at the funeral inspired the overflow mourning party in St James's Park to cheers which flooded in through the doors of Westminster Abbey. The villain was the Conservative leader William Hague, whose perfectly sensible response was deemed to be a public relations disaster by Britain's totalitarian tabloids.

To those who tried to go about their normal business at that time, thinking that Diana's death was certainly tragic but not really a pressing personal concern, it seemed that the nation would never recover its collective wits. It was estimated that 15,000 tons of flowers – or 'floral tributes' in the preferred media term – were scattered across the nation as a whole. People lining the route to Diana's burial place at the family seat bombarded the funeral car with bouquets. After two decades of selfish individualism the public had been craving any opportunity to show that, after all, there was such a thing as society. It might have chosen a more constructive outlet; and of course there was still a strong element of individualism, because the mourners often fantasised that they had enjoyed a personal relationship with the deceased princess. The mood passed away fairly quickly; but lasting damage had been done. A similar wave of irrationality swept the country three years later, when a 'popular' protest against fuel taxes endangered essential services. The reaction to the death of

the **Queen Mother** in 2002 was much more decorous, dashing the ◀
hopes of some **national daily newspapers** for Diana II. ◀

Although for a time it looked as if the British monarchy would
never recover from the divorce and Diana's death, actually the whole
episode was a bitter blow for republicans. As people reflected in tranquillity, it began to dawn on them that it might have been more digni-
fied to keep a stiff upper lip after all – like Prince Charles, whose
conduct in the face of a crushing personal tragedy had been exemplary. More seriously, a country that could behave in that fashion was
certainly not fit for a rational debate about its head of state; and one
could only shudder at the likely outcome of any presidential contest
decided by this electorate.

■ Disabled

'I am not an animal. I am a man,' cried John Hurt in *The Elephant Man*
(1980), a film adaptation of the life of Joseph Merrick (1862–90). Until
the 1950s, physically disabled people, especially those who were handicapped from birth, were regarded by the rest of society with a
mixture of condescension, disgust, pity and fear. Unable to work, they
were of little use to ordinary families; while the better off simply
regarded them as an embarrassment. Consequently, most were given
over to residential institutions run by churches, charities and the
state, where they languished in appalling conditions, often with the
insane and mentally handicapped. Those who did take an interest in
the disabled either yearned for their demise, like the **social Darwin-** ◀
ists of the eugenics movement, or they exhibited them in freak shows
(the fate that befell Merrick). A gradual change of approach took place
after the Second World War.

The expansion of the social services enabled poorer families to care
for disabled relatives at home; while the less severely handicapped
were given the chance to lead relatively independent lives in their own
accommodation. The introduction of Sickness Benefit in 1948 was a
crucial landmark in both respects. A more generous version, Invalidity
Benefit, replaced it in 1971, following surveys exposing the **poverty** in ◀
which most disabled people continued to live. The number in receipt
of state assistance nearly trebled as a result, from 922,000 in 1971 to
2,406,000 in 1995. Dismayed at the cost of the care, the governments
of John Major and **Tony Blair** introduced stricter 'means testing' to ◀
root out malingerers with Invalidity Benefit (1995) and Disability
Living Allowance (1998).

The disabled were partly compensated by legislation that granted
them more rights. The 1970 Chronically Sick and Disabled Persons Act,
made it compulsory for local authorities to provide basic amenities

D

such as special toilets and wheelchair ramps in public buildings. It also gave them a theoretical right to equal treatment in employment, ▶ housing, services and entertainment, although in practice this was not enforced and rarely volunteered. The 1995 Disability Discrimination Act strengthened the law by making it a criminal offence to treat disabled people less favourably. The Disability Rights Commission Act of 1999 set up a semi-independent state body, similar to the Commission for Racial Equality, in order to promote equal opportunities, monitor discrimination and advise the government on policy. Among its achievements was a new Disability Discrimination Act. This compels the private sector to improve disabled access to buildings, something it has been reluctant to do because of the costs involved and the fact that they are difficult to recoup because the income of disabled people tends to be far lower than that of the able-bodied.

A change of perception was also brought about by the public awareness campaigns of charities like Scope. Founded by a group of parents in 1952, it changed its name from the Spastics Society to Scope in 1994 in response to the fact that 'spastic' had become a popular term of ridicule. The British Council of Disabled People was formed in 1981 by the disabled themselves. An umbrella group, it included some militant organisations whose members' direct action included chaining their wheelchairs to buildings (including the gates of Downing Street) then hurling themselves to the ground. Their cause was helped by the scandal over Thalidomide. Celebrities also helped to change attitudes, in particular the Cockney artist and singer Ian Dury (1942–2000). Crippled and disfigured by polio from the age of 7, Dury was the first British entertainer to make disability part of his persona without inviting either pity or voyeurism. To mark the World Health Organisation's 'International Year of the Disabled' in 1981, he released the single 'Spasticus Autisticus' which proudly proclaimed his condition. ▶ It was banned by the BBC for being offensive. All Dury's songs celebrated the full life he led, notably 'Sex & Drugs & Rock 'n' Roll' (1977) which offered the startling revelation that disabled people enjoyed coitus.

Britain's 8.6 million disabled people remained second-class citizens. But their standard of living did improve, as did the attitudes of the able-bodied majority towards them. A measure of the latter was ▶ that the England football team manager, Glen Hoddle, was sacked as a result of comments he made in an interview with *The Times* in February 1999, in which he expressed the view that the disabled were paying for sins they had committed in a previous life. Though Hoddle's beliefs were commonly held by Hindus and Buddhists, he was seen to have degraded a section of society who now deserved respect as well as consideration.

■ DIY

Unlike **gardening**, with which it was closely associated, the do-it-yourself craze did not emerge until after the Second World War. It was imported from **suburban** America in the 1950s when rising levels of home ownership gave more people the freedom to make improvements to their habitats that ranged from the erection of shelves to the re-wiring of an entire building. DIY was a testosterone-fuelled hobby, the frequent botching of which led to more domestic injuries than any other household activity (on average, a quarter of a million per year). It also epitomised the home-loving, private and apparently peaceful nature of the British in the age of affluence.

The appeal of DIY was threefold. First, it was cost-effective, particularly as the building, electrical and plumbing trades were notorious for ripping off customers. Second, by giving men the chance to display artistical skills, it helped to compensate them for the Fordist production methods used in modern factories, in which they were stuck at one point of an assembly line with little sense of creating a product. DIY had a similarly compensatory appeal for Britain's growing number of office workers. Third, it reprieved the traditional masculinity which came under threat as a result of feminism. DIY enabled men to meet female demands that they pull their weight around the house, while maintaining the separate spheres of labour which they, and a good many **women**, deemed to be natural. In 2001, 84 per cent of men did DIY compared to only 54 per cent of women, while the figures for washing and ironing were 59.5 and 93.5 respectively.

The hobby was further popularised by the creator of DIY TV, Barry Bucknell (1912–2003), whose programmes *About the Home* (BBC, 1951–8) and *Do-It-Yourself* (1957–72) attracted 6 million viewers. His reassuring, fatherly manner made him as well-loved as Percy Thrower was to gardeners. By the 1960s, a DIY manual could be found in most working- and lower-middle-**class** households, much as the Bible had once been. That decade also witnessed an explosion in the supply of DIY materials. New out-of-town self-service superstores (modelled on those in America) began to replace small high-street builders' merchants by offering a larger and cheaper range of products. Richard Block and David Quayle opened their first store in Southampton in 1969. Renamed 'B&Q', their empire expanded rapidly during the 1980s. By the end of the century it comprised 300 stores, making it Europe's biggest DIY supplier (rivalled only by Homebase, founded in 1981). In 1994, B&Q became one of the first British retail chains to open on a Sunday, the success of which confirmed that secular leisure pursuits had become more popular than organised religion.

■ Drink

'Lacte et carne vivant' ('they live on milk and meat') wrote Julius Caesar of the ancient Britons. That became less true of modern Britons as a result of the Industrial Revolution and by the 1960s their drinking and eating habits had changed beyond recognition. Most of what they now drink – instant coffee, soft drinks, lager, wine and bottled water – did not become commonplace until the last quarter of the twentieth century. Like the shifting patterns of **food** consumption, those of liquid have been driven by affluence, by revolutions in technology and retailing, and by the power of the modern advertising industry to stimulate demand.

The one constant is tea. For over two centuries after its introduction to Britain in 1612, it was a predominantly upper- and middle-class beverage. It only became common among the working classes after governments and the **monarchy**, lobbied by the temperance movement, promoted it as a healthier alternative to beer (which many people then drank for breakfast). Produced cheaply in the colonies, import duties on tea were slashed in 1863, making it cheaper still, and by the 1880s it was acclaimed as the national drink, with brands like the Manchester-based Brooke Bond (1869) leading the market. Tea shops, a uniquely British social institution, helped to spread the habit. The most famous was founded by a Jewish tobacconist, Montague Gluckstein, and his relative Joseph Lyons (1848–1917). They opened the first Lyons Tea Shop in Piccadilly in 1894 and by 1914 their catering business was one of the largest in the UK, with over 200 branches frequented by people of all **classes**.

A peak of consumption was reached between 1929 and 1932, during the worst years of the **Great Depression**. Tea was considered so important to national morale that during the Second World War **Churchill**'s government made strenuous efforts to maintain supplies in order to ration it generously, as a result of which consumption fell only slightly. The teabag, an American invention introduced to the UK by Tetley's in the mid-1950s, made tea-making a faster process. But consumption fell by half between the 1960s and the 1990s, to less than a fifth of its pre-war level. Seventy-five per cent of Britons still drank tea daily at the century's end (compared to 55 per cent soft drinks, 53 per cent coffee and 32 per cent alcohol). But the heaviest drinkers were now pensioners and most was consumed in the home, the drink having lost its place to coffee as the daytime social lubricant of choice.

Although coffee houses were fashionable in the eighteenth century, it had been unable to compete with tea because, despite attempts by the Exchequer to stimulate demand for it, coffee didn't go as far (tea leaves could be re-brewed more effectively than ground coffee). It was also harder to make. Affluence erased the first concern and technology erased the second. Freeze-dried 'instant' coffee granules, invented by the Swiss firm Nestlé in 1938, began to be imported in large quantities after 1965 when Nestlé improved its quality and launched Gold Blend. The invention of the modern coffee-making machine by the Italian firm Gaggia in 1946 formed the basis of a boom in coffee bars that reached a peak in the 1990s when the largest chain was that of the American firm Starbucks. The words *espresso* and *cappuccino* entered the English **language**. More importantly, the coffee ◀ shop replaced the tea shop as the main rival to the **pub** as the place ◀ where Britons met for business or pleasure. The mass adoption of the Continental practice of restaurant-going meant that more people saw coffee as the natural accompaniment to a meal. All of this trebled the British intake between 1950 and 1993 when, for the first time, they spent more money on coffee than tea.

One of the peculiarities of tea-drinking in the UK is the British fondness for pouring milk into it. Pasteurisation had made milk safer in the late nineteenth century. Concern about the physical fitness of the British race led to it being dispensed to schoolchildren from 1906. In 1933 the Milk Marketing Board was set up to ameliorate the **agricul-** ◀ **tural** depression by holding down the price of milk and stimulating public demand. Consequently, between 1914 and 1945 consumption doubled to five pints per head a week. This jump was assisted by the arrival of American breakfast cereals and by dehydrated milk drinks, notably Horlicks from the US in 1908 and Ovaltine from Switzerland in 1913. The fashion for American milk bars also helped. Between 1935 and 1955 around a thousand were opened in the UK. Selling fruit-flavoured milkshakes in Art Deco chrome, glass and leather interiors, they offered adolescents the chance to meet and court in morally acceptable, alcohol-free surroundings. Bottled milk deliveries became common during the interwar period and by the 1950s the milkman was as integral to British household life as the postman.

'There is no finer investment for any community than putting milk into babies,' declared Winston Churchill during the 1943 broadcast in which he belatedly endorsed the **Beveridge Report**. In 1968 the **Labour** ◀ government ended the provision of free milk for secondary schools and in 1971 the **Conservatives** ended it for primary schools, earning ◀ Education Secretary **Margaret Thatcher** the nickname 'milk-snatcher'. ◀ But this was one public service cut that actually stemmed from falling demand and one, moreover, that met with the retrospective approval of nutritionists concerned by the high fat content of milk. From 1984, when skimmed and semi-skimmed milk became nationally available, to 1993 consumption rose from 9.2 per cent to 53.3 per cent of all milk sold. Milk continued to be a staple part of the British diet but drinking it became much less common. The main challenge to it came from soft drinks.

Cheaper imports of fruit and sugar from the UK's Caribbean colonies from the 1870s onwards, together with growing knowledge of fruit's healthy properties and approval from the temperance movement, caused a rise in the consumption of soft drinks in the late Victorian era. But it was the explosion of the mass leisure industry in the following century, and the influence of America, that made the drinks so popular. Consumption increased from 2 million gallons in 1900 to 110.2 million in 1938, rising to 9.6 billion litres in 1995, representing the biggest change in British drinking habits of modern times. Companies continued to stress the health benefits of their brands. But by the interwar period the claim was bogus because they contained more sugar and water than fruit. Their appeal was heightened by the addition of carbon dioxide, first utilised by the father of fizzy drinks, Jacob Schweppe, in 1792. Some were British. Irn Bru (Iron Brew), invented in Scotland in 1901 by Robert Barr and marketed as 'Scotland's second national drink', continues to be the best-selling non-alcoholic beverage north of the border.

However, most fizzy drinks were American – notably Coca-Cola, which came to symbolise the creeping **Americanisation** of Britain. It was actually based on a French drink: Vin Mariani, a mixture of wine and coca leaves popular in Europe and America from the 1860s until it was superseded by its US rival (Queen Victoria was a regular imbiber). Coca-Cola was invented in 1886 by John Pemberton, a teetotaller who substituted wine with the West African kola nut, although cocaine was not removed from its ingredients until 1906 when **drug** use became a concern. Regular shipments to the UK of Coca-Cola began in 1901, the year of Queen Victoria's death – a coincidence, but one that was a contraction in the birth of modern Britain. A company executive sent to assess the UK market potential in 1924 reported that, because of Britain's cold **weather**, its people favoured the consumption of hot beverages. However, by the mid-1950s, the aggressive marketing of Coke as an elixir of youth, promising vitality, friendship and sexual conquest, had made it the most popular soft drink in Britain, its American-ness adding to its appeal in the age of rock 'n' roll.

The 1964 Soft Drinks Regulations Act restricted the use of dangerous chemical additives and, as the public became more health-conscious, they drank more fruit juices and mineral water. Bottled spa water had been used as a tonic by the wealthier classes since the eighteenth century, and the Victorian realisation that pump and tap water carried fatal diseases like typhoid added to its appeal. The introduction of cleaner urban water supplies turned mineral water from a necessity into a luxury, as a result of which it became even more of a status symbol. This, as much as health concern, was responsible for a dramatic rise in consumption during the 1980s – from 25 million litres in 1980 to 619 million in 1995. Most of it was drunk by professionals under the age of 45 – advertisers successfully associating brands like Perrier with beauty, affluence and cultivation – although some of the rise was attributable to the fact that Ecstasy users consumed water to offset the dehydrative effects of their drug. None of these changes lessened the dominance of the artificial soft drinks market. Just as tobacco manufacturers responded to health-consciousness by producing low-tar cigarettes, so drink manufacturers responded by producing low-sugar, 'diet' variants of their products, and a host of 'energy' drinks that would have been familiar to a seller of quack tonics in the centuries before mass **education** and healthcare. ◄

The British drank less alcohol than their forebears. Between 1875 and 1935, the nation's total alcohol consumption halved, from 83 million gallons a year to 40 million. This was partly the result of government action: the shortening of pub licensing hours and restrictions on the sale of alcohol in places like the **music hall** and **cinema**. ◄ It was also the result of greater public awareness that alcoholism was a disease and not a series of social faux pas (Britain's first drying-out clinics were sanctioned by the Inebriates Act of 1898). Between 1900 and 1939, the amount of beer drunk per head each year fell from approximately 34.3 gallons to 14.6. The fashion for fizzy **German** lager ◄ beers that started in the 1970s revived the industry somewhat, with 21.9 million gallons being drunk by 1995. The consumption of spirits also picked up after the war, in this case as a result of the American fashion for cocktails (the first recorded cocktail party in Britain was held by the artist C.R.W. Nevinson in 1924). But consumption was still well down on earlier levels (5.9 pints per head a year in 1995, compared to 1.04 gallons in 1900). Soft drinks containing alcohol, known as 'alcopops,' grew in number during the 1990s in a controversial effort to stimulate under-age drinking. Consumption of the original 'alcopop', cider, rose from 18 million gallons in 1963 to 123 million in 1995.

The greater leisure opportunities open to people were primarily responsible for the overall decline in British drinking; but the same factor was also responsible for the biggest change in alcohol consumption and the one that did most to keep the trade profitable: wine. For centuries it had been the preserve of the upper classes, with the exception of cheap, sweet varieties like port and Madeira. Duties were cut in the 1860s and 1940s but this had little effect on drinking habits and by the time that Raymond Postgate's *The Plain Man's Guide to Wine* was published in 1950, wine was more likely to pass the plain man's lips at an altar rail than at the dinner table. It remained beyond the purse of most working people and its class associations were such that many people felt intimidated by the apparent necessity of possessing a connoisseur's knowledge of the drink.

That changed in the 1960s as a result of three things. First, wine became cheaper and more widely available thanks to bulk-buying by supermarkets. Sainsbury's were the first to stock it on open shelves in 1962 and the company also pioneered the practice of providing clear labels to guide the consumer and remove the mystique surrounding the drink. The creation of wine bars and the cosmopolitanisation of the British pub in the 1980s also made it easier to find. Second, cheaper foreign **holidays** brought Britons into contact with cultures where wine was drunk by all classes, and many took the practice home with them, as they did Continental food. Third, demand was stimulated by the growth of restaurant-going. Between 1960 and 1995, British wine consumption rose ten times, from 3.6 pints a head per year to 32.1 pints, with over half the country – 30.45 million – drinking it regularly by the year 2000.

The British are known as one of Europe's heaviest drinkers of alcohol, a reputation based largely on the fact that so many of the holidaying Britons that Continentals encounter are drunk. In fact, while their consumption of drugs is the highest in Europe, that of alcohol is around the EU average. What has changed is their liking for coffee and wine, both of them Continental practices – a development which indicates that a Europeanisation of British tastes took place alongside the Americanisation that excited so much controversy.

■ Drugs

Although mind-altering substances have been used as means of enlightenment and recreation since antiquity, it was the British who established the international drugs trade in the late eighteenth century when the East India Company developed a lucrative traffic in opium with India and China. By the time Queen Victoria ascended the throne, Treasury revenue from the trade was equivalent to half the annual cost of the **monarchy** and the **civil service**. So lucrative was the trade that the British went to **war** with China in 1856 in a successful bid to gain a monopoly of the opium trade (one of the spoils of that war was the ceding of Hong Kong to Britain). By 1900 the British consumed more drugs than any other European people, at a time when they ruled a quarter of the planet. A century later, after **parliament** had imposed the most draconian anti-drugs laws in Europe, they still consumed the most.

At the turn of the twentieth century, most narcotics were freely available and attracted little opprobrium in comparison to alcohol. Sherlock Holmes' frequent use of cocaine worried Dr Watson and it was expunged in cinematic adaptations of his exploits. But the drug habits of Arthur Conan Doyle's (1859–1930) fictional detective hero did not affect his popularity with the Edwardian public. Cocaine was used as a pick-me-up in a range of cheap tonics, the most famous of which was Coca-Cola, until it was dropped as an ingredient in 1906 in favour of caffeine. Amphetamines ('uppers'), first synthesised in 1887 for the treatment of asthmatics, became popular in the 1930s among better-off party-goers, as did barbiturates ('downers') with which they were often used.

Opium was usually smoked in special 'opium dens' situated in Britain's seaports and staffed by Oriental immigrants. Laudanum (opium dissolved in alcohol) was extremely popular among all classes and was bought in small penny vials from pharmacists to relieve everything from menstrual pain to a bad day at work, while 'Mrs Winslow's Soothing Syrup for Children' was one of the products used to calm noisy infants. Heroin, which was created in 1874 as a non-addictive substitute for opium, was just as easy to obtain. So too was cannabis, though Queen Victoria's regular use of the drug did not commend it to her subjects. Until the 1950s it was mainly popular with jazz musicians and people who had diseases like multiple sclerosis, for whom it offered some pain relief.

Pub opening times were severely restricted in 1916, a law that marked the high point of the Victorian temperance movement. But the war on **drink** gave way to a new war on drugs. It was led by the United States on moral grounds and formally prosecuted through the League of Nations. At the League's inaugural meeting in 1920, the first of several Conventions was set up in a bid to limit the recreational drug trade. America had tried to prohibit narcotics since 1875, banning cocaine and opiates in 1915. But the federal government had only driven drug use underground, and in doing so it laid the foundations of organised crime in the US.

Britain was at first reluctant to follow. When the young Mahatma Gandhi denounced opium as 'that other oppressor' his followers were arrested on charges of 'undermining the revenue'. But the British also had benign reasons for their opposition. A commission under Sir Humphrey Rolleston, set up by the Ministry of Health in 1914 to examine American policy, concluded that **crime** and misery were its inevitable outcome and he recommended that serious addicts should be prescribed a maintenance dose of their drug so that they might lead 'a useful and fairly normal life'.

However, while the **Lloyd George**'s government resisted America's prohibition of alcohol in 1920, in the same year it bowed to pressure over narcotics and parliament passed the Dangerous Drugs Act, which made cocaine and opiates illegal. Cannabis followed in 1939. US political muscle was strengthened by the public campaigns of Britain's own moralists and by the more insidious desire of industrialists and politicians to exert greater control over the lives of a newly enfranchised population.

Pragmatists feared that workers would not be fit to staff the factories and offices that generated the nation's wealth, nor the **armed forces** with which that wealth was defended. Ideologues argued that the British race would become morally as well as physically degenerate. **Women** were thought to be particularly vulnerable. It was feared that people of colour used narcotics to overcome the 'natural' resistance of white women to having sex with other races. This view became more pronounced during the 1950s when Afro-Caribbean **immigrants'** use of cannabis became popular among white youths engaging in black music and **fashion**. For example, a Home Office report on London's nightclubs in 1964 concluded that where drugs were available, 'there is a great deal of "necking" with coloured people. In this atmosphere, any young person is obviously in serious moral danger.' The first prosecution for possession took place in 1952 and in 1964 more whites than blacks were convicted for the first time; by 1970 annual prosecutions had risen to 7,500. Like the Chinese before them, Afro-Caribbeans were blamed for the nation's entire drug consumption when in fact they were only indirectly responsible for a fraction of it.

The burgeoning youth culture of the post-war era and a growing number of synthetic narcotics maintained consumption. Amphetamines became the favoured drug of **Mods**. During the Second World War, 72 million tablets had been given to Allied soldiers to keep them alert in battle and Prime Minister Anthony Eden took them throughout the **Suez crisis**. But it was mass recreational use by teenagers that prompted amphetamines to be banned in the Dangerous Drugs Act of 1964. The same was true of LSD, or 'Acid', which was banned in the corresponding act of 1966. A Swiss research chemist, Dr Albert Hofmann, invented LSD in 1938 and after experimenting on **animals**, he took the first trip in 1943. In the 1950s, the psychiatric profession used it on **homosexuals** and schizophrenics in an effort to cure them, and during the same period, the CIA experimented on volunteers with a view to winning the **Cold War** by disorientating communist troops. It was then adopted by the Hippie movement and inspired the associated trend in Psychedelic music, which reached an apogee with the **Beatles'** *Sgt Pepper* (1967) and Pink Floyd's *The Piper at the Gates of Dawn* (1967). Novelist Aldous Huxley's

(1894–1963) account of his experiments with the natural psychotropic drug mescalin, *The Doors of Perception* (1954), became a bible for LSD users in the same period.

Altogether, from 1950 to 1970 the number of proscribed narcotics rose from 33 to 106. This, and not a rise in consumption, drove up the annual number of drug offences – from 6,911 in 1969 to 93,631 in 1995, of which 84.2 per cent of the total over that period (773,581) were marijuana-related. Celebrity drug-busts like that of Mick Jagger and Keith Richards in 1967 made drug-taking more glamorous for British youths. But, as a consequence, the state became more determined to fight what was now seen as an epidemic. Baroness Wootton's 1968 Report on Drug Abuse called for a relaxation of drug laws. It was met by further proscriptive legislation in 1970 and again in 1988, when even tranquillisers were placed under strict controls. In the same year, pub-opening hours were extended for the first time since 1916.

The arrival of Ecstasy led to another increase in recreational drug taking. Its compound, MDMA, was first synthesised in the USA in 1914 as an appetite suppressant and it began to be used by American youths in 1981. Ecstasy came to Britain in 1988, where it became the drug of choice in the Rave scene. By the end of the century, half a million clubbers in the UK were consuming approximately 1 million tablets every week. **Tony Blair's** use of D:Ream's Ecstasy anthem 'Things Can ◄ Only Get Better' in **Labour's** 1997 general election campaign did not ◄ signal a more intelligent attitude to the issue.

A national consensus emerged over cannabis use. Scientists, police and even Tory politicians (some of whom admitted to having used the drug) pressed for reform, on the grounds that British law was being made an ass of. In 2002 cannabis was reclassified as a class C drug, as a result of which it was no longer an offence to be in possession of small amounts of the drug, and doctors were also able to prescribe it to the sick. However, government attempts to suppress the wider drug culture continued, for example by restricting the licensing of **music** ◄ **festivals**.

For a few people, drugs were a temporary, toxic escape from **poverty** ◄ and not the path to enlightenment or the means to a good night out. This was particularly true of heroin use. The number of addicts rose tenfold between 1955 and 1968, and thereafter they accounted for most drug-related deaths, shattering heroin's early promise as a safe alternative to opium. The wider social effects could be appalling. Drug use accounted for about a third of all property crime in the UK. However, this continued to be mainly due to the fact that the illegality of narcotics kept prices so high that addicts were forced to steal for a fix, which they bought from dealers supplied by organised crime syndicates. By 2001, the United Nations had proscribed over a hundred psychoactive compounds, the illegal trade in which amounted to 10 per cent of the world's commodities market, more than food or oil.

The political potential of drug use was never as great as radicals during the 1960s suggested. As the British cultural commentator Jeff Nuttall put it, 'drugs are an excellent strategy against society but a poor alternative to it'. But nor were they as toxic as their detractors claimed. Although annual deaths from illegal drugs trebled in the second half of the twentieth century (to 2,063 in 2001), the numbers continued to be far lower compared with deaths from legal ones. While approximately 8,300 smokers and 625 drinkers per million died each year as a result of their habit, only 7 per million Ecstasy users did. Statistically, a British citizen was more likely to be killed by an avalanche than by taking Ecstasy.

In *The Sign of Four* (1890), we read that Sherlock Holmes 'thrust the sharp point home, pressed down the tiny piston and sank back into the velvet-lined armchair with a long sigh of satisfaction'. 'I abhor the dull routine of existence, I crave for mental exaltation,' declares Holmes, explaining both his intellectual vocation and his penchant for injecting cocaine. The vast majority of British drug users approached narcotics with the same outlook, and on the whole they did so responsibly. The only difference between the manner and the extent to which modern Britons chose to use recreational drugs is that they were subject to less hypocrisy than their Victorian forebears had been.

■ Ealing Comedies

A group of eight critically and commercially successful comedy dramas produced by Ealing Studios in west London between 1947 and 1953. They affectionately captured key elements of the national character and in doing so came to symbolise what a confident, independent British film industry could achieve.

Ealing Studios were established by the producer Michael Balcon (1896–1977) in 1938 and made a total of 95 features before their demise in 1955. His autobiography records: 'My ruling passion has always been the building up of a native industry in the soil of this country . . . [for] films to be international, [they] must be thoroughly national in the first instance . . . there is nothing wrong with a degree of cultural chauvinism.' After cutting his teeth at Gainsborough Studios and Gaumont British, where he produced the film adaptation of J.B. Priestley's *Good Companions* (1932), Balcon took charge of Metro- ◄ Goldwyn-Mayer's UK operation in 1936. But he was unhappy with the tenor of the movies he was asked to make by the American giant and left for Ealing. There, he gathered around him some of the best directors in the country, primarily Alexander Mackendrick, Robert Hamer, Harry Watt, Charles Frend and Charles Crichton, who helped to realise his vision.

The Studios made their reputation during the Second World War, with quality patriotic features, notably *Went the Day Well?* (1942). Set in an English village, the members of which unite to defeat a Nazi fifth column within its midst, the film established one of the Studios' defining characteristics: the importance of community life.

Ealing Comedies share a horror of bureaucracy, authoritarianism, selfishness and violence. They celebrate virtues that the British most like to see in themselves: eccentricity, tolerance, gentleness and a love of liberty. The heroes of Ealing Comedies are canny, self-reliant people who struggled against injustice, whether it comes in the shape of villains in *The Ladykillers* (1955), aristocratic snobbery in *Kind Hearts and Coronets* (1949), civil servants and politicians in *Passport to Pimlico* (1949), the military in *Whisky Galore* (1949) or business and **trade unions** in *The* ◄ *Man in the White Suit* (1951).

Some were subversive in the way that they challenged authority. But crime is never shown to pay, however just the motives – be it murder in *Kind Hearts* or theft in *The Lavender Hill Mob* (1951). Sometimes Ealing films could be dark, surreal even, like the chiller *Dead of Night* (1945) or gritty like *It Always Rains on Sunday* (1947). But most, like *The Titfield Thunderbolt* (1953), were consensual, striving to show that men and women of different personalities and **classes** can work ◄ together if they share common values. The genre is, therefore, very

E

165

much a product of the 1940s, when British society was relatively
▶ united in order to prosecute **war** and establish **welfare**.

Although the Studios continued to make films until 1959, they had
▶ begun to lose the plot by the time Balcon sold up to the **BBC** in 1955.
Or rather, they had hung on to the plot too long. Younger British film-
makers like Lindsay Anderson and Tony Richardson of the so-called
'Kitchen-Sink' school saw Ealing's cosy, hierarchical world not as an
expression of democratic vigour, but one of torpor that bore little relation to the aspirations and conflicts that were beginning to change
▶ Britain. 'The no man's land between **Establishment** and Outsider
never began to be trodden,' observed the critic Kenneth Tynan
(1927–80), 'good taste intervened to prevent action.'

Which is precisely why Ealing Comedies remain so popular, especially in England. Their humorous picture of social harmony and
cultural homogeneity appeals to those distressed by today's more frag-
mented world. Yet their popularity also resides in the fact that there
are traces of Ealing's world left in Britain. *The Full Monty* (1997), in
which a group of unemployed Sheffield steelworkers and their boss
overcome their plight by becoming male strippers, is one of several
films that critics have called 'Ealingesque' despite their contemporary
settings. When the Studios were sold, Balcon had a plaque erected on
their walls that read: 'Here during a quarter of a century many films
were made projecting Britain and the British character'. However
short the Ealing legacy turns out to be, the epitaph that its founder
gave it is an apt and deserved one.

■ Easter Rising (1916)

On 24 April 1916 the British government was taken by surprise by an
insurrection in Dublin. Twelve hundred republicans, whose leaders
included members of the Irish Volunteers, Sinn Féin and the Irish
Republican Brotherhood (IRB), seized the post office in Sackville Street
along with other buildings. But their fledgling independent republic
was snuffed out by British troops within four days. There had been no
assistance from Germany, which was currently at war with Britain,
and the rebels failed to capture either Dublin Castle or the government's arsenal in Phoenix Park. In the fighting, around 100 British
soldiers and 450 republicans were killed; sixteen of the leaders were
subsequently executed after being court-martialled.

Initially, there was little sympathy in Ireland for the insurrectionists.
▶ In the *New Statesman*, the Irish playwright **G.B. Shaw** lamented 'a piece
of hopeless mischief'. Home Rule had been promised after the war, so it
made sense for nationalists at least to remain neutral so that the British
could get the conflict with Germany finished as quickly as possible. In

recognition of this logic the British had not treated the republican Volunteers as potential fifth columnists before the Rising; they were allowed to keep their arms. But the nationalists had split after September 1914, when their leader John Redmond had appealed to his supporters to fight on the British side. For a radical faction numbering more than 10,000, Home Rule was inadequate in the first place. For them the war offered the chance of immediate independence.

The executions, carried out after private hearings with no chance of appeal, transformed nationalist opinion. They might have had some justification in normal circumstances, since casualties had been high and there was extensive damage to the centre of Dublin. But in 1916 it was an act of political madness, sure to turn the victims into martyrs – a status which some of the leaders had actively sought. Sir Roger Casement, who had travelled to Germany to raise a force from Irish prisoners of war, was captured and killed despite international calls for clemency; the selective release of diaries which revealed his **homo-** ◄ **sexuality** might have seemed a clever way of smearing his reputation at the time, but with hindsight it makes the authorities seem even more sordid. And having acted ruthlessly in the first instance, the British over-compensated by releasing all the remaining rebel leaders in the following year. One of them, Eamon de Valera, subsequently became Taoiseach on three occasions, ending as President of the Republic.

Given the continuing opposition to Home Rule in Ulster, the postwar **partition of Ireland**, with full independence to the South, would ◄ have happened with or without the Rising. But while the incident underlined the urgent need for a peaceful compromise, it also excluded any possibility that a resolution could be found without bloodshed. The British repression destroyed the career of John Redmond, who condemned the Rising as a German plot. The constitutional nationalists were virtually extinguished as a political force, and Sinn Féin took their place. At the 1918 general election the party won 73 seats. One of their number, Countess Markiewicz who had been court-martialled in 1916 but reprieved because of her sex, was the first **woman** ever elected to the House of Commons although she ◄ never took her seat (she boycotted that imperial institution along with all of her Sinn Féin colleagues). Perhaps the most damaging legacy of the violence was a feeling in Ireland that the option of armed resistence, however bloody and futile, would ensure a lasting fame for the perpetrators.

■ Economic growth

The health of a nation's economy is normally measured by changes in

E

the level of its gross domestic product (GDP) – its overall output of goods and services. Economic growth is the result either of an increase in the number of workers in productive employment, or a rise in the productivity of those already employed. During the post-war period the rate of growth has been regarded as a crucial indicator of a government's performance; the political ideal is to preside over a healthy rate of growth (i.e. a respectable annual increase in GDP by international standards), coupled with relatively low **inflation**.

The obsession with growth is a product of the second half of the twentieth century. After 1945, governments were more closely involved in the management of the economy, and were happy to take the credit in good times. When growth was stagnant or worse, they habitually tried to shift the blame on to problems in the world market; but they were rarely believed. In any case GDP is a crude and abstract measurement of economic wellbeing as it relates to the 'average' citizen. Rapid growth in one sector can coexist with a marked decline elsewhere. A surge in productivity can mean that the economy grows significantly while **unemployment** rises. And even at times of 'full' employment, the rewards of growth can be distributed in a fashion which increases existing inequality.

In 1964 (a time when the growth obsession was particularly strong) the economist Samuel Brittan suggested that the figures should be revised to exclude products which no one really wanted, and to bring in developments which contributed to the nation's 'happiness', such as a better environment and shorter working hours. Although happiness is obviously difficult to quantify, some statistics (like the proportion of people on anti-depressants) might be used to build up a broad picture, and it could be argued that with all its faults a more inclusive index would be more relevant to voters in a general election.

When evaluating economic growth there is an obvious danger in choosing the evidence to suit the hypothesis. But it is indisputable that the period from 1945 to the oil crisis of the mid-1970s was one of almost continuous growth in the developed Western economies: and that Britain's performance was markedly worse than that of comparable nations. For example, in real terms the British economy was at its peak between 1960 and 1964, when the average annual growth rate was 3.4 per cent. But during those years the figure for Japan was nearly 12 per cent. Between 1955 and 1960 Britain did outperform the United States (2.5 per cent growth compared to 2.4 per cent). But this was merely a temporary breach of the overall post-war pattern. **Governments** tried to stimulate domestic growth through the techniques of **Keynesian** demand management; but because other countries were better at satisfying the growing **consumerist** culture – with more attractive goods and lower prices – in the long term the strategy was more beneficial to Britain's competitors.

Britain's relative economic decline, compared with other European ◄ countries, was an obvious stimulus for the application to join the European Economic Community (EEC) at the beginning of the 1960s. But it also inspired a search for explanations within the domestic economy. Thus in the 1960s policy-makers devised plans to reform the **trade unions**. Both **Labour** and the **Conservatives** adopted forms of ◄ **economic planning**. Despair at being outstripped by countries like ◄ France, West Germany and even Italy provoked the conclusion in some quarters that Britain's vitality had been sapped. The **welfare state** was ◄ usually identified as the culprit here, although this overlooked the fact that Britain's successful competitors had adopted similar social policies. A more sensible answer would have focused on Britain's excessive concern to protect the value of its currency, which led governments to jump on to the economic brakes after applying the accelerator (a sequence of events aptly known as 'stop-go'). Here, as in so many areas, the country was hampered by the legacy of its pre-war role. Ironically, the same people who frantically searched for economic scapegoats at home generally lamented the erosion of Britain's international status, and prevented more rational politicians from explaining the new realities to the electorate.

Up to the mid-1970s Britain had relied on economic growth to fund the expansion of its social provision. Thus the oil shock, which actually caused a reduction of GDP per head in 1974–5, induced something like a collective nervous breakdown. **Thatcherism** promised a radical ◄ break with recent practice. Lower direct taxation, trade union reform, and a retreat from detailed economic intervention seemed to have produced a 'miracle'. Average growth between 1983 and 1988 was 3.7 per cent, compared to 2.6 per cent for the post-war period as a whole. Yet the 'miracle' claim could only be substantiated if this 'boom' had continued. Instead, by the end of the 1980s Britain was gripped by a new recession, creating an unfortunate symmetry with the slump at the beginning of the decade. The recovery after 1992 looked to be more sustainable, since a more modest rate did not seem to threaten a fresh outbreak of inflation, and to keep up the momentum in February 2003 interest rates were cut to 3.75 per cent – the lowest since 1955. By the end of the twentieth century British GDP per head was around twice its 1963 level.

Overall, despite the regular prophecies of doom, Britain's economy performed respectably during the twentieth century. In 2003, it was the fourth biggest in the world. Almost everyone had benefited from economic growth to some extent, if living standards are accepted as the sole criterion. The 'happiness' index might tell a different story, though. And some commentators were beginning to question the

whole idea of 'growth', which already seemed to have taken a deadly
▶ toll on the global **environment**. The concept of 'zero growth', coupled
with a more equitable distribution of income, could alleviate (if not
entirely solve) many of the problems which governments had promised to tackle through ever-increasing prosperity for the nation as a
whole. For example, a crisis was looming over the cost of pensions. By
the end of the twentieth century politicians were hinting that the
retirement age would have to be increased, as pensioners made up an
ever-rising proportion of the workforce as a whole. Yet most middle-
aged people were longing to retire as early as possible. Only a radical
change in working practices could alter this mood; yet the obsession
with growth implied that people should work harder than ever, under
the constant threat of redundancy. Something, eventually, would have
to give.

■ Economic planning

Throughout the twentieth century economists and politicians argued
about the proper role of the state. But very few proposed that it should
do nothing at all, and to that extent most would have agreed that the
ability to predict the future performance of the British economy
would be a considerable asset for governments. Even if the state were
to provide nothing more than a system of workhouses for the poor, it
would be helpful for it to be able to anticipate changing levels of
unemployment. The chief concern for economic liberals like Friedrich
von Hayek (1899–1992) was that the state would move from making
predictions to trying to turn that guesswork into reality by direct
intervention in the economy. Such efforts, they felt, would inevitably
be self-defeating, and the attempt to rectify initial mistakes would
lead to even further, ham-fisted interference. The final result would be
a totalitarian state, like the Soviet Union, where production was
geared to the meeting of targets rather than the fulfilment of 'real'
market demand.

The economic liberals detected alarming trends in Britain during
the 1930s, when governments made half-hearted attempts to promote
▶ **economic growth** in depressed regions. More worrying for people who
were fixated with intellectual trends, independent policy institutes
such as Political and Economic Planning (PEP, 1931), and the National
Institute of Economic and Social Research (1938) were established to
provide specialised advice for a more active state. Inevitably the
Second World War brought an influx of planners into Whitehall,
initially to ensure the efficient allocation of resources and then to
devise a strategy for post-war reconstruction.

For the economic liberals, Britain was moving rapidly down what

Hayek called 'the road to serfdom', just as it was fighting a war to preserve its liberties. The election of a **Labour** government in 1945 ◄ provoked some hysterical attacks; in his 1948 book *Ordeal by Planning* John Jewkes went so far as to describe the process as a 'moral sickness'. Rationing came to an end, albeit slowly, but the experience of wartime control had encouraged the 'man in Whitehall' to think that he knew better than the consumer, and the public accepted Labour's initial programme of **nationalisation** with hardly a murmur. Other state ◄ agencies, like the Milk Marketing Board, stayed on to regulate and bully producers. The stated objective of 'full' employment committed the state indefinitely to the support of failing companies, whether through subsidies or state ownership. Targets were also set for the growth of exports, to close the 'dollar gap' with America.

E

If anything, the economic liberals were most worried by politicians like Harold Macmillan, who had spoken out between the wars for a British 'middle way' between the extremes of socialism and *laissez-faire* capitalism. For liberals like Hayek, such compromises were just as illusory as **J.M. Keynes**'s view that if planning proved to be necessary, civil- ◄ isation would still be safe so long as the planning was conducted by people who valued freedom in other fields. After Macmillan became Prime Minister in 1957 there was a definite move towards economic planning, in response to Britain's relative economic decline. In 1961 the **Conservative** government instituted a National Economic Development Corporation (NEDC), a forum for **government**, employers and ◄ **trade unions**. Simultaneously, the Chancellor Selwyn Lloyd called for ◄ a 'pay pause'. It seemed that Britain was already a 'corporate state', in which the key decisions were taken by a handful of people who aspired not simply to second-guess the operation of the market but rather to forestall it. Elsewhere, planners like Dr Richard Beeching redesigned the railway network according to projections of likely demand; Lord Robbins reached more optimistic conclusions with regard to future expansion of the **universities**. ◄

Thus when Labour returned to office in 1964 the Conservatives had already prepared the ground for a further advance by the state. In September 1965 the government unveiled its National Plan, which envisaged an accelerated growth rate of 4 per cent. In fact, the Plan was undermined by balance of payments problems which induced devaluation of the pound, and a policy of deflation, in 1967. The Plan had not been backed by any new powers; from the outset it had seemed like nothing more than a wish-list. As Britain's economic plight deepened, machinery was introduced to control prices and incomes. But experience showed that this only worked in the short term, and in its extreme form it really did smack of totalitarianism.

By the end of the twentieth century the ill-starred National Plan

▶ looked like the high-water mark of planning in Britain. During the
▶ **Thatcher** years the chief targets were set for inflation, which could be
▶ controlled by government action according to **monetarist** theory.
▶ **Thatcherite** ministers were actively hostile to the concept of planning,
▶ and claimed that it had failed. But the preservation of the **welfare
state** meant that they had to eat their words to some extent. Expensive
state programmes, like hospital building and weapons procurement
▶ for the **armed forces**, had to be planned on the basis of demographic
projections and developments in foreign policy; but they also had to
be drawn up with at least half an eye on the likely availability of
resources. Chancellors continued to forecast economic growth in their
budget statements, and even if these were very informal targets,
governments remained hopeful of fostering economic growth, for
electoral reasons. Meanwhile, at the micro level private companies
crucially depended on their own growth forecasts. Instead of waiting
for booms and slumps, entrepreneurs had to be forewarned; some
▶ even employed long-term **weather** forecasters, when the prospects of
their businesses were seasonally sensitive.

▶   The end of the **Cold War** promised a more objective debate on the
subject. Some argued that rigorous economic planning had never
been given a fair trial in Britain, compared to countries like France.
Even those who lacked an ideological commitment wondered
whether it might have been applied too weakly, particularly in the
cases of transport and the unsustainable growth of the capital city. But
while the fears of the economic liberals could now be exposed as an
ideological over-reaction unworthy of people who claimed that their
subject was 'scientific', more practical objections had emerged.
Society was increasingly complex, so forward planning of any kind
was increasingly hazardous. Even individuals could hardly plan their
own futures with safety, with their jobs and pensions more vulnerable
than ever to unpredictable fluctuations in the world economy. Despite
all the hopes of the 1960s, government and people alike would have to
go on living with uncertainty.

■ Education Act (1902)

Over the second half of the nineteenth century the British state
exerted increasing influence over the nation's schools, making attendance between the ages of 5 and 10 compulsory in 1880, providing
more of the funds (depending on results) and virtually guaranteeing
free (elementary) schooling in 1891. Although the original concentration was on the rudiments of reading, writing and arithmetic (the
'three R's'), concern about slipping standards in industry led to the
passage of the Technical Instruction Act (1889). The demands of a new

century required something more advanced than the old system, under which secondary education had been almost the exclusive preserve of affluent families. A new **government** Science and Art ◀ Department was created alongside the existing Department of Education. Ten years later the increasingly complex administrative machinery was rationalised under a Board of Education.

In 1900 more than half of Britain's schools were administered by elected Boards which had been established after the 1870 Education Act. They were funded by a mixture of local rates and central government grants to cover building costs, but the School Boards varied in size and many were struggling to fulfil the new standards expected by the state. There were also 'voluntary' schools, which were largely funded by various religious bodies, including the established **Church** ◀ **of England**, although they also received some government aid. By 1895 these voluntary schools were also struggling, and asked the government for increased help. A Board of Education official, Robert Morant, saw the chance of turning the funding problems to advantage, and instigating a thorough reform. He was supported by the Leader of the House of Commons, the aristocratic, sceptical Arthur James Balfour.

The 1902 Education Act inspired by Morant and pushed through parliament by Balfour abolished the School Boards. Responsibility passed to county and borough councils which were authorised to establish secondary schools. At the same time, while the voluntary schools would still be responsible for building maintenance, the burden of their other running costs was transferred to local ratepayers. This section of the Act was always likely to provoke a furore, even if the cause of the dispute seems obscure a century later. Many voluntary schools might have disappeared without ratepayer support, and they were still free to provide religious instruction as they saw fit. But education was already a burning issue for many Nonconformists, who resented the fact that in some areas their children had no alternative but to attend Anglican schools. At least they had not previously been asked to subsidise what they saw as indoctrination in a false creed – or rather they had been able to overlook the small amounts which came to the schools through general taxation. The terms of the Act also meant that devout Anglicans would now have to support the propagation of Nonconformist (and **Roman** ◀ **Catholic**) doctrines through the rates. In short, the measure was calculated to upset everyone whose religious fervour exceeded their desire for better instruction in other subjects, and in 1902 this element within the UK population was substantial enough to have deterred most orthodox politicians. Balfour, though, was out of the ordinary. As his notorious **Declaration** of 1916 was to show, his judgement ◀ occasionally deserted him on religious questions. But the author of

A Defence of Philosophical Doubt (1879) could not be moved by unseemly squabbles among Christian sects.

There was, though, a heavy political price for Balfour's party. The legislation offered the **Liberal Party**, the traditional home of Nonconformity, a chance to reunite after recent bitter divisions over Irish Home Rule. Opposition to the reform was particularly strong in Wales, and **David Lloyd George** enhanced his reputation within his party with some withering attacks on the legislation. Outside parliament, a Passive Resisters' League withheld part of their rates in protest; in 1904 alone there were more than 7,000 prosecutions. The cry of 'religion on the rates' also proved very potent in the general election of 1906. But although the Liberals were swept back into power (and Balfour himself lost his Manchester seat), their subsequent attempts to amend the hated Act were stymied by the House of Lords. Morant and Balfour had taken an essential first step towards a modern education system, allowing gifted children from all backgrounds a much improved chance of expanding their knowledge instead of being fed untutored into the world of work. Serious anomalies remained, and secondary education (up to the age of 14) was not made compulsory until an Act of 1918 which also provided that at least a quarter of grammar school places would be given to children who competed for scholarships. But continuing religious sensitivities ensured that new reforms on the 1902 scale had to wait until R.A. Butler's **1944 Education Act** more than forty years later.

■ Education Act (1944)

Richard Austen Butler (1902–82) was the son of a distinguished colonial official who later became Master of Pembroke College, Cambridge. 'Rab' Butler will probably be best remembered as a man who could have seized the **Conservative Party** leadership on two occasions (1956, after **Suez**, and 1963, on the resignation of Harold Macmillan), but missed his chances. His other chief claim to the notice of posterity was the Education Act of 1944, which is often referred to as the 'Butler Act' as if it were his unaided achievement.

In reality, as even Butler freely admitted, the Act merely built on existing practices, and on educational ideas which had become commonplace in the inter-war period. Free milk, meals and transport for children, and the complete abolition of tutorial fees in state schools, rounded off the logic of Balfour's **1902 Education Act**. Another provision of the Act, to raise the school-leaving age to 15, had been foreshadowed in legislation of 1936, and was merely delayed by the war. The Hadow Report of 1926 had backed this idea, and also urged that 11 was a suitable age for appraising the relative ability of children. The 'eleven-plus' examination was the most notorious legacy of Butler's Act, although this arbitrary rite of passage for **children** had been accepted by many local authorities before the war and was supported by the current vogue for 'IQ' tests. The system of local authority supervision was also rationalised – 400 responsible bodies were reduced to 146 – but this was the kind of bureaucratic tinkering which rarely won headlines.

Butler was originally appointed to the Board of Education (outside the Cabinet) in July 1941. **Churchill** had every reason to suspect Butler, who had supported **appeasement**. Education would keep him as far as possible from foreign affairs: to Churchill's mind, indeed, it would distance him from interesting work of any kind. Yet Butler had other ideas. Although he was the product of a privileged background himself, he was passionately committed to the levelling-up of standards. Remembering the factional furore over the 1902 Act, Churchill was unenthusiastic at the prospect of any major reform. However, Butler was not to be deterred. Intensive preparations began within his department, in the hope of finding a suitable opportunity once the fortunes of war had turned.

Butler's chance came after the publication of the **Beveridge** Report in December 1942. 'Ignorance' had been one of Beveridge's fearful 'Giants' ripe for slaying. Yet education was not a specialist area for Beveridge himself, and Treasury officials formed the view that a move against ignorance would steal some of the great man's thunder. For them the clinching point was Butler's reassurance that the cost would not be prohibitive. A White Paper, 'Educational Reconstruction', was issued in July 1943, and during the crucial debates in the following January Butler was praised from all sides of the Commons. There was an unexpected hitch at the last minute, though. Tory rebels combined with **Labour** to force through an amendment which would have guaranteed **women** teachers equal pay with their male counterparts. Churchill ensured that this vote was quickly nullified; it was the only parliamentary defeat ever suffered by his coalition government.

The next obstacles were the churches. At the beginning of the war more than half of the schools in England and Wales – the 'voluntary schools' – were run by the various religious denominations. Sectarian sensitivities over education had helped to bring down a Conservative government in 1906. But the voluntary schools lacked the financial resources to ensure satisfactory secondary education. Patiently diplomatic, Butler offered them a choice. The expense of their schools could be taken over entirely by local authorities; although the churches could still provide religious instruction, in other respects, henceforth, these schools would be indistinguishable from the rest of the state sector. The alternative was to plump for 'aided' status, which meant that the churches would retain most of their managerial power while local councils settled the bills, except for 50 per cent of the bill for structural improvements (most of the substandard buildings at the time were in schools in the voluntary sector).

▸ Butler quickly won over the Archbishop of Canterbury, **William Temple**, who had no reason to fear the change since Anglicanism as currently practised was already difficult to distinguish from secular

▸ life. Of the 9,000 **Church of England** schools, a third accepted the 'aided' option – far more than Butler's department had expected. The

▸ **Roman Catholic** hierarchy proved more resistant, although in arguing that the proposed 50 per cent buildings grant for their schools was insufficient they tacitly admitted that they lacked the financial resources to provide a satisfactory education. All of the Roman Catholic schools (which numbered around 2,000) took 'aided' status. Ultimately, Churchill's fears proved unjustified; unlike Butler, he had failed to gauge the decline of religious fervour over the intervening period.

▸ For Butler the real problem was not religion, but **class**. Privilege

▸ was embodied in the independent **public schools**, but he made only token gestures at a time when those institutions were financially weak. He had missed a chance for radical reform which might never be repeated. As it was, the parents of children in public schools remained outside the state system. The public schools did agree to reserve at least a quarter of their places to children who won local authority scholarships, but this actually strengthened the independent sector by improving its financial position and giving it a veneer of democratic respectability. Fearing state interference, some of the elite semi-independent grammar schools promptly went private, so that the new system lost its 'beacons of excellence' which might have driven up standards.

Butler himself hoped that class differences would not be reflected in the state schools. His Act consolidated a tripartite division which already existed in many places, between grammar schools, technical schools and what were now called secondary moderns. Butler suggested that children of differing abilities should be found suitable schools, which would enjoy 'parity of esteem'. But when the legislation was put into practice by the local authorities it became clear that Butler had been too subtle and large-minded for his fellow creatures. Very few technical schools were ever established. Since these were designed to accommodate children who showed a real aptitude for technical work, as opposed to the traditional 'academic' subjects like Latin and Greek, the failure to expand this sector was a lamentable

▸ failure of **local government** after 1945. Instead, the secondary moderns made half-hearted efforts to equip children for the life of manual labour which seemed to be their inescapable destiny.

Ultimately, perhaps the most notable achievement of the 'Butler Act' was to add extra impetus behind the drive to raise the school-leaving age. This was duly increased to 15 in 1947, and the Attlee government largely succeeded in recruiting the extra teachers and providing new buildings. Elsewhere, the Act did improve the life-chances of those who failed the eleven-plus. But grammar schools were still much better funded than their poor relations, the secondary moderns. In these schools children almost invariably left at the first legal opportunity, 15, while their grammar-school counterparts usually stayed on for three additional years.

Thus the stigma of failure was not lifted completely from those who underperformed at 11, for all of Butler's hopes for 'parity of esteem'. This was not Butler's fault; the Education Minister relied on local authorities and educationalists for the implementation of his Act, and it was they (for one reason or another) who ensured that the secondary moderns were regarded as dumping grounds for failures. The abolition of fees did lead to a marked increase in the number of talented working-class children who made their way into grammar schools. But this bold step towards real equality of opportunity only encouraged demands for more radical action, since children from middle-class homes still had a far better chance of passing the eleven-plus. 'Progressive' educationalists argued that true equality of opportunity was impossible unless every child could be guaranteed a similar (high) standard of teaching. The scene was set for a protracted debate over the virtues of a '**comprehensive**' system, under which children of ◄ all backgrounds and abilities would be taught in the same school.

■ Edward VIII (1894–1972)

The most controversial of modern British monarchs, whose forced abdication highlighted nascent tensions within the **Establishment** ◄ caused by the dawning of mass democracy. He was christened 'David' and was starved of affection by his father, George V, and mother, Queen Mary, who believed that instilling fear in their son would fit him to be king. In fact, the emotional damage it caused contributed to his spectacular downfall.

For a time, he promised much. Despite his unhappy childhood, he grew up to be an intelligent, articulate, good-looking and charming young man; his installation as Prince of Wales at Caernarvon in 1911 was a spectacular success, and he seemed set to continue the regeneration of the British **monarchy** which his father had begun during ◄ the First World War. He spent two years at Magdalen College, Oxford (1912–14), and was then commissioned into the Grenadier Guards, spending the First World War touring the front line to raise the morale of British and Commonwealth troops. David loathed the stuffy formality of royal protocol and he attempted with some success to modernise the monarchy. On a series of domestic and international tours between 1919 and 1936, he created a more stylish, accessible and politically engaged institution which combined glamour and social concern in equal measure. He symbolically dispensed with top hat and tails, preferring to meet his people in fashionable lounge suits. And, whereas previous British monarchs were content to patronise charities, he believed that the state had a duty to improve social conditions and publicly said so on a visit to the South Wales coalfield in 1936.

His sexual conduct alarmed the court as early as 1920. While his grandfather, Edward VII, had had a penchant for unattached actresses, David preferred to seduce married women, and he did so without discretion, brazenly cuckolding scores of aristocratic worthies, especially on his tours around the **Empire**. One of his lovers, Lady Thelma Furness, introduced him to the wealthy American divorcee, Wallis Simpson in 1932. In Wallis he found the maternal affection denied him by Queen Mary; the Prince was also, reputedly, the beneficiary of imaginative sexual techniques which Wallis had gleaned from amatory adventures in the Far East. Hopes that he would tire of her were dashed when, on the morning his accession as Edward VIII was proclaimed on 30 January 1936, the two lovers were filmed watching the proclamation from a nearby window. In November 1936 he told Prime Minister **Stanley Baldwin** that he was determined to marry the woman he loved rather than keep her as a mistress in accordance with royal protocol. Baldwin refused the King's offer of a morganatic marriage, in which Wallis would be his wife but not his Queen, on the grounds that the romance would not be morally acceptable to the public.

In fact, the public response to the abdication crisis highlighted the change in sexual mores since the First World War. There was some anti-American hostility to Mrs Simpson among sections of the middle and upper **classes** who saw her as the symbol of a vulgar nation that was corrupting not only the King but society as a whole. However, most Britons warmed to the romance of the affair, saw it as evidence of the King's modernity and did not think he should be forced to choose between love and power.

The Simpson affair was little more than a pretext for the British Establishment to rid themselves of a troublesome monarch. Edward admired Continental fascist leaders whom he secretly courted in an attempt to further the cause of **appeasement**. He was also an ardent Germanophile who regretted his father's Anglicisation of the Saxe-Coburg-Gotha dynasty, and he aimed to restore Anglo-German relations through an anti-Communist alliance. Although appeasement was official British foreign policy, the government worried that Edward's fascist sympathies made him a threat to national security. Aware of the public sympathy for his personal predicament, Baldwin denied his request to make a direct appeal to the nation via the radio. No 'King's Party' emerged in parliament, and with political support for the King coming only from the maverick **Winston** ◄ **Churchill** and the fascist leader **Oswald Mosley**, the King reluctantly signed the instrument of abdication on 10 December 1936. Edward's more malleable brother Bertie was crowned George VI on 12 May 1937 and he gladly set about restoring the probity of their father's old court. Edward was created Duke of Windsor and married Mrs Simpson in France the following spring (Wallis was denied the title of Royal Highness, a snub that caused lifelong bitterness). Thus, what is commonly termed an abdication was, in reality, more of a *coup d'état*.

E

Over the following decade, the Duke confirmed the Establishment's fears. A visit to Hitler in October 1937 reputedly secured a promise that, in the event of war and a Nazi victory, he would be restored to the British throne. When war came, Edward maintained contact with Nazi officials, first in France where he was posted as a military attaché, and later in Spain where he fled after Dunkirk. This treasonable conduct forced Churchill, as Prime Minister, to remove him to the Bahamas, where he was appointed Governor (1940–5). He continued to cause trouble by attempting to broker peace between Britain and Germany at a meeting with President Roosevelt. Although he was greeted with enthusiasm in the United States, his mission failed and he never again exercised influence in British or international affairs. The Duke and Duchess spent the rest of their lives devoted to each other but listless and bored in their chateau outside Paris.

Edward was keen to return to Britain after the war, but Queen Elizabeth (later the **Queen Mother**) feared that even as Duke he would ◄ outshine her uncharismatic husband; and she helped to ensure that Edward remained in exile for the rest of his life. He was allowed to return for his brother's funeral in 1952 but not for the subsequent Coronation of Elizabeth II, and Wallis was forbidden to accompany him. The next time Edward returned to the UK was in a coffin, after his death from throat cancer. He was interred at Frogmore near Windsor. With her husband dead, Wallis was no longer a threat and the Windsors felt sufficiently confident to invite her to her husband's funeral, at which she publicly met the royal family for the first time. She died in 1984.

Edward VIII was a vain, misguided man, whose political beliefs can

only be explained in part by the tyranny of the Windsor nursery. Nevertheless, his attempt to create a more informal, 'Art Deco'
▶ monarchy prefigured the attempt by **Diana, Princess of Wales** to modernise the institution. His removal from the throne saved Britain from having a quisling king at a time of national crisis. However, in the long term, the abdication arrested the development of the British monarchy, preventing it from keeping in step with social change. The unexpected departure from a strict line of succession, together with the end of press silence on the personal lives of royalty, also robbed the institution of some of the mystique which had protected it since the 1880s.

■ Elgar, Sir Edward (1857–1934)

Edward Elgar was born near Worcester, the son of an organist and music teacher. At first it seemed that he would become a solicitor, but he gave that up after only a year. He had already learned to play most instruments, and showed a particular aptitude for the violin. To support himself he began to follow his father's profession, and his first source of regular income came from an appointment as bandmaster to the Worcester City and County Pauper Lunatic Asylum.

Elgar was still giving lessons to supplement his income as late as 1901. But even at the lunatic asylum he had been producing original music of his own, and by the 1890s his compositions (mainly religious
▶ music, reflecting his **Roman Catholicism**) were attracting attention. The oratorio *The Dream of Gerontius* (1900), following the more secular *Enigma Variations* (1899) which commemorated Elgar's friendships, won him an international reputation. For the first time since the premature death of Purcell in 1695 England had produced a composer of the first rank.

Carping critics often explained away this unexpected revival by pointing out the echoes of foreign composers (notably Brahms) in Elgar's output. But there was something unmistakably English (and
▶ rural) about Elgar's work. Like **Thomas Hardy**, he was socially insecure and only felt comfortable in the provincial surroundings of his childhood. He also resembled Hardy in over-reacting to criticism. In both men, a thick layer of Victorian repression struggled to contain a highly passionate soul. The internal conflict brought them deep personal unhappiness, and gave the world works of art which might never have been produced if they had lived at peace with themselves. While Elgar's marriage was happy, he found an emotional outlet in a prolonged flirtation with Dora Penny, the daughter of one of his wife's friends. The tenth *Enigma Variation*, 'Dorabella', is an exquisite evocation of the joy Elgar found in this platonic relationship. The

mood is in telling contrast to the solemn opening variation, dedicated to his wife.

Elgar was knighted in 1904, and joined the Order of Merit in 1911. By that time he had produced the *Pomp and Circumstance* marches (1901 and later) for which, regrettably, he is best known today. 'Land of Hope and Glory', which exercised the lungs of generations of exhibitionists at the **Last Night of the Proms**, was a throwaway piece compared with Elgar's best work. A.C. Benson was the lyrical culprit; although Elgar's own imperial sympathies were demonstrated by his public opposition to Irish Home Rule, an unquestioning idolatry of his country would be unexpected in a close friend of **George Bernard Shaw**.

Elgar composed little after 1920, when his religious faith was shaken (if not entirely destroyed) by the death of his devoted wife. But he had consolidated his reputation with unforgettable concertos for violin and cello, and two marvellous symphonies (he started a third at the request of the **BBC**, but left only a few sketches). Some of his shorter pieces were of equal merit; for example, *Sospiri* sounds like the perfect elegy for the generation slaughtered in the First World War, even though it was premiered before the worst of the carnage. He continued to conduct his own works, and various recordings of these performances still exist. An obsessive devotee of the gramophone, in 1931 Elgar opened the Abbey Road studios later immortalised by the **Beatles**.

Although he would have been somewhat unsettled by the worldwide impact of Lennon and McCartney, at the time of his death it could be claimed that Elgar had heralded a wave of notable English music-makers. Elgar's near-contemporaries Frederick Delius (1862–1934) and Gustav Holst (1874–1934) sounded like reversions to the old model of imported music-makers, but they were both English-born. At the time of Elgar's death, Ralph Vaughan Williams (1872–1958) and Benjamin Britten (1913–76) were well placed to pick up the master's baton. Despite their undoubted achievements they never quite matched the quality of Elgar's output. His enduring popularity was reflected in the interest aroused by the 'completion' of his Third Symphony, by Anthony Payne in 1994.

■ Environmentalism; Green Party

Britain has a long history of environment protection, dating back to the thirteenth century when a decree was issued prohibiting the burning of sea coal. It could be argued, though, that as the first industrial nation the British have had more to be concerned about than most countries, and for much longer. The unplanned exodus of the rural population to the towns during the nineteenth century resulted in a two-pronged attack on the environment, since they added their own waste products to the toxic emissions from the factories which enslaved them. Thus although Britain created the world's first agency specifically designed to control air pollution – the Alkali Inspectorate, established in 1863 – considering the scale of the problem, in London and in industrial towns, the governmental response was relatively slow and small-scale.

In the second half of the twentieth century rising affluence, and the British love affair with the internal combustion engine, added to the problem. MPs were exposed to a cocktail of fumes in London – where the 'smog' was a perennial hazard during the winter months – but even the deaths of around 4,000 people in December 1952 was not enough to spur them into urgent action. Only in 1956 did the **Conservative** government pass a comprehensive Clean Air Act, but the environment was still not regarded as an important political issue.

Yet diverse voluntary groups dedicated to the preservation of the environment had been thriving in Britain for many years. The Society for the Prevention of Cruelty to Animals (later the RSPCA) was founded as early as 1824; a similar body for bird-lovers followed in 1889. The National Smoke Abatement Institution emerged in 1880; in 1958 this joined other bodies in the National Society for Clean Air. Even so, campaigners were regarded as worthy but eccentric, riding their own hobby-horses while most people were preoccupied with 'bread and butter' issues. Only those with adequate leisure time, such as the retired and the affluent, were likely to become involved.

In the 1960s, several factors coincided to push environmentalism up the political agenda and to grab the attention of younger people. In part, the more general concern was a by-product of the anti-war movement. Opposition to nuclear weapons, in particular, was likely to produce greater interest in an endangered planet. Other technological innovations, such as pesticides, drew attention to the possibility that the environment might be destroyed more gradually, and people slowly poisoned by pesticide on the apple a day which was supposed to keep the doctor away. New techniques were available to evaluate this environmental damage. The electronic media, and improvements in transportation, brought the problems of the outside world closer to home. But the most important stimulus to environmental concern was the general rise in living standards. More people could afford to turn away from 'bread and butter'; there was a growing feeling that affluence might have been achieved at too high a price.

By the end of the 1960s the older organisations had grown markedly, and new ones had sprung up. Friends of the Earth (1969) and Greenpeace (1972) were both founded in North America, but they soon attracted support in Britain. The Worldwide Fund for Nature had been established in Switzerland (as the World Wildlife Fund) back in 1961. There was at least a token recognition of the new awareness in the British government's decision to reorganise the Ministry of Housing and Local Government as the Department of the Environment in 1970. The fuel crisis of 1973–4 induced a campaign to conserve energy. Patrick Jenkin, the Energy Minister, even urged his compatriots to brush their teeth in the dark.

Emerging evidence that the 'developed' world had been heaping up potentially lethal problems for itself in its obsession with **economic** ◄ **growth** was increasingly recognised by the British public in opinion surveys during the 1980s. But it was easy to say that protection of the environment should be an overriding priority; it was quite another thing to renounce the trophies of affluence, such as the motor car. In 1982 the Campaign for Lead-Free Air was established, reflecting concerns about the chemical components of exhaust fumes. Before the end of the decade the government had begun to subsidise lead-free petrol through the tax system. But even without lead, petrol was still a major pollutant, affecting asthma sufferers in particular. It seemed that successful campaigns on specific issues could even prove counter-productive, since consumers tended to think that they could safely undertake unnecessary car journeys if they filled their tanks with 'environmentally friendly' fuel. Even some of the environmentally aware apparently regarded a donation to Greenpeace as an adequate alternative to a radical change of lifestyle.

There was, in short, a feeling that although 'green' pressure groups were expanding fast (membership estimated at around 4.5 million in Britain by 1990), too many people were satisfied with only token gestures at a time when the consequences of industrialism were becoming increasingly clear. No one could be ignorant of 'global warming' and the depletion of the ozone layer, even if the science was disputed. In response, politicians from the major parties could allay **consumerist** consciences by introducing marginal 'green' taxes rather ◄ than asking voters for meaningful sacrifices. But in the 1989 European elections – three years after the Chernobyl nuclear accident – the British Green Party won almost 15 per cent of the British vote. The first 'green' party had actually been founded in New Zealand in 1972, and similar groups in Switzerland and Germany had won seats in their respective parliaments earlier in the 1980s. But the British 'People' Party (founded in 1973) had been Europe's first environmental organisation committed to winning votes rather than just hoping to influence established politicians. In 1975 the 'People' party was renamed the 'Ecology' Party, taking the Green label ten years later. At first it had appeared to be a fringe outfit, apparently condemned to an endless series of lost deposits. But its sudden surge in 1989 pushed the **Liberal** ◄

Democrats into fourth place. A new wave of idealism seemed to be sweeping Britain, threatening to tap into the growing disillusionment with the core assumptions of modern life.

By the end of the century, though, the crisis seemed to be over for the major parties – if not for the world, which was faced with growing evidence of climate change. In part, the Greens were the victims of their own success. Under intense media scrutiny it became clear that even some of their leading spokespeople were unsure whether they should conform to the traditional British model of political parties, or continue to act more like a pressure group. In the 1992 general election the familiar pattern re-asserted itself: the campaign was dominated by the old bread-and-butter issues, and although the Greens ran candidates in almost half of the seats none came close to winning.

▶ They did, though, pick up two seats in the **European** Parliament in the 1999 election held under proportional representation, and their focus on specific local issues helped them to perform creditably in council elections.

Even so, the environment was still essentially a secondary political issue. There was a series of 'scares' – salmonella in eggs, BSE in cattle, genetically modified crops, and so on – which showed that the subject could dominate the headlines provided that the issue had an immediate relevance to human health. But to the most committed campaigners – the 'dark' Greens – the outcry against these problems overlooked the general picture: it was as if Noah had gone around grumbling about the miserable weather instead of working on his ark. The affluent West needed a fundamental and immediate rethink. Those who imagined that it was possible to square the circle with the notion of 'sustainable growth' were indulging in wishful thinking. Even the existing level of consumption was *un*sustainable; and it was also radically unjust, because it rested on the exploitation of the developing world. The logic of this position drew many environmentalists towards direct action, joining with other radicals to oppose the globalisation of the capitalist economy and to force governments to take action against climate change. Politicians did at least hold summits on the issue, starting with the UN conference at Rio de Janiero in June 1992. But they tended to wind up with grubby deals which shirked the real issues. None of this fooled the campaigners. In 2000 it was estimated that 5 million Britons were members of environmental groups. With the decline of Marxism, environmentalists and their allies in the anti-globalisation movement were likely to provide the most serious challenge to prevailing orthodoxies, in Britain and elsewhere, for the foreseeable future.

■ Establishment

Pejorative term for the network of power that maintains Britain's ruling elites. The novelist Ford Madox Ford (1873–1939) used the term in 1920 and the historian A.J.P. Taylor in 1952. But it was popularised ◄ by a liberal journalist of Scottish descent, Henry Fairlie (1924–90) in an article he wrote for the *Spectator* on 23 September 1955. The catalyst was the revelation, in a White Paper published five days earlier, that two senior Foreign Office officials – Guy Burgess and Donald Maclean – had fled to the Soviet Union in 1951 after spying for it. The public's realisation that successive governments had failed to detect Burgess and Maclean, and had then covered up their failure, provoked fury that Britain's rulers were more concerned to protect their own reputation than they were with the safety of the realm. The press condemned the quasi-Masonic 'old school tie' network which had its roots in the nation's **public schools**. But it was Fairlie's phrase that ◄ entered the lexicon of British life.

Etymologically, the word derives from the ecclesiastical establishment of the **Churches of England and Scotland** in the sixteenth ◄ century, by which the oligarchic rulers of the British Isles harnessed the Protestant Reformation for political and economic ends by making the churches subject to state control. Fairlie – an alcoholic womaniser who spent his life in debt – had personal reasons for detesting the Calvinism of his parents' native land. But the originality of Fairlie's article lay in his detection of the Establishment beyond the traditional arenas of church, **parliament**, military and judiciary. What he called ◄ the 'whole matrix of official and social relations within which power is exercised' also included 'such lesser mortals as the Chairman of the Arts Council, the Director-General of the **BBC** and even the editor of ◄ the *Times Literary Supplement*'. It was this broader, unaccountable network which in 1955 apparently stopped Princess Margaret marrying the **Battle of Britain** hero, Squadron Leader Peter Town- ◄ shend, because he was a commoner and a divorcé. Preventing royal love matches was the least of its crimes. An entire nation, said Fairlie, was being held back through snobbery and prudery, traits which had ossified during the Victorian era and were now being maintained by a ruling elite which had yet to face up to Britain's decline as a world power.

What ensued was, in essence, a battle between public-school boys and grammar-school boys. The cohorts of the latter had been expanded and emboldened by the Butler **Education Act (1944)** and ◄ their critique was elaborated upon in a best-selling collection of essays edited by the grammar-school educated Oxford historian Hugh Thomas, *The Establishment* (1959). Thomas concluded, 'It is Victorian

England, with all its prejudices, ignorances and inhibitions, that the Establishment sets out to defend. The Establishment is the present-day institutional museum of Britain's past greatness.' Fairlie's contribution to the book attacked his *bête noir*, the BBC: 'A population which can erect its own idols, even if they are only the idols of Wembley, is a population that will not be predisposed to idolise those whom the Establishment would wish it to. It is far safer to brainwash the mass of the population in a middling, middlebrow, middle-class culture; and it is the task of brainwashing an entire population which the Establishment entrusts to the BBC.'

Two events then popularised the term in the 1960s. First, the
▶ **Profumo** scandal of 1963 and, second, the undemocratic elevation of Sir Alec Douglas-Home to the premiership in October 1963, in which
▶ the **Conservative Party** compensated for the loss of power at home and abroad by clinging to its stereotyped semblance in the form of a grouse-shooting aristocrat with a rudimentary grasp of economics.
▶ The **Labour Party**'s subsequent election victory in 1964 was partly due to Harold Wilson reinforcing the public's association of conservatism with inherited privilege by using the new buzzword. He did so most famously in his 'white heat of technology' speech of 19 January 1964, during which he declared, 'We are living in the jet-age but we are governed by an Edwardian establishment mentality.'

Yet Harold Wilson helped to ensure that the term became detached from its liberal moorings. His strategic celebration of a new meritoc-
▶ racy of creativity, which included pop stars, photographers, **fashion**
▶ designers and **footballers**, briefly won the Labour Party some kudos among younger Britons. But it soon became apparent that a new Estab-
▶ lishment was being created – more working **class** in composition and more liberal in outlook, perhaps, but equally dependent on extant
▶ power structures. Indeed, by helping the Medusan **cult of celebrity** to grow more heads, the so-called 'pop aristocracy' arguably strengthened those power structures. At the very least, it re-legitimised them by providing a veneer of sexy fashionability and by once more associating Britain's elites in the public mind with national progress rather than national decline. It was fitting that the headquarters of the satire boom was Peter Cook's nightclub 'The Establishment' which opened in 1961. But, as Cook himself said, when reflecting on its closure two years later, 'Our satire did as much to topple the British ruling classes as the Berlin cabarets of the Weimar period did to prevent the rise of Hitler.'

Moreover, as in 1920s Germany, it was the right and not the left who benefited from disillusionment with the pace of change. During the 1970s, conservatives began to blame what they called the 'liberal Establishment' for the failures of British social democracy. Teachers,

doctors, town planners and **trade unions** were among those who were ◄
castigated for limiting the professional aspirations and consumer
choices of the working and lower-middle classes, either through venal
self-interest or condescending paternalism. The successful identifica-
tion of liberalism with unaccountable power underpinned **Mrs** ◄
Thatcher's attack on key institutions of state – among them the BBC,
Fairlie's view of which was echoed by the Conservative Party Chairman
Norman Tebbit in 1987 after a US raid on Libya. Indeed, one measure
of how much the 1950s critique of the Establishment was inverted
during the 1980s was the fact that intellectuals involved in the original debate, like Hugh Thomas and Kingsley Amis, became ardent
Thatcherites. It is symbolic, too, that when Fairlie was forced to flee
the UK in 1965 after libelling Lady Antonia Fraser on the BBC radio
show *Any Questions?* he chose America. For it was America's less class-
ridden society which appealed to liberals who sought to make Britain
a more meritocratic place.

The ease with which the term 'Establishment' was distorted by the
right was partly due to the failure of its original critics to address the
question of gender and race. Few Establishment-baiters were interested in how **women**, still less ethnic minorities, were deliberately ◄
excluded from positions of influence and the effect this had on British
society. Therefore, the weakness of their critique of power was not
simply that it was descriptive rather than prescriptive, but that the
original description was inaccurate, failing as it did to confront how
much Britain had already changed.

Still, it cannot entirely be dismissed. By providing a non-Marxist,
portmanteau term for power during a period in which the decline of
deference was on everyone's lips, its originators opened up Britain's
ruling caste to further, critical scrutiny. In the twenty-first century,
the term 'Establishment' still denotes for most Britons a set of
undemocratic power relations designed to perpetuate an overtly
conservative agenda of self-interest.

■ Europe; European Union

When the Treaty of Rome was signed on 25 March 1957 by France,
West Germany, Italy, Belgium, the Netherlands and Luxembourg the
British government was content to hold aloof. It had sent an observer
to the preliminary talks, which began at Messina in June 1955. But
that official withdrew after a few months, declaring that the developing plan to place European co-operation on an institutional basis
was unworkable and rather frightening.

This was the least defensible decision in twentieth-century British
diplomacy. After all, if the experiment had failed the UK would hardly

have gone under, while the failure to participate in a successful venture from the outset meant that it could never hope for an equal share of the spoils. And the British had been given plenty of warning; if they had not known of ambitions for European co-operation before the visionary speech of May 1950 by France's Foreign Minister, Robert Schuman, they were well apprised afterwards. For those who were not blinded by an anachronistic assessment of Britain's true international status, the lesson of Messina was quickly learned. While the Six went ahead with the European Economic Community (EEC), Britain established a rival European Free Trade Area (EFTA) along with Austria, Denmark, Norway, Portugal, Sweden and Switzerland. But the EEC quickly proved its worth – as its predecessor, the Iron and Steel Community, had done before Messina. By contrast, EFTA arguably worsened Britain's trading position.

Britain's relatively poor economic performance persuaded Harold
▶ Macmillan's **Conservative** government to begin negotiations with the EEC in July 1961. The belated courtship was rebuffed by France's General de Gaulle in January 1963. Harold Wilson's second attempt in 1967 met a similar fate, although this time de Gaulle put an end to the talks after only seven months. De Gaulle might have been exercising a
▶ personal grudge, given his treatment by **Churchill** during the Second World War. A more serious objection was his knowledge that Britain felt much closer to the US than to its near neighbours across the Channel.

When Edward Heath became Prime Minister in May 1970 the omens were far more propitious. De Gaulle had resigned, Heath himself had made a favourable impression when he conducted the
▶ talks of 1961–3, and the French had negotiated a Common **Agricultural** Policy (CAP) which ensured protection for its inefficient farmers whatever competition might arise in future. Agreement on all the main points was reached by the summer of 1971, and in October, after a lengthy debate, the terms of membership were accepted by the House of Commons. The majority was more than 100, despite the fact
▶ that Wilson had tried to mobilise **Labour** against entry. Heath had indicated that Britain should only join if membership received the 'full-hearted consent' of the people; since parliament had voted so decisively it seemed to him that this condition had been satisfied. Others paid more attention to opinion polls which showed consistent majorities opposed to entry. But Britain joined, along with Denmark and Ireland, on 1 January 1973.

In the two general election campaigns of 1974 Labour pledged itself to a referendum on continued membership. This was a typical Wilsonian manoeuvre, which effectively disguised the divisions within the party. During the campaign leading up to the referendum (an unprecedented poll for the UK as a whole, held on 5 June 1975) Cabinet collective responsibility was suspended. Although the main campaigning work was left to others, both Wilson and the Conservative leader **Margaret Thatcher** supported a 'Yes' vote. The controversial ◀ personalities of the most prominent advocates of withdrawal, **Enoch** ◀ **Powell** and Tony Benn, tended to overshadow the issues, and the pro-EEC campaign was far better funded. It could also be argued that holding a vote after Britain had joined loaded the dice against the 'No' camp, which found it harder to motivate the electorate against the new status quo. Even so, the result was an impressive endorsement of membership, with almost two-thirds of voters approving the move and majorities in favour everywhere in the UK except Shetland and the Western Isles.

E

For more than a decade the issue of 'Europe' slumbered in the background. The Foreign Office stepped in quietly to negotiate a rebate on Britain's contribution to EEC funds, reducing the net figure by around £3 billion between 1981 and 1984. In December 1985 Mrs Thatcher signed the Single European Act, which set a deadline for the removal of trade barriers within the Community but also pointed the way towards deeper integration by increasing the powers of the European Parliament. Since Mrs Thatcher's main argument against the Community was (and continued to be) its undemocratic institutions, her agreement to the terms of the 1985 Act testified to her preference at the time for economic arguments over the **sovereignty** debate. ◀

But in 1988 there was a sudden reversal of priorities. For some time Thatcher's Chancellor of the Exchequer Nigel Lawson had been arguing that membership of the Exchange Rate Mechanism (ERM) of the European Monetary System (EMS) would provide a reliable check on domestic **inflation**. The Prime Minister gave her sweeping response ◀ at Bruges in September. In a defining moment of her premiership, she claimed (without adequate justification) that her government had succeeded in 'rolling back the state' in Britain, and had no desire to see the good work undone by the developing Community. The precise motivation for the speech is a little obscure; probably Mrs Thatcher was riled by the ideas of the socialist President of the European Commission, Jacques Delors, but a Prime Minister who enjoyed defining herself against powerful enemies may also have been casting around for a new bogey after the establishment of warmer relations with the Soviet leadership.

On this occasion the 'Iron Lady' had selected her foe unwisely. Her stand cost her the services of Lawson and of Sir Geoffrey Howe, her longest-serving Cabinet colleague. Howe's resignation speech in November 1990 precipitated Thatcher's own departure from office. Her successor John Major came into office promising a more construc-

E

tive relationship with the EEC, and since he had finally secured British membership of the ERM during his period as Chancellor he was briefly popular with his European colleagues. At the Maastricht Summit of December 1991 he secured concessions over social policy and the proposed single European currency. Unfortunately for him, his backbenchers were now so restive on the European issue that the Maastricht Treaty could only be ratified after bitter debates which threatened to bring down his government. Britain's humiliating exit from the ERM in September 1992, after frenzied selling of sterling, was celebrated by Major's critics even though it destroyed the credibility of their party. In May 1996, faced with a Europe-wide ban on British beef, Major tried to restore his popularity by threatening to withdraw co-operation in Europe. Within a month he had tacitly admitted defeat in this futile 'Beef War', adding further fuel to the anger on his back-benches.

The European issue played a decisive role in the Conservative defeat in the 1997 general election. The government had seemed hopelessly divided, and was unable to expose remaining differences within the Labour Party, which had moved away from its 'Eurosceptic' stance since 1983 but still contained many opponents of deeper integration.

▶ Like Major, **Tony Blair** initially promised a more constructive relationship with what was now (since 1993) the European Union (EU). But the new government was committed to a referendum before Britain joined the single currency. Pro-Europeans had argued ever since the 1950s that belated British membership of European institutions had robbed the country of influence over key developments, and despite the warmer words there was no real variation in the pattern under Blair. The only cause for relief was that, unlike the Tories and the

▶ tabloid press, 'New' Labour did not resort to cheap rhetoric about the (much exaggerated) size of Brussels bureaucracy, nor complain unduly about the burden of European regulation (most of which would have been imposed anyway through national legislation).

More than any other issue, 'Europe' best exemplifies Britain's failure to live up to its boasted democratic credentials. On the one hand the 'Euro-sceptics' were justified in arguing that the British electorate had been beguiled; the 1975 referendum was a perfect example of the 'political classes' uniting behind a project which enjoyed, at best, the half-hearted consent of the public. The real issues involved – at first the need to tie Germany into a wider union in order to prevent a new war, then the urgent necessity of forming a trading bloc to rival Britain's most determined and effective twentieth-century enemy, the United States – were never presented with sufficient clarity. On the other hand, if the 'Euro lobby' was somewhat devious, the 'sceptics' were at best naive. Meaningful British sovereignty had been ceded in the decade and a half after the Second World War. Before the 2001 general election, the new Conservative leader William Hague thought that he could rally the public against the EU (and Labour) by urging that they vote to 'save' a small piece of metal which was itself of recent provenance (ironically, on one side of that pound coin was the head of a monarch who had been widely reviled in the 'Euro-sceptic' press after the death of **Diana, Princess of Wales**). ◄

E

At least in part, the anti-European argument was based on a fear that Britain would end up being dominated by European states which would somehow retain their (unpleasant) identity while Britain lost its own distinctiveness. The only interesting aspect of this argument was its unwitting testimony to British insecurity. At its most respectable, the argument accepted the inevitability of further economic decline in a country which distanced itself from both Europe and the US (though some followed the logic of the post-war surrender of sovereignty to the latter, and hoped to make Britain into the 51st state of America). Unfortunately, many British voters really did imagine that such a development would allow their country to resume the grandeur which it had lost for ever as a result of the Second World War. Here the argument became entangled with a xenophobia which was the most enduring legacy of the war (mainly directed against **Germans** by those who had not actually fought them). ◄

By the end of the twentieth century the British were providing over £10 billion to the EU budget, around three-quarters of which returned to the country through various subsidies. But the argument about British involvement in an alleged 'Federal Superstate' could not be resolved by reference to economic statistics. If Britain still had an adverse trade balance with the Continental mainland, that proved nothing at all: the situation would have been far worse if the country had pulled out in 1975. A new referendum, this time on membership of the euro, was looming. Euro-sceptics who thought that the government would delay the poll until it was sure of a positive outcome were right. But whatever the result, it still seemed most unlikely that rational argument would play much part in deciding the outcome. *Plus ça change*, as French politicians might have reflected.

■ Fabian Society

Founded in 1884, the Fabian Society began as a small discussion group. Its name commemorated the Roman General Fabius Cunctator, who preferred to wear down his opponents through delays and limited actions rather than throwing all his resources into an all-out attack. The Society aimed at the gradual introduction of socialism in Britain, taking the path of legislative reform rather than agitation among the working population. Its early members included such middle-class intellectuals as the colonial civil servant Sidney Webb, ▶ the playwright **George Bernard Shaw** and the tireless campaigner for women's rights and Indian independence, Annie Besant. The philoso-▶ pher **Bertrand Russell** also joined in the 1890s.

▶ Instead of standing for **parliament** themselves the early Fabians hoped to influence policy-makers, either through personal contact or through their numerous lectures and publications, including *Fabian Essays* (1889) which sold over 20,000 copies in little over a year. A typical Fabian production would mix polemical argument and constructive proposals for reform with detailed research, particularly into the living conditions of the poor. They were prepared to work with any political party, in the belief that socialism would be universally accepted at some point. Eventually, though, the Society affiliated to ▶ the **Labour Party** and Webb played a prominent role in the drafting of the 1918 constitution which committed the party to 'the common ▶ ownership of the means of production' – a policy of **nationalisation** which later aroused much controversy.

The Fabians did not deal in grand theories. But while Marxists thought that the state would eventually 'wither away', the Society's members shared a paternalistic belief in the virtues of sound admin-istration. Sidney Webb and his wife Beatrice acclaimed Stalin's Soviet Union in the 1930s. But this was an aberration inspired by wishful thinking. Webb was a democrat, who had advocated universal suffrage and annual parliaments in his contribution to *Fabian Essays*. Although Webb later became a Cabinet minister (as did another founder-member, Sydney Olivier), the Fabians preferred to work for piecemeal ▶ change through **local government**, rather than hoping that a national dictator would impose rational policies by force.

The Fabians were undoubtedly influential over domestic policy in ▶ their heyday. The historian **A.J.P. Taylor** claimed that the 1943 ▶ **Beveridge** Report represented the fulfilment of the Webbs' pre-war planning. Their influence over local government, witnessed (for example) in the idea that municipal utilities should be run in the interests of the general public rather than for profit, was testified by the sneering label of 'gas and water socialists' applied by their critics.

Later the Society's Colonial Bureau played a part in assisting Britain's retreat from **Empire**. But the practical experiences of two world **wars** ◄ provided the essential catalyst for the advance of Fabian ideas. In the last quarter of the twentieth century the Society's arguments and earnest egalitarian outlook seemed outdated, as politicians of all parties exploited a widespread distrust of public officials and even the Labour Party leadership began to tolerate rising social inequality. Ironically, the **Conservative** government of **Margaret Thatcher** was ◄ advised by several independent 'think tanks', such as the Institute of Economic Affairs, which had been founded with the deliberate aim of emulating the success of the Fabians.

In 1947, under the first majority Labour government, the optimistic Shaw claimed that the spirit which animated his fellow Fabians would still be alive in sixty years' time: 'the name may perish, but not the species'. He could not have been more mistaken. The Society itself continued to meet, and boasted several thousand members in 2000. But its vitality had died long before, and its main purpose now was to provide an 'alternative' platform for any Labour Party politicians looking for a costless way to establish a reputation for profound thinking.

■ Falklands War

On 1 April 1982 the US President Ronald Reagan spent almost an hour on the telephone pleading with the Argentinian military ruler, General Galtieri, to call off an invasion of the Falkland Islands in the South Atlantic. Despite the close ties between the two countries, Galtieri refused. The invasion went ahead, and the British governor of the Falkland Islands surrendered to Argentine forces on the following day, along with the garrison of only 80 troops.

On 14 June the capital city, Port Stanley, was recaptured by a British task force. Although the conscripted Argentine army put up less resistance than British strategists had feared, there had been several hard-fought engagements and the British **armed forces** carried out their ◄ mission with remarkable skill and courage. More than a thousand were killed or wounded; many of the casualties were incurred on board the six vessels sunk by the Argentine air force. For a time the whole British fleet had seemed to lie at the mercy of the lethal 'Exocet' missile; the outcome might have been different had the Argentines possessed more of these weapons.

The Falklands had been a British colony since 1833, after several decades of disputation involving Spain, the US and Argentina. By 1979 the islands had limited strategic value and even less economic importance to Britain. Yet the 1,800 islanders had no wish to be ruled by

Argentina, which was more than a thousand miles away even if maps of the vast, empty South Atlantic made it look like a near neighbour.
► During an invasion scare in 1977 the **Labour** government had dispatched a nuclear submarine to warn off the Argentines. Three years later Tory backbenchers expressed outrage at a Foreign Office plan under which the British would continue to govern the islands
► while **sovereignty** was ceded to Argentina. Negotiations for a
► handover immediately stalled. But **Margaret Thatcher** was anxious to cut naval expenditure, and a White Paper of July 1981 envisaged the withdrawal of HMS *Endurance*, the most visible symbol of British commitment to the islands.

Well aware that Argentina was being sent conflicting signals, British officials could only hope that the problem would quietly resolve itself in the future. But a military adventure was highly attractive to Galtieri, and the Argentines were keen to take over the islands before the 150th anniversary of British rule. The circumstances leading up to the invasion meant that the British government had no alternative but to prepare for action, despite the considerable logistical problems involved in an operation 8,000 miles away. A negotiated settlement would obviously be best, but despite intensive efforts by the US (and a UN resolution ordering an Argentine withdrawal) talks came to nothing.

The reaction to the Argentine invasion provided fascinating insights into the outlook of the British in 1982. To some extent the bellicose response of the British public was conditioned by a natural affinity for the underdog. The fact that the Argentine government was a military junta helped to clarify the issue (although it raised the awkward question of why the British and the Americans had previously been so friendly with the regime and its equally unsavoury neighbours). The same dislike of bullies helped to inspire a prolonged and passionate outcry when a British nuclear submarine sank the elderly Argentine cruiser, the *General Belgrano*. Yet at the time these views were held by a small minority of dissidents. The *Sun* newspaper saw fit to celebrate the same event under the banner headline 'Gotcha!'. Britons who previously had hardly registered the existence of South America began to speak disdainfully of 'the Argies', but this animosity would only resurface in future whenever England played Argentina at football.

Critics on the left liked to present the war as a late outburst of the colonial spirit. Yet since the Thatcher government had been prepared to cut a deal over the Falklands this seemed implausible, and the Labour leader Michael Foot offered wholehearted support to the
► government. The spirit of **Empire** was not lacking in some of the outspoken Tory backbenchers, and naturally they were delighted

with the eventual outcome. But the recapture of the Falklands was hardly seen by ministers as a springboard for a new era of overseas acquisition. Rather, they were left with the problem of preparing the ground for an eventual handover, while reluctantly meeting the considerable financial burden of defending the islands until the stubborn inhabitants could be persuaded to accept the inevitable. Even the possibility of finding oil significant reserves in the area, which would have provided some icing on an indigestible cake, proved to be illusory.

F

Among those who took the key decisions, partisan considerations were paramount. The Thatcher government was deeply unpopular when the invaders arrived. But the war was not an attempt to deflect attention from rising **unemployment**. Rather, the task force was ◀ assembled to compensate for the errors which had led up to the invasion. If it had been decided that a counterstrike was too risky – and if the Argentine government refused to hand back the islands through diplomacy – Mrs Thatcher could not have survived. British prestige would have been damaged, but given the obvious hazards of the operation the blow would not have been fatal. Indeed, the very fact that the majority of the British public felt an influx of self-confidence as a result of a war fought against shivering conscripts was tacit testimony to the widespread recognition that the glory days were over. The armed forces had certainly proved their capacity, but the world still knew that the British were prepared to divest themselves of their remaining possessions, like Hong Kong, when the conditions were right.

When the Americans invaded the Commonwealth state of Grenada in October 1983 Mrs Thatcher did not order her military advisers to prepare a new task force to bring the **'special relationship'** to a spec- ◀ tacular close. Indeed, by her own account she even spared Reagan the kind of difficult phone call which he had endured with Galtieri. By that time the 'Falklands Factor' had helped to ensure a landslide victory for the Conservatives in the 1983 general election, and Grenada made no lasting dent in the Iron Lady's armour. Probably the party would have been re-elected with or without the Falklands. But rarely can a government have derived so much political benefit from a grievous and avoidable mistake.

■ Fashion

'If there is no copying, how are you going to have fashion?' the Nazi-sympathising French couturier, Gabrielle 'Coco' Chanel (1883–1971), once said when asked how she felt about her designs being reproduced for working people. Whether she was speaking for democracy or fascism is still being debated. What is certain is that until the twentieth century, only the middle and upper **classes** could afford to copy the latest trends, most of which were generated by royal courts. The fashion industry as we know it today is the combined result of British and French creativity and American production and retailing techniques.

An Englishman, Charles Worth (1825–95), laid the foundations of the industry by grasping the revolutionary potential of the sewing machine, invented by an American, Isaac Singer, in 1851. Utilising the machine's ability to produce high-quality clothes at speed, Worth set up the first large-scale fashion house in Paris in 1858. By the time of his death, he had established French haute couture as the stylistic leader of the Western world. Still, fashion remained beyond the reach of most working people. Their clothes, drab in colour and made by necessity from hard-wearing cloth, conformed to a generic style that spanned a generation rather than a season.

Mass-produced, ready-to-wear fashion clothing, based on standard sizes agreed by manufacturers, was pioneered in the United States during the 1900s. Britain was initially slow to follow because the much smaller size of its domestic market precluded the long production runs necessary to make ready-to-wear profitable. However, by the late 1920s, Britain had caught up, thanks to three things: **war**, affluence and feminism. The First World War created a more organised clothing industry. The state had begun to take it more seriously when clothing was included within the remit of the Board of Trade in 1911. But it was the wartime need to avoid wastage of materials and manpower that led to a wider use of machinery and Fordist assembly-line techniques. The shift from the craft-based world of the tailor and seamstress to factory production was consolidated by the creation of the Tailors and Garment Workers Union in 1915. Its attempt to regulate working conditions did not prevent sweatshops remaining a feature of British industrial life, especially in the East End of London where first **Jewish** and then Asian immigrants ran and staffed them. But the Union did accept the process of standardisation.

By galvanising the **women**'s movement the war also accelerated a stylistic revolution in women's clothes. The constricting 'S-shaped' raiment of the Victorians, which had been designed to enlarge the appearance of the buttocks and the bust, was first loosened by the linear designs of the French couturier Paul Poiret in 1908. The growing number of women in the British workforce after 1914, especially those in clerical and retail employment, created a need for stylish yet practical clothing that allowed the wearer to move more freely. The growth of female participation in sports like tennis and golfing, together with pastimes like motoring and cycling, was another factor. In 1909, the

British firm Aquascutum, which invented a unisex version of the military trench coat, declared: 'Coats for women lead naturally to votes for women.'

There was never a causal link between fashion and the franchise. But women's demand for more practical clothes was compounded by a real desire to shake off the constraints that men had placed on the female form for centuries. Although the bobbed-haired boyish look of the 'flapper girl' only lasted from 1925 to 1929, and again from 1963 to 1967, clothes generally became straighter and looser fitting, with lower necklines and higher hemlines. The handbag, usually seen as an icon of conventional femininity, became ubiquitous during the interwar period because women required somewhere to put personal items that had once been stowed in pockets under the frills and folds of traditional costume. Similarly, the initial purpose of the brassiere, introduced in 1912 and standardised with cup-sizing in 1939, was to support the breasts discreetly in the absence of corsetry. The invention of cheap, hard-wearing synthetic fabrics like rayon (1926), nylon (1935) and polyester (1941) made clothing more affordable, as well as fostering the invention of stockings and tights which enabled women to wear shorter dresses in all weathers.

Growing affluence and the retail revolution that accompanied it drove the fashion revolution. The American-based *Vogue*, launched in the UK in 1916, was one of many magazines that suggested not only new styles, like the padded shoulder, but also entirely new forms of clothing that challenged gender boundaries, like the trouser suit. Both became staples of female 'power-dressing' following their launch in 1933 by the Italian designer Elsa Schiaparelli (1896–1973), a close associate of the Surrealist art movement. The cinema also had a great ◄ influence on taste, with Hollywood stars helping to gain acceptance for daring modes like trousers (Marlene Dietrich) or by popularising more conventional ones like the 'little black dress' (Audrey Hepburn). Department stores were the first outlets to make ready-to-wear fashion more widely available. They had been a feature of British life since the mid-nineteenth century (Worth began his career in one), but they did not become commonplace until Debenham's opened a palatial new store in London in 1909. Mail-order shopping, pioneered by Debenham's in the 1870s, catered for less affluent women.

The Second World War briefly made fashion a harder thing to pursue. The introduction of utility clothing in 1941 forced manufacturers to make 85 per cent of their clothing in regulation fabrics and styles, and in the same year, clothing became a rationed item. The government's 'Make Do and Mend' campaign encouraged people to recycle anything from blankets to curtains and parachutes, the latter prized for the scarce silk they provided. The 1947 launch of Christian

Dior's flamboyant 'New Look', followed by the end of rationing two years later, brought relief from the dourness of wartime clothing. So too did the designs of the British couturiers Norman Hartnell (1901–78) and Hardy Amies (1909–2003), dressmakers to both the ▶ **Queen Mother** and the Queen. But the real change in post-war clothing began with the development of youth culture in the mid-1950s.

Denim jeans, patented by Levi Strauss in 1873, made the transition from blue-collar work wear to fashion when they were controversially marketed in the United States in the 1950s as 'right for school' and then adopted by adolescent followers of rock 'n' roll. The t-shirt, originally developed during the 1930s by the US military as a sweat-absorbing undergarment, was also adopted. The training shoe, pioneered by the American company Nike in 1971, completed a trinity of casual unisex clothing that formed the basis of youth apparel, their essential form retained while their styles are periodically adjusted. And though all three came to be worn by most age groups, for the first time a real gap appeared between what the generations wore.

'Fashion,' said Chanel, 'does not exist unless it goes down into the streets. The fashion that remains in the salons has no more significance than a costume ball.' From the 1960s onwards, the street began ▶ to invade the salons. Members of youth cults like **Mod**, **Punk** and Rave pioneered a plethora of styles and fads, the origins of which became less precise as the customary one-way journey from catwalk to chain store became a more symbiotic one. A new breed of designers, based in their own boutiques rather than fashion houses, and more in tune with pop culture, challenged the dominance of elite couturiers. The most famous, Mary Quant (b. 1934), declared, 'snobbery has gone out of fashion, and in our shops you will find duchesses jostling with typists to buy the same dresses . . . the voices, rules and culture of this generation are as different from the past as tea and wine. And the clothes they choose evoke their lives . . . daring and gay, never dull . . . They represent the whole new spirit that is present-day Britain, a classless spirit that has grown out of the Second World War.'

Quant was blamed by some feminists for encouraging the objectification of women with the miniskirt that she popularised. So too was the contrasting style of Laura Ashley (1925–85). Her work, inspired by ▶ patchwork quilts made for charity by the **Women's Institute**, promoted a traditional, rustic femininity through long, floral cotton dresses. Her Victorian milkmaid look, sold in over a hundred shops in Britain's towns and cities, also highlighted the perennial tendency of the British middle classes to romanticise the countryside.

Women's clothing never stopped being shaped by the sexual imperatives of men. The bra that feminists publicly burned in protest had been re-designed in the 1950s artificially to emphasise the bust as much as any Victorian corset (a process that accelerated with Gossard's launch of the 'Wonderbra' in 1969). The bikini is another example. Patented in 1946 by a French mechanical engineer, Louis Reard, it achieved notoriety when Ursula Andress stepped out of the sea in one to meet Sean Connery in the **James Bond** film *Dr No* (1962). ◄ It became common apparel when the cult of sunbathing exploded a decade later thanks to the affordability of Mediterranean **holidays**. ◄ The ability to wear a bikini was seen as a benchmark of female beauty – a belief encouraged by the bikini round of the Miss World contest, which began in 1951.

Nonetheless, fashion became an important element of British post-imperial culture. The establishment of London Fashion Week in 1959; the recasting of fashion imagery by working-class photographers like David Bailey (b. 1938) and the first black supermodel, Naomi Campbell (b. 1970); the pioneering creativity of designers from Vivienne West-wood (b. 1941) to Alexander McQueen (b. 1969); and the international recognition they all received were a source of national pride for many people. In 1909, the wife of the British Prime Minister, Herbert Asquith, brought Poiret over from Paris to show his latest collection at 10 Downing Street. She was attacked in the press for betraying her country and questions were asked in parliament. Half a century later, British designers were regularly given state honours, and by the time they were invited to the court of **Tony Blair** by his wife, it was a tight ◄ squeeze to get them all into Downing Street.

Another key change of the 1960s – the transformation of men's clothing – testified to fashion's continuing ability to undermine social convention. Retail chains like Burton were established in the 1930s, catering for the white-collar male workers' demand for inexpensive, smart clothes. Some chains had couturiers design for them, such as Hepworth's who commissioned Hardy Amies in 1959. But men's fash-ions, from Hepworth's to Savile Row, changed little. The one exception was the declining popularity of the hat after 1918. As **John Betjeman** ◄ wrote describing the accession of **Edward VIII**, 'Old men stare at the ◄ new suburb stretched beyond the run-way / Where a young man lands hatless from the air.' Otherwise, men's clothes continued to revolve around the suit, shirt and tie in brown, black or navy. Colourful, flam-boyant clothes were associated with **homosexuality**. ◄

From the 1960s, however, they were more widely accepted and sometimes consumed with gusto, a fact satirised in the Kinks song 'Dedicated Follower of Fashion' (1967). British men continued to eschew the male handbag, which became common on the Continent, but they did embrace a more nuanced masculinity that was evident in the ranges sold by chain stores like Next. It was also apparent in men's use of cosmetics, beginning with the introduction of 'Old Spice' in 1957 and accelerating with the launch of 'male' moisturiser in the 1980s, a change driven by women's insistence that grooming was as much an ingredient of successful courtship as solvency.

The fashion industry is, as its critics argue, the prime example of how mass-production techniques have combined with the marketing power of the media and the supply networks of corporate retailers to stimulate demand for products most of which are not, strictly speaking, needed. Furthermore, the elitism of fashion survived its descent to the street. When English **football** hooligans rioted in Paris in 1984, the French were amazed to see that the shops favoured by looters were those selling 'designer' clothes like Lacoste. The obsession with labels among all classes from the 1970s onwards reflected the fact that fashion was now so affordable that those desperate to display their affluence could only do so by further undermining their individuality.

However, changes in British clothing styles do reflect wider forms of social emancipation relating both to **class** and gender. 'Wow! Look at me! Isn't life wonderful!' was how Mary Quant described the feeling that her miniskirt generated. That may not be the best foundation for individual happiness or social justice. But fashion in Britain has frequently transcended the narcissism and herd instinct upon which it is based, to enrich and even transform lives. In 1952, one fashion writer observed, 'the English, alas, hate fashion. The same Puritanical streak that ordains our licensing hours . . . makes the island race despise clothes, fear personal beauty and feel shame in all colours except beige.' It was an exaggeration at the time, and a complete misconstrual half a century later.

■ Folk music

British folk music stems from the pre-literate medieval era when song was a way to pass on history, myth and **morality** as well as personal experience. The emergence of the modern entertainment industry between 1880 and 1930, especially the growth of **music halls**, the gramophone and American popular music, caused a sharp decline in the fortunes of folk music. Yet, that decline provoked a concerted effort to retrieve the genre by artists and intellectuals, most of whom were driven by a sentimental view of British rural life. The most influential of these figures in the first half of the century was Cecil Sharp (1859–1924) who spent his life travelling around Britain collecting more than 3,000 tunes and over 200 dances from any peasant he could find. In 1898, he formed the English Folk Song Society (from 1932, the English Folk Dance and Song Society). Similar organisations were formed in Scotland, Wales and Ireland. Ralph Vaughan Williams (1872–1958) was among several twentieth-century British composers who incorporated traditional melodies into their work, for example the *English Folk Song Suite* (1923). The movement's rural romanticism, together with its musical purism prevented it from gaining a mass audience. Its hostility to any form of **Americanisation** was particularly ◄ damaging. During the craze for US line-dancing that followed the success of the musical *Calcutta* (1946), attempts were made to reform the Society but its leaders decided that morris dancing was a superior activity and membership fell away once more.

Since the Middle Ages, there had been a subversive political strand within folk music. From the 1950s to the 1970s, the genre gained a large following among the left/liberal middle classes when it became ◄ allied with protest songs of the CND and anti-Vietnam campaigns, and ◄ with the Hippie movement in general. A new generation of American musicians, influenced by blues and country, inspired by Woody Guthrie and led by Bob Dylan and Joan Baez, wrote their own songs about contemporary Western life as well as rearranging traditional ones. As with that of earlier revivalists, their work was shot through with rural romanticism and ersatz paganism – an outlook that was apparent in the movement's best-known song, Joni Mitchell's 'Big Yellow Taxi' (1969), the chorus of which was 'They sold paradise and put up a parking lot'. But this trend was tempered by a more cosmopolitan outlook than that of Cecil Sharp and his ilk, and the emergence of folk rock, following Bob Dylan's switch to electric guitar in 1966, won the genre a wider audience. Groups like Jefferson Airplane and the Byrds in the US, Steeleye Span and Fairport Convention in the UK, together with mainstream acts like Donovan and the Seekers, were popular until the mid-1970s. The establishment of the Cambridge Folk Festival in 1971 testified to the success of the revival.

However, the use of electric guitars was condemned by a new generation of purists, who soon returned the genre to its antediluvian roots and condemned it once more to relative obscurity. In Britain, the leader of this reaction was Ewan MacColl (1915–89). The son of an ironworker and char lady from Manchester, MacColl was a lifelong Communist who was heavily involved in left-wing theatre with his wife, the director Joan Littlewood, from the 1930s until their separation in 1952. It was during his subsequent relationship with the singer Peggy Seeger that he emerged as the driving force behind UK folk. His *Radio Ballads* broadcast on the BBC (1958–64) dealt with the everyday lives of British people, from steelworkers to fishermen. Like Cecil Sharp, he and Seeger collected extant folk, published in their *Travellers' Songs from England and Scotland* (1977), as well as writing their own songs in folk styles. They also established the Singers' Club in London and estimated that by 1957 there were 1,500 such clubs around Britain. At first, MacColl welcomed American folk styles but, in common with most leftists of the time, he grew concerned that Britain was becoming too Americanised, and at the Singers' Club he introduced a policy that artists could only perform work from their own native traditions. MacColl only once made money from a song – 'The First Time Ever I Saw Your Face', a version of which was a no. 1 hit for US soul singer Roberta Flack in 1972.

Despite several revivals, folk music never recaptured a mass audience in Britain, for two reasons. First, it was associated in the public mind with a political radicalism that few shared outside the **university** campus and Hippie commune. Second, it remained earnestly rural in outlook, dominated by badly-dressed men and women singing in West Country accents with a nasal whine that they took to be the authentic voice of rustic Britain. To the urban ear of the twentieth century – be it working, middle or upper **class** – folk music was regarded as the pastime of harmless eccentrics. The revival had more longevity in Scotland, Wales and Ireland, where the music was taken up by nationalists as a vehicle for protests about English misrule. The Celticity that consequently dominated the genre in the second half of the twentieth century appealed to its English enthusiasts (MacColl was born James Miller before a name change gave him stage credibility). There was also a brief fashion for the Irish folk rock group, the Pogues, and for their English counterparts, the Levellers. In general, however, the Celticity of folk minimised its appeal in England where it remained a minority pursuit.

■ Food

British cooking is renowned the world over for its lack of imagination – a stodgy melange of fat, sugar and salt epitomised by dishes like toad-in-the-hole and jam roly-poly with custard, to which is added a range of toxic chemicals. However, until the second half of the twentieth century, the nutritional poverty of the people was more the result of their low incomes than it was due to the failings of their cuisine or the quality of its ingredients.

Until the Boer War, Britain's rulers took little interest in the effects of poor diet. As long as the working classes had enough in their stomachs to enable them to work long hours in field and factory and not riot (or, worse still, start a revolution), nutrition was considered to be the eccentric concern of soft-headed philanthropists. Imperial insecurity changed all that. When the Director-General of the Army Medical Service discovered that 38 per cent of all volunteers for the Boer War were unfit for combat (despite a reduction in the minimum height requirement for recruits to five feet) there was a national outcry. How would Britain defeat a makeshift army of Dutch farmers, never mind the might of the German military machine in a future war? Two of the immediate results of this concern were the 1906 Education Act (Provision of Meals) which provided free school meals for the poorest children and the setting up, in 1913, of the Medical Research Committee (later the Medical Research Council), which established nutrition as a science and made doctors more aware of its importance.

These advances were built on during the First World War. In 1916, severe food shortages as a result of German submarine attacks on merchant shipping, coupled with industrial unrest, led to the creation of a Ministry of Food with compulsory powers under the Defence of the Realm Act to subsidise and distribute essentials like bread and milk. The Bolshevik Revolution in Russia a year later concentrated minds at Westminster still further. On 1 January 1918, civilian rationing was introduced to the UK for the first time and industrial canteens were set up which, by the end of the war, were serving a million cheap meals a day. The result was a lower sickness rate and increased productivity. The difference between the health of the classes was still stark. During the final round of conscription in 1917–18, 41 per cent of working men were graded unfit for military service, compared to only 10 per cent of Cambridge undergraduates. Despite government campaigns like 'Eat More Fruit', the Great Depression made the situation worse, with 62 per cent of army volunteers unfit for service in 1935. However, in areas less affected by the Depression, new patterns of food consumption emerged in the interwar era, influenced largely by the United States.

Grocery chain stores – the forerunners of today's supermarkets – expanded, making food retailing one of the UK's biggest businesses. The number of Sainsbury's branches, for example, rose from 123 in 1919 to 244 in 1939. Small, independent stores remained a prominent feature of British life but large conglomerates selling branded goods increasingly supplied them. America influenced the type of food Britons bought as well as the way they bought it. Processed breakfast cereals, invented by Kellogg's (1906), replaced porridge as the nation's favourite start to the day, while canned foods, pioneered in America during the 1870s, became more ubiquitous thanks to the Heinz company (1888) and British imitators like Crosse & Blackwell. Dehydrated food, of which Bird's custard and Oxo meat stock cubes were the most popular brands, was another thing to cross the Atlantic. Health foods and processed vitamins also arrived, closely linked to the craze for outdoor exercise that swept the Western world in this period. The first British health food shop opened in 1923, though as George ◄

Orwell noted in 1939, vegetarianism was then a fad of the left-leaning middle classes.

There were exceptions to this transatlantic rule. The potato crisp was invented by the French at the turn of the century and by the 1920s it had become a popular snack in Britain. Fish and chips was invented ▶ by a combination of London **Jews** and Lancashire Gentiles in the mid-nineteenth century and by the 1900s, a visit to the 'chippie' had replaced the Victorian hot pie shop as the favourite form of eating out for industrial workers. During the 1920s fish and chips came to be celebrated as Britain's national dish (although it never entirely replaced roast beef in England nor haggis in Scotland as symbols of the UK's constituent nations). Its patriotic reputation was cemented by the role that fryers played in feeding munitions workers during the First World War and by the fact that the prosperity of Britain's fishermen (and, by association, its seafaring tradition) depended on the public's appetite for cod and haddock. Still, wherever British culinary customs hailed from, the British diet was initially improved as a result of scarcity, not abundance.

Second World War rationing was one of the most effective state interventions in British life during the twentieth century. Tinned American processed ham, known as 'Spam', flooded the country after the introduction of Lend-Lease in 1942 (its prevalence was later ▶ satirised by the **Monty Python** show). But on the whole, fat and sugar intake was reduced while that of fibrous cereals and fruit and vegetables increased. Although the British were not as well fed as the ▶ **Germans**, the system worked better than it had in the previous war, for three reasons. First, the UK depended less on food imports, thanks ▶ to state subsidising of British **agriculture** since the 1930s. Second, the government was better prepared than before, introducing rationing as soon as war broke out rather than waiting for shortages to occur. Third, rationing was, and was seen to be, more equitable. A points system for non-vital foodstuffs, introduced in 1941, gave every citizen some purchasing freedom, while the government's power to set a product's value helped nutritionists to stimulate consumption of healthy options.

Nutritional science had also advanced since 1918 and its leader, Professor J.C. (Jack) Drummond (1891–1952), was Chief Scientific Adviser at the Ministry of Food from 1940 to 1946. Drummond's career was brought to a premature end when he was murdered with his wife and daughter while camping in the French Alps, but not before he had made a significant contribution to British health. As well as overcoming the vested interests of the food trade in order to maximise the nutritional content of what the nation ate, Drummond utilised the wartime propaganda machine in order to improve nutritional knowledge. The main result was a long-term decline in red meat consumption in favour of pork and chicken. Fish consumption fell despite the invention of the fish finger in 1955 (although this was largely because fish became more expensive as a result of North Sea stocks being ravaged by over-fishing). The British still ate less fruit and vegetables than any other European people (the Scots less than anyone), but consumption did rise after the war.

Many ignored Professor Drummond's advice. The consumption of cheese – a cheap source of protein but also a source of artery-blocking fat – rose tenfold between the 1950s and 1980s. Sugar consumption also rose, thanks to the popularity of American-style confectionery and soft **drinks**, which together did much to undermine the cheap ◄ dental care offered by the **National Health Service**. Britons still ◄ preferred white bread to brown by almost two to one. From 1901, when flour-bleaching by nitrogen peroxide was patented, mass-produced white bread was a minor status symbol of the British working classes, its supposed purity denoting a departure from the roughage of brown bread and with it an escape from the rougher life endured by their forebears. Yet bread only began to be rationed in 1947, and it was this event which discredited a peacetime rationing system that was unpopular in a nation anxious to be rewarded for victory. Rationing was not abolished until 1953, two years after the **Conservative Party** returned ◄ to power. But their ending of it came to symbolise the transformation of **Labour**-led Austerity Britain into Tory-led Consumption Britain. ◄

For the rest of the century, rising average earnings meant that people spent a smaller proportion of their income on food than ever before and, for the first time in the Isles' history, a majority of the people had access to a nutritionally adequate diet. The notion that British food was less natural than ever before is a myth. Food adulteration in pursuit of commercial profit is a phenomenon of urban society, which has taken place since the classical era, and it was common in nineteenth-century Britain, often with poisonous effects (the use of lead and mercury was widespread). The 1875 Sale of Food and Drugs Act established the basis of modern food safety legislation and a system of local authority inspectors. Only by the 1900s had a limited culture of responsibility been established among producers and retailers.

Furthermore, the public appetite for fast food stems from social change that to some extent has been beneficial. The greater leisure opportunities that affluence and moral liberalism made available from the 1950s onwards, meant that people, especially the young, spent more time socialising outside the home. Snatching a quick meal maximised the proportion of that time used for pleasures like drinking, dancing and having sex. Our fast-food society is also a

▶ product of the greater number of **women** in work. The evening meal and Sunday roast, cooked using natural ingredients by an obliging wife and mother for a happy family all present and correct around the kitchen table, owed more to adverts for Bisto than it ever did to the reality of British domestic life. The decline of the family meal, such as it is, has taken place against a background of female liberation in which women spend more of their time pursuing careers and less of it shackled to the oven. By 2001, 85 per cent of British men cooked regularly, not a great deal less than the 97 per cent of women who did so, although the change was partly due to the realisation that preparing a meal could facilitate seduction, a trend encouraged by Michael Caine's culinary expertise in *The Ipcress File* (1965).

Female neurosis about body weight is also a sign of material progress. In previous, more patriarchal centuries, a fuller figure was a status symbol because it denoted a fuller larder. While that remains the case in the Third World, elsewhere affluence is now so common that being slim denotes how much income a person can shed on

▶ things like **fashion** wear. The cult of slimming crossed the Atlantic in the early 1920s. Over the next half-century it spread from the pampered upper classes to the poorest workers, so that by the end of the twentieth century, half a million British women were estimated to be on a rigorous diet at any one time. Slimming was partly a response to male demands; it brought emotional misery to many women and, as anorexia nervosa showed, physical trauma and even death. Although categorised in Britain in 1874, the disease did not become

▶ prevalent until the advent of **consumerism**, incidence of it doubling between 1960 and 1976. Yet slimming also highlighted the fact that few Britons were now malnourished. However much women might be in urgent need of more fruit and vegetables and less chips and choco-late, they were clearly not starving as so many of their forebears had been. In short, fat was not so much a feminist issue as a fiscal one.

The British diet became more varied in the second half of the twen-tieth century, partly as a result of black, Asian and Oriental immigra-tion. Between 1948 and 1998, the number of Indian restaurants in the UK rose from half a dozen to 5,300, while the number of Chinese restaurants rose from a dozen to just over 5,000 (many of them take-aways). Greek and Turkish kebab takeaways also became a feature of British life. Cheap foreign travel, and a subsequent engagement with other gastronomies, intensified the demand for foreign dishes, from lasagne to stir fry. Demand was also stimulated by a new breed of cookery writers like Elizabeth David (1913–92), whose *French Provincial Cooking* (1960) helped popularise Continental food; and by those who became celebrity TV chefs, like Philip Harben (1906–70), Delia Smith (b. 1941) and Jamie Oliver (b. 1972). The ubiquity of the restaurant was a direct result of these developments. A French invention of the mid-nineteenth century, the restaurant as we know it today was imported into Britain after Acts of Parliament in 1861 and 1921 made it easier to sell alcohol with meals (the latter allowed alcohol to be sold after 11 p.m. in restaurants, thereby making them an attractive option for those shut out of **pubs**). The huge success of Raymond Postgate's *Good* ◀ *Food Guide*, first published in 1951, was a testament to the restaurant's growing popularity and by 2001, three-quarters of the British people ate out regularly.

F

However, all these advances were undermined by the fact that the overall quality of food in Britain declined after 1945. The popularity of American fast foods, with their high fat, sugar and salt levels, was of especial concern of nutritionists and accelerated when the first British hamburger 'restaurant' was opened by Wimpy in 1962. Another concern was the use of chemical fertilisers and pesticides in agriculture, and processed convenience foods with their heavy reliance on chemical preservatives, flavourings and colourings. Over 3,000 such chemicals were legally in use by the end of the century, despite legislation banning some and limiting others, beginning with the Food Safety Act of 1955. American freezing techniques, developed just before the war, facilitated the growth of processed food. Bird's Eye set up its first UK base in 1945 and by the end of the century, 75 per cent of households had a freezer.

Awareness that these developments might be responsible for the post-war rise in cancer and heart disease rates shook public confidence in the 1980s. A decade later confidence in the safety of meat was further hit by the BSE scandal and that of crops by genetic modification, the latter pioneered by the American food giant Monsanto. All of this led to the setting up of a national Food Standards Agency in 2000 and to the growth of the organic food movement. The name of Cranks' vegetarian restaurants, established in 1961, no longer reflected either the number of non-meat eaters or the way that most carnivores viewed them. However, the higher price of organic produce prevented it from undermining agri-business, while the reluctance of supermarkets, still less chemical companies, to challenge the practices of the processed food industry helped to maintain its grip on the British body.

Supermarkets made a huge range of foodstuffs available in one convenient place (between 1970 and 2000, the number of items that Sainsbury's stocked rose from 4,000 to 23,000). But in doing so they crushed the small grocery store and specialist stores like butchers and bakers. Supermarkets became firmly established in the 1960s, and their sociological effects became fully apparent after a French company, Carrefour, opened the first out-of-town 'hypermarket' north of Caerphilly, in 1972. Between 1995 and 2000, the UK lost 30,000 local outlets, a fifth of the total. Whereas the traditional grocery or specialist store had been a hub of community life where people met to exchange news and gossip, the supermarket epitomised Britain's more atomised society. Romance may sometimes blossom in its aisles, but personal contact is usually limited to the struggle for a parking space and a shopping trolley. Moreover, the huge purchasing power of supermarket companies that helped to keep food prices low largely did so by enabling them to extort low prices from producers. This made small farmers more dependent on state subsidies, so that in effect the consumer was subsidising supermarket giants through their taxes, for food that was slowly poisoning them.

In 1946, the Hungarian-born Jewish émigré and student of the English character, George Mikes wrote: 'On the Continent people have good food; in England people have good table manners.' Half a century later, the difference was less stark. Food in Britain became more abundant and varied as a result of greater affluence and engagement with foreign cultures. The changes in food consumption, like those wrought on drinking habits, proved that America was not the only cultural influence on the British. But change came at a higher price. In 2003, a third of Britons were clinically obese. If we are what we eat, then the British have become, like others in the West, a nation of gluttonous self-abusers.

■ Football

Most popular sport in the UK and arguably Britain's most visible legacy to the world next to the Industrial Revolution, out of which the modern game grew. It seems to have emerged in England during the twelfth century but it only achieved a mass following in the late Victorian era when it became a leisure pursuit of the northern industrial ▸ working classes, third in importance to the **pub** and the **music hall**. Rules were first drawn up at Cambridge University in 1848; a further standardisation followed at a meeting in London in 1863, out of which the English Football Association (FA) was formed. Thereafter, the game was officially known as association football and, more popularly, as 'soccer', the latter term stemming from the word 'association'.

The FA was run by the metropolitan propertied classes who attempted to stamp an amateur ethos on the game. Although they were less successful in doing so than in other sports invented by the ▸ British like **cricket**, **rugby** and tennis, amateurism arrested the technical and commercial development of football and so allowed other nations to overtake the British. Still, the Football Association did much to promote the modern game, especially with its creation of the

FA Challenge Cup, which was first competed for in season 1871–2. A Scottish Football Association (SFA) was formed in 1878 and a Scottish League followed in 1890. Welsh and Irish leagues were also set up in 1890, although rugby continued to be the most popular sport in Wales and Gaelic football the most popular in Ireland (moreover, unlike Celtic and Rangers, the leading Welsh clubs – Cardiff and Swansea – played in the English league).

Professionalism was accepted by the British FAs in 1885, clubs like Old Etonians began to fade, and in 1888 the English Football League was established with 44 clubs. By 1914 there were 156. Based in Lancashire, it was run by self-made northern businessmen and only one of its members was a southern club: Royal Arsenal (later Arsenal) based in Woolwich. The division of responsibilities between governing body and league, each with different outlooks, was, and is, unique in the world. For the first two decades of the century, southern English clubs were amateur outfits which played in their own league, established in 1894. However, as the game grew in popularity and professionalism spread south, in 1920 all 22 clubs in the first of the Southern League's two divisions were elected to the Football League. The latter's Third Division then split into two sections – North and South – until in 1958 they were reconstituted to form the Third and Fourth Divisions, so ending the formal **North–South divide** in the ◀ sport.

During the Second World War, League competition was suspended, though exhibition matches were popular, with scratch teams made up of star players who were on leave from the forces at the time. The hunger for entertainment after the rigours of war culminated in the ◀ highest attendance for a season – 41 million in 1948–9. Subsequently, television ate heavily into gates, particularly after the start of ITV in ◀ 1955; by season 1964–5, only 27.6 million people went to matches. The British male did not lose his interest in the sport; he simply became more of an armchair fan. Moreover, TV fostered a commercial revolution in the sport which helped to turn football from a leisure pursuit of the urban, male working classes into a mass phenomenon which embraced virtually all sections of society.

After a campaign led by the head of the Professional Footballers Association Jimmy Hill (b. 1928), which culminated in the threat of a players' strike, the maximum wage for players and the restrictions on them transferring to other clubs were abolished in 1961. This had two negative consequences. First, rising wage bills widened the gap between clubs in the upper and lower divisions of the British leagues and contributed to the extinction of the smallest ones. Similarly, as fans became more affluent, and mobile thanks to car ownership, they were less restricted to local teams and could travel to the nearest glamour club in order to watch better football if they chose (the rise to prominence of Manchester United in the 1950s was a product of that trend). Second, Hill's revolution began a steady export trade from Scotland to England. Because few clubs other than Celtic and Rangers could afford the new wage levels, the best Scottish players went south to earn more money (their departure formed part of a larger exodus of skilled Scots, as the country's industrial economy began to decline in the late 1950s). By the 1970s, virtually every major English club had a backbone of Scottish talent.

For all its drawbacks, Hill's victory benefited the men who played the game. As power began to shift from the boardroom to the locker room, football became one of the few ways that semi-educated working-class men could obtain wealth and fulfilment. The top professionals, like **George Best**, acquired lifestyles comparable to film and pop stars, while the majority now earned enough in their brief sporting life to start a second career when the day came to hang up their boots (running a pub was a favoured, though not always wise, option). The highest wages were sometimes criticised by the upper and middle classes who did not like to see a lack of education being so handsomely rewarded. But the majority of Britons, however jealous they might be of their heroes, did not think their earnings were immoral, and increasingly looked to them as role models.

As British football became more commercial it also became more international. The first international match to be played anywhere in the world took place on 1 November 1872 between England and Scotland at the West of Scotland Cricket Club ground at Partick, near Glasgow (from 1924, the fixture alternated between national stadia at Hampden Park and Wembley). The Scots took the fixture more seriously than the English, beating England being one way to prove that they were worthy partners of their much larger neighbour in the Union. The 128,810 supporters who cheered on Scotland at Hampden in 1931 set a new world record for attendance at a sporting fixture. From the 1930s onwards, it became a biannual tradition for tens of thousands of Scots – known as the Tartan Army – to travel south and occupy the streets of London with drunken, banner-waving revelry before and after the match at Wembley. During the Silver Jubilee Year of 1977, the Tartan Army tore up the pitch after their team had won, an event that reflected the rise of Scottish nationalism; and the fixture was abolished in 1989 because it was thought to be souring Anglo-Scottish relations. Between 1872 and 1989 the Scots won 40 matches, compared to England's 43 out of 118 played.

Both countries remained complacent about the developing skills of foreign countries, despite the fact that most clubs around the world had either been set up by British expatriates, or else were coached by them. An international governing body, FIFA, was created in Paris in 1904. Until 1954 it was run by a Frenchman, Jules Rimet, who in 1930 set up the World Cup which initially bore his name. Chafing at the Gallic cheek of it, the British FAs did not join FIFA on a permanent basis until 1947 and did not compete in the World Cup until 1950, when England lost to the United States. The first defeat to a foreign team had taken place in 1929 against Spain, in Madrid (Scotland first lost to Austria in Vienna in 1931). But the humiliation of losing to a country that barely played the sport and one, moreover, that was superseding Britain as the superpower of the West, was far greater. It was compounded in 1953 by the first defeat on British soil, against Hungary. These defeats galvanised the Football Association into taking international competition more seriously. Scientific coaching techniques were imported from abroad and in 1962 Alf Ramsey (1920–99) was appointed England manager with the power to choose the team himself (previously selection was made by an FA committee). This enabled England to win the World Cup at Wembley in 1966, which in turn helped to transform football from a working-class entertainment into a national obsession.

Victory also galvanised England (and Scotland) into competing for the European nations tournament in 1968, from which the British FAs had remained aloof since its inception in 1958. European club football also became more popular. Like FIFA, the European Cup was a French initiative, started in season 1955–6. The Football League prevented English champions Chelsea taking part, and it was not competed for until the following season when Matt Busby's Manchester United side defied the League. By the time that Celtic became the first British club to win the competition in 1968, it had become an accepted feature of the sport.

Unfortunately, international football also became a source of hooliganism, which brought the British game into disrepute. At club level, the violence culminated with the Heysel Stadium disaster before the European Cup Final of 1985 between Liverpool and Juventus, in which 39 spectators were killed; and at international level with a riot at the 1995 match between England and the Republic of Ireland in Dublin. There had always been fighting at spectator sports (including cricket) but organised violence at football matches, driven by racism and xenophobia, is a recent phenomenon. It first emerged in the 1960s when the loosening of family, community and gender structures created a vacuum in the lives of insecure men that football tribalism filled; greater affluence enabled them to travel more widely to battle with opposing groups; and anxiety about Britain's decline as a superpower, coupled with hostility towards black immigration and the European Union, gave the violence an ideological purpose that disguised its

F

primary psycho-social causes. The trend was captured in Peter Howson's (b. 1958) painting *Just Another Bloody Sunday* (1987), the braying faces and pointing fingers of its spectators in sharp contrast to the peaceful demeanour of those in L.S. Lowry's (1887–1976) *Going to the Match*.

However, few British football fans were ever hooligans and the problem was gradually stamped out by tougher policing and government action, primarily the licensing system for stadia introduced by the 1989 Football Spectators Act. This, coupled with the 1990 Taylor Report which led to the introduction of all-seater stadia, restored the sport's reputation and attendance rose once more with a growing

▶ number of **women** present. The 1994 Bosman Ruling, which did for the restrictive practices of the EU what Jimmy Hill had done for those of the UK, allowed more foreigners to play in Britain. The first foreign professional was a Dane, Nils Middleboe, who signed for Chelsea in 1913; and it was Chelsea who fielded the first all-foreign team, in 1999. By then they accounted for a third of the Premiership's playing force. Most came from Continental Europe, as did a number of leading managers. In 2000 the English happily accepted a Swede as the first foreign coach of their national side, and the Scots followed suit in 2001 with a German. To some extent, football remained, in the words

▶ of **George Orwell**, 'war minus the shooting', even for the most peaceable fans. Yet the new European dimension of the sport fostered a greater cultural engagement between the British and the Continent

▶ that was second in importance only to the foreign package **holiday**.

As in most areas of national life, the commercialisation of the sport was a mixed blessing. The stock market flotation of top clubs, starting with Tottenham Hotspur in 1983, made them more remote from fans but it also generated funds which helped to pay for better stadia and youth training programmes. So too did the income generated from TV coverage and the sponsorship of competitions (1970) and teams (1981). Later, though, the collapse of ITV Digital in 2001, after it paid too much for football coverage, demonstrated that the sport's popularity was not infinite and it resulted in a financial downturn in the game which hit the smaller clubs hardest.

However, football retained a quasi-religious place in British life. Within half a century, it had forged a bond between classes, races, sexes and even nations, providing the foundation for a global popular culture that was unparalleled in human history. Juvenal's second-century dictum that Romans and the people under their yoke needed *panem et circenses* is just as true for those living under the American empire of the twenty-first century. But if bread is still hard to come by for millions of people, their favourite circus is at least not of America's making.

■ Freud, Sigmund (1856–1939); Freudianism

Sigmund Freud only arrived in Britain in 1938, and died just a few days after the outbreak of the Second World War. But news of his work had long preceded him. Indeed, few people rivalled his influence on twentieth-century Britain, for good or ill. *The Interpretation of Dreams* (published appropriately in 1900) attracted many disciples, not just in Vienna where he worked but also abroad. Building on an existing interest in the 'unconscious', rather than the superficial manifestations of neurosis in individual patients, Freud emphasised the role of non-rational urges – primarily sexual, but also a more general survival instinct – in producing guilt and anxiety from childhood onwards. Difficulties arise for individuals when the usual checks on these urges fail to develop or cease to function.

From an early stage Freud's theories created dissension. Two early admirers, Alfred Adler (1870–1937) and Carl Jung (1875–1961) broke away in search of more nuanced approaches. But among laymen in general – and the artistic community in particular – Freud was much discussed and widely accepted. The carnage of the First World War seemed to invite the idea of a collective outbreak of savage, primeval impulses (the response of Freud himself was to switch his focus from the 'life instinct' to the 'death instinct'). In reality these emotions mainly affected the outlook of non-combatants, including the numerous artists and writers who escaped **conscription**; the soldiers themselves generally went to their futile deaths with quiet resignation. The survivors were often racked with guilt, ensuring a steady supply of new patients whose symptoms seemed to validate Freud's ideas.

Before 1939 Freud's theories had already inspired the Surrealist movement; artists like Pablo Picasso (1881–1973) were also influenced. Faced with almost any unfathomable abstract painting, the pedantic observer would invariably try to explain it by referring to the 'Freudian' unconscious. On behalf of these artists it could be argued that any work which provokes thought is of some merit – even if the thoughts in question are idiotic. It might even be claimed that Freud saved **art**, in the era of the photograph. But as his theories filtered out of the scientific community and into the general marketplace of ideas, they threatened more serious consequences.

Leaving aside the demands of empirical science, Freud's methodology even failed to satisfy the rudiments of common sense. His early work relied heavily on the examination of disturbed individuals under hypnosis. The tendency to attribute all of their problems to a single cause – and to claim that this had now been discovered – was quite understandable for a man with Freud's high ambitions. But by definition Freud's subjects were idiosyncratic, providing no basis for theories of universal application. And the results of his speculation could not be refuted, either as a theory or a therapy. The excitable 'id', the practical 'ego' and the conscience-stricken 'superego' could be wheeled out to explain everything; and anyone who protested that they had no awareness of these things could be met with the crushing answer that this was the whole point. Even the silliest Freudian deductions – such as the idea that all **women** suffer from 'penis envy' – could not be gainsaid. People who took all this seriously might even develop neuroses on discovering that they had never had the slightest inclination to kill their fathers or rape their mothers, as 'normal' people should. Intensive psychoanalysis might produce positive results; but then in an anonymous world most people are likely to take comfort from an attentive listener.

Despite all the sound and fury, Freud's work seems little more than an extended and pretentious commentary on Oscar Wilde's quip: 'I can resist everything except temptation.' Most people seek pleasure – although they find it in very different things – and the main problem of a civilised society has concerned the means of keeping this drive within sustainable boundaries. These are always culturally conditioned, so that a hanging offence in one century is regarded as the reason for no more than a friendly admonition in the next. To the extent that Freud's work helped to relax some of the more rigid or spurious 'taboos', its effects were welcome and consistent with his own conscious desire to promote rational thinking by stripping away harmful illusions. But in the cultural context of the twentieth century the chief constraints – religion, the feeling of community and the concept of reason itself – were being rapidly eroded. While Freud might be said to have helped to *explain* this process, it was all too easy to claim that his work *justified* (or encouraged) it. In particular, the advertising industry seized on Freud's ideas, so that (for example) images of sex became all-pervasive, regardless of the commodity in question. The net result was a further erosion of social and economic constraints, and a spurious endorsement of decadence.

■ Gambling

In their study of *English Life and Leisure* (1951), B. Seebohm Rowntree and G.R. Lavers considered the **morality** of gambling. From their self-proclaimed vantage point, that of open-minded investigators who had 'knocked about the world a lot', they concluded that 'nobody should gamble who is a Christian, or who has a well-developed cultural background'. They felt that the moral argument against gambling was 'unanswerable', anathematising the activity as 'a rejection and betrayal of the long and painful progress of man from his primitive animal state'.

The most obvious moral argument was actually an economic one, applying to people with dependants. The likely losses could impoverish a family – or, what was more often the case, make its existing **poverty** a great deal worse. But Rowntree and Lavers went further, claiming that, 'Gambling is unethical because it is an attempt to obtain property without effort, whereas the true ethical basis for the acquisition of property is effort followed by satisfaction.' In the wrong hands this argument might have inspired revolutionary thoughts. Does the landlord make much 'effort' when he collects rent from properties which he has inherited? Is the successful City investor more entitled to his profits than the man who studies the racing form for hours before striking his bets? In fact, gambling on the stock exchange was far more vulnerable to moral criticism than the desire to win the pools, because the livelihood of millions could be at stake. Yet Rowntree and Lavers went out of their way to justify gambling in shares. In so doing they revealed their real purpose, and that of all their kind. The real fear of the anti-gambling brigade was not that losses would worsen the plight of the poor – but that a run of good luck might make some of them rich.

Although the Quaker Rowntree represented a fading tradition within British liberalism, such views were surprisingly common even in 1951. Before 1900, self-appointed moral custodians of the poor thought that gambling on organised sporting events ranked as highly as **drink** among the enemies of a sound social order. The difficulty was to clamp down on such activities without looking too hypocritical; but this had been achieved before, when through legislation of 1845 and 1854 MPs who spent their evenings hazarding vast sums at cards in London's clubs voted to prosecute poor people who opened their houses to venture a few shillings. Before the First World War it had looked as if the new battle might be won. Acts of 1899 and 1906, passed under the influence of the National Anti-Gambling League, outlawed off-course cash betting. This promised to attack the problem without disturbing wealthy people who wanted to gamble on their own nags while watching them perform, or to place bets through their credit accounts with 'Turf Accountants'. Such double-think would have impressed even **George Orwell**, and indeed it outlived him. In their absurd anxiety to draw some concrete distinction between the harmless pastimes of the rich and the vices of the poor, in 1951 Rowntree and Lavers echoed government policy at the time by convincing themselves that horse-racing at least had one practical spin-off in improved horse-breeding, overlooking the fact that racehorses have no practical use outside racing.

The self-satisfaction of the League was misplaced. It would have been difficult enough to prevent people from striking surreptitious wagers within the narrow confines of a racecourse. Even when news of results travelled slowly, gamblers across the whole country could put down their money in advance and wait a couple of days for the outcome. But with the introduction of the Post Office telegraph in 1870, racing devotees hundreds of miles away could learn their fate seconds after the beasts had crossed the line. After the birth of the *Sporting Chronicle* newspaper (1871) those who preferred black-and-white evidence could see not only how their selections had fared (and the odds of return), but also pit their wits against an array of tipsters. Attempts to apply the law in these circumstances were futile at best, and threatened to discredit the whole legal system. Enterprising bookmakers, assisted by 'runners' who collected stake money from punters, could reduce their risks by making a pact of mutual benefit with corrupt local policemen, who in any case had far more important work to do. In 1913, annual betting turnover was estimated by one well-informed observer at around £100 million, and an Anglican clergyman who researched the problem guessed that no less than 80 per cent of the working-class population were regular gamblers.

In the mid-1920s technology struck against the moralists from a different direction. Dog-racing had been a source of alarm to the nineteenth-century reformers: its most common form of 'coursing' was objectionable because spectators enjoyed betting on it, but it also involved the death of many hares. Unfortunately, the rich liked it almost as much as horse-racing, so there was no chance of an outright ban. After 1921, when the mechanical hare was patented in America, greyhound racing tracks sprang up in almost every large British town or city. Unlike horse-racing, this sport readily lent itself to evening meetings under floodlights, making it possible for the working poor to attend as often as they wanted – along with their wives and children, to the horror of the righteous. The first large stadium, at Belle Vue in Manchester, attracted an audience of 1,700 for its first meeting in 1926: soon the best tracks could expect 20,000 visitors every race night, and the rage for sporting distractions in an age of austerity pushed the overall number of paying customers up to 45 million in 1946. The sudden popularity of 'going to the dogs' was symbolised by the sport's first **celebrity**, the greyhound Mick the Miller, who appeared in films and earned the quaint compliment of being stuffed and put on display at the National History Museum.

Many would have liked to abolish this proletarian form of racing, but the surge in popularity came in the wake of the **General Strike**, and the nation's legislators had no intention of reminding ordinary people that they had lost the class war. Instead, after a Royal Commission the sport was regulated in 1934. Agitators against the **football** pools (which emerged in its modern form in the 1920s with the creation of the Littlewoods company) were to be equally disappointed. This game was particularly abhorrent to the moralists, because many people refused to accept that it was a form of gambling at all and many women took part, sometimes raiding the housekeeping budget to join in (and concealing the fact from their husbands). By the late 1930s around 10 million people were trying to guess the weekend's football results, and Orwell noted that in 1936 an attempt to wreck the system, by preventing the publication of fixtures until two days before kick-off, provoked a much greater public stir than Hitler's reoccupation of the Rhineland. In fact, the approach of a new war, with all that this implied for the civilian population, was a further stimulus to the gambling instinct ('housey housey', now better known as Bingo, seems to have been invented by soldiers preparing for action in the First World War).

In 1936 it was estimated that gambling had become the nation's second biggest industry, with an annual turnover of around £200 million. In these circumstances even Oliver Cromwell would have found it difficult to resist the argument that, if the people refused to turn away from vice, the state should help itself to some of the proceeds. A betting tax had been introduced in 1926, but was abolished three years later. The measure proved ineffective because as the Chancellor of the Exchequer, **Winston Churchill**, tacitly recognised, it would barely cover the costs of administration unless it could be extended to off-course betting, which would have to be legalised before it could be taxed. This was a step too far for Churchill who (rather surprisingly, given his robust attitude to life) considered gambling to be an 'evil'. Instead, rich racehorse owners were allowed after 1928 to administer the 'Tote', a form of licensed pool betting, on the understanding that profits were to be applied to the improvement of bloodstock.

The historian Paul Addison has described post-war gambling as 'the irrational supplement to the **Beveridge Report**'. In fact, policy-makers now saw it as a way of helping to finance the **welfare state**. In 1947 –

when gambling expenditure reached an incredible £800 million – a 10 per cent duty was imposed on the football pools. This was a heavy blow for the moralists, since taxation is equivalent to official tolerance. In 1956 they suffered a more serious blow. Five years earlier Rowntree and Lavers had been sufficiently worried by the prospect of a state-run lottery to warn that this would be 'a retrograde and unfortunate step'. Yet there had been such lotteries in Britain during the eighteenth century, and private 'sweepstakes' had never gone away. This was a tricky area for the moralists, who could hardly complain when the proceeds were ploughed into 'good causes', particularly hospitals. The law was relaxed by a private member's bill just before the 1956 budget, in which the Chancellor Harold Macmillan scandalised 'respectable' opinion by introducing 'Premium Bonds'. Macmillan claimed that this was a form of saving rather than gambling, because the investor

▶ could not lose his or her money. No one was fooled; **Labour**'s Harold Wilson lambasted a 'squalid lottery'. But the Chancellor's confidence in the British gambling instinct bore fruit, netting the state more than £100 million in 1957–8. Here, too, technology played a part. Since the numbers were selected by a computer, players could feel more secure against cheating (although in fact the game was rigged to ensure that the holders of large blocks of bonds won a high proportion of the big prizes).

In 1856 such a move would have cost a Chancellor his career (and possibly even his life, so deep were the feelings of the moralistic mob). A century later Macmillan's success led inexorably to the 1960 Betting and Gaming Act, which finally allowed off-course bookmakers to trade legally. Back in 1926 Churchill had suggested that if bookies' shops were to be permitted, they should at least be made as uncomfortable as possible. This advice was followed in the 1960 legislation, so that the residue of moralists in the Commons could square their votes with their consciences. To the respectable middle-class householder, the dens of iniquity were the nearest twentieth-century equivalent to a scene from Hogarth's *Rake's Progress* – a bleak landscape of overflowing ashtrays and discarded betting slips, even lacking seats in case any loafers were tempted to sleep off the effects of lunchtime drinking. Normally, though, the casual shopper could only imagine these scenes; in an apparent attempt to increase the sense of shame for regular punters, the shop-fronts had to be designed so that the interior could not be seen.

The 1960 Betting and Gaming Act is not usually seen as a landmark in social legislation, but given the hysteria of the anti-gambling lobby – and the popularity of betting, despite all the opprobrium – its effect

▶ in paving the way for a decade of **'permissive'** liberalisation should not be underestimated. Housewives who previously had to seek out a bookies' runner for their annual 'flutters' on the Grand National and the Derby could now do the deed of darkness without fear, particularly since they were likely to meet many of their neighbours when they popped into William Hill or Ladbrokes. By 1962 there were more than 13,000 such shops in Britain. At first the firms tended to be small and locally-based, as previously illegal operations turned 'legit'. But by the late 1970s a handful of big companies had cornered nearly a quarter of the market. In other words, instead of undermining capitalism as the moralists habitually claimed, gambling was becoming just another arm of the burgeoning service sector, displaying the familiar tendency to monopoly and restrictive practices. The only difference was that the terms and conditions for workers tended to be less attractive than most other occupations, in the absence of **trade unions**. ◄

By 1990 it was estimated that Britons were staking an annual £10 billion on various forms of gambling (excluding arcade machines). Around 3 million people were playing bingo, the game of choice for housewives and the retired. It might have been a symptom of continuing misgivings in high places that this information was always placed last in the government's annual digest of statistics. But it could not be denied that Britain was a nation of gamblers, and the old argument for an undisguised state lottery began to resurface. It was a natural step for a **Conservative** government which had promoted ◄ 'casino capitalism', encouraging small investors to risk their savings on stocks and shares, and presiding over the transformation of the **housing** market into the biggest lottery of them all. A National Lottery ◄ was foreshadowed in the 1992 Queen's Speech, and started running two years later.

By this time there were few moralists left to offend. But the associated advertising campaign seemed intent on smoking them out, by using the slogan 'It could be you' without adding a touch of disheartening realism, '. . . but it probably won't'. The idea of 'undeserved' riches which Rowntree and Lavers had deplored was now being used to entice new punters. At least there were two certain winners – the lottery operator, which was guaranteed a percentage of the proceeds, and the government, which promised to use the money for 'bread and circuses', like sport and the arts. Its record in this respect was somewhat patchy – there was a storm in 1995 when Churchill's private papers were bought for £12.5 million thanks to the kind of gambling which he had deplored, and the millennium celebrations were widely regarded as a waste of money. Not everyone who bagged the jackpot – a sum invariably in excess of £1 million – realised their dreams. There were regular tidings of **marriage** break-ups, and an unemployed ◄ carpenter who won in 1999 bought a mansion, a Bentley and a Rolls-Royce before drinking himself to death in December 2001. In the following year an habitual petty crook netted a fortune, which suggested that the nineteenth-century moralisers might have had a point after all. Sales peaked at £5.5 billion in 1997–8; in 2000–1 they fell to £4.8 billion, despite changes in the format and increasingly desperate advertising. But even if the Lottery's popularity was fading by the end of the century, Britain's gamblers were fully occupied, with the internet providing exciting new opportunities to lose.

■ Gardening

Britain's favourite hobby. Gardening for pleasure, as opposed to husbandry, first became popular among the **aristocracy** during the seventeenth century. By the nineteenth century, the middle **classes** had also taken it up and a new garden style developed out of their enthusiasm, one that was deliberately rambling and which was said to symbolise the pragmatic English character, in contrast to the more formal styles of Continental Europe. But gardening only became a mass pursuit at the start of the twentieth century, when shorter working hours and the establishment of British summer time in 1916 enabled people to spend more time outdoors on summer evenings.

Edwardian social reformers saw gardening as a form of responsible recreation that kept the working classes away from the **pub** and **gambling**. The Society for the Promotion of Window Boxes (1869) was one manifestation of that trend; another, more successful one was the Allotments Act of 1885. This made it compulsory for local authorities in England and Wales to provide land for cultivation at a rent afford-able to most citizens. The male urban poor took to the scheme because it enabled them to grow cheap fresh **food** and because it gave them socially acceptable space and time to escape their families whenever they wished. Another manifestation of the trend was the garden city movement. Led by Ebenezer Howard, and inspired by American exper-iments in Chicago and Boston, a new generation of town planners saw gardens as the basis of a healthier, more communal urban life. The Garden City Association was inaugurated in 1899 (renamed the Town and Country Planning Association in 1941) and it led to the creation of towns like Letchworth (1903) and Welwyn (1920) that were designed around green spaces, from the humblest cottage rose bed to the grandest civic lawn. Elsewhere, the number of private gardens grew during the interwar period thanks to rising wages, cheap mortgages and **suburban** development. These trends enabled many working- and lower-middle-class people to move out of city centres and into new houses with ready-made plots, often at the front as well as the rear of the property. Between 1918 and 1939 150,000 acres of garden were laid out in Britain. The growing of flowers rather than fruit and vegetables became part of the status of suburban life, denoting an ability to afford decoration over function.

Those who could not afford to grow their own lilies were still able to consider them, thanks to the creation of public parks and gardens. **Parliament** began to augment philanthropic ventures by purchasing Primrose Hill in London in 1836. But most of Britain's parks were laid out between 1907, when the Public Health Act of that year instructed local authorities to do so, and 1929, when the start of the **Great Depression** made them less of a priority. By 1920, Manchester alone had 57 parks. Often graced with bandstands, ponds, bowling greens, tennis courts and **football** pitches, they became an arena of respectable public resort, as well as a source of civic pride, flowers being the focus of regional and national competitions to find the most beautiful park. During the Second World War, flower beds in private and public gardens were turned over to vegetables as part of the Dig For Victory campaign, and this became a symbol of the sacrifice made by the British in order to defeat Germany. When flower beds resumed their decorative purpose in 1945, they were a symbol of peace and of pride in victory, it being common for red, white and blue species to be planted together. The aristocracy had a direct influence as a result of the huge rise in stately home visiting after the war. Their gardens were one of the main attractions for day-trippers, who borrowed designs and bought cuttings from the originators of the pursuit.

By 1950, gardening was central to how the British defined their way of life. Polemicists of all political hues claimed that it proved the national soul still resided in the countryside despite two centuries of urbanisation, and they claimed it often enough for the idea to gain some currency in the population as a whole. In *The English People* (1947) **George Orwell** wrote: 'Nearly everyone who can afford to do so sets up as a country gentleman, or at least makes some effort in that direction. The manor house with its walled gardens reappears in reduced form in the stockbroker's weekend cottage, in the suburban villa with its lawn and herbaceous border, perhaps even in the potted nasturtiums on the window-sill of the Bayswater flat. This widespread daydream is undoubtedly snobbish, it has tended to stabilise class distinctions and has helped to prevent the modernisation of English **agriculture**; but it is mixed up with a kind of idealism, a feeling that style and tradition are more important than money.'

It was also common to attribute the conservative character of the British to gardening, on the grounds that cultivation required patience, a sense of nature's slow evolution, and a dislike of sudden changes in the **weather**. At the height of the **Cold War** in the 1950s it was even claimed that gardening was a bulwark against communism. Here too, the daydream had some basis in reality. For, although

gardening became a truly common pursuit in the post-war era, it was based more than ever before in the private sphere; and in particular on the idea of Britain as a property-owning democracy. Few public parks were opened after 1939; and much of the remainder fell into
▶ disrepair, blighted by vandalism, budget restraints and civic **apathy**. The number of allotments tended in Britain reached a peak of 1.03 million plots in 1950, but by 1970 the figure had halved. During the same period, the number of household gardens more than doubled to 14 million. Four-fifths of British homes had one. They covered 620,000 acres, an area equal in size to the county of Dorset, and an estimated 29 million people were active gardeners, making it officially the UK's most popular leisure activity after watching television, and occupying four times as many hours as drinking or watching sport.

Like most recreational trends of that era, the garden explosion was
▶ driven by two things: a further rise in **home ownership**, and the media boom powered by the mass purchase of television sets. *Gardeners' Question Time*, first broadcast on BBC radio in 1947, was followed on TV in 1954 by *Gardeners' World*, which made a national celebrity out of Percy Thrower (1913–88). Thrower's calm manner and West Country burr denoted the peaceful, quasi-rural domesticity with which gardening was associated in the public mind. Yet, during the 1950s a revolution took place with the arrival of the garden centre, a companion to the supermarket, where customers could buy ready-grown plants that required no cultivation. This instant Eden was an American invention, as was the craze for patios and barbecues, which helped to turn the garden into a second living room for six months of the year.

Gardening was never quite as popular in Scotland, Wales and Northern Ireland as it was in England, partly because of the more inclement weather in those countries but mainly because property ownership was, on average, at half the level of the south. It is also important to note that by the end of the twentieth century, the number of active gardeners had almost halved, down to 15 million from its peak in 1970. But this reflected the middle-class exodus from the suburbs and their return to city centres, which were fashionable once more but still lacked the necessary space for the hobby. Its continuing popularity was evidenced by the success of the garden 'makeover' programme *Ground Force* (BBC2/1, 1997–). Fronted by Percy Thrower's successor, Alan Titchmarsh, it was pitched at young married home-owners. It also brought sex into the garden, in the shape of Titchmarsh's flame-haired and bra-less assistant Charlie Dimmock. The greening of the nation's fingers was more than skin-deep and the British remained Europe's most passionate gardeners.

■ General Strike

Between Tuesday 4 and Thursday 13 May 1926, life in Britain was seriously disrupted by a General Strike. A long-running dispute over pay and conditions in the coal industry developed into a direct challenge to the **Conservative** government of **Stanley Baldwin**. In the face of ◄ aggressive competition from abroad and an overvalued pound, the mine owners planned to implement wage cuts, in some cases amounting to half of the current pay packet. The prospect of widespread disruption made the government contemplate surrender, by appointing a commission which recommended temporary subsidies to employers and workers alike. The findings also pointed to a radical restructuring of the coal industry, encouraging the miners to think that they had seized the initiative. But when this arrangement expired after nine months no more money was forthcoming, and the owners locked the miners out on 1 May 1926. Attempts to find a compromise broke off when printers refused to lay out the type for the next issue of the *Daily Mail*. The Lord Chancellor, Birkenhead, spoke for many by muttering 'bloody good job' when he heard what the printers had done; after all, the *Mail* was something less than an ornament to Britain's democracy, having published the forged Zinoviev Letter in a successful attempt to discredit the **Labour Party** before the 1924 ◄ general election. But the incident could still be presented as a threat to free speech, giving the government an excuse for intransigence. Although there had been little or no advance planning, workers in all the key industries responded when the General Council of the **Trades** ◄ **Union** Congress (TUC) called for a wider stoppage.

When after nine days the TUC General Council agreed to call off the strike, the *Mail* marked the restoration of free speech by crowing that the 'revolutionaries' had 'surrendered'. In fact, although some had undoubtedly hoped to destroy the existing order – and the miners' leader A.J. Cook often spoke as if he welcomed a confrontation – the vast majority of strikers were merely motivated by the wish to preserve their own living standards. The main symptoms of **class** hatred were evinced by the mine owners and other employers, who found a venomous supporter in **Winston Churchill**, the Chancellor of the ◄ Exchequer. Churchill's decision in the previous year to return Britain to the gold standard, leaving the pound grossly overvalued, had been one of the main causes of the crisis in the mining industry (and eventually of the **Great Depression**). Yet as editor of the temporary news- ◄ paper the *British Gazette*, Churchill stirred up feelings against the strikers and denounced any idea of compromise. At the **BBC** John ◄ Reith helped in the propaganda war, preventing the Archbishop of Canterbury from delivering a conciliatory broadcast.

G

Under different leaders, the strikers might have verified Churchill's lurid rhetoric, and justified his deployment of armoured cars. But the TUC was terrified by the possibility that feelings might run out of control. Many of the union leaders had only thrown their weight behind the miners in the first place because of a defensive sense of solidarity – a hangover from the spirit of the trenches. It was no accident that one of the most memorable images of the strike was a ▶ replica of the impromptu England–Germany **football** matches held during the short-lived wartime truce of Christmas 1914. Whatever their differences, the strikers and the opposing policemen had no desire to fight each other. Faced with proof that Marx's critique of capitalism had much to recommend it after all, the TUC contradicted the rest of his theory by deciding not to throw off their chains. They grasped at Baldwin's vague promise to work for a fair settlement for the miners, in order to close the Pandora's box which they had opened themselves.

The country was not quite brought to a standstill by the strike. Enthusiastic volunteers maintained most essential services. If the railways had retained their monopoly of rapid inland transport the government would have been in more serious trouble. As it was, the lorry drivers were far less organised and militant than the rail unions, and where they did join the dispute affluent car drivers had both the means and the motivation to take their places (up until 1931 it was not even necessary to declare oneself physically fit before beginning to drive, so in 1926 anyone over 17 could be a motorised 'strike-breaker'). One well-off citizen who felt the call of duty was the novelist Evelyn Waugh, who eagerly enrolled with the Civil Constabulary Reserve just before the strike ended. He found the company uncongenial, describing some of his fellow volunteers as 'the dregs of civilisation'. A week earlier he and his cronies had indulged in an all-day drinking spree, which ended with Waugh seeing double. This doughty fighter for British civilisation had spent £3 on alcohol, at a time when a mineworker was lucky to earn more than £3 per week.

There were some violent clashes as well as friendly sporting rivalry, and under the government's emergency powers troops were called out. But a final tally of just over 3,000 prosecutions (and around 1,000 prison sentences) reflected the fact that, in general, the government had been sparing in its use of powers which showed that the right to free speech and assembly existed only on sufferance. Baldwin himself was no class warrior, but he was acutely aware of strong feelings among Conservative backbenchers. Even those who sympathised with the miners' case were exercised by their fear of the 'Red Peril'. In the year after the strike the government passed the Trades Disputes and Trade Union Act, which outlawed sympathetic strikes and attacked the financial link between the unions and the Labour Party. Many Conservatives would have gone further, and made the unions legally responsible for losses incurred during any dispute; but although the Act avoided extreme measures it was still an unequal compromise.

The TUC had capitulated on 12 May without the approval of the miners. This led to allegations of 'betrayal' – an inevitable charge on these occasions, which for once seems fully justified. For a few days some workers in other industries joined the miners in defying the call for a return to work. If anything, this renewed outbreak had the greater potential for provoking a concerted revolutionary attempt. But it soon petered out. The miners were left to carry on the struggle alone, and by the end of 1926 the strike was over. The employers secured everything they had wanted. Many miners were laid off, either because of victimisation or the deepening depression in the industry. Those who were fortunate enough to resume working did so for longer hours, and for less pay.

■ The Germans

A people with whom the British became obsessed during the twentieth century and against whom they largely defined themselves. Until the First World War, German culture was an accepted part of British life. It was no longer as fashionable as it had been during the mid-nineteenth century when the cult of Prince Albert was at its height. But Germany continued to have a cultural influence which the British found convenient and necessary to ignore, as two world wars for which the Germans were wholly blamed fostered a pathological dislike of them.

The decorated Christmas tree was established as a custom by Albert himself in the 1850s; so too was the nation's favourite Christmas carol, 'Silent Night', based on the German one 'Stille Nacht'. And long after Karl Marx vacated his seat at the British Library, German influence on the British left was apparent in the song 'Keep the Red Flag Flying'. Adopted by the **Labour Party** as its anthem in 1918, it was based on the tune of a German carol, 'O Tannenbaum' ('O, Christmas tree'). The craze for recreational camping and hill-walking, which began during the Edwardian era owed much to the influence of the German *Wandervogel* movement, as did the Youth Hostels Association, formed in 1930. German idealist philosophy had less influence on British intellectuals than it had in the nineteenth century, giving way to home-grown positivism. But in theology Karl Barth (1886–1968) and Paul Tillich (1886–1965) dominated British Protestant thought. Both men were vocal opponents of the Nazi regime and were exiled. During the 1930s, many other, mostly **Jewish**, intellectuals escaped to the UK. Notable

225

among them was the architect Erich Mendelsohn (1887–1953), who helped to introduce the Art Deco style to Britain; and the architectural critic Nikolaus Pevsner (1902–83). Pevsner, whose monumental guide-book *The Buildings of England* (1945–74) was based on the German *Handbuch der Deutschen Kunstdenkmäler* (1906), is the only person to have received both a knighthood and an Order of Merit from the Federal Republic of Germany.

The influence of refugees from Nazi Germany was acknowledged, but mainly so that the British could congratulate themselves on their greater tolerance of minorities, rather than to rekindle a sense of affinity with Germany. The most prominent early victim of Germanophobia was the most Teutonic British institution of all, the
▶ **monarchy**. During the First World War, families of German origin long resident in the UK were attacked and interned as spies and some had their businesses looted. Among the better-off it became unaccept-
▶ able to keep dachshunds or to drink German wine (when **Winston Churchill** was rebuked for downing a bottle of hock at dinner one night, he replied, 'I'm interning it'). Scare stories circulated by the British press about nuns being raped and babies murdered by the Kaiser's troops whipped up public feeling, which spilled over into doubts about the loyalty of the Kaiser's first cousin, George V. The Secretary of State for War, Lord Kitchener, was forced to assure the Cabinet that lights seen flashing near the palace at Sandringham during a German zeppelin raid was the local vicar driving home and not the King signalling to his relatives.

George V was certainly fond of his German relatives and regarded the dynastic European network established by the fecundity and diplomacy of his grandmother, Queen Victoria, as a kind of benevolent royal trade union. Nevertheless, he was stung by rumours of treachery and when he heard that the writer H.G. Wells (1866–1946) had denounced his 'alien and uninspiring court', he barked, 'I may be
▶ uninspiring but I'll be damned if I'm an alien.' Still, he accepted **Lloyd George**'s advice to change the royal family's name from Saxe-Coburg-Gotha to Windsor in 1917, after the royal palace in Berkshire that was built following a successful French invasion of England in 1066. Members of the royal family were ordered to relinquish their 'German degrees, styles, dignities, titles, honours and appellations'. The news was welcomed by the public and so began a lengthy process of naturalising the British monarchy.

The Second World War intensified hostility to the German people. Any sympathy they had gained as a result of their harsh treatment following the Treaty of Versailles in 1918 evaporated as the full force of German military might was turned against Britain in 1940–1. Internment was again introduced, among its victims some of the émigrés who had escaped to Britain during the 1930s. There was less of the knee-jerk jingoism of the previous war, with Britons being encouraged by government propagandists to distinguish between the German culture of Beethoven and the Nazi regime against which Britain was at war. But few distinguished between that regime and the German people. The death and suffering caused by the war was wholly blamed on them, and although anti-semitism was rife in Britain, when news arrived of the Holocaust, for many it seemed to confirm that the scare stories of German atrocities in 1914–18 had in fact been true.

In the early post-war period, the British people were reluctant to learn the lessons of Versailles and Weimar. There was considerable hostility to the Allies' policy of helping to rebuild West Germany, of nurturing democracy by giving the country **Marshall Aid** instead of beggaring it by demanding reparations. Despite sympathy for those trapped in Communist East Germany, which reached a peak during the Berlin airlift of 1948–9, most Britons wanted the dismemberment of Germany to be permanent. They were nervous about the creation of the Federal Republic in 1949, even though Allied troops remained in the country and despite the fact that its first Chancellor, Konrad Adenauer (1876–1967), had been imprisoned by the Nazis between 1933 and 1944 for opposing the Third Reich.

The Federal Republic became locked into the NATO alliance but the British were still opposed to German rearmament during the **Cold War (Nye Bevan**'s 'No Guns for the Huns!' was a popular cry) because they continued to see the Germans as old enemies rather than new allies. This tendency was apparent in Peter Sellers's satirical portrait in Stanley Kubrick's *Dr Strangelove* (1964), of a German scientist whose right arm keeps lifting involuntarily into a Nazi salute while discussing Cold War strategy with his new British and American bosses.

The United Kingdom's first application to join the Common Market may have been vetoed by the French in 1963, on the grounds that Britain was still more interested in the remnants of **Empire**. But it was Germanophobia, and not Francophobia or imperialism that fostered hostility to the nascent **European Union** and continued to do so for the rest of the century. Even Prime Minister Harold Macmillan could not exorcise the ghosts of his time as an officer in the trenches during the First World War. At a Downing Street dinner during the negotiations, he remarked to the Duke of Edinburgh: 'the Huns are always the same. When they are down they crawl under your feet, and when they are up they use their feet to stamp on your face.' The Duke, whose brother-in-law, Philip of Hesse, had been an SS colonel on Himmler's personal staff, said nothing.

During the 1960s, he and the Queen began to proclaim the monarchy's German origins in order to improve public attitudes and assist Britain's EEC application. The first speech of that nature was made by the Queen in 1958, and in 1965 she made the first visit by a British sovereign to Germany since George V attended the wedding of Princess Victoria of Prussia in 1913. Other reconciliatory initiatives included inviting German officials to the consecration of the new Coventry Cathedral in 1962 (the old one had been destroyed during the **Blitz**) and the opening of a new German Parliament building in Berlin in 1999, designed by the British **architect** Norman Foster. When the UK finally joined the European Community in 1973, the practice of town-twinning became common, and by 2000, 463 German towns were twinned with British ones. The Anglo-German Association was formed in 1951 with government assistance by a group of academics led by the philosopher Gilbert Murray.

Official initiatives did not prevent Germanophobia dominating British culture. In **children**'s comics, like *The Victor* (1961–92), and in the plethora of war films produced in the 1950s and 60s, the Germans were shown to be innately militaristic and authoritarian in contrast to good-humoured, phlegmatic British action heroes. Ironically, the schoolboy passion for war-gaming that reached a peak of popularity at this time was a German invention – *Kriegspiel* – introduced into the British army after the Franco-Prussian war of 1870. **Women** were not ideologically immune to Germanophobia. But its cultural forms were primarily male pursuits that reflected its origins in military conflict. In fact, without Germany, British masculinity would have had little with which to define itself during the century in which feminism launched its first successful assaults on male power.

Football was another important strand of the phenomenon, especially for the English after they finally became champions of the sport they had invented by beating West Germany in the World Cup final of 1966. They had already played West Germany in four 'friendlies' since the war, winning every match. But doing so in official international competition was treated as a re-run of the Second World War with less bloodshed but no less passion. Subsequent defeats by Germany in the World Cups of 1970 and 1990 merely exacerbated that tendency. Even after they eventually won another match, in 2000, the victory of 1966 had a totemic hold on the English, because it convinced them that Britain had not 'lost the peace'.

In fact, they had. The German 'economic miracle' of 1950 to 1990 won Britain's defeated enemy a higher standard of living. To the dismay of the British, Germany became the world's strongest economy after the United States and another defeated enemy, Japan, while at the same time maintaining good industrial relations *and* a better

welfare state than the British. Germany excelled in mechanical engineering. The point was drilled home by the success of the tool company whose name recalled the term used to insult Germans in the First World War: Bosch. But the ultimate humiliation was the extent to which the British car industry was taken over, culminating in the sale of Rolls-Royce to BMW in 1998.

The most visible sign of German affluence was the number of German tourists roaming the world. The Foreign Office noted the trend in the 1950s, and the hostility of British tourists towards them. By the 1970s, the Germans' legendary efficiency was being located in their supposed ability to annex poolside chairs before anyone else, so denying the British their rightful place in the sun. Aside from taking football matches and sunbeds too seriously, the British reaction to German economic supremacy was to ignore their own failings and instead mock the Germans for their efficiency. A composite Teutonic stereotype was constructed which explained German peacetime success through the traits they had displayed in war: humourlessness, arrogance, ruthlessness and blind obedience.

This caricature and the general British obsession with the Second World War was satirised in 1975 in 'The Germans' episode of the **sitcom** *Fawlty Towers*, in which John Cleese's rude and bigoted hotelier Basil Fawlty insults German guests at dinner. Although at first determined not to 'mention the war', he says, 'I'll just take your orders . . . orders . . . orders must be obeyed at all times!' Their requests are then translated as 'Egg mayonnaise, a prawn Goebbels and a Hermann Goering', before Fawlty starts goose-stepping around the dining room. The understandable reluctance to talk about the war by Germans who had lived through it was succeeded by a generation who, weighed down with collective guilt, felt the need to apologise for the sins of their fathers. This tendency was satirised in the *Harry Enfield and Chums* (1994) sketch character of Jürgen the German, a young tourist who apologises for 'what my country did to yours' at every opportunity. The embarrassed reaction to Jürgen illustrated a change in British attitudes.

At a dinner in 1990 to celebrate Anglo-German friendship, **Margaret Thatcher** told a former German ambassador, 'We need another forty years before we can forget what you have done.' In fact they only needed another ten. As the wartime generation began to die off and the conflict became a distant memory for those who had grown up in its shadow, Germanophobia gradually declined. The popularity of war comics and films fell sharply, as did fears that the EU was merely a cover for Teutonic domination. And when the German Chancellor's request to participate in the fiftieth anniversary celebrations of D-Day and VE Day was rebuffed by the British and

French governments, there was a widespread feeling (even among veterans) that these should be the last celebrations of their kind. The Germans were still seen as arch-rivals and the delight on 1 September 2001 when England beat their football team 5–1 in Munich was immense. But despite the attempts of the tabloid press to re-ignite wartime passions, it was a rivalry which now mirrored that between the British and the French: sometimes testy, but usually good-humoured.

■ Government

In 1900 the 3rd Marquess of Salisbury presided over a Cabinet of 19 members (9 of whom were peers). Including junior ministers, there were 60 men in Salisbury's government (to keep himself busy Salis- ▶ bury was his own Foreign Secretary). In 2000 **Tony Blair** had a 22-strong Cabinet. But the overall strength of the government was 106, leaving aside the 47 unpaid Parliamentary Private Secretaries drawn from the House of Commons. Over the century, there was a threefold increase in the number of MPs who could be appointed to a government office of some sort.

Some of the Cabinet positions in Salisbury's government have long disappeared. In 1900 the First Lord of the Admiralty sat alongside the Secretaries of State for India and the Colonies, and the Lord Chancellor of Ireland. Over the century other offices came and went. Prices and Consumer Protection was a Cabinet post for only five years (1974–9). Trade was combined with Industry in 1970, decoupled in 1974, and recombined in 1983. After twenty-two years of short-lived titular experimentation, in 1992 Michael Heseltine resumed the title of President of the Board of Trade, which had been sported in turn by ▶ Salisbury's son, then by **David Lloyd George** and **Winston Churchill** between 1905 and 1910.

The increase in the number of ministerial positions ensures that the government can (usually) rely on the support of a significant proportion of its MPs. But it also reflects the increasing scope of governmental functions. Lord Salisbury would have been perplexed by the advent of a Minister for Sport (1964), and as the owner of Hatfield House he would have been astonished when a Secretary of State for National Heritage infiltrated the Cabinet (1992), with the preservation of stately homes as part of the ministerial brief. As the government took on more and more responsibilities – including, apparently, the duty to protect its citizens from heartbreaking defeats for national sporting teams, and the imperative for British films to win Oscars – its revenues inevitably expanded. Lord Salisbury had £140 million to spend; Tony Blair's piggy bank contained more than £250 billion. Even ▶ allowing for **inflation** this was an extraordinary increase. In 1900 the

British were not immune from the tax collector – between them, the Inland Revenue and Customs and Excise employed 9,000 people at that time. But not until the First World War did the standard rate of income tax reach the shocking level of 30 per cent, and even this was only levied on the relatively affluent.

The two major wars of the twentieth century help to explain the growth of British government. A cynic or a **Thatcherite** ideologue might argue that once the state had begun to absorb a high proportion of the national income it found it impossible to kick the tax-raising habit, so after 1918 and 1945 its only problem was to find new things to do with the money. In fact, after both **wars** there was a strong demand that government should step in to alleviate some of the insecurities of life; and ministers were willing to satisfy the clamour, since a discontented (and undernourished) population is unlikely to meet the challenges of 'total war'. Even the social reforms of the **Liberal** government elected in 1906 were partly inspired by the unfitness of many working-class volunteers for the Boer War. Correspondingly, since modern wars can be entrusted to a relatively small number of highly-trained troops, the incentive to guarantee a decent standard of living for all has rapidly receded.

By 1974, the British government was heavily involved in economic management, even to the extent of restraining prices and incomes by law. It also owned a significant proportion of industrial concerns, including coal, gas and electricity, iron and steel, and the railways. All of these were vital elements of the national infrastructure, and their fortunes in private hands had been distinctly mixed. It could be argued, indeed, that far from pointing the way towards 'socialism', Britain's **nationalised** industries only existed to subsidise private investors in 'secondary' productive enterprises. After 1974 the **Labour Party** turned its attention to vehicle and aircraft production. From the socialist perspective this was no advance on the general post-war approach; since it was still reluctant to acquire any profitable concerns, the government was far from revolutionary. But to capitalists, it looked as if the state was trying to usurp the functions of an entrepreneur. Even the uncommitted wondered whether **civil servants** were the right people to decide between competing designs of motor car.

In hindsight, however, the ambitions of the 1974–9 Labour government look like the last hurrah of the British state. The 1973–4 oil price rise induced a crisis of confidence throughout the West, but its effects were felt most keenly in Britain, where it became fashionable to speak of government 'overload'. Rampant inflation, coupled with rising **unemployment**, brought the prevailing **Keynesian** system of economic management into discredit. The real point was not that the government was doing too much (though that was undoubtedly true); rather, faced with a new range of insoluble problems, the failing state was damned the more because people remembered its wartime success. Politicians like Edward Heath and Harold Wilson had rightly been impressed by the performance of the British state between 1939 and 1945. But in drawing on the same resources in the mid-1970s, they forgot that their country was no longer at war, and

▶ appeals to the 'Dunkirk spirit' were misplaced. In the **consumerist** era after 1945, the idea even of trivial and temporary material sacrifice was anathema to most people. Voters were not anxious for a radical alternative – certainly the skilled working classes courted by

▶ **Mrs Thatcher**'s **Conservatives** were not hankering after a government which would remove favourable subsidies like the mortgage tax allowance. But they were more receptive to ideas which suggested

▶ cuts in benefits for the **unemployed** – so long, that is, as they remained secure in their own jobs.

When Labour lost power in 1979 it seemed that the era of 'big

▶ government' was over for ever. Even under **'New' Labour** after 1997 state assets were sold off wherever possible; if civil service numbers could not be reduced very significantly, the ethos of the bureaucracy was eroded by 'hiving off' specific functions to semi-autonomous agencies. Even ministers who rejected Thatcherism in other respects could rejoice at this development, which allowed them to deny personal responsibility where previously they might have been forced into resignation. But the attempt to 'roll back the frontiers of the state' amounted to little more than rhetoric so far as it concerned the average citizen. In reality, the state continued to absorb a fairly constant proportion of the national income (around 40 per cent); the money was simply collected in different ways, most of which reduced the relative burden on the wealthy. And the British would have remained a highly regulated people whether or not they remained

▶ within **European** institutions (which served as a handy scapegoat for Thatcherite ministers and their 'New' Labour successors).

At the beginning of the twenty-first century 'government' had negative connotations for most British voters, even though they depended upon it to safeguard at least the possibility of civilised life. Despite numerous petty scandals in the 1990s the British state was less corrupt than almost any of its counterparts. The most serious threat to this state of affairs was a hyper-critical public opinion, abetted by Thatcherite ideas and whipped up by some irresponsible

▶ **national newspapers**. If the servants of the state lived down to general expectations in future years, its victims would have only themselves to blame.

■ Great Depression

The economic hardships of the 1930s were perhaps the most influential memories for British politicians between 1945 and 1979. MPs of all parties felt that **governments** could have done more to prevent mass ◀ **unemployment**, and they were determined not to allow a repeat. For ◀ some, this feeling persisted even after the election of the first **Thatcher** government, which acted on the view that attempts to curb ◀ unemployment had only served to make the problem worse.

In fact, some popular impressions of the 1930s are inaccurate. Often the slump in Britain is associated with the Wall Street Crash which began on 'Black Thursday', 24 October 1929. While America had been enjoying a boom until that rude awakening, unemployment in Britain was already such a problem that before the general election of that year **Lloyd George** published *We Can Conquer Unemployment*, strongly ◀ influenced by **J.M. Keynes**. Academic commentators had been ◀ studying the problem since the economy took a sharp downturn soon after the First World War. British unemployment was over 2 million in 1921; after that it never fell below 1 million until 1940, peaking in 1932 when, according to some estimates, it was around 3.5 million. Economic historians usually pinpoint Chancellor **Winston Churchill's** ◀ decision in 1925 to return sterling to its pre-war parity of $4.86 as a grievous self-inflicted wound. Increasing the value of the pound relative to the dollar by around 10 per cent overnight certainly did not help, since it made exports more expensive and also necessitated a policy of high interest rates which choked off investment. But a severe dose of the wrong medicine cannot account for the patient's underlying illness.

Also, the problem was localised. It mainly affected long-established, labour-intensive industries such as coal-mining, steel-making and shipbuilding. Other areas were barely affected. In 1933 **J.B. Priestley** ◀ published *English Journey*, contrasting the thriving suburban areas of the south with the grim northern towns dominated by a single employer, whose failure would mean the end of employment prospects for many (particularly older) workers. At the time that Priestley was writing about this **North–South divide**, 480,000 people ◀ had been out of work for a year or longer. And this figure applied only to *insured* workers; the true impact of long-term unemployment must have been somewhat greater, bringing with it a growing sense of apathy and alienation. The other common response was to migrate, either to the south of England or abroad. Between 1931 and 1938 the population of South Wales fell by more than 100,000.

Had television been more widely available, the vivid contrast between the older industrial areas and the prosperous south might

have provoked wider social discontent, or at least pricked a few consciences. For those in secure employment, the 1930s was a decade of rising living standards. Although average earnings fell slightly, low worldwide demand meant that prices declined much faster, despite the welcome decision to abandon the gold standard in 1931 (the currency lost a quarter of its value against the dollar in the first 12 months, though subsequently it rebounded). The availability of new consumer goods added to a 'feelgood factor'. Between 1930 and 1939 the number of motor vehicles on British roads doubled, to around 3
▶ million by the outbreak of war. There was a boom in seaside **holidays**
▶ and other leisure activities; by 1939 there were 5,000 **cinemas** in
▶ Britain. **Housing** of reasonable quality was also cheaper, as the stock increased under slum-clearance programmes and a relaxed interest-rate regime encouraged home ownership.

The worst of the slump was over by the end of 1933, as the terms of trade moved back in Britain's favour and borrowing became cheaper. But some of the most vivid memories of the decade come from later events. The march of 200 jobless men from Jarrow to London took place in October 1936, by which time national unemployment had fallen to about 1.6 million. Jarrow in the north-east was over-reliant on shipbuilding, and more than two-thirds of its insured workers were unemployed by 1934. Although Jarrow was a special case even in the depressed north-east, the famous march was only one of many; the protests were at their height in 1932, when demonstrations often led to violence and arrests.

The charge against the National Government (which was formed
▶ after **Labour** ministers failed to agree on economic measures in 1931) was that it took inadequate measures to combat the problem, despite being fully aware of viable alternatives. Keynes's ideas were well known, and in the US Roosevelt's New Deal provided concrete evidence that extensive public works could reduce unemployment. The British government did designate the worst-affected regions as Special Areas, but resources were pitifully small. At the same time, the Unemployment Act of 1934 was well intentioned, introducing national standards of assistance in place of the old patchwork system. But it was widely resented for its reliance on a 'means test' which accentuated the psychological effects of unemployment.

From one perspective the government certainly stood condemned. Lloyd George's post-war promise of 'Homes for Heroes' had not been fulfilled – to be more accurate, he should have said 'Homes for Heroes who live in the south-east of England'. When it came to the manufacture of munitions – or the organisational effort required to conscript the nation for slaughter – the government had shown itself to be highly competent during the First World War. It was inevitable that inactivity in the face of misery at home would be deeply resented. The only wonder was that when the supine state called on its people for fresh sacrifices in 1939, the men of Jarrow responded once again. The reckoning only came later. Despite his wartime leadership, during the 1945 general election campaign Churchill was interrupted by cries of 'What about jobs?' Harold Macmillan, who had been among the few **Conservative** MPs to point the way to recovery through public works ◄ in his books *Reconstruction* (1933) and *The Middle Way* (1938), was crushed in his north-eastern seat of Stockton. But he was not lost to the House of Commons; he quickly found a refuge in the leafy London suburb of Bromley.

G

■ Great Exhibitions

The British invented large, spectacular displays, designed to showcase the collective talent and might of a nation, when Queen Victoria's husband, Albert, organised the Great Exhibition at the Crystal Palace near London in 1851. Over 6 million people of all classes visited from around the country to see 100,000 exhibits in categories ranging from 'Machinery and Invention' to 'Plastic Arts'. As well as fostering a sense of pride and progress, the broader purpose of such events was to prove that **education** and entertainment, culture and commerce, were not ◄ antithetical but dependent upon each other. 'The public are benefited educationally, socially and morally by such displays, and the manufacturers derive a direct profit from them,' declared the organisers of the Great Exhibition held at South Kensington in 1862.

Over the next century and a half, the world's other superpowers – France, Germany, Japan, Russia and the United States – put on their own events. They sometimes had a progressive international result, like the 1925 Exposition Internationale des Arts Decoratifs et Industriels Modernes in Paris which launched the Art Deco style. Sometimes they were joint ventures, such as the Franco-British one of 1908, staged in the wake of the 1904 'Entente Cordiale', which was signed by the two countries in order to counter **German** power. Occasionally, they ◄ were even used by one country to celebrate another, as when an American Exhibition was staged in London in 1887 and again in 1914. The venue of the first of these, Earls Court, later hosted the Ideal Home Exhibition (1927–) an annual event that aimed to stimulate consumption by displaying the latest gadgets and interior designs for **home-** ◄ **owners**.

Most exhibitions, however, sought to aggrandise the host nation. One of the largest was the British Empire Exhibition, staged in the London **suburb** of Wembley in 1924 and 1925 with the aim of main- ◄ taining the public's enthusiasm for **Empire**. Costing £10 million, it ◄

attracted 27.25 million visitors to displays covering 220 acres. 'Walk up, Walk up and Hear the Lion Roar' was its motto. Famous defeats of native armies were re-enacted for the delight of spectators, while semi-naked black women demonstrated native handicrafts. The British lion roared loudest at the Exhibition's centrepiece, Wembley Stadium. Neo-classical in design and compared by the organisers to the Coliseum of ancient Rome, Wembley hosted the opening ceremony at which

▶ 100,000 armed servicemen and Boy **Scouts** took part in a mass torchlit parade, accompanied by 1,000 military bandsmen playing music by

▶ **Edward Elgar** especially composed for the occasion. The event was one of the inspirations behind Hitler's Nuremberg rallies and the last British Empire Exhibition did not take place until 1938, in Glasgow.

▶ Meanwhile, Wembley achieved longevity as the English national **foot-ball** stadium, from 1926, when it first hosted the FA Cup Final, until its demolition in the first years of the twenty-first century.

Concern at the way great exhibitions were being used for nationalist ends grew after the First World War and in 1928 a Convention was signed in Paris by 92 countries in which they pledged to make the events more international. One result was the 1939 World's Fair in New York, though it did not prevent the Second World War starting a few months later. The UK staged the first major post-war exhibition, the Festival of Britain, in 1951, breaking the 1928 Convention by making it 'a national display illustrating Britain's contribution to civilisation'. The Royal Society of Arts had conceived it as an international event to

▶ mark the centenary of Prince Albert's Great Exhibition. But the **Labour** government saw an opportunity to raise public morale and its own standing during a period of economic austerity and the outbreak of the Korean War in 1950. The Cabinet Minister Herbert Morrison (1888–1965) was appointed to oversee a project which he described as 'a tonic to the nation', at a cost of £11 million.

Unlike the British Empire Exhibition, the Festival of Britain made little mention of the nation's still considerable Empire, for fear of antagonising both colonial nationalist movements and the ostensibly

▶ anti-colonial United States, whose **Marshal Aid** was keeping the British economy afloat. The Festival also made no mention of the UK's Conti-nental links because the government, which had recently rejected the

▶ Schumann Plan, did not want the issue of **European Union** raised. Instead, the Festival celebrated British cultural, scientific and polit-ical achievements, from the work of Shakespeare to the discovery of penicillin and the development of parliamentary democracy. The centrepiece of the event was the South Bank Exhibition in London, which included daring architectural structures like the Dome of Discovery and the Skylon. Separate exhibitions were held in Scotland, Wales and Northern Ireland in order to demonstrate the plurality of the United Kingdom and to placate growing demands for **devolution** in Scotland and Wales. Travelling exhibitions toured England's provincial cities and 900 local authorities staged events in 2,000 towns and villages. The Festival was a success. The main events attracted 18 million visitors, of whom 8.5 million went to the South Bank while a further 7 million went to locally organised events. In total, this constituted around half the population.

For all the diversity on display, the Festival was the last of the great exhibitions to celebrate Britain as a homogeneous society. It was also seen as a high point of twentieth-century social democracy, lauding as it did Labour's idea that the 'nation' was synonymous with 'the people'. Yet the Festival was also the death knell of the era that gave birth to the **welfare state**. By displaying so many goods for home and garden, the exhibitions reminded the British what they were missing materially and what, as victors in **war**, they felt they deserved. A month after the Festival closed, they voted the **Conservatives** back into office and a period of unprecedented **consumerism** began. In 1973, a smaller event, 'Fanfare for Europe', was staged by the government of Edward Heath (b. 1916) to celebrate the UK's entry into the Common Market by displaying the cultural heritage which the British shared with their Continental partners. But it was not popular in a country that remained deeply sceptical about **European** integration.

Still, Fanfare for Europe was a success in comparison to the Millennium Exhibition, staged in 2000 and commonly known as 'the Dome', after its centrepiece designed by the Richard Rogers Partnership. The Dome was built at Greenwich, London, the Meridian of which had been universally adopted as the measurement for longitude in 1884, and as such it recalled a time when Britain was the commercial centre of the world. Prime Minister **Tony Blair** declared, 'This is our Dome, Britain's Dome. And believe me it will be the envy of the world.' The design consciously echoed that of the Dome of Discovery and the exhibition was organised in part by Herbert Morrison's grandson and **'New' Labour** guru, Peter Mandelson. But there the comparison between 1951 and 2000 ends.

Costing over £300 million of National Lottery money, the Dome was an expensive, poorly executed and unpopular project that came to stand as a symbol of the pragmatic vacuity of the Blair government. It made a noble attempt to celebrate the racial diversity of the UK, describing the British as a 'creative' and 'tolerant' people. But it failed to address the different cultures of England, Scotland, Wales and Northern Ireland. In addition, left/liberal critics saw corporate sponsorship of the Dome as typical of Blair's courting of the private sector. Conservatives objected to the fact that, while the millennium marked Jesus Christ's 2000th birthday, Christianity was merely one of many religions displayed in the 'Faith Zone'. Only 6.5 million people visited, a third of the number who had seen the Festival of Britain and only a quarter of those who had visited the British Empire Exhibition. In April 2000, the Dome's Director, Jennie Page, was sacked and replaced with 'P-Y' Gerbeau, a Frenchman who had previously managed Euro Disney.

All the great exhibitions attracted criticism about their financial cost and political intent. Furthermore, there had always been corporate involvement in them – often of a foreign nature that exposed the extent to which capitalism undermined national **sovereignty** long before 'globalisation' became a buzzword (America's Ford Motor Company had sponsored a display of its revolutionary car-assembly techniques at the British Empire Exhibition in 1924). However, when Elizabeth II claimed that the Dome was 'an inspiring vision of life in Britain in the new millennium' her words had a hollower ring than the bombast that accompanied earlier events of its kind. When the 1851 Exhibition closed, Elizabeth's great-great-grandmother, Queen Victoria, wrote in her diary, 'To think that this great and bright time is past, like a dream, all its success and triumph [gone], and that all the labour and anxiety it caused for nearly two years should now be only remembered as a "has been" seems incredible and melancholy.' Victoria's conclusion could stand as an epitaph for the age of relatively unfettered British power that such exhibitions symbolised and then, vainly, tried to reclaim.

■ Hardy, Thomas (1840–1928)

Born in the tiny village of Higher Bockhampton near Dorchester, Wilt-shire, Thomas Hardy was the son of a master stonemason and trained as an architect. Addicted to poetry but unable to find a market for his work, he turned to the novel, publishing his first book, *Desperate Reme-dies*, at the age of 31. Although his sales were never spectacular, by the mid-1870s his income and reputation were sufficiently secure to allow him to become a full-time 'man of letters'.

The circumstances of Hardy's birth were in fact a great boon. They enabled him to provide snapshots of a vanished rural life which moved nostalgic urban readers, and he could draw on his stock of memories to inject some humour into his tales. Yet a more sombre tone had always been present, and in *The Return of the Native* (1878) the beautiful landscape of 'Wessex' was presented as a hostile force. *Tess of the d'Urbervilles* (1891) presents a harrowing picture of the social impact of mechanisation in **agriculture**. Both *Tess* and *Jude the Obscure* (1895) ◄ were unrelentingly morbid, as Hardy broke his leading characters like butterflies on the wheel. Both books were attacked by critics, among whom was numbered Hardy's own eccentric wife Lavinia. The problem was not a falling-off of literary power, but the subject matter. Tess's melodramatic career provoked the subversive thought that the death penalty ought not to be automatic when a woman killed a man. In *Jude* Hardy moved on to address the topic of incest. The narrative voice of both books was that of an author who had moved beyond questioning the existence of God, and was now intent on proving that human life was a brief, cruel interlude between two indefinite periods of merciful oblivion.

Thanks largely to the influence of **Freud**, by the end of the twen- ◄ tieth century the attacks on sexual taboos which had caused outrage among the critics seemed rather tame. Hardy was never taken very seriously by **cultural elitists**, partly because of his relatively humble ◄ origins and his over-anxiety to compensate for the lack of a **university** ◄ education. But his enduring popularity rests on more than the enforcement of his books on schoolchildren. Sometimes the plot-lines were too contrived, and Hardy's pomposity makes some passages read like geological treatises. Even so, characters like Gabriel Oak, Eustacia Vye and Michael Henchard stuck in the memory. Both *Tess* and *Jude* were made into successful films (1979 and 1996 respectively), following *Far from the Madding Crowd* (1967), which had been Hardy's first major success when the novel was published in 1874. But it was probably in Hardy's own interests that after the storm aroused by *Jude* he decided to return to poetry. In fact, he had never stopped writing in a genre which he considered far superior to the novel, so he had a formidable stockpile to publish under such bitter-sweet titles as *Time's Laughingstocks* (1909).

Hardy's shorter poems often addressed his feelings about Lavinia, who had died in 1912. Having been at loggerheads with his wife for much of their life together, Hardy indulged himself in a passionate posthumous love affair and scarcely wrote a word about his second wife, Florence Dugdale, whom he married in 1914. Despite the lugubrious message of his work Hardy's remarkable gift for the melody of language made him a particular favourite of other poets. But his poetic ambitions stretched beyond his poignant lyrical pieces. In 1904, 1906 and 1908 he brought out his epic-drama of the Napoleonic Wars, *The Dynasts*, a brilliant but barely stageable presentation of his fatalistic philosophy. Hardy's universe was gloomy enough, but after the First World War he expressed regret that he had allowed himself to end the play on an up-beat note. By 1922 he had come to feel that Britain was threatened with 'a new Dark Age', because the 'dark madness' of the war had combined with existing philistine tendencies – 'the unabashed cultivation of selfishness in all classes, the plethoric growth of knowledge simultaneously with the stunting of wisdom'.

▶ Even before the carnage of 1914–18 Hardy had become an **Establishment** figure, as if to demonstrate that his only fault in writing *Tess* and *Jude* was to sound gloomy a few years before the mood became
▶ prevalent. He was given the Order of Merit in 1909. The **Liberal** Prime Minister H.H. Asquith even considered granting the childless Hardy a peerage during the 1911 constitutional crisis over the House of Lords, along with an assorted bag of worthies which included the philoso-
▶ pher **Bertrand Russell** and the **Scout** leader Baden-Powell. In fact, Hardy never courted honours; initially he turned down the offer of the OM. Although much of his poetry is intensely personal and his novels occasionally autobiographical, he was a shy man who burned his papers before his death and only authorised the publication of his posthumous memoir on the understanding that it should masquerade as the work of his second wife. His ashes were buried in Westminster Abbey, but his heart was interred with Lavinia in Dorset – unless the story is true that this organ was devoured by the surgeon's cat, in an ironic twist which might have provoked a grim smile from the author himself.

■ Holidays

'Passports,' declared the 1887 edition of the German guidebook Baedeker approvingly, 'are not necessary in England, except for the purpose of retrieving a letter from a [postal depot].' Until 1914, a

British citizen could travel abroad without one. But this freedom was an irrelevance to most Britons, since few of them could afford to travel unless they enlisted in one of the armed services or obtained work in one of the colonies.

Foreign package holidays, pioneered in 1841 by Thomas Cook (1808-92), a Baptist preacher from Derbyshire, enabled the middle classes to experience some of the delights of the Grand Tour that the ◄ aristocracy had enjoyed since the eighteenth century. The creation of ◄ Bank Holidays in 1871 provided statutory paid breaks for the first time. But until 1939 less than half the population left home for a single night in the year and those who did took domestic breaks. They paid for them through saving clubs run in **pubs**, factories and offices ◄ until parliament passed the 1938 Holidays with Pay Act which gave Britons the right to extended holidays for the first time. In 1931, only 1.5 million people received a paid holiday; by 1946 over 12 million did (about 80 per cent of the workforce).

H

Most British holidaymakers travelled by railway to seaside resorts, the most popular of which was Blackpool. From the 1870s to the 1970s, the seaside offered a winning combination of clean air and exercise, **drink**, sex, dancing and **gambling**, the latter provided by the amuse- ◄ ment arcades which scattered seafronts and piers. In 1936 a new attraction was added when Billy Butlin (1899-1980) opened his first holiday camp at Skegness. Butlin was born to English parents in South Africa; his mother belonged to an old circus family and when he came to Britain in 1921 he made a living as a fairground huckster in the West Country. His holiday camps – advertised as 'AN EDEN-ON-SEA, almost an earthly paradise' – offered a more regimented version of the traditional seaside holiday, with food, accommodation and entertain- ment all provided at one price in one complex. By 1947, he had five of them, which received half a million visitors every year. 'Redcoats – the men and women who organised camp entertainment like Knobbly Knees and Glamorous Granny contests – often went on to successful TV careers in light entertainment, among them such talents as Des O'Connor (b. 1932). Butlins was particularly successful at attracting married **women** and adolescents – women, because they could escape ◄ the drudgery of domestic chores, and adolescents because the camp's chalets provided a space to enjoy sex away from the prying eyes of family members and the legendary censoriousness of the seaside land- lady.

Those who fancied more of a challenge ventured into the British countryside. The cycling, rambling and camping crazes, which began in the 1900s, grew rapidly after the First World War. As elsewhere in Europe, such holidaymakers often had a romantic, nationalistic view of the countryside that was encouraged by guidebooks of the time, like H.V. Morton's *In Search of England* (1926). Morton argued that the land contained the essence of the British people; the Industrial Revolution had been a tragic interlude; and a country holiday was the best way to restore the virility of the nation, short of returning permanently to till the land, which few people were keen to do. Many landowners were reluctant to grant recreational public access to their property, and the refusal of governments to legislate effectively to make them do so provoked a 'mass trespass' at Kinder Scout in the Peak District in 1932. However, access to rural areas was improved by the rise of car ownership and by the creation, in 1949, of ten National Parks in England and Wales, and others, subsequently, in Scotland (1967) and Northern Ireland (1983).

The most popular pursuit was stately home visiting. Heavy post-war taxation forced more aristocrats to open their properties to the public to pay for their upkeep, and by 1960 over 300 were open, attracting 6 million visitors a year. Some augmented the aesthetic appeal of their
▶ homes and **gardens** with miniature railways, wild **animals** and the re-enactment of famous British battles. Lord Montagu of Beaulieu even
▶ staged a jazz festival, which laid the foundation of the rock **music festivals** that became such a feature of British life from the 1970s onwards. Less enterprising aristocrats left their houses to the nation in lieu of death duties. The property was usually then managed by the National Trust for England and Wales, a charity founded in 1895 by the middle-class philanthropist Octavia Hill to 'preserve places of historic interest and natural beauty for the benefit of the nation' (a National Trust for Scotland was formed in 1926). Like many of Britain's cultural institutions, by the 1920s the Trust had come to be governed by aristocrats and was criticised for helping to bale them out. However, between 1945 and 1965, it became one of the most popular British institutions. During that time, its membership rose from 8,000 to 157,000 and by the end of the century the figure had reached 2.2
▶ million, more than the active membership of the **Church of England**.

The public appetite for national heritage was supplied by a growing number of privately owned historic monuments. When parliament passed the Ancient Monuments Act in 1882, it deemed 68 worthy of preservation. A century later, the figure had risen to over 12,000, in addition to which there were 330,000 buildings and 5,000 conserva-
▶ tion sites. In 1985, the **Thatcher** government privatised the state's holdings, setting up English Heritage to run them. The increasingly commercial way in which such attractions were run led to criticism that the 'heritage industry', as it was now called, was pandering to conservative nostalgia by sanitising the past.

However, neither seaside resorts nor country houses could compete with foreign travel, which finally became affordable to the masses during the 1970s. In 1951 only 1.5 million foreign holidays were taken each year; in 1971 the figure had risen to 4.2 million while the number of passports issued each year rose from 470,000 to just over a million. By 1981, 13.13 million foreign holidays were taken and by 1997 the figure had risen to 29.14 million. The most popular destination was Spain, followed by France, Greece and Italy. Most people went on package holidays, which became steadily cheaper as a rash of new airlines and travel agents competed for customers. Older people, who were at first suspicious and reluctant to leave Britain's shores, were catered for by Saga Holidays, set up in 1970 by Sidney de Haan (1919–2002), a Jewish Cockney entrepreneur and veteran of Dunkirk. ◄

The development of safe, efficient jet travel in the 1950s was a catalyst in expanding a travel industry which by the 1980s was worth twice as much as the arms trade to the global economy. Another factor was the invention of the credit card, which made it easier to 'take' money abroad as well as encouraging working people to increase their debt burden. Ironically, it was invented in America, the nation that had the lowest proportion of passport holders in the world. The first was the American Express card, launched by the Bank of America in 1958, which sixty years earlier had developed travellers' cheques. By 2001, 62 per cent of the UK population were in possession of a credit card.

Despite early hopes that foreign travel would help to 'civilise' the working class, most holidaymakers simply replicated the fairground fun of the traditional British seaside resort. They swapped windbreaks for suntan lotion but usually disdained the **language** and culture of ◄ the places they visited, although the xenophobia of the British tourist was mostly directly towards **German** ones whom they encountered ◄ wherever they went. 'Travel narrows the mind,' concluded the Catholic moralist Malcolm Muggeridge (1903–1990) in 1966, though he also believed that 'tourism today is a more dynamic force than revolution, swaying as it does crowns and thrones; Thomas Cook and American Express, not the "Internationale" unite the human race'.

Muggeridge exaggerated on both counts. Tourism did not change political systems, something highlighted by the fact that the favourite sunspot of British holidaymakers was Europe's last surviving fascist dictatorship. But nor did travel narrow the mind. Gradually, recreational engagement with foreign cultures had an impact on British tastes and customs, notably in the liking for Continental **food** and ◄ drink. The American cult of sunbathing, popularised in Europe during the 1930s by the French **fashion** designer, Coco Chanel, led to an ◄ increase in skin cancer rates. But it also encouraged the British to be less puritanically self-conscious of their bodies; and it highlighted a less pathological attitude to the whiteness of Caucasian skin that perhaps reflected their more relaxed view of racial differences within

Britain's multi-cultural society. Foreign travel had a particularly liberating effect on women because female sexual promiscuity was stigmatised less when they were abroad. Their liaisons with Continental men prompted a moral panic about the threat from supposedly more
▶ potent Mediterranean men, a panic that echoed older fears of **miscegenation** between British women and the coloured subjects of the
▶ **Empire**. Meanwhile, some men indulged in a less savoury form of sex tourism, particularly in the fleshpots of South-East Asia, although prostitution had always been a feature of 'respectable' travel.

A second wave of foreign tourism began in the late 1980s, when the British 'Rave scene' was exported to Mediterranean islands like Ibiza and Aya Napa by nightclub promoters and DJs. The consumption of
▶ recreational **drugs** on such holidays, to the accompaniment of what became known as the 'Balearic Beat', together with youth's perennial appetite for casual sex, led to further condemnation of the British holidaymaker – a view that would have been shared by Thomas Cook had he lived to see what his invention spawned. The middle classes tried to escape the hordes by going to ever more remote and exotic places to seek out picturesquely 'authentic' cultures, economically impoverished by global capitalism, yet relatively untouched by its homogenising forces compared to more developed countries.

However, the storming of the bourgeois summer veranda could not be repulsed. An irreversible revolution in British holidaymaking had taken place that on the whole amplified personal freedom. 'My foreign policy,' declared the Labour Foreign Secretary Ernest Bevin in 1951, 'is to be able to take a ticket at Victoria Station and go wherever I damn well please.' For all the restrictions imposed on the individual by the expanding remit of the British state, by the twenty-first century Bevin's wish had come true for all but the poorest Britons.

■ Homosexuality

A sexual orientation less tolerated in Britain than on the Continent until the twenty-first century. Between 1533 and 1861, buggery was punishable by death, although the last execution for it took place in 1836. It was re-criminalised in 1885 by the Criminal Law Amendment Act, with punishment restricted to a custodial sentence of five years' hard labour. The Act originally made no reference to homosexuality but was designed to prevent anal sex between man and wife, amid fears that Britain's racial stock was declining as a result of 'unnatural' practices. Henry Labouchere MP moved a further amendment extending the law to homosexuals and it was this that led to the 'martyrdom' of Oscar Wilde in 1895. Wilde's high-profile trial and subsequent imprisonment briefly made homosexuality a talking point in the salons of London, and in 1898 the Criminal Vagrancy Act outlawed homosexual importuning. But by the turn of the century it was once more a practice that the British pretended did not exist. In 1921, an attempt was made in parliament to proscribe lesbianism, but it failed and lesbians like the writer Radclyffe Hall (1880–1943) escaped the fate that befell so many of their male counterparts – although her gay classic, *The Well of Loneliness* (1928) was banned until 1949.

A more sympathetic attitude to homosexuality emerged in the Edwardian era with the advent of professional psychiatry. But the belief that men and women could be cured of their condition was based on the traditional assumption that they were dysfunctional in the first place. The absurdity of the 'cure' was described by E.M. Forster in his novel *Maurice* (written in 1917 but not published, at his request, until after his death in 1970). Moreover, the **police** still investigated ◄ and regularly prosecuted men for homosexual acts. Notable defendants included the actor John Gielgud, the **music festival** impresario ◄ Lord Montagu of Beaulieu and the Tory MP Ian Harvey, who was forced to end a promising career at Westminster after an encounter with a guardsman in St James's Park in 1950. Prominent members of the **Establishment** like Noël Coward (1899–1973) and his wartime lover ◄ the Duke of Kent had their activities covered up. Less well-connected people not only had to contend with prison; they also had to run the gauntlet of 'queer-bashing' by street gangs of homophobic men, a trend captured without self-pity in Quentin Crisp's memoirs *The Naked Civil Servant* (1978).

After the Second World War, homosexuality continued to be blamed for a perceived decline in Britain's fortunes. It was even argued that homosexuals were prone to treason because their primary allegiance was to those who shared their proclivities and because they wanted to take revenge on a society which marginalised them. There was no substance to these claims, although it may be true that the homosexual's enforced tendency to live a secretive life was good preparation for a career as a double agent. Sir Roger Casement's death sentence for involvement in the 1916 **Easter Rising** was secured partly thanks to ◄ government revelations that he was homosexual. In 1955, the Foreign Office officials Guy Burgess and Donald Maclean, who had defected to the Soviet Union four years earlier, were simultaneously exposed as Communist spies and homosexuals. The fact that their co-conspirator, Kim Philby, who defected in 1961, was a married hetersosexual, did not prevent the link between perversion and subversion gaining ground in the public mind, especially since the next agent to defect, John Vassall in 1962, was homosexual. It was ironic that national security could be endangered because of the bigotry of the man on the street.

In 1957 a committee chaired by Sir John Wolfenden recommended that homosexual acts between consenting adults over 21 should be legalised. Wolfenden, a stern Nonconformist whose son was homosexual, had no more liking for sodomy than did Henry Labouchere. He made his recommendation on the expedient grounds that the law was encouraging the organised blackmail of men terrified of prosecution and of the social leprosy that exposure brought with it. This fact was brought to the public's attention again in the film *Victim* (1961), starring Dirk Bogarde – the first in British cinema to deal openly and sympathetically with the subject of homosexuality. The Wolfenden Report was condemned by the press as 'a pansie's charter'. After several failed attempts to legislate, Leo Abse's 1967 Private Member's Bill finally legalised homosexual acts in England and Wales. However, in Scotland and Northern Ireland the churches led fierce public opposition to the Bill and Abse was forced by the Labour government to amend it. As a consequence, the Act did not apply to Scotland until 1980 and Northern Ireland until 1982.

Throughout the UK, homophobia was rife until the 1990s. The British had a sneaking fascination, even fondness, for homosexual 'characters', a fact evidenced by their love of camp humour. Kenneth Williams made his name as the king of camp with the character of 'Sandy' in the BBC radio comedy series *Round the Horne* (1954–60), in which he spoke 'palare', a coded patois current in homosexual circles at the time. Williams transposed his act to the Carry On films and then on to TV, where he was followed by a succession of similar entertainers, notably the Lancashire comedian Larry Grayson (1923–95), whose catchphrase was 'What a gay day!' Grayson was the first celebrity to use the term 'gay' in its modern context and, largely thanks to him, it was adopted by the public. However, homosexual practice was less readily accepted and the term 'gay' – coined by political activists in the 1960s – never entirely replaced offensive euphemisms like 'poof', 'homo' and 'shirtlifter'. Ultimately, camp comedy made homosexuality palatable by de-sexing it and by reinforcing the popular view that gay men were naturally effeminate, just as gay women were seen to be naturally butch. When buggery was simulated on stage at the National Theatre in Peter Shaffer's play *The Romans in Britain* (1980) a national outcry followed, with calls for censorship of the theatre (abolished in 1968) to be restored.

Like feminism, homosexuality became associated with left-wing militancy in the 1970s – an impression which groups like Peter Tatchell's 'Outrage' did not dispel when they cruelly 'outed' closet homosexuals such as Mervyn Stockwood, the Bishop of Southwark. In 1986, John Giffard's amendment – popularly known as 'Section 28' – passed into law, preventing schools from organising pastoral discussions of sexuality for adolescents. More seriously, the AIDS epidemic that came to notice in 1985 led to a new wave of homophobia. Openly gay people were shunned as potential carriers of the disease, a practice encouraged by conservative moralists who claimed that AIDS was God's judgement on sodomy. In 1998, the **Blair** government's attempt ◄ to equalise the gay age of consent at 16 was scuppered by **Conservative** ◄ peers in the House of Lords. Homosexuality was still widely equated with pederasty, transsexuality and transvestism. Lesbianism was more accepted, but only on salacious grounds by heterosexual men who were aroused by the sight of women having sex with each other, a taste amply supplied by the **pornography** industry. ◄

However, by the end of the century, gay people were no longer seen as a threat to national security or to the British way of life as a whole. Gay characters were a regular feature of TV **soap operas** like *EastEnders* ◄ and *Brookside*, while pop stars like George Michael and Will Young were able to come out without their record sales falling. And although revelations about Michael Portillo's homosexual past helped to scupper his bid for the leadership of the Conservative Party in 2001, four years earlier Chris Smith became the first openly gay politician to obtain a senior ministerial post. In 1998, a survey showed that for the first time a majority of the population did not believe homosexuality to be immoral nor that it should prevent a person from holding public office. The journey from hanging, imprisonment, psychiatric treatment and ostracism through to acceptance was a long and painful one. But British homosexuals made it with courage, dignity and, eventually, pride.

■ Housing; home ownership

In the second half of the nineteenth century there was a belated recognition that the Industrial Revolution in Britain had produced desperate social problems. As usual, it took a little longer for policymakers to realise that something could, and should, be done about them. Many of the evils could be traced to a single source. The unplanned, unregulated building of houses, particularly in industrial areas, had created vast slums. The most obvious effect of poor sanitation and chronic overcrowding was the promotion of contagious disease; but they also threatened to nullify other efforts to improve the condition of the working **class**, notably through education. At first ◄ **government** action took the form of 'permissive' legislation, giving ◄ local authorities the power to improve houses and to clear the slums. After the First World War there was a shift towards compulsion. The 1919 Housing Act required local authorities to undertake surveys of their housing stock, and provided government subsidies for remedial action. At the same time the state introduced restrictions on the rents charged by private landlords. But the promise of 'homes fit for heroes' was unfulfilled, as economic depression succeeded the immediate post-war boom.

▶ Between the **wars** housing became one of the key issues of contention between the political parties. If nothing else, the wartime promises had raised expectations; possibly the curious British obsession with home ownership should be dated from that time. Until the late nineteenth century a mortgage had usually been a way for a rich family to raise money on the security of its existing property. Now, instead of paying rent to a landlord, the upwardly mobile joined the 'property owning democracy' by means of a loan from a building society. Although there were clear differences of emphasis – the
▶ **Conservatives** favoured building by the private sector, while **Labour**
▶ preferred to work through **local government** – in general policy was dictated by a pragmatic assessment of economic conditions. House-building was subsidised whenever help was required, regardless of the party in power, and there was general agreement that slum clearance, at least, should be assisted out of public funds.

In total, between the wars nearly 4 million new houses were built in England and Wales. More than half of these were provided by the private sector, without subsidy (greatly assisted by the low interest rates which prevailed for most of the period, and by the growth of building societies). But the local authorities built over a million homes, so that by 1939 council housing accounted for 10 per cent of the total stock. At the same time it was claimed that the housing shortage was over; on some estimates, indeed, there were more than half a million more homes than families. However, the housing boom had mainly benefited families above the poverty line. As the upwardly mobile moved into better houses, the poor could occupy the properties which they had left behind. So there was a general improvement reinforcing inequality, rather than a genuine 'levelling-up' of conditions; and as the better-off moved out to the suburbs, conditions in the towns deteriorated. Many slum areas remained, in London itself but also in the old industrial towns of Scotland and the north of England. The squalid conditions uncovered by a series of investigators,
▶ including **George Orwell** whose *Road to Wigan Pier* (1937) chronicled in lavish detail the misery arising from poor housing, proved that the overall statistics left no room for complacency.

During the Second World War the housing stock was reduced by around 500,000, as a result of enemy action. Many of the remaining homes were unsatisfactory; about two-thirds lacked hot water, and a 1947 survey of rural areas found that more than half of houses had no separate bathroom. Before the 1945 general election Labour promised 'five million homes in quick time', to make up the deficiencies and to

248

provide better housing for the poor. It was a popular pledge; nearly two-thirds of voters named housing as the most pressing issue facing a post-war government. But an initial shortage of building materials, followed by the demands of economic 'austerity', meant that the number of completions during six years of Labour government was only around 1.2 million. Around 160,000 of these were 'prefabricated' houses, which were supposed to be temporary. Yet many hundreds still existed fifty years later.

The great majority of these new houses were built by local government, and nearly a fifth of families now lived in council accommodation. The proportion of owner-occupiers continued to rise; no more than 10 per cent before the First World War, it had increased threefold by 1950. In 1951 the Conservatives returned to office, helped by a pledge of 300,000 new houses a year forced on the leadership by its party conference. The target was met in 1953, thanks again largely to building by local authorities. Over half the population still rented privately. But this sector had begun a marked decline, in the face of additional rent controls. The controversial Rent Act (1957) introduced by the Conservatives did little or nothing to arrest this trend; its most notable product was the scandal of 'Rachmanism' in the early 1960s, when some unscrupulous landlords took full advantage of the new right to increase the rent on a change of tenancy. In 1965 Labour legislated to increase security of tenure, and allowed local councils to impose a 'fair rent' on private landlords. Before then, the Conservatives had hit on a more promising way of boosting the private sector, though this time the electoral bonus took longer to collect. In 1963 the Schedule 'A' tax on home-ownership was scrapped, but the mortgage interest allowance which had previously been set against liabilities was allowed to continue. Overnight, the penalty on house-buyers had been turned into a bribe.

In 1968 new house building reached a post-war peak, at 426,000 – almost equally divided between the public and the private sector. But from the mid-1960s there was a new concern with the homeless, reflected by the foundation of the charities Shelter (1966) and Crisis at Christmas (1967, later Crisis). Such glaring evidence of **poverty** in ◄ the midst of plenty was impossible to ignore, particularly when so many houses were left unoccupied (in 1977 almost 750,000 properties were vacant). Another development before the end of the decade was the retreat from high-rise accommodation, after a gas explosion at Ronan Point in the East End of London. These flats had been built with special government subsidies, since they promised to provide relatively cheap accommodation in spite of high land values. But in too many cases they only offered squalor in the sky.

The Conservatives made Labour's indifferent record on housing a key campaign issue at the 1970 general election. They were particularly interested in the development of voluntary housing associations as alternative landlords to the councils, and they also promised to encourage council house sales. Back in the 1950s Anthony Eden had envisaged Britain as a 'property-owning democracy'; under Edward Heath the party argued that the policy would not only help to realise this vision, but the elderly and the disabled could also benefit if councils built special accommodation for them with the receipts from sales. While the Heath government made only limited progress, the party continued to believe that housing was a vote-winning issue. In

▶ October 1974 **Margaret Thatcher** attracted attention by (reluctantly) suggesting a guarantee of low mortgage interest rates.

Britain's economic problems after the mid-1970s ensured a slower rate of house-building. By 1982 new completions had fallen below 200,000 per year for the first time since 1947. By that time, though, the new Conservative government had begun to benefit from the party's ability to forget its ideological dislike of subsidies when it came to (private) housing. Under the 1980 Housing Act council tenants who had occupied their houses for three years or more were given the right to buy at a generous discount. The legislation promised to create a reliable constituency of support for the Tories. Actually, Conservatives had frequently complained in the past that council house tenants were being subsidised even if they were comfortably off. These affluent tenants were most likely to benefit from the right to buy; and the fact that the properties were grossly undervalued could be seen as a parting gift for people who had already done very well out of the public sector.

In 1982 more than 200,000 council houses were sold. By 1985 the figure had more than halved, for understandable reasons. The most prosperous tenants had pounced on the bargains at the first opportunity, so continuing council tenancy now really was a reasonable indication of poverty. But there was another surge of sales at the end of the decade, as Britain embarked on an unprecedented housing boom. This was fuelled by several factors, not least of which was family break-up (the average household contained 2.9 people in 1971, but only 2.3 in the year 2000). Another powerful incentive to buy was the increased subsidisation of mortgage holders at the taxpayer's expense. The ceiling for mortgage interest tax relief had been raised from £25,000 to £30,000 in 1983. In tandem with other cuts in direct taxation, this was a powerful stimulus. In 1984 customers took out more than 1 million mortgages from building societies for the first time ever – an increase of more than 300,000 in only six years. In 1969 the average price of an English house was £4,674; in 1983 it was £28,500.

By 1990 housing tax relief was costing around £8 billion per year. In his 1988 budget the Chancellor Nigel Lawson took action to halt the boom, restricting the relief to only one person per household. Unfortunately, this had to be phased in over several months; in the interim hesitant buyers took the plunge. During that year prices rose by an average of around 30 per cent. Then, inevitably, the new restrictions pricked the bubble. Less than twelve months later some prices were falling by £2,000 per month, and many of those who had mistimed their scramble on to the property ladder found that their homes were now worth less than the value of their mortgages. This phenomenon – 'negative equity' – brought an abrupt end to the long profitable run for the Conservatives in housing policy. Ideally, the unfortunate owners could have sat out the storm, waiting for a revival in the market. But when the general economic boom turned into a recession, rising unemployment meant that many could not afford to keep up ◄ their monthly payments. Some were forced to sell at a loss; for others the dream of property ownership ended with their houses repossessed by building societies which had helped to bring about the disaster through their indiscriminate lending.

Even through the recession new house building continued at a respectable rate. But restrictions on council spending meant that, for example, in 1992 only 17,000 out of nearly 150,000 new houses were built by the public sector. Council tenancy continued to decline, too, falling to around 14 per cent by the end of the century. There were still bargains to be found. In 2001 an enterprising firm bought Blackburn's entire council stock of 10,000 houses for an average of £3,600 each. There was a minor revival in private tenancies, but by this time more than two-thirds of England's housing was occupied by its owners (although the figure was below 50 per cent in Scotland; in Germany it was less than 40 per cent).

Given the poor state of Britain's housing back in 1900, the twentieth century saw remarkable improvements for almost everyone. The general pattern, of increasing state intervention up to 1950 followed by an accelerating retreat, might be taken by some as ample proof that the free market always does these things best. But that would be highly misleading. Ironically, the state had always acted as an enabler for the private sector; either indirectly through subsidies, or directly as slum-clearer, builder and landlord, it had erased the most scandalous blots on the landscape and helped to bring private ownership within the reach of most people.

Towards the end of the century repeated reductions in interest rates sparked off another boom, amid signs that many buyers were regarding the property market as a one-way ticket to quick prosperity rather than an investment for life. By 2002 there were clear signs that the operations of the market would once again bring undesirable

H

results. The average price of a house soared to almost £115,000 in the autumn of 2002. At the time, the average annual wage was less than £24,000.

In part, the spiralling costs were being fuelled by loneliness. By 2002 the proportion of single-occupied houses was just over 30 per cent; it had been only 17 per cent in 1971. It was estimated that by 2010 40 per cent of houses would be occupied by single people. First-time buyers were finding the first step on the ladder increasingly difficult; and the strains arising from the financial burdens were likely to increase the incidence of broken relationships, thus fuelling demand in the most miserable of circumstances. Even more seriously, housing was so expensive in certain areas (notably the south-east) that the public services were unable to match recruitment targets. The market itself offered no short-term solutions, and adequate state subsidies would be ruinously expensive. The problem was exacerbated by restrictions on new building in the most desirable 'green belt' areas. Meanwhile, in a stark illustration of the **North–South divide**, it was difficult even to give houses away in towns like Salford. Roads of derelict and deserted buildings, long abandoned by anyone who could afford to leave, offered adventure playgrounds for vandals – and for political groups opposed to **immigration**, since poor housing exacerbated interracial tensions in the deprived urban areas. Although governments were at last beginning to pay some attention to the problem of empty houses, around 700,000 UK properties were still vacant in 2002. Only 1,200 Britons slept on the streets, for various reasons, but it was estimated that almost 1.5 million households occupied properties which were unfit for habitation. Home ownership remained a dream for most people; but it looked set to provide policy-makers with plenty of nightmares in the years ahead.

■ Immigration and race relations

As I went to the steamer, I asked myself with anxiety, 'Under which flag does she sail, – Norwegian, German, English?' Then I saw floating above the stern the Union Jack, – the flag under which so many refugees, Russian, Italian, French, Hungarian and of all nations, have found an asylum. I greeted that flag from the depth of my heart.

Prince Peter Kropotkin, 1876

At the beginning of the twenty-first century immigration was a major political issue in Britain, as it had been since the early 1960s. Popular feeling was whipped up by the tabloid press at the prospect of hordes of asylum seekers flooding an already overcrowded country. The public was encouraged to assume that all refugees were 'bogus', merely seeking a better life at the expense of the over-generous British taxpayer. Applicants with important skills were denied the right to work, while they waited for their claims to be processed. Politicians made no attempt to explain that this state of affairs had come about, at least in part, because the more rational routes to immigration were blocked by laws which had been progressively tightened over the previous four decades.

The situation would have made more sense had British politicians not been so loud in denouncing human rights abuses across the world, when it suited them to pick quarrels with regimes in the Balkans, Afghanistan and Iraq. If any asylum seekers really were pulled in to Britain rather than other EU states by the hope of a decent ◄ future, rather than pushed out from their homes by dread of torture, it was because of the worldwide dominance of the English language – something which in other contexts was turned to profit by British businessmen, and exploited as an excuse for belligerent condescension by tourists. Research, as opposed to media mischief-making, suggested that immigrants were also attracted by positive images of Britain created by its **football** teams, pop stars and politicians like ◄ **Margaret Thatcher** (who, ironically, had played on fear of foreigners ◄ more than anyone since **Enoch Powell**). ◄

If Britain really was overcrowded, the problem would have been a good deal worse without the movement of peoples. Between 1900 and 1984 the United Kingdom suffered a net loss of 2.4 million people. This figure was rarely publicised in the early stages of the debate; the overall statistics were only bandied about when the trend was reversed after the mid-1980s. When it was mentioned at all, outward migration was referred to as a 'brain drain', implying that only the most intelligent and dynamic Britons went abroad. The same logic should have made politicians receive those who wanted to settle in Britain as precious economic assets. They did not, because the argument was about skin colour and culture, not skills or overcrowding.

Before the First World War most immigrants came from Ireland or from Eastern Europe. The latter group were undoubtedly refugees
▶ from persecution; the majority were **Jews**, fleeing anti-semitic violence. For most of them Britain proved to be a safer haven, although the concentration of many Jewish immigrants in the East End of London provided an easy target for rabble-rousers. A Royal Commission reported in 1903 that the immigrants quickly adapted to British society, but an Aliens Act was passed two years later to appease racist sentiment. For the first time since 1826 restrictions were imposed, and the real motivation for the Bill proved to be an ominous precedent. One provision allowed the exclusion of any immigrants without obvious means of support. A further Aliens Act was passed in 1919,
▶ reflecting anti-**German** hysteria.

During the 1930s, more than 50,000 Jewish refugees fled to Britain from Central Europe. Despite the unequivocal evidence of persecution, their arrival helped to stir more anti-semitism and attracted
▶ numerous recruits to **Oswald Mosley**'s British Union of Fascists. Immediately after the war around 120,000 Poles who had fought the Nazis were resettled in Britain. This compassionate decision also aroused resentment in some quarters.

But post-war immigration in Britain has been dominated by arrivals from the 'New Commonwealth' – notably India, Pakistan and the West Indies. Under the 1948 British Nationality Act immigration from these areas was unrestricted. The legislation met little resistance, because it appealed to left-wing ideas about equal citizenship throughout the emerging Commonwealth, while reassuring the right
▶ that the old ties of **Empire** would be maintained. As the economy recovered from wartime dislocation, shortage of labour – particularly unskilled – meant that migration to Britain was encouraged. The increase in the black populaton was dramatic; in 1951, for example, only 17,500 British residents had been born in the West Indies, but by 1971 the figure was 548,000. In 1961 alone more than 60,000 West Indians moved to the UK. As in the case of Jewish immigrants, the newcomers tended to congregate in specific areas. By the mid-1980s, for example, more than half of the West Indian-born immigrants lived in Greater London. For their part, many Asians settled in towns like Oldham and Bradford, where the declining textile industries were pulling in cheap labour before throwing it back out on to the dole queues.

Governments began to consider legislation to reduce immigration from the New Commonwealth in the mid-1950s. While the over-generous 1948 Act had been passed at a time of optimism about

Britain's continuing world role, it was now widely felt that the British Empire had been produced by something worse than a fit of absent-mindedness. In 1958 racial tensions came to a head, with serious riots in Notting Hill and Nottingham. The response was typical of the British attitude to race. Although a majority of respondents to a Gallup poll correctly blamed the riots on white troublemakers, they still overwhelmingly favoured controls on future immigration. Such attitudes were reflected in what became a common position voiced by individual politicians – that while the speaker was not himself a racist, unfortunately most of his constituents were prejudiced, so 'coloured' immigration should be halted immediately, for the good of the immigrants themselves. Unfortunately, racism was so prevalent by the mid-1960s that it was impossible to dismiss such opinions out of hand as the products of simple hypocrisy. The problem was so serious that the central figure in the 1960s television comedy *Till Death us do Part* was regarded as a plain-speaking man on racial issues, even though his creator was trying to satirise ignorant bigotry.

Whether or not the majority of MPs were racist, legislation was rushed through in 1962 to satisfy the clamour for restrictions. The Commonwealth Immigrants Act restricted entry by introducing a voucher system for unskilled workers. Further legislation was passed by Harold Wilson's **Labour** government, in 1965. Gallup reported that nine out of ten Britons approved of the measure, but as a sop to residual liberal opinion the government also enacted the first (tooth-less) race relations legislation. A more punitive Bill was passed in 1968, but only after the government had introduced further immigration restrictions in response to the expulsion of Asians from Kenya. Not to be outdone, the Heath government passed the 1971 Immigration Act, which guaranteed entry only to people with at least one UK-born grandparent. To the credit of ministers, after the psychopathic Ugandan dictator Idi Amin forced out 50,000 Asian residents more than half were allowed to settle in Britain. But by now it was difficult for anyone from the New Commonwealth to gain entry unless they had close relatives already living in the country; and even this loop-hole was attacked by further legislation of 1983 and 1988. Particular attention was paid to those who hoped to embark on 'arranged marriages' with UK residents, but legislation to outlaw this practice seemed likely to fall foul of the European Court of Human Rights.

After 1980, immigration from the New Commonwealth never exceeded 30,000 per year. Generally, this represented less than half the total of new entrants, although the relative extent of white immigra-tion never registered in the public debate. In 1991 around 7 per cent of UK residents had been born outside the country, and the overall tally of black and Asian Britons was estimated at 3.5 million. Those who hoped to stimulate prejudice against black people could still emphasise differential birthrates. But this was based on an ironic premise: namely that cultural influences in Britain were so weak that black children born in the country would retain an 'alien' identity. Actually, they were most likely to act and think like Americans; their youthful white counterparts certainly did.

Worries about the 'assimilation' of black Britons were reinforced by the rioting which affected many urban areas in 1981. Enoch Powell, whose 1968 'Rivers of Blood' speech prophesied anarchy on the streets, was encouraged by this evidence to imagine that his visions were about to come true. Actually, although race was undoubtedly a factor in many incidents the causes of the rioting were far more complicated; racial tension could hardly explain the outbreak in Cirencester, for example. Insensitive policing was blamed for further disorder in the mid-1980s, in Birmingham and Tottenham. While some of the violence was inexcusable under any circumstances, many black people had reason to feel that they were far more likely to attract the atten-
▶ tion of the **police** than whites, whether or not they had done anything illegal.

By the end of the twentieth century racial tensions were still high in some areas of the country, particularly in the north-west of England
▶ where feelings were accentuated by **poverty** and poor **housing** among both blacks and whites. The murder of the black teenager Stephen Lawrence in 1993 finally gave publicity and credence to the perception among the black community that racially-motivated crime was only tackled with sufficient diligence by the police when the victim was white. Black sportsmen were cheered by their own supporters – so
▶ long as they performed well – and the cast of many popular **soap operas** began to reflect the true composition of British society. More than a third of Britain's GPs were non-whites. Black people were seri-
▶ ously under-represented in most **Establishment** occupations, and in
▶ **parliament**. But these were always bound to be the last bastions of prejudice to fall. Meanwhile, politicians who seemed prepared to 'play the race card' were still sure to win a positive response in some quarters, but their opportunism was also likely to cause widespread offence.

Even so, at the beginning of the twenty-first century it was still over-optimistic to describe Britain as a healthy 'multi-racial' society. Decades of discrimination had been followed by the advent of 'political correctness', which was (almost) as mistaken. The feeling – even shared by some black community leaders – that the police were becoming reluctant to stop and search suspects from the ethnic minorities threatened to re-ignite tensions at a time when statistics
▶ showed that the perpetrators of street **crime** were predominantly

black. But opinion polls indicated a gradual decline in the proportion of people ready to admit to feelings of racial prejudice, down to little more than a quarter by 2002. The fact that the clear majority of these were old or poorly educated was no surprise, and it offered hope for the future. The country was moving on, and only its tabloid press and politicians could hold it back.

■ Inflation

Inflation can be regarded as a sustained increase in prices, or a decline in the purchasing power of a given sum of money. It can be seen as the product either of a rise in consumer demand relative to supply, an increase in costs independently of demand, or indeed as a mixture of all these things and more. Instead of being a first step to resolving their other differences, an agreement on the definition of inflation would in itself settle most arguments among economists; the various definitions point to an array of causes, and a host of different remedies.

For most people in Britain, the key measure of inflation is the Retail Price Index, which reflects fluctuations in a wide range of consumer prices. While this convenient guide often reinforces public impressions, like most headline-catching economic figures it can be misleading. The price of a few essential commodities can be rising steeply while others are declining, in which case an average cannot truly reflect 'the cost of living'. At the beginning of the twenty-first century **housing** costs were soaring while many consumer goods were ◄ actually becoming cheaper. Even though the overall rate of inflation was low by post-war British standards, it remained a headache for the newly-independent Bank of England and government ministers.

There was a significant rise in inflation between 1915 and 1921, and another during the Second World War. But in the 1930s the real problem in Britain was *de*flation, resulting from the worldwide **Great** ◄ **Depression** which produced a slump in trade. Inflation became a problem for peacetime ministers after 1950–2, when there was a steady rise in prices mainly due to increasing consumer demand. Until the oil crisis of 1973–4 fears of inflation were partly responsible for the pattern of economic management which was criticised as 'stop-go'. **Economic growth** would be encouraged up to a point where the ◄ economy seemed to be overheating, whereupon the Treasury would introduce a package of disinflationary measures (normally expenditure cuts plus an increase in interest rates). But it was generally understood that a moderate rise in inflation was an acceptable by-product of a policy designed to ensure 'full' employment. It discouraged saving, and obviously reduced the living standards of people on fixed incomes. On the other hand, it encouraged borrowing, since the cost

of a loan in real terms would fall before repayment was due. For a
▶ **consumerist** society already becoming addicted to credit, this made
inflation a price well worth paying.

This situation was transformed by the oil shock. By 1975 inflation
was running at an annual rate of over 25 per cent. Economists
disagreed about the causes: was the inflation a direct result of raised
import costs, had it been fostered by higher wage settlements, or (as
▶ the **monetarists** argued) had it arisen from an unsustainable increase
in Britain's money supply? At least almost everyone agreed that policy
▶ priorities must switch. Inflation, rather than **unemployment**, was
now the main evil. At the time politicians assumed that it was impossible to bring one of these indicators down without provoking an
increase in the other. Direct controls on incomes and prices were
introduced in an attempt to square the circle, but they proved impossible to sustain in the face of opposition from employers and unions
▶ alike. The policy's failure helped to discredit the ideas of **J.M. Keynes**,
▶ and even James Callaghan's **Labour** government adopted the rival
▶ monetarist remedies. Callaghan's successor **Margaret Thatcher** was
an enthusiastic advocate of a theory which Labour had adopted with
deep reluctance. By the time of the 1983 general election inflation had
fallen below 5 per cent. Yet nothing had been proved, since the government had found it difficult in practice to define the money supply, let
alone control it. The only indisputable facts were that unemployment
▶ was over 3 million, and that the **Conservatives** were re-elected.

Inflation resurged briefly towards the end of the 1980s, and once
again the price was paid in lost jobs. But by the end of the century it
seemed that Britain had entered an era of stable prices. In part this
may have been due to increased competition between producers in an
increasingly complex global economy, but consumers were also more
willing to shop around for bargains. Indeed, in some countries it
seemed that the attack on the inflationary culture had succeeded *too*
well. Falling prices were a serious problem in Japan, and governments
across the world were hacking down their interest rates in a bid to
resuscitate demand. After fifty years of rising prices a new field of
speculation was opening to keep the economists in work, while their
fellow citizens braced themselves in expectation of a new era of
unemployment.

■ Ireland, partition of

In 1886, W.E. Gladstone's Bill to give Home Rule to the whole of Ireland
was defeated on its second reading in the House of Commons by 30
▶ votes. The Bill had proposed an extensive measure of **devolution**, but
▶ the Westminster **government** would have kept control of the policy

areas normally associated with national **sovereignty** – defence, ◄
foreign relations, external customs duties and the coinage. A second
attempt to introduce Home Rule was repulsed by the House of Lords
in 1893, and Gladstone retired shortly afterwards.

The controversy provoked numerous defections from Gladstone's
Liberal Party to the **Conservatives**. Although the latter party was fully ◄
committed to the maintenance of the United Kingdom, it had a
particular affection for the largely Protestant North of Ireland, the
area known as Ulster. Before the introduction of the first Home Rule
Bill the Conservative Lord Randolph Churchill proclaimed that if the
legislation was passed 'Ulster will fight and Ulster will be right'. He
pledged that in the event of trouble powerful elements on the British
mainland would be ready to join the struggle to uphold the power of
a religion which, to the majority **Roman Catholic** population, was ◄
synonymous with rapacious absentee landlords and other forms of
social injustice.

Between the fall of Gladstone and the election of the next Liberal
government in 1906 the Conservatives tried to govern Ireland through
a mixture of coercion and concessions over the crucial question of
land-ownership. Feelings in Ulster remained high against Home Rule,
and the passage of the 1911 Parliament Act raised the temperature still
further because now the House of Lords could only delay legislation,
not veto it entirely as it had done back in 1893. In preparing a new Bill
the Liberal government watered down Gladstone's proposals even
further, and they were prepared to discuss compromise over Ulster.
But arms and ammunition had been flooding into Ireland in preparation for a fight, and after the second reading had been approved by a
comfortable majority in May 1912, Unionists prepared for action. In
July the Conservative leader Bonar Law told a rally of supporters that
'there are things stronger than parliamentary majorities'. Two
months later Unionists signed a Solemn League and Covenant,
protesting their loyalty to the Crown and their determination to resist
the government. Among the signatories were **Rudyard Kipling, Sir** ◄
Edward Elgar, and Britain's best-known constitutional lawyer, A.V.
Dicey. Zealous guardianship of the constitution was one of the
unquestioned assumptions of Conservative tradition. Despite Dicey's
presence on the Unionist side of the argument, their stand was now
threatening to plunge part of the kingdom into civil war.

The Liberal Prime Minister, Asquith, was in an impossible situation.
He could only buy off the unionists at the cost of his parliamentary
majority, since he was dependent on Irish Nationalist votes. In 1914 he
offered a compromise, suggesting that any Irish counties which
rejected Home Rule could opt out for six years. This was not enough
for the Unionists, and their power to extract further concessions was

I

revealed when 58 serving British officers resigned their commissions rather than face the prospect of coercing Ulster into acceptance of Home Rule. This 'Curragh Mutiny' should have come as no surprise to the government, since Britain's most famous soldier, Lord Roberts of Kandahar, had signed the Covenant and hand-picked the leader of the Ulster rebels.

In September 1914 the Home Rule Bill finally became law, including provisions for separate parliaments in the north and the south of Ireland. Historically, Ulster had consisted of nine counties; the Northern parliament was based upon six of these, with the highest concentration of Protestants. Partition was thus given official

▶ recognition of a kind. But by that time war had broken out in **Europe** and the Act was suspended for the duration of the conflict. Asquith had also promised an Amending Bill, which would allow for changes in the final settlement. But some radicals in the south of Ireland could not wait for the fulfilment of such a vague promise. The effects of the

▶ abortive Dublin **Easter Rising** of 1916 were that the defeated republicans became heroes in the South, and the moderate nationalist party led by John Redmond, which had kept Asquith in office, was discredited. At the 1918 general election, 72 members of the republican Sinn Féin party were elected to Westminster, but boycotted the Imperial parliament. Instead, they constituted themselves into a breakaway Irish parliament (the Dáil), and in January 1919 claimed independence for their country.

Of the votes cast in the whole of Ireland in 1918, just over a fifth had gone to candidates favouring the continuation of the union. But although democratic principles suggested that limited Home Rule was now a dead letter, for the British government Sinn Féin's defiance had to be treated as being different in kind from the earlier threats of

▶ rebellion in the North. The new Liberal Prime Minister **Lloyd George** was now in coalition with the Conservatives, and whatever his personal feelings as a Welshman who had formerly stood up for nationalist movement he readily accepted the case for repression. A

▶ brutal guerrilla war ensued, with the **Irish Republican Army** (IRA) inflicting serious casualties on the British forces, which included not only the regular army but also the notorious 'Black and Tans', paramilitary reinforcements for the official police force.

As the underdog in this struggle, the IRA was sure to have the better of the propaganda war, and its own atrocities were greeted with particular acclaim in the US, Britain's erstwhile ally. Amid all the carnage, in 1921 elections were held for the parliaments of the North and the South. Sinn Féin won almost all of the 128 seats in the South, and took 12 of the 52 Ulster constituencies. Opening the Belfast parliament, George V appealed for an end to the conflict. A truce soon followed, then negotiations between the British government and what was now the *de facto* republican administration of the South. Although the British claimed to be impressed by the Irish delegation, and in particular by Michael Collins, a tactical genius in guerrilla war whose instinctive approach to politics was no match for the machinations of the British, the terms were left vague as far as they concerned Ulster. But in December 1921 a treaty was signed, creating an Irish Free State in the South which would be an independent member of the British Commonwealth. Significantly, the terms demanded that people who had recently been in arms against Britain still had to swear an oath of loyalty to the Crown; and Britain's strategic interests were served by the guarantee that its navy could still use three 'treaty ports' in the South. When the border between the Free State and Northern Ireland was finally drawn, it was clear that the British had tried to make Ulster as economically prosperous as possible. Although the Dáil ratified the treaty, serious grievances remained and the new Free State was plunged into a civil war which cost Collins his life. But the deplorable sacrifice of this able and charismatic man should not obscure the fact that the new Irish government proved as unflinching as the British had been in exterminating its enemies, either through normal court procedure or by courts martial. Indeed, Collins had pleaded for British help in his attempt to suppress a republican uprising in Dublin.

The Irish Free State was renamed 'Éire' in 1937, when the country adopted a constitution which did not recognise partition. Éire remained neutral throughout the Second World War. This position made a mockery of its continuing status as a dominion of the British Crown, but only in 1949 did it become a republic. For their own part, the British passed a law which promised that partition could not be brought to an end without the consent of an electorate which had a built-in Protestant majority. Not even Dicey could have explained why, while British politicians claimed that no **parliament** could bind its ◄ successors, this legislation was held to be an immovable obstacle to reunification. Meanwhile, citizens of Éire who were resident in Britain were allowed a vote in Westminster elections, implying that the final break of 1949 had never happened. It was a surreal stand-off across the Irish Sea, utterly incomprehensible to any Briton who lacked detailed historical knowledge (and baffling enough even to experts in the subject). By the 1970s, when regular IRA bombs were killing and maiming people on the British mainland, few of the victims had any idea why they were being targeted. It was hardly surprising that the British regarded anyone with an Irish accent as a potential assassin, and that several innocent people were singled out and imprisoned merely because they were visitors from Belfast.

Ever hopeful, after helping to negotiate the 1922 treaty **Winston** ◄

Churchill, son of Lord Randolph, had felt able to tell the House of Commons that it might prove possible 'to reconcile the spirit of the ▶ Irish nation to the **British Empire** in the same way as Scotland and Wales have been reconciled'. This could form the basis of an interesting undergraduate essay on the history of the United Kingdom. Whatever the British might have hoped in 1922, continued conflict was guaranteed by the creation of the Northern Ireland 'statelet' which contained a substantial Catholic minority. Among the Protestants, raucous 'loyalty' to the UK was just another way of spitting defiance across the border. More than a hundred years after Gladstone tried to solve the 'Irish Question' in the only way that stood a realistic chance of success, the hatreds persisted even when the guns were silent.

■ Irish Republican Army (IRA)

In the 1918 British general election, Ireland voted decisively for independence. Out of 105 Westminster seats, supporters of the Union won only 25. The main republican group, Sinn Féin, was by far the largest party, with 73 MPs (nearly half of whom were currently in prison). ▶ They had no intention of sitting in the imperial **parliament** at Westminster even if they should be released. Instead, all the available MPs met at the Mansion House in Dublin, and declared national independence on 21 January 1919. On the same day, two policemen were murdered by the Irish Volunteers, soon to be renamed the Irish Republican Army.

The IRA was well funded, and brilliantly organised by Michael Collins, a former London bank clerk who had taken part in the 1916 ▶ **Easter Rising**. It has been estimated that the IRA could call on around 15,000 volunteers; against them, the British government deployed more than 50,000 troops and policemen. Atrocities were committed on both sides. On the first 'Bloody Sunday', 21 November 1920, the IRA dragged 14 men from their beds and shot them. That afternoon, at Dublin's Croke Park, the notorious 'Black and Tans', who had been recruited by the British government to assist the Royal Irish Constabulary (RIC), murdered 12 people at a football match. Overall, around 1,000 people were killed between 1919 and the truce of July 1921.

When Ireland was partitioned at the end of 1921 Collins became Prime Minister in the provisional government of the new Irish Free State. But he was regarded by most of the IRA as a traitor, for having accepted the continuance of British rule in the northern counties of Ulster. In August 1922 he was ambushed and shot dead, aged just 31 and a perfect candidate for immortalisation by the movie industry. Two months earlier the IRA had claimed another celebrated victim in the newly-retired British Chief of the Imperial General Staff, Sir Henry

Wilson, who was assassinated on the steps of his Belgravia home. Wilson had been a strong advocate of partition (once the old Union was no longer tenable); he had disliked the violence of the 'Black and Tans', but only because of its piecemeal, semi-official nature.

The Irish civil war officially ended in May 1924, after a campaign of ruthless repression by the government of the Irish Free State. But the IRA did not disband, and began a new campaign of terrorism on the British mainland in 1939. An explosion in Coventry killed 5 people. There were a few minor incidents in the 1950s, but it then seemed that the IRA was no longer a serious threat either on the mainland of Britain or across the Irish Sea. Although it retained its commitment to a united Ireland, many of its members had embraced Marxism, which promised to transcend the religious hatreds which divided the North from the South, and the residents of Ulster against each other.

All this changed as a result of the civil rights movement, which emerged in the late 1960s. The Protestant majority had manipulated electoral boundaries to secure its political dominance, Catholics were grossly under-represented in bodies like the Royal Ulster Constabulary (RUC), and **housing** policy was heavily skewed towards the Protestants. The Ulster Catholics, in short, occupied a position which was comparable to that of American blacks in the Deep South; and their new determination to assert their rights as human beings was just as likely to be resisted. In August 1969 the IRA resumed its activities, in response to attacks on the Catholic population. This decision coincided with the dispatch of British troops, who were assigned to restore order in Northern Ireland. But heavy-handed tactics, including the adoption of internment without trial, soon convinced even moderate Catholics that the army intended to uphold, by force, the Protestant ascendancy which had inspired the civil rights movement in the first place. On a new 'Bloody Sunday', 30 January 1972, members of the Parachute Regiment fired on demonstrators in Londonderry, killing 13 unarmed civilians. In retaliation the IRA bombed a Parachute Regiment barracks in Aldershot, but succeeded only in killing ancillary staff and a Catholic priest. Soon afterwards the IRA announced a ceasefire, which proved to be permanent.

But a new, more militant organisation already existed to prosecute the war with Britain (which assumed direct responsibility for governing the Province in March 1972). This 'Provisional' IRA had split from the 'Official' wing in 1969. Growing hostility towards the British presence ensured a steady supply of young recruits, including Martin McGuinness. On 21 July 1973 20 bombs exploded in Belfast, with inadequate warnings. Eleven people were killed on what was dubbed 'Bloody Friday'. In November 1974, 21 people were killed by bombs in Birmingham pubs. Other IRA 'spectaculars' included the assassination of Lord Mountbatten, who was murdered by a bomb planted aboard his fishing boat off County Sligo in August 1979, and the killing of 18 soldiers in an ambush at Warrenpoint, County Down on the same day.

The IRA's strategy was conditioned by the awkward fact that a clear majority of the population of Northern Ireland would not contemplate the prospect of unification with the 'priest-ridden' South. The existence of the border might be a matter for regret, particularly for British ministers; but partition had happened for reasons which were quite understandable at the time, and the majority population in the North regarded it as the only security for their way of life. Under these circumstances the only hope for Irish Republicans was that the people of Great Britain would become so embittered in the face of constant acts of violence that they would pressurise their government into forcing the Unionists in Northern Ireland to surrender.

This approach was not completely irrational. The average Briton
▶ was entirely ignorant of the underlying causes of the 'Troubles', and the typical response to outrages on the mainland was a paroxysm of hatred (Irishmen were attacked indiscriminately after the Birmingham bombs), followed by a wish that the government would wash its hands of the whole problem. But the main political parties were united behind the proposition that the Union should be sustained unless the majority declared otherwise. Only a steep escalation in the violence would put that consensus under strain. But it would also make the prospect of unification far less enticing to the people and parties in the south of Ireland. Direct attempts to assassinate members of the Cabinet, at the Grand Hotel in Brighton in 1984 and in Downing Street itself in February 1991, were quickly followed by new attempts by Westminster politicians to involve the Éire government in the
▶ affairs of the North. It was almost as if **Margaret Thatcher** and John Major felt that the South should be given timely reminders of the hazards involved in unification.

From this perspective, the 'armed struggle' apparently persisted merely because the IRA equated a lasting peace with the unpalatable idea of 'surrender'. The renewed 'Troubles' had also developed their own momentum; to retaliate against an atrocity by an opposing paramilitary group was a matter of professional pride, and if organised crime began as an efficient means of raising funds for the struggle, it could soon become a way of life for people who were not ideally qualified for many civilian occupations. The only way to break the dreary logic of events was for the IRA to pursue a dual strategy of politics and violence. The by-election victories of the jailed hunger-striker Bobby Sands, and of Owen Carron, at Fermanagh and South Tyrone in 1981, gave a considerable boost to this new initiative; Sands was the first

Sinn Féin candidate to win a seat since 1955. Martin McGuinness and his colleague Gerry Adams were both elected for Westminster constituencies in 1997; although they clearly retained intimate links with the IRA, most impartial observers were satisfied that they were now sincere in their adherence to peaceful change.

Ostensibly, at least, the IRA declared a ceasefire in October 1994 because it had been impressed by official hints that British troops were no longer in Northern Ireland to sustain a policy of self-interest. But this had been obvious to any neutral observer since the army arrived in 1969. Although John Major was determined to achieve a lasting breakthrough if possible, his precarious parliamentary position proved an insuperable handicap. The ceasefire was broken on 9 February 1996, when an IRA bomb exploded outside London's Canary Wharf.

In the following year, when **Labour** was elected with a crushing ◄ majority, talks could resume. A new ceasefire was announced on 20 July, and the Good Friday Agreement signed on 10 April 1998. The terms allowed for the staged release of convicted terrorists from both sides, but there was much dispute about the process of 'putting arms beyond use' and until a few days before the end of the century there was little evidence even of a desire to talk about this. Adams and McGuinness could hardly press too urgently for the 'decommissioning' of IRA weapons; as it was, critics in republican circles were able to compare their recent activities with the 'betrayal' by Michael Collins. From this perspective, at least, the bomb outrage in Omagh on 15 August 1998, perpetrated by a new splinter group which called itself the 'Real IRA', had the beneficial effect of tying Sinn Féin more securely into the political process. However, the Provisionals were ready for a resumption of hostilities, and were accused of carrying out 'punishment beatings' and other criminal acts. Even if the war was over, it had been succeeded by a very strange kind of peace.

■ ITV

The first commercial television network in Britain, it became synonymous with light entertainment, a burgeoning advertising industry and the **consumer** culture of the post-war era. It came into being as a ◄ direct result of agitation within the **Conservative Party** for the ◄ monopoly of the **BBC** to be broken in order to stimulate competition. ◄ There was opposition from all quarters of the **Establishment**, most of ◄ it based on a fear that commercial TV would exacerbate the **Americanisation** of Britain that Hollywood had already effected. Despite this, the Television Act was passed on 31 July 1954. It set up six regionally-based franchises and a governing body, the Independent Television Authority (ITA), to monitor the quality of their output, chaired by the art historian Sir Kenneth Clark.

The network began broadcasting on 22 September 1955 and the first advert to be aired was for Gibbs' toothpaste. ITV trounced the BBC, stealing half its viewers overnight, and within two years it had 76 per cent of audience share. Its success was partly the result of its populist approach of 'giving the people what they want', by offering more variety shows, and by adapting American formats like the ► sitcom and quiz show. As audience share rose, so did advertising revenue, a trend that seemed to confirm predictions that the market would determine programming and influence taste. Between 1950 and 1960, the amount of money spent on advertising in the UK almost trebled, from £162 million per year to £454 million, most of it the result of ITV. The system was, announced the gleeful owner of Scottish TV, Sir Roy Thomson, 'a licence to print money'.

However, the network's success was also the result of a more imaginative broadcasting strategy – for example, having newsreaders appear on camera and in a more informal manner, while also encouraging a more interrogative approach to interviewing, a trend personified by Robin Day (1923–2000). Consequently, ITV was seen as emblematic of the less deferential British society that emerged in the second half of the 1950s. It also pioneered the more discursive, barroom approach to sports coverage, using retired sportsmen as pundits. The ITV companies also made more effort to reflect regional cultures than the BBC, although in order for programmes to be networked they had to appeal to a nationwide audience.

The Pilkington Inquiry of 1962 condemned the output of the commercial network as 'trivial' and praised the BBC for maintaining standards. The Macmillan government rejected its recommendation that the ITA should take over programming and the selling of advertising time, and instead added eight further franchises to the network. The debate revolved, as it still does, over the question of whether culture, like other forms of consumption, is led by demand or supply. In 1960, the ITA chairman, Sir Robert Fraser, stated that it was the former. 'People of superior mental constitution are going to find much of television intellectually beneath them . . . If in their hearts they despise popular pleasures and interests, then of course they will be angrily dissatisfied with television. But it is not really television with which they are dissatisfied. It is with people.'

Although the BBC was invigorated by the competition, ITV continued to beat it in most areas between the 1960s and 80s. Commercial television even stole a lead in the field of arts and other minority programming when Channel 4 was launched in 1982. ► Channel 4's radical approach, for example its celebration of **homo-**

sexual culture, earned it the opprobrium of religious moralists. But it also won 10 per cent of audience share and, as a consequence, enough advertising revenue to prove that the 'Hidden Persuaders' were sometimes capable of being persuaded themselves. For a time, the channel was even able to sponsor the ailing British film industry, through its subsidiary Film Four (1998). However, its reliance on the success of the reality TV show *Big Brother* (2000–) pointed to a more mainstream programming future.

By the 1990s, the glory days of ITV were over. It was neither offering the quality of broadcasting provided by the BBC nor the quantity offered by competitors in the commercial sector. The network initially saw off the threat unleashed by a new wave of Conservative free-marketeering under **Margaret Thatcher**. Cable TV, launched in 1984 ◄ and dominated by American companies, had persuaded only 3.5 million homes to connect by 2002. Even the Australian Rupert Murdoch's Sky TV, launched in 1989 and getting 6.1 million direct subscribers, had still only won a 6 per cent audience share by 2002. A third terrestrial station, Channel Five, was launched in 1997. But it too only gained 6 per cent, despite initially basing its appeal on the quantity of soft **pornography** that it showed. ◄

Ironically, ITV lost most ground to its original adversary. In 2002, the BBC took 38 per cent of audience share and ITV only 24 per cent – 50 per cent less than it had taken at its peak in the 1950s. One of the network's early boasts, that its regionally-based franchises offered more diverse programming, was less true than it had been because ITV became something of a monopoly itself. In 1992, the 16 franchises had 16 owners; a decade later there were only 5, with the big two – Carlton and Granada – snapping up all the English franchises and that of Wales. This did not prevent the collapse of the Carlton/Granada-sponsored ITV digital platform six years after the 1996 Broadcasting Act gave the go-ahead for digital television. Here, too, the collapse was laden with irony. **Football** coverage, which ITV had struggled to wrest ◄ from the BBC since the 1950s, formed the basis of the excessive costs that led to the collapse, and it took place in the same year, 2001, that the number of UK homes with multi-channel TV passed the 50 per cent mark.

The launch of ITV began a media revolution that, for better or worse, transformed British life. The network profited for half a century, but in the end discovered that the market always eats its own children. 'From now on,' said the controller of one company in 1957, 'what the public wants, it's going to get.' In a world of over 200 channels where over half of 4–9-year-old **children** have their own TV sets, ◄ what the public wanted was no longer something that ITV could deliver on its own.

■ Jews

Jews have been less systematically persecuted in Britain than in most European countries, although anti-semitism remains a feature of British society. In 1290, Edward I became the first European monarch to expel the entire Jewish population from his realm. Cromwell re-admitted them in 1650, but the prominent role they played in establishing the country's financial institutions during the eighteenth
▶ century cemented ancient stereotypes of them as usurers. **Roman Catholic** emancipation in 1829 left them as the only religious group to be legally denied access to institutions of state.

Their plight was highlighted when Lionel Rothschild was elected to
▶ **parliament** in 1847 but prevented from sitting because he would not take a Christian oath of allegiance. The law was changed in 1858; the
▶ first **government** minister of Jewish faith was appointed in 1871 and the first judge followed two years later. The community also became more organised in this period. The 1870 Jewish United Synagogues Act placed Britain's synagogues under the authority of a Board of Guardians, later known as the Board of Deputies. Its religious leader was created Chief Rabbi, a sort of semitic Archbishop of Canterbury, but a post modelled on those of the Continental *landesrabinner*. The Board's President (usually a Rothschild) became the *de facto* lay leader of British Jewry.

Thousands of poorer Jews, seeking asylum from pogroms in Eastern Europe, settled in the UK between 1881 and 1914, mainly around the East End of London. As a result, the Jewish population rose from an estimated 51,000 in 1876 to a peak of 430,000 in 1950. They were instrumental in developing Britain's retail trade, two examples of which stand out. The first was the founding of Marks and Spencer's in 1884 by Michael Marks and Thomas Spencer. Initially it was a chain of penny bazaars, but Michael's son Simon Marks (1884–1964) established what is now a British institution, following a visit to the US in 1924 where he absorbed American techniques of selling quality goods at reasonable prices. (The company's trademark, St Michael, registered in 1928, is one of the stranger examples of Jews adopting Christian names in order to be accepted.) The second was the founding of Tesco by Sir John Cohen (1898–1979), whose cheap, self-service food stores helped to establish the American supermarket concept in Britain during the 1960s.

As in America, Jews of this generation also helped to create the
▶ modern entertainment industry – from the **cinema** mogul Alexander Korda (1893–1956) to the commercial television owners and impresarios, Sid Bernstein (1899–1993) and Lew Grade (1906–98). Among
▶ their many achievements was Bernstein's launch of the **soap opera**

J

Coronation Street, and Grade's commissioning of the first **Morecambe** ◄
and Wise TV series.

A smaller but influential wave of Jewish asylum seekers came to escape Nazi persecution. Between 1933 and 1939, 50,000 arrived, their passage assisted by refugee funds set up by Simon Marks and by **William Beveridge**. A large proportion were intellectuals, many of ◄ whom, like the Austrian artist Oskar Kokoschka (1886–1980), the German architect Walter Gropius (1883–1969) and the pioneer of psychoanalysis, **Sigmund Freud** (1856–1939), made a lasting contribu- ◄ tion to British cultural life.

Neither the role of Jews in creating a **consumer** society, nor their ◄ role in the artistic world that usually critiqued it, improved attitudes towards them as a race. Whereas hostility to black, Asian and Oriental immigrants was based on their supposed failure to integrate, hostility towards Jews was based on a belief that they integrated rather too well. The influx of Eastern Europeans and their disproportionate represen- tation in politics, business, the professions and the arts led to a revival of anti-semitism. Riots took place in Bethnal Green in 1903, prompting the 1905 Aliens Act, which the **Conservative** Prime Minister ◄ A.J. Balfour commended to parliament thus: 'It would not be to the advantage of the civilisation of the country that there should be an immense body of persons who, however patriotic, able and indus- trious . . . remained a people apart and not merely held a religion differing from the vast majority of their countrymen but only inter- married among themselves.' This contrasted sharply with public hostility towards **miscegenation** with coloured races. ◄

The attitude of religious Jews to intermarriage was not the only thing that provoked suspicion of their loyalty to Britain. So too did the secular movement for a Jewish state. Zionism was incubated in the United Kingdom (Israel's first President, Chaim Weizmann, spent most of his working life as a pioneering chemist at Manchester Univer- sity). Although intellectual Zionists like Weizmann were admirers of British democracy, the movement grew in popularity as a result of disillusionment with the ability of that system to protect them in the face of continued rejection by fellow Britons. The movement also bene- fited from the support given to it by the oldest Jewish newspaper in the world, the London-based *Jewish Chronicle* (1841) which became a Zionist organ in 1906, although the Board of Deputies was not won over until 1939. Ironically, Zionism's most significant backing came from Gentiles who disliked the Jewish presence in Britain – notably A.J. Balfour who saw it as a solution to the problem with which he had wrestled in 1905. His support culminated in the so-called **Balfour** ◄ **Declaration** of 1917.

Further anti-semitic riots took place in Tredegar in 1911 and

London in 1917, prompting a second Aliens Act in 1919 that was rigorously implemented from 1924 to 1929 by the most anti-semitic British Home Secretary to date, William Joynson-Hicks. The publication in 1920 of an English translation of *The Protocols of the Elders of Zion* – the notorious tract warning of an international Jewish conspiracy to take

▶ over the world – caused alarm. So too did the rise of **Oswald Mosley**'s British Union of Fascists. Jews had always been prominent among the upper echelons of the British left, the most notable of whom was the

▶ ideological architect of **nationalised** industry, Harold Laski

▶ (1893–1950). But, as a result of fascism, the **Labour** and **Communist** movements attracted many more Jewish followers during the interwar period (they constituted a tenth of CPGB national membership and a third in parts of London). As one Jewish activist noted in 1937, 'it is not the Jews who make the East End "Red", but the East End which made the Jews "Red".'

▶ However, Mosley's attempt to scapegoat Jews for the **Great Depression** and, paradoxically, to associate them with international Communism, met with little success. Indeed, the BUF's bullish anti-semitism was one of the reasons why fascism was still-born in a country where racial prejudice is usually expressed with a sneer rather than a punch. Sympathy for the Jews grew when the Holocaust became public knowledge after the liberation of Nazi concentration camps in 1945, although four years later polls showed that half the UK population still had strong anti-semitic views. Anti-semitic riots occurred in London, Manchester, Liverpool and Glasgow in 1947. They were motivated by a belief that Jews were exploiting austerity by running the black market, and by anger at the murder of British soldiers by Zionist terrorists in Palestine.

The end of the UK's Mandate in Palestine and the subsequent creation of the state of Israel on 14 May 1948 had two consequences for British Jewry. First, emigration to Israel reduced the Jewish population to 300,000 by the end of the twentieth century. Second, the Jews' apparent contempt for the Arabs they now ruled alienated Britons who had sympathised with the Jews when they had been underdogs. The socialism of Israel's founding leaders, David Ben-Gurion and Golda Meir, briefly endeared Zionism to the British left. Despite

▶ Israel's collusion in the **Suez crisis**, sympathy did not evaporate until it won the Six Day War of 1967, which followed a pan-Arab attempt to invade and destroy the country for good. Israel's subsequent occupation of the West Bank in Jordan, and later southern Lebanon, its generally more aggressive defence policy, and America's growing role in financing the entire state, led Zionism to be seen as a facet of Western imperialism in the Middle East.

That attitude, culminating in the 1983 Labour Party manifesto which endorsed the aims of the Palestine Liberation Organization (PLO), together with the party's increasingly anti-business outlook, drove more and more Jews into the welcoming arms of the **Conservative Party**. Their influence on the development and implementation of **Thatcherism**, notably in the work of Keith Joseph and former socialist Alfred Sherman, was as profound as their influence on the left had been a generation or two earlier. The number of Jewish Labour MPs reached its peak (38) in 1966, a year before the Arab–Israeli war. By 1987 this was down to 7, the lowest figure since 1935, while the number of Jewish Tory MPs rose to 16. In 1988 the Cabinet contained 5 of them, more than any previous government. All of this prompted *Sunday Telegraph* editor Peregrine Worsthorne to proclaim that Judaism was 'the new creed of Thatcherite Britain'.

The rightward shift of British Jewry soured their relationship with black Britons. Jews benefited from post-war black **immigration** because the presence of people considered more alien than them (and, because of skin colour, more recognisable) diverted British racism away from its traditional domestic focus. It is probably no coincidence that the last anti-semitic riots in Britain occurred a year before the arrival of Jamaican immigrants on board the *Empire Windrush* in 1948. Sometimes, Jews benefited from this process as much by design as by default. Although they came under the protection of race relations legislation, most objected to being defined as an ethnic minority and some blamed the black population for the growth of racial conflict in the UK. This culminated in the response of Chief Rabbi Emmanuel Jakobovits to the Church of England's 1986 report on urban poverty, *Faith in the City*. Criticising blacks for giving British society 'a multi-ethnic form', he said they were too dependent on the state, concluding that, 'Self-reliant efforts and perseverance eventually pay off.'

Like other forms of racial prejudice, anti-semitism in Britain is no longer expressed as overtly as it once was. Often, it hides behind anti-Zionism, although the two are not, as zealots claim, the same thing. But it has declined, and that is due in part to the determination of Jews to integrate as far as they possibly can with British society. Fagin, Charles Dickens's unscrupulous money-grabber, has achieved greater longevity than most of his characters, thanks to film adaptations of *Oliver Twist* in 1948 and 1968. But although his caricature of the Jew still resonates in Britain, it is not because Gentiles feel threatened by them.

■ **Keynes, John Maynard** (1883–1946); 'Keynesianism'

▶ John Maynard Keynes was born in Cambridge. His father was a **university** don; his mother, who had also been educated at Cambridge, was an energetic philanthropist. The young Keynes was a brilliant student, at Eton and at King's College, Cambridge. Here he met Lytton Strachey and Leonard Woolf, who became lifelong friends and fellow members of the so-called 'Bloomsbury Group'. Although an economist might seem out of place in the company of aesthetes, Keynes had a remarkable range of interests, and the capacity to pursue each of them with a passion more characteristic of a monomaniac. Among many other things, he became President of the Cambridge Union.

Instead of finishing his degree, Keynes began his distinguished career in public service by joining the India Office. At the same time, he was writing a *Treatise on Probability*, which was published in 1914. This work led to the offer of an economics lectureship in Cambridge; later he was elected to a fellowship at King's. He revealed a remarkable talent for administration, but an even greater propensity for establishing influential connections. At the age of 29 he was appointed to a Royal Commission on Indian Finance. In May 1915 he was recruited into the Treasury, where he rapidly became a prominent figure, taking part in many discussions on war finance with the French and the Americans.

In 1919 Keynes headed the British Treasury delegation to the Paris peace conference. But he left before the signature of the Versailles Treaty, having tried unavailingly to soften the terms of reparations from Germany. The 'wickedness' of the settlement induced nervous exhaustion, but he recovered to dash off his counterblast – *The Economic Consequences of the Peace* – in two months. This dazzling
▶ polemic, including an uncompromising portrait of **Lloyd George**, made Keynes world-famous. It was also vindicated by later events. On paper the Versailles terms were a humiliation for Germany, and helped provoke the desire for revenge; but they also proved far too harsh to impose in practice, leaving the defeated nation with both the means and the motive to rebuild its economy and its armies.

At the time there were some hostile reviews of Keynes's book, but they could not damage his glittering prospects. The brilliance of his writing ensured lucrative journalistic commissions. He was also in demand for directorships, and became Second Bursar at King's in 1920. At around this time he also began a remarkable career as a speculator in stocks and currencies; although his judgement was not infallible his instinctive feel for the operations of the market made him a rich man. He also used his money-making talents to the benefit of his college. Like everything Keynes did, he took to this activity with gusto; but it was still rather like a skilful surgeon moonlighting in an abattoir.

In 1923 Keynes returned to economic theory, publishing *A Tract on Monetary Reform*. But even here he caused a public stir, by attacking the gold standard which was widely regarded at the time as the hallmark of economic stability. With the British economy faltering after a post-war boom, he also upset orthodox opinion by claiming that deflation was a greater evil than **inflation**. When the Chancellor of the Exchequer, **Winston Churchill**, returned Britain to the gold standard in 1925 Keynes produced a blistering retort in his pamphlet *The Economic Consequences of Mr Churchill*. The decision was as disastrous as Keynes expected, crippling Britain's exporting industries and contributing significantly to the **Great Depression**. With **unemployment** mounting Keynes helped Lloyd George to devise an ambitious programme of public works; but although the **Liberal** vote increased in the 1929 general election **Ramsay MacDonald** formed his second **Labour** government, which proved notoriously unequal to the economic crisis.

Just before the publication of his *Treatise on Money* – a work which has been overshadowed by Keynes's other productions – he served on the Macmillan Committee formed to give economic advice to the Labour government. The Committee's report has been seen as a turning point in Britain's economic history, and Keynes's influence was obvious in the conclusion that the maintenance of a high level of employment should be a key factor guiding the management of the currency. He also demonstrated his sensitivity to contemporary developments by abandoning his previous commitment to free trade, arguing that a measure of protection would help the economy at least in its short-term predicament.

For the next few years Keynes worked on a comprehensive statement of his evolving views. His *General Theory of Employment, Interest and Money* (1936), along with the **Beveridge Report** of 1942, provided the foundation for economic and social policy in Britain until the 1970s. Far from arguing that capitalism should be superseded in the wake of recent troubles, Keynes set out to save it. It was clear to him that the old orthodoxy, under which the market acted as a self-correcting mechanism, had been disproved; or at least, if the market did correct itself in the long run that was not much comfort, because, as he put it, 'in the long run we are all dead'. The main threat to the social order, mass unemployment, could only be avoided through the skilful manipulation of 'effective demand'. Public works, and low interest rates, would alleviate the effects of a slump. Employers would also have to curb their natural instinct to reduce wages at a time of high unemployment. By doing so, they were reducing aggregate demand

K

and thus perpetuating the slump. They had to be saved from themselves; and Keynes would be the saviour.

In 1937 Keynes was struck down by the heart trouble which eventually killed him. But he was recalled to the Treasury in 1940. He influenced the 1941 budget, which included the innovative idea of extending taxation to the working class in return for the promise of post-war compensation. Again this showed how much of Keynes's thought was based on psychological insight. As well as reducing demand at a time of scarcity, the measure would bind the workers into the common struggle. Despite his uncertain health Keynes became a governor of the Bank of England in the same year; he was raised to the peerage in 1942.

Keynes continued to influence British economic policy, and his ideas also bore fruit in the creation of the Arts Council (1945). In June 1944 he flew to America to take part in the Bretton Woods conference, which created the economic framework of the Western world until the early 1970s. The discussions led to the formation of the International Monetary Fund (IMF) and the World Bank, ostensibly as agents of global economic stability. In practice, these institutions imposed American ideas on any country which mismanaged its affairs badly enough to need help. Keynes was also forced to agree to the erection of a system of currency management which looked uncannily like the notorious gold standard, but this time with the dollar at its centre. His recognition of US hegemony was also evident in the negotiations for a post-war loan, which was criticised for its lack of generosity.

Worn out by his exertions, Keynes died back in England on 21 April 1946. Yet his influence became more potent than ever, and the exact meaning of his work was disputed up to the end of the century – proving that in the long run we are all misinterpreted. In fact, Keynes's approach invited distortion. He actively sought disciples, among professional economists and laymen alike. Yet his was essentially an empirical outlook, demanding new solutions in ever-changing circumstances. He was that rarest of beings – a transcendent genius working in the service of common sense. His followers might have had some of the latter quality, but none of the former (which was more important). Hence while Keynes's changing views were almost invariably expressed in a dogmatic tone, the 'Keynesians' were usually dogmatic without the capacity to change.

Keynes's best-known writings were composed in response to a worldwide depression. In the 1970s the problem was how to prevent runaway inflation leading to mass unemployment. Those who tried to implement a 'Keynesian' approach in the mid-1970s were at an obvious disadvantage if they turned to the master's works. More seriously, by that time his legacy had been twisted by a generation of supposed followers who had used his doctrines in order to manipulate the economic cycle for electoral advantage. This political – or more accurately 'bastardised' – Keynesianism could only be applied to the detriment of the underlying health of the British economy. It meant that hard decisions were endlessly delayed, ensuring that the final reckoning would be much heavier than it needed to have been. Ironically, since the 'Keynesians' failed to act in time it was left to the **monetarists**, who had never ◄ accepted his theory, to do the work; their botched remedies proved that Keynes had at least been right in his strictures against 'classical' economists. At the beginning of the twenty-first century it was unclear whether Keynes had emerged from his coffin, despite the election of a **'New' Labour** government pledged to attack the legacy of **Thatcherism**. ◄ At some point, though, his reputation was certain to revive.

■ Kipling, Rudyard (1865–1936)

Joseph Rudyard Kipling was born in Bombay, the child of an artistic official in the Indian civil service and an ebullient mother of Celtic ancestry. Kipling was sent to be educated in England, and the prolonged absences of his parents undoubtedly caused lasting psychological damage. At the age of 16 he returned to India, where he worked as a journalist. In the time that was free from the mundane chores of his trade, he established a literary reputation with a steady stream of poems and short stories.

With hardly any Anglo-Indian competitors, Kipling might have inhabited a tiny pond but his work caused a terrific splash. He was already well known in Britain on his return there in 1889. Very different authors, including Oscar Wilde and **Thomas Hardy**, were ◄ then in vogue. But whatever he thought of Wilde's flamboyance and Hardy's brooding grandeur, Kipling knew that there was a mass market for his own distinctive, colloquial voice. He consolidated his popular appeal with *Barrack-Room Ballads* (1892), influenced by a new-found love of **music hall** entertainment. His *Jungle Book* (1894) of short ◄ stories was once riotously successful with children (it was made into a Disney cartoon in 1967, following a less successful wartime film). Although critics dispute his aptitude for the novel, his most notable foray into that genre, *Kim* (1901), provided a vivid and deeply sympathetic portrait of India. But today Kipling is mostly remembered for individual poems, notably 'If', a Baedeker's Guide to the stiff upper-lip which even at the end of the twentieth century was voted the nation's favourite, and 'Recessional', a moving and profound commemoration of Victoria's Golden Jubilee.

Kipling ought to be a hero for the opponents of **cultural elitism**, ◄ since he wrote in order to be understood by any literate reader. The

K

fact that most of his work is deeply unfashionable today shows that style (and skill) are unavailing when much of the subject matter is outdated. During his rise to fame Kipling's commercial trump card was an uncanny (and instinctive) sympathy with the ordinary British soldier. But his archetypal 'Tommy Atkins' is no longer a figure representative of society as a whole, or even of the army rank-and-file. His short stories about boarding-school life, *Stalky & Co.* (1899), appealed to

▶ adults no less than **children**. But they portrayed childhood as a preparation for the military life, and most modern parents will shun them as tales of torture and tobacco.

▶   Kipling's celebration of the **British Empire** was anachronistic even
▶ before his death. **George Orwell** recognised that in Kipling's prime it had 'been possible to be an Imperialist and a gentleman'. But his gift for memorable, easily distorted phrases – his attack on 'lesser breeds
▶ without the law' (by which he seems to have meant the **Germans**), and his prayer that Americans would share 'the White Man's Burden' – transformed him from a national treasure into an unwanted heirloom as the Union Jacks were hauled down across the world. Orwell had 'worshipped' Kipling when he was 13, and had come to admire him again at the time of his death; in between he regarded him as 'a kind of enemy, a man of alien and perverted genius'. Orwell's was the last generation to wrestle with these complicated feelings. After the
▶ Second World War members of the Boy **Scouts**' movement continued to draw on Kipling's vocabulary. But most of them probably had no idea what they were doing, and the list of names could have been drawn at random from anybody's books.

    Whatever the fate of his literary output Kipling continues to attract the attention of biographers. After years of speculation about his repressed personality, more profitable recent studies have concentrated on his politics. But this revisionism runs the risk of defending his brand of imperialism under the guise of a perfectly laudable attempt to understand it. Kipling himself seemed to sense the danger of becoming an anachronism; a good hater, he lashed out against the trends that disturbed him, unperturbed by the prospect of making enemies or committing crimes against logic. He became a Vice-President of the India Defence League, formed to maintain the
▶ awesome duty of governing distant peoples; he opposed the **partition**
▶ of Ireland, reform of the House of Lords, and women's **suffrage** (although Kipling wrote that 'the female of the species must be deadlier than the male', he echoed the die-hard chauvinist view that
▶ women should not participate in politics because they were too compassionate to be trusted with influence over defence policy).

    Kipling was awarded the Nobel Prize for Literature in 1907, having spurned all of the domestic honours that were dangled before him.

He would never have been a candidate for the Peace Prize, and after that year much of his output was disfigured by fulminations at what he regarded as a British loss of resolve. He was a strange, neurotic character, whose inner drives elude even skilful and sympathetic commentators. His later life was overshadowed by the death of his son in the First World War – a conflict that the Germanophobic Kipling had long expected. This grievous personal blow followed the early loss of his favourite daughter. At least he was spared the verification of his doleful prophecies about Hitler's intentions, dying two months before the latter re-militarised the Rhineland. As the nation absorbed the news of Kipling's death, the life of his friend George V was also drawing to its drug-induced close. After Kipling's imperial dreaming it was time for the reality of **Edward VIII's** abdication, and ◄
appeasement. ◄

■ The Krays

The twin brothers Ronnie (1933–95) and Reggie (1933–2000) were the most notorious British gangsters of the twentieth century whose fame highlighted a Western tendency to romanticise organised **crime**. The ◄
twins were born in London's East End to a feckless father, Charlie, and doting mother, Violet, who came from Irish, Jewish and Romany stock. After some success in the boxing rings of the East End, they spent their national service assaulting officers, going AWOL and, as a result, being incarcerated in military prison. Their reputation for ruthlessness was established in 1954 when they took over the Regal billiard hall on the Mile End Road and Ronnie cutlassed members of a Maltese gang who tried to get protection money from them. By the time they bought their own club in 1957, naming it the 'Double R', the twins were making a healthy living extorting money from others. Their gang's name – The Firm – entered the English **language** as the euphemistic ◄
term for a criminal organisation.

But, unlike other gang leaders, the Krays were not content to turn over a profit. They longed to be Cockney James Cagneys and courted fame. When they extended their operation into the West End of London, celebrities from the worlds of film, TV, music and sport queued up to rub tuxedoed shoulders with them, attracted by the frisson of danger and deviance that surrounded the 'Glamour Gangsters'. They were particularly attractive to stars with an East End background, who perhaps felt that socialising with the Krays kept them in touch with their working-class roots. Barbara Windsor, a luminary of ◄
the **Carry On films**, was one such friend. Another East Ender, the ◄
photographer David Bailey, captured the twins' dashing menace in a 1963 studio portrait. Exhibited in art galleries and reproduced on

countless t-shirts and posters, it became one of the most iconographic images of modern Britain, and it helped the Krays to become folk

▶ heroes, their careers seeming to epitomise the anti-Establishment mood of the time.

In 1965, Reggie married Frances Shea, who committed suicide two

▶ years later. Ronnie was a voracious **homosexual**, whose lovers ranged from pretty cosh boys to the corpulent Tory peer Bob Boothby. He also had a lifelong enjoyment of violence which, Broadmoor psychiatrists later concluded, stemmed from paranoid schizophrenia. This was the source of the Krays' strength and of their downfall. Although they terrified rival gangs for more than a decade, their reckless sadism enabled the police to convict the twins for two murders. The first, George Cornell, was shot by Ronnie in the Blind Beggar pub, Bethnal Green, in 1966 after he called his assailant a 'fat poof'. The second, Jack 'The Hat' McVitie, was stabbed to death in 1967 by Reggie in a Stoke Newington flat after Ronnie told his brother, 'I've done mine. About time you done yours.' The twins were pursued by Inspector Leonard 'Nipper' Read, who persuaded enough of their criminal associates to testify against them at the Old Bailey in 1969. Passing sentence, Mr Justice Melford Stevenson recommended that they serve no less than thirty years and expressed the hope that this would be enough to erase them from the public mind.

In fact, their long incarceration only added to their mythic status.

▶ As organised gangs progressed from robbing banks to dealing **drugs**, as the crime rate rose and the nature of criminal acts seemed to grow ever more perverse and arbitrary, the Krays came to represent a Golden Age of the Gangster. They 'only hurt their own' (i.e. other gangsters), loved their mother and, like feudal warlords, looked after the

▶ communities in which they lived. Their lampooning by **Monty Python** as 'the Piranha Brothers' during the 1970s, a 1989 hit single by Morrissey ('The Last of the Famous International Playboys'), and a graphic 1990 film biography, *The Krays*, all failed to dent that roseate image. When the twins were allowed out of jail for their mother's funeral in 1982 more than 60,000 people lined the streets of East London to do homage. When Ronnie died eight years later, a similar number paid their respects. Reggie lingered on in Parkhurst where he protected homosexual inmates from bullying, became a born-again Christian, produced an autobiography (*Born Fighter*, 1990) and got married again, to one of the many women attracted by the Kray legend. Roberta Kray was a public relations expert who led the growing calls for her husband's release.

The refusal of Home Secretaries to parole Reggie when he was plainly no longer a threat to society was a political decision that testified to the Krays' cult status and to the Establishment's fear of

condoning the libertarian impulse which they represented. **Myra** ◀
Hindley was imprisoned longer than necessary because the British
demonised her; Reggie Kray was denied his freedom because the
British romanticised him. Justice was not done in either case. Reggie
was finally released on compassionate grounds in August 2000 after
being diagnosed with terminal cancer. A macabre deathbed interview
with him by the **BBC** only attracted 5 million viewers and when he ◀
died two months later, only 2,500 turned out for his funeral. Mr Justice
Melford Stevenson's wish was starting to come true.

K

■ Labour Party

The Labour Party was founded after a meeting of **trade unionists** and socialist bodies, including the **Fabian Society** and the Independent Labour Party (ILP), in February 1900. Initially known as the Labour Representation Committee (LRC), its purpose was to secure the election of working-class candidates to **parliament**. During the years between the passage of the Second Reform Act (1867) and 1900 several working men had been elected, but they had fought under the **Liberal** label. Now the trade unions, with a membership of around 2 million, had a party of their own. But the new organisation got off to a relatively slow start. At the general election of 1900 only 15 LRC candidates were nominated. Two of them were successful, including the Glaswegian trade unionist and ILP stalwart Keir Hardie who had first entered the Commons in 1892.

After this modest beginning, the Law Lords' ruling in the Taff Vale case of 1901 that trade unions could be sued boosted the number of LRC-affiliated unions from an original 41 to 158. Labour's official membership rose to nearly 1 million. There was another important advance in 1903 when a limited electoral pact was negotiated with the Liberals. As a result, 29 MPs were elected in the 1906 general election and the Committee adopted its more familiar name. By the outbreak of the First World War the tally had increased to 42, and in May 1915 Arthur Henderson became the first Labour Cabinet minister, in the Asquith coalition.

Labour's Leaders

Keir Hardie (1906–8); Arthur Henderson (1908–10 and 1914–17, 1931–2); George Barnes (1910–11); Ramsay MacDonald (1911–14 and 1922–31); George Lansbury (1932–35); Clement Attlee (1935–55); Hugh Gaitskell (1955–63); Harold Wilson (1963–76); James Callaghan (1976–80); Michael Foot (1980–83); Neil Kinnock (1983–92); John Smith (1992–4); Tony Blair (since 1994).

The war confronted Labour with a choice between nationalism and an idealistic yearning for pan-European unity among workers. Its chairman, the pacifist **Ramsay MacDonald**, resigned from his post, bequeathing a divided party to his successor, Henderson. At the 1918 general election 18 Labour candidates stood on behalf of **Lloyd George**'s coalition government, while 63 opposition Labour MPs were elected. But these setbacks were less damaging than the wounds which the Liberals were inflicting on themselves. When the coalition dissolved, Labour won 142 seats at the 1922 general election, beating the Liberals for second place. After an even stronger performance in December 1923 it formed a government for the first time. This administration, led by MacDonald, left office after only a few months. But it added to the party's prestige, and allayed any serious fears about its intentions, so soon after the Bolshevik Revolution in Russia. The party's constitution, adopted in 1918, pledged to secure 'common ownership of the means of production' for the 'producers by hand or by brain'. At the time its phrases were ambiguous enough to win endorsement from an organisation which included few committed socialists, and MacDonald's ministers lacked the parliamentary power to put **nationalisation** into practice even if they had wanted to. ◀

Although Labour was still unable to match the total vote for the **Conservatives**, it formed another government in 1929. Thus the party ◀ was in power during the **Great Depression**, and in the autumn of 1931 ◀ it was faced with an agonising decision over government expenditure. The majority of the Cabinet was unwilling to accept cuts in **unem-** ◀ **ployment** benefit demanded by the Treasury. Partly under the influence of King George V, MacDonald agreed to remain in office and implemented the measures. He remained as Prime Minister until 1935, but his coalition government was dominated by the Conservative Party; only three of his old Cabinet colleagues agreed to stay on with him. Henderson, who had served as Foreign Secretary, resumed his caretaking role as the bulk of the shattered party returned to opposition. MacDonald's name became synonymous with betrayal, and his ghost continued to haunt Labour for the rest of the century.

At the 1931 election the divided party returned only 65 MPs in total, 13 of whom stayed loyal to MacDonald. But in part this result reflected the distorting effects of the British electoral system. Altogether the party polled nearly 7 million votes, a higher percentage of the electorate than it had attracted in 1923. The revival continued in 1935. Under its new leader Clement Attlee Labour was ambivalent, at best, on the subject of rearmament. But **Churchill**'s wartime coalition ◀ included Labour ministers, such as Ernest Bevin, Stafford Cripps and Attlee himself, who were widely credited for efficient and dynamic leadership on the 'Home Front'. The landslide Labour victory of 1945 surprised most observers, but the Conservatives were associated with economic depression and the **appeasement** of foreign dictators. By ◀ contrast, Labour seemed to offer a fresh start for the country.

The Attlee governments of 1945–51 have always been regarded as a positive (if not sacred) model for Labour, to contrast with the bugbear of 'MacDonaldism'. The party achieved much, at a time of economic stringency. Key industries, such as coal and the railways, were nationalised, and the fiery Welsh orator **Aneurin ('Nye') Bevan** ◀ established a comprehensive **National Health Service** (NHS). But ◀

L

there was an ambiguity in the government's record. The industries selected for nationalisation had been struggling badly before the war, and their unwieldy new management structures were dominated by private-sector veterans. Meanwhile, in order to establish the NHS, Bevan was compelled to offer concessions to the British Medical Association (BMA), allowing consultants to continue the 'private' treatment of affluent patients. Like the absurd first- and third-class compartments of state-owned railway carriages, medical provision was an everyday reminder of a divided society.

Although Labour was re-elected in 1950 its leading ministers were exhausted. Despite attracting a record vote of almost 14 million in October 1951, the party lost office and remained in opposition for the next thirteen years. After 1955, under the leadership of the middle-class intellectual Hugh Gaitskell, there was almost continuous argument about the true nature of the party. The 'Gaitskellite' revisionists tried to reform the party's constitution, arguing that the commitment to nationalisation had become an unnecessary handicap. They claimed that, contrary to Marxist theory, capitalism had been transformed and state ownership was now irrelevant at best. Gaitskell also urged his party to accept Britain's nuclear arsenal. On this subject he eventually prevailed, with Bevan's surprising support. To other socialists Gaitskell seemed like a new incarnation of MacDonald, this time seeking to enforce his 'betrayal' of socialism on the party as a whole.

Labour lost two elections under Gaitskell, but by 1963 the Conservatives were losing popularity and a change of government was looking increasingly likely when the opposition leader suddenly died at the beginning of that year. The new leader, Harold Wilson, won left-wing support in the leadership election, partly because he had resigned from the Attlee government (along with Bevan) over the imposition of NHS prescription charges. As Prime Minister between 1964 and 1970, however, he proved a bitter disappointment to socialists. After a protracted struggle the steel industry was nationalised, but Wilson seemed more interested in managing his divided party than in driving it decisively towards the left. An experiment with detailed **economic planning** was quickly abandoned, and before the party lost office in 1970 it had introduced proposals to curb trade union power. Although this idea was dropped in the face of union opposition, it helped to convince the left that without a radical transformation of the party it would never live up to the original intentions of 1900. When Labour subsequently opposed the Heath government's package of very similar measures of trade union reform, Wilson merely looked opportunistic.

Wilson himself was surprised when Labour returned to office in February 1974, and after narrowly winning a further election that October he seemed to have lost his appetite for power. He resigned in

April 1976, amid rumours of 'dirty tricks' by the security services. Under his successor James Callaghan Labour had to establish another pact with the Liberals in order to hang on. High **inflation** forced ◀ Callaghan to adopt a policy of pay restraint, and the International Monetary Fund (IMF) imposed deep cuts in public spending. The government fell, unlamented, in May 1979.

Labour was out of power for another 18 years. Although this gave it ample time for internal debate over its real purpose, it also allowed successive Conservative governments to attack the legacy of the Attlee years. At first Labour moved to the left, adopting a manifesto for the 1983 election which opposed membership of **Europe**, promised unilat- ◀ eral disarmament and envisaged a significant extension of public ownership. A morale-shattering defeat provoked further soul-searching. Neil Kinnock, who succeeded his mentor Michael Foot as leader, decided that the party could never regain power unless it returned to the centre-left. Members of the Trotskyite Militant Tendency were expelled, and the party's radical policies were gradu-ally discarded.

In effect, Kinnock had accepted the general argument of the **Social** ◀ **Democratic Party** (SDP), which had split from Labour in 1981. While socialists claimed that Labour had betrayed its principles in order to win and retain power (at least since 1951), the resurgent 'modernisers' accepted Gaitskell's view that capitalism could be humanised and its wealth-creating powers harnessed to the cause of social justice. On this view, Labour's previous leaders had been handicapped, rather than helped, by the unrealistic visions of the left. The aim of the party should be to work for justice within the existing economic order, effecting a modest redistribution of wealth through the tax system, securing full employment, and ensuring high-quality public services.

Had Kinnock won in 1992 – or if his successor John Smith had survived to win the 1997 general election – this broad programme might have been given a trial run in government. Instead, before Labour regained power its leadership had fallen into the hands of a group which made even the SDP look like the Militant Tendency. At best, they mistakenly believed that **Thatcherism** had exploited a ◀ genuine mood across all Britain's classes. Others, one suspects, were simply relieved that they could embrace ideas which would increase their own prosperity, and enrich their families. **Tony Blair**, elected ◀ leader in 1994, gave the impression of belonging to the latter faction. He endorsed economic inequality in principle, and developed an infat-uation for the private sector which owed more to his hatred of trade unions than any objective assessment of economic performance. The commitment to public ownership was duly dropped from the party's constitution, and replaced with a form of words which made the vague original formulation seem as clear as the Ten Commandments.

In hindsight, it is difficult to avoid the conclusion that Labour was a victim of its own success; or rather, that its troubles have arisen from success in uncongenial circumstances. When it adopted its constitution in 1918 power was a distant prospect; at best, in the near future it seemed possible that it would form part of a Liberal-dominated government. Universal suffrage would give a clear preponderance to the working class, but even before the franchise was extended in 1918 the party's leaders already knew that this could not guarantee electoral success. If capitalism entered a crisis it was possible that workers would begin to vote as one for 'their' party, but in the meantime Labour would have to be something like a parliamentary pressure group, retaining its separate identity because in the final analysis the Liberals could not be trusted to prioritise the interests of working people.

Ironically, the precipitate and unexpected decline of the Liberal Party confronted Labour with a dilemma from which it has never recovered. The party had always attracted middle-class intellectuals, but these activists had tended to outflank the mass trade union membership on the left. After the Liberal eclipse, however, Labour became highly attractive to ambitious people (like Harold Wilson) who would surely have worked within the older party had it retained its position as the natural alternative to the Conservatives. The notion of
▶ well-heeled, vaguely well-meaning **public-school** products like Gaitskell and Blair emerging as party leaders would have been quite unthinkable to Keir Hardie. But with the Liberals ruled out as a vehicle for self-promotion, the only question of interest is why they did not
▶ join the Conservatives who themselves embraced **consensus** politics after 1945.

Judged by the intentions of its founders, then, it would be reasonable to argue that the Labour Party only enjoyed real power for the six Attlee years. The first two minority administrations were too weak and short-lived to achieve much. Between 1951 and 1994 Labour MPs dragged out an uneasy existence, as a Liberal (or Social Democratic) Party in all but name, almost entirely funded by workers who had little or nothing in common with their supposed parliamentary representatives. Only since the advent of Tony Blair has this unsatisfactory arrangement begun to unravel. Despite some modest window-dressing, Blair has verified Keir Hardie's analysis. There is a conflict between the interests of capital and labour, and only a workers' government can be trusted to carry through a determined programme in the interests of 'the producers by hand or by brain'. Unfortunately for socialists, hardly anyone in Britain is 'producing' any more; and those that do produce work in conditions which promote individualism rather than solidarity of any kind.

For many years young liberals had been forced to join the Labour Party because there was no other political home to go to. At the beginning of the twenty-first century, by contrast, the trade unions were forced to stick with 'New' Labour for precisely the same reason. The ◄ introduction of state funding for the political parties, or a system of proportional representation, might remove these strange anomalies and promote a more realistic political alignment in the future. The most logical outcome would be a reunion of Labour and the Liberals. Only a recognition by the leadership that many party members retain tribal loyalties has prevented this from happening already, and eloquent commentators have long lamented a split without which Thatcherism would probably have never happened. But for anyone who dreams of reversing the political and social trends of the past few decades, the merger will probably come too late.

■ Language

The English language unites the world but it continues to divide the British. Observing the extent to which class dominates their culture, ◄ the American sociologist Lewis Mumford observed that 'the English are branded on the tongue at birth'. It was not always so. Lingual hierarchies are a creation of the mid-eighteenth to mid-twentieth centuries, and in particular of the Victorian reformation of manners. Previously, regional accents denoted simply the regional origins of the speaker and not his or her status. Only royalty, aristocracy and senior ◄ clergy spoke what was popularly known as 'the King's/Queen's English – what phoneticians now call 'standard English' or 'received pronunciation' (RP). Based on the speech patterns of the southern elite, its main characteristics are the short *r* so that harbour becomes *hahbah*; and the long *a* so that path becomes *pahth* (in contrast to the north of England where the *a* is short).

Cockney is the prime example of that cultural transformation. It was once spoken by virtually all Londoners from doctors to chimney sweeps. Hence the fact that the phrase 'born within the sound of Bow Bells' refers to St Mary Le Bow in the heart of the City of London and not, as some assume, the Bow of east London. The late-Victorian romanticisation of Cockneys as cheery, patriotic working people was made possible by the fact that the London accent had recently become exclusive to the slums of the East End. Cockney rhyming slang is also a modern phenomenon and it highlights the mass media's ability to influence linguistic developments. A certain amount of slang was spoken in previous eras, especially associative phrases like *trouble and strife* (wife). But most of it, especially euphemistic phrases like *Bristols* (Bristol City = titty) was invented by music hall, radio and TV ◄

scriptwriters, then disseminated by popular entertainers like the comedian Max Miller (1895–1963) who specialised in sexual innuendo.

▶ Cockney also illustrates the effect that foreign cultures have had on the English language. The large number of **Jewish** immigrants who settled in the East End as a result of Continental pogroms between the 1860s and 1930s brought with them Yiddish expressions, some of which remain in use, like *nosh* (food). The verb *gazump*, meaning to sell a property to one buyer having verbally accepted a lower price from another one, comes from the Yiddish word *gezumph*, meaning to swindle. Cockney was also a conduit for words and phrases picked up

▶ around the **British Empire**. For example, the common word for friend – *mate* – is Australasian in origin and *trek* (journey) is Afrikaans. India had the biggest influence, for two reasons: first, because, thanks to William Jones (an eighteenth-century colonial judge and amateur philologist) we know that the origins of English, like that of other European languages, lie partly in the ancient Indian language of Sanskrit. Second, because, by the time Jones made his discovery, India had become Britain's most populous and prestigious colony, with a concomitant impact on the speech of its rulers. The Cockney term 'Let's have a *shufti*' (look) is Hindustani in origin, while *doolally* (demented) stems from Deolali, a town near Bombay that contained a mental hospital for British troops. A Victorian glossary of Anglo-Indian words ran to 26,000 entries and today the *Oxford English Dictionary* (*OED*) still lists around 900.

The *OED* – first compiled between 1884 and 1928 by two Scottish philologists, Sir James Murray and Sir William Craigie – codified the grammar, vocabulary and pronunciation of the English language. So too did the introduction of state education between 1870 and 1944 which placed the teaching of standard English at the heart of school curricula. A leading textbook of the early twentieth century, *The Pronunciation of English* (1909), stated, 'It is necessary to set up a standard and the standard selected is the pronunciation which appears to be most usually employed by Southern English persons who have been educated at the great public boarding schools.' The work of schoolteachers was augmented by private elocution tutors, the numbers of whom grew during the Edwardian era. They catered for ambitious men and women of humble origins who saw a refined accent as a pass-

▶ port to success. **George Bernard Shaw** (an advocate of phonetic spelling) satirised the practice in *Pygmalion* (1916) when Eliza Doolittle is shown how to speak 'proper' by the phonetician Henry Higgins. In real life, those whose careers benefited from elocution lessons were

▶ the **Conservative** Prime Ministers Edward Heath and **Margaret Thatcher**.

The most influential policing of English in the first half of the twentieth century was carried out by the **BBC**. Lord Reith believed that ◀ 'you cannot raise social standards without raising speech standards', and in 1926 he set up a Committee on Spoken English which monitored the accents and diction of announcers and performers. By the 1930s, the term 'Queen's English' had given way to 'BBC English' to denote the ideal way for Britons to speak, and 'well-spoken' had become a popular term of approval for those who actually used it. Among the Committee's members was the art historian Sir Kenneth Clark. A scion of Scottish textile magnates educated at Eton and Oxford, Clark's clipped English accent evidenced the extent to which national as well as regional ones had been ironed out among the upper classes. However, accent remained a distinguishing feature of the majority. Indeed, throughout Britain, the standardisation of English was more of an ideal than a process; one that people were encouraged to aspire to, and often admired, but which had little effect on their patterns of interlocution.

Furthermore, nationalist claims that the Scottish and Welsh *languages* declined as a result of English hegemony are bogus. Whereas in Ireland, the British state actively discouraged the use of Gaelic, in Scotland and Wales native languages went into decline when industrialisation linked each country more closely to England and the wider world, and people freely chose to learn the lingua franca in order to improve their lot. By 1961, only 3 per cent of Scots could speak the Scottish variant of Gaelic (most of them in the Highlands and Islands of western Scotland). Despite state-sponsored attempts to revive it, by 2001 the number had fallen to 0.7 per cent. Simultaneous Gaelic translations of Scottish parliamentary debates following **devo-** ◀ **lution** in 1998 symbolised for many the rebirth of a nation but concealed the fact that there were more Gujerati-speaking MSPs than there were Gaelic-speaking ones. Lallans, a dialect of Lowlands English, was championed by **Hugh MacDiarmid** and other luminaries ◀ of the Scottish literary renaissance during the mid-twentieth century; but it too was eschewed by their compatriots.

Unlike Scotland, Wales does not have its own education system. Yet, precisely because it lacks this and other institutions of state, revivalists had more success, arguing that its language was a necessary way for the Welsh to mark themselves out from their larger neighbours. The revival began in 1962, when the **Plaid Cymru** founder, Saunders ◀ Lewis, started Cymdeithas yr Iaith Gymraeg (the Welsh Language Society) to press for Welsh to be offered in all secondary schools and for it to be given the same legal status as English. It achieved both aims in 1967 when **parliament** passed the Welsh Language Act. In 1961, the ◀ number of speakers had fallen to 23 per cent of the population (down from 54 per cent at the turn of the century), most of them residing in the rural areas of north and west Wales. By 1991, the figure had begun to stabilise at 19 per cent and a larger proportion of the bilingual population lived in urban areas than at any time since the Industrial Revolution. Some chafed at nationalists' insistence that bilingualism was a test of nationality. Eventually, however, the Welsh language came to be seen, by speakers and non-speakers alike, as a distinguishing feature of the Welsh people and a source of pride for all. The same was true to a lesser extent in the county of Cornwall. A pressure group, Tyr ha Tavas (Land and Language), formed in 1932, secured the creation of a Cornish Language Board in 1967 and the provision of optional courses in secondary schools. Though less than 1 per cent of the population spoke Cornish by the end of the century, here too it became a source of pride.

For the majority of Britons who remained monolingual, hierarchies of speech became less rigid in the second half of the twentieth century. In order to mobilise the population during the Second World War, the BBC relaxed its linguistic rules, notably by allowing Wilfred Pickles to read the news in his Yorkshire accent in 1940, an event that ▶ shocked millions of listeners. Post-war competition from the ITV ▶ network – in particular the launch of Lancashire **soap opera** *Coronation Street* in 1961 – encouraged the Corporation to broadcast more regional accents in drama and current affairs as well as in light entertainment, where they were traditionally confined. Ultimately, what caused the authority of standard English to be undermined in the 1960s was the unprecedented social mobility effected by affluence and ▶ better access to **education**, together with the decline of deference ▶ brought about by the **Suez crisis** and the **Profumo Affair**. By 1970, it was once more considered acceptable to speak in a regional accent, as a result of which the link between accent and class became more ambiguous. The surge of working-class pop stars had a particular impact. The Liverpudlian accent was heavily influenced by Irish immigrants to Merseyside in the nineteenth century and had been despised ▶ as a consequence ever since. Yet, when spoken by the **Beatles**, it became instead a marker of wit and intelligence and an emblem of a resurgent, more democratic, British culture.

Such was the power of that revolution that the urban middle classes began to adopt the speech patterns of the working classes, while members of the upper classes adopted those of the middle classes, leaving few except the Queen herself in command of the ▶ Queen's English. **George Orwell**'s observation in *The Road to Wigan Pier* (1937) that 'We of the sinking middle classes . . . have nothing to lose but our aitches' was audibly taking place throughout the UK. Working-class speech patterns changed too. America had some influence, for example in the adaption of the term 'cool' from the jazz scene of the 1950s. But black immigration had more influence, and Jamaican English the most. It first received scholarly attention in F.G. Cassidy's *Jamaica Talk* (1953). Its adoption by white, Asian, African and Oriental British youth was effected through music of Jamaican origin, primarily reggae and rap. The street culture of sex, drugs and violence that black music celebrated added to the allure of the accents, dialects and language contained within its lyrics.

The phonetician who first studied the linguistic blurring of class boundaries – Professor J.C. Wells – noted in *Accents of English* (3 vols, 1982) that a softer variant of Cockney dominated. What Wells termed 'Estuary English' was characterised by the dropping of 'l's as well as 'h's – hence 'milk' became 'miwk'. More importantly, Wells observed that this accent was leaving its base in London and spreading not only to the Thames Estuary but throughout the south and even into the Midlands. The fact that the working-class accent of south-east England was the most prevalent of those adopted by the downwardly mobile middle classes, rather than, for example, that of Merseyside, was a testament to the continuing economic and cultural dominance of that region within the UK. If standard English was based on the historic nexus of London, Oxford and Cambridge, and Estuary English on that of London, Harlow and Croydon, then, one might ask, how much had really changed since Wilfred Pickles made his historic radio broadcast?

Of all the changes wrought by the Victorian reformation of manners, that of speech had the least practical effect on the British. Whereas sexual Puritanism damaged thousands of lives by stigmatising any who broke its codes, received pronunciation was only ever spoken by a minority of the population, and the majority who chose not to use it were tolerated, even if the branding of their tongues contributed to the frustration of their ambitions and the stunting of their lives. However, one cannot ignore the power of ideals. It is surely significant that RP was established as a linguistic standard at precisely the moment in British history when oligarchy was giving way to democracy.

■ Last Night of the Proms

Annual concert of classical music held in London, which became a popular vehicle for Anglo-British nationalism. The Promenade concert season, which lasts from mid-July to mid-September, was founded in 1895 by the impresario Robert Newman and the conductor Henry Wood (1869–1944). They conceived it as a way of improving public taste by slipping 'difficult' modern works into the nightly programme of crowd-pulling popular classics. Tickets were cheap and its founders created an informal atmosphere by allowing people to eat, drink and smoke during performances (though patrons were asked not to strike matches during arias).

From the start, the season was used to promote British composers like **Elgar**, Vaughan Williams and Delius. Yet, the Proms were, and still are, an international festival, with orchestras and soloists from around the world performing a vast repertoire. When the First World War led to a dislike of all things **German**, Newman and Wood stood firm against jingoism, declaring that 'the greatest examples of Music and Art are world possessions and unassailable even by the prejudices of the hour'. In 1927, the **BBC** took over the sponsorship of the Proms from the music publishers Chappell and Co., and in 1930 Henry Wood's musicians became the BBC Symphony Orchestra. Like Wood, the BBC was committed to sponsoring native composers, thanks to which a new generation flourished, led by Benjamin Britten (1913–76). The Queen's Hall, which had staged the Proms since their inception, was gutted by a German air raid in May 1941 and the season was moved to the Royal Albert Hall. It was there, in the 1950s, that the Last Night of the Proms became a national institution.

The season had always ended with patriotic musical favourites like Arne's *Rule Britannia* (1740), not to mention Wood's own arrangement of traditional British sea songs. But it was under Sir Malcolm Sargent (1895–1967; BBCSO Chief Conductor, 1950–67) that the programme fossilised into an unapologetic celebration of British majesty, climaxing with the audience singing along to Elgar's *Pomp and Circumstance March No. 1* ('Land of Hope and Glory') while waving Union Jacks, blowing whistles and hurling streamers and balloons. In the year of Elizabeth II's Coronation, the BBC tried to make the Last Night programme less bombastic and was forced to back down in the face of a public outcry. The event's sanctity was assured when it was televised for the first time in 1954. Sargent's gift for showmanship helped to bring in audiences of 15 million, an extraordinary feat for a concert of classical music. The enduring popularity of the Last Night was such that in 1996 the BBC launched Prom in the Park, an almost identical event staged simultaneously in nearby Hyde Park for those who could not get tickets for the Albert Hall.

For many people, the Last Night was simply a chance to express their patriotism in a more informal way than was possible at state occasions, and the imperial echoes it contained were for them incidental. Ultimately, however, the popularity of the event was based on nostalgia for a pre-war Britain in which the **Empire** was still intact, the working **class** and blacks knew their place and the Scots and Welsh were content. In some respects, therefore, it was fitting that the Promenaders should finally be humbled by America. In 2001, as a tribute to the 3,000 victims of terrorist attacks on the United States, the programme was amended to include American music and *Rule Britannia* briefly gave way to Samuel Barber's *Adagio*.

■ Lawrence of Arabia (1888–1935)

The most mythic of Britain's twentieth-century national heroes, whose extraordinary but short-lived career as a soldier and writer symbolised the romance and fragility of the **British Empire** in the run- ◄ up to its dissolution. Thomas Edward Lawrence was born in North Wales, the illegitimate son of a man from the Anglo-Irish gentry. Like many people with a talent for leadership and a will to power, he was short and not physically attractive. He was also a **homosexual** whose ◄ taste for sado-masochistic sex perhaps reflected the lifelong guilt he felt about being gay.

Lawrence studied at Jesus College, Oxford, where he obtained a first in history in 1910. He had a passion for medieval **architecture** and ◄ contemporary politics; and from 1911 to 1914, he was given the chance to pursue both when he was sent to spy on Ottoman military bases while assisting with archaeological excavations at Carchemish for the Ashmolean Museum. As well as giving him the opportunity for **miscegenation** with an Arab boy called Mustafa, the experience ◄ provided two things that made him useful when the First World War broke out: an expertise in cartography and a belief that the Arab people must unite to throw off the Ottoman Empire. Britain's rulers were pro-Arab because Turkey was a German ally and because the discovery of large oil deposits in the Middle East during the 1900s had made the region economically vital.

Lawrence was put to work as an intelligence officer in the Arab Bureau based in Cairo from 1914 to 1916, helping to undermine Turkish forces. At a meeting in the Hejaz desert in 1916, he won the confidence of Faisal (son of the Grand Sharif of Mecca) and left his desk job to lead the Arab Revolt. Swapping fatigues for the white and gold robes of an Arab prince, he turned Faisal's troops into a swift and ruthless guerrilla army. They disrupted Turkish communication lines by attacking railways, and in 1917 they captured the Red Sea port of Aqaba in a daring assault launched from the desert and not, as the Turks had expected, from the sea. Impressed, General Allenby promoted Lawrence Colonel and got him half a million pounds from the War Office to raise a bigger Arab force, which smashed the Turkish Fourth Army. On 1 October 1918, Lawrence led triumphant Arab troops into Damascus.

He attended the Paris Peace Conference of 1919, where his lobbying helped to install Faisal as King of Iraq (1921–58) and Abdullah as Prince of Trans-Jordan (1921–51). Ultimately both were assassinated by anti-monarchist Arab radicals, but in the short term Lawrence's problem was the British. He belatedly discovered that his compatriots were more interested in extending their own empire on the ruins of the Ottoman one than empowering Arabs. He obtained a Fellowship at All Souls, Oxford, in 1919, and became a political adviser to the Middle Eastern Department of the Colonial Office (1921–2), thanks to the

▶ patronage of **Winston Churchill** who had a lifelong admiration for
▶ him. But the military and political **Establishment** were by now suspicious of Lawrence as one who had 'gone native', and as a result his influence at the Colonial Office was limited.

Disillusioned, he joined the RAF as an ordinary aircraftsman, spending most of his service (1922–3; 1925–35) testing high-speed
▶ watercraft in Poole Harbour, site of the first Boy **Scout** camp. His earthy memoir of this time *The Mint* was published in 1955 and remains his best work. Lawrence also wrote a highly poetic and inaccurate account of his Arabian exploits, published as *The Seven Pillars of Wisdom* (1926; abridged as *Revolt in the Desert*, 1927). It began 'The dreamers of the day are dangerous men, for they may act out their dream with open eyes, to make it possible. This I did.' The book, coupled with ongoing press attention, made him into a national sensation and the legend of 'Lawrence of Arabia' joined those like Clive of India and Gordon of Khartoum in the British Empire's hall of fame.

▶ However, like many people who become the object of a **cult of celebrity**, Lawrence was scared of the legend he had helped to create and he became even more reclusive, changing his name to T. E. Shaw by deed poll in 1927 and moving to a tiny, spartan cottage at Clouds Hill, Dorset, where at night he entertained men from the Tank Corps who were based nearby. He was also befriended by the military theorist
▶ Basil Liddell Hart (1895–1970), **George Bernard Shaw**, and the novelists E.M. Forster (1879–1970) and John Buchan (1875–1940). But at the same time he became interested in fascism and in the spring of 1935, the
▶ novelist and **Mosley** supporter Henry Williamson (1895–1977) became an associate. Lawrence was returning by motorbike from a post office having telegrammed Williamson when he crashed into a tree. He died six days later on 19 May. There has since been journalistic speculation that he was assassinated by the secret services.

He was buried in Moreton churchyard, after the local vicar refused to inter him within the church because of his sexual activities in the parish. A marble effigy of him in Arab dress by Eric Kennington lies instead in an Anglo-Saxon church at Wareham that Lawrence restored during his retirement. David Lean's Oscar-winning film *Lawrence of Arabia* (1960) perpetuated the legend for another generation, though scenes illustrating his sexuality and his disputes with the British Establishment over the future of the Middle East were cut by the censor. Speaking in St Paul's Cathedral at the memorial service to Lawrence in 1936, Churchill said, 'He was a prince of our disorder.' It remains the best epitaph to a tortured, misunderstood and, perhaps, overrated man.

■ Liberal Party; Liberal Democrats

At the beginning of the twenty-first century, most Western democracies were governed by parties which fell clearly within the liberal ideological tradition. Key liberal ideas, such as equality of opportunity and of treatment under the law, free speech, tolerance and representative government, were enshrined in theory almost everywhere, even if they were commonly breached in practice. Admittedly in the USA 'liberal' was a term of abuse in Republican Party circles. But from the British perspective this was a terminological eccentricity, since in Presidential contests the line-up usually seemed to be cuddly liberal (Democratic candidate) versus nasty liberal (Republican). In Britain itself after 1990 at the latest the familiar partisan rancour could not conceal the shared underlying assumptions of all the major participants; indeed, the fact that the battle for power was no more than a squabble between branches of the same ideological family was a significant reason for the growth of political **apathy** in Britain and elsewhere.

L

> **Liberal Leaders**
> Sir Henry Campbell-Bannerman (1900–8); Herbert Henry Asquith (1908–26); David Lloyd George (1926–31); Sir Herbert Samuel (1931–5); Sir Archibald Sinclair (1935–45); Clement Davis (1945–56); Jo Grimond (1956–67); Jeremy Thorpe (1967–76); David Steel (1976–88); Paddy Ashdown (1988–99); Charles Kennedy (since 1999).

Yet a superficial reading of party conflict in twentieth-century Britain would suggest that conservatism had alternated with socialism as governing ideologies, while liberalism had been impotent since the Second World War. The Liberal Party last held office independently in 1915, when Herbert Asquith invited the **Conservatives** into a wartime coalition. In 1906 – before **women** and most workers were included in the electorate – the party won almost half of the national vote, and with 400 seats enjoyed an overall majority of 130. Despite the serious distractions of Irish Home Rule and reform of the House of Lords, the government led by Campbell-Bannerman and Asquith (after the former's death in office) was

▶ arguably the most creative of the century, laying the foundations of the modern **welfare state**. But by 1924 Liberal representation in the Commons had been reduced by 90 per cent from its peak. A slight revival in 1929 brought 59 seats, but despite frequent rumours of a Liberal rebirth the party fell below this level at all of the remaining twentieth-century general elections. Between 1945 and 1974 it never had more than 12 MPs.

Three general factors explain the 'Strange Death of Liberal England': events, individuals and institutions. The key event was the First World War. Liberal governments had presided over conflicts before, but even brief naval engagements, fought in distant oceans, had troubled a party which nursed a strong streak of pacifism. Many Liberals assumed that free trade would bring universal peace as well as prosperity; for them a war between 'civilised' nations was an

▶ unpalatable prospect, even before **conscription** was introduced in 1916. Although Asquith himself was no pacifist, three senior ministers resigned at the outbreak of war in August 1914. The Liberals already relied on the support of other parties for their parliamentary majority. Once Asquith had been compelled to govern in coalition, it was always likely that parties which were fully committed to all-out struggle against the enemy would benefit more than the Liberals from a successful outcome.

After this polite disagreement over principle came a bitter clash of

▶ egos. In 1916 Asquith's Liberal colleague, **David Lloyd George**, toppled the Prime Minister with Conservative support. Lloyd George proved a remarkable war leader. But his *coup* further tarnished a reputation which was shaky enough already. A significant group of Liberals remained loyal to Asquith, and in the general election at the end of the war these independent Liberals polled almost equally with Lloyd George's supporters. Between them the two groups only returned 161 MPs in 1918, compared to 335 Conservatives. Lloyd George remained as Prime Minister, but only at the convenience of the Conservatives, who found him surplus to requirements by 1922.

The party reunited (uneasily) in 1923, and 159 Liberals were returned in the election of that year. But the political landscape had been transformed by a second unfortunate 'event' for the Liberals –

▶ the rise of the **Labour Party**. In its early days Labour had seemed a natural ally for the Liberals, and won many of its seats because the older party agreed not to run candidates against it. After the First World War the balance of power was very different. In the 1923 election Labour won 191 seats, and formed its first government. The Liberals offered support, but there was no coalition. When that support was withdrawn on a flimsy pretext, the Liberals were the main losers. Labour had proved that it could govern without realising the nightmare visions of its opponents, while the Liberals lost vital goodwill in working-class constituencies.

In 1929 the Liberals were confronted for the first time by the institutional obstacle which would hamper them for the rest of the century. After a dynamic election campaign inspired by Lloyd George, the party received nearly a quarter of the popular vote – but returned only 59 MPs, less than a tenth of the total. Under the 'first past the post' electoral system the Liberals, like any third party, would always find it difficult to break through. From that time on it was possible for Labour and the Conservatives to deride support for the Liberals as a 'wasted vote'. In fact, since the Liberals clung tenaciously to the 'middle ground' which reflected majority opinion, most of the people who supported them as a protest against the other two parties were unwittingly registering their true preference. But they tended to save such gestures for parliamentary by-elections, hoping that the Conservatives or Labour would learn the lesson in time for the next national contest.

In these circumstances, the survival of the Liberal Party has been quite remarkable. It was represented in the coalition governments of the 1930s and 1940s, but only on a token basis. In 1951 it fielded only 109 candidates, who received 2.5 per cent of the popular vote; but still its indomitable members struggled on. Under the charismatic Jo Grimond its national profile was raised, but this only posed another awkward problem. By the early 1960s it was at least starting to win some by-elections, and to pick up numerous **local government** seats. ◄ In many other constituencies it was running second. But this meant that for the national leadership schizophrenia was a tactical necessity. When the party was challenging Labour it had to exaggerate its left-wing credentials, while against Conservative incumbents it was well advised to tone down its radicalism. It was no surprise that voters found it hard to say what the Liberals really stood for.

For a succession of leaders the only reason for perseverence was a love of the party; there was no chance of winning outright, and usually the prospect of a 'hung' parliament was unappetising, since it would require the party to support either Labour or the Conservatives in government, with the inevitable risk of outraging half of the grass-roots membership. The people who attended Liberal Party conferences were beloved by political commentators as the 'beards and sandals brigade', and were always ready to air their quirky views. Some took the idea of permanent, futile opposition as proof of their own virtue – for them, even the theoretical possibility of power was a contaminating thought. But in a media age leaders still had to talk as if a sensational victory was possible.

The election of February 1974 crystallised the Liberal dilemma. Many voters were disillusioned with both the major parties, and the

Liberals achieved their highest vote (almost 20 per cent) since 1929. Yet there were still only 14 Liberal MPs, and even if the leader Jeremy Thorpe had been able to negotiate a deal with the Conservatives this would still not have been enough to keep Edward Heath in office. Later in the decade the Liberals under David Steel entered a pact with James Callaghan's minority Labour government, but the failure of this arrangement was reflected in the return of only 11 Liberals at the 1979 general election.

▶ In 1981, however, it seemed that the Liberals would benefit from another major political upheaval. The formation of the **Social Democratic Party** (SDP), after a schism in the Labour party, was quickly followed by an electoral alliance and opinion poll ratings which supported Steel's contention that the Liberals could once again 'prepare for government'. Given the prevailing moderation of the British electorate it should have been a winning combination. But the old political 'mould' soon reasserted itself. At the 1983 election the Alliance tally of 7,780,000 votes was easily the highest for any third party in history, but it was not enough to dislodge Labour as the official opposition. The effect of the electoral system was worse than ever, yielding only 23 Liberal/SDP seats. The very popularity of the Alliance made it even less likely that either of the major parties would contemplate proportional representation.

After a similar disappointment – and protracted, often bitter, debate – the Alliance parties merged in March 1988. At first the new party took the name 'Social and Liberal Democrats', but its opponents relished the opportunity of dubbing its members 'Salads' and in 1989 it became the Liberal Democrats. Under another dynamic leader, Paddy Ashdown, the party quietly built up its parliamentary representation. There were 46 MPs after the 1997 general election, with the prospect of better to come as support for the two main parties continued to decline. But the electoral system was still punishing the Liberal Democrats, and with Labour securely in power hopes of a deal (which might have given the party seats in the Cabinet for the first time since 1945) were dashed at least for the immediate future.

Ashdown resigned as party leader in 1999. His amiable successor Charles Kennedy had an enviable inheritance, compared to most Liberal leaders throughout the twentieth century. Helped by the new popularity of tactical voting, he could hope for a healthy parliamentary contingent for years to come, and at some stage a 'hung' parliament could force a change in the electoral system. At the 2001 general election the Liberal Democrat vote-share rose slightly, to just over 18 per cent, and the party won 52 seats. Yet the key dilemma remained. Under Ashdown the Liberal Democrats had moved closer to Labour, which was only natural given the widespread unpopularity of the

Conservatives. But Kennedy could not afford to sound like an impotent echo of the government. His party had to be distinctive, without alienating anyone. In the short term, at least, the Liberal Democrats were still stuck with schizophrenia.

■ Lloyd George, David (1863–1945)

Born in Manchester, David Lloyd George was brought up in Llanystumdwy, north Wales, after his father's early death. It was a romantic setting in which he eventually chose to be buried, and although there was a great deal of poverty in the area Lloyd George's thrifty relatives ensured that he was never in want. Through his uncle Richard, a Baptist lay preacher, the boy was introduced to the central issues of late Victorian liberalism, notably temperance. From the age of 15 he began to train as a solicitor, which further honed his natural skills in the arts of persuasion. By 1885 he had set up his own legal practice, and five years later he was elected **Liberal** MP for Carnarvon Boroughs ◄ (with a majority of just 18 votes).

In **parliament** Lloyd George quickly won a reputation as a fiery ◄ orator, not least in his opposition to Balfour's **1902 Education Act,** ◄ and to the Boer War. He became a hero to many, but a devil to his opponents. In December 1901 he narrowly escaped with his life when a 30,000-strong mob of jingoistic warmongers surrounded Birmingham Town Hall when he was speaking. As President of the Board of Trade from 1905 to 1908 he established the credentials which underpinned his later success. His speeches identified him as a determined, even reckless radical; but in his official capacity he applied his energies to the causes of prosperity and industrial harmony. As Chancellor of the Exchequer (1908–15) he precipitated a constitutional crisis by introducing a new tax on land, and helped to lay the foundations of the **welfare state** by supporting Old Age Pensions and ◄ National Insurance. But he continued to arouse controversy; although he survived the **Marconi** scandal of 1913, his reputation was ◄ badly tarnished. The impression of an untrustworthy operator was reinforced by his colourful private life, which earned him the nickname of 'the goat'.

Although Lloyd George had initial doubts about the First World War, once it had begun he devoted himself to its efficient prosecution. Since the Treasury was no longer at the centre of the political action, he became successively Minister for Munitions and Secretary of State for War. Before the war his partnership with the Prime Minister, Asquith, had been a creative one. But Asquith was no war leader, and Lloyd George saw no reason to restrain allies in the press (notably **Lord** ◄

L

▶ **Beaverbrook**) who pressed for his elevation to the premiership. In December 1916 he succeeded Asquith, and immediately reformed
▶ **government** institutions to reflect the needs of the moment rather than traditional departmental divisions. While Asquith had been hampered in directing the war effort by his respect for traditional liberalism, Lloyd George was a pragmatist who had no hesitation in imposing state control, even over prices and the deployment of labour. His lack of military experience did not prevent him from bullying British generals, and his instincts sometimes proved sounder than their textbook training. But while his mistrust of the British commander, Sir Douglas Haig, seems amply justified, his attempt to undermine him by lying about the number of troops at his disposal created a distracting political furore.

During the negotiations leading up to the Treaty of Versailles (June 1919), Lloyd George used his influence to moderate the peace terms with Germany. But his later ventures into foreign policy were less successful, and his promises of 'homes for heroes' after the war began to look hollow during the post-war economic depression. The replacement of Asquith had produced lasting bitterness within the Liberal Party, and Lloyd George's preference for practical men, rather than party loyalists, deepened the split. Always ready to discard people who had outlived their usefulness, Lloyd George tacitly invited others to follow his example. After the 1918 general election he presided over a
▶ government dominated by **Conservatives**, and held his position only through their permission. This was withdrawn in October 1922, and Lloyd George never held government office again.

Lloyd George's sale of honours made him a byword for political corruption; knighthoods were available at a knock-down £10,000, and, since it was not just for Christmas but for as long as the family could sustain it, a peerage was a marvellous present at just £50,000. But given his impatience with the restraints of party, it was far-sighted to build up a personal fighting fund of over £2 million to guarantee his survival on the political scene. The proceeds of corruption promised to establish a political dynasty; his son Gwilym and his daughter Megan were elected to parliament at an early age.

After Asquith's retirement in 1926 Lloyd George became Liberal leader once again, but the party was no longer a promising vehicle for his ambitions (after his death his son and daughter would defect, to
▶ the Conservatives and **Labour** respectively). Always searching for
▶ practical ideas, he campaigned in 1929 for a **Keynesian** programme of
▶ public works to combat **unemployment**. The result was an improved share of the vote, but only 59 MPs. Another chance of office passed him by in 1931, when he was seriously ill at the time that another all-party National Government was founded. The fact that he was not

called to the colours even after his recovery is testimony to the general relief at the timing of his malady.

Later in the 1930s Lloyd George took a sympathetic interest in the German economic recovery, and if the Second World War had been lost by Britain he might have been earmarked as the leader of a puppet government. Whether he would have accepted the post is another matter; certainly he was too shrewd a gambler to do more than flirt with Britain's would-be Hitler, **Oswald Mosley**. As it was, Lloyd George ◄ was ailing when his old friend **Winston Churchill** established his new ◄ government in 1940, and turned down the suggestion of a posting to America. He died of cancer in 1945, shortly after accepting an unlikely (but cost-free) peerage. That decision closed an unbroken career of fifty-five years in the Commons.

At the time of Lloyd George's downfall **Stanley Baldwin** described ◄ him as 'a dynamic force'. Baldwin may have been right in thinking that this was a 'terrible thing' in peacetime politics; but for the purposes of war Lloyd George could hardly have been bettered. Objective comparisons with Churchill are difficult, since the direct threat to national survival was far greater in 1940–5 and this ensured that Churchill would be regarded as the ideal embodiment of the bulldog spirit. The crucial difference, perhaps, was that while both were essentially romantic visionaries, Churchill's dreams revolved around his contribution to the nation's destiny, while the Welshman Lloyd George hoped that Britain would prosper only so long as this redounded to his personal credit.

The complicated circumstances of 1916 have ensured a lasting controversy about the precise role of Lloyd George in the destruction of the Liberal Party as a major force in British politics. While Asquith proved unfit to lead the government, Lloyd George was highly unsuitable as a leader for any party. His performance as Prime Minister showed that his connection with Liberalism had been little more than a biographical accident. It was asking too much of a man of Lloyd George's temperament for him to acknowledge these points, and retire to his estate like a dictator of Republican Rome once his work was finished. As a result, he must bear the prime responsibility for the decline of the Liberal Party; but it is unlikely that he would have found this a troubling legacy.

■ Local government

In 1935 a group of experts published a volume of essays which celebrated *A Century of Municipal Progress*. One of the authors, William Robson, predicted a significant expansion of local government in the near future. The various authorities would have different priorities, but he confidently expected that somewhere in the country before too long there would be 'a municipal milk supply, municipal bakeries, municipal laundries, municipal publishing departments (for school books at least), municipal brickworks, clothing factories, restaurants, hotels'. He felt that such developments would merely be a logical extension of the accepted principles of UK local government, which was already responsible for a large and lengthening list of services to the general public.

On this view the prestige and civic pride reflected in the elegant town halls built during the Victorian era would be further bolstered; by contrast, most departments of the central state could wither away. Yet Britain's unwritten constitution meant that there was nothing to
▶ stop **parliament** from abolishing its rival. Westminster had already struck back, through Neville Chamberlain's Local Government Acts (1928 and 1929). As well as rationalising the functions of local admin-
▶ istration, Chamberlain (in co-operation with **Winston Churchill** at the Treasury) introduced new government grants to replace local revenue
▶ lost by the complete exemption of **agriculture** from local taxes, and the partial 'derating' of industry. Already the central government was
▶ providing subsidies through general taxation for education, **housing**,
▶ **police** and other services. The question was whether the relationship would remain amicable, with local government obediently following legislative guidelines laid down by the centre, or whether the two institutions would fall out. If the latter, then Westminster's increasing control of the purse-strings was bound to prove decisive.

In part, at least, the new concern reflected the increasing 'politicisation' of local government. A challenge to the traditional control of councils by well-to-do businessmen and local worthies had begun in
▶ the nineteenth century, and the rise of **Labour** presented an additional threat. But the tension between Whitehall and Town Hall seemed to affect all national politicians, regardless of party allegiance.
▶ There was a sign of further trouble ahead in **Nye Bevan's National Health Service** (NHS), which created separate health authorities rather than working exclusively through the existing councils. Even a patriotic Welshman like Bevan could not resist entirely the tendency
▶ of MPs to adopt the Westminster world-view. The **nationalisation** of gas and electricity also reduced local responsibilities (undermining among other things the idea of small-scale, 'gas and water' socialism
▶ promoted by the **Fabian Society**). In this battle, policy-makers in London were assisted by technological change, and an increasingly mobile population whose support for local sporting teams did not imply a similar respect for other civic institutions.

Local government scarcely surfaced as an issue in national elections until the 1960s. Increasingly, it was felt that the 'two-tier' system of local government based on county and district administrative units needed updating (it had been introduced in 1888). Large and expanding metropolitan areas had sprawled over county boundaries, so competing authorities now provided services in different suburbs. As a preliminary 'modernising' move, in 1963 the Greater London Council (GLC) was set up by the **Conservatives**. This included parts of ◄ Essex, Kent and Surrey as well as Middlesex and the domain of the old London County Council (LCC). A more rational framework of local government, reflecting the changing demography of Britain, would increase the powers of the various authorities, which apparently contradicted the centralising trend of previous decades. But something had to be done to increase voter interest if democracy in the UK were not to die from the roots upwards; the turnout in the 1960 borough elections had been a miserable 35 per cent.

Unfortunately the full-scale reorganisation, conducted by the Heath government in 1972, proved deeply unpopular. The minuscule county of Rutland disappeared from the map, and new Metropolitan districts severed large cities from the counties. Some of these changes were perfectly defensible, but the reformers overestimated the power of abstract logic in this context. Following the Joni Mitchell principle ('You don't know what you got till it's gone'), residents who had only noticed their local councils to the extent of complaining about the level of taxation suddenly discovered an atavistic longing for the old county boundaries. The Conservative Party, supposedly the natural protector and beneficiary of outdated attachments, undoubtedly lost support because of the reorganisation in the run-up to its disastrous 1974 election defeats. Even radicals were outraged. 'To Hell with Merseyside,' fumed the historian A.J.P. **Taylor**, a proud Lancastrian ◄ who found his Birkdale birthplace transplanted into that 'misbegotten' Metropolitan county.

But the controversy over the structure of local government proved far less damaging to the councils than the problem of finance. In May 1975 the Labour Environment Secretary, Anthony Crosland, warned councillors that 'the party's over, at least for the moment'. Public expenditure had to be curbed in the wake of the 1973–4 oil crisis, and government ministers began to worry that unless they took firmer control of local authorities their own cost-cutting measures might be futile. The idea that local government might become a bottomless pit was underlined by the 'Winter of Discontent' in which low-paid ◄ council employees brought services to a standstill.

By 1980 local government was spending around £28 billion per year overall. The new Conservative attack on the councils started slowly, focusing on the right of tenants to buy council houses. But in May 1981 the local elections reflected the government's general unpopularity, giving Labour control of all six Metropolitan Councils and impressive gains elsewhere. In the GLC the Conservatives had won a comfortable majority in the previous (1977) election. Now Labour bounced back, and after an internal party *coup* the charismatic left-winger Ken Livingstone became GLC Chairman.

▶ The centre and the localities were now more sharply divided than ever before. If this gave the central **government** a clear incentive to strike, some useful weapons were provided by the tabloid press, which suddenly discovered a fascination with local government which it had previously kept well hidden. In particular, stories about generous council grants to minority groups proved irresistible. To some readers it must have seemed that these causes monopolised councillors' attention, and that they were determined to fritter away the whole of their burgeoning budgets on spurious projects. Clear signs that councils were genuinely feeling the financial pinch – notably the sales of facilities like municipal swimming baths and school playing fields, which invariably disappeared to make way for office blocks – were ignored, or used as further evidence that councillors had perverse priorities.

It was relatively easy for the central government to cut its grants to the councils, but the main object of the exercise was to reduce overall spending; and this would not be achieved if the councils merely increased local taxes. An Act of 1984 introduced 'rate-capping', and also instructed councils to give residents more information about their expenditure. In the following year, the Metropolitan Councils and the GLC were abolished. Leaving aside the naked partisanship of these measures – which imposed far-reaching constitutional change for short-term reasons – they resolved any lingering doubts about the nature of British government. The centre had triumphed over the localities. Later, the government forced councils to allow private firms to compete for business against their own employees, hoping that this
▶ would further reduce bills while undermining the power of the **trade unions**. The 1988 Education Reform Act gave schools the right to 'opt out' of local government control; and in the same year the Local
▶ Government Finance Act introduced the **Poll Tax**. This helped to bring
▶ down the **Thatcher** government, but its replacement by a compromise Council Tax did nothing to decelerate the process of centralisation in Britain.

By 1992 local government was still accounting for around a quarter of all public expenditure – £57 billion. The failure of the Poll Tax had increased further the proportion of funding provided by the central government; now the local councils raised only a fifth of the money they spent (down from more than half in 1989/90). They still enjoyed some autonomy. But increasingly they were being seen merely as agents of the centre, and the scope of their activities was being whittled away as the Conservatives introduced a range of unelected 'quangos' to do the jobs instead. If the ballot box was no longer a reliable method of choosing businessmen to run local affairs, the electorate would have to be bypassed.

Predictably enough, turnout in the contests for the remaining elected positions declined further (from a level which was low already). The old stories of controversial grants to local pressure groups and the banning of allegedly racist nursery rhymes gave way to more disturbing tales of serious corruption. After all, since local authorities had been reduced to the status of business subsidiaries, it seemed logical for councillors to adopt business ethics. In the vicious circle generated by **Thatcherite** legislation, there was less likelihood ◄ that voters would be sufficiently motivated to expel the offenders.

'New' Labour's victory in the 1997 general election might have been ◄ taken as a signal for a local government revival; after all, the party had regularly protested against bullying from the centre, and some ministers (notably the new Education Secretary, David Blunkett) had made their reputations at council level. In practice, the new government was thankful for the Tory reforms. The logic of the changes meant that local authorities only retained any meaningful functions on sufferance. If they were deemed to be 'failing' by some arbitrary standard dreamed up by ministers, the dreaded 'private sector' could be brought in to manage things instead.

The introduction of elected Mayors (beginning with Livingstone's return to office in London in May 2000) might at one time have spurred a local government revival: but not in the prevailing atmosphere of political **apathy**. The policy had been inherited from the ◄ Conservative minister Michael Heseltine, whose ambitious plans for revitalising local politics had dwindled away into yet another half-hearted reorganisation. The thinking behind **devolution** to Scotland, ◄ Wales and Northern Ireland (and similar developments within the **European Union**) pointed to a new system of regional government in ◄ England. But for understandable reasons enthusiasm in Whitehall was muted, and the policy was bogged down in endless consultation exercises. In hindsight, 'Municipal Progress' had barely outlived its first century; after that it had been downhill all the way.

■ Lynn, Vera (b. 1917)

Popular female singer during the 1940s, famous for raising morale among British troops during the Second World War. She was born Vera Welch, in the East End of London, the daughter of a plumber and seamstress of **Jewish** extraction. She came to notice singing in local ◄ working men's clubs, adopting her grandmother's maiden name as

▶ her stage name. In 1935, she performed on the **BBC** for the first time, singing with the Joe Loss Orchestra, the most popular dance band of the time. Thereafter, she became a regular, also dueting with Charlie Kunz for the Ambrose Orchestra.

The war turned Vera Lynn into a national institution. In 1939, she was voted 'Forces Sweetheart' in a *Daily Mirror* poll, an epithet that stuck. A year later, she married a saxophone player, Harry Lewis, to whom she remained devoted until his death in 1998. Unlike American stars of the time such as Betty Grable, Vera Lynn was not glamorous or overtly sexual. Nor did she have the vocal skills of, say, Ella Fitzgerald. But her pretty, girl-next-door looks and her warm, homely sincerity appealed to men stationed abroad, for whom she became a surrogate girlfriend, offering reassurance that they would survive the ordeal and return to the country they loved. Some of her output was conventionally patriotic, notably 'There'll Always Be an England' (1939) and her popular recording of 'Land of Hope and Glory' (1942). But it was her softer, sentimental songs like 'White Cliffs of Dover' (1940), 'When the Lights Go on Again' (1941) and her most famous, 'We'll Meet Again' (1941) that best characterised her work.

In 1941, she got the first of her own radio shows, *Sincerely Yours*, of which BBC executives said, 'deplored but popularity noted'. While recording and broadcasting made Vera Lynn a star, it was her troop concerts that made her truly loved and which established her reputation as the symbol of wartime female pluck. Between 1939 and 1945 she regularly toured theatres of war, often staying in harsh conditions and singing to men on hospital wards as well as in makeshift concert halls. She packed one set of khakis and one pink chiffon dress, which cost her a year's clothing coupons and became her trademark apparel. 'Home can't be that far away 'cause you're here,' was, she reported, a typical response from the troops she called 'my boys'. It was typical of her that the men to whom she was most attached were those who served in Burma – one of the least glamorous and least successful of British operations.

Vera Lynn was briefly a star in the United States. Indeed, she was the first British artist to have a number one in America, with 'Auf Wieder-
▶ sehen Sweetheart' (1952), preceding the **Beatles**' 'She Loves You' by a decade. But she remained an essentially British figure. Her post-war
▶ charitable work for the **British Legion**, at which she constantly reprised wartime favourites for veterans, helped to make her a nostalgia act, trapped for ever in the 1940s. Yet it also cemented her reputation as the personification of the nation's Finest Hour, preceded
▶ only by **Churchill** and the **Queen Mother**. In 1967 she was made a Dame of the British Empire by Harold Wilson.

■ MacDiarmid, Hugh (1892–1978)

Scotland's most significant poet since Robert Burns and the intellectual founder of modern Scottish nationalism. He was born Christopher Murray Grieve into a farming community in Dumfriesshire, where his father was a postman. After serving in the army during the First World War, he forged a shaky career in journalism while editing three anthologies of contemporary Scottish poetry, *Northern Numbers* (1920, 1922 and 1923). These, together with his epic poem *A Drunk Man Looks at the Thistle* (1926), formed the basis of what became known as the Scottish Literary Renaissance.

The trend was first identified in a leading article of that title by the *Glasgow Herald* on 31 December 1923 amid what the newspaper identified as 'discontent with London standards and with the submersion of Scottish literature' in English manners and outlook. Aside from MacDiarmid, the movement's prominent members were Lewis Grassic Gibbon (1901–35), Sorley MacLean (1911–96) and Neil Gunn (1891–1973), with several others like Naomi Mitchison (1897–1999) on the fringes. They were influenced by Continental literature and realised that the romantic cult of Robert Burns had hampered the development of their own country's output. The cult, MacDiarmid wrote, 'has been largely responsible for landing the Scottish muse in the horrible mess it has occupied since'. Yet he and his followers remained determined to write about Scottish life. Inspired by the nation's Gaelic traditions, they used a lyrical style that celebrated the rural world of the Highlands. Much of their work explored the tension between their love of the land and the call of urban, cosmopolitan life – an exemplar of which is Gibbon's *Sunset Song* (1932), the first of his *Scots Quair* trilogy of novels.

Some, like Sorley MacLean, wrote in Gaelic. Others employed 'braid' Scots to add authenticity. A literary language, it combined the speech patterns of modern Scotland with the idioms of earlier Scottish authors. MacDiarmid accused poets like Edwin Muir (1887–1959) of betraying their country by writing solely in English. In the 1923 poem 'Gairmscoile' (Gaelic for 'school-call') he wrote: 'For we ha'e faith in Scotland's poo'ers / The present's theirs, but a' the past and future's oors'. MacDiarmid's faith in Scotland's powers was buttressed by a lifelong dislike of the English (he listed 'Anglophobia' among his recreations in *Who's Who*). He regarded the English as an innately aggressive and corrupt people who had colonised and exploited Scotland over several centuries. As the **British Empire** began to falter, he argued that ◄ the Scots had a historic opportunity to shake off southern rule. 'The English are finished as a world power,' he wrote in 1949, 'surely there is no need to slobber kisses on the feet that are trampling us down.'

His politics were an amalgam – unusual in Britain at the time – of nationalism and socialism that led him close to what he himself described as 'a kind of Scottish fascism'. Like **Oswald Mosley**, he was influenced by the Social Credit movement of the anti-semitic Scottish thinker C.H. Douglas (1879–1952), which aimed to counter capitalism (and the Jewish usury on which it was thought to be based) through state loans to the poor. At the same time, MacDiarmid saw the close community structure of the Highlands as a proto-Communist society and was influenced in this respect by the political activist John MacLean (1879–1923). MacLean was appointed Soviet Consul on the Clyde after the Russian Revolution and was imprisoned by the British government for sedition for his part in the 'Red Clyde' strikes of 1916–23. But, wary of Russian influence on the **Communist Party of Great Britain**, he set up the Scottish Socialist Party, the outlook of which owed more to Irish republican nationalism, especially that of James Connolly (1868–1916), the Scots-born revolutionary executed for his part in the **Easter Rising**. Although frequently penniless, MacDiarmid lived a less dangerous life than either MacLean or Connolly. He spent most of it secluded in the Highlands with his Cornish-born second wife, Valda. There, he was appointed a Justice of the Peace and was elected a **Labour** member of Montrose town council. He also served in the Merchant Navy during the Second World War and in 1950 he accepted a Civil List pension for his services to British literature.

However, MacDiarmid did more than cheer from a safe distance behind the barricades. In 1927–8, he helped to found the National Party of Scotland (forerunner of the **Scottish National Party**) together with the writer Compton Mackenzie (1883–1972). The two men represented the radical and moderate wings of the SNP that continued to do battle into the twenty-first century. Whereas Mackenzie wanted Home Rule within a United Kingdom bound together by the monarchy, MacDiarmid argued for an independent Scottish republic within a united Europe. After frequent disputes, MacDiarmid was expelled from the party in 1933 for being too left-wing. His poem 'Hymn to Lenin' (1931) had not impressed nationalists and he joined the Communist Party in 1934. Unfortunately, his new comrades saw his belief in Scotland's uniqueness as a distraction from the class struggle and in 1937 they expelled him for 'national deviation'.

Undeterred, he stood as an Independent Scottish Nationalist at the 1945 general election. In 1957, he rejoined the Communist Party, at a time when most left-wing British intellectuals were deserting it, their disillusionment with Stalinism heightened by the Soviet invasion of Hungary in 1956. In 1964, he stood as the Communist candidate against the **Conservative Party** leader, Alec Douglas-Home, in the

Highland constituency of Kinross. He attacked Douglas-Home on the grounds that he typified a Scottish **aristocracy** that was historically a ◄ Trojan horse for English imperialism. 'He is a zombie,' declared MacDiarmid, 'personifying the obsolescent traditions of [a] big land-lord order . . . All his education and social affiliations are anti-Scottish. Sir Walter [Scott] warned long ago that a Scotsman unscotched would only become a damned mischievous Englishman, and that is precisely what has happened in this case.' He won 127 votes; Douglas-Home won 16,659.

Like **George Orwell**, for most of his life MacDiarmid tried to recon- ◄ cile two ideologies that were at loggerheads. Unlike Orwell, he had an authoritarian temper that led him to flirt with the far left and the far right. But the main difference between the two is that, whereas Orwell's radicalism had little direct influence on English political culture, MacDiarmid's helped to shape that of Scotland. Although he played no active part in the post-war development of the SNP, he was acknowledged as the intellectual conscience of the nationalist move-ment. The SNP's leftward shift, its increasingly firm commitment to independence, and the popular support this attracted from the 1960s onwards, vindicated the stance he had taken as a young idealist in the 1920s. So too did the party's fresh enthusiasm for **European Union** in ◄ the decades after his death.

MacDiarmid also had a long-term impact on the literary culture of his homeland. As a cohesive movement, the Scottish Literary Renaissance was short-lived, its last testament being *Scottish Scene* (1934), a collection of poetry and essays written jointly by him and Gibbon. But its influence was apparent in a new generation of writers that emerged in the 1980s to challenge the dominance of the English scene. Irvine Welsh (b. 1961) and James Kelman (b. 1946) were among those who wrote vividly about dispossessed and transient lives in contemporary Scotland. They too used Scottish dialect, the validity of which was formally acknowledged in England when Kelman won the Booker Prize for the novel *How late late it was, how late* (1994). MacDiarmid's influence extended beyond literature. He helped to set up the Edinburgh Fringe Festival with other Scottish Communists in the 1950s, having criticised the city's main festival, established in 1947, as 'a snob culture jamboree for the delectation of the decadent bourgeoisie'.

Hugh MacDiarmid personified the strengths and weaknesses of Scottish nationalism. His resolute belief in the cultural uniqueness of Scotland, his ability to express it and inspire others to do so embold-ened Scots in an era when their country's economic decline, and English indifference to it, was denting their confidence. Yet his viru-lent Anglophobia and his tendency to blame England for all his

M

country's failings found its way into the nationalist movement, further souring Anglo-Scottish relations and undermining the attempt to make Scotland a cosmopolitan European nation. Towards the end of his life he wrote that his job had been 'to erupt like a volcano, emitting not only flame, but a lot of rubbish'. It remains an accurate summary of the cultural and political movements to which he contributed in over sixty years of passionate activity.

■ MacDonald, Ramsay (1866–1937)

James Ramsay MacDonald was born in the Scottish fishing village of Lossiemouth, the illegitimate son of poor agricultural labourers. He never knew his father; according to one story his mother once helpfully pointed him out working in a distant field. But a local schoolmaster spotted his potential and urged him to extend his horizons. After travelling to London he joined the Independent Labour Party (ILP) in 1894; previously he had tried to win selection as a **Liberal** candidate. When the ILP joined the Labour Representation Committee (LRC) in 1900 he was appointed the first secretary of what became the **Labour Party**. In this capacity he negotiated an agreement with the Liberals which gave the new party the chance to boost its parliamentary representation at the 1906 general election. He himself became MP for Leicester in that contest.

In 1911 MacDonald was elected Chairman of the Parliamentary Labour Party (PLP), which now had 42 members. In the same year he lost his wife Margaret, who had provided him with some economic independence, and more important emotional support. But this only spurred him to greater efforts. He was a prolific author, expounding a 'revisionist' or evolutionary brand of socialism which in practice was difficult to distinguish from the 'new' liberalism exhibited by **Lloyd George** and **Winston Churchill**. Before war broke out in August 1914 Lloyd George offered him a seat in the Asquith coalition government, but he refused, rightly sensing a trap. A convinced pacifist, he relinquished the party leadership at the start of the conflict, and was widely abused for his stance; in a shameful foretaste of later tabloid tactics, the bellicose newspaper *John Bull* exposed his illegitimacy and denounced him as a traitor who deserved to be executed. He lost his seat at the 1918 general election.

If Lloyd George had delivered his promise of 'homes for heroes' after the years of wartime sacrifice, MacDonald's career might never have recovered. Instead, disillusionment with the government quickly restored his reputation. His original flirtations with the Liberals were (briefly) forgotten; he now seemed to be an heroic figurehead for the working class, ready to put his principles before his own interests. In

1922 he returned to parliament as MP for Aberavon, and was re-elected as Labour's leader.

When Labour was given the opportunity of forming a minority government after the general election of December 1923 MacDonald was faced with a difficult decision. Even if he had been committed to radical change, his reliance on Liberal support meant that he would have little room for manoeuvre as Prime Minister. Yet the formation of a Labour administration would arouse unrealistic expectations among its supporters. In the end it was felt that a refusal of office would amount to a confession of incompetence. On MacDonald's insistence, when his ministers went to Buckingham Palace they conformed to the approved dress code. It was an accurate indication of their intentions; the government attempted little, and achieved hardly anything, before it fell in October 1924 amid various manufactured 'Red scares'. The ensuing election was dominated by the forged 'Zinoviev Letter', in which the Soviet President of the Communist International supposedly advised his British comrades to stir up an insurrection. Although this incident rightly convinced Labour supporters that some elements within the **Establishment** would stop at nothing to discredit the ◄ party, its limited impact on the voters is suggested by the fact that Labour's support actually increased in 1924. But MacDonald himself was exposed to further smears, because a childhood friend had given him financial support and the use of a Daimler car. It was pretty small beer compared to Lloyd George's recent sale of honours, which the Tory press had tolerated while the Liberal leader remained useful to them.

M

Although it lost the 1924 election, Labour recovered well and formed a second government in June 1929. However, once again MacDonald was dependent on Liberal support, and handicapped by inadequate colleagues like the Chancellor Philip Snowden whose economic outlook owed more to Adam Smith than to Karl Marx. In the face of economic depression MacDonald had no answers; and those who offered workable alternatives (like **Oswald Mosley**) were rebuffed. ◄ Unable to accept a 10 per cent cut in **unemployment** benefit, the ◄ government resigned in August 1931. MacDonald agreed to stay on as head of a National Government, and Snowden duly imposed the cuts. The pound was devalued anyway, leaving the gold standard in September. MacDonald's former colleagues felt (probably rightly) that the authorities would never have allowed them to take this step, which inevitably improved the prospects for Britain's exporters.

MacDonald remained Prime Minister until June 1935. After handing over to **Stanley Baldwin** he stayed in the Cabinet until May ◄ 1937, by which time he was regarded as a broken old man. In November he died, during a sea journey undertaken to restore his health. In his last years he had concentrated on foreign policy, but the failure of his efforts was registered by the beginning of British rearmament from 1935. His only tangible legacy was a bitter split in his own party, which was crushed at the 1935 general election (MacDonald himself lost Aberavon and had to sneak back into parliament courtesy of one of the anachronistic university constituencies).

With hindsight, MacDonald's decision to form a government in 1924 had proved a fatal miscalculation. In theory, the establishment of Labour as a party of government, prepared to abide by constitutional practice, was a reasonable strategic move. But emerging so soon after the Bolshevik Revolution (and MacDonald's own troubles during the First World War), the government was bound to be attacked by the vermin of Fleet Street. After this experience it was understandable that senior party figures should develop an aversion to bold policy initiatives; and in this sense the second failure, of 1929–31, was merely a new instalment of the first one.

Whatever his qualities as a political organiser and a diplomat – and his ability to move an audience with high-sounding rhetoric – MacDonald himself was not equipped to lead a major party. As Prime Minister, he was aptly characterised by Churchill in January 1931 as a 'Boneless Wonder'. Vain and oversensitive, with an incongruous preference for aristocratic society, he was unlucky to have the chance of greatness thrust upon him and to die in the certain knowledge that his tireless work for his party in its early years would count as nothing against the odium produced by his 'betrayal' of 1931.

■ Manufacturing; services

At the beginning of the twentieth century Britain was still a manufacturing superpower, but it was no longer dominant. The United States had recently surpassed it in production of the sinews of modern society – coal and steel. Germany overtook Britain's overall manufacturing output just before the First World War. Once a source of national pride (if not complacency), the league tables for manufacturing production were awaited with apprehension at that time. By the end of the century they were hardly noticed at all. Even the
▶ Labour Party, which had traditionally drawn much of its support from the heavily unionised manufacturing sector, was apparently unconcerned. Instead, academics conducted a post-mortem on British industry. Some historians attributed the decline to cultural factors,
▶ notably an antipathy to 'trade' which was a hangover from aristo-
▶ cratic society. In the universities, an overreaction against traditional subjects helped to inspire a dash towards 'vocational' courses. No one seemed too troubled by the fact that the boom areas for the new

courses were tourism and catering rather than engineering.

By the year 2000 Britain was not exactly a 'post-industrial society'. For example, despite this industry's various vicissitudes, it was still producing twice as much steel per year (around 17 million tons) as it had done before the Second World War. But the other 'staples' of 1900, based on coal and cotton, had almost disappeared. At its peak before 1914, British coal production approached 300 million tons per year; by the end of the century it was less than 50 million. There were almost 1,000 mines in 1947, when the state took over the industry; in 2003 there were 13. The cotton mills of Lancashire, once the busiest in the world, accounting for around a quarter of British exports by value in 1900, were now silent; in 1959–60 alone 300 factories had closed. Before the First World War Britain was responsible for around three-fifths of the world's shipbuilding; by 1977, when Labour **nationalised** ◄ the few remaining yards, it was down to 4 per cent. Manufacturing as a whole accounted for 43 per cent of employees in 1955. By 1990 this proportion had fallen to a fifth. In the same period, employment in the service sector rose from 36 to 69 per cent of the total. Between 1995 and 2002 the service sector expanded by a quarter, ten times the rate for manufacturing. And at the end of the twentieth century more people were employed in Indian restaurants than worked in steel and coal production combined.

M

The decline was most marked between 1979 and 1987, when 2 million manufacturing jobs were lost. Among other things, the concentration of the old manufacturing industries in specific areas accentuated the **North–South divide**. The **Thatcher** government did ◄ not entirely withdraw its support from manufacturing – for example, in its early years it poured subsidies into steel and car-making – but other elements of its economic policy overwhelmed any palliative effect from these measures. Some had thought that the extraction of North Sea oil, which virtually coincided with Mrs Thatcher's first election victory, might herald an industrial renaissance in Britain. Instead, it merely helped to pay for cuts in direct taxation, and to compensate for the yawning disparity between the value of manufactured imports and exports.

In the boom of the late 1980s Britain developed an insatiable demand for consumer goods which were no longer produced by domestic industry, and at the same time the value of oil exports declined sharply. Even 'invisible earnings' – which seemed to increase the influence of the City of London and the financial sector in general precisely because they were invisible – could not plug the gap. Thus in 1989 Britain's overall balance of payments was in deficit by more than £20 billion. Although the next few years showed a slight improvement, the overall figure for 1990–3 was -£60 billion. Twice since the war, trade deficits of less than £1 billion had plunged Labour governments into crisis and induced devaluations of sterling. Although nemesis eventually caught up with him, Mrs Thatcher's Chancellor Nigel Lawson initially brushed aside figures which would have been greeted by the right-wing press as symptoms of national bankruptcy (if not the

▶ end of civilisation) only a decade earlier. After 'New' Labour took over in 1997 the press continued to ignore the balance of payments. When in 2002 the 'visible' deficit turned out to be a new record of £46.3 billion the tone of the coverage suggested that this was merely an historical curiosity.

In hindsight the dramatic shift from manufacturing to services could be justified – and even praised – under the general argument

▶ deployed by admirers of the Thatcherite revolution. By 1979 British industry was undoubtedly suffering from chronic overmanning, and instead of feeling gratitude for the generosity of misguided governments who kept them in work, truculent employees in the manufacturing sector had not hesitated to bring production to a halt in their self-defeating pursuit of higher wages. Thatcherites argued that the nation was faced with two alternatives – ruin, or a recognition of reality. The traditional industries should be exposed to market conditions, and if they failed the test, they should be allowed to die. Whatever the temporary inconvenience, in the end Britain would have to pay its own way: whether the recovery came from manufacturing or services, so long as the government stopped interfering it would come eventually. As it happened, the developed world as a whole was switching from manufacturing to services, so if its policies discriminated against the former this meant that the government had backed the winning side. And insofar as Britain continued to make things, at least it did so more efficiently.

At the beginning of the twenty-first century the jury was still out on this *post-facto* rationalisation. Certainly during the 1980s many qualified observers doubted that Britain could survive without manufacturing, and the shift towards services was as marked as ever after 2000. But one interesting feature of the debate was rarely noted. The idea that Britain should continue to prop up manufacturing industry was inspired partly by the desire to maintain 'full' employment. But it also reflected national self-esteem: even if Britain had slipped down the league tables, it would be wrong to admit defeat and drop out of the competition entirely (in this respect attitudes to manufacturing

▶ were rather like the national view of cricket).

More seriously, the government's indifference to manufacturing decline contradicted the presuppositions of people who had been

▶ affected by the wartime experience. Between the wars, the staple industries might hit hard times; but no government could stand idly by if they looked like going out of business entirely. If the worst came to the worst, Britain would have to aim for industrial self-sufficiency. Equally, no government could have allowed overseas firms to take over key industries. Hence, at least in part, the angry response to attempts in the 1980s to sell off the car-maker British Leyland on commercial, rather than 'patriotic', criteria. Consciously or not, in this respect (like their attitude towards the **welfare state**), the ideologues in the ◄ Thatcher governments were taking for granted that there would never be another prolonged war. In these circumstances the loss of manufacturing was bearable, because there was no longer a connection between mass production and national survival. The government would only have to make sure that the arms industry remained prosperous enough to develop high-tech weapons. Thanks to their efforts Britain is the second largest arms exporter in the world, although the strategy involves an endless round of demeaning ministerial sales pitches to overseas buyers, who have on occasion returned the compliment by using their purchases against British **armed forces**. ◄

Possibly the general decline of manufacturing all made good sense, and it really was time for the British to shake off old assumptions about being 'the workshop of the world'. But a future dominated by services – perhaps ending up with neighbours taking in each other's washing (or, more likely, listening to each other's complaints in 'call centres') – was still an unsettling prospect. The continuing unease was reflected in the bizarre tendency of service providers, like banks and even travel agencies, to refer to their offerings as 'products'. This abuse of the English language would have fascinated **George Orwell**, who wrote in 1938 that almost every aspect of British ◄ life depended on coal. Half a century later, after Mrs Thatcher's victory over the National Union of Mineworkers (NUM), this attitude seemed hopelessly outdated. But at least one can understand why it was widely held, whereas the inherent logic of the service sector looks far more vulnerable.

M

■ Marconi Affair

In March 1912 the English Marconi Company was provisionally awarded a lucrative government contract to establish radio links between Britain and its **Empire**. The utility of radio had already been ◄ demonstrated by its role in the capture of the celebrated murderer, Dr Crippen; soon afterwards it preserved the lives of 700 victims of the *Titanic* disaster. Within a week of that spectacular aquatic advertisement the Chancellor of the Exchequer, **David Lloyd George**, ◄ purchased 1,000 shares in the American parent company of English Marconi. The vendor was his ministerial colleague, the Attorney-

General Rufus Isaacs (later Lord Reading), who had helped himself to 10,000 shares just before the *Titanic* met the iceberg. Isaacs also passed on a block of shares to the Liberal Chief Whip, who invested £9,000 on behalf of his party (and prudently took ship to Bogata when the scandal broke).

Rumours about financial skulduggery were soon circulating, but when the story appeared in a French magazine the ministers brought a successful libel action. The perverse code of honour among lawyers meant that the MPs F.E. Smith and Edward Carson, who were currently taking their opposition to the government's Irish policy beyond the limits of treachery, were perfectly happy to act for the

▶ complainants. When **parliament** debated the Marconi contract in October 1912, Isaacs and Lloyd George denied that they had used inside knowledge to buy any shares in *English* Marconi, the direct beneficiary of the government contract. Technically this was correct, but they omitted to mention that they had bought into the parent company, which was unlikely to have suffered from its connection with the new contract. Doubts persisted, and the government was forced to set up a select committee to investigate further. Eventually the truth emerged, and both Lloyd George and Isaacs offered to resign. The Prime Minister, Asquith, allowed them to continue in office and the (Liberal) majority on the select committee exonerated them.

Overall, the ministers made a loss from their dealings in Marconi shares – but only because they made the mistake of re-investing, after selling their original tranche of shares at a considerable profit. In other respects they were more fortunate; their careers continued to prosper. There was a fragmentary element of justice in this, because

▶ their chief persecutors in the press (including **Rudyard Kipling**) exploited anti-semitism to whip up feelings against Isaacs. Probably if

▶ Isaacs had not been **Jewish** – and Lloyd George had not made so many enemies – the incident would have been a one-day wonder. But their involvement had been at best a major error of judgement, inspired by reckless greed. Isaacs's brother held a senior post in English Marconi, and he had suggested the investment opportunity just before the company embarked on a major share issue. Even without the *Titanic* and the radio contract, the deal was a one-way bet for Isaacs; the fact that the privileged information came from family contacts, rather than his ministerial position, did not make him less culpable. As Chancellor of the Exchequer, Lloyd George was the last person who should have accepted the certain prospect of short-term gain when government investment was even indirectly involved. Their subsequent 'economy with the truth' is eloquent testimony to ministerial guilty consciences.

By international standards British political corruption remained fairly petty throughout the twentieth century. But the Marconi Affair would not be the last demonstration that the same venal motives were at work, even if they were less remunerative in Britain. Until the year of the scandal MPs and ministers were unpaid; henceforth, given the importance of their role, they were paid inadequately. It was a typical, unsatisfactory British compromise. Relatively poor salaries implied that MPs should continue to earn money through extra-parliamentary activities, and the House would benefit from this knowledge of the 'real world'. Yet it was increasingly difficult to square the demands of constituents, and the obligation to scrutinise legislation, with an outside career. In these circumstances it was not surprising that allegations of 'sleaze' among MPs came to dominate British politics in the mid-1990s. The temptation to 'earn' extra money through minimal effort had been too much for Lloyd George; and since human nature had not changed, at least some of his successors were sure to follow suit.

■ Marriage; divorce

The decline of marriage was one of the major social themes of twentieth-century Britain, and some commentators traced all of the country's ills to that single source. Social conservatives, who liked to blame the 1960s for everything, argued as if the process had begun in that decade. But, as usual, its origins lay much further back. The historian Lawrence Stone was perfectly justified in using 1530 as a convenient starting point for his fascinating study of the *Road to Divorce* (1990), thus including the spectacular marital misdeeds of Henry VIII.

Until the 1920s people trapped in unsatisfactory marriages still faced more serious obstacles than those swept aside with such aplomb by Bluff King Hal. In trying to resolve the problem, MPs were guided by pragmatism rather than any desire to undermine a cherished institution. A limited reform of the divorce laws was approved by **parliament** in 1923. The annual rate increased, from less than a thousand in 1910 to 4,522 in 1928. But this legislation and the ensuing upsurge both undoubtedly reflected a new desire for freedom among **women**, ◄ which also fostered the **Suffragette movement**. This was not reform ◄ imposed from above; rather, it was an inadequate response to a cry from the nation's kitchens.

In 1937 the author and independent MP for Oxford University, A.P. Herbert, introduced a Private Member's Bill on divorce along the lines of the majority findings of a 1909 Royal Commission. Before Herbert's reform husbands seeking a divorce would normally have to provide the courts with concrete evidence of their adultery; usually this could only be done by means of a ridiculous collusive charade. There were also many 'judicial separations', which seemed a fairly pointless half-way house to divorce. In the 1937 debate Herbert was able to argue that the present law was making adultery seem respectable. In 'fashionable' circles, such as that of the prolific

▶ **Oswald Mosley**, it was almost *de rigueur*. In his best-selling 1929 book
▶ *Marriage and Morals* the libertarian philosopher **Bertrand Russell**
▶ had argued that couples should at least stay together until their **children** came of age, but in 1932 even he had begun divorce proceedings against his second wife Dora because she insisted on having children with other men.

Herbert also pointed out the injustice of a situation which provided at least the theoretical possibility of painless divorce for the rich, but made it almost impossible for anyone else. When the Bill was passed, insanity and (more importantly) desertion were added as grounds for divorce, bringing England and Wales into line with Scottish practice since the sixteenth century. The price of the Bill's passage was the concession that there could be no divorce within the first five years of

▶ a marriage; and until 2002 clergymen of the **Church of England** had no obligation to allow divorced people to remarry within their precincts.

Herbert's timing was unfortunate. His Bill provided a much-needed release from marriages which had come under 'natural' strains, and between 1937 and 1939 the divorce rate almost doubled. But it also loosened ties on the eve of a conflict which would tear apart thousands of otherwise contented couples. In 1938 there were fewer than 10,000 divorce petitions. The effect of prolonged absences from home (and, in part, the importation of virile American servicemen) meant that by 1947 the figure had increased fivefold.

Thus the much-maligned generation which made law in the 1960s had itself been brought up by parents who no longer felt instinctive reverence towards marriage. The decade did see two additional measures, in 1967 and 1969; but these reforms were preceded by another Act, of 1950 – at the beginning of the decade which social conservatives hail as a moral paradise. Admittedly, less than 26,000 divorces were made absolute in 1960, which marked a drop of nearly 7,000 compared with 1950. But the greatest increase actually came during the 1970s (62,000 divorces at the start of the decade, 158,000 ten years later). And perhaps the most significant move towards liberalisation was the Matrimonial and Family Proceedings Act, passed

▶ under the supposedly moralistic **Thatcher** government in 1984. It allowed people to sue for divorce after just one year of marriage. The
▶ **Conservative** reaction was delayed until 1996, when the Major

government's proposal for 'no fault' divorces was rejected by its own backbenchers.

The forces ranged against the institution of marriage during the twentieth century were so powerful that its survival is more surprising than its decline. In fact, the idea of marriage, at least, seemed to be as popular as ever; in a survey of 10,000 young women conducted in 1980 more than three-quarters refused to accept that marriage was outdated. This seemed to be a triumph of optimism over other people's experiences – or perhaps a testament to the power of fictional romances over real life. Certainly the trip to the altar was coming later, if at all. In 1972, 1.25 million women between the ages of 16 and 24 got married. The corresponding figure for 1996 was 250,000. The proportion of married women between 18 and 50 was almost three-quarters in 1979; in 2000 it was just over a half. Many of these were likely to be repeat offenders; re-marriages accounted for more than a quarter of the total, and there were four times as many as in 1961.

Although marriage was not entirely dependent on religious belief, the secular spirit was bound to undermine it. Civil weddings had been introduced as far back as 1836 – reflecting worries even at that early stage that the decline in piety might erode the attraction of wedlock. As late as 1962 only 32 per cent of marriages took place in register offices; by 1978 the proportion had soared to 57 per cent. Feminism was another obvious factor; men divorced women who were no longer ready either to 'honour' or 'obey', and women contacted their lawyers if their spouses tried to enact a literal interpretation of the repellent wedding vows. In this respect, at least, the female proved to be the more deadly of the species. By the mid-1970s, nearly three-quarters of all divorce petitions were being filed by women.

M

But even these factors were merely symptoms of the real enemy of marriage – individualism. By the end of the twentieth century all forms of cohabitation were looking increasingly vulnerable to the urge for self-expression, and the reluctance to share even the temporary misfortunes of another. Couples who lived together for a 'trial period' before getting married were faring no better than those who had stayed in the family home – quite the contrary, in fact. Ironically, individualism also helps to explain why weddings were still taking place in their traditional form. For the proud parents, they provided excellent showcases for their personal wealth – the average marriage costs £13,000 – while the happy couples were sure of being at the centre of attention at least for a few brief hours.

Rather than blaming the well-meaning politicians who rightly regarded the old laws as an offence against reason, social conservatives would do better to lament the **cult of celebrity**, and the media ◄ which was gleefully reporting the details of marital breakdown long

before the Second World War. Just before Herbert introduced his Bill
▶ **Edward VIII** had helped to remove some of the stigma from divorce by
treating Mrs Simpson as if she retained human characteristics,
notwithstanding her failed marriage. By the beginning of the twenty-
first century most celebrity marriages were going through a repetitive
dreary cycle: wedding; glossy magazine photographs; birth of child;
glossy magazine photographs; divorce; serialised autobiography
showing that the marriage had always been a sham. In those pages
break-ups were glamorised just as much as romance, so that couples
who thoughtlessly grasped at the latter were likely to be equally ignorant of the real consequences of the former. At least for the average
couple the process of divorce was relatively inexpensive, particularly
for those who qualified for Legal Aid (introduced by the Attlee government in 1949). Prior to this, despite Herbert's efforts, adultery had
been a luxury for the upper classes; now the state ensured equality of
opportunity. As Lawrence Stone noted, by 1985 the divorce rate for
unskilled workers was four times the level for professionals. Rather
than suggesting that professionals were more uxurious than low-paid
workers, this reflected their marked tendency to delay the first
marriage for longer.

One of Stone's most interesting insights is the effect of declining
mortality on marriage. In the nineteenth century, when so many
wives died in childbirth, the idea of keeping a series of promises 'till
death us do part' did not necessarily imply a protracted commitment.
From this perspective, the 1920–50 period, with its relatively low
divorce rate at a time of decreasing mortality, really does seem to be
one of amazing amity between the sexes. What one cannot know, of
course, is the number of marriages that persisted despite bitter resent-
ments nursed by one partner or both. All one can say is that the
successive Acts still seem to have been responses to increased demand,
but that the progressive relaxation of the laws has meant that many
(if not most) marriages are now contracted with the spectre of a
divorce lawyer loitering in the background.

By the end of the twentieth century the increase in the divorce rate
at least seemed to be slowing (more than 167,000 were finalised in
1995). But this still left policy-makers with significant headaches. In a
▶ fantasy world where couples mated for life, the **housing** problem
would be solved at a stroke; presumably there would also be fewer
▶ suicides, and less **crime** (although experts continued to argue over this
link). More than a third of all live births now took place outside
marriage, and many of these children would be brought up by a single
parent, joining others who had been born within a union which was
subsequently dissolved. If anything, the social consequences of
marriage break-up were worse than those of the unprotected one-

night stand; those who never knew their fathers were less likely to suffer from the corrosive sense of loss.

In 1991 the Major government established a Child Support Agency to force errant parents to contribute towards the support of their offspring. Inevitably, this body was soon mired in controversy. As so often in British social policy, it had been introduced when the problem had already lurched beyond rational control. But by this time it was more than just counter-productive for politicians to think of preaching to an individualist audience. It was impossible for them to find the right words, because they were individualists themselves.

■ Marshall Aid

In June 1947 the US Secretary of State, General George Marshall, proposed a scheme to assist post-war European economic recovery, which was being hampered by a shortage of dollars. Substantial financial assistance would be made available to all European nations, to promote a revival of production and international trade. The only condition was that the scheme should be administered by European states in co-operation. Originally, the offer was extended to the Soviet Union, but this suggestion was quickly spurned by the Soviet Foreign Minister, Molotov. For their part the British agreed, after protracted debates within the **Labour** government. ◀

M

In accordance with Marshall's proposal, sixteen European nations established a permanent Organisation for European Economic Co-operation (OEEC) in April 1948. The plan would last for four years, disbursing a maximum of $17 billion. Long before 1952 it had been hailed as a great success. The French and West German economies recovered rapidly, and the British actually withdrew from the scheme in December 1950, in the belief that the aid was no longer necessary. However, in June 1949 the government had decided to devalue the pound by almost a third, from $4.03 (its level since 1940) to $2.80. The British economy was still geared towards exporting to the US, rather than prioritising **consumer** demand at home. Post-war 'austerity' ◀ continued in Britain.

Winston Churchill had described US aid during the Second World ◀ War as the most 'unsordid' act in history. Yet the benefits which accrued to the American economy were hardly an accidental by-product, and similar mixed motives were at work in the Marshall Plan. US officials were worried that European states might turn to Communism if economic recovery were postponed for too long. If the Soviets had agreed to participate in the plan, it would almost certainly have been aborted. Thus, at minimal cost (relative to its resources) the US government secured a major propaganda *coup*. Accelerated recovery in

▶ **Europe** would also ensure a swift restoration of 'normal' world trade, offering new opportunities for American exporters while potential competitors were recovering.

The US government also saw the OEEC as a stepping stone to a united Europe. For the British, this was an unpleasant aspect of the plan and a good reason for a hasty withdrawal. But other governments were happier with the hint. In May 1950 the French Foreign Minister Robert Schuman put forward a plan which led two years later to the formation of the European Coal and Steel Community. In the short term British ministers felt that they could remain aloof from the increasing drive towards European economic and political unity. But since the Americans remained convinced that such a development would keep the world safe from Communism (and the threat of a resurgent Germany) the British would not enjoy the luxury of indifference for very much longer.

■ Matthews, Sir Stanley (1915–2000)

Stanley Matthews was born near Stoke-on-Trent, the son of a small tradesman who was himself a notable sportsman, nicknamed 'the Fighting Barber of Hanley'. Preferring to prosper through his feet ▶ rather than his fists, Stanley made his debut for the local **football** team at the age of 17, and scored in his first game for the senior English side two years later. Although the war and some peculiar decisions by England selectors meant that he did not win as many caps (only 54) as his abilities deserved, he was still representing his country in his forties.

Matthews joined Blackpool in 1947, and played in three FA Cup Finals for the team. Blackpool lost the first two, and seemed to be heading for another defeat in 1953 when Bolton led them 3–1 with only twenty minutes left. But with his dazzling dribbles and accurate crosses, Matthews inspired the most famous fightback in the history of the competition. Blackpool won 4–3. Although the centre forward Stanley Mortenson scored a hat-trick, the match became known as 'the Matthews final'. In fact, Matthews rarely scored (only 71 goals in around 800 games), but he was invaluable as a provider of chances for other players, usually by swerving around the opposing left-back and crossing from the goal line.

In 1961 Matthews rejoined Stoke City. In that year the cap on wages (at £20 for each week of the season) had finally been lifted. This development might have tempted some ageing players simply to go through the motions a little longer. But the wiry, 46-year-old Matthews was a fitness fanatic, and his positive contribution was far from over. In 1963 he was named Footballer of the Year for the second time (he had been the first recipient of the award, back in 1948). He finally retired from the first-class game in 1965, having become Britain's first-ever footballing knight. Such was his international reputation that a tribe in Ghana asked him to become a chieftain.

Matthews tried his hand at management, but after a few unsuccessful ventures he spent most of his time coaching abroad. By the time of his death football had been transformed, not least in its wage structure. Even the commentators were much more excitable, so that film footage of the Matthews final looked and sounded like a kick-around among amateurs in oversized shorts. Almost certainly, though, a superb athlete like Matthews, with total dedication to the game, would have excelled if he had reached his prime in the modern era. Yet he might have landed on the transfer list if he had refused to modify his approach, which ruled out activities like diving to win penalties.

Although the critics complained that Matthews often declined to pass to better-placed colleagues, his was not the crude kind of individualism which marked the closing years of the century. As the *Guardian* reporter put it, his death 'marked the passing of a different kind of England . . . a country in which modesty was respected or worshipped almost as much as popular virtuosity'. The fact that Matthews had possessed both of these qualities won him a final accolade, when an estimated 100,000 people lined the streets of Stoke on the day of his funeral.

■ Mini

Britain's most famous car, which became a symbol of creative innovation and mass democracy. Like so many accepted features of British life, the Mini was invented by an immigrant, Alec Issigonis (1906–88). He was the son of a British man of Greek descent and a German woman, resident in Turkey. As a consequence of the First World War, the family was evacuated by the Royal Navy and arrived penniless in the UK in 1922, minus Alec's father who died *en route*. Despite lacking an aptitude for mathematics, Issigonis trained as an engineer and draughtsman, after which he took a job at Humber (1934) and then at Morris Motors (1936).

There, between 1942 and 1947, he created the practical but dowdy Morris Minor. The chairman, William Morris (Lord Nuffield, 1877–1963), disliked it at first, saying it looked like 'a poached egg'. But the car went into production in 1948, and over the next twenty-four years 1.6 million were produced. Issigonis was made Chief Engineer in 1950. Disliking big corporations, he left for Alvis in 1952 when Morris was merged with Austin to form the British Motor Corporation (BMC).

But the car he designed for them was not put into production and he returned to BMC in 1955.

The petrol-rationing and general insecurity about oil supplies ▶ caused by the **Suez crisis** led manufacturers to intensify their search for fuel-efficient cars, in addition to which rising car ownership, and ▶ the **transport** gridlock it was beginning to cause, made size and manoeuvrability more important. In 1957, BMC set Issigonis to work on producing a successor to the Morris Minor. Two years later, the Mini was launched, with a revolutionary design, surpassed only by the Volkswagen 'Beetle'. A transverse-mounted engine enabled the small amount of space provided by its ten-foot-long chassis to be fully utilised, providing room for four people, a boot and a glove compartment.

In an age when cars were beginning to look indistinguishable, with personalised number plates the only way to assert the driver's individuality, the Mini seemed truly distinctive. It was marketed especially at the young, independent 'girl-about-town' and it achieved cult status from the mid-1960s when it became popular with celebrities like the model Twiggy (b. Leslie Hornby, 1949) as a symbol of urban chic. The car's appeal to men grew after its racing variant, the Mini Cooper, won the Monte Carlo rally in 1964 and again in 1965, the year that the millionth Mini was sold.

M

What elevated the Mini into an icon was its starring role in the film *The Italian Job* (1969), in which three of the cars – red, white and blue – are used by Michael Caine and his gang to complete a gold bullion robbery from the Italian car giant, Fiat. Thereafter, the Mini became for ever associated in the public mind with the 1960s, and the more meritocratic post-imperial culture that was forged in that era. The car was in continuous production for three decades, with 5 million produced by 1986. A total of 5,387,862 had been made by the time the last one rolled off the production line in 2000 with 'GB' bolted in chrome to its boot. Fittingly, it was driven away by the 1960s pop star Lulu (b. Marie Lawrie, 1948).

Yet beneath this apparent success story lay the British failure properly to capitalise on their inventions. The Mini was not a comfortable car and, despite its spatial manoeuvrability, it was a physical effort to drive. Like most British motor vehicles, it was also unreliable (early models often conked out in the rain). The car industry was hit ▶ by the militancy of British **trade unions** in the 1970s, but long before that, it suffered from the same executive complacency that scup-▶ pered the development of **Alan Turing**'s computer. When, for example, BMC were asked by the makers of *The Italian Job* to supply 16 Minis for the film, they refused, saying that they couldn't see any publicity value in doing so. In 1950, the UK exported more cars than

France, Germany and the United States. A decade later, it had been overtaken by all of them, and the Mini's failure to do anything about it was driven home when the German **manufacturer**, BMW, bought ◄ the parent company in 1995.

By the time the **Germans** decided to end a British legend five years ◄ later, the Mini had become a much-loved object of national nostalgia. But, unlike the Volkswagen Beetle, it was not one that many people still wanted to buy. 'When you're designing a new car for production,' Issigonis once said, 'never, never copy the opposition.' Unfortunately, a motto that seemed to work in the design room was less successful when adopted in the boardroom.

■ Miscegenation

Term used to denote interracial sexual relationships, from the Latin *miscere* (meaning to mingle) and *genus* (meaning race), it was coined by the British in the 1860s when pseudo-scientific theories about white supremacy hardened attitudes towards a practice which had taken place in all civilisations since the dawn of humanity. Numerically, miscegenation reached a peak during the era of slavery when black people were seen to be chattels, as duty bound to satisfy their white owners in the bedroom as in the field. These unions were usually no more than systematic rape. After the abolition of the slave trade (1809) and the emancipation of slaves (1833), colonists had more consensual unions with the races over which they ruled. Relationships were still unequal, framed as they were by the fact that economic and social advancement depended on the approval of the white partner, and because that approval was often based on an objectified exoticisation of the black female. Moreover, black men were denied reciprocal access to white women; indeed, the mythic fear of rapacious libidos and oversized genitals became more central to racist discourse after slaves were freed and attained a degree of mobility.

Nonetheless, by the start of the twentieth century, mixed common-law **marriages** were such a standard feature of colonial life that ◄ Britain's rulers became worried that they were undermining white authority and, ultimately, destroying the British race. Two steps were taken to stamp out the practice of 'going native'. The first was to encourage white women to emigrate to the colonies. This they did in increasing numbers from the 1880s onwards; not only providing men with racially correct sex, but also creating a hierarchical social world which mirrored more exactly that of the middle and upper classes in Britain. Second, in 1909, the Colonial Office issued the so-called Crewe Circular, which forbade men from having relationships with black women (although the visiting of brothels was still allowed, since this

M

was not thought to generate emotional attachments). Thousands were forced to make a painful choice between love and career, and when they attempted to maintain both the consequences could be severe, even for the most senior officials. Some resigned, like J. Stephenson. A District Commissioner in northern Rhodesia, he refused to give up his Ngoni wife and eight children, and started a new life as an orange grower.

Meanwhile, women who were abandoned – either as a result of the Crewe Circular, or because their white partners simply tired of them – were usually left destitute, with no right to compensatory financial maintenance for themselves or their mixed-race children. This was unsurprising, since black women were generally blamed for miscegenation, their supposedly pronounced sexuality trapping otherwise decent men into a life of degradation – a theme present in imperial popular culture, notably the film *White Cargo* (1929; 1942). Mixed-race children fared a little better than their parents. The belief that they were physically and morally degenerate declined steadily in the second half of the twentieth century and ever since slavery days they had been accorded a higher status than black people, gaining access to better employment as a result. However, these benefits flowed mainly from an imperial strategy of divide and rule, and the hierarchy of colour which it established remains strong in former European colonies to the detriment of their social cohesion.

Back in Britain, hostility towards miscegenation was always
▶ stronger, for two reasons: first, because more rigid **moral** codes
▶ operated at the core of the **Empire** than on its periphery; and second, because, until the 1960s, most black people in Britain were male. Whether they were merchant seamen settling with working-class women in Britain's seaports, or domestic servants having
▶ affairs with **aristocrats**, moral panic ensued. Every race riot that took place in Britain, from that in Liverpool in 1919 to that in Notting Hill, London, in 1958, was sparked by hostility to miscegenation, with mixed-race couples being the focus of mob violence,
▶ a theme explored in the film *Flame in the Streets* (1960). **Class** did matter. Even in an age when the British were more concerned with social equality, high-profile cases (like the marriage of Peggy Cripps – daughter of Labour politician Stafford Cripps – to a Ghanaian chief, in 1950), caused the most alarm, since leadership was still expected of the upper classes on what were deemed to be key moral issues. Throughout the twentieth century, the fear of miscegena-
▶ tion also fuelled hostility to recreational **drug** use in the UK. The belief that narcotics lowered the natural resistance of white women to other races was a feature of debates about the Chinese peddling of opium and the Afro-Caribbean trade in marijuana. It may be no

coincidence that the UK's most draconian drug laws were passed shortly after those debates reached their respective peaks, in the 1920s and 1960s.

Still, the British were more sympathetic to miscegenation than the Americans. Black/white sexual relationships were first banned in Maryland in 1660 and the last imprisonment of a couple took place as late as 1960 in Virginia. By 1971 a fifth of all Americans claimed to have experienced interracial sex. But the practice remained taboo with harsh social consequences for anyone of either race who broke it; a fact reflected in the continuing reluctance of US film and TV companies to screen a kiss between a black person and a white one. Although the British still had a voyeuristic fascination for interracial sex that was surreptitiously underpinned by imperial pathologies, by the end of the century they had begun to accept miscegenation as a natural form of human interaction. The increased number of black British women played an important part in that process (in the largest group, West Indians, the number of females had matched that of males by 1965). In an ironic reversal of the policy which had sent Britannia's daughters out to the colonies, black women were encouraged to come to the UK by **Labour** and **Conservative** governments in order to ◄ provide male immigrants with sexual partners and so keep them away from indigenous females. Although initially successful in its aim, what this policy did in the long run was to give white Britons greater opportunities for interracial love, sex and procreation.

Miscegenation is not a black and white issue. Races of all kinds commingled in Britain, its Empire and the rest of the world, and hostility to the practice was present within every society. Sometimes the desire to preserve black purity was a defensive reaction to white racism; but more often than not it sprang from existing phobias about the degenerative impact of miscegenation – a theme especially apparent within Asian, Arab and Jewish culture, where arranged marriages are still regarded as an essential bulwark against contamination by Western culture.

However, hostility to interracial sex – from wherever it hailed – could not banish **Winston Churchill**'s fear that Britain would become ◄ a 'Magpie society'. Mixed-race pop stars – from Shirley Bassey to Mel B – proliferated; as did footballers like Rio Ferdinand; while the presence of mixed-race couples in advertising testified to the fact that they were common enough and affluent enough to warrant attention by corporate executives. A 1997 survey estimated that half of all British Afro-Caribbean men and a third of British Asian men had a white partner, while a third of Afro-Caribbean and a tenth of Asian women were in mixed relationships. These figures were approximately double those of a decade earlier. Their white partners constituted one per cent of

M

the UK population. A conservative estimate of the total mixed-race population put it at 350,000, of which 80 per cent were born in Britain and over half of whom were under 18 years of age. By the start of the twenty-first century, people of mixed race were the fastest growing ethnic group in the country, and Britain (or rather, England, where most ethnic minorities resided) had become the most ethnically diverse country in Europe.

The British Empire was largely responsible for that transformation. Like most empires it contained a contradiction which helped to destroy it: namely the impossibility of engaging with colonised peoples sufficiently in order to exploit them, while maintaining the moral distinctions ascribed to race that were used to justify colonisation in the first place. If, as some scientists now believe, the survival of *Homo sapiens* depends on biological hybridity, then apologists for the British Empire seeking to pinpoint its contribution to world civilisation should look no further than the mixed-race face.

■ Mods

The largest and most long-lasting British youth cult, which originally flourished between 1962 and 1966. It began in London in 1958 among followers of modern jazz, most of them art students, who called themselves 'Modernists' and who adopted Continental **fashion** and an obsession with style that was then rare among British men. The Italian look predominated: a short, bouffant haircut known as the 'Roman'; narrow ties and lightweight, shiny two-tone suits, known as 'Toniks'; with a Vespa scooter for travelling between the coffee bars, discotheques and boutiques they frequented. Female followers had sharp, angular haircuts, heavy, contrasting make-up, and wore short, tight-fitting dresses adorned with geometric patterns.

In early 1962, the image was taken up by Italian and Jewish youths in Soho and the East End, who shortened its name to 'Mod'. They were soon joined by other Londoners assimilating the black music upon which the British Beat boom was based – soul and rhythm 'n' blues from America, ska and bluebeat from Jamaica. Most gathered at the Marquee Club in Soho, London's rival to the Cavern in Liverpool. The **Beatles** adopted much of the Mod style, and when they crashed into the public consciousness in 1963, the cult spread rapidly beyond the capital, helped on its way by a national press eager to catalogue the roots of Beatlemania. At its peak in the summer of 1965, the Mod movement's nucleus of a few hundred trendsetters, known as 'Faces' or 'Stylists', had swelled to an estimated following of 500,000 people with many more on the fringes, known as 'Mids'.

The movement's musical nucleus consisted of three groups from the London area: The Who (1964–89) led by Pete Townshend (b. 1945) and managed by Kit Lambert, son of the avant-garde composer Constant Lambert; The Kinks (1964–2001) led by Ray Davies (b. 1944); and The Small Faces (1965–9) led by Steve Marriott (1947–91) and later, as The Faces (1970–5), by Ronnie Lane (1946–97). In 1965, The Who provided their collective anthem, 'My Generation'. Described at the time by Townshend as 'anti-middle age, anti-boss class and anti-young marrieds', it captured the adolescent's desire to be misunderstood, although the lyric 'Hope I die before I get old' became a stick with which to beat ageing rock stars ever after. The Who's auto-destructive stage act (inspired, according to their manager, by the Dadaist artist Gustav Metzke) thrilled audiences and inspired similar acts by **Punk** ◄ bands a generation later.

The Who-Kinks-Faces triumvirate, together with lesser groups like The Pretty Things (1965–71) and The Dave Clark Five (1964–71) appeared regularly on what was effectively the movement's own TV show *Ready, Steady, Go!* (ITV, 1963–6). It was hosted by Kathy MacGowan, a young fan plucked from obscurity who was the first of a new breed of 'youth presenters' on British TV. She also edited the magazine *Mod's Monthly* (1964–6) which charted a dizzying succession of fads, the least tasteful but most enduring of which was the parka, a hooded American army jacket. Michelangelo Antonioni's cinematic hymn to Swinging London *Blow Up* (1966), based loosely on the life of fashion photographer David Bailey, also did much to immortalise the Mod style.

Mods achieved notoriety in May 1964 as a result of bank **holiday** ◄ skirmishes with Rockers in Hastings, Brighton and other south-coast resorts, which were repeated the following year and were later portrayed in the film *Quadrophenia* (1979). The battles were motivated by a rejection of Rockers' continuing allegiance to American rock 'n' roll and its rougher clothing fashions, and also by the perennial need of young men to burn surplus testosterone by fighting each other. The demands of testosterone were fuelled by synthetic chemicals, notably amphetamine pills, known to Mods as 'Blueys'. The widespread use of these pills brought recreational **drug** use to the attention of Alec ◄ Douglas-Home's **Conservative** government and led to the increasingly ◄ draconian proscription of narcotics in the UK.

More than any other British youth cult, Mod highlighted the emancipation of the working- and lower-middle-class adolescent from the dictates of pre-war mores, thanks to the spending power that relative affluence provided in an age of full employment. The movement's subversive effect was blunted by its aspirational spirit. Driven by their own totems of consumption, Mods were narcissistic, apolitical and, as Townshend lamented in 1966, 'just as conformist and reactionary as anyone else'. Yet the movement's fragmentation a year later into other sub-cultures like Skinheads and Hippies was partly a response by its followers to the process of commercialisation that feeds then neutralises all such movements. Similarly, its popularity in later decades cannot be explained merely by reference to the commercial value of nostalgia.

The phenomenon illustrates, and is seen to illustrate, the extent to
▸ which British popular culture challenged **Americanisation** in the 1960s. Mod was always cosmopolitan. Its musical influences were American and Caribbean; its signifying symbols like the target were
▸ borrowed from Anglo-American Pop Art (especially the work of Jasper Johns) while its clothing fused Continental and US styles. But the determination of many Mod groups to sing about British life in native accents and in a musical style that became utterly distinctive, coupled with the ubiquitous use of national symbols like the Union Jack and the RAF roundel, vindicates its claim to be 'a very British phenomenon'. And it was Mod's eclectic authenticity which inspired subsequent generations of musicians and designers.

The Mod revival of 1978–82 incorporated a brief Ska one (1979–81) that was a reminder of the link between the two genres and the multiracial origins of both. The revival often descended into pastiche. But the group at its centre, The Jam (1977–82) were an original force, combining harmonics inspired by their 1960s heroes with the aggression of their Punk contemporaries. The group's songwriter Paul Weller (b. 1958) became one of the most popular figures in British music, a consistent champion of the Mod sound and style whose successful solo career formed a bridge with the next revival and earned him the sobriquet 'The Modfather'.

The Britpop phenomenon (1993–9) contained a greater depth of talent. Moreover, its leading groups – Blur, Oasis, Supergrass and Pulp – were unfettered by Punk's affected distaste for the 1960s, acknowledging their debt to the music of that era and thus helping to establish a cultural lineage in the public's mind. Britpop coincided with a brief
▸ post-**Thatcher** optimism in the UK that was also apparent in the Britart movement led by Damien Hirst and a newly vigorous British fashion industry led by Ozwald Boateng, all of which led *Vanity Fair* to proclaim 'LONDON SWINGS AGAIN!' in 1997. But Britpop never crossed the
▸ Atlantic and an attempt by the **'New' Labour** government to co-opt it in a PR ploy called 'Cool Britannia' curtailed its popularity in the UK.

The pretensions of 1960s British culture and its imitators were satirised in the Mike Myers film *Austin Powers* (1997). But successful satire depends on the object of mirth being recognisable; and the fact that so much of the culture on display in the film was familiar to people not even born in the 1960s testified to the iconic longevity of the era and that of Mod in particular. The cult got old before dying but with much of its style and some of its dignity intact.

Monarchy

Nothing exemplifies the transformation of British society since 1900 better than the fortunes of its monarchy. Leaving aside the uncrowned **Edward VIII**, the five individuals who occupied the throne carried out ◄ their official role in a manner which compared very favourably with any of their predecessors. Yet by the end of the century the monarchy was endangered as never before. As in so many cases, the change was most dramatic in the two closing decades; while the Silver Jubilee of Queen Elizabeth II (1977) was widely celebrated, the approach of her Golden Jubilee in 2002 provoked concerns that the public would have to be cajoled into paying its respects. Although the event was seen as a modest success, its appeal was much exaggerated by the **spin** ◄ **doctors** who now surrounded the throne. An opinion poll at the end of the jubilee year suggested that the abolition of the monarchy would be regretted by only 43 per cent of the public.

It had all looked very different when Queen Victoria died at Osborne House on 22 January 1901, attended by her devoted grandson Kaiser Wilhelm II. Victoria had shown alarming signs of human feeling in her response to the death of Albert, the Prince Consort, in 1861, and attracted adverse comment for secluding herself. But in her last years she resumed her public role, acting as a focus for loyal sentiment during the Boer War and paying an extended visit to Ireland shortly before her death.

Despite her motherly image – which befitted someone who produced nine children – Victoria was far more astute than her adoring subjects could have guessed. Her successor Edward VII (1901–10) endured a prolonged apprenticeship. He was 59 when he ascended the throne, and by that time he was best known for his romantic dalliances. Yet the royal love-maker was also hailed for his prowess in the pursuit of peace, after a visit to Paris in 1903 which reduced tensions between Britain and France. During the constitutional crisis of 1910 he refused Asquith's request to create new peers to overpower the **Conservative** majority in the House of Lords, unless the **Liberal** govern- ◄ ment's stance was first endorsed by a general election. Republicans might regard this as a gross interference in the political process, but it provided the best way out of the *impasse* for all concerned.

Unfortunately, Edward died suddenly with the crisis unresolved, and his son George V (1910–36) was wholly inexperienced. He was relieved to be absolved from carrying out the promise of a mass creation of peers – the Lords finally passed the Parliament Bill which

M

had provoked the crisis – but the unpleasant incident confirmed his existing conservative instincts. Another enforced decision came in June 1917, when the royal surname of Saxe-Coburg-Gotha was changed
▶ to Windsor in the face of anti-German feeling (if he had lived Edward VII might have been advised to take elocution lessons; throughout his life he retained a strong German accent).

After the war George showed that he had inherited some of his father's peacemaking skills. His speech on 22 June 1922, at the opening of the Stormont Parliament in Belfast, was an eloquent plea for an end to violence; the positive public reaction encouraged the government to open serious negotiations for a truce in the continuing
▶ war over the **partition of Ireland**. During the **General Strike** he curbed his real feelings and made public appeals for moderation, and in 1931 he remitted £50,000 from the Civil List as a gesture of solidarity with the poor (although previously he had negotiated tax concessions which ensured that the royal family avoided the economic decline of other landowners). More controversially, in the
▶ same year George helped to persuade **Ramsay MacDonald** to stay in
▶ office, to push through **unemployment** benefit cuts and other economic measures which had been rejected by the majority of his
▶ **Labour** cabinet colleagues. The King had already performed a similar role, when he named Andrew Bonar Law's successor in 1923; on that
▶ occasion he canvassed widely before promoting **Stanley Baldwin** instead of the more experienced Lord Curzon, so it could hardly be classed as a naked reassertion of monarchical power.

In his final years George was troubled by evidence that his eldest son and heir would prove unequal to the demands of his position. George's trick was to give the impression that despite all the temptations of his position and the public pomp and pageantry, he himself spurned all the obvious gratifications. In fact, he denied himself nothing – it was just that he wanted very little in the first place (unlike his Queen, Mary of Teck, who visited friends to pilfer their jewellery collections). Unfortunately, the Prince of Wales (later Edward VIII) had more exotic interests. He was the first heir formally to be given his title – an example of George's uncanny ability to introduce innovations without seeming to change anything. But 'Prince of Wales' lacked a job description, so that Edward had no set role to liberate him from his sense of unworthiness.

The abdication crisis after George's death overshadowed his reign, so that by the end of the twentieth century he was barely remembered. Yet at the time he inspired great affection, as testified in the response to his Silver Jubilee of 1935. The ceremony – the first to mark this particular anniversary – was held to remind Britons that they were lucky to live under a constitutional monarchy, unlike the inhabitants of Germany and Italy; and for all his limitations George could not have presented a more agreeable contrast to Hitler or Mussolini. In 1932 he had delivered the first Christmas radio broadcast, which enhanced the feeling that he cared personally for the welfare of his subjects. George was, indeed, a far more satisfactory father-figure to the nation than to his own immediate family. A stickler for precedent in all matters domestic, he equated parental duty with the bullying practices of his own father. His death, on 20 January 1936, was induced by doctors in order to coincide with press deadlines. This example of a 'spin-doctored' royal demise had been anticipated; a photograph of Edward VII's corpse had been published in the *Daily Mirror*, with the permission of his widow. But it was an illegal act. The special privileges of the royal family extended even to the manner of their deaths.

If George V's combination of common sense and narrow-mindedness had saved the British monarchy, these qualities came naturally to him. For more gifted or sensitive successors, his example imposed a strait-jacket which was barely tolerable. George VI (1936–52) who succeeded after his brother's abdication, was a shy man who struggled to overcome a speech impediment. But his broadcast to the nation after the outbreak of war in 1939 was well received, and although he hoped that Lord Halifax would replace Neville Chamberlain as Prime Minister this preference seems far more eccentric now than it did in 1940, when **Winston Churchill** was widely suspected as a divisive ◄ influence. After the election of the Attlee government in 1945 George was alleged to have influenced the Prime Minister's choice of Ernest Bevin, rather than Hugh Dalton, as Foreign Secretary, but that seems unlikely. The King was once heard to complain that the US President Roosevelt spoke to him more openly than his own ministers. But like the most recent 'unexpected' monarch, William IV, George was not one to overrate his own importance. He and his formidable wife Elizabeth refused to abandon Buckingham Palace for their own safety during the **Blitz**, and toured the worst affected areas. Even so, at the ◄ time, and ever since, Churchill has rightly been regarded as the true symbol of national defiance. Although constitutional purists continued to attack the residual powers of the monarchy, this was probably the moment when the long struggle between the Crown and **parliament** came to an end, and prerogative power passed to prime ◄ ministers who enjoyed the position of elected dictators so long as they could command a majority of MPs.

Judged by the popular acclaim which greeted Elizabeth II at her Coronation in 1953, the British monarchy was utterly secure. Yet only a decade later the critic Malcolm Muggeridge could compare the activities of the royal family to a **soap opera**, and predicted that its days ◄

were numbered. This comparison with trivial television drama became a dreary commonplace before the end of the twentieth century. What had happened? The Queen herself had behaved impeccably by previous standards. But there was a growing feeling that she was too 'remote'. Tellingly, this complaint had nothing to do with the kind of physical withdrawal exercised by Queen Victoria after 1861. Elizabeth, and her outspoken consort the Duke of Edinburgh, were punctilious in performing their tedious public duties at home and abroad. Instead, the criticism concerned the monarchical lifestyle, when the Queen was not on duty. Most of the remaining European monarchies (they had been cut down to seven) had 'adapted' themselves to modern life. Yet British courtiers were apparently dismissive of these examples of 'bicycling royalty', and with some reason. Less than a hundred years after Victoria was hailed as 'Empress of India', the idea of Queen Elizabeth II waiting in a bus queue seemed to overturn the logic of the British monarchy (of course, other monarchs were also less likely to attract the attention of passing terrorists). In ▶ any case, for a **consumerist** society, a monarchy has value precisely in so far as it deviates from the norm.

In part, the royal family's troubles were self-inflicted. While other ▶ members of the **aristocracy** had been forced to open their stately homes to the public in order to meet their tax bills, the Queen was a stranger to the Inland Revenue until 1993. At the time she was receiving more than £10 million from taxpayers, via the Civil List. Although monarchists could claim that this represented an excellent bargain for the country – and in real terms it was considerably less than the grant bestowed upon Edward VII – the extent of the Queen's personal wealth remained unclear. There was a feeling that the 'concession' over tax had been wrung from the Queen by public pressure; if a deal had been struck earlier – at the time of the Silver Jubilee, perhaps – it would have been taken as a positive sign, not an indication of weakness.

Yet the focus on the Queen's wealth reflected the general hypocrisy of the British on this subject. In the modern world, it was widely held, material rewards should reflect intrinsic merit. On these grounds the Queen obviously stood condemned, along with the rest of the hereditary aristocracy. As an abstract ideal, this argument was unimpeachable. But the idea that every rich Briton without a title must have somehow 'deserved' their affluence was laughable. From time to time British anger could be stirred against the inflated salaries of 'fat cats' on company boards. But these characters usually managed to slink away from the limelight after a few critical headlines. By contrast, the royal family was stuck in full public view. It was not that their inherited privilege was uniquely unjustified. Rather,

M

being uniquely publicised, it was subjected to persistent sniping, often from overpaid media commentators.

The marital problems of the Queen's sister Margaret, who divorced her photographer husband Lord Snowden in 1978, and those of her children Charles, Anne and Andrew, also caused serious damage to the monarchy. On this score, too, the obsessive interest of the media, particularly with the ill-fated **Diana**, played its part. Yet the monarchy had survived the public humiliation of George IV's wife Caroline, who was left outside Westminster Abbey at her husband's coronation. Traditionally, monarchs had lived in defiance of the standards which the **Church of England** tried (unavailingly) to impose on everyone else. In recent decades the roles have been reversed; the royal family is expected to conform to 'Victorian' morality while the general public emulates George IV at his most decadent.

It might be argued that this is another instance of the royal family perpetrating its own downfall. Yet the promotion of the family as an ideal of domestic harmony was quite understandable. After all, once the monarchy had lost its constitutional power there were few other constructive roles available, and despite the spectacular lacuna of Edward VIII both his father and his brother were 'orthodox' family men. In the year of George V's accession there were fewer than 1,000 **divorces**; he was not to know that the annual figure would be approaching 200,000 by the end of the twentieth century. Even if every member of the family had lived in connubial bliss, it would have seemed a discomforting exception in such a society, merely adding a gloss of *ersatz* communitarianism in the age of the hedonistic individual.

The royal family, then, were partly the products but chiefly the victims of developments in British society during the second half of the twentieth century. Like the House of Lords, the institution had been made to look ridiculous because it was impotent. At the end of the century monarchists were clinging to a final fig leaf – the idea that the institution might act as a final redoubt in the face of any attempt at a military *coup*. They can also argue that although the idea of an elected UK president might sound good in principle, in practice it would lead to the choice of a professional **footballer**, while any President of **Europe** would have to be a colour-free compromise candidate. But it cannot be taken for granted that the younger members of the 'firm' will want to carry out such a thankless job for much longer, simply for the sake of a theoretical constitutional duty. Muggeridge was slightly premature, but his prophetic powers were sound. The only mourners for the monarchy when it finally falls will be the tabloids and the tourist industry.

■ Monetarism

During the 1980s 'monetarism' was often used as a blanket term for the
▶ domestic policies of the **Conservative** government. It could be described
▶ as the sheet-anchor of **Thatcherism**, and for its opponents the word was
a term of abuse. The idea that the quantity of money in circulation must
▶ have a significant effect on the rate of **inflation** is a basic assumption
for all economists; after all, the way money is used is an expression of
supply and demand. But monetarists go further, arguing that the
money supply is the *only* significant factor affecting the rate of inflation.
Wage increases, for example, cannot cause inflation; they merely result
in job losses for overpaid workers. The first (if not the only) economic
▶ duty of **government** is to keep monetary growth under control, broadly
matching fluctuations in national economic activity.

Monetarist ideas can be traced back at least as far as Adam Smith
(1723–90), the Scot who founded modern economics with his treatise
The Wealth of Nations (1776). The importance of the money supply was
never ignored by governments, but it tended to be downplayed in the
post-war era while both main British political parties concentrated on
▶ delivering **economic growth** to demanding voters. Even in America,
▶ the prevailing **Keynesian** orthodoxy urged extensive economic intervention on governments. In the 1960s interest in monetarism was
revived, largely due to the work of the Chicago academic Milton
Friedman. The new monetarists argued that Keynes's ideas had
produced a vicious inflationary cycle, in which ill-advised state intervention in response to weak economic performance had only made
matters worse. Since policy-makers were unable to think outside the
Keynesian paradigm, whenever the economy hit fresh trouble they
instinctively applied even stronger doses of the medicine which had
aggravated the condition in the first place.

In itself, monetarism had nothing to say about the redistribution of
wealth. Provided that the stock of money remained stable, governments could still take from the rich and give to the poor. But in the
▶ **Cold War** context the theory became part of a general attack on
'socialism', and in the 1960s it was yoked to a claim that high taxation
for any purpose reduced incentives to work harder. Like all ideologues,
this school of monetarists also presented a moral case. They claimed
that anything beyond the bare minimum of state economic activity
was a threat to freedom in every sphere of life. In combination, these
ideas offered the starkest possible contrast with practice in the Soviet
bloc, where every element of economic life was controlled by the
government. Some monetarists went further, arguing that Keynes's
attempt to mark out a 'middle way' between capitalism and socialism
was not only self-defeating in its economic effects; it also entailed an

ever-increasing encroachment on cherished liberties. Most obviously, it denied individuals the freedom to spend the money that they earned. If governments should do less, there was no reason for them to tax so much. In so far as the prevailing political **consensus** rested ◄ on Keynes's ideas, it stood condemned.

To support their argument, monetarists frequently invoked the name of Adam Smith. Actually, by the standards of his time Smith had been a raging 'Keynesian' *avant la lettre*, advocating public works to boost employment at a time when governments really did believe in the 'minimal state'. He also regarded **manufacturing** as the source of ◄ wealth-creation, and the service sector as merely parasitic. This was inconvenient for Thatcherites, who disliked the manufacturing sector as the bastion of the **trade union** movement. The anachronistic appro- ◄ priation of Smith was typical of the monetarist approach to history, which was based on selective forgetting. After all, Keynes had only ever produced his theory because the old orthodoxy had clearly proved unequal to the challenges of the interwar period. But few academic monetarists were prepared to give Keynes credit for anything. His main crime in their eyes was that he had combined acute anxiety about the value of freedom with a confidence that Western civilisation could survive active state intervention in the economy.

The first full-scale attempt to implement monetarist ideas was General Pinochet's Chile after 1973. The policy was accompanied by a brutal policy of ideological cleansing backed by US intelligence operatives. But whereas Western commentators equated Communism with violent repression, the Pinochet experiment attracted little attention from Britons, at a time when the Vietnam War, the Watergate scandal and domestic industrial unrest dominated the headlines. By the mid-1970s the British economy was in crisis, in the face of huge hikes in world commodity prices, particularly that of oil. Monetarists noted that the government of Edward Heath (1970–4) had allowed the money supply to rise sharply; they argued that this, rather than the higher cost of vital imports, was the source of the ensuing inflationary surge. Keynes's followers lacked the imagination to amend his (highly flexible) approach to meet unforeseen circumstances, and politicians panicked at the prospect of having to abandon their usual practice of bribing the electorate. The monetarists stepped into the void – or, more exactly, the International Monetary Fund (IMF) strode into Britain to impose monetarist prescriptions. Under the pressure of events, key economic journalists such as Peter Jay (*The Times*) and Samuel Brittan (*Financial Times*) abandoned their Keynesian views and became enthusiastic advocates for monetarism. Friedman was awarded the Nobel Prize for economics in 1976. But it remained an open question whether Keynes had 'failed',

M

or whether his admirers had betrayed his legacy by making only muted objections to irresponsible decisions by successive governments since the war.

▶ **Labour's** Chancellor Denis Healey claimed that he published monetary targets only to appease the international money markets. Although the government did reduce public spending, ministers still pinned their faith in the 'Keynesian' policy of curbing inflation by
▶ controlling prices and incomes. In the **'Winter of Discontent'** of 1978–9, this approach broke down and the stage was set for radical alternatives. When the Conservatives regained power in May 1979 at last the monetarist theory could be tested by true believers.

▶ The economic record of the **Thatcher** governments will always be
▶ fiercely contested. Inflation fell sharply, but **unemployment** soared under the impact of high interest rates. The relationship between inflation and unemployment was well known to Keynes and his followers, and illustrated as a 'trade-off' in the work of A.W.H. Phillips. In their attempts to argue that the conquest of inflation was a victory for their ideas rather than proof that 'Keynesian' demand management could deepen recessions as well as moderating them, the monetarists were handicapped by one awkward piece of evidence. It had been difficult even to get to first base – to produce an agreed measurement of 'money' – let alone to control its supply or its rate of circulation. In one respect, at least, the government had brought this difficulty on itself. One of its first decisions was to abolish exchange controls, so money could flood in and out of the economy unchecked. Nigel Lawson, the charismatic ex-Keynesian who became Chancellor in 1983, quietly downgraded monetary targets in the autumn of 1984, and selected the UK exchange rate as his chief weapon against inflation. Once so triumphant, less pragmatic monetarists now scoured the statistics to explain how their theory had really worked after all (or been betrayed by politicians, a class of people who had never found much favour with them).

Since the end of the monetarist experiment in Britain, and the 1992 departure from the European Exchange Rate Mechanism (ERM), governments have generally muddled through without following any specific economic prescription. They have learned their lesson. They do keep a close eye on the money supply, as any prudent government should do, and they remain over-reliant on interest rates rather than taxation as an instrument of economic policy. The main legacy of the experiment was political. Governments still tried to take the credit in the good times, and continued to be blamed by the public when things went wrong. But their new concentration on piecemeal interventions made them a much more modest source of good or evil; and they even jettisoned direct control over monetary policy, leaving it in the hands of a committee of economists after 1997. Despite the patchy post-war record of the profession this did not seem unduly risky. After all the sound and fury since 1945, even the economists had now surfeited on theoretical disputation.

■ Montgomery, Bernard Law, first Viscount Montgomery of Alamein (1887–1976)

The greatest British general of modern times; disliked by most of his colleagues but known fondly by the public as 'Monty' for leadership skills that were matched only by **Churchill**. He came from an unusual ◀ ecclesiastical family: his father was Bishop of Tasmania, while his maternal grandfather was Frederick Farrar, Dean of Canterbury and author of *Eric, or Little by Little* (1858), a novel that recounted the prevalence of homoerotic masturbation in British **public schools**. Mont- ◀ gomery saw Farrar as evidence of a genetic moral weakness in the family and he spent most of his life sublimating his own sexual desires in military service and Protestant fundamentalism. He was educated at St Paul's School, London, and at Sandhurst, where he was disciplined for setting fire to a fellow cadet's shirt tails, badly burning his buttocks in the process. In 1908 he was commissioned in the Royal Warwickshire Regiment and posted to the North-West Frontier of India.

The young Montgomery made his name during the First World War, at the first Battle of Ypres (1914). He came away with a serious wound, the DSO, Croix de Guerre, and a belief that attritional trench warfare had been a terrible mistake, made worse by the fact that the slaughter was ordered by generals in the chandeliered comfort of their commandeered chateaux miles behind the front line. His answer was the rapid deployment of men and machines, backed up by sophisticated intelligence-gathering and led by officers who valued their men and were capable of showing it.

He developed these ideas while rising steadily through the ranks of the Imperial Army during the interwar period. He was Instructor at the Staff College, Camberley (1920–1; 1926–30), served in Ireland (1921–4), India (1924–5), Egypt (1931–3), Afghanistan (1934–7) and Palestine (1938), reaching the rank of Major-General by the outbreak of the Second World War. To everyone's surprise, in 1927 he married Elizabeth Carver, a widow whom he courted after becoming friendly with her two sons. The marriage was passionless but companionable and to his delight, she produced a son for him before her premature death from septicaemia in 1937. From 1939 to 1940, Monty commanded the 3rd Division of the British Expeditionary Force (BEF) under a former

M

colleague at Camberley, Alan Brooke (later Viscount Alanbrooke, 1883–1963), and distinguished himself during the retreat to, and evacuation from, Dunkirk. On his return to Britain, he was appointed Commander-in-Chief Southern Command, responsible for organising
▶ the resistance to **German** invasion.

Throughout his career, Monty alienated his peers by his vanity and arrogance. He also acquired a reputation as a stern disciplinarian, a trait he extended into the sexual lives of his troops. During his posting to Egypt before the war, he had clamped down on the brothels of North Africa. In 1939 he issued a circular warning BEF men of the dangers of venereal disease; yet, throughout the war he restricted the distribution of condoms and even tried to restrict his troops' access to wives and girlfriends. His actions earned a reprimand from Alan Brooke, the only British military commander he ever respected. 'It is a great pity,' wrote Brooke, 'that he spoils his very high military ability by a mad desire to talk or write nonsense.'

Faith in Montgomery's military talent, coupled with an extraordinary piece of luck, gave him another chance to prove himself. In August 1942, Churchill replaced Claude Auchinleck (1884–1981) as Commander-in-Chief North Africa with Harold Alexander (1891–1969). A vacancy on Alexander's staff suddenly appeared when an undistinguished lieutenant-general, W.H. Gott, was killed in a plane crash. Monty was flown out from Britain to replace him and put in command of the Eighth Army – a division known as 'the Desert Rats' that was poorly supplied and dispirited after being forced to retreat by Erwin Rommel's Afrika Korps.

Monty quickly regrouped the Eighth and at a speech in Cairo on 13 August 1942 he declared, 'I have ordered that all plans and instructions dealing with further withdrawal are to be burnt, and at once. We will stand and fight *here*. If we can't stay here alive, then let us stay here dead.' Despite being unable to pronounce his 'r's, he inspired troops with similar speeches on regular tours of the front lines and when the Germans attacked at Alam Halfa on 30 August 1942, they were successfully repelled. Monty resisted pressure to counter-attack until the Eighth had been rested and reinforced. On the night of 23 October, German and Italian forces were hit at El Alamein. By 7 November Rommel had been routed, at a cost of 13,500 British casualties, and the Axis powers were subsequently swept out of Africa.

El Alamein was Britain's first land victory in the war. It boosted morale on the Home Front, relieving the pressure which had been building up on Churchill's position as Prime Minister, and it made Montgomery a national hero. He was appointed KBE and promoted full general on 11 November 1942. He was forced to play a minor role in the invasion of Italy in the summer of 1943, describing the plan which the Americans executed as 'a dog's breakfast'. During a brief return to London in July of that year he discovered just how popular he was with the British public, which intensified his arrogance. Describing his victorious commander, Churchill remarked, 'In defeat unbeatable; in victory unbearable.' For the rest of the war, Monty's personality damaged relations with Britain's American allies, not least his oft-expressed opinion that he, and not Dwight D. Eisenhower, should be Supreme Allied Commander.

In December 1943, he returned to Britain as Commander, 21st Army Group, to help prepare for the invasion of Europe. He was Commander-in-Chief of all ground forces for the Normandy landings, reluctantly handing over to the Americans once a bridgehead had been established. Convinced that they were not advancing fast enough, he persuaded them to adopt his own daring plan, codenamed 'Operation Market Garden'. The first major paratroop attack in military history, it was designed to capture key bridges in Belgium and the Netherlands, landing the newly-formed 1st British Airborne Division behind enemy lines on 17 September 1944. A series of logistical errors meant that the 1st was not properly supported, so that while the American 82nd and 101st airborne divisions captured their objectives at Eindhoven and Nijmegen, the British were trapped by the **Germans** ◄ at Arnhem and forced to surrender.

Monty's haste was as much ideological as vainglorious, since he was desperate to prevent the Russians conquering Germany. Eisenhower subsequently ignored his advice to launch a single thrust into northern Germany, advancing instead on a broad front. This almost certainly cost the Western Allies time and allowed the Soviet Union to occupy more of Eastern Europe. The error was compounded by the willingness of US leaders to placate Stalin's imperial ambitions at the Tehran and Yalta peace conferences, as a result of which millions of Europeans were condemned to half a century of totalitarian Communist rule.

Monty was promoted Field Marshal (1944) and made viscount and KG (1946). He succeeded Alanbrooke as Chief of the Imperial General Staff (1946–8), during which time he was responsible for introducing National Service, the first peacetime **conscription** in British history. ◄ He was then Chairman of the Western Union Commanders-in-Chief Committee (1948–51) before ending his career as Deputy Supreme Commander, under Eisenhower, of NATO forces in Europe (1951–8). His *Memoirs* (1958) were critical of American war strategy, in which respect they were partly motivated by his longstanding jealousy of 'Ike', who in 1952 strengthened his leadership of NATO by also becoming the 34th President of the United States and the first to lead it as a superpower. Whatever Monty's motives were, the book's anti-American tone helped it to become a best-seller in the period ▶ following the **Suez crisis** when Britons were still smarting about the United States' manifest supremacy.

Montgomery attracted controversy throughout his retirement, and at times was a sad caricature of a reactionary old general. He was ▶ vehemently opposed to the **European Union**, seeing it as a vehicle for ▶ German domination (even though a far greater loss of UK **sovereignty** had taken place with the formation of NATO over which he had presided). Like Churchill, he had a romantic attachment to the white Commonwealth, based on what he called 'ties of blood', that would have made most Germans blush. Indeed, Monty detested the idea of a multi-racial society so much that he became a vocal champion of South African apartheid, visiting the country and describing his love for it in the travel memoir *Three Continents* (1962).

▶ His hatred of **homosexuality** also took an unusual turn. He formed attachments to a series of boys, whose school fees he paid in return for looking after them in the summer holidays. No physical abuse took place, though one boy, the son of a Swiss doctor, recalls being made to bathe then perform military drill, naked, before dinner each night. Yet when the House of Lords debated the legalisation of homosexual acts in 1967, Monty was furiously opposed, describing sodomy as 'the most abominable bestiality any human being can take part in', and claiming that it was a Continental practice which had been imported into Britain.

Like most British generals, Monty died with his slippers on and not his boots, although that was not a reflection of his military career. He was a courageous man with a rare ability to inspire courage in others and his unwavering self-belief was as crucial to his success as it was to his failures. He came to stand in the British imagination as a personi-fication of just and democratic warfare, in much the same way that Douglas Haig (1861–1928), Monty's commander at the Battle of Ypres, personified the opposite. But despite Monty's common touch, he belonged like Haig to a Victorian generation of commanders for whom the military were a fourth estate. Distrustful of politicians, contemp-tuous of women and other races, Monty believed that military men of his ilk were best placed to lead the country. He was sensible enough not seriously to consider a political career, because unlike the Duke of Wellington, he lived in a democratic age and, unlike Eisenhower, he had no talent for conciliation. It is with Eisenhower and not other British generals that Montgomery must, ultimately, be compared. Their interwoven careers tell the story of the supplanting of Britain by the United States during the twentieth century even if the benefits of that shift in global power are open to question.

■ Monty Python's Flying Circus

Anarchic comedy sketch show (BBC, 1969–74) written by and starring
Graham Chapman, John Cleese, Terry Gilliam, Eric Idle, Terry Jones
and Michael Palin. Although heavily influenced by the pioneering
radio show *The Goons* (1951–60), its origins lay in Oxbridge university
revues and the anti-**Establishment** satire boom that they generated in
the 1960s. Other landmarks of the genre were *That Was The Week That
Was* (BBC, 1962–3), *Not Only But Also* (BBC, 1965–6) and *Not the Nine
O'Clock News* (BBC, 1979–82). What made *Monty Python* different was that
it broke the rules of programme construction. Sketches were often
interrupted by Terry Gilliam's surreal animations, a reprise of the
theme tune (Sousa's *Liberty Bell*), or by a premature rolling of credits.
Also, sketches were merged when a character from an earlier piece
wandered into the current action, sometimes in order to make an
interesting juxtaposition but usually just to disorientate the viewer. If
the task of 'ending' a sketch fell to John Cleese, he would utter the
catchphrase 'And now for something completely different', which
encapsulated the show's ethos.

Its content was almost as innovative as its structure. While other
sketch shows sometimes gave the impression of schoolboys being rude
to their headmaster, *Monty Python*'s cerebral wit and surreal slapstick
combined fearlessly to mock a range of taboos. For example, in one
animation sequence a cancerous spot kills a man but itself survives,
gets married and lives happily ever after (cancer was changed to
gangrene on the orders of BBC executives). Musical routines included
'The Lumberjack Song', which celebrated an apparent prevalence of
transvestism among Canadian woodcutters. Classic sketches include
the self-explanatory 'Upper Class Twit of the Year'; the 'Blackmail'
gameshow, in which a naked, piano-playing Terry Jones threatens to
show compromising film of stockbrokers having extramarital sex
unless the victims phone in with cash pledges; and, most famously but
least amusingly, the 'Dead Parrot' sketch in which Cleese attempts to
return a patently deceased bird to Michael Palin's stubborn pet-shop
owner.

Although its influence is apparent in many of the satirical TV
shows which followed it, *Monty Python*'s historical, philosophical and
artistic allusions were lost on most people, and its viewing figures
rarely matched those of the formulaic **sitcoms** which remained
Britain's staple comedy entertainment. Naturally, that added to its
cult status. *Monty Python* began life on a Sunday-evening slot previously
reserved for religious programmes. So it was entirely fitting that the
team only reached a mass audience with their feature film *The Life of
Brian* (1979), which told the story of an ordinary Jewish boy in the time

M

341

of Jesus who is mistaken for the Messiah. Funded by the Hindu-
▶ worshipping **Beatle**, George Harrison, it was condemned by the
Vatican and caused outrage throughout the Christian world. But its
brilliant satire of the absurdities of religious belief spoke to millions
of cinemagoers and its closing sequence, with a crucified Brian
singing 'Always Look on the Bright Side of Life', is a modest epitaph for
a series that revolutionised British comedy.

■ Morality; moral relativism

The fact that Queen Victoria scarcely outlived the nineteenth century
should have provided a very convenient chronological marker for
historians of British morals. But 1914 seems to be a more significant
date. At the beginning of the twentieth century Britons were still
strongly influenced by the moral earnestness associated with the
Victorian period, although the evangelical world-view had been
buffeted by Darwin's evolutionary theory (and, perhaps, even more so
by the country's relative economic decline). But after the slaughter in
the trenches, which affected all classes, it was difficult to envisage a
benevolent God bestowing his rewards on the thrifty and the self-
reliant. Even those thoughtful survivors who retained their faith
tended to become inward-looking, while the general public sought
catharsis in symbolic acts of vengeance ('Hang the Kaiser!') or more
constructive (if over-optimistic) visions of the future ('Homes for
heroes').

With the religious sanction losing its potency as a bastion of public
morality, those Britons who thought deeply on such matters were left
searching for ethical reinforcements. None have been forthcoming.
The remainder of the century can be read as a period in which moral
relativism gradually asserted itself, undermining all the institutions
which had thrived in the age of faith. Almost the only remaining relic
was a hollowed-out version of the Enlightenment idea of progress.
Since contemporary Britons were clever enough to expose the
undoubted hypocrisy of the Victorians, it seemed to follow that their
thinking was an improvement on their ancestors'. But if hypocrisy is a
backhanded compliment to virtue, at least the Victorians had some
standards to be hypocritical about. In the twentieth century, scoffing
at the Victorians became a substitute for constructive speculation in
ethical matters. Professional philosophers were no help in this
respect; they tended to retreat into arid investigations of the nature of
▶ language, and only exerted any influence at all on the wider public
▶ when (like **Bertrand Russell**) they indulged themselves in some off-
duty speculations for the benefit of the electronic media.
▶ Between the wars, many Britons rallied around the ethical idea of

pacifism, resulting in the Peace Pledge Union, which achieved a remarkable membership of 100,000 in the mid-1930s, and the vote of the Oxford Union in February 1933 (by 275 votes to 153) that rejected the idea of fighting 'for King and Country'. Yet even this mood was difficult to distinguish from active complicity in evil, once Hitler's intentions had become too obvious to overlook. The shared privations of the Second World War induced some sense of community – the ethos of the **Blitz** and the 'Dunkirk spirit' – but this was never likely ◄ to survive the return of peace and what seemed to be a more secure prosperity. From the ethical perspective the student activism of the 1960s might be seen as a predictable reaction against the dominance of **consumerist** thinking. Equally, though, it conforms with a general ◄ trend towards rootless individualism, which was sure to return to the materialistic mainstream once the dreams of a better world had been thwarted by the world's stubborn refusal to improve. Afterwards, memories of sit-ins and brief hunger strikes made an ideal topic for wistful dinner-party conversation among guests who hated the 'rat race' but lacked the wit to escape from it.

By the beginning of the twentieth century moral relativism was as dominant as 'Victorian Values' had ever been. Tolerance was in vogue, and in the right context this really would have been a sign of 'progress'. Unfortunately, though, in hollowed-out Britain the word was used without discrimination. So, for example, people habitually spoke of 'racial toleration' as if there was something about diverse ethnic origin which needed to be 'tolerated'. Social conservatives in Britain or America who understood the difference between token gestures and genuine enlightenment found it easy to scoff at 'political correctness'. In more relevant cases, such as attitudes towards private lifestyle choices, there was undoubtedly a welcome relaxation. Between 1985 and 2001, for example, the proportion of people who thought that **homosexuality** was 'always' or 'mostly' wrong fell from ◄ 70 to 47 per cent. Probably not many people had changed their minds; more likely, the findings reflected a demographic shift, as the older generations faded out of the picture. For the same reason, in the mid-1990s the **Conservative Party**'s attempt to stigmatise unmarried ◄ mothers backfired badly; at worst, the rise in single parenthood, and the increase in the divorce rate, were symptoms of deeper problems which the party had no intention of addressing. Yet there were signs that this change, at least, was only 'skin-deep'. Private sexual behaviour could still be used to denigrate people who were in disfavour for other reasons. In this respect, as in most other things, the tabloid press took the lead.

In previous centuries social conduct had been too closely governed by rigid rules, but living without a moral compass of any kind faced people with a much greater challenge – making things up as they went along. The French philosopher Jean-Paul Sartre (1905–80) had accused those who flunked the ordeal, by conforming to accepted norms, of 'bad faith'. Yet what happens when there is nothing to conform to? In such circumstances the conformist emerges as a greater social innovator than the Sartrean exhibitionist. The dilemma was cleverly echoed by the poet Philip Larkin – in his own private life an interesting subject for moral speculation – in *Church Going* (1954): 'what remains when disbelief has gone?' For too many people, the answer was to retreat entirely from any meaningful social encounter – to move to and from work, and to act during the interval, as a machine. In the workplace, at least, there were formal rules to obey, relating to the smooth operation of the firm, not the dealings of people with each other. Anyone who travelled on commuter trains in the London area would have recognised the effects. It was a hollowed-out form of individualism – the social counterpart of political **apathy**.

The process seemed to be self-perpetuating. The new generation, after all, was being taught by people who had lived through the period when there was nothing positive to believe about the human condition – and precious little even to react against. In some quarters, though, it was realised that an amoral population might be attended with some unpleasant consequences. The omnipresent **cult of celebrity** seemed to offer a way forward. Suitable 'role models' could be identified for emulation by the young. To qualify as a role model, a celebrity had to be wealthy, youthful, self-denying and (most importantly) instantly recognisable by the target audience.

But even where such paragons could be found, the message could easily become confused. The sanitised celebrities had earned their status by resisting the pressures which accompany widespread adulation (it was asking too much for them to transcend the temptations of conspicuous consumption). By contrast, the people they were supposed to coax into the path of righteousness had to withstand the stresses of anonymity. Their only perceived escape route from this lamentable condition was to become famous themselves, even if only for fifteen minutes. Once that had been achieved, they would decide for themselves whether or not to conform to the approved model. It was evident enough that there was no necessary connection between celebrity and conformism; indeed, since the media was constantly seeking sensational stories about 'stars' behaving badly, the quickest route to fame was to perform a well-publicised act of depravity.

The real need was for some dissident voices. Those who still believe in 'progress' habitually pointed to previous eras, rightly suggesting that gloomy appraisals of moral conduct are nothing new. At the beginning of the twenty-first century there were plenty of doom-mongers – judging by the letters page of the *Daily Telegraph*, at least. But it was difficult to identify any public figure who was willing to don the mantle. The 'sixties generation' had Mary Whitehouse (1910–2001), who chaired the National Viewers and Listeners Association (founded in 1964). Her strongly-expressed views usually struck a chord with the public. But her frequent absurdities made her an easy target for the 'liberal' press, revealing the limits of its own 'tolerance'. Perhaps Whitehouse's fate has discouraged anyone from taking on her role, which would be bad enough; but the media might have adopted an unwritten rule denying anyone the chance of a full-scale blast against social trends, which would be even worse. In spite of his constitutional and personal disqualifications, the Prince of Wales has sometimes dipped his toe into these turbulent waters. For many, his interventions merely confirmed that he was 'out of touch' and unfit to inherit the crown.

The election in 1997 of a **'New' Labour** government, with **Tony Blair** ◄ as a prime minister who obviously took a serious interest in moral matters, briefly promised a shift in mood. But these hopes were extinguished even before the government's 'ethical' foreign policy was revealed as a drive to sell offensive weapons to regimes of any kind, so long as they opposed 'our' enemies. The best chance of a thorough, rational debate about contemporary life now lies with the **environ-** ◄ **mentalist** movement. The discovery that people born in 1970 are twice as likely to be depressed than the children of the late 1950s is far from being the only indication that the easy life promised by consumerism is actually a good deal harder. Environmentalists are ideally placed to present the public with these connections. Yet the urgency of their critique, and the radical nature of the changes needed to halt the destruction of the planet, makes it less likely that they will win a proper hearing. Few media outlets can be keen to advertise views on the costs of **economic growth** which are so much at odds with the ◄ interests of their commercial backers. Despite the opportunities opened up by the internet, developments in the world's climate might have to get a great deal worse before the chances of a sensible public debate on 'the way we live now'.

■ **Morecambe and Wise**

Eric Morecambe, né Bartholomew (1926–84), and Ernie Wise, né Wiseman (1925–99), formed the most popular comic double act in Britain, matched only by Laurel and Hardy. Eric's persona was that of a savvy, sexually experienced and down-to-earth wisecracker. Ernie's was that of a vain, puritanical and pompous fool. The humour rested on Eric's debunking of Ernie's pretensions, especially those of an artistic nature: Ernie: 'My mother's got a Whistler.' Eric: 'Now there's a novelty.' Wise never cracked; indeed, like Oliver Hardy, he was a funny-straight man upon whom the whole act depended. Eric regularly slapped 'Little Ern' condescendingly on the cheeks; yet a crucial part of their dynamic was Eric's supposed insecurity. Whenever his friend got applause, he walked forlornly off stage in his shabby cap and raincoat, clutching a carrier bag.

They formed a rare cross-Pennine alliance. Eric was born in Morecambe, Lancashire, from where he took his stage name; his parents were shopkeepers. Ernie was the son of a railwayman from Leeds and went on stage at the age of 7, joining his father at local working-men's clubs where, as Carson and Kid, they performed sentimental songs. He met Eric in 1941 at an audition for *Youth Takes a Bow*, a child talent show, and they immediately hit it off. The pair were separated for the rest of the Second World War (Wise served in the navy, Morecambe as a 'Bevin Boy' in the mines) but their partnership was renewed by chance in 1947 when Eric auditioned for the role of feed to a comic in Lord Sangster's variety circus at Godalming in Surrey. The comic was Ernie Wise and a 44-year-long partnership began with them borrowing routines from the American duo Abbott and Costello. By 1950, they were topping the bill at variety shows around the country and in 1954 they moved into television. Their first show, *Running Wild*, was not a success. But when they joined forces with the writers Sid Green and Dick Hills at ATV in 1961 to produce *The Morecambe and Wise Show*, they began to develop their unique style.

What made Morecambe and Wise different was the tangible depth of their friendship. This allowed them virtually to dispense with joke-telling and slapstick and base their act on the free-flowing banter between two caricatures of their real selves. Their sketch routines usually had them sharing a flat, including a double bed, though there
▶ was never a suggestion of them being **homosexual**, and in reality they lived in different parts of England with their devoted wives. The pair made three films – *The Intelligence Men* (1965), *That Riviera Touch* (1966) and *The Magnificent Two* (1967) – which were modest box-office successes but which failed to convey the intimate simplicity that TV audiences warmed to. Somehow, Eric flicking an imaginary pebble into a paper bag lost its ability to amuse when shot in exotic locations.
▶ In 1968, they moved to the BBC and began to work with a third scriptwriter, Eddie Braben. There, over the next ten years, they produced the work that turned them into legends. A regular feature of the show was a performance of one of Ernie's dreadful plays based on literary classics like *Wuthering Heights*. Guests ranging from Prime Minister Harold Wilson to actor John Mills and newsreader Angela Rippon appeared on the show to perform in them, enduring ritual

humiliation from Eric's philistinism on the one hand and Ernie's arrogance on the other. An average of 18 million people tuned in, from all ages and social backgrounds, among them the Queen. The *Morecambe and Wise Christmas Show* became as much a part of the British festive season as the Queen's Christmas message; and in 1977 over 26 million people watched – still a record for a light-entertainment programme.

The following year they returned to ITV, but Eric's heart trouble, ◄ which had plagued him since 1968, grew worse and in 1984 he suffered a fatal heart attack. Although Ernie was professionally as well as personally bereft as a result of his friend's death, he continued to be respected, such was the esteem in which the pair were held. Unlike many performers of their generation who translated **music-hall** ◄ variety to TV, the reputation of Morecambe and Wise never fell victim to the more politicised humour that emerged in the 1960s. 'Don't say that – you make us sound like a cheap music-hall act,' Ernie would snap; to which Eric would reply, 'But we are a cheap music hall act.' They were always much more than that. The *Morecambe and Wise Show* ended on Saturday nights with Eric and Ernie singing their signature tune, 'Bring Me Sunshine'. It captured their ability – rare for any performer – to make an audience feel truly happy as well as entertained. They were awarded OBEs in 1976, and in 1994 the Queen unveiled a bronze statue of Eric on the seafront at Morecambe.

M

■ Mosley, Sir Oswald (1896–1980)

Oswald ('Tom') Mosley was the son of a feckless Staffordshire baronet. After an education at Harrow and Sandhurst, he joined the army, seeing action at the first battle of Ypres in 1914. But he had already volunteered for the Royal Flying Corps, and left the trenches to train as a pilot. Showing off his skills to his mother, he crashed his plane and broke an ankle. Although he returned to the army his wound had not healed, and he was sent home in March 1916. It looked for a time as if he would lose the leg; instead, surgery left it more than an inch shorter than the other. The addition of a limp to his dark good looks and commanding presence rounded off the appearance of a Byronic hero. Although Mosley's character was a very shabby version of the original model, in interwar Britain the second-rate proved to be quite good enough, particularly after he inherited his father's title in 1928.

On a sudden whim Mosley stood as a **Conservative** in the 1918 ◄ general election, winning the Harrow seat. From the start it was clear that his party label was merely a flag of convenience. He first made a mark by attacking the Conservative-dominated **Lloyd George** coalition ◄ over the semi-official policy of repression in Ireland. By the time of the 1922 general election he had broken with his constituency association,

▶ and defeated an official Conservative candidate. After a further victory in 1923 he joined the **Labour Party**. The glamorous new recruit (who had shored up his finances by marrying Cimmie, a daughter of Lord Curzon) attracted admiration and envy in roughly equal measure. But he was found a winnable seat, at Ladywood, Birmingham, only to be narrowly defeated at the 1924 election by Neville Chamberlain.

▶ Banished from **parliament**, Mosley published a pamphlet, *Revolu-*
▶ *tion by Reason*, which drew on the economic ideas of **John Maynard Keynes**. As an ex-serviceman Mosley was disgusted by the govern-
▶ ment's inaction in the face of mass **unemployment**, and he advocated
▶ an expansion of credit to stimulate **consumer** demand. These ideas,
▶ and his active support for the workers during the **General Strike**, marked Mosley as a dangerous class traitor in the eyes of many Conservatives. In December 1926 he won a by-election at Smethwick despite a barrage of press criticism. His popularity with ordinary Labour members was signalled by his election to the party's National Executive Committee (NEC) in 1927. He developed a strong following in the
▶ Midlands – rather like **Enoch Powell** in the 1960s – and in the 1929 election his wife joined him in the Commons, winning Stoke-on-Trent.

▶ **Ramsay MacDonald** admired Mosley and even considered making him Foreign Secretary in the second minority Labour government. Instead, he was made Chancellor of the Duchy of Lancaster (outside the Cabinet) with special responsibility for unemployment. But he was not given a free hand, being yoked together in this key policy area with the Lord Privy Seal, J.H. Thomas. By the end of 1929 Sir Oswald had drawn up a memorandum advancing a variety of radical proposals. Again he urged the expansion of demand, partly through more generous pensions, and envisaged the restructuring of industry under state direction. Imports would be rigorously controlled. This was far too much for MacDonald's orthodox ministers to swallow, and by May 1930 the programme had been rejected. Mosley resigned, but instead of quitting his party he continued to fight for his ideas; a motion supporting the memorandum was narrowly defeated at the 1930 party
▶ conference. A number of MPs, including **Nye Bevan** and **Stanley Baldwin**'s son Oliver, associated themselves with a manifesto published in December 1930. Two months later Mosley announced the formation of the New Party (at this point Bevan prudently backed away).

In the general election of 1931 the New Party fielded 24 candidates. None were successful, and only 3 (including Mosley himself) saved their deposits. Neither Labour nor the Conservatives had any answer to unemployment – thus apparently vindicating Mosley's abandonment of both parties. But Mosley's admirers had begun to suspect his real intentions, and his public meetings were often disorderly. A visit to fascist Italy after the election convinced Mosley that a similar movement was sure to succeed in Britain, and that he was the man to lead it. The British Union of Fascists (BUF) was founded in 1932. It never won a parliamentary seat, but it did provoke a series of anti-semitic riots, mainly in the East End of London. The government was slow to act against a movement which was at least vigorously anti-Communist, and thousands of **police** protected BUF marches against anti-racist protestors.

But after the 'Battle of Cable Street' of October 1936, which resulted in almost 100 injuries to police and rival demonstrators, the government moved against Mosley. The Public Order Act, which prohibited the kind of political uniforms sported by Mosley and his 'blackshirts', effectively killed off the BUF. By 1938, when the novelist P.G. Wodehouse portrayed Mosley in the guise of Roderick Spode in his book *The Code of the Woosters*, it was possible to laugh at the movement. Spode's supporters, the 'Saviours of Britain', are nicknamed the 'Black Shorts', because the shops had sold out of shirts. Wooster tells Spode that he is mistaken in regarding the shouts of his followers as the Voice of the People: 'What the Voice of the People is saying is, "Look at that frightful ass Spode swanking around in footer bags!"'

But by 1940, when the country was engaged in a life-and-death struggle against fascism, satire and British common sense had to be reinforced by other weapons. The BUF was proscribed by the government in 1940. Mosley himself was interned for three years, along with his second wife Diana (née Mitford). Like **Bertrand Russell** in the First World War, Mosley won sympathy from people within the **Establishment** who thought that **aristocratic** birth was in itself a certificate of good conduct. The difference was that Russell was a dissident living in a country which was supposed to be fighting for traditional British values, while Mosley was a traitor who wanted to extinguish them. His eventual release from detention in November 1943 – on 'humanitarian grounds', ironically enough – marked an interesting contrast with the fate of his pre-war follower William Joyce, who was hanged in retribution for the taunting broadcasts from Germany which earned him the nickname 'Lord Haw-Haw'.

In 1947 Mosley founded the 'Union Movement', but was no more successful under that banner. Ever the opportunist, he now supplemented his earlier anti-semitism with hostility towards **immigrants** from the 'New Commonwealth'. But Mosley also warmly embraced the concept of **European** unity, which must have made some sympathisers suspect that his hatred of foreigners was only skin-deep. By the time of his death in Paris, Mosley was irrelevant enough to allow a reassessment which erred on the side of generosity – assisted by Robert Skidelsky's brilliant biography (1975) more than by

M

the subject's own unapologetic memoir (1968). From this rosy-tinted perspective it was possible to dwell on the constructive, far-sighted ideas of Mosley's early years, rather than the personal cruelty and vaulting ambition which inspired the pernicious BUF.

■ Music festivals

Large, open-air concerts, usually taking place over two to five days in the English countryside between May and September. They emerged in the mid-1950s as modern successors to the country fairs of spring and harvest time, which had declined with the urbanisation of Britain or which, having been re-born in towns, were then proscribed from the mid to late nineteenth century as fears of working-class revolution grew. Although influenced by American ventures like the Newport Jazz and Folk Festival (1954–), the Monterey Pop Festival (1967) and the legendary Woodstock Music and Arts Fair (1969), British music festivals became one of the country's prime contributions to Western
▸ popular culture and one in which, unusually, the **aristocracy** played a leading part.

Strictly speaking, the first such event was the Glastonbury Festival (1914; 1918–26), organised by Rutland Boughton, a socialist composer of little note who saw it as an English Bayreuth and he its Wagner.
▸ Despite support from **George Bernard Shaw**, his financial backers pulled out on the grounds that he was encouraging Communism among the locals. The Glyndebourne Opera (1934–9; 1950–) was started by John Christie (1882–1962) on his country estate in Sussex
▸ with the **German** émigré Rudolf Bing as its first director and with a contrasting political outlook to that of Boughton. Glyndebourne soon became a feature of the upper-class social calendar and when it was successfully resumed after the Second World War, for many patrons it was a reassuring sign that the old social order had not entirely collapsed. However, these are exceptions. Most events were devoted, like their pre-industrial antecedents, to popular music.

The first of these was the Beaulieu Jazz Festival held by Edward (Lord) Montagu in the grounds of his stately home in Hampshire, in 1956, to cater for the jazz craze that was then sweeping middle-class youth. Montagu was one of the first aristocrats to realise that the cost of maintaining his property could be met through tourism and that the Inland Revenue, demolition gangs and the National Trust could all be kept at bay by offering visitors more than a suit of armour and a formal garden. 'I did have in the back of my mind a British version of the Newport Jazz Festival,' said Montagu, 'but I think I saw the festival, ideally, as the Glyndebourne of Jazz.' The 1956 event consisted of just two bands – the Dill Jones Trio and George Melly with the Mick Mulligan Band – playing for an evening in front of a polite audience of a few hundred people. But by 1958 Beaulieu had most of the features now familiar to festivalgoers – a two-day event, with half a dozen big-name acts, attended by 4,000 people with a car park, on-site camping, toilets and fast-food stalls. In 1960, when the ◄ Festival was televised by the BBC, fights broke out between supporters ◄ of modern jazz, who had come to hear Johnny Dankworth, and supporters of trad jazz who had come to hear Acker Bilk (the rivalry between the two cults prefigured that between Mods and Rockers). ◄ The incident, together with mounting opposition from local villagers about the number of visitors, led Montagu to make 1961 the last of his pioneering events.

But that year, under the aegis of the National Jazz Federation, Harold Pendleton started the Richmond Jazz Festival and it was there in 1965 that rock music began to dominate the phenomenon. Beat and rhythm 'n' blues bands (led by the Rolling Stones) outnumbered jazz acts for the first time, and 30,000 turned up to hear them, prompting the organisers to describe it as 'a teenagers' Ascot'. At Windsor in 1967, Pendleton held a 'Summer of Love' festival at which Donovan and The Nice played, but love did not seem to be in the air when a fire was started and an attendant fire engine was pelted with bottles. Though only a minority were involved, few festivals passed without some disturbance. That, coupled with the unashamed sex and drug-taking ◄ that took place at them, made festivals a focal point of moral opprobrium towards youth culture (the main objection lodged by the residents of Windsor was that unmarried men and women were sharing tents). Security guards and the police became a permanent feature; ◄ the national press took up the cause of disgruntled locals; and the state began to legislate.

The Night Assemblies Bill 1972 and the Local Government (Miscel- ◄ laneous Provisions) Act 1982 restricted festival culture. They did so mainly by establishing a licensing system similar to that which had been imposed on fairs, pubs, music halls and cinemas earlier in the ◄ century, with the aim once more of containing a perceived threat to social order from the communal pursuit of pleasure. But, like those other sources of entertainment, the music festival adapted to its new conditions and continued to grow. In 1971, Harold Pendleton moved his festival to Reading, at the invitation of enlightened local councillors who wanted to celebrate a thousand years of the town's existence. Still surviving today, the Reading Rock Festival is the longest-running event of its kind. Many others came and went but among those that achieved longevity were the Knebworth Rock Festival (1974–), WOMAD (1982–), devoted to world music, and the Fleadh (1990–), which showcased Celtic music. By the 1970s, people could choose from a dozen events that stretched across half the year. This helped to turn the phenomenon into a platform for alternative lifestyles.

The association of music festivals with the Hippie movement, which began during the 'Summer of Love', was cemented by the Isle of Wight Festival (1968–70) and then perpetuated by a new Glastonbury Festival (1970–71; 1979–87; 1989–). The movement first appeared in California in 1965, the name being coined by the San Franciscan columnist Herb Caen. Hippies' enthusiasm for psychotropic drugs, an *ersatz* Gypsy travelling lifestyle, and radical politics (usually anarchism) was underpinned by a penchant for Amerindian, Asian and Oriental mysticism. Shamanism – an Amerindian cult involving ritual group drumming designed to foster a trance-like state – was especially popular among festivalgoers, their drums playing long into the night after the last professional act had left the stage. Hippies with a darker bent dabbled in the European occult, with the result that Aleister Crowley (1875–1947) regained some of the notoriety he had enjoyed in the 1920s. What British Hippies added to this intoxicating mélange was a pagan form of rural romanticism, based on two things: a fascination for Celtic folklore (especially the Arthurian and Druidic cults of ▶ ancient Britain) and **environmental** campaigns that ranged from sabotaging fox hunts to saving trees from road developers.

The Glastonbury Festival was remade by Michael Eavis, a Wiltshire landowner who shared Rutland Boughton's left-wing sympathies, declaring, 'It's a kind of utopia, something outside of the normal world we all live in.' The proximity of his annual utopia at Pilton to the Arthurian site of Glastonbury Tor and to the Druidic temple of Stonehenge made the festival popular with a fresh generation of 'New Age' Hippies, or 'Crusties' in the 1980s. Eavis's profits were given to organi- ▶ sations like the United Nations and the **Campaign for Nuclear Disarmament**. At the same time, his insistence on booking mainstream pop acts like Robbie Williams, veteran performers like Johnny Cash and 'Rave' dance-music DJs, widened Glastonbury's appeal, making it the best-loved of Britain's music festivals.

They became huge commercial ventures in the 1990s. Their six-figure attendances attracted corporate sponsorship or, like Richard Branson's 'V' event, were staged by the corporation itself. Even the free festivals of the 1970s, with their motto 'Fuck All For Sale', had seen a brisk trade in everything from tarot readings to tie 'n' dye t-shirts. But now, every event had an open-air market with a stall offering mobile phone cards (an essential accessory for the modern festivalgoer who had lost friends amid the vast crowds). The dance-music explosion, which began in the so-called 'Second Summer of Love' in 1988, was transformed from unpublicised all-night raves with minimal facilities in any field that could be hired, to mass events staged by the 'superclubs' and record companies, like Creamfields outside Manchester. Furthermore, the narrowing 'generation gap' as a result of pop and rock's longevity, was evident in the wider age range of festival audiences.

However, neither commercialism nor family attendance ended the disquiet that festivals caused. The Increased Penalties Act 1990, the Criminal Justice and Public Order Act 1994 and the Entertainments Licences Act 1997 placed further restrictions on organisers. That of 1994 even defined the subject of its proscription as 'sounds wholly or predominantly characterised by the succession of repetitive beats', thus proving that cultural taste, and not noise in itself, was the motive behind legislation. Nonetheless, the survival of music festivals and the central place they won in British culture was a testament to the failure of conservatives to contain the moral freedoms unleashed by mass affluence in the second half of the twentieth century. And even if the typical festivalgoer was a city-dweller who rarely ventured into the countryside and cared little about it, the phenomenon was also a posthumous victory for the rural people whose bawdy summer revels had been curtailed in the streets of industrial Britain.

■ Music halls

M

The most popular non-domestic entertainment of the British working classes between 1880 and 1920 which, like vaudeville in America, ◀ offered song, dance, comedy and magic in one show. Music halls originated in taverns of the early nineteenth century, when landlords began to hire professional song-and-dance acts to draw custom. The first purpose-built auditorium was probably The Star at Bolton (1832) and the first to call itself a music hall was The Rotunda in Southwark (1838). They began to spread rapidly after the impresario Charles Morton spotted their potential. Morton established the first of his halls – The Canterbury – at Lambeth in 1851; and by 1900, almost every town in Britain had one.

Like the taverns from which they sprang, music halls were a meeting place for prostitutes and their clients as well as for friends and lovers, and the atmosphere was bawdy, drunken and often riotous, a feature captured by the artist Walter Sickert. Although the sale of alcoholic **drink** in auditoria was banned in 1902, audiences ◀ remained boisterous, heckling the worst acts and joining the better ones in song. The 'Queen of the Halls' was Marie Lloyd (1870–1922). Her saucy songs, like 'Oh, Mr Porter', and even saucier private life were condemned by Britain's moral guardians but they helped to make her the country's first modern celebrity-entertainer. Harry Lauder (1870–1950) – the 'Laird of the Halls' – epitomised the more

respectable side of the phenomenon. An ex-miner, Lauder mixed jocular patter with quaint Scottish airs and ballads like 'I Love a Lassie'. His knighthood in 1919 was a reward for entertaining troops
► during the First World War and for years of touring the **Empire**. The Empire figured strongly in songs of the Edwardian music hall. But Marxist criticism that they induced jingoism in an otherwise revolutionary proletariat is debatable, since owners could not afford to impose taste on their clientele, especially when they had to compete with new forms of entertainment.

Music halls began to decline in popularity during the 1920s with
► the advent of radio and **cinema**. The last great stars were the comedian/singers Gracie Fields (1898–1979) and George Formby (1904–61). Lancastrians both, they saw the change coming and moved into film, where they had successful careers that lasted into the 1940s. The development of television after the Second World War finished off the halls. Over a hundred closed down between 1945 and 1958 and by the early 1960s only a handful were left – most of them at seaside resorts where they catered to a dwindling audience of elderly summer holi-
► daymakers. One venue of that kind provided the setting for **John Osborne**'s play *The Entertainer* (1957). In it, the music hall was used as a metaphor for the decline of the British Empire, its anti-hero Archie Rice delivering songs, jokes and patriotic rants to half-empty stalls with growing bitterness and ennui.

However, the style of entertainment survived long after the auditoria had gone. Many music-hall stars took their acts on to the small
► screen. In shows like *Sunday Night at the London Palladium* (ITV, 1955–67; 1973–4), music hall transmogrified into 'variety' and got a second wind that lasted until the 1980s (Gracie Fields performed in the first show). Such was its enduring appeal that one programme –
► *The Good Old Days* (BBC, 1953–83) – replicated the whole experience, with performers and audience dressed up in Edwardian clothes. Variety was supplied with a new generation of entertainers from working-men's clubs. These dingy venues, most of which were found in the north of England, may have lacked the rococo splendour of the music halls, but their bullishly discerning audiences blooded many TV stars like the comic Les Dawson (1933–93), whose inspiration was 'Old Mother Riley', a stalwart of the halls during the 1920s. The
► Redcoats of Butlins **holiday** camps also provided a rich source of talent in the TV era. The greatest testament to the endurance of the
► phenomenon was that the **monarchy** associated itself with variety through the Royal Command Performance. It was attended by the Queen, and like *Sunday Night at the Palladium*, combined traditional acts with pop groups of the day. First instituted in 1912, and an annual event since 1921, it was first televised on ITV in 1960. Several

outstanding pop groups were heavily influenced by music-hall song, a tendency notably manifest in the **Beatles'** *Sgt Pepper's Lonely Hearts* ◄ *Club Band* (1967), the Small Faces' *Ogden's Nut Gone Flake* (1968) and Ian Dury and the Blockheads' *New Boots and Panties* (1977).

Together with seaside holidays and the **pub**, music halls formed the ◄ basis of British industrial working-class culture for at least half a century. Their influence was felt around the world and in most social strata. Ironically, what led to the eventual decline of the variety format was the very respectability which had allowed it to make the transition from auditoria to cinema, radio and TV. As a new generation of Britons demanded more sexually explicit and politically pointed entertainment, variety shows came to be seen as conservative nostalgia for a more supine society. In fact, 'alternative' comics, musicians and chat-show hosts owed more to the original music hall than they knew.

■ Muslims

The fastest growing faith group in twentieth-century Britain. By 1900 there were approximately 10,000 Muslims in the UK; by 2000 the number had grown to 1.5 million, 3 per cent of the population. The first British mosque appeared in Cardiff in 1860, and the first purpose-built one in Woking in 1894. But it was not until 1944, when George VI opened the Islamic Centre in Regent's Park, London, that mosques started to become a familiar sight in Britain. The idea for the Centre came from Lord Headley, an English convert to Islam. In 1916, Headley suggested to the Secretary of State for India, Austen Chamberlain, that the state should pay for one 'in memory of Muslim soldiers who died fighting for the **Empire**' during the First World War. Eventually, in ◄ 1940, the British government allocated £100,000 to the project and the King donated 2.3 acres of land in the royal park. It was rebuilt as the Central Mosque in 1977, to a design by Sir Frederick Gibberd, **architect** ◄ of Liverpool's Roman Catholic Cathedral, at a cost of £6.5 million, most of which came from oil sheikhs in the Gulf States.

The surge in the Muslim population was largely a result of **immi-** ◄ **gration** from former British colonies in Asia, which took place between the 1950s and 1970s. The majority – 640,000 – came from Pakistan and Bangladesh. Numbers were boosted by converts from the Afro-Caribbean population who associated Christianity with imperialism. But such converts, and organisations like The Nation of Islam where they found inspiration, were few in number compared to their counterparts in the United States. Like **Roman Catholicism**, Islam's ◄ new strength in Britain was based more on the growth of separate faith schools. Two reasons for their popularity among Muslim

M

parents were the desire, on religious principle, for boys and girls to be educated separately, and the fact that, whereas 40 per cent of other faith schools taught a multi-faith syllabus, Islamic ones did not. State funding for them was controversially introduced in 1998. Only four schools were in receipt of funding by 2001, compared to 551 Christian ones, 32 Jewish and 2 Sikh. But Ofsted inspectors had already censured one for its limited curriculum.

Two further controversies marked out the religion as a cause of tension. The publication of Salman Rushdie's (b. 1947) *Satanic Verses* in 1989 led to a *fatwa* issued by the Iranian leader Ayatollah Khomeini which placed a duty on Muslims everywhere to kill the writer for blasphemy. Many British ones supported the *fatwa* and thousands burnt copies of Rushdie's book and effigies of him in public demonstrations. Throughout the 1990s, Islamic leaders called for Britain's blasphemy laws to incorporate their religion. The extant Blasphemy Act of 1698

▶ only protected the doctrines of the established **Churches of Scotland and England**. But prosecutions were rare, thanks both to a culture of religious tolerance and the growth of secularism (the last execution for blasphemy took place, under Scots law, in 1697, and the last imprisonment in 1842). The Islamist terrorist attacks of 11 September 2001 in America, when planes were crashed into the Pentagon and New York's 'twin towers', were condoned by some Muslims, including the leader of the mainstream Association of British Muslims. A few even went to fight for the al-Qaeda movement in the subsequent Afghan war.

Islamic fundamentalists remained a minority. But they were a vocal minority; and their abuse of religious tolerance in the UK damaged relations between the sane Muslim majority and their counterparts in

▶ other faiths, especially Christians and **Jews**. Anxious to avoid racial
▶ conflict, the **'New' Labour** government claimed that Islamic fundamentalists were not really Muslims at all but merely terrorists; just as the IRA had once been dismissed. The Ouseley Report for the Commission for Racial Equality on the riots between Asian and white youths in Bradford in 2001 was a landmark. Although it blamed the neo-fascist British National Party for inciting the white population to riot, the

▶ report found that Muslim separatism, particularly that in **education**, was also responsible for poor race relations in the area.

Throughout the world, Islam was put on trial after the 11 September attack. Ignorance of Islamic history, culture and philosophy had always accounted for most of the hostility that Muslims endured in the UK. It was therefore unjust that the peaceful majority should have the burden of proof thrust upon them to establish their innocence of crimes committed in their name. But, rightly or wrongly, it was an inescapable burden.

■ National daily newspapers

At the start of the twentieth century a jaundiced observer, Sir Francis Petrie, stormed that the articles in British newspapers were as much 'a revelation of the vacuity of the public mind, as the advertisements are a testimony to its imbecility'. Petrie was reacting to the new explosion of 'popular' national newspapers – the *Daily Mail* (founded in 1896), the *Express* (1900) and the *Mirror* (1903). By the time of the First World War all of these were owned by 'press barons'. Viscount Rothermere controlled the *Mirror*, which in 1904 became Britain's first paper of convenient 'tabloid' size, with numerous photographic illustrations. Over the century, this format came to mark out the boundary between unabashed entertainment and serious news, so that when 'quality' broadsheet newspapers followed the general trend towards lowbrow news they added a tabloid supplement. Rothermere's brother Viscount Northcliffe (who had originally designed the *Mirror* as a newspaper for **women**) owned the *Mail*; and the Canadian-born **Lord** ◄ **Beaverbrook** acquired the *Express* in 1916.

Although the provincial press hung on, the ultimate dominance of London-based newspapers had been inevitable since the dawn of the railway age, facilitating overnight distribution. Even at the end of the twentieth century local newspapers retained a serious tone, as if afraid of alienating a bedrock of God-fearing readers whose complaints might damage circulation. But the national press knew no such inhibitions; its proprietors guessed that for every reader it offended with moronic tittle-tattle, it would probably attract two more.

The *Mail* was by far the most influential of the new breed of popular national papers. By 1900 it was bought by more than half a million people – the biggest sale anywhere in the world. Northcliffe brilliantly exploited the new opportunities for press entrepreneurs: a growing literate audience – with little time or inclination to brood over 'heavy', impartial news reports – was likely to relish lively snippets which reduced complex issues to simplistic moral propositions. At the same time, such people would also be most vulnerable to the materialistic urge. This was held to be particularly true of women, who were regarded at the time as too irrational to vote and likely to be free-spending for the same reason. At Northcliffe's insistence the *Mail* had a special section for women; it has survived to this day, usually in the form of features on underwear which are clearly intended to edify the men.

Thus potential advertisers could be confident that many readers would rush out to the shops to buy their products as soon as they caught sight of their brand names in the *Mail*. A low cover price would be subsidised by the advertisers. The Prime Minister Lord Salisbury scoffed that Northcliffe's newspapers were 'written by office boys for office boys', but that fastidious judgement had actually touched on the reason for the *Mail*'s success. In 1908 Northcliffe also acquired *The Times*, which was languishing at the time. He cut the price and brightened up the paper, without quite reducing it to the approved level for 'office boys'.

Over the century the *Mail*'s fortunes were slightly uneven. For many years Beaverbrook's *Express* outsold it by around two to one (at its height in the 1950s the *Express* was shifting more than 4 million copies per day, while the *Mail* barely rose above 2 million). The battle
▶ raged most fiercely between the wars, when the rivals, grasping the true nature of their readers' loyalty, scattered free gifts (including life insurance policies) in order to keep them faithful.

The papers were squabbling over the same sector of the market –
▶ broadly speaking, they appealed to **Conservative** supporters (or rather, people who hated socialism). This left an opening for the *Mirror*, which moved to the left smartly enough after 1940 to claim part of the credit
▶ for **Labour**'s 1945 landslide. The photograph of a soldier, captioned 'Vote for Him' was certainly a clever stroke for that election; the *Mirror*'s 1950 follow-up ('Whose finger on the trigger?') was equally
▶ evocative, portraying **Winston Churchill** as a reckless warmonger. By that time the *Mirror* had the largest circulation, at 4.6 million: and the overall figure of 16.6 million for the 'dailies' was the highest ever. But by far the most successful paper of all was the *News of the World*, which had captured an audience of around 8.5 million on Sundays. It was estimated that around 80 per cent of the adult population saw at least one newspaper every day, although whether or not they absorbed very much of the content was another matter.

▶   As newspaper proprietors became **celebrities** in their own right, they could not resist the temptation to interfere with editorial lines. Beaverbrook and Rothermere even set up their own political vehicle,
▶ the short-lived United Empire Party which campaigned for **tariff**
▶ **reform** at the end of the 1920s. **Stanley Baldwin**, whose leadership of the Conservative Party was threatened by the press lords, hit back against those who exercised 'power without responsibility'. This justified rebuke did not prevent Rothermere from publishing an article in the *Mail* (which he took over from Northcliffe after the latter's death),
▶ saluting **Oswald Mosley**'s blackshirts.

Later in the century Rupert Murdoch (*Sun, News of the World, Today, Times*) and Robert Maxwell (*Mirror, Sunday Mirror*) were generally accredited with a similar ambition to move the political agenda to suit their own preferences. The key question, though, was whether newspapers changed the thinking of their readers, or merely reflected and reinforced an existing bias. The motives of the proprietors themselves were not always transparent. For example, Murdoch's decision to switch from the Conservatives to 'New' Labour before the 1997 general ◄ election might have reflected a desire to join what was clearly the winning side, a recognition that Labour was now a 'business-friendly' party, or a mixture of both.

Murdoch was a hate-figure on the left long before he revolutionised the newspaper industry by moving his operation from Fleet Street to London's docklands in 1986, and crushing the power of the trade ◄ unions in an industry which had been badly affected by over-manning and restrictive practices. The *Sun*, which he purchased in 1969, had until 1964 been the Labour-supporting *Daily Herald*. Murdoch caused offence not just because he changed the politics of the paper; more seriously, the *Sun* championed 'permissive' attitudes, particularly on ◄ the subject of sex. The topless pin-up girl became a regular feature on page 3 after November 1970. The exploitation made a mockery of recent advances towards sexual equality. But the paper claimed that the models were 'liberated' because the work paid well (and in a world dominated by materialism it was difficult to gainsay the argument). Meanwhile, the *Sun*'s stablemate, the *News of the World*, profiteered by exploiting British confusion about sex. Back in 1843, the newspaper's first edition included an 'inviolable compact with the public' that the price would never be raised from threepence. The sacred pledge proved violable after all: but the newspaper certainly continued to be cheap. Late twentieth-century readers were encouraged to think that if their 'love lives' were mundane they were somehow inadequate. Yet celebrities were exposed 'in the public interest' if they sought consensual gratification with anyone prepared to sell their story. The press had won the right to peddle smutty stories in the 'public interest' after the Profumo Affair of 1963, when sensational tales about members of ◄ the Establishment were passed off under the shelter of a general ◄ panic about national security. After this politicians were understandably reluctant to interfere with press 'freedom', because they were likely to be exposed if they put a foot (or other body parts) out of line. This egregious formula was still winning around 4 million paying customers for the *News of the World* in the summer of 2002. In the more competitive daily market the *Sun* enjoyed a similar dominance, now selling a million more copies than its closest rival, the *Mail*.

While the tabloid press dominated the overall market, several 'quality' broadsheets held their own throughout the century. *The Times* was a prestige acquisition for Murdoch as it had been for Northcliffe; its sales were apparently rising in the last years of the century, but like his predecessor Murdoch resorted to price-cutting to lift the figures over 750,000. The *Daily Telegraph* was more successful, with an audience of over 1 million. The stereotype of a *Telegraph* reader – taken from its much-parodied letters page – was that of an elderly retired military man, anguished by most contemporary trends and clinging more defiantly to traditional British institutions as a result. The newspaper remained true to the Conservative Party throughout the century. By contrast, the *Guardian* (until 1959 the *Manchester Guardian*) was denounced by its opponents as a bastion of woolly-minded liberalism. Indeed, such was the right-wing bias of most of the press in the 1980s that readers of Conservative newspapers tended to assume that the paper was a subversive organ of the extreme left. In reality, over the century it rarely went so far as to support Labour – and even when it did, it was a critical friend. The paper did, though, uncover several stories of genuine public interest in the 1990s, as corruption ate away at a government which had been in power for too long. In 1986 its insubstantial niche in the market was invaded by the *Independent*, but both newspapers managed to survive, selling around 800,000 copies between them every day.

At the end of the century Britons still read – or at least bought – more newspapers than any of their contemporaries in the developed world. But the circulation of the 'nationals' was declining – down more than 3 million from the peak in the 1950s – and editors were faced with several dilemmas. Even the broadsheets were affected by the phenomenon known as 'dumbing down'. Some tabloid stories – like the *Sun*'s front-page allegation that an entertainer had consumed a pet rodent – were too infantile to report at length. But the 'qualities' were happy to pass on most celebrity gossip, presumably on the assumption that their readers had a right to know what 'the man in the street' was talking about. When these stories had anything more than a marginal relevance to attractive stars, prominent photographs were printed (even *Guardian* readers could be assumed to share the frailties of human flesh). At the end of the millennium a rash of spurious opinion surveys broke out, providing the excuse for a lasting trend (the 'greatest' figure in almost every category turned out to be of recent vintage, unsurprisingly). The temptation to fill newspaper columns with such low-cost ephemera masquerading as weighty historical judgement, instead of encouraging serious (but expensive) investigative journalism, was far too great.

Meanwhile, the tabloids fed off the general post-war British neurosis. This marked a subtle change from 1900, when Northcliffe had based his *Mail* on the insight that most people enjoyed a few minutes of hatred every day. Popular hatred was still exploited for profit – figures like **Ian Brady** and (particularly) **Myra Hindley** served this purpose when Britain was not at war with some moustachioed dictator – but fear was now the predominant emotion. Asylum seekers and paedophiles were the most alluring targets at the end of the century, but the **crime** figures were a reliable stand-by and the decline ◀ of confidence in public servants, like teachers and doctors, provided a steady stream of flesh-creeping copy.

Did the British simply get the newspapers they deserved? Judging by **public opinion polls**, it would seem not. At the end of the century ◀ one organisation found that although around half the population claimed to read a newspaper every day, only 15 per cent (well below half of the EU average) put much trust in the printed word. The decline in sales might be explained away by the proliferation of the electronic media, but it was just as likely to reflect a growing resentment against the tendency of all newspapers to operate on the assumption that human nature can be reduced to a few basic tendencies. There was a suggestion of unease in the creation of a Press Complaints Commission in 1991; even the Conservative Party, which had done so well out of the press, had been forced to recognise that the free market was an inadequate custodian of standards. But the Commission's limited powers were generally exercised in the most appalling examples of press 'intrusion' into the lives of the rich and famous; the poor were left to fend for themselves.

Had Milton or John Stuart Mill been alive at the beginning of the twenty-first century and read the *Mail* or the *Sun*, they might have thought twice before advocating a free press. But amid general confusion about **morality**, this was one idea too sacred to question. In any ◀ case, it would be facile to demonise Northcliffe, Murdoch and their less fortunate competitors for having corrupted British taste. The 'media moguls' might have upset as many people as they pleased, but had they not existed the prevailing economic system would have invented others to take their place.

■ National Front (NF); British National Party (BNP)

The National Front was founded in February 1967, as a result of a merger between the British National Party and the League of Empire Loyalists. This new (and temporary) unity on the far right of British politics was in part a reflection of public disquiet at **immigration** from the ◀ 'New Commonwealth'. Large immigrant populations, in areas of high **unemployment**, provoked a reaction which offered obvious recruiting ◀ potential to the new party, which advocated forcible repatriation. Both **Labour** and the **Conservatives** had accepted that immigration should ◀ be controlled. But for the NF the passage of the integrationist Race Relations Act (1965) was an additional spur, allowing agitators to claim that white Britons should unite against the prospect of being reduced to the status of 'second-class citizens' in their own land.

NF supporters tended to be unskilled workers fearing for their jobs,
► rather than 'toffs' bemoaning the loss of **Empire**. The latter group
found their natural home in the Monday Club, within the Conserva-
► tive Party. But the Conservative MP **Enoch Powell** added respectability
to the National Front's arguments with his 1968 'Rivers of Blood'
speech, which looked like an attempt to appeal beyond the saloon-bar
racism of the Monday Club and build support for himself and his party
among the workers. His gambit failed, and when the Conservatives
returned to office they accepted an obligation to allow the settlement
of Asians expelled from Uganda. This humane gesture, in 1973,
inevitably boosted the NF. At the West Bromwich by-election in May
the party's candidate, Martin Webster, won 16 per cent of the vote.
Although the Front flopped in the two general elections of 1974, it
polled relatively strongly in the 1976 local elections, winning two
council seats in Blackburn and securing nearly 20 per cent of the vote
in Leicester. At the 1977 Stechford by-election the NF pushed the
► **Liberals** into fourth place.

In the 1979 general election the NF ran more than 300 candidates.
They were rewarded with an average of just over 1 per cent of the vote.
Some potential NF voters were siphoned off by the Conservatives,
► whose new leader **Margaret Thatcher** had pledged to restrict (if not
entirely to prevent) future immigration. But the NF was also associated
► with public disorder, like the supporters of **Oswald Mosley** in the
1930s. The Front's marches – almost invariably routed through inflam-
mable areas – were often attacked by the Anti-Nazi League (ANL). These
clashes came to a head during the 1979 election campaign, when one
► ANL protestor was killed by the **police** in Southall, London.

The National Front split in the wake of the 1979 debacle. By the end
of the century it was virtually extinct. But one splinter group, headed
by the ex-NF leader John Tyndall, joined forces with other groups to
resurrect the old British National Party label in 1982. After a faltering
start the BNP was confident enough to field more than 50 candidates
for the 1997 general election. On average, its performance was no
improvement on the NF in 1979. But there were signs of a new strategy
for the party, combining the old attempt to exploit racial tensions
► with a more 'acceptable' image in the era of 'New' Labour. At the 2001
general election support rose, especially in Oldham, the scene of
recent rioting. There was still no sign of the BNP actually picking up a
parliamentary seat, but in 2002–3 it won several council seats, notably
► in Blackburn and Halifax. Elsewhere in **Europe**, anti-immigrant
parties benefited not only from the problem of asylum seekers, but
► also from a pervasive feeling of **apathy** among the voters. As ever, the
major parties in Britain were ready to appease this mood. The notion
that this was a price worth paying if it prevented the rise of extremist

parties was unworthy of serious examination. By going even halfway to meet the likes of the BNP, the other parties were increasing the credibility of racist ideas and allowing them far more influence over policy than they were ever likely to achieve through the ballot box.

■ National Health Service (NHS)

Between the wars, healthcare in Britain was widely recognised as a symptom of a more general social inequality. Most workers were covered under a National Health Insurance scheme, but their families were not. Private insurance was available, but the premiums were high. The standard of hospital care was extremely uneven. In 1945 there were more than 1,300 'voluntary' hospitals, traditionally funded through private donations but now increasingly reliant on the state, and more than 1,750 institutions under the control of various local authorities. The voluntary hospitals were far more prestigious, and medical staff felt a sense of obligation to undertake some unpaid duties; but they tended to concentrate on 'kill or cure' cases rather than chronic conditions, which were almost exclusively treated in the municipal hospitals. The affluent could afford private care in nursing homes, but even in the voluntary hospitals they tended to enjoy preferential treatment. Meanwhile there was a powerful incentive for general practitioners (GPs) to work in areas in which there was a high proportion of residents able to pay for their services.

In a 1935 book celebrating the record of **local government** over the ◄ previous century, a rise in life expectancy from 39 to 60 was attributed to the excellence of the existing health services. But the inequities of the system were obvious, and in the previous year the **Labour Party** ◄ had committed itself to a comprehensive national health service. In 1941 the **(Liberal)** Minister of Health in the coalition government ◄ promised post-war reform, although he held out the prospect of more consistent standards of care rather than a free service. At the time, the British Medical Association (BMA) was also strongly in favour of reform, in the interests of greater efficiency. In the following year the **Beveridge Report** came out in favour of a free and universal service, ◄ after identifying Disease as one of the 'Five Giants' which had to be attacked.

By the end of the war there was something like a cross-party **consensus** on health. *A National Health Service*, issued in 1944 by the ◄ **Conservative** minister Henry Willink, followed Beveridge's prescrip- ◄ tion. Faced with entrenched vested interests, Willink retreated from some of the more ambitious plans for reorganisation. In particular, the idea of placing all hospitals under local authority control ran up against the traditional prejudice in favour of the voluntary sector.

Compared to what another Conservative, R.A. Butler, had envisaged in
▶ his **1944 Education Act**, the scheme was a step forward but only part
▶ of the journey. After the 1945 general election Willink's successor **Nye
Bevan** came up with a different solution – bringing all the hospitals
under the control of the central state. Under the 1946 National Health
Act 14 Regional Health Boards were created, run by nominees of the
Minister of Health. From the start this system was criticised for being
over-centralised. Yet arguably the real problem was poor co-ordination;
the 38 teaching hospitals had separate managements, and some services (like the ambulances) were left to the existing local authorities. As
a conciliatory gesture towards the doctors, Bevan agreed that, as
before, the bulk of their income would be related to the number of
patients. Finally, private practice was not banned, so that medical staff
could still supplement their earnings by attending to patients in 'pay
beds'. Although this compromise was forced on Bevan, it ensured the
continuation of a 'two-tier' health system. Since Butler had also missed
▶ the chance of abolishing **public schools**, life-chances from cradle to
grave were still incomparably better for the rich.

The guiding principle of the NHS was that treatment should be
free, as in Butler's schools. Millions took advantage of this generosity.
Among other things, Bevan announced that more than 8 million pairs
of spectacles had been ordered in the first year of the service, which
was inaugurated on 5 July 1948. But in 1951 charges were introduced
for dentures and spectacles, provoking the resignations of both Bevan
and Harold Wilson. The official justification for this policy departure
was the need to increase Britain's defence expenditure during the
Korean War. In fact, the charges amounted to about 0.5 per cent of the
rearmament bill, which suggested that the Chancellor, Hugh
Gaitskell, had pushed them through for reasons which were personal
and political rather than financial. His action implied that his rival
Bevan had been too optimistic in believing that Britain could afford a
generous NHS. Yet the Guillebaud Committee, set up by the Conservatives two years later to audit the NHS, found that the cost could be
sustained, even though it had proved greater than Bevan expected.
▶ Under such dynamic ministers as Iain Macleod and **Enoch Powell** the
Conservatives embarked on an ambitious programme of hospital-
building. The expansion led to staff shortages; increasingly, vacancies
were filled by recruits from the 'New Commonwealth', laying Powell
▶ open to the claim that his own policies had fostered the **immigration**
which he later attacked.

When Labour returned to office in 1964 prescription charges were
abolished, only to be re-imposed (with numerous, bureaucracy-
breeding exemptions) in response to an economic crisis four years
later. By now it was becoming clear that the NHS was a victim of its

own success. Life expectancy for both men and women increased by around eight years between 1938 and 1970, and the proportion of people over 80 in the British population had more than doubled. Alternative methods of funding the service, such as a 'boarding charge' for hospital patients, were canvassed. But it proved impossible to devise a scheme which would be both cost-effective and politically acceptable. Even the free-market radical Sir Keith Joseph had to admit defeat in a search for new funds during his spell as Secretary of State for Social Services from 1970 to 1974.

When **Margaret Thatcher** became Prime Minister in 1979 the NHS ◄ seemed ripe for reform. By 1982 health was absorbing nearly 6 per cent of Britain's gross domestic product (around £11.5 billion), and many NHS staff had taken industrial action during the '**Winter of** ◄ **Discontent'** of 1978–9. Yet before the 1983 general election Mrs Thatcher affirmed that the NHS was 'safe' in Conservative hands. Only in her third term did her government undertake a far-reaching review. The result was the 'internal market', which made hospitals into self-governing trusts and gave doctors control of their own budgets. The split between 'purchaser' and 'provider' was designed to make hospitals compete with each other, as if they were businesses in a free market. While treatment would still be free, the government also introduced incentives for pensioners to take out private medical insurance.

The British Medical Association (BMA) had strongly opposed Bevan's original plan. Now it spoke out in defence of his system. While for the **Thatcherites** this was ample proof that health professionals consti- ◄ tuted yet another entrenched group intent on protecting its own interests, the BMA could argue that the reforms were an unworkable compromise between the free market and state control. The results tended to support its strictures. In theory, the ability of GPs to refer their patients to hospitals outside their areas ought to have driven up standards across the board. In practice, the only thing driven up was the number of health service bureaucrats. According to one estimate, there were 18,000 administrators in 1989; three years later the ranks had swollen to almost 135,000. Over the same period, the number of nurses and midwives hardly changed (on some calculations it actually fell). Thus, although the health budget was more than £30 billion in 1992, much of the increase was being frittered away on non-essential services. Meanwhile, the government's policy of running down institutions for psychiatric patients, under a policy of 'care in the community', was blamed for some widely-publicised attacks on members of the public. Although the old system had been deeply unpopular, it seemed that the government had only seized on these arguments as another way of cutting costs.

▶   In the run-up to the 1997 general election 'New' Labour attacked the Conservative record on health, and promised that it would 'save' the NHS. It argued that underfunding of the NHS had been a deliberate strategy; rather than face the prospect of a prolonged delay before receiving treatment, anyone who could afford to pay would take out private insurance. By 1992 over 3 million people were taking this option, suggesting that privatisation would come in through the back door. To reverse the trend, 'New' Labour promised to scrap the Conservative reforms. But the extent of the subsequent change was debatable. Certainly by the end of the century the NHS was under more pressure than ever. Staff were overworked and unhappy, harassed on the one hand by government-imposed targets and on the other by a new culture of litigation if their treatment fell short of perfection. The media added to the pressure, constantly seeking evidence of new 'scandals' in the wake of the real atrocities committed by the GP Harold Shipman, who murdered more than 200 of his patients over 24 years. By the beginning of 2003 a fifth of GPs wanted to leave their jobs, at a time when the government was trying to boost the numbers entering the profession.

As the NHS celebrated its first half-century, health was still generally regarded as natural Labour territory. Yet it is doubtful whether Nye Bevan or William Beveridge would have been very happy with the situation. The institution itself still upheld the public service ethos, although the all-pervasive spirit of commercialism meant that it devoted far too much time and money to spurious activities such as the designing of new logos and 'mission statements'. The real problem lay with the public themselves, but no politician was proposing a reform of their attitudes. As originally designed, the NHS was part of a framework of institutions intended to insulate the public from avoidable misfortunes. By the end of the century the British wanted more than this. Their definition of 'misfortune' had been revised. When they fell ill – even with the most trivial of maladies – they were satisfied with nothing less than an immediate and complete cure. GPs were constantly being asked to write reports for patients who had suffered minor injuries, in the hope that this would help their claims for compensation. A refusal to co-operate could lead to an official complaint. Much of the daily routine was occupied by problems relating to the general unhappiness of contemporary life, notably stress-induced illness; but the doctor dishing out anti-depressants would often need help far more than the patient. In short, while Bevan and Beveridge saw the NHS as a springboard to a better future, by the end of the century it was a piece of tattered sticking plaster.

■ Nationalisation

In 1918 the **Labour Party** adopted a new constitution, largely drafted ◄
by the **Fabian** Sidney Webb. The document included a commitment to ◄
public ownership of the means of production ('distribution and
exchange' were added more than a decade later). It is commonly
assumed that a history of nationalisation in Britain should start with
this development, and that the next landmark was the election in
1945 of the Attlee government, which gave Labour an overall parliamentary majority for the first time. In fact, by the time of the 1918
conference the first 'nationalisations' had already taken place; and
there were to be several more by 1939.

The Post Office (founded in 1657) could be regarded as the first
ominous step in the process; it was run directly by civil servants until
it was made into a public corporation in 1969. But a more plausible
account might begin in 1870, when the Postmaster-General took
control of private telegraph services. In 1875 the Disraeli government
acquired shares in the Suez Canal Company, for £4 million. The Port of
London Authority was set up by statute in 1909; a similar body, the
Mersey Docks and Harbour Board, dated back to 1874. Worries about
fuel supplies led the government (in the formidable shape of the First
Lord of the Admiralty, **Winston Churchill**) to purchase a majority ◄
stake in the Anglo-Persian Oil Company in 1914. The British Broadcasting Company (**BBC**) was given a temporary licence in 1922; a ◄
committee of inquiry recommended that it be given permanent form
as a public corporation, and this step was taken in 1926. In the same
year the Central Electricity Board (CEB) was set up, although generation remained in private hands. After some delay – and opposition
from **Conservatives** who denounced a 'socialist' measure – in the ◄
1930s the National Government created the London Passenger Transport Board (LPTB), with authority over buses and trams as well as the
underground railway. As a concession, while the members of the CEB
were appointed by the minister, the LPTB was chosen by an independent group.

Thus by 1939 – when the British Overseas Airways Corporation
(BOAC) was established by the government of that frequent flyer,
Neville Chamberlain – the state had encroached far enough into
ownership of the means of production to cause distress among doctri-
naire opponents of nationalisation. The fact that the process had been
driven not by ideology, but rather by pragmatic calculation, was no
comfort to them. Basing their own opposition to state intervention on
faith instead of facts, they tended to see anyone who took a contrary
view as a 'socialist'. Within the Conservative Party in particular, this
was a source of trouble into the 1990s.

From this perspective, the programme of the Attlee government begins to look like a more systematic application of pre-war principles, rather than a radical new departure. During the Second World War the state had apparently proved its competence, and the 'shopping list' presented in Labour's 1945 manifesto was relatively uncontentious. The Bank of England, nationalised in 1946, was already a quasi-state body; and the rest of the financial sector was left intact. The railways and canals (1948) had been struggling for many years in private hands, and the same was obviously true of coal (although the romanticised history of this industry led many workers to exaggerate the importance of state ownership, which was authorised in 1946). Gas was also nationalised in 1948, and in the next year the Iron and Steel Corporation was established. In the latter case there was clear evidence that the drive for nationalisation was running out of steam; while core production could be centralised and controlled, small-scale specialised steel-making concerns stayed privately-owned.

On the whole, then, the Attlee government confined itself to the state ownership of long-established, generally declining and labour-intensive industries. Understandably, it was a backward-looking exercise. Industries which provided essential goods in wartime were obvious candidates for nationalisation so soon after Britain had been fully mobilised for the struggle against Germany. There was no suggestion that the state would try to meddle with the industries which could thrive in a **consumerist** future. In fact, it could be argued that the programme of nationalisation was a help to private industry, rather than a 'totalitarian' threat. If raw materials and energy were subsidised under state ownership, private manufacturers would find it easier to undercut foreign competition.

Critics also pointed out that the members of the boards, even when these were directly appointed by a 'socialist' minister, tended to be businessmen with long experience of the private sector. They were the obvious candidates – unless one took the radical step of placing control of each industry in the hands of the workers. Although even the Conservatives were beginning to flirt with the idea of worker participation, Labour backed away from the challenge. And, of course, the old owners were generously compensated.

Until the mid-1970s, the nationalisation debate centred on iron and steel, denationalised by the Conservatives then reclaimed (with some trouble) by the Wilson government in 1967. Labour fought the general election of February 1974 with a radical new programme to storm the 'commanding heights' of the British economy. But even if senior figures had been determined to carry this into effect they would have been thwarted by the party's slender parliamentary majority. The ailing British Leyland was rescued in 1975, and British Aerospace and British Shipbuilders were both established in 1977. Labour's National Enterprise Board (1975) provided new scope for intervention, but the most publicised initiatives concerned failing (or 'lame duck') industries, like the Meriden motorcycle firm.

Although at first the Conservatives proceeded cautiously with **privatisation** after their re-election in 1979, their **Thatcherite** philosophy was antagonistic to the very idea of a 'mixed economy'. And one of the best pragmatic arguments for state ownership – the need to mobilise the economy during a protracted all-out conflict between powerful nations – had apparently disappeared for ever. Socialists might persist with the argument that full-scale nationalisation had never been given a trial, so the case for capitalism had 'won' by default. That was certainly true; but the British experience had raised a serious question. In the mid-1970s the great nationalised industries, like coal, iron and steel, could no longer run on an economic basis without radical restructuring. But at a time of general economic decline, governments which hoped to maintain high levels of employment could not lay off large numbers of workers without courting defeat at a general election. At the same time, **trade unions** in the ◄ state sector felt that their government paymasters would always back down whenever they felt like striking for higher wages.

Thus the sorry story of mounting losses in the state sector looked certain to perpetuate itself unless something dramatic was done. If nationalisation had spread across the economy, it could only be assumed that the process would have been much worse. Ultimately, those who argued for state ownership had to fall back on their socialist faith in human nature: in other words, they had to assert that the destruction of the profit motive would liberate workers from the mental chains which made them bid up the price of their labour regardless of their real needs, and cling to outdated methods of production instead of adapting to technological advances. But at the end of the century this proposition looked more dubious than at any time since the Industrial Revolution. Even Labour had accepted that 'private is good, public is bad'. **Tony Blair's** determination to trans- ◄ form the party into **'New' Labour** hinged on the issue of state owner- ◄ ship. In April 1995 the historic commitment was duly ditched, and when the party returned to office two years later it was anxious to prove the sincerity of its conversion. In 2002, when the failure of the privatised railways was obvious to even the most besotted Conservatives, the government tried every expedient to avoid describing its rescue of Railtrack as an act of nationalisation.

N

■ **'New' Labour**

▶ **Tony Blair**'s comfortable election as leader of the **Labour Party** in July 1994 marked the triumph of a 'modernising' faction which had been growing in influence since the party's second consecutive election defeat in 1983. This group, which also included Blair's Shadow Chancellor Gordon Brown, was convinced that Labour would keep losing elections so long as it was associated with apparent electoral liabilities, like its commitment to public ownership and its umbilical link
▶ with the **trade unions**. The modernisers could argue that the first of
▶ these was an unnecessary burden; **nationalisation** had been discredited by developments at home and abroad, yet Labour governments had been criticised by the left for failing to carry out their manifesto promises in this area. Far better to face the electorate with a more realistic (and honest) programme, accepting the central role of capitalism which no Labour governments had seriously challenged in practice.

The unions were still a vital source of funds, at least to keep the party going until it could attract significant support from the business community. But they would have to be kept at arm's length; and
▶ thanks to **Conservative** reforms they would acquiesce, given that they had no other political home available. But this was more than just a tactical decision. The modernisers disliked the unions on principle, since they had helped to bring down the Callaghan government in 1979 and had generally failed to engage in constructive co-operation with Labour administrations. In any case, 'New' Labour leaders were obsessed by 'wealth creators'; and whatever their negotiating skills, most contemporary union leaders were mere apparatchiks, much like the politicians themselves, rather than dynamic entrepreneurs.

When he took the party leadership in 1983 Neil Kinnock was determined to make Labour 'electable', and whatever his private feelings this meant accepting the broad outlines of the modernisers' case. By the time of the 1992 general election party policy had been transformed, and left-wing militants had been purged. But it was left to Kinnock's successors to push through the key institutional changes. Before his premature death in 1994 John Smith moved against the union 'block vote'. But Smith was genuinely divided between his affection for 'Old' Labour, with its theoretical commitment to social justice, and his desire to hold office. Had he lived, he would certainly have moved more slowly than Blair subsequently did to reform Clause IV of the party constitution, which enshrined the commitment to public ownership. Although Smith had been criticised by the left as at best a lukewarm socialist, after his fatal heart attack he was sincerely mourned by many of the same people, as the last obstacle in the path of 'New' Labour.

Smith would almost certainly have become Prime Minister in 1997. But for the left, that will remain a maddening 'might have been'. Like Smith, Blair was determined to build an anti-Conservative coalition. But while Smith would probably have tried to mobilise existing opponents of the government under Labour's banner, Blair directly appealed to disillusioned Conservatives. Although he posed as a 'One Nation' politician, there was little mileage in that slogan; most left-wing Tories had abandoned their old party long before. Blair's real purpose was much more radical: to draw into his 'Big Tent' economic individualists who had benefited from **Thatcherite** policies, but now ◀ felt that the Conservatives had lost their way under John Major. By the 1997 general election, a resolution to avoid frightening these disgruntled Tories with radical policy alternatives had turned into a hope of winning their active support, by accepting the broad Thatcherite framework.

The ensuing 'New' Labour landslide, bringing a majority of 179 seats, certainly owed its scale to Blair's strategy. Ironically, it also cemented it. Although commentators were already writing off the chances of a significant Tory comeback at the next election, no government likes to have its majority cut. 'New' Labour had won many seats in Conservative heartlands, and these would be endangered by a serious deviation from Thatcherism. By the end of the century, Blair's promise not to govern like 'Old' Labour could not be questioned even by his most dogmatic right-wing opponent.

But what did 'New' Labour stand for? To some extent, it marked the rebirth of the defunct **Social Democratic Party** (SDP). That party had ◀ been thwarted by the lack of a significant electoral base. But Labour's modernisers had no need to build a party machine from scratch; they simply seized the existing one, and introduced additional methods of central control. They could also depend on a core of support; even if they were increasingly disgruntled, 'Old' Labour voters continued to support the new leadership, because like the unions they had nowhere else to go. The SDP could never count on this kind of loyalty; it was exclusively for fair-weather friends.

After 'New' Labour's second electoral landslide in 2001 questions about the party's future revolved around Blair's intentions. If he chose to step down in favour of Brown after two terms 'the project' might survive, since the Chancellor had retained some of his credibility with the left. But as in the case of the SDP 'New' Labour was badly affected by faction-fighting; and if Brown's place in the succession were to be usurped by one of Blair's colourless acolytes, the emptiness at the heart of the reformed party would be exposed. Blair

▶ also faced the old SDP dilemma of what to do about the **Liberal Democrats**. Some even wondered if the first landslide had upset his strategy, since a narrow win would have given him the excuse to launch his own version of the SDP/Liberal Alliance. In short, although 'New' Labour had redesigned the electoral map of Britain and transcended the old 'left–right' divisions, there was no reason to think that the achievement would be lasting.

■ North–South divide

When Benjamin Disraeli identified 'two nations' in his novel *Sybil* (1845), he had in mind the gulf between the rich and the poor. Yet when he made a fictional Chartist agitator describe a country whose inhabitants were like 'dwellers in different zones or inhabitants of different planets', he was hinting at a geographical dimension to the problem which also features in the works of Charles Dickens and Elizabeth Gaskell, who pulled no punches in *North and South* (1855). It was never quite as simple as that title suggested, and the phrase 'North–South divide' has survived at least in part because Southern-based commentators have an eccentric idea of what counts as 'the North'. But the short-hand generalisation is as good as any, and
▶ cultural commentators now have the rival **soap operas** *Coronation Street* (1960–), set near Manchester, and London's *EastEnders* (1985–) to illustrate the phenomenon.

During the nineteenth century the main fascination for social observers was the grim working environment for the inhabitants of
▶ **manufacturing** towns. If Britain's unrivalled status as the 'workshop of the world' had lasted longer, provincial cities like Birmingham, Leeds, Manchester and Newcastle might have emerged as rivals to London. As it was, the civic pride symbolised by the great public buildings of the North and the Midlands began to drain away as soon as the country's economic performance was surpassed by the USA and Germany. For almost all of the twentieth century, the most striking contrast was between conditions in the generally affluent south-east of England, and the plight of the unemployed as the great, labour-intensive industries elsewhere fell into decline. The geographical element was under-
▶ lined by **J.B. Priestley** in *English Journey* (1933) and **George Orwell's** *The*
▶ *Road to Wigan Pier* (1937). Orwell was well aware of **poverty** in London. But there was something different about the experience in the North,
▶ mainly because of the **class** solidarity which added dignity to poignant protests such as the march of Jarrow's unemployed in October 1936. Orwell criticised northerners for being unduly proud of their alleged virility: but this was an understandable attempt to find psychological compensation for their relative economic deprivation.

The **unemployment** figures in the 1930s proved the existence of a divide, although despite the impact of the **Great Depression** in places like Jarrow ('the town that died'), the blight was actually at its worst in South Wales. In 1932, unemployment among insured workers in Wales as a whole was 36.5 per cent, but in some areas it approached 100 per cent. London and the south-east were by no means unaffected, but the rate there (13.7 per cent) was around half of the figure in Scotland, Northern Ireland and the North of England.

Even in the 1930s governments were trying to redress the imbalance, with policies designed to attract new businesses to the 'depressed areas'. But emerging industries, like the manufacture of motor cars and electrical goods, tended to concentrate in the South and the Midlands. In so far as these firms catered for affluent **consumers**, the depressed areas were trapped in a vicious circle. Manufacturers might as well locate close to their markets; they could be sure that skilled workers would gravitate towards the best-paid work, thus increasing the incentive for other businesses to follow their example. 'Full' employment after the Second World War had a moderating influence, but did not reverse the trend; during the 1960s, for example, governments felt that they should move some of their offices out of London to alleviate pressure on **housing**.

During the economic slump of the 1980s the North–South divide once again became a favourite topic for commentators. The country was polarised politically, with **Labour** winning most seats in its crumbling industrial 'heartlands' and the ruling **Conservatives** almost impregnable in the South; after the 1983 general election Labour and the **SDP/Liberal** Alliance held only 8 seats between them in this area, compared to 168 Conservatives. To opponents of **Thatcherism** the Prime Minister herself seemed to epitomise the divide with her cut-glass accent; it was difficult to remember that she actually hailed from Lincolnshire, which might as well be in the Arctic Circle so far as many southerners were concerned.

Again the contrast was reflected in the unemployment statistics. Yet for most of the post-war period unemployment in the north of England, in Scotland and in Wales, had been around double the rate in the south-east. The relative proportions had hardly changed; it was just that the level was now much higher (around 23 per cent in the north, less than 12 per cent in the south-east). Within regions, the pattern was more diverse than it had been in the 1930s; oil-rich Aberdeen, for example, compared very favourably to the experience of most south-eastern towns. A new complication was the extent of unemployment among ethnic minority groups, regardless of where they lived. Thus the 1981 riots in many English towns, the South no less than the North, were chiefly the product of poverty and alienation.

N

Northerners could regard the second slump of the Thatcher years, at the end of the 1980s, as a belated visitation of poetic justice. It affected all regions of the UK, but the south-east fared worst, suffering around half of the new job losses. Even in the mid-1980s house prices in the favoured region had been about double that for the North of England. But the bursting of the subsequent bubble did not mark the end of the divide. By 2000 house prices were soaring again, and if the effects of the boom were felt almost everywhere the contrast between the south-east and the rest of the country was still unmistakable because the prices there were rising from a much higher base. In 2001 the average house price in London was £180,000; in the North it was just over £60,000. The average house price in London's most deprived borough (Tower Hamlets) was nearly the same as the overall average for Manchester (£67,000 compared to £68,300). Between 1995 and 2001 more than 8,000 houses in London and the south-east were sold for over £1 million each, compared to less than fifty for the North. Meanwhile, the average wage in central London was more than 50 per cent higher than in the West Midlands. Long-distance commuting into London was now an attractive option for many, who imagined that the chance of spending higher wages at home over the weekend would somehow compensate for the exhaustion of working days. But it was increasingly difficult to recruit public-sector workers in some parts of the South, opening the prospect that London would soon provide a perfect example of public squalor amid private affluence.

Culturally, the North–South divide was underlined by the London bias of the media. Although regional accents were common on radio and television – indeed, by the end of the century this seemed to be an essential qualification for a broadcasting job – only the most tough-minded could fail to absorb the prevailing ethos, which dictated that a news story like a murder or a flood was a trivial event unless it occurred south of Watford. In itself, of course, the ubiquity of northerners in the media reflected the pragmatic migration of many talented people to the South; they could still flaunt their regional ▶ identity in the capital, and support their favourite **football** teams at a safe distance.

At a time of generally rising living standards, all this could be rated as one of life's minor irritants. But it did have some serious implications. For example, the media were very interested in issues such as the election of a London mayor. But there was little reporting of the demand for regional government – because, as a poll in 2002 discovered, the south-east of England was the only area which did ▶ not want it. Political **apathy** as a general phenomenon seemed to be ▶ worse in the North; although few senior 'New' Labour figures were southerners themselves, it was widely felt that they were preoccupied with Islington rather than Immingham. In short, Labour's victories in 'natural' Conservative territory like Guildford did not suggest that the North–South gap was disappearing: rather, they marked the final triumph of the South, and the North would have to like it or lump it.

N

■ Orwell, George (1903–50)

Radical patriot, novelist and essayist who challenged left-wing ortho-doxies, raised modern political writing into an art form and effectively founded the study of popular culture in Britain.

Orwell was a renegade from his social background, as maverick figures so often are. He was born Eric Arthur Blair in Motihari, Bengal, where his father worked in the Opium Department of the Govern-
▶ ment of India, managing the **drugs** trade with China. At 13, Blair was sent to England to attend Eton College (1917–21). His contemporaries there included future luminaries of the English literary world like Cyril Connolly (1903–74). He made friends and at first shared their
▶ taste for **George Bernard Shaw**, H.G. Wells and the fashionable socialism that was based more on a dislike of their fathers – whom they held responsible for the First World War – than it was on any
▶ knowledge of or affinity for the working **classes**. 'At the age of eighteen', he wrote, 'I was both a snob and a revolutionary. I was against all authority.' But unlike others of that generation who
▶ affected to despise the Victorian **Establishment** while reaping the benefits of it, Orwell's radicalism became a sincere and lifelong passion that led him into as much conflict with the left as it did with the right. His beliefs were primarily shaped by three experiences.

After leaving Eton, he served in the Indian Imperial Police (1922–27). Based in Burma, he witnessed at first hand the poverty and brutality caused by British rule, an experience that left him with a
▶ detestation of the **Empire** which he later recalled in the novel *Burmese Days* (1935). To the dismay of his parents, he resigned his commission and returned to England, where he embarked on his second formative odyssey: life as a tramp. From 1928 to 1930, he wandered the streets of London and Paris staying in doss-houses and speaking with their inhabitants.

Orwell's record of this time, *Down and Out in Paris and London* (1933) established his reputation as a writer (it also occasioned his name
▶ change). Its impact as a document of the **Great Depression** era is comparable only to Walter Greenwood's novel *Love on the Dole* (1933).
▶ Orwell never romanticised **poverty** or the people who suffered it, whether they were overworked Burmese peasants or unemployed European labourers. His frank observation in *Down and Out* that many comfortably-off people think that 'the working-classes smell' has often been taken as proof that the snobbery of Eton never left him. What it actually testifies to is the fact that, having got near enough to smell them, he was able to grasp the degrading effects that unsanitary living conditions have on human beings.

Orwell's third defining moment was the Spanish Civil War, in which Communism and fascism locked horns in a violent prelude to the Second World War. Most supporters of the Republican government either pontificated from afar or paid brief observatory visits to Spain. Those who actually fought usually joined the Communist-led International Brigade. Orwell was already suspicious of Stalin and his sympathisers so, when he arrived in Barcelona in January 1937, he joined the anarchist POUM militia for which he fought bravely before being shot in the throat. His account of the war, *Homage to Catalonia* (1938), highlighted the deliberate undermining of anarchist forces by their allies and it established the aspect of his work for which he is most famous: exposing the authoritarian nature of Communism and the regimes it spawned.

Orwell's suspicions were confirmed by the Nazi–Soviet Pact of 1939 and by the support it received from the **Communist Party of Great** ◀ **Britain**. He attracted more leftist criticism during the Second World War by making propaganda broadcasts for the **BBC**. His belief that, for ◀ all its faults, liberal democracy was preferable to fascism inspired *The Lion and the Unicorn: Socialism and the English Genius* (1941), a celebration of English life and a treatise on the virtues of patriotism. Orwell attacked the reactionary nature of the conservative ruling class, characterising Britain as 'a family with the wrong members in control'. But he also criticised the internationalism of left-wing intellectuals and the snobbery towards English working people that so often lay beneath it. 'It is a strange fact,' he wrote, 'but unquestionably true, that almost any English intellectual would feel more ashamed of standing to attention during "God Save the King" than of stealing from a poor box.' *Animal Farm* (1945), an allegory about Soviet totalitarianism, was followed in 1949 by his most famous work, the dystopian novel *Nineteen Eighty-Four*. Set in a totalitarian, technocratic Britain of the future, ruled by the all-seeing dictator, 'Big Brother', its phraseology of oppression has become familiar throughout the world, with 'Newspeak' associated with political manipulation of the media, and 'doublethink' a rhetorical technique by which lies are presented as truth.

Though less well known by the general public, Orwell's essays – collected in his lifetime as *Inside the Whale* (1940) and *Shooting an Elephant* (1950) – are among his greatest achievements. Their bracing lucidity, withering irony and deadly invective invite comparison with the great essayists of previous centuries, William Hazlitt and Jonathan Swift. Orwell's subject matter was, however, thoroughly modern. He was the first political writer to take British popular culture seriously. 'The Art of Donald McGill', for example, celebrated bawdy seaside postcards and the working-class **holiday** patterns which they ◀ reflected. Like the poet **John Betjeman**, whom he admired, Orwell was ◀ scathing about the soullessness of the **consumer** society that emerged ◀

▶ between the wars, an outlook that shaped his critique of **suburban** life in the novel *Coming Up for Air* (1937). Broadly speaking, he welcomed the material advances of the era and the freedoms that they spawned. But had he watched the TV show *Big Brother*, he would have detested the trivialisation of his concept. More importantly, he would have

▶ recognised in today's world of 'reality' TV and **spin doctors** a new threat to individuality that could be as potent as the totalitarian regimes of his day.

Orwell could sometimes be naive about the people with whom he empathised, like his belief that the Home Guard, which he joined in 1940, would become a revolutionary militia. And his insistence on drinking tea out of a mug rather than a cup because he thought it more proletarian revealed an enduring guilt about his background. As for those he detested, his condemnation of Communist totalitarianism was manipulated by the right as a stick with which to beat all

▶ radical aspirations during the **Cold War**. *Animal Farm*, for example, became widely known because it was animated in 1949 for propaganda purposes by the reactionary American Walt Disney (1901–66).

However, Orwell's international renown is justified. His death from tuberculosis in middle age prevented him scrutinising the vast changes wrought on Britain by the 1950s and 1960s. But he provided a model for others to do so – notably the novelist and essayist Colin

▶ MacInnes (1914–76) who celebrated the influence that black **immigration** had on the country. The enduring hostility of many on the British left towards Orwell, especially his justification of patriotism, merely confirms his continuing relevance. As the novelist V.S. Pritchett (1900–97) remarked when reviewing one of his books, he 'wakes one up suddenly like cold water dashed in the face'.

■ Osborne, John (1929–94)

The most influential British playwright of the later twentieth century.

▶ Osborne was born into a lower-middle-class **suburban** London family; his father was an advertising copywriter and his mother a barmaid. When his father died in 1941, Osborne invested the legacy left to him in a boarding-school education in Devon. Still heartbroken over his father's death, Osborne could not concentrate on his studies and was expelled after hitting the headmaster. He returned to London, lived briefly with his mother and, after escaping National Service on the grounds of ill-health, in 1950 he took a job tutoring a touring company of young actors. He then served as actor-manager for a string of repertory companies in provincial England, during which time he wrote the first of his plays, *Epitaph for George Dillon* (1954), with his lover Anthony Creighton.

In January 1956, he answered an advert in the *Stage* calling for new plays, which had been placed by George Devine, director of the progressive English Stage Company based at the Royal Court Theatre in London. The work Osborne submitted, *Look Back in Anger*, was accepted, performed and changed the face of British theatre almost overnight. The protagonist, Jimmy Porter, captured the rebellious mood of a new generation of lower-middle-class youths: the first beneficiaries of free secondary and higher education, angry at the **class** ◄ prejudices that still stood in their way and frustrated by the perpetuation of Victorian sexual mores. 'Don't be afraid of being emotional. You won't die of it' was a typical Porter line. It was a far cry from the mannered plays about upper-middle-class drawing-room life which then cluttered the British stage. Osborne never liked the epithet 'Angry Young Man' which bracketed him with other writers of his background and generation like Kingsley Amis and Colin Wilson. But it did suit him, and for almost a decade he benefited from it.

Osborne's next play, *The Entertainer* (1957), confirmed his status. Set in a shabby English seaside resort, its protagonist was Archie Rice, an embittered **music-hall** singer and comedian (played by Laurence ◄ Olivier), who performed tired routines to shrinking audiences. Osborne used the decline of the music hall as a metaphor for that of the British **Empire**, a device that spoke directly to a country still ◄ divided by the **Suez crisis**. While *The Entertainer* was playing to packed ◄ houses, Osborne met the film producer Tony Richardson, who was to become his greatest friend and creative partner. In 1958, they set up Woodfall Films together, which came to form the vanguard of the UK **cinema**'s 'New Wave', not only adapting Osborne's first two plays for ◄ the screen but also the best work of similar writers. Most of Woodfall's films were commercial successes and so brought the 'Angries' to a wider audience. In 1963, Osborne won an Oscar for the screenplay of Richardson's adaptation of *Tom Jones*. He also wrote three more classic plays: *Luther* (1961), about the Reformation leader; *Inadmissible Evidence* (1965), about a frustrated city solicitor; and *A Patriot For Me* (1967) about a nineteenth-century Prussian officer victimised for his **homosexuality**. ◄

In 1964, Osborne wrote, 'Whatever else, I have been blessed with God's two greatest gifts: to be born English and heterosexual.' Attitudes such as this, compounded by his vocal disillusionment with left/liberal causes he had once espoused (he was an early CND activist), ◄ led Osborne to be characterised in later life as a reactionary. In fact, he simply loathed **establishments** wherever he found them. However, his ◄ turbulent private life (he was married five times) did contribute to a decline in the quality of his plays and by the time *A Subject of Scandal and Concern* flopped at the National Theatre in 1971, Osborne's rage

O

had begun to grate with audiences. His last play, *Déjà Vu* (1992), found an ageing Jimmy Porter in defiant mood. Porter, said his creator, strikes 'a churling, grating note, a spokesman for no one but myself, with deadening effect, cruelly abusive, unable to be coherent about my despair'.

Osborne's death from diabetes at the age of 65 led to a predictable but necessary reassessment of his work. His life-long friend and creative heir, playwright David Hare (b. 1947), wrote, 'Nothing bewilders the English more than someone who exhibits great feeling and great intelligence. When, as in John's case, a person is abundant in both, the English response is to take in the washing and bolt the back door.' Osborne's lifetime achievement was to wash England's dirty linen in public. His legacy was to inject realism into the British theatre. Osborne wrote two volumes of classic autobiography, *A Better Class of Person* (1981) and *Almost a Gentleman* (1991). His essays and journalism were collected in *Damn You, England* (1992).

O

■ Paisley, Revd Ian (b. 1926)

Described by Lord Carrington as 'the bigot of all bigots', Paisley came to represent the narrow-minded intransigence of Ulster's Protestant majority during the era of the 'Troubles'. Paisley was born into a ◄ working-class community in Ballymena, County Antrim. He was ◄ ordained into the Free Presbyterian Church by his father, a dissident Baptist. His illiberal education continued at the South Wales Bible College, Belfast's Reformed Presbyterian College and the Bob Jones University in South Carolina. He married and had two children, who discerned a loving man with a warm sense of humour. But in public he modelled himself on the Loyalist demagogue Edward Carson (1854–1935) who had secured the **Partition of Ireland** by armed force. ◄ Paisley had a mountainous frame, a booming voice and, like most fire-and-brimstone preachers, he had a gift for public speaking. It was not long before these attributes were mobilised to serve his militant Unionism.

Paisley's political career began in 1959, when he formed the Ulster Protestant Association in Belfast, a ginger group devoted to shoring up sectarian prejudices among the city's industrial workers. He was jailed for three months in 1964 for attacking the 'Romish tendencies' of mainstream Presbyterians and again, for six weeks, in 1968 for blocking a Catholic civil rights march. He was always careful in public to distance himself from the violence of Protestant paramilitaries. In 1970, Paisley formed the Protestant Unionist Party and at the general election that year he captured Antrim North from the official Unionist MP, Henry Clark – a result that shocked the Heath government and brought him squarely to the attention of the British public. In 1971, the PUP changed its name to the DUP (Democratic Unionist Party). By then, it had become the political voice of Ulster's Protestant working classes.

Paisley's hatred of **Roman Catholicism** was matched only by his ◄ hatred of the landed, patrician Unionist establishment and its main-land masters in the **Conservative Party**. At Westminster, he regularly ◄ voted with **Labour** MPs on social legislation. Yet, he believed that the ◄ Westminster-sponsored liberal reform programme of Northern Ireland governments during the 1960s had encouraged nationalist insurgence and so led to Direct Rule. He has devoted the rest of his life to opposing any further concessions to Irish nationalists and their British appeasers. In 1974–5, he helped organise the Ulster Workers' Council which brought down the Power Sharing Executive established by the Sunningdale Agreement. When challenged, he argued that 'the British constitution is founded on sectarianism' because the Queen had promised to uphold the Protestant faith at her Coronation. It was

P

not a point that impressed mainland Britons and it highlighted the gulf between Ulster and the relatively secular societies of Scotland, Wales and England. A decade later, he organised mass opposition to
▶ the Anglo-Irish Agreement. 'Ulster says no!' he told **Margaret Thatcher** in December 1986. The prime minister shared many character traits with Paisley and probably agreed with his views. But this could not overcome the British desire for peace.

▶ Despite a detestation of the **European Union** (which he saw as a ramp for Continental Catholicism) he was elected to the European Parliament in 1979. By 1997, he found himself and the DUP marginalised by a new consensus for power-sharing that embraced even loyalist paramilitaries. Paisley refused to take part in the negotiations that led to the 1998 Good Friday Agreement; and he described the Agreement itself as 'the greatest betrayal ever foisted by a Unionist leader on the Unionist people'. Still, the DUP won 20 seats in the first election to the Northern Ireland Assembly in June 1998, and did all they could to wreck its operation. When Sinn Féin's Martin McGuinness was appointed Education Minister for the province in November 1999, Paisley described him as a man 'whose hands drip with blood'.

Paisley was often described as paranoid. In fact, his frequent claim that the British were pursuing a policy of unification by consent was absolutely true. The problem was that he framed his opposition to it with a fundamentalist Protestantism which the majority of British people found bizarre, and he expressed his opposition to it in a manner they found distasteful.

P

■ Parliament; elections

At the end of the twentieth century the proceedings of the British parliament were televised, and the whole population over 18 years of age had the right to vote in general elections. It would be hard to say which of these developments would have been more startling for a late-Victorian Prime Minister like Lord Salisbury. The most ambitious of the
▶ **Suffragettes** might have been slightly disappointed with the situation, but at least there had been a female Prime Minister, out of 659 MPs there were now 120 women in the House of Commons, and they formed a majority of the electorate. Ethnic minorities were still chronically under-represented – over the century, only 13 from their ranks had reached the Commons – but even here there were slow signs of improvement. Political leaders were also far more anxious to keep abreast of public opinion. Regular surveys kept MPs informed of the public mood; and parties had established their own 'focus groups' to study voters' thinking in more detail.

Yet the British parliament was in serious trouble at the end of the century. Despite all their efforts there was a widespread feeling that MPs were 'out of touch'. Public attention could be drawn by sexual scandals, or evidence of financial misdeeds; but the political process itself was strictly a minority interest. Fewer people voted in the 1997 general election than had turned out in February 1974, even though the electorate had expanded by more than 4 million in the interim. The downward trend was continuing at the end of the century; the turnout for the **European** election of June 1999 was less than a quarter of those entitled to vote, and the 2001 general election established a record low (59.4 per cent) for such a contest in the democratic era. Membership of political parties was in even steeper decline; the **Conservatives**, who had boasted of more than 2 million members in the 1950s, now had to admit that the figure was down to around 300,000. **Labour** had no reason to brag; its tally was even smaller.

The British electorate had been expanded over the century in four stages. In 1918 a Representation of the People Act gave the vote to almost all adult males over 21, subject to a six-month residency requirement (previously this had been fixed at one year). The requirement was abolished entirely by a further Act of 1948, which also removed the right of plural voting which had been enjoyed by some businessmen and graduates of Oxford or Cambridge **universities**. **Women** over 30 had been given the vote in 1918; the Equal Franchise Act of 1928 reduced this age to 21. With a few trivial exceptions, all men and women over 18 were entitled to vote after the 1969 Representation of the People Act. As a result of all these measures, the 1900 electorate of around 6,700,000 had swollen to 47,000,000 by the end of the century.

There were other changes designed to broaden the social composition of the Commons. From 1911, MPs were paid (£400 at first; by 1996 the salary had increased to £55,000). Since Labour members could also draw on sponsorship from **trade unions**, an important obstacle for working-class aspirants had been removed. The state contributed to MPs' office expenses after 1969. Similarly, expenditure on election campaigns was controlled by law.

Even so, the average MP was still very different from the average UK citizen. The composition of the parliamentary Conservative Party remained fairly stable over the century; in 2000, as in 1900, members of the working **class** were almost wholly absent, while around a third of Tory MPs had a background in business. In the Labour Party only 13 per cent came from the working class; within the 'workers' party' the proportion had receded far more quickly than within the **population** as a whole.

The feeling that MPs were different from the electorate was partly a reflection of the rise of the career politician. It was easy to scoff at people who had sought election to the Commons after an apprentice-ship of political activism at university, followed by a few years' experience as a political adviser. But MPs who had pursued other careers were also attacked. Successful businessmen were often associ-ated with 'sleaze', while **Margaret Thatcher** ridiculed Labour's exces-sive reliance on former polytechnic lecturers. Ultimately, the provenance of MPs is a secondary issue. They will remain unrepresen-tative of the electorate so long as the average citizen has no interest in politics. Probably they will also continue to suffer the classic symp-toms of excessive stress. A survey of 1995 found that 45 per cent of MPs admitted that they smoked and drank too much; more than a third said that they were deprived of sleep; and 38 per cent found that their sex drive had dwindled since entering the Commons. This last finding, at least, was in sharp contrast to the popular image of Britain's politicians in the 1990s.

Throughout the century the House of Lords caught the attention of would-be reformers. A clash between the Conservative-dominated chamber and the **Liberal** government of Herbert Asquith inspired the 1911 Parliament Act, which laid down that a Bill would become law if the Commons passed it in three successive sessions, even if the Lords continued to oppose it. Another Act of 1949 reduced this 'delaying power' to two sessions. Having curtailed the power of the Lords, reformers turned to its composition. The Life Peerage Act of 1958 provided a means of rewarding retiring MPs, and increased the patronage of the Prime Minister without challenging the dominance of the hereditary peers. More radical ideas foundered in the late 1960s – ironically, due to opposition from the Commons – but after 1997 the **Blair** government promised a thorough overhaul, which it embarked upon before it had any idea of how it should finish. The demand for a fully elected Upper House – which would bring Britain into line with most Western democracies – was resisted by a government which prized its powers of appointment. In February 2003 the Commons (and the government) showed how seriously they really took the ques-tion of Lords reform by rejecting every single one of the various options for change. The real point of the exercise had been to win cheap applause from party activists by removing the automatic right of hereditary **aristocrats** to sit in the Lords, and at least that had been achieved.

Reform of the Lords – and the televising of the Commons, which began on a permanent basis in 1991 – seemed to arrive with typical British timing. When these measures might have made a difference they were resisted; the arguments only seemed incontestable when they could no longer help anyone except, perhaps, political corre-spondents. Westminster – called 'the Mother of Parliaments' in a familiar misquotation – had suffered a three-pronged attack during the twentieth century. In 1900 it was at the centre of a mighty **empire**, ◄ and speeches could affect the lives of millions of people. As Britain's power declined, key political decisions were taken by supranational bodies, usually meeting in Washington or Brussels rather than London. **Devolved** institutions set up in Wales and Scotland in 1999, ◄ following the establishment of a new Northern Ireland Assembly in the previous year, at least brought government closer to the people of those countries. But their powers were restricted, so that they barely differed from existing **local government** which was regarded with ◄ indifference by most voters, attracting a turnout of less than 30 per cent in 2000.

In theory, at least, British governments could still be broken in the House of Commons. During the crisis over the ratification of the Maastricht Treaty in 1992–3, for example, John Major was fighting for his political life on more than one occasion. But comfortable majorities meant that neither Margaret Thatcher nor Tony Blair felt it necessary to attend or vote very often. Under Blair, in particular, the Cabinet became a rubber-stamp rather than a forum for discussion and collective decision-making. There was a tendency to regard the television studio as more important than the Commons' dispatch box – even as a proving-ground for potential ministers. Increasingly, the British system was coming to resemble America, and other models of 'Presidential' government. The parliamentary committee system was overhauled, beginning in 1966, theoretically allowing backbenchers the resources to scrutinise executive decisions. In response, the political parties merely exerted tighter control over the membership of such committees. Since the government seemed to hold the Commons in contempt, it could hardly be surprised when voters adopted the same attitude.

This second factor was more potent because it coincided with a general loss of confidence in traditional British institutions. After a century of education reforms, it might have been expected that well-informed citizens would provide new impetus for democratic bodies, holding them to account when representatives made avoidable mistakes, while acknowledging that politics is 'the art of the possible'. Instead, the public tended to make unrealistic demands on government, and in response politicians turned election campaigns into undignified auctions. The resulting cynicism meant that by the end of the century ministers were more likely to survive professional incompetence – which voters assumed to be a universal trait – than personal frailties which could still sell **national newspapers**, if reported in ◄ lurid detail.

Thus the cliché that the public 'gets the politicians it deserves' contains far more truth today than at any time since the whole public was given a choice. It could be argued that this was always a predictable result of democracy. Given that most people would always be too busy to pay detailed attention to politics, the successive expansions of the electorate were likely to create an ever-increasing majority

▶ of the **apathetic**. Ironically, the most common recommendation is to make Britain's politics even more democratic, exploiting technological innovations such as the internet. Some politicians remained optimistic, on behalf of their ideals if not of the institutions they had served. Before the 2001 general election, for example, the veteran Labour MP Tony Benn declared that he was giving up his parliamentary seat in order to 'go into politics'. Whether or not he would gain a hearing for his views out of the Commons, independent thinkers of his stamp were right to feel that they could spend their time more profitably than in constant struggles with the party whips. And as Benn and his type left parliament, that magnificent, inconvenient building and its over-stressed occupants were sure to decline further in public esteem.

■ 'Permissive society'

From the late 1960s the phrase 'permissive society' was most commonly used to signify disapproval of recent developments in British life. Strictly speaking, it referred to the relaxation of censorship

▶ of the theatre and **cinema**, which 'permitted' the public exhibition of behaviour (mainly sexual) which had previously been prohibited. But later it was used to identify a more general trend, under which alleged

▶ 'do-gooders' in **parliament** removed legal obstacles to a range of practices which would otherwise have taken place covertly. Thus in 1967 a

▶ Private Member's Bill decriminalised **homosexuality** in England and Wales (although the age of consent was set at 21), and abortion was legalised under certain conditions. Even more controversially, legisla-

▶ tion allowed free contraception on the **National Health Service** (NHS), and the 1969 Divorce Reform Act meant that marriages could be dissolved after five years even if one partner withheld their consent. Even the very moderate Race Relations Acts of 1965 and 1968, and the Equal Pay Act of 1970, were often included in the indictment, insofar as they vindicated the general clamour for civil rights during the

▶ 1960s. And 'permissiveness' was also taken to refer to the use of **drugs** which remained illegal at the end of the century. 'Permissiveness', in short, stood for 'anything goes'; even though some of it was not allowed to 'go' at all.

Those who spoke bitterly of a new 'permissive society', like Mary Whitehouse (1910–2001), argued that such measures actively fostered

what they saw as a sudden breakdown in traditional **morality**. The ◄
case of the social conservatives ultimately rested on a pessimistic
assessment of human nature. On this view, most human beings are
oblivious to the barriers which separate liberty from licence; and
those 'liberal' politicians who had expanded social freedoms were
unsuitable legislators, because while they might be perfectly 'rational'
themselves they had no conception of the primeval instincts which
drive the average person. Their position resembled that of the
Austrian Chancellor Metternich, who said that he would abolish
capital punishment as soon as murderers adopted the same evaluation of human life. For the social conservatives, the final abolition of
the death penalty in 1969 was the crowning insult in a decade of
disaster.

The conservative position was frequently caricatured and criticised,
and lurking behind it was a reactionary social agenda, since many of
the 'new' freedoms were merely being extended to the general population, instead of being restricted to the rich. Thus, when the poet
Philip Larkin claimed that sexual intercourse only began in 1963, he
was reflecting his middle-class origins; the remark would certainly
have perplexed D.H. Lawrence (1885–1930), whose tale of frenzied
couplings across the social divide, *Lady Chatterley's Lover*, provoked the
most idiotic trial of the century in 1960. But the general argument
certainly had more intrinsic merit than its 'permissive' opponents
tried to make out. The most damaging riposte was that while the
conservatives were quite certain that the liberal chicken had laid the
egg, in reality the link between cause and effect was more complicated. It could be argued that in every case the reformers were merely
responding to public demand, rather than creating it. Thus between
1960 and 1970 the divorce rate more than doubled. Did that mean that
an additional 45,000 contented couples had heard about divorce
reform on the radio and immediately telephoned their lawyers? The
number of legal abortions doubled in a single year, after the passage
of David Steel's Bill. Almost certainly the increase would have been
smaller without the legislation; but did that mean that 27,000 children had been deprived of what was sure to be a happy life, or would
the pregnant women have sought backstreet abortions instead?

For pragmatists, the theoretical arguments had to give way before
the indisputable fact that society had already changed and the law
would have to follow suit if it were not to start looking like an ass.
Moral preaching had never been very popular among twentieth-
century politicians, and to stand out against evident changes in public
morality would have been tantamount to preaching. In any case, there
was not so much of a theoretical 'debate' as a shouted exchange of
slogans. The insuperable obstacle to clear thinking was the wider

P

social context. Even allowing the (mistaken) argument that the population was generally law-abiding and God-fearing in 1959, in an increasingly atomised world under bombardment from the forces of commercialism traditional moral codes would have burst asunder
▶ anyway. A single piece of evidence seems decisive. If the **Profumo Affair** had occurred in 1933 rather than thirty years later it might have been hushed up. But in the different circumstances of 1963, once the story was out it inspired a stream of press rumours about sexual skulduggery in high places. This happened before all of the major legislative changes of the 1960s – and largely because of the desire of newspaper editors to boost their sales.

Even the apostles of permissiveness must have been slightly taken aback at the extent of the ensuing changes. In part, this arose because of an obvious 'generation gap' – between those who had experienced
▶ the fear, and, more particularly, the privations of **war**, and their **children** who had been brought up in the hope that there would never be another one. There had been a similar mood after 1918, but it was bound to have a more lasting effect in the new media age. Even the parents had chafed against the continuation of rationing into the
▶ post-war period, and in 1951 they had turned to the **Conservative Party** which deployed the rhetoric of 'freedom' and promised to drive away the clouds of austerity. By 1951, 'freedom' was no more than a synonym for 'materialism' – the same force which expelled the last residue of Victorian morality in the following decades. Confusingly enough, those who demanded more freedom in the economic sphere tended to be those who wanted less of it in other respects. To that extent, at least, those who raged against 'permissiveness' had merely reaped their own harvest: and they raged the more because they were only dimly conscious of what they had done.

■ Plaid Cymru

Welsh nationalist party founded in 1925. Its dominant figure and President from 1926 to 1939 was Saunders Lewis (1897–1972), a writer, dramatist and lecturer at University College, Swansea. Unusually for a
▶ Welshman he was also a **Roman Catholic**. His romantic view of medieval Christendom was the basis of his belief that Wales belonged in a community of small European nations. Lewis typified the intellectual basis of pre-war Welsh and Scottish nationalism, but he was not afraid of direct action. On 7 September 1936, he and two other leading party figures, the Revd Lewis Valentine and D.J. Williams, burnt down the Ministry of Defence bombing school at Penyberth in the Llyn peninsula. The 'Penyberth Three' stood trial at Caernarfon but the Welsh jury was unable to return a verdict and the National

Government had them retried at the Old Bailey in London, where they were sentenced to nine months in prison. Welsh nationalism had its first 'martyrs' and 350,000 people signed a petition protesting at the verdict. Plaid contested its first parliamentary election when Lewis Valentine stood at Caernarfon in the general election of 1929, winning 609 votes. Like the Scottish National Party, Plaid rarely polled more than 5 per cent of the vote, although its General Secretary, J.E. Jones, steadily turned it into a more professional outfit.

The party had a bad Second World War. In 1939, it sent a delegation to Berlin which offered Hitler full co-operation in the event of a successful German invasion of Britain, in return for which Wales would get Home Rule. The proposal did not excite Hitler but it did anger the British government, as did Plaid's opposition to **conscrip- ◄ tion** on the grounds that Wales had not declared war on anyone. Party members applied to be exempted as conscientious objectors, but most were turned down and their stand damaged Plaid's cause. After the war Plaid became more pragmatic, thanks to a new President, Gwynfor Evans (1945–65). Evans supported the successful cross-party campaigns to designate Cardiff a capital city (1955); to have the Welsh flag recognised by the British state (1960); and to obtain a Welsh Office (1964). The party grew in strength from the late 1950s onwards as economic decline spread disillusionment with the **Labour Party**, the ◄ dominant political force in the principality since the 1930s. Evans won Plaid Cymru's first seat in **parliament** at a by-election in Carmarthen ◄ on 14 July 1966. From 1959 to 1974, its share of the vote rose from 0.2 to 20 per cent, returning 3 MPs at the general election of October 1974 (it contested all Welsh seats for the first time in 1970).

Like the SNP, Plaid learnt to disguise its republican element, ◄ knowing how popular the **monarchy** still was. In 1969 the party ◄ actively co-operated with the investiture of Charles Windsor as Prince of Wales (a Plaid parliamentary candidate, Edward Millward, tutored him in Welsh history and language in the run-up to the ceremony). In 1962, Saunders Lewis had come out of retirement calling for 'revolu- tionary methods' to be used in defence of the Welsh **language**. The ◄ language issue provoked a new wave of militancy, both non-violent (the defacement of English road signs) and violent (bomb attacks on police stations) which Plaid found hard to control but managed even- tually to distance itself from. The 1967 Welsh Language Act, which gave Welsh the same legal status as English, was a victory for moderate nationalism.

Between 1974 and 1979, Plaid joined forces with the SNP to pressure the Labour government into granting **devolution**. However, the refer- ◄ endum held in Wales on 1 March 1979 resulted in defeat, with only 11.8 per cent of the principality in favour of change, and 46.5 against,

on a poor turnout of 58.3 per cent of the electorate. Welsh nationalism was in disarray for the next decade, despite public fury over the
▶ collapse of the Welsh mining industry. While **Margaret Thatcher**
▶ inflicted the full force of **monetarism** on Scotland, believing the Scots to be naturally thrifty and entrepreneurial, she allowed her Welsh Secretary, Peter Walker, to ring-fence the principality with high-spending corporatist policies that ameliorated its economic problems. In 1980, Gwynfor Evans went on hunger strike, demanding a Welsh language TV channel. S4C began broadcasting in 1982, and by 1984, there were 466 organisations that were wholly Welsh or semi-autonomous branches of those based outside the country.

This large measure of devolution did not prevent a revival of Welsh
▶ nationalism following the **Conservatives'** third successive election victory in 1987. As in Scotland, dislike of Tory rule, compounded by disillusionment with Labour's inability to prevent it, helped Plaid to gain four seats at the election of 1992 – its best showing since 1974. Three things contributed to the revival. First, Plaid moved further to the left; a process begun in the 1960s and accelerated under the leadership of Dafydd Wigley (b. 1943; 1984–2001). As the Labour Party became more right-wing in an attempt to win over 'Middle England', Plaid was better able to appeal to disaffected Welsh voters. Second, in 1989 Wigley committed the party to a policy of 'independence within Europe'. Despite the Continental outlook of its founder, Plaid had
▶ traditionally been suspicious of the **European Union** as a capitalist, Catholic organisation, membership of which would further marginalise Wales. The new policy of autonomy within an integrated but devolved 'Europe of the Regions' removed the bogey of navel-gazing isolationism which had always dogged its ultimate aim of independence from the UK. The policy also made that aim more viable, since it was hoped that the EU would pay for the start-up costs of independence. Third, in 1986 Plaid signed a formal pact with the SNP, making them a single grouping at Westminster for the first time and burying much of the traditional Welsh/Scottish rivalry which had previously hampered the nationalist assault on the British state.

▶ Devolution in the 1990s was a mixed blessing for Plaid Cymru. **Tony Blair** only offered the Welsh an Assembly with none of the tax-raising powers given to the Scots and, therefore, with little to do except dispense Treasury money. Even this was too much for them. At the referendum on 18 September 1997, on a miserable turnout of 51.3 per cent, only 50.3 per cent voted in favour, although this did represent a swing of 30 per cent since the referendum of 1979. But once again, complacency got the better of the British government. A Blair loyalist, Alun Michael, was named First Minister of Wales in preference to the more popular Rhodri Morgan, which signalled the government's intention of tightly controlling what little autonomy Wales had. As a direct consequence, at the first elections for the Assembly, in June 1999, Plaid got 28 per cent of the vote – double its previous best performance in any election. This made it the second largest party in Wales and placed it on a par with the SNP for the first time in its history. Although it did less well in the elections of 2003, Welsh nationalism had clearly come of age and a party once dismissed by Edward Heath as 'flower politics for flower people' could begin to claim that it was power politics for empowered people.

■ Police

Between 1900 and 2000 the UK **population** increased by a half. In the same period the numbers of police more than trebled (46,800 for England, Wales and Scotland in 1900, nearly 141,000 in 1999). On its own a comparison of these figures provides eloquent testimony to the change in British society over the century. But while **crime** was a problem throughout the period, the average person was far more fearful in 2000 than a hundred years before. The most popular remedy was even more police – or, at least, more 'Bobbies on the Beat', just like the old days.

Despite the widespread impression that Britain was becoming a lawless country, public confidence in the police was very high for most of the century. In 1962 a Royal Commission detected 'an overwhelming vote of confidence' from the public; this followed a survey of the mid-1950s which backed the idea that the police embodied a national sense of 'fair play'. In this era a gentle programme like *Dixon of Dock Green* (1955–76) could be screened as an approximation of reality rather than an exercise in nostalgia. As late as 1982 an official government publication observed that 'British police action in enforcing the law rests mainly upon common consent'. But in the last decades of the twentieth century it seemed significant that the television cops became tougher; John Thaw and Dennis Waterman in *The Sweeney* (1977–8) were far more pugnacious than the petty villains apprehended by PC Dixon. The specific nature of their work, perhaps, made them unrepresentative. But their more mainstream counterparts in programmes like *The Bill* (1984–) would still have been more than a match for the cast of *Z-Cars* (1962–78) or *Softly, Softly* (1966–76).

No police force can be immune from general developments in a society; and in post-war Britain it would have been a miracle if the much higher incidence of crime had left the police untouched. In 1977 it was announced that 400 London officers had been forced to resign after investigations into corruption. During the 1980s there were frequent allegations of police brutality during riots or strikes; in

P

particular, some of the inner-city rioting of 1981 was attributed to heavy-handed tactics against ethnic groups. Although the police were reluctant to accept interference from outsiders, a Police Complaints Board was established in 1976 and the legislation was toughened after the 1981 riots and a critical report by Lord Scarman. The Macpherson Report (1999) into the murder of Stephen Lawrence six years earlier unearthed evidence of 'institutional racism' within London's Metropolitan Police. Macpherson reported two years after a parliamentary investigation into the links between the same force and Freemasonry. In 1987 it had been estimated that around 5,000 Metropolitan policemen were members of the secretive organisation. Whatever the true figure, it was likely to be much higher than the proportion of ethnic minorities in the country-wide force as a whole, which was only 3 per cent.

Although the police still seemed unlikely to take industrial action – as they had done in 1919 – they became increasingly disillusioned with successive Home Secretaries and often made their feelings plain at the annual conferences of the Police Federation (which had been formed after the 1919 dispute). Morale was unlikely to be improved by the Macpherson Report; officers already felt that they were so burdened with paperwork, often designed to ensure that proper procedures had been followed, that they had very little time for crime prevention and detection. When they did get the chance to perform their real functions, they were better equipped than ever to track down criminals. In the 1990s they secured the right to take DNA samples, and suspects lost the unconditional right to silence. The police still had the power to stop and search on suspicion, even though this had caused much friction at the time of the riots; and in the last resort they could use CS gas and firearms.

Britain still prided itself on its independent police forces – only the Metropolitan Police were under the supervision of the Home Secretary – but there were several reorganisations over the century, which reduced the number of forces. In 1920 there were nearly 244 of these in the UK as a whole; by 2000 there were only 52. Information technology allowed much better co-operation between these forces. The tough police response to the miners' strike of 1984–5 could not have been better co-ordinated even if every officer had taken orders directly from London.

At the beginning of the twenty-first century the police were trying to re-establish links with their communities. They were still trusted by around two-thirds of the population. But social and technological changes left them with serious handicaps. Criminals are more mobile than ever; so the police will continue to rely on cars and helicopters, ruling out a mass revival of pedal power and shoe leather. Increasingly, the police relied for information on television programmes like *Crimewatch*, because so many witnesses were likely to be passing the scene of an incident on their way to distant destinations. Even the fictional Chief Inspector Morse occasionally had to stray outside Oxford to track down his prey. More seriously, in few parts of Britain was there an identifiable 'community' with which the police could make contact. In an anonymous society crime was more likely, the faces of the culprits would be unknown even to their neighbours, and when the local bobbies conducted house-to-house inquiries they risked being treated as suspicious strangers. It was unsurprising that clear-up rates were pitifully low – about 1 prosecution for every 30 crimes in 1994 – and when targets were introduced for the police many people expected that the figures would have to be fiddled. Although Britain in 1900 had been a long way from Utopia, it had been very different from this.

■ Poll Tax

The Community Charge, better known as the Poll Tax, was seen by the Thatcher government as the answer to the problem of **local government** finance. Heralded by a Green Paper of January 1986, it proposed a breach of the historical link between local taxes and (notional) property values. The existing rating system was widely resented by many **Conservative** voters, who often cited the example of a poor widow living alone in a big house having to pay as much as a whole family of wage-earners in a similar property. The obvious free-market solution to the widow's plight would be to move into a more modest home; but in this instance, at least, **Margaret Thatcher** was prepared to overrule the harsh dictates of economic liberalism.

The Poll Tax was to be a flat-rate charge levied on all residents, regardless of income (although people in certain categories would pay only 20 per cent of the levy). At the same time, local councils lost the right to set a different rate for businesses; from now on this would be calculated by the government. The motivation behind the scheme was the alleged tendency of local voters who paid no rates to choose the party which offered the most generous services, without paying attention to a cost which would be borne by others. In theory, the new tax would make such 'free riders' switch their support to candidates who proposed the most cost-effective provision. Normally these would be Conservatives unless the other parties changed their ways, in which case local authorities everywhere would be run like a business and the central **government** could finally leave them alone.

Under any regime, and at any time, the proposal would have been controversial – like the fourteenth-century Poll Tax which inspired the

Peasants' Revolt. But the Thatcher governments had already drawn electoral dividends from promises of tax cuts which mainly benefited the rich. Many of the party's MPs – and members of the House of Lords who were encouraged to turn out to vote down rebellions against the measure – were fully aware that personally they would be much better off as a result of the change. When the idea had been suggested at an earlier stage it had been rejected out of hand – 'Try collecting that in Brixton,' one official had quipped. The fact that it was revived and pushed through as official government policy suggested that after two successive election wins the government was taking its dominant position for granted. In final acts of hubris, it decided that the new tax should be imposed on Scotland in 1989, a year before it affected the rest of Britain; and a prudent plan to phase it in gradually was scrapped.

▶   In the 1987 general election campaign **Labour** failed to capitalise on the issue, partly because the bills had yet to be sent out but also because for the opposition it was simply part of a general indictment
▶   of the government. But even hardline **Thatcherites** realised before the official introduction of the tax that it would be extremely unpopular. As early critics had predicted, switching local taxes from property to individuals who could evade registration meant that levels of non-payment were far worse than they had been for the rates, thus pushing the charge even higher for those who did pay. Attempts were made to soften the blow through subsidies. But this allowed some Labour councils to turn Conservative logic on its head, increasing expenditure in the knowledge that the higher costs would either be borne by the Treasury or blamed on the government. In March 1990 the Conservatives lost the Mid-Staffordshire by-election on a swing of 22 per cent, and at the end of that month an anti-Poll Tax demonstration in London turned into a riot. Although most people deplored the violence, there was no loss of sympathy for the cause.

By the end of the year Mrs Thatcher had been deposed by her own party, and although the opportunity arose because of disagreements
▶   over **Europe**, fears that the Poll Tax had made the government unelectable – and that it could never be abolished while Mrs Thatcher remained in Downing Street – was probably the main reason for her downfall. Her successor John Major immediately announced a review, and the tax was pronounced dead in March 1991. In its place the Conservatives introduced a Council Tax, which reintroduced the old notion of a property tax while retaining the idea of taxing individuals. Although it was still regressive, it was better related to the ability to pay. It was a messy solution – and expensive, since the Treasury had to pour out more subsidies to make it more palatable than its predecessor. Now responsible for raising only 20 per cent of the money they

spent, local councils were more than ever the creatures of central government. They did start to adopt more 'businesslike' methods, regardless of the party in power. So the Poll Tax might have cost the Conservatives their leader, but something valuable had been dragged from the wreckage.

■ Population

The population of the UK continued to rise in the twentieth century but at a third of the rate of the nineteenth. Altogether, it grew by just over 17 million from 41.5 million in 1901 to 58.9 million in 2001. England accounted for 90 per cent of this growth, and in the process it became the most densely populated country in Europe. In 1901 there were 32.53 million people in England and Wales, 4.47 in Scotland, 1.24 in what became Northern Ireland and 3.22 in the South. In 1951, England had 41.2 million people, Wales 2.6, Scotland 5.1 and Northern Ireland 1.4. By 2001, the figures were 49.2 million, 2.9, 5.1 and 1.7.

England's larger growth sprang from its economic supremacy over the rest of the Isles. Because living standards were higher there, **death** ◀ rates were lower; in addition to which millions of Scots and Welsh migrated to England, either to escape **unemployment** or to improve ◀ their professional opportunities. Migration from Ireland partly compensated the Scots, as it had during the nineteenth century. Thanks to civil war in the 1920s and 1970s, the Irish were now as likely to be escaping violence as they were **poverty**. Their ability to do so was ◀ not hampered by the granting of independence to southern Ireland, because its people retained their dual British/Irish citizenship. Scottish, Welsh and Irish migration within the Isles was part of a general drift towards the rich south-east which included northern England. Between 1924 and 1939 alone, 1.75 million people moved from the north and west of Britain to the south-east. The southern drift was only temporarily reversed during the Second World War and its social effects made a substantial contribution to the rise of Scottish and Welsh nationalism.

The overall living standard did rise throughout the UK and this led to greater longevity, particularly after the Second World War when the **welfare state** augmented affluence to give the working **classes** better ◀ **housing**, diet, **education** and healthcare. The annual death rate in ◀ England and Wales fell from 16.1 per thousand people in 1901 to 11.4 in 1991. In Scotland it fell from 17.5 to 11.7, and in Ireland from 18.1 to 10.4. Average life expectancy for men rose from 52 years in 1901 to 74.6 in 2000; for women it rose from 54 years to 79.6. Infant mortality fell too from 150 per thousand in 1901 to 30 in 1950 and then to 9 by

P

2001 (the biggest drop took place in the 1940s). After the Second World War, medical advances like keyhole surgery, transplants and
▶ inoculation – all provided by the NHS – had a major impact. Tuberculosis, typhoid and polio were virtually eradicated; and despite a rise in the number of Britons getting cancer and heart disease, death rates from both diseases began to fall in the 1960s. However, life expectancy differentials between the classes actually rose proving just how severe inequality still was in the age of affluence. In 1976 a male professional lived on average 5.5 years longer than a manual worker and females 5.3 years longer. By 1999 the difference was 7.4 and 5.7 years respectively.

What prevented a population explosion was a parallel fall in the national birth rate. In England and Wales, it dropped from 28.2 per thousand people in 1901 to 13 in 1991; 29.4 to 13.6 in Scotland and even in Ireland, from 23 to 17.6. Two factors were responsible: better
▶ access to contraception and the growing independence of **women**. The vulcanisation of rubber in the 1900s made sheaths cheaper and more effective. Marie Stopes's (1880–1958) *Wise Parenthood* (1918) helped millions to understand that coitus interruptus was not reliable and her birth control clinics, started in 1921, made contraceptives like the Dutch cap and coil more widely available. The Pill, introduced in 1961 and freely prescribed after the 1967 Family Planning Act, revolutionised birth control. So too, to a lesser extent, did the legalisation of abortion in 1967, although it was not until 1986 that government statisticians stopped counting abstinence as a form of contraception –
▶ a reflection perhaps of concern about the '**permissive society**'.

Women's biological urge for children did not abate. But they were better able to choose when, and how many, children they had. Most chose to have fewer, because they wanted to pursue careers and/or because they wanted to enjoy the greater number of leisure activities now available to them. In 1901, the average family size was 4.5 people, much the same as it had been since the eighteenth century; by 2000 it was 2.4. Despite a brief 'baby boom' when troops returned from the
▶ war of 1939–45, the biggest fall in the birthrate took place after 1950, when it shrank by 12 per cent. This, coupled with the falling death rate meant that the British population was getting older. All of this put huge strains on the NHS and called into question the viability of
▶ **William Beveridge**'s national insurance system, because there were not enough working people making contributions at one end to pay for the care needed by the retired at the other.

▶ Contrary to popular belief, black **immigration** did not make a significant contribution to the population rise of the twentieth century. First, Irish newcomers outweighed black ones. During the period of highest black immigration, for example, an average of 60,000 southern

Irish people came to the UK each year compared to an average of 48,000 black Britons. Second, although the black population of Britain rose from approximately 100,000 in 1900 to 3.5 million in 2001 (5.5 per cent of the population), as a result of higher emigration Britain suffered a net loss of 1.31 million people in the same period. From 1980 onwards there was a small net gain of approximately 150,000 – but that was *after* laws restricting black immigration had taken effect. The main cause of the overall loss was emigration to the **Empire** and, following decoloni- ◄ sation, to America and the Commonwealth, particularly Australia. It is a fact that reiterates our first point: that the population history of the UK reveals little unless it is studied as the history of four nations not one; and preferably that of many more beyond.

■ Pornography

The word 'pornography' first appeared in the *Oxford English Dictionary* in 1864. The timing of its appearance reflected the fact that, like pros- titution, it became more common in Britain during the second half of the nineteenth century. To some extent, this was because the Vic- torian reformation of manners forced people to obtain sexual satis- faction in more furtive ways. Addressing the Sexual Reform Congress in London in 1929, **Bertrand Russell** said that the appeal of pornog- ◄ raphy was 'due to the indecent feelings concerning sex which moral- ists inculcate in the young'. However, the liberalisation of British society led to greater consumption not less, thus proving that auto- stimulation was as much of a desire as a need.

Until the mid-twentieth century, pornographic literature was prohibitively expensive and was enjoyed mainly by the middle and upper **classes** who imported it from the Continent through specialist ◄ dealers. Most people had to make do with earnest sex manuals like Marie Stopes's *Married Love* (1918), Leslie Weatherhead's *The Mastery of Sex* (1931) and Anthony Havil's *The Technique of Sex* (1939), all of which were best-sellers running to several editions. *Men Only*, first published in 1937, was the first affordable, legally distributed, British magazine to carry pictures of naked women, although the display of genitalia and pubic hair was forbidden. During the 1950s, a flurry of more explicit magazines appeared and **government** concern about the ◄ nation's **morals** led to the passing of the Obscene Publications Act in ◄ 1959. Although the Act strictly codified what was permissible, it also introduced the defence of literary merit. It was this that enabled Penguin Books to win the 1960 *Lady Chatterley* trial, in which the Crown failed to halt the publication of the unexpurgated version of D.H. Lawrence's novel. The Act was amended by the Wilson govern- ment in 1964 to permit more sexually explicit material. That move,

▶ together with a wider '**permissive**' relaxation of mores and growing affluence, fostered a revolution in British pornography which turned it from an underground cottage industry into a corporate enterprise worth billions of pounds.

By the mid-1970s, the magazines *Escort* and *Mayfair*, published by Paul Raymond, together with American publications like *Penthouse*, were stocked by W.H. Smith and were each selling a million copies a month. *Forum*, a pocket-size magazine containing more
▶ stories/fantasies than pictures, sold 200,000 a month. **Cinema** remained strictly controlled by the British Board of Film Censors. In America and Europe, 'hardcore' pornography, featuring coitus in close-up and every kind of deviance from sado-masochism to bestiality, was rife. British cinema chains could only offer softcore films like the *Emmanuelle* series or sex comedies like the *Confessions* series which contained all the eroticism of a seaside postcard. A few specialist porn cinemas showing imported films secured licences by designating themselves 'private members' clubs'.

The advent of video in 1980 made it easier to view hardcore films, including illegal material deemed too obscene for public screening. Video had the additional attraction of enabling films to be watched in the privacy and comfort of one's home rather than in the more public and seedy arena of the porn cinema. The growth of sex shops further increased the supply of videos, magazines and mass-produced accessories like the vibrator and blow-up doll. The sex shop was invented by
▶ a **German** woman, Beate Uhse, in 1954; the first British one was opened in London's Soho in 1961, and by 1980 there were over a hundred in the capital. During the 1970s local authorities began to grant more licences, making the sex shop a common feature of the high street, most of them run by the David Sullivan empire.

Two government-sponsored reports on pornography took
▶ contrasting views of the industry's growth. That of the **Roman Catholic** Labour peer Lord Longford in 1972 argued for a clamp-down. Longford's main proposal was that obscenity should be legally defined as that which outraged 'contemporary standards of decency or humanity accepted by the public at large'. This was vague enough to include the *Sun*, which, after its launch in 1969, became Britain's biggest-selling newspaper thanks to its daily picture of a topless girl on page 3. Longford was supported by an unlikely alliance of religious moralists like Mary Whitehouse and by militant feminists who regarded pornography as an inducement to rape (a plausible link which has yet to be proved). A 1979 report by the Oxford philosopher Bernard Williams recommended further liberalisation – primarily that the Obscene Publications Act be abolished and that sex shops need not be licensed. Neither report was implemented. But the

coming to power in 1979 of a female **Conservative** Prime Minister ◄ determined to revive Victorian values did lead to a tightening of restrictions.

Legislation was passed limiting the display of 'indecent literature' in newsagents and bookshops (1981) and the showing of films in cinema clubs (1982). The 1984 Video Recordings Act introduced a special licensing system for videos and the 1990 Broadcasting Act made TV subject to the Obscene Publications Act in an attempt to curtail the increasingly explicit documentaries on sex and sexuality being broadcast by Channel 4. In an echo of the interwar period, the restrictions on video led to a wave of mild erotica sold as educational aids, notably the *Lover's Guide* (1987). However, all these measures failed to arrest the public's appetite for porn. Indeed, it grew, thanks to a new breed of feminists who argued that women had to 'reclaim' pornography rather than reject it. Nancy Friday's collection of women's fantasies, *My Secret Garden* (1973), was a landmark in that respect, running to 15 editions by 1990. The internet also unleashed more porn which accounts for around 40 per cent of net usage.

Although the British were still more uneasy about pornography than Continentals, by the end of the century it had become an accepted part of national life. The basis for that acceptance was, first, a belief that masturbation was a healthy activity and not a sin that led to degeneracy; and, second, a belief that sexual fantasies were an integral part of a fulfilling sexual partnership. Conservatives who saw pornography as part of a moral decline that included divorce failed to see that, while rising levels of each were accelerated by moral liberalisation, what really drove the change was the ability of ordinary Britons to gain access to that which they had always desired but which had previously been the preserve of the propertied classes. Their bedfellows on the left argued that pornography was an example of how capitalism commodified sex, largely at the expense of **women**. ◄ Sex certainly pervaded the advertising industry in order to sell goods and services; and women were exploited in pornography as ruthlessly as in other sectors of the sex industry. But that does not explain why rates of rape and molestation were lowest in countries whose sex industries were allowed to flourish legally under state regulation; just as rates of **drug** addiction were lower in those that did not proscribe ◄ narcotics outright. Sex sold in modern Britain; but it didn't always corrupt.

P

■ Poverty; inequality

Four of the 'Five Giants' targeted by the 1942 **Beveridge Report** – Want, ◄ Disease, Ignorance and Squalor – were obviously connected with

poverty. The fifth – Idleness – stalked the very rich rather than the working poor. But like most liberals William Beveridge felt that the rich could look after themselves. His concern was to avoid the invol-
▶ untary idleness resulting from high **unemployment**, which had produced the worst poverty in Britain before the war.

At the end of the twentieth century important progress had been made in the battle against disease, ignorance and squalor. But the attack on 'idleness' had stalled in the mid-1970s, when 'full' employment ceased to be a government priority; and although there was a marked improvement in the 1990s there was no room for complacency. This left the fate of the first and most important giant – Want – open to question. Opinion was divided, between those who claimed that poverty had been eradicated, and others who emphasised the growing gap between various income groups. For them, at least, poverty was as great a problem as ever; and they thought that they had the statistics to prove it.

'Poverty', of course, is an emotive word and it is no surprise that people should still wish to use it. But in the contemporary British debate it can only mean *relative* poverty. By historical standards, or international comparisons, *absolute* poverty – an inability to afford the real necessities of life, leading to serious malnutrition and even death from starvation or hypothermia – is almost unknown. Thus the debate in Britain is really about *inequality*. On this score, the emergence of the
▶ post-war **welfare state** did make some difference. In 1949, for example, the top 10 per cent of the UK population earned around 27 per cent of total income after tax. By 1982 this was down to about 23 per cent. However, the bottom *half* of the population earned little more than the top 10 per cent in 1982 – and its share (around a quarter) had scarcely
▶ changed since 1949. The period of **Conservative** government after 1979 reversed the previous trend, so that by 1989 the share of the poorest 10 per cent had declined by half a per cent, while that of the richest 10 per
▶ cent *grew* by nearly 5 per cent. Between the election of **Margaret Thatcher** in 1979 and the fourth consecutive Conservative general election victory in 1992 the number of people living on less than half of the average national income rose from 5 million to over 14 million.

At the end of the century it was claimed that more than 4 million
▶ **children** were living in households classed as 'poor'. In line with internationally-accepted standards, poor households were identified as those which received less than 60 per cent of median incomes, with adjustments for other factors such as the size of families. In a civilised society, this was a sober standard – lower than it would have been if the figure had been calculated on the basis of average earnings. On
▶ that reckoning, Portugal was the only EU country with more poverty than the UK. However, talk of 'children in poverty' only evoked memo-

ries of the 1930s, when barefooted urchins scavenged for coal on the unsightly dumps that loomed above grim industrial towns. At the end of the century, among the **consumer** goods widely claimed as 'necessities' were television sets. The use of the word 'poverty' in this context was highly dubious; but those very devices were now churning out endless 'lifestyle' programmes on cars and **housing** which emphasised the gulf between the 'haves' and the 'have-littles'. In short, cultural pressures were making *inequality* more relevant than ever.

The widening of inequality after 1979 was a deliberate aim of the Conservative governments, who believed that previous attempts to redistribute wealth through the tax system had stifled 'incentives'. No real evidence was ever produced to substantiate this claim; all one could say was that if the modest post-war redistribution really had driven dynamic entrepreneurs out of the country, their emotional attachment to Britain must have been pitifully weak. **Thatcherite** theory claimed that if they could only be persuaded to stay, they would create so much extra wealth that everyone would benefit through a 'trickle-down' effect. But by the end of the century the poor were still waiting for these refreshing rivulets.

The Thatcherites also argued that attempts to bring about absolute equality could only succeed at the expense of freedom. This might have been less plausible if the Soviet Union had not been available to illustrate the story. But in any case it completely missed the point. No major politician had seriously tried to impose economic equality in Britain; the aim had been to reduce inequality to acceptable levels, and even that had not been achieved. By the end of the twentieth century 'New' Labour was directing its efforts towards the poorest – a long overdue initiative. It introduced a minimum wage (albeit at a ludicrous level), and even aspired to abolish child poverty entirely by the year 2020. However, no one had really tackled head-on the Thatcherite arguments (flimsy as they were); and in the absence of a serious public debate there was every chance that the disappearance of *absolute* poverty would be used in the future as an argument for allowing inequality to grow even further.

■ Powell, (John) Enoch (1912–98)

Enoch Powell was born in Birmingham, the son of a schoolteacher whose forebears had migrated to the area from Wales. He was educated locally, at the King Edward grammar school, before going up to Trinity College, Cambridge, to read Classics. He was a brilliant student, and became a Cambridge don before being offered the Chair of Greek at Sydney University in 1937. As soon as the war broke out he returned to volunteer in the Royal Warwickshire Regiment. In the autumn of 1944 he became (briefly) the youngest brigadier in the British army. His wartime career included a spell in India, which he loved; characteristically, he taught himself Urdu.

▶ After the war Powell joined the **Conservative** Research Department, and became MP for Wolverhampton South-West at the 1950 general election. Even among the many remarkable Conservative newcomers – who also included Edward Heath and the later Chancellors Iain Macleod and Reginald Maudling – Powell stood out for his intellectual ability. But he had always impressed his contemporaries as an eccentric. To his admirers he was a charming companion, but others were either irritated by his apparent self-sufficiency, or intimidated by his uncompromising outlook. Presumably the sense that Powell was not 'clubbable' explains his prolonged wait for government office. He was made Financial Secretary to the Treasury in 1957.

This first ministerial stint lasted only one year. In January 1958 Powell resigned along with the Economic Secretary, Nigel Birch, and the Chancellor of the Exchequer, Peter Thorneycroft. The *casus belli* was a cut in welfare spending. The majority of the Cabinet, including the Prime Minister Harold Macmillan, hoped to reach a compromise, but Thorneycroft stuck to his full demands and resigned. Powell was widely blamed for his intransigence.

But the errant minister was too able – or potentially dangerous – to leave out for long. In July 1960 he was made Minister of Health, and was promoted to the Cabinet in the same capacity two years later. His strategy was to keep costs down as far as possible – and to raise additional revenue by increasing prescription charges – while being more generous than his predecessors in such areas as mental health. He also launched an ambitious programme of hospital-building, which seemed inconsistent with his image as an enemy of 'planning'.

While his decisions were sometimes controversial, at least it looked as if Powell had mellowed into a 'team player'. But in October 1963 he abruptly resigned, along with his friend Macleod, in protest at the appointment of Alec Douglas-Home as Macmillan's replacement in Number 10. Powell was recalled to the front bench after the Conservatives lost the 1964 general election. But two resignations within six years had fully confirmed the fears of those who had always regarded him as a likely source of instability.

After Douglas-Home's resignation from the leadership, Powell stood in the first-ever Conservative ballot held to choose a successor, in 1965. However, he received only fifteen votes. The winner of the election, Edward Heath, retained Powell in the Shadow Cabinet, as spokesman on Defence. But there was little personal rapport between them, and Heath had been irritated by some of Powell's comments even before April 1968, when the latter was sacked for his 'Rivers of

Blood' speech on **immigration**. Powell's intemperate rhetoric,   ◄
conjuring visions of 'the River Tiber foaming with much blood' unless
even stricter controls were introduced, left Heath with no alternative.
In suggesting that immigrants would always remain an alien (if not
positively dangerous) element in British society, Powell threatened to
burst the developing parliamentary consensus, which envisaged mild
legislation to improve race relations while barriers were erected to
limit new immigrants. Yet Powell enjoyed strong public support,
reflected in more than 100,000 fan letters, and demonstrations in
London. He became a folk-hero in his Wolverhampton constituency,
where an immigrant population of less than 5 per cent was made the
scapegoat for pre-existing economic difficulties.

Later in 1968 Powell launched a further attack on 'orthodox'
thinking with his 'Morecambe Programme' which proposed slashing
cuts in taxation and public expenditure without affecting the central
planks of the **welfare state** or embarking on a radical programme of   ◄
privatisation. But he left his listeners in no doubt that he harboured   ◄
even more radical ambitions for cost-cutting. In the following year he
indicated that he had changed his mind about **Europe**, now feeling   ◄
that Britain had no need of any foreign entanglements which would
reduce national **sovereignty**. The same logic reinforced his antipathy   ◄
to America – one aspect of his thought which was rarely emphasised
by his right-wing admirers.

When the Conservatives regained office in 1970 Powell was at odds
with his leader over almost every important issue. Yet his popularity
in the Midlands was widely held to have helped ensure the Conservative victory. He became a regular and outspoken critic of the government, particularly over Europe and economic policy. Even so, it was
still a major surprise when, just before the general election of
February 1974, he announced that he would not contest his seat and
had, in fact, already cast a postal vote for a **Labour** candidate.   ◄

Since Powell had always hoped to lead his party, this was a quixotic
gesture even by his previous standards; and the error seemed to be
compounded when he fought and won a seat for the Ulster Unionists
in October 1974. But Powell may well have calculated that before very
long support for the Union would be the only principle which could
bind the Conservatives together. When **Margaret Thatcher** toppled   ◄
Heath he could not conceal his chagrin. She had played something
like a 'Powellite' hand, but reversed the priorities attributed to him in
recent years, by emphasising economics rather than nationalism. Even
if Powell had stayed in the party he could not have seized the leadership on an anti-European platform as early as 1975.

Powell remained an MP until 1987, when he lost his South Down
seat. Despite increasing frailty, he remained active until his death,

adding biblical scholarship to his numerous intellectual distinctions. It would be easy to regard his career as a tragic waste, but his difficulties were caused by poor judgement, not bad luck. Even so, his admirers could advance a plausible argument for ranking him among the most influential of post-war politicians. His economic thinking had much in common with **Thatcherism**, although it took similar principles even further. On Europe, he marshalled the case for British sovereignty with far greater skill than any of his disciples (this was characteristic of Powell on almost every subject – except race, where he never convinced his critics that he lacked the prejudices of his admirers). His prophecy of social breakdown in the wake of mass immigration had not been fulfilled, but he articulated fears which were still widespread at the close of the twentieth century. And if they were honest, many of the politicians who spoke out against his views would have to admit that they tacitly accepted them when voting on immigration after 1968.

■ **Priestley, J.B.** (1894–1984)

Prolific left/liberal playwright, novelist and essayist, popular from the 1930s to the 1950s. John Boynton Priestley was born in Bradford, the son of a prosperous schoolmaster. He attended Bradford Grammar School until the age of 16, then left to work as a junior clerk in a local wool firm (1910–14). During this time, he began to write poetry for his own pleasure and contributed articles to newspapers in Bradford and London. In the First World War he served in the Duke of Wellington and Devon regiments, surviving the front line at Flanders and rising to the rank of Lieutenant. In 1919, he secured an ex-serviceman's grant to study literature, history and political science at Cambridge, receiving his BA in 1921. During the 1920s he established himself as a journalist in London, working for the *London Mercury* and *New Statesman*, and in 1922 he published his first book, the essay collection *Brief Diversions*. His first novel, *Adam in Moonshine*, appeared in 1927 but it was his fourth, *The Good Companions* (1929), that won him national acclaim.

Staged in 1931 and filmed twice (1932; 1956), *The Good Companions* tells the story of a group of travelling players. Their cheery, stoical communality was not an accurate picture of British repertory theatre even at its height in the 1900s. The novel was a nostalgic tribute to Edwardian liberalism and, more generally, a call to social harmony, as a result of which it caught the mood of the **Great Depression** era and became a literary expression of the National Government. Priestley's only other novel of note was *Angel Pavement* (1930), which depicted the office clerks of London, and the changes wrought upon them by the visit of a mysterious stranger. He also used that device in his best play,

An Inspector Calls (1946), in which a middle-class family are visited by a man claiming to be a policeman investigating a murder. In the course of questioning the family, he draws out hidden scandal and exposes the terrible consequences their actions have had on ordinary people. Playing as it did on middle-class guilt, the work was a metaphor for the moderate social democracy that Priestley championed, and it captured the mood of the Attlee era as surely as *The Good Companions* had done that of the **Baldwin** era. ◄

Priestley's reputation was secured during the Second World War. His Sunday-night **BBC** broadcasts during the **Battle of Britain**, ◄ collected in *Postscripts* (1941), were patriotic celebrations of everyday British life and the ordinary heroes and heroines who were fighting to save the country. The broadcasts received audiences second only to **Churchill**'s and were instrumental in fostering the legend of 'The ◄ People's War'. In one of the Postscripts, Priestley called for a state-driven redistribution of wealth and this reputedly led to him being withdrawn from the air. Unbowed, he elaborated his views in *Out of the People* (1941), one of the best political tracts of the era. He was a founding member of Richard Acland's Commonwealth Party in 1942, switching his allegiance to **Labour** when it folded in 1947. He joined ◄ **William Beveridge**'s Europhile think-tank, Federal Union, in 1940; was ◄ active in the **Campaign for Nuclear Disarmament**; and in various ◄ campaigns for state subsidy of the arts, a case he argued in *The Arts Under Socialism* (1947).

Priestley succeeded **George Bernard Shaw** as the intellectual voice ◄ of the British literary left and held the position for a quarter of a century. Like Shaw, he had a compendious brain, a belief that he could solve all the world's problems, and left a huge body of work which proved that he could not (in total 120 books and 50 plays). He resented the posthumous reputation of **George Orwell**, complaining that ◄ Orwell merely echoed what he had already said. There was some truth in this, but Orwell said it so much better and with more radical bite. In the 1960s, Priestley's verbose style and relatively conservative views on the social issues of the period lost him readers and led to him being satirised by **Monty Python** as a pompous has-been. His opposition to ◄ Anglo-American mass culture weighed especially heavily on people. In *Thoughts in the Wilderness* (1957), Priestley coined the phrase 'Admass' to describe a Britain in which 'people would cheerfully exchange their last glimpse of freedom for a new car, refrigerator and a TV screen'. His influential travelogue *English Journey* (1934) had made similar criticisms and been applauded for it. But in a post-war world of cultural plurality, fewer people were receptive to his essentially Edwardian view of British working-class life. The novel *Lost Empires* (1965) refracted that change through the fading fortunes of a **music-hall** performer. Like ◄

▶ **John Osborne**'s *The Entertainer* (1957), *Lost Empires* contains a sentimental view of music halls, their world apparently shattered in the last
   scene by a girl dancing to pop music blasting out of a record player.

   Priestley was married three times: to Emily Tempest, Mary 'Jane'
Wyndham Lewis and the archaeologist Jacquetta Hawkes, with whom
he co-authored several books, the best of which was *Down a Rainbow*
(1955), an account of their travels in Mexico. He refused a knighthood
and a peerage but accepted the Order of Merit in 1977. His memoirs
were published as *Margin Released* (1962).

■ Privatisation

▶ The selling off of Britain's **nationalised** industries was a key aim for
▶ **Thatcherites** before the 1979 general election, although one would
   never have guessed it from the party manifesto which included a very
   modest prospectus. But the failure of the Heath government (1970–4)
   to do more than dispose of a few incongruous state assets – notably
   the Thomas Cook travel agency and the Carlisle breweries – was seen
   in hindsight as a serious failing. Instead of 'rolling back the state',
   Heath had allegedly spurred it forward by acquiring the aero-engine
   division of Rolls-Royce after the parent company went bankrupt. Actually, Rolls-Royce was a very special case and the company was restruc-
   tured with a view to a speedy return to the private sector. Thatcherites
   also forgot that there had been a general lack of confidence within the
   private sector at that time; and the preparatory work in opposition
   before 1970 had been inadequate. But they were determined to make
   up for this lost opportunity as soon as they were given another chance.

   Although planning for privatisation on a grand scale began at an
early stage (particularly within Sir Keith Joseph's Department of
▶ Industry), the first **Thatcher** government made little more progress
   than Heath had done. It disposed of Amersham International and the
   British Freight Corporation, and a start was made with Britoil and
   Cable and Wireless. But only in 1982–3 did receipts from state sales
   exceed £1 billion.

   In the second Thatcher term the pace quickened. The sale of British
Telecom (BT) began in November 1984. This was the real breakthrough
for the Thatcherites; the flotation was heralded by a series of advertisements to lure the small investor. The overwhelming response,
more than matched when British Gas was sold off (1986–8), suggested
that Britain was about to embrace 'popular capitalism'. Millions of
ordinary shareholders bought into the Thatcherite dream (although
many succumbed to the temptation to cash in a quick profit from the
shares, and during the 1980s the proportion of shares held by individuals actually fell by a third). The government would not be deflected

by criticisms, including some from within its own ranks. The ex-premier Harold Macmillian, now the aged Earl of Stockton, chided those who were selling off 'the family silver'. But the critics could make no headway against what was seen as a recipe for repeated **Conservative** electoral successes – at least while stocks lasted. In the ◄ meantime, the policy paid other dividends. In tandem with the creation of high **unemployment**, and direct legislative measures, it ◄ curbed **trade union** power, since negotiators would no longer be cush- ◄ ioned from market forces by a bountiful state employer.

In 1987–8 receipts from privatisation rose to more than £7 billion. But now the government was straying into controversial territory – just as **Labour** had done when it began to target unsuitable candidates ◄ for nationalisation. There had already been some disquiet about the extent to which the Conservatives were handing monopolies over to the private sector as licences to print money. Water, which was sold off between 1988 and 1991, was an obvious problem. Once the native-based profiteers had sold out, many of the controlling interests were based abroad. Conservative rhetoric invited citizens to wrap them-selves in the Union Jack; but they were having to wash in foreign water. Elaborate safeguards were designed to prevent the abuse of dominant market share by new private electricity companies. But in order to satisfy the critics the government was having to impose regu-lators on the rapacious privatised sector. This threatened to create a new bureaucracy, although Mrs Thatcher had promised to 'roll back the frontiers of the state'; and if the regulators were over-zealous the market would never be truly 'free'.

Ironically, though, privatisation only became an issue of wide-spread public concern after John Major succeeded Mrs Thatcher. Sales peaked at over £8 billion in 1991–2. But by 1990 the real plums had all been picked; Major was left with unappetising leftovers, notably the railways. One Conservative MP warned that this flotation would prove to be 'the **Poll Tax** on wheels'. That was a slight exaggeration, ◄ but the sell-off was particularly scandalous; in the three years after privatisation the level of government subsidy to the railways actually doubled. Electricity generation from nuclear power was another grievous headache. Decommissioning the ageing reactors would be a drain on the public purse for decades to come. The allegation that the 'family silver' had been flogged off at firesale prices began to take hold, as the public lost confidence in the general Conservative handling of the economy. The inflated salaries enjoyed by a new class of private sector bosses inspired damaging headlines, and it was noted that many ex-ministers had found their way into the privatised boardrooms. It generally went unremarked that Britain's remaining public services were crumbling because, instead of investing the proceeds of privatisation in constructive projects, the Thatcherites had frittered them away in tax cuts. But insofar as this was realised it certainly increased the wave of public contempt for the government.

By 1997, then, privatisation was far from being a vote-winning policy, and it was a contributory factor in the Conservative defeat. But ▸ 'New' Labour had accepted that the process would not be reversed, ▸ and Tony Blair himself seemed happy for it to proceed further. Controversial new plans, including the sale of air-traffic control, were pursued even though this prospect caused understandable disquiet. Blair and his Chancellor, Gordon Brown, were attracted by the concept of public–private partnerships, under which (for example) hospitals would be built by the private sector then leased to the government. The rationale behind this was that the state would no longer be forced to pay large lump sums for capital developments, and the responsibility for timely completion would fall on the contractors. The overall bill for the taxpayer would be considerably higher, but the expense would be spread over decades. It was felt that under this system everyone would gain – or at least the public would be able to feel that it had secured a generous deal, because direct taxation would not have to rise.

On its own, this line of argument seemed conclusive, given 'New' Labour's self-imposed policy constraints. But there were other reasons for the survival of privatisation. Chief among these was the scope it allowed for ministers to avoid responsibility. In a complex world, where politicians could hardly be asked to undertake the detailed supervision of their departments, there was some justification for a revision of constitutional conventions which had evolved in a different age. But this was revision by stealth. Voters could not deliver a verdict on the standard of public services when these were no longer the direct concern of ministers; and they could not 'vote' by withdrawing their custom from the monopolistic water companies. By the end of the century, in short, an alarming 'democratic deficit' was widening; and this was apparently being reflected in collapsing electoral participation.

▸ It also seemed that the entire machinery of **government** had become addicted to the proposition that the private sector was invariably efficient, while the opposite was true of anything run by the state. The evidence for this claim was distinctly mixed. Indeed, many of the 'utilities', like the railways, had originally been taken into state ownership because the private sector had manifestly failed, so it was no surprise when the pattern began to repeat itself. Yet no evidence seemed capable of shaking ministers and their officials. Ironically, the ▸ willing collaboration of **civil servants** in the privatisation process disproved one of the key 'Thatcherite' assumptions – that the denizens of Whitehall were insatiable empire-builders, who saw the expansion of the state as a matter of professional pride.

Thus, with **parliament** impotent, by 2000 there was no institutional check on the runaway train of privatisation. The state still ran key public services, such as the **National Health Service** (NHS), and it continued to dominate education. But the logic of privatisation suggested that these monolithic structures would have to fall eventually. The **police** and the **armed forces** might prove more resilient, but they stood condemned by the same dogmatic principle.

■ Profumo Affair

On 22 March 1963 the wealthy **Conservative** Minister for War, John Profumo, denied in the House of Commons that there had been any 'impropriety' in his relationship with a costly call-girl, Christine Keeler. This statement contradicted a common and well-founded rumour; there had indeed been a brief affair, in 1961. At almost the same time Keeler had begun a dalliance with Colonel Eugene Ivanov, the Soviet Military Attaché. The security services were alerted, and Profumo's denial was prompted by the Prime Minister, Harold Macmillan, who knew the broad outlines of the story (if not the real extent of his minister's involvement).

Keeler's involvement in a much-publicised shooting incident gave the press an irresistible excuse to speculate. Since she was also a model, the story could be illustrated with titillating photographs, and her sharp-witted friend Mandy Rice-Davies furnished some memorable quotations. The whole business was a fabulous gift for Fleet Street, which had been rebuked just a few months earlier in the wake of another scandal, this time involving John Vassall, a homosexual Admiralty clerk. It was in any case a time of increasing irreverence, coinciding with a boom in political satire and a vogue for attacks on the **Establishment**. Profumo's timing was even less adroit than his choice of partner.

Gradually, more details were revealed to Macmillan, and at the end of May 1963 an inquiry was set up under the Lord Chancellor. Hauled back from a Venetian holiday to face the inquiry, Profumo preferred to make a private confession to Macmillan's aides on 4 June. He resigned both his government position (which had not carried membership of the Cabinet) and his parliamentary seat.

Yet the scandal lost little momentum. Macmillan set up a new inquiry, under **Lord Denning**; his subsequent report concentrated on sex rather than national security, and became an instant best-seller. Denning's report laid much of the blame on Stephen Ward, an osteopath who had introduced both Profumo and Ivanov to Keeler. On

3 July, while a judge was directing a jury to convict him for living on immoral earnings, he took a fatal overdose. At the time the press gloated over Ward's downfall, but the film *Scandal* (1988) rightly portrayed him as a convenient (if somewhat unpleasant) scapegoat.

▶ Meanwhile, other politicians, **aristocrats** and even senior members of the royal family had been mentioned in rumours of sexual 'improprieties'. It seemed that the Establishment hardly had time to be running the country, such was its orgiastic appetite. Since Profumo, Britain's

▶ **national newspapers** have never relented in their quest to catch politicians in compromising situations, hoping to expose them in the national interest.

Macmillan survived the immediate aftermath of the Profumo scandal, but at best he seemed naive and out of touch. In fact, as a man who had coped for many years with his wife's infidelity, he was

▶ arguably better attuned to the emerging '**permissive society**' than the prurient public. He resigned through ill health in October 1963. At the beginning of the year Britain's application to join the EEC had been vetoed by the French. Since this destroyed the main plank of Macmillan's strategy for Britain's economic revival, it might have been expected to dominate discussions of his subsequent problems. Instead, the British obsessions with sex, the rich and espionage ensured that the main focus fell on Profumo. The disgraced minister himself retired into obscurity; unlike Ward he retained most of his friends, and he raised money for charities. Apparently, he felt that certain aspects of the affair had been grossly distorted. But he refused to take any steps towards correcting the record, at least during his lifetime.

■ Pub

Colloquial term for the public house, which first appeared in the seventeenth century when inns and taverns were forced by the Cromwell regime to obtain licences for the sale of alcohol. By the start of the nineteenth century it was the standard term for a drinking place and by the 1870s pubs had become the epicentre of British popular culture. As well as the historic trinity of alcohol, sex and equine transport, they offered meeting rooms for people engaged in everything from antiquarianism to revolutionary politics; they staged

▶ 'singalongs' which gave birth to the **music hall**; and they provided a discreet venue for cock-fighting and bare-knuckle boxing after each

▶ was made illegal; while the more reputable sport of professional **football** owed its creation to far-sighted landlords who sponsored clubs like Liverpool and Everton in their formative years as amateur pub

▶ teams. Pubs also provided essential services for working-class people. Those who were unable to obtain a bank account could usually borrow or change money at their 'local'; and before the introduction of labour exchanges in 1911, pubs were the best place to find employment.

The type of pub which the world associates with the British – gloomily ornate and organically convivial – emerged between 1880 and 1930 after breweries took direct control of premises in order to counter the influence of the temperance movement. The 1869 Beer Act gave more power to magistrates to refuse licences and reduce opening hours. This began a legislative trend that culminated with the 1915 Defence of the Realm (Amendment) Act which closed all pubs before 11 a.m., from 2 p.m. to 5 p.m. and after 11p.m., a supposedly temporary measure that was strictly enforced for another seventy years. MPs were rallied by fears about the moral and physical decline of the British race, together with more pressing concerns about the effect that drink was having on the productivity of munitions workers. The **nationali-** ◀ **sation** of the entire liquor trade was seriously considered by the wartime government of **Lloyd George** and in 1916 it experimented by ◀ taking over the Carlisle area, acquiring four breweries and over 200 pubs, half of which were swiftly closed down. The scheme was not extended due to public hostility, but the 1921 Licensing Act made other wartime measures permanent, with the result that total opening hours in the UK were slashed to half those of 1914.

Faced with this unprecedented assault on their business, larger breweries like Courage floated on the Stock Exchange to raise the capital to buy independently-run 'free houses'. By 1900, most of Britain's 100.000 pubs were brewery-owned and publicans were no more than managers with tied houses (although they were still called 'landlords' in common parlance). As well as ensuring that their own products were consumed on the premises and not those of rivals, breweries used their new power to change the whole way that the British drank alcohol. First, table service was rejected in favour of counter service in order to accelerate turnover during the ever-decreasing hours that were available to sell liquor. This time-and-motion revolution – as significant as the Fordist techniques that were simultaneously implemented in Britain's factories – marked out British pubs from Continental bars. It also had an important side effect: by bringing publicans and their regular customers into closer contact around the counter, it rescued some of the intimacy lost by the demise of the free house. Second, the breweries attracted more middle-class customers by making their premises more luxurious. Frosted glass, wood panelling, brass rails, chandeliers and carpeting replaced the 'spit and sawdust' atmosphere known for centuries; and although fewer new pubs were built than before, they were lavishly executed in the Dutch-influenced 'Queen Anne' style that dominated Edwardian architecture. Eminent **architects** like Norman Shaw (1831–1912) – ◀

P

▶ creator of New Scotland Yard for the Metropolitan **Police** – were among those commissioned to design the new buildings. If the medieval inn had become a public house, it was the splendid town house of a professional gentleman to which the public were invited – except that, once inside, every customer was asked not to forget their place.

The third change designed to make the pub a more respectable institution was the partitioning of its interior. Saloon, or 'lounge', bars invited white-collar workers to drink in more luxurious surroundings, while the rest of society was confined to the more spartan public bar, and often on condition that they were not wearing soiled clothes. Some premises also had small private bars, or 'snugs', which usually seated half a dozen of the wealthiest regular customers. They were sectioned off from the counter by 'snob screens' which stopped bar

▶ staff seeing the customer and under which **drink** and money was exchanged. Snugs disappeared in the interwar period, mainly because they were being used for illicit sex, though other types of partition remained in place. Throughout the 1930s, smart saloon bars were

▶ built into the mock-Tudor 'roadhouses' that were erected on **suburban** ribbon developments in order to catch passing trade from the rising number of middle-class car owners. Intellectuals as diverse as G.K.

▶ Chesterton and **George Orwell** celebrated the British pub as a unique institution which fostered social harmony and an evolutionary political tradition. In fact, it symbolised the sharp class divisions on the island, in contrast to the bars of America and Europe which continued to be relatively open spaces. The point was well-made in Joseph Losey's 1963 film *The Servant* about a London manservant, played by Dirk

▶ Bogarde, who usurps the authority of his **aristocratic** employer, played by James Fox. In a pivotal scene at their local pub, Bogarde crosses into the saloon bar to speak to Fox, a moment intended to symbolise his subversion of the class system.

Despite the conservative motives behind the remaking of the British pub, what aesthetes derided as 'Brewer's Tudor' was genuinely popular. Customers welcomed a more luxurious drinking environ-

▶ ment which, like the ornate **cinemas** of the day, reflected the aspirations and fantasies encouraged by the product on sale. So much so that a Royal Commission on Licensing (1929–32) concluded that further legal restrictions on drinking were unnecessary because those imposed from 1916–21, together with the more respectable pub culture fostered by the breweries, had halted the nation's slide into decadence (annual beer consumption fell by 50 per cent in the decade up to 1932, when it reached an all-time low of 10.7 gallons per person). Thus, through a typically British compromise, the UK escaped both

▶ **nationalisation** of the drinks trade and, more importantly, the complete prohibition of alcohol which so divided American society from 1920 to 1934 and which laid the foundation of modern organised **crime** in the US. ◄

This compromise held during the Second World War. Fewer worries about the health and volatility of the working classes meant that the **Churchill** government regarded beer, like tea, as an aid to national ◄ morale. In order to ensure that there were reasonable supplies of alcohol at all times, and to make distribution more efficient, the UK was divided into 88 self-contained drink zones. Pubs had to take their supplies from the nearest brewery, even if that meant breaking a tied house agreement. The strength of alcohol was cut by an average of 15 per cent during the war, though more out of profiteering than puritanism, and beer consumption rose again to 25.6 gallons per person, not far off the post-war peak of 27.1 gallons reached in 1979.

The 'traditional' British pub survived the explosion of leisure opportunities after the Second World War by continuing to adapt, ironically by mimicking the marketing strategies of the temperance movement. In 1901, Earl Grey had formed the Public House Trust Company in his native Northumberland which eventually acquired over 200 properties (later the Trust House Forte empire). Northumberland aimed to minimise inebriation by making pubs more family-oriented – admitting **children** and serving food, beverages and soft ◄ drinks as well as alcohol. His idea was first copied by commercial breweries in the roadhouses of the 1930s and by the 1960s such premises were commonplace. An enduring dislike of children in drinking places meant that by the end of the century less than 3,000 children's licences had been applied for in England and Wales. But scampi and chips, Black Forest gateau and coffee became as common a feature in pubs as a pint of bitter – a development assisted by the microwave oven, which made it possible to offer a wider range of fast **foods**. ◄ (Invented in the US 1945; introduced to the UK 1959).

Other adaptations worth noting include the greater choice of alcohol that became available during the 1970s. The legendary British taste for warm, mild beer gave way to a preference for colder, sharper, foreign (mostly German) lager beers which were initially tasted and enjoyed while on foreign package **holidays**. Most lager was produced ◄ using chemicals, as were a growing number of 'traditional' British ales. Discontent led to the creation of the Society for the Preservation of Beers (1963) and the Campaign for Real Ale (1971). The campaign appealed to people who had practical concerns about the environment and those who wished to save a Britain of the imagination. As a result, breweries began to stock organic beers made by their smaller competitors, which for many years had only been available in Britain's surviving free houses. Music also made a reappearance. The American jukebox had begun to enliven pubs during the 1950s; in the 1980s it

P

was joined by the Japanese karaoke machine, an electronic singing aid that allowed the talentless to be three-minute pop stars. Pubs still produced real stars, staging concerts by aspiring groups (the British ▶ **Punk** movement began life in the pubs of west London). More controversially, the 1970s saw a growth in the number of landlords offering striptease in a short-lived attempt to cash in on the burgeoning sex ▶ industry. Appropriately, therefore, it was **women** who changed the face of the British pub in the last decade of the century.

▶ **Margaret Thatcher** relaxed Lloyd George's drinking laws in the 1988 Licensing Act, which once more allowed pubs to open all day, for up to twelve hours, though it shied away from the late-night opening which a majority of the population wanted. More importantly, the corporate barrage that Thatcher's deregulation of the City unleashed during the 1980s hit a complacent brewing industry with takeovers from entertainment conglomerates who had a firmer finger on the pulse of British society. They were especially aware that ambitious women were entering full-time employment in greater numbers than ever before, and these women wanted a less masculine, more sophisticated environment in which to drink, both professionally and socially. Enough young men were prepared to follow; and so, a generation after gloomy overwrought Victorian interiors were ripped out of the British house in favour of bright, simple modern decor, they were similarly extirpated from the British public house. The most significant event was the disappearance of separate bars. Just as Protestant reformers had torn down rood screens during the Reformation so that congregations could once more kneel at the altar, late twentieth-century interior designers encouraged drinkers to lean at the bar in unison by removing the glass and wood partitions erected by Victorian social engineers.

By the year 2000, the word 'pub' had largely been replaced by 'bar', the former denoting a passing tradition rather than a way of life. Chains of redesigned premises, of which Whitbread's 'All Bar One' was the largest, also offered a better choice of food and drink. While pubs tended to maintain a stolid British fare of steak and kidney pie, bars offered world cuisine, often cooked on site by a resident chef. Wine also became more common. Specialist wine bars were briefly fashionable among women in the early 1980s, but lost their appeal as pub landlords learnt to distinguish between a Merlot and a Bordeaux. The traditional British pub still dominated rural areas and every town had at least one. Some remained integral to the communities in which they were ▶ located, a fact highlighted by the darts and **football** teams and charity events that many publicans still sponsored. The communitarian aspect ▶ of pub life featured heavily in **soap operas**, from the Rover's Return in *Coronation Street* to the Queen Vic in *EastEnders*. Both were Victorian in design, and were shown to be the warm, convivial meeting places of a close-knit community. The popularity of soap pubs showed how much late nineteenth-century urban culture still possessed the imagination of a nation that, in all essentials, had left it behind.

■ Public opinion polls

After 1928 almost everyone in Britain over the age of 21 had the right to vote. But in the eighteenth century Jean-Jacques Rousseau had jeered that the British were only free at election time. The emergence of British public opinion polls in the 1930s offered the possibility of an effective (if belated) refutation. If properly conducted, opinion surveys could predict the outcome of the elections. But they could also force governments to focus on the clearly-expressed wishes of the people in the intervening period.

In America there had been polling of a kind almost since the birth of the republic, and by the time of the 1928 presidential election there were more than eighty polling organisations. But a more professional Institute of Public Opinion began work in 1935, to provide statistics for the press. For the first time, the Institute tried to identify a representative cross-section of the electorate and posed carefully-worded questions. A similar British body officially opened on 1 January 1937. Apparently, no one paused to ponder on Plato's distinction between 'opinion' and 'knowledge'. After all, this argument had been used to discredit the idea that ordinary people should have a say in political decisions, and Britain was now a fully-fledged democracy. Yet when asked for her opinion of the Munich crisis in 1938 one woman inadvertently suggested that Plato might have been on to something. 'Of course it takes educated people to understand it all,' she told her earnest inquisitor.

At the beginning of the twenty-first century the Institute (known as 'Gallup' after 1952 in honour of the American who founded the parent group) was still publishing monthly bulletins on a wide variety of questions, extending far beyond politics. Rival organisations had emerged since the war, including National Opinion Polls (NOP, 1957), Opinion Research Centre (ORC, 1965), and Market & Opinion Research International (MORI, 1969). Originally, Gallup's findings had been exclusively published in the *News Chronicle*, and after the war there was an obvious incentive for other newspapers, political parties and commercial companies to help fund these bodies. In turn, the various organisations competed with each other, trying to improve their methods in the hope of producing results that were as accurate as possible.

The 'Peace Ballot' of 1935 could be cited as the first British opinion poll. Eleven and a half million people took part, producing a crushing

P

majority in favour of disarmament and the resolution of international crises by peaceful means. Undoubtedly, this finding strengthened the
► hand of the supporters of **appeasement**. But the phrasing of the questions had left little room for a negative answer. Mass Observation, founded in 1937 by a poet, Charles Madge, and Tom Harrisson, a bird-watcher and anthropologist, also depended on a large volunteer army of canvassers to produce its reports. But the organisation was concerned to produce 'scientific' findings, reporting the words of its subjects rather than simple 'yes/no' answers. There remained the problem of reducing these to statistical form; but at least Mass Observation could claim to be objective.

By the end of the twentieth century public opinion polls were a familiar feature of British life. But their role continued to be controversial. In 1970, for example, almost all of them wrongly predicted an
► election victory for Harold Wilson's **Labour Party**. The **BBC** began to commission 'exit polls', hoping that people would disclose their real preferences after casting their votes. But in 1987 this technique backfired in spectacular fashion, predicting something close to a dead heat
► when in fact the **Conservatives** had won by more than a hundred seats. Concluding that some respondents were concealing their allegiance to the Conservatives – perhaps out of guilt, given that party's
► indifferent record on **unemployment** – many researchers tried to allow for an element of deception in future calculations. This only underlined the fact that, contrary to initial hopes, opinion pollsters could never fulfil 'scientific' criteria. The political parties preferred to rely on 'focus groups', which allowed in-depth analysis of opinion movements. Yet such groups were necessarily small, and even if they were designed to reflect the nation's social diversity this could only be based on highly questionable, mechanistic assumptions about the
► relationship between gender, ethnic background, **class** status, etc., and party preference.

By the end of the twentieth century, then, the prestige of political opinion polls had faded as the electorate became more volatile (and cynical). Yet the pollsters could still find plenty of work. The media had an insatiable demand for surveys on almost every conceivable subject: they could fill gaps in newspapers or news bulletins; they were relatively cheap; and, even if the findings were dubious, editors could always commission further polls to contradict them. Meanwhile, people were badgered for their views, in shopping centres, on the telephone, or at home. It was doubtful whether they knew any more about the issues than the self-deprecating woman back in 1938. But for those few seconds, at least, they could feel that their opinions really mattered to somebody.

■ Public schools

Popular term by which independent, fee-paying schools are known. The public schools grew in number and stature during the nineteenth century as a direct result of the rise of the commercial and professional middle classes. Some, like Winchester, concentrated on intellectual achievement. But most, like Eton, fostered a cult of unreflective discipline and atheleticism based around the school chapel, playing field and cadet corps. By the time universal suffrage was granted in 1920, the public schools still provided the bulk of the country's governing classes, were credited with the success of the **British Empire** and were one of the things Adolf Hitler most admired about the English. But during the interwar period they were criticised for perpetuating social apartheid and, following the defeat of the Third Reich, two attempts were made to integrate them with Britain's state schools.

Both failed. The mild, gradualist proposals of the Fleming Report (1944) were ignored by the **Labour** government of 1945–50, mainly because Clement Attlee believed in the ethos of an education system of which he, a former Haileybury boy, was a successful product. 'The first-class carriage was shunted on to a safe siding,' lamented R.A. Butler, who had commissioned Fleming and saw public-school reform as a vital adjunct to his **Education Act** of 1944. Twenty years later, a Royal Commission on Public Schools, appointed by Harold Wilson, resulted in the Newsom and Dennison Reports (1968; 1970). Collating the statistical evidence of half a century, Newsom demonstrated beyond any doubt that the effect of private education was to create two nations. He recommended that public schools should be gradually taken over by local authorities – in effect municipal **nationalisation**. Prior to that, he argued, their charitable status should be abolished and half their places should be given to state-school pupils. Wilson rejected the plan as unworkable. In reality, he too lacked the desire and political will to act. Dennison diluted Newsom's proposals, but his report shared the same fate and the issue of public-school reform was not raised again.

For the rest of the century, Labour and **Conservative** governments instead concentrated on reforming the state sector by introducing **comprehensive schools**. The only beneficiaries of that policy were the public schools. As the quality of the state sector declined, thousands of middle-class parents moved their children back to the private sector. By 1996 there were 2,540 independents in the UK, linked by the Headmasters' Conference (formed in 1869 to resist state intervention in their affairs) and serving 7.5 per cent of the population. An assisted places scheme, run between 1981 and 1996, enabled 70,000 poorer

P

417

children to access them, but made little difference to the system as a whole. In the national league table, public schools comprised on average 170 of the 200 top-rated schools in the UK. Pupil–teacher ratios were twice that of comprehensives and the money spent on equipment for each child was twice as high. The results were plain. Entry to

▶ higher education ran at 88 per cent of public-school **children**, compared to 27 per cent of state school children. The representation of the former in almost every area of power and influence was correspondingly higher. For example, when Margaret Thatcher became Prime Minister in 1979, only 2 of her 22 Cabinet colleagues had not attended a public school.

Public schools improved a lot in the second half of the century. Establishments like Roedean, which had once done little beyond 'finishing' girls to make them suitable marriage partners, began to prepare them for professional life as well. And, although libertarian experiments never caught on (like A.S. Neill's Summerhill where children chose whether or not to study), the brutal culture of beating and buggery that once characterised male public-school life became less evident. However, nothing fundamental changed from the time when the public schools were satirised in Evelyn Waugh's *Decline and Fall* (1928).

While Continental elites invested their faith and taxes in a more integrated education system, Britain retained one that actively prevented equality of opportunity and, in doing so, perpetuated the most rigid class system in the Western world. The economic result was a pool of untapped talent and the social consequence was the stunting of millions of lives. Lindsay Anderson's film *If . . .* (1968) in which a group of boys subvert, then destroy, their boarding school, with the help of machine guns, hand grenades and local working-class girls, remained an engaging fantasy.

■ Punk

Short-lived, nihilistic youth cult of the late 1970s which set itself
▶ against the optimistic pop culture generated by the **Beatles** and came to symbolise – for supporters and opponents alike – the death of
▶ Britain's post-war **consensus**. It was generated in the United States in 1975, amid the bohemian milieu of New York. The name came from a rock fanzine, *Punk*, which aired the views of poet/musicians like Richard Hell. Inspired by the anti-bourgeois philosophies of Rimbaud and Nietzsche, Hell and others attacked 'pomp' rock which was then in vogue, blaming a corrupt, capitalist entertainment industry for betraying the revolutionary ideals of the 1960s. Musically, the revolt was manifest in the work of the New York group The Ramones, who

took the melodies of 1960s Beat and stripped them down to three chords, then speeded them up into a fast, aggressive howl against authority. Their unkempt hair, black leather jackets, dark glasses and torn jeans established the basis of the punk look.

Punk emerged soon after in the UK, where it became the biggest youth phenomenon since Beatlemania, as a result of which it came to be seen as a wholly British invention. The catalyst for its British manifestation was Malcolm MacLaren (b. 1946) – a boutique owner and the partner of **fashion** designer Vivienne Westwood, who was familiar ◄ with the New York scene and realised its commercial potential. In December 1975, he formed a band, The Sex Pistols, made up of four working-class London teenagers: guitarist Steve Jones (b. 1955); drummer Paul Cook (b. 1956), bass guitarist and songwriter Glenn Matlock (b. 1956) and singer John Lydon, known as 'Johnny Rotten' (b. 1956). By September 1976, when they headlined a Punk rock festival at the 100 Club in London, they had become the movement's musical and stylistic vanguard. Lydon's spiky dyed hair, body piercing and angry sneer was copied by groups like The Damned, The Clash, The Buzzcocks and Stiff Little Fingers. The Pistols' best songs, 'Anarchy in the UK' (1976), 'God Save the Queen' and 'Pretty Vacant' (1977), together with their album *Never Mind the Bollocks – Here's the Sex Pistols* (1977), are landmarks in the history of popular music. But their influence, and that of Punk as a whole, was curtailed by two things. First, the band's sacking of Glenn Matlock in February 1977 and his replacement with a violent, talentless caricature, John Ritchie, alias 'Sid Vicious' (1957–79); and second, the extreme moral panic that the group provoked.

To some extent Punk was an authentic expression of the **class** and ◄ racial conflicts which rent the United Kingdom in this period. Those conflicts – intensified by the virtual collapse of the British economy in 1976 – produced a morbid, despairing outlook among a generation of young people for whom anarchism seemed to be the only solution. Indeed, the difference between the youth culture of the 1960s and that of the 1970s is captured in the fact that while the Beatles sang 'All You Need is Love', the Pistols sang 'There ain't no future in England's dreaming'. Their angry republican anthem – 'God Save the Queen' – from which the lyric came, reached no. 2 in the same week as Elizabeth II's Silver Jubilee celebrations, despite attempts to suppress it which included the arrest of MacLaren and the band after an impromptu concert on a riverboat facing the Houses of Parliament. The song's success was the first cultural event to serve notice that monarchism could no longer be relied upon to unite the British people. At their most organised, punk bands and fans were closely involved in the Anti-Nazi League, which led popular resistance to the

P

▶ **National Front** in the 1970s; several bands (notably The Clash and The Ruts) were also heavily influenced by Jamaican reggae and helped it to reach a white audience.

However politicised Punk became, like all youth movements, it depended on the commercial system it was spitting at in order to reach a wide audience, and it relied upon a wide catchment of adolescents for whom Punk's rebel yell was not the start of an anarchist revolt but merely the latest vehicle for their hormonally challenged assault on parents and teachers. Moreover, the hippie-baiting indulged in by Punk's hardcore followers may have been a justifiable disillusionment with the 1960s, but it was peppered with contradictions. MacLaren was a self-proclaimed Situationist, one of the most risibly ineffective, if entertaining, political movements of the 1960s. Glenn Matlock was loathed by the other Sex Pistols for liking the Beatles; yet it was Matlock's Fab Four-inspired melodies which underpinned their success. And it was the *New Musical Express* and Richard Branson's Virgin Records – both products of the Beat and Psychedelia booms – which championed the Punk cause while the mainstream media were pouring vitriol on it. If, as The Clash claimed in their classic song 'London Calling' (1979), 'phoney Beatlemania has bitten the dust', it was not apparent to the more astute observers of the day. Still, Punk's antisocial outlook hastened its implosion. On 1 December 1976 The Sex Pistols appeared on London Weekend's *Today* programme, where they were invited by interviewer Bill Grundy to utter expletives. Cook responded with, 'You dirty fucker.' This taboo Anglo-Saxon word had first been uttered on TV by the Oxford-educated theatre critic Kenneth Tynan in 1965, causing mild consternation, but when uttered by a scruffy working-class youth it was seen to symbolise the decline of a nation. As a consequence, the group were dropped by EMI, local authorities across the UK banned them from playing, and radio stations refused to air their music. Lydon left the group in early 1978. Jones and Cook flew to Brazil where they were filmed singing with exiled Great Train Robber, Ronnie Biggs. This publicity stunt formed part of Julien Temple's film *The Great Rock 'n' Roll Swindle* (1979) which portrayed MacLaren as the Punk movement's Svengali. If MacLaren swindled anyone, it was not, as he claimed, the record companies but the four men whose talents he lived off, a fact later upheld by the courts. The death of Sid Vicious from a heroin overdose in New York on 2 February 1979, while on bail for murdering his girlfriend, marked the official end of the Punk movement, appropriately in the city where it had begun four years earlier.

Punk lived on in various guises during the early 1980s, but largely through the more sophisticated groups who had ridden its new wave while developing a style of their own, primarily The Jam, The Stran-

P

glers and Siouxsie and the Banshees. Punk's long-term influence on British youth culture was muted. During the 1990s, its angry, guitar-based whine echoed in the American Grunge movement led by Nirvana and in the Britpop band Oasis, who justly claimed to have fused the music of the Beatles and the Sex Pistols. Meanwhile, Punk's anti-corporate, do-it-yourself aesthetic was discernible in the electronic dance music of the 'Rave' scene which, like Oasis, emanated from Manchester.

Punk's legacy is this: for an all too brief moment it challenged the entertainment industry, and even political leaders, to examine their complacent assumption that Britain's young people were passive consumers whose fads, fashions and cults could be commercially exploited, and in doing so be smoothly incorporated into the canons of national culture. 'The middle classes,' declared Malcolm McLaren in 1971, 'invented the commodity. It defines our aspirations, our quality of life. Its effects are repression, loneliness and boredom.' Six years later the Stranglers modestly lamented that there were 'No More Heroes'. In reality, they helped to provide some for a generation of young Britons.

P

■ **Queen Mother** (1900–2002)

Informal title by which Elizabeth Bowes-Lyon, Queen Consort of George VI, was known from his death in 1952 until her own. The term 'Queen Mother' in its modern, symbolic, sense was first applied to Mary of Teck (1867–1953), the wife of George V, when she was widowed in 1936 and her unruly son, David, became **Edward VIII**. The press proclaimed her to be 'Grandma England', an epithet which the dour Queen Mary did not like but which stuck and proved useful to the monarchy. Within a year of her second son, George VI, dying and Bowes-Lyon becoming 'Queen Mother' of Elizabeth II, Mary fortuitously died herself, thus avoiding the need to promote the idea of 'Queen Grandmother'.

Elizabeth Angela Marguerite Bowes-Lyon was the ninth of ten children born to Lord and Lady Strathmore, Scottish aristocrats whose family seat was Glamis Castle where, according to folklore, Macbeth killed Duncan. As a young debutante, keen on gin, dancing and horse-racing, she dated James Stuart, the Earl of Moray, a war hero, womaniser and equerry to Prince Albert, who introduced her to the Prince at a society ball then left to work on an oil rig in Oklahoma. 'Bertie', as he was known to his family, had none of the dash of her former lover. The Windsors' parental techniques had left him shy, awkward and with a stutter. But she agreed to marry him on the second time of asking and, after a ceremony at Westminster Abbey on 26 April 1923, she became the Duchess of York. 'It was my duty to marry Bertie,' she later remarked. 'I fell in love with him afterwards.'

It was no idle boast. Bowes-Lyon had a deep sense of duty which she instilled in her children, and which led her to despise Edward VIII (she and her husband often had to cover royal engagements for him while he made love to Wallis Simpson). She also gave Bertie the emotional support which he desperately needed in order to fulfil his public duties as a Duke and, later, as the King. But behind her stoically beatific smile, she was a canny and ruthless woman and it was those characteristics which helped to ensure that the monarchy recovered from the abdication crisis. She and her husband were crowned King George VI and Queen Elizabeth on 12 May 1937. She had played no part in the abdication, except to comfort a husband distraught at the prospect of becoming King. But thereafter, she kept the Duke of Windsor in exile, overruling her husband's affection for a brother he had always admired. She correctly judged that the Duke's popularity with the public would overshadow their attempts to establish a new reign.

They made the **monarchy** respectable again through a return to the homely probity of George V, a mood captured by her husband's description of the royal family as 'us four'. That they became four was, allegedly, thanks to Bowes-Lyon's willingness to submit to artificial insemination (then a difficult procedure), since the King was impotent. But the greatest achievement of her career took place on the morning of 13 September 1940, when the Ministry of Information sent forty journalists and a film crew to cover the King and Queen's inspection of the minor damage caused to Buckingham Palace by a bombing raid the night before, on the theme 'The King with his People in the Front Line'. After leading her husband over the rubble in a Norman Hartnell dress, then speaking to workmen clearing it up, she announced, 'We can now look the East End in the face.' Though probably sincere, the comment was a sublime piece of royal propaganda which came to represent the bond between Crown and People in the British mind over the next forty years.

The Queen's comment was clever for two reasons: first because it paraded an equality of sacrifice with working-class subjects that was ◄ entirely bogus but utterly necessary for morale. Second, the comment accelerated the process by which the British distanced themselves from **appeasement**. Like most of the country, George VI and his Queen ◄ had supported the policy, partly because fascism seemed preferable to Communism but mainly because those who remembered the First World War did not want a repeat of it (the Queen had lost two brothers in the trenches). The royal couple had stood next to Chamberlain on the balcony of Buckingham Palace after he foolishly announced 'Peace in Our Time' on his return from Munich. Pictures of the event had flashed across the media but were rarely published again, in contrast to those taken of the couple standing next to **Churchill** on VE Day ◄ which became a stock image of the monarchy.

In her incarnation as Queen Mother she remained a power behind the throne and used that power to maintain the appearance of royal probity. She helped the Queen to keep Prince Philip's many affairs secret; she pressurised her younger daughter, Margaret (1931–2002) into giving up the divorced commoner with whom the Princess had fallen in love; and she ensured that her two retarded nieces – Katherine and Nerissa Bowes-Lyon – were kept hidden in a mental hospital in Surrey, even listing them in *Debrett* as deceased. Like most royals, she was politically an arch-**Conservative**. Throughout her life, ◄ she held unsavoury views about **Jews**, blacks (whom she referred to in ◄ private as 'nig-nogs') and the **Empire** ('it was nice while it lasted' was ◄ her comment when British rule in India ended) – views which she handed down to her children. She was also a keen admirer of **Margaret Thatcher**. ◄

By the 1980s, the Queen Mother had become the best-loved member of the royal family after **Princess Diana**. Though initially sympathetic ◄

423

towards her granddaughter-in-law, she came to despise her for much the same reason she had once despised Wallis Simpson as 'the lowest of the low': namely a refusal to put the Windsors first. 'A traitor entered our house,' she once said of Diana's marriage to Charles, whose side she took in their marital disputes. To most Britons, unaware of her animus towards 'the People's Princess', she was the 'Queen Mum' and 'everyone's favourite granny' (an epithet coined by the photographer Cecil Beaton). Although in old age she dominated the court less, her popularity increased as the private lives of the younger Windsors brought the monarchy into disrepute. Partly, this was because her sheer longevity fulfilled one of the key functions of any monarchy: continuity with the past, and especially with an episode that remained dear to the British. After Churchill's death, for many she became the living embodiment of the nation's heroism during the Second World War. But more than that, her enduring popularity sprang from her ability to play the role of moral matriarch without ever appearing to be fusty like the Queen.

Her final contribution to the monarchy was the timing of her death. In the early months of 2002, there was little interest in the Golden Jubilee of Elizabeth II. The Queen Mother's passing, shortly after that of Princess Margaret, invoked enough public sympathy for the Windsors to make the Jubilee a success. Over four days 200,000 people filed past her catafalque at Westminster before her funeral on 9 April. However, claims that the British had rediscovered monarchism as a defining ideology of their national life were exaggerated, and fresh scandal involving theft and homosexual rape in royal palaces reminded the British why they had grown disillusioned with the institution. Elizabeth Bowes-Lyon was widely mourned. But she may yet be remembered, in the words of Princess Diana, as 'the chief leper in the leper colony'.

■ Roman Catholicism

In most parts of Britain, centuries of conflict between Protestants and Roman Catholics were a distant memory by 2000, and the fact that Catholics had been denied basic civil rights until 'Emancipation' in 1829 must have been a surprise to most schoolchildren. Oliver Cromwell was safely sanitised as a 'Great Briton', rather than a psychopath who could have given lessons in bigotry to the Taliban. Britons continued to burn the effigy of the Catholic would-be regicide Guy Fawkes on every 5 November of the century, but by the year 2000 many Protestants sympathised with Fawkes' objective of blowing up the House of Commons. The **monarchy** refused to contemplate a ◄ Catholic on the throne, so there was no chance that the rightful heirs, descendants of Bonnie Prince Charlie, would regain their inheritance, or that the Prince of Wales would marry anyone but a co-religionist. But most Catholics could endure this anachronistic prohibition. **Immigration** from Ireland helped to keep up Catholic numbers on the ◄ mainland, and produced pockets of ill feeling in places like Liverpool and Glasgow. But in the latter city, the restoration of relative peace in Ulster after 1998 forced the sectarian supporters of the rival football teams, Rangers and Celtic, to express their hatred by identifying with the Israelis and the Palestinians. It was a tacit recognition that **Muslims** versus the Rest was the new game in town. ◄

If the old cries of 'No Popery!' no longer swayed many voters in Great Britain, Northern Ireland was a spectacular exception. At the end of the millennium seventeenth-century grievances were still a living memory, nursed within a sectarian education system. Yet the exception underlined the rule, since the sources of the conflict, and the rhetoric of protagonists like **Ian Paisley**, were incomprehensible to ◄ a majority of Britons outside Ulster.

A more logical threat to the survival of Catholicism was its refusal to genuflect to contemporary social trends. Modern individualism seemed almost ludicrously at odds with the Church's traditional attachment to hierarchy. On the other hand, the continued emphasis on ritual was attractive to people who disliked the spirit of the age. Throughout the century Catholicism won high-profile converts, such as the authors G.K. Chesterton and Graham Greene. The attachment of the latter might not have been very sincere, but this merely emphasised the extent to which Catholicism could now be embraced as a fashion accessory. By 1961 there was an annual conversion rate of 14,000. At the same time, there was a better chance of retaining the allegiance of children born into the Catholic faith, because religion remained integral to their education while the input of the Protestant churches was declining. The authors of *English Life and Leisure* (1951), admittedly not impartial observers, went so far as to describe the atmosphere in Catholic schools as one of 'spiritual totalitarianism'. The same antagonistic spirit had informed Anglican and Nonconformist resistance to the 1902 **Education Act**. But forty-two years later 'RAB' Butler encountered much less trouble smoothing the path for legislation under which most of Britain's 2,000 Roman Catholic schools retained their managerial autonomy but had most of their running costs paid by **local government**.

Towards the end of the twentieth century there was a new influx of recruits from the **Church of England**, provoked by the ordination of **women**. The Prime Minister, **Tony Blair**, had married a Catholic and at times he seemed likely to fall into temptation. Even so, the figures suggested a decline in membership. Most religious statistics need to be taken with a pinch of salt. But while at its peak in 1990 the Catholic population in Britain was estimated at over 5.5 million, only six years later it had fallen to around 4,900,000. Even so, the statistics suggested that after 1980 active Catholics, as opposed to occasional communicants, outnumbered their Protestant counterparts.

The church continued to reject the idea of contraception. The priestly vow of celibacy endeared Catholicism to opponents of the 'permissive society', like the **Conservative** MP Ann Widdecombe. But the Catholic attitude to sex had been complex, to say the least, long before Flaubert wrote *Madame Bovary*. Sceptics had good reason to suspect that Catholic clergymen were composed of flesh and blood like their sinful flocks; they only lacked what were still regarded as 'normal' outlets for their feelings. So it was no great surprise when a series of paedophile scandals rocked the Church, leading to calls for the resignation of the Archbishop of Westminster, Cormac Murphy-O'Connor, in 2002. At least things were not so bad as they had become in the US, where compensation claims from the victims threatened to bankrupt the Church entirely.

Meanwhile, a long-running battle over the ordination of women threatened to balk what had been a thriving ecumenical movement in both the major British churches. While Basil Hume was Archbishop of Westminster (1976–99) and Robert Runcie held the Anglican see of Canterbury (1980–91) it seemed that the rival congregations were led by eminently reasonable men – to non-believers their faith was the only unreasonable thing about them – who really belonged under the same umbrella. But ordination underlined the fact that while the Anglican Church felt that it must 'move with the times', the strongest selling point of Catholicism was its unwillingness even to come to terms even with the **Suffragette movement**. Only a further deep decline in church attendances on both sides seemed likely to inspire a new approach to unity.

■ Rugby

Rugby, wrote the Welsh dramatist Gwyn Thomas in 1962, is a distillation of 'sensuality, rebellion and revivalism'. In Wales, where it is the national sport, that is true to some extent. In most other parts of Britain rugby plays second fiddle to **football** and is mainly followed by ◄ the middle **classes** to whom it represents machismo, conformity and ◄ unionism. The sport was invented in England at Rugby School in 1841 when a pupil, William Webb Ellis, picked up the ball and ran with it during a soccer match. The game that resulted was anarchic, sometimes involving 300 players in a massive, rolling and often violent scrimmage. Other **public schools**, grammar schools and **universities** ◄ took it up over the next thirty years and doctors at Guy's Hospital, London, formed the world's first adult club in 1855.

Rugby was considered to be a mere variant of soccer until the late nineteenth century. The creation of the Football Association in 1863 started the formal divergence of the two sports. But the rules of rugby did not begin to be codified until a group of Scottish teams challenged England to an international match, prompting the formation of the Rugby Football Union (RFU) at a meeting in London on 26 January 1871. Its most important decision was to outlaw the practice of 'hacking' (kicking a player to the ground) which had maimed hundreds of players since the birth of the sport. The Scottish, Irish and Welsh RFUs accepted the rules when they formed in 1873, 1874 and 1880 respectively. Purged of its more violent tendencies and better organised, rugby grew in popularity, the number of clubs affiliated to the English RFU rising from 31 in 1872 to 481 in 1893. Counties began to compete against each other in 1870, a proper county championship following in 1890. An English national stadium was built at Twickenham in 1909. Rugby was exported abroad by British businessmen and soldiers to New Zealand (1892), Australia (1903) and France (1919).

The boom in rugby, like that in football, made it harder for the game's governing bodies to enforce the principle of amateurism on which the Victorians based their organisation of British sport. In 1895, 22 clubs from Yorkshire and Lancashire broke away from the RFU after it refused to allow them to compensate players for wages they lost while away from their jobs playing. The renegade clubs formed the Northern Rugby Football Union (from 1922 the Rugby Football League) and in 1898, their sport became fully professional. In 1896, the Challenge Cup was established, modelled on the FA Cup with its final tie played at soccer's headquarters, Wembley, from 1929. The rules of the game were repeatedly amended to make it more entertaining, from 1897 when line-outs were abolished to the 'four-tackle' rule introduced in 1966.

R

The immediate result of the split was a decline in the number of clubs affiliated to the RFU (down to 244 by 1903) and a decline in the fortunes of the England team, shorn of its northern talent by the permanent expulsion of professionals. In the long term, the intransigence of the RFU created a fissure within the sport along class lines that hampered the best efforts to challenge the popularity of soccer. For half a century, rugby league was a central and defining aspect of northern working-class culture, though not always to its benefit. While the game offered a few talented men another way out of poverty it also fostered an aggressive, monolithic masculinity that was no different to that which rugby union fostered among the middle and upper classes, a fact illustrated by the film *This Sporting Life* (1963). Based on the eponymous novel by David Storey (a Yorkshire-born former player) and directed by Lindsay Anderson (a privately-educated Scot), it de-romanticised the brutal and commercial world of rugby league by highlighting the destructive effect that it has on the love life of a top player, Arthur Machin (Richard Harris in his first starring role). An international rugby league competition was started in 1934, and the sport became especially popular in Australia, where it was founded in 1908 in similar circumstances to those that gave birth to it in Britain. However, the British game was hit hard by the rising popularity of football – by 1972, attendances were down to a third of their 1952 level – as a consequence of which rugby league had become a minority pursuit by the end of the twentieth century.

Meanwhile, rugby union had retained some of its cross-class support in the Borders region of Scotland, where it was played by all elements of the farming communities, and in Cornwall, where the county side was regarded by Cornish patriots as a quasi-national one. But it was only in Wales – the last British country to adopt rugby – that it remained a truly popular sport. There were three reasons for this. First, the small size of most Welsh industrial towns made commercial football clubs less viable, so soccer never gained a foothold in the principality except in the cities of Cardiff and Swansea. Second, most of those who migrated to Wales in the late nineteenth century to work in its coalfields came from the rural west of England where, for similar reasons, soccer did not have a mass following. Third, the Welsh RFU bent the rules of amateurism in order to remunerate poorer players, compensating them for lost wages, awarding win bonuses and giving the best men testimonial matches on retirement. Wales was also the first British country to appoint a full-time professional coach for its national team, in 1967. At the same time, the Welsh RFU paid just enough lip service to the amateur ideal to prevent a split within its ranks or with other RFUs, despite frequent protests from them that sometimes resulted in international matches being suspended.

Many working-class Welsh players still defected to rugby league, especially during the interwar **Great Depression**, when they joined a ◄ mass migration of 400,000 of their compatriots to England in search of employment. But rugby union retained enough of its men to continue competing at international level. From 1900 to 1912, and again from 1964 to 1980, the Welsh team was the best in the world. Foreign countries sent coaches to the principality to learn the fast pass-and-run style perfected by the Welsh. Players like the miner's son Barry John (b. 1945) attracted adulation as intense as that experienced by soccer stars like **George Best**, and it caused him, like Best, to retire ◄ early from the game. Cardiff Arms Park, the national rugby stadium completely refurbished in the 1970s, became as much an icon of Welsh culture as Wembley was of English culture (no British team beat them there between 1968 and 1982). Mass singing at sporting events was invented by Welsh rugby fans, the male-voice choirs of Nonconformist chapels adapting their hymns for the terraces to help intimidate visitors to Cardiff Arms Park.

Success reinforced the quasi-religious status that rugby union acquired in Wales. The Welsh RFU's defence of its independence formed part of a broader assertion of Welsh identity that led to various forms of **devolution** and to the electoral success of **Plaid** ◄ **Cymru**. But *the* focal point of Welsh national pride was to beat the English at the sport they had invented, just as beating them at football fulfilled that role in Scotland, and beating them at cricket fulfilled it for the Anglo-West Indian minority of England. It was ironic, therefore, that the decline of Welsh rugby effectively began with a defeat at Twickenham in 1980 and deepened with the gradual professionalisation of the sport in England.

Pressure for rugby to be professionalised came initially from Australia during the 1980s, beginning with corporate sponsorship of national teams and of the Rugby World Cup, following its launch in 1987. The English RFU reluctantly accepted these changes but could not stem the demand from players for a complete transformation of the game. In 1995, it created a league system based on that of football, and in 2000, it accepted professionalisation.

Yet rugby has retained its uniqueness. It remains one of the few team sports that links Britain simultaneously to Europe and the Commonwealth, since rugby is as popular in France as it is in New Zealand; it is also one of the few in which the English, Welsh and Scots compete in a united team, the British Lions, for overseas tours (the first in 1888); and it is one of the few in which Ireland, north and south, play together as a national side. And, however boorish the culture of the rugby club may be, it has generated less hooliganism among spectators than cricket and football have traditionally done. These benign characteristics owe much to the middle-class dominance of rugby and they illustrate its central paradox: that Britain's most violent sport after boxing is also the one that retained for longest a gentlemanly ethos.

■ Russell, Lord Bertrand (1872–1970)

Bertrand ('Bertie') Russell could hardly have been born in more auspicious circumstances. He was the grandson of Lord John Russell, a younger son of the sixth Duke of Bedford who served Queen Victoria as Home Secretary, Foreign Secretary and (twice) as Prime Minister. With such a pedigree, money was unlikely to be much of a problem for Bertrand. Even though he himself was only a second son, he inherited £20,000 at the age of 21. In any case, his intelligence was evident from an early age, as befitted a boy whose parents had enlisted the philosopher John Stuart Mill as a (strictly secular) godfather.

Yet Russell's good fortune was short-lived. He lost both of his parents before his fourth birthday, and was brought up by his grandmother and an unmarried aunt. These surrogate parents did not exactly conform to the strait-laced stereotype of Victorian prudery, but they came close enough to induce a marked reaction in young Bertie as soon as he was free to act on his private thoughts. However, for all his theoretical endorsement of unconventional lifestyles, Russell's adult outlook retained some of the flavour of his stifled childhood.

At Trinity College, Cambridge, Russell studied mathematics and immersed himself in philosophy. He also joined the elite conversation group, the Apostles. Despite this distraction, and that of his first serious love affair which led to marriage at the age of 22, Russell achieved first-class honours and in 1895 was elected to a fellowship at Trinity.

To philosophical purists, Russell's greatest achievements were registered before he was 40. *The Principles of Mathematics* (1903) and *Principia Mathematica* (co-written with A.N. Whitehead and published in three elephantine volumes between 1910 and 1913) were indeed brilliant expositions of symbolic logic. But the relevance of this work to the daily lives of Russell's contemporaries was somewhat obscure, even if the *Principia* was helpful in the development of computers. Russell was originally attracted to geometry because it seemed to offer unquestionable truths in a world full of uncertainty. Yet the conclusions were true by definition; they revealed nothing profound about the world of 'real' experience. Russell's attempts to wrestle with these larger questions were no more availing than the efforts of his predecessors. Even on the secondary problems of philosophy he was prone to dramatic intellectual U-turns. But at least his early analytical work had an impact on his profession; it encouraged followers like Ludwig Wittgenstein and the Viennese School of 'logical positivists' further to recede from the questions which concern ordinary people, and into such momentous matters as the logical structure of sentences.

Although twentieth-century philosophy marked something like a return to the cloistered world of the medieval schoolmen, in the two centuries leading up to Russell's birth the great philosophers like Locke, Descartes and Hume had deserved the status of international celebrities and from an early age Russell was identified as an up-and-coming public intellectual. He himself was attracted to a life of action, and it seems that he only returned to his philosophical work at times when he was disgusted by the business of living. However, rather than applying himself to the emulation of his illustrious grandfather, he made only a half-hearted attempt to win a 1907 parliamentary by-election in support of the cause of women's **suffrage** (he stood on two ◄ other fruitless occasions). Nevertheless, during the crisis over reform of the House of Lords in 1910–11, the **Liberal** government included his ◄ name on a list of worthies who might be given peerages if it proved necessary to overturn the inbuilt **Conservative** majority. Presumably ◄ Russell featured on the list because his childless brother was an earl already; but the example shows how easy it was for a rich man to win attention in that pre-democratic age. In his turn, 'Bertie' inherited the family title in 1931.

Ironically, Russell first came to the notice of the general public because of a stance which isolated him from most of his fellow Britons – namely, his outspoken opposition to the First World War. In August 1914 he joined a group of intellectuals, including the **Labour Party** ◄ leader **Ramsay MacDonald** in the Union of Democratic Control (UDC), ◄ which argued that the war had largely been the product of secretive, selfish diplomacy. To support the case, Russell published a pamphlet, *The Policy of the Entente, 1904–1914* (1915). It was an early sign that however nit-picking in his philosophical arguments, Russell was addicted to sweeping generalisations when he turned his mind to events in the outside world.

In 1916, when the outrage of **conscription** was added to the ◄ grievous injury of a needless conflict, Russell's feelings could no longer be contained. After an inflammatory speech on behalf of conscientious objection, he was prosecuted under the draconian Defence of the Realm Act (DORA). Though he was not imprisoned (much to his disappointment), he was stripped of his Trinity lecture-ship. In February 1918 he was prosecuted again, for having claimed that American troops would be used to suppress militant **trade** ◄

► **unions** in Britain. In an early demonstration of the new **'special relationship'** between the freedom-loving transatlantic cousins, he was originally sentenced to six months' jail without privileges. Eventually, the conditions were eased and Russell was able to catch up with reading and writing; his only discomfort in Brixton prison was the thought that his current lover might be unfaithful in his absence.

After the war Russell travelled to the new Soviet Union and to China with his second wife, Dora. Although nominally a socialist, Russell was
► repelled by Soviet repression, and unlike Dora (and his **Fabian** friends Sidney and Beatrice Webb) he returned with his illusions shattered. But he was deeply impressed by China, predicting that it would
► become the world's last refuge from **consumerism**.

After his dismissal from Trinity, Russell's financial situation became more precarious. Always a prolific writer, he set about supporting himself through a stream of books and articles, written for the popular market. He had already written a book for the educated general reader – *The Problems of Philosophy* (1912), a volume which was suspiciously slender. Absurdly, academic philosophers took this as their cue to question Russell's intellectual credentials.

Nevertheless, the author might have profited from the most salient remark in Wittgenstein's enigmatic *Tractatus Logico-Philosophicus* (1921): 'Whereof one cannot speak, thereof one must remain silent.' Russell's contributions to political thought were disappointing, but his work became downright dangerous when he turned his attention to education. His advice on the subject was compiled into a best-selling book, and in 1927 he and Dora tried to put it into practice, setting up a private school. Unfortunately, Russell was unduly impressed by behaviourism, and his recipe for a sound preparation for adult life would have been better suited to Pavlov's dog. Russell himself was no administrator, and he soon lost interest in the school. But, forgetting that J.S. Mill had become an emotional wreck thanks to the excessive zeal of his own father, Russell inflicted his doctrines on his son, John (born in 1921), and his daughter Kate (1923). John's adult life was ruined by an unavailing struggle against his homosexual impulses; far from sympathising when his mental health deteriorated, John's indulgent father was determined to see him committed to an asylum. The suicide of one of his granddaughters can also be attributed directly to Russell's failed experiment in rational parenthood.

Undaunted by his own patchy performance in this sphere, Russell turned his attention to *Marriage and Morals* (1929). This book returned to haunt him years later, when he was driven from an academic post in the US as an advocate of adultery. In fact, the book was really a stoical appeal for greater tolerance in relationships between the sexes, and Russell included a plea that parents should try to stay together for

the sake of their young **children**. Unfortunately for Russell, this ◄
commendable outlook was tested to destruction at the end of 1929,
when Dora told him that she was pregnant by another man. After a
repeat performance in 1932 Russell sued for what proved to be a very
unpleasant divorce. By 1935 he was ready for a new venture, with a
woman who was his junior by almost forty years. This marriage went
the same way, but not before the new Lady Russell had given birth to
a son, Conrad, who later became the 4th Earl Russell and a notable
historian.

The Second World War provided Russell with the chance to return
to the Cambridge fold. He had never been a pacifist, and this time he
approved of the conflict. At the beginning of 1944 he was re-elected to
a Trinity fellowship. Ironically, he returned to academic life in
England armed with the manuscript of his *History of Western Philosophy*,
which might have dished his chances of a fellowship if it had already
been published. At its best, the book provides an engaging, broad-
brush introduction to the work of the great philosophers. But at other
times Russell's personal prejudices lead not so much to condensation
as to caricature. It was a tragic missed opportunity; instead of
inspiring a new generation of philosophers who wanted to understand
the world in their various ways (and, perhaps, even to change it),
Russell's text gave the impression that his subject had no constructive
future, and that its eminent practitioners had all been deluding
themselves.

By this time Russell's was a household name, and as a prodigal son
he was a welcome contributor to **BBC** broadcasts. But the atomic ◄
bombs which ended the war rekindled his rebellious streak. As a fish
out of water in the modern, consumerist age – in outlook he was really
a belated flower of the Enlightenment, straddling the supposedly
impassable divide between science and the arts – Russell was appalled
by the possibility that civilisation might be extinguished. In February
1958 he became President of the newly-founded **Campaign for** ◄
Nuclear Disarmament (CND). Unable to stumble on a manger without
acting the dog's part, he grew impatient with those within the movement who retained their respect for the law. Ultimately, he broke away
to serve as a venerable figurehead for the 'Committee of 100', whose
penchant for direct action brought the whole anti-nuclear movement
into discredit in the early 1960s.

By this time Russell's ego (which had never been quiet) was raging
out of control. A gaunt figure with a windswept mane of grey hair, he
could be an inspiring platform speaker and he was idolised on the left.
In 1950 he had been awarded the Nobel Prize for Literature, a decision
which was scarcely justified despite his accessible prose style. While
his name could lend prestige to his chosen campaigns, there was

precious little dignity in his pronouncements. His interventions in the Cuban missile crisis of 1962 produced replies from Khrushchev and Kennedy; this convinced him that his unaided efforts had dragged mankind from the brink of oblivion. Later, like an overheated student activist, he backed the peripatetic revolutionary Che Guevara. By that time, it appears, he had indeed resigned his judgement to younger men who bought his friendship with their flattery.

For the sake of his posthumous reputation, Russell would have been well advised to destroy all of his copious and self-revealing correspondence. This has recently been quarried brilliantly in Ray Monk's two-volume biography (1996 and 2000). Few people have left such a complete record of their dealings with their immediate family; and hardly anyone has dealt so disastrously. But Russell himself had previously displayed some of his least edifying warts, in an autiobiography which he began to write some forty years before his death. Trying his hand at fiction, he hinted at a thorough-going misanthropy, which would welcome (if not bring forward) the extinction of the human race. A scintillating conversationalist, he befriended many of the century's notable characters (including D.H. Lawrence and J.M. Keynes), but he alienated most of them, and outlived the others. Such an erratic individualist cannot be made to stand as a satisfactory symbol of any deep historical trend, but Russell's career does say something about the dilemmas facing public intellectuals in an increasingly trivial world.

R

■ Scottish National Party (SNP)

Formed in 1934 as the result of a merger between the National Party of Scotland (NPS; 1938) and the Scottish Party (SP; 1930), the SNP has been the main political voice of Scottish nationalism since the mid-1950s, seeking an independent parliament for Scotland with control over the nation's domestic and foreign affairs.

As in the case of the Welsh nationalist party, **Plaid Cymru**, the SNP ◄ was partly inspired by the creation of the Irish Free State in 1922. Unlike its Irish counterpart, however, the SNP has rarely advocated republicanism. Instead, it has aspired to 'independence under the Crown' in order to gain equal status with England – initially as a 'Mother Nation' of the **British Empire** and latterly as a partner in ◄ **Europe**. Nor (unlike Plaid Cymru) has the SNP shown much interest in ◄ the revival of Gaelic culture, as advocated by intellectual nationalists such as the poet **Hugh MacDiarmid** (although he was instrumental in ◄ setting up the party). The main reason for this difference is that the Protestant majority in Scotland led the SNP to sympathise with the Unionism of fellow Presbyterians in Ulster, while the Presbyterian Church itself opposed the disestablishment that would result from republican separatism.

The SNP's main aim has been to reverse Scotland's economic decline. This began after the First World War when the British economy began to shift away from the heavy **manufacturing** indus- ◄ tries of the nineteenth century upon which Scotland depended. The decline was exacerbated by Scottish financiers choosing to invest in the new light industries of the south for short-term profit rather than diversifying in Scotland itself. For many years, the party was divided between left-wing radicals from the NPS, who wanted complete inde-pendence, and moderates from the SP who merely looked for **devolu-** ◄ **tion** along the lines advocated by the Scottish Home Rule Association in the nineteenth century. In 1942, this led to a formal split with the party's leader, John MacCormick (1904–61), breaking away with other moderates to form the Scottish Convention (later Covenant).

In a by-election at Motherwell in 1945, the SNP's new chairman, Robert Macintyre, won the party's first parliamentary seat. However, at the general election later that year the seat was returned to **Labour**, and the SNP had little support for the next twenty years as ◄ the Labour and **Conservative** parties delivered **welfare** and affluence ◄ to the country. In 1950, a group of Covenantors stole the symbolic Stone of Scone from Westminster Abbey, on which the kings of Scot-land are reputed to have been crowned; and the movement enjoyed brief popularity, with 2 million people signing a petition demanding a Scottish parliament. However, by 1954 support for the Covenant had

S

▶ also dwindled: MacCormick joined the **Liberal Party** (the only party consistently in favour of devolution) and the movement was disbanded.

The affluence of the 1950s had only slowed Scotland's economic decline, and regional aid given by the Macmillan, Home and Wilson governments failed to improve the situation. Professional and economic opportunities which the British Empire had offered to Scots since the eighteenth century had also disappeared, further denting the appeal of Union. The main political parties lost support, and there was a corresponding revival for the SNP in the 1960s. This was sustained over the next decade by the controversy over North Sea oil. Despite the boost which the refining industry gave to the Scottish economy after it was first brought ashore in 1975, the SNP exploited resentment over the multi-national ownership of the oil.

In November 1967, Winnie Ewing captured Hamilton from Labour. Success in local elections followed in 1968 and the revival culminated with the SNP winning eleven seats in the general election of February 1974, with over 30 per cent of the Scottish vote. In this period a more distinct Scottish popular culture also emerged, centred on vociferous

▶ support for Scotland's **football** team, while the Bay City Rollers, a tartan-clad pop group, took Britain by storm in 1972.

The new nationalist spirit north of the border had concentrated minds in Westminster. In 1973, a Royal Commission on the Constitution, recommended the creation of a Scottish Assembly; this was accepted by the main parties and by the SNP on gradualist principles. In July 1978 a Bill passed through parliament but in a referendum held on 1 March 1979 only 32.8 per cent of the electorate supported devolution instead of the 40 per cent needed to make it law. This cost the Labour government of James Callaghan the vital support of SNP MPs. Over the next decade, support for the party slumped once more.

▶ However, by 1990, **Margaret Thatcher**, who in opposition had ditched the Conservative commitment to devolution, inadvertently restored SNP fortunes. Basing her anti-devolutionist views on traditional Tory Unionist grounds and on her admiration for the eighteenth-century Scottish economist Adam Smith, Mrs Thatcher used Scotland as a

▶ testing ground for a series of unpopular policies, notably the **Poll Tax**. The result was that the country's economic decline began for the first time in the twentieth century to be popularly associated with English nationalism.

The election of Alex Salmond as leader of the SNP in 1990 confirmed the party's left-of-centre position and the Labour Party, worried that its Scottish heartlands would turn towards the nationalists, once again took up the cause of devolution while other radical positions were abandoned. Thatcher's successor John Major believed that his negative stance on the issue played a significant role in securing the Conservative election victory of 1992. In 1997, however, the Conservatives lost all of their remaining Scottish seats, and **Tony** ◄ **Blair** carried out his promise of a new referendum, which was supported by the SNP. On a 60.2 per cent turnout in September 1997, the vote was 74.3 per cent in favour of a Scottish parliament with tax-raising powers, subject to the Crown and the **parliament** of Westmin- ◄ ster, and with the Act of Union therefore intact. The parliament opened on 1 January 2000, with a governing coalition between Labour and Liberal Democrats to keep out the SNP, now the second largest party in Scotland.

■ Scouting

The most successful of Britain's youth movements, founded in 1908 by Major-General Robert Stephenson-Smyth Baden-Powell (1857–1941). Baden-Powell was a committed imperialist who made his name paci-fying South Africa, notably during the Boer War when, in 1900, he became a national hero defending Mafeking. Reconnaissance was his special military skill and in 1899 he imparted it in *Aids to Scouting*, which was an unexpected success among the civilian population of the UK. In 1908, he held the first scout camp at Brownsea, a wooded island in Poole Harbour, Dorset, where he took a small group of London boys for a week of fresh air. The same year, he wrote *Scouting for Boys* and publicly expressed the wish that it might distract them from masturbation and girls by highlighting the virtue of neighbourly 'good deeds', outdoor pursuits and military discipline, all of which were underpinned by Christianity and patriotism. It became the fourth best-selling book of all time, after the Bible, the Qur'an and Mao Tse-tung's *Little Red Book*.

By the time Baden-Powell left the army in 1910 to devote his life to the movement, it had over 100,000 members aged between 11 and 18, organised into scout troops led by adult volunteers; a uniform modelled on that worn by reconnaissance troops in the African bush; and an award scheme for competence in activities ranging from first aid to knot-tying. His sister, Agnes, and wife, Olave, were keen for girls to join. However, public opinion – then concerned by the **Suffragettes** ◄ – was against young ladies tearing their dresses on bramble bushes and guy ropes; and Baden-Powell did not want them mixing with his boys. Consequently, in 1910, he set up the Girl Guides, a separate organisation with a more domestic ethos but one with sufficient outdoor activity to make it exciting for girls desperate to escape the dolour of sewing circles. In 1916, Baden-Powell added the Wolf Cubs (later Cub Scouts) to cater to the demand from boys aged 6 to 11 and, in 1918, the Brownies for girls in the same age group.

S

Scouting during the First World War usually involved crawling through mud, barbed wire and severed limbs. But this did not dent the appeal of Baden-Powell's sanitised version for children, which survived by falling between two extremes. It was less militaristic and less religious than the Boys' Brigade, which had been founded in 1883 by a Glaswegian Presbyterian minister to keep slum children on the straight and narrow; yet it was more conventional than the Woodcraft Folk, a socialist, pagan and sexually mixed outfit set up by members of the arts and crafts movement in 1894 to foster free spirits.

▶ Scouting's early appeal was based on and around the **Empire**.

▶ **Rudyard Kipling** was a close friend of Baden-Powell and the characters of his *Jungle Books* provided the names, like Akela, that troop leaders were given. Scouts and Girl Guides formed a central part of Empire Day ceremonial throughout British territories, and in 1924 massed ranks of flag-waving Scouts paraded before George V at the opening of the Wembley Empire Exhibition – an event which inspired the Nazis to create the Hitler Youth and the Nuremberg Rallies and which helped to condemn scouting in the Communist world. Later in 1924, Baden-Powell proclaimed himself Chief Scout at the first World Scout Jamboree in Copenhagen.

Over the next decade, with the help of his wife and an exhausting round of book and lecture tours (the profits from which he ploughed back into the movement), he transformed scouting into a truly international phenomenon. By the end of the century, the International Federation of Scout Groups had 25 million members, and the World Association of Girl Guides a further 9 million. Altogether, an estimated half a billion people had been involved since its inception. The collapse of Communism in Europe and Asia during the 1990s led to an increase in membership and by the year 2000 only five countries in the entire world did not have Scout groups – three Communist dictatorships: China, North Korea and Cuba; one fascist regime, Burma; and an Islamic one, Turkmenistan.

Eventually, scouting became more popular abroad than it was in Britain. From 1940 to 1960, its UK membership rose from 343,000 to 588,000 (Girl Guide numbers rose from 400,000 to 595,000). But thereafter, membership began to decline steadily as God, Queen and Country came to have less appeal than the Anglo-American youth
▶ culture centred around music, **fashion**, sex and gadgets. The movement was also undermined from within by sexual abuse scandals, most involving young boys. The term 'Scout leader', once a byword for the British voluntary spirit, became instead a euphemism for predatory paedophilia. In 1967, reforms were pushed through. Out went shorts and the 'lemon-squeezer' hat; in came long trousers. 'Boy' was dropped from the title of the organisation, which became simply 'The

Scouting Association' and guidelines on child protection were issued. In 1989, the first move was made towards sexual integration, as a result of which about 10 per cent of Scout troops were mixed by the year 2000. But this did not halt the movement's decline. Scouting's strength now lay in America. The new superpower may have generated the youth culture which undermined British scouting. But it was also the country where muscular Christian patriotism still pervaded civil society and where parents welcomed the chance to have their children inculcated with Baden-Powell's Edwardian values. An American businessman, William Boyce, had established scouting in the US in 1909 after being directed back to his hotel through a London smog by a boy claiming to be a Scout 'doing his duty'.

Baden-Powell was made a Baron in 1929 and received the Order of Merit in 1937. When his health began to fail in 1938, he returned to Africa, living in Kenya until his death three years later. In his last message to the world's Scouts he wrote, 'God put us in this jolly world to be happy and enjoy life. One step towards happiness is to make yourself healthy and strong while you are a boy so that you can be useful when you are a man. Nature study will show you how full of beautiful and wonderful things God has made the world for you. Be contented with what you have got and make the best of it.' The Baden-Powells never had any children of their own.

■ Shaw, George Bernard (1856–1950)

Born in Dublin, the child of an impoverished alcoholic from a genteel Protestant family, G.B. Shaw came to London at 20 and initially scraped a living as a critic of art and music. When he moved on to drama criticism his work for the *Saturday Review* made the initials 'G.B.S.' as familiar as 'GBH' would become in a later era. A brilliant socialist pamphleteer (as well as a vegetarian, non-smoker and tee-totaller) he was an early member of the **Fabian Society**, and edited ◄ *Fabian Essays* (1889). Later, when his own plays and marriage to an heiress had brought him affluence, he provided financial support when his fellow Fabians Sidney and Beatrice Webb founded the left-wing journal the *New Statesman* (1913).

Shaw despised an economic system where reward bore no relationship to personal effort, as befitted a man who had experienced poverty despite working up to 18 hours a day. But he combined his visions of a socialist future with unashamed political elitism. Admirers can point to occasional positive remarks about democracy as a principle, but he clearly doubted that the majority of his contemporaries were fit to vote. As he put it in the play *Man and Superman* (1903), 'Englishmen never will be slaves: they are free to do whatever

S

the government and public opinion allows them to do.' The only
▶ problem was that **government** and public opinion were both
misguided. The solution, Shaw felt, was the rule of a specially-trained
bureaucracy. Like many thinkers of both left and right at this time, he
▶ also espoused a form of **social Darwinism**, believing that progress
could only be assured through selective breeding.

Shaw's ideas were expounded in a steady stream of polemical
books, pamphlets, articles and letters to the press. But his adopted
persona of ironic iconoclast made it difficult to take him seriously.
This impish outlook undermined the effect of some courageous writings, such as *Common Sense About the War* (1914), which argued that
although Britain was right to declare war on Germany it should accept
some of the blame for the conflict, and an unsuccessful plea for
clemency for Roger Casement, who was executed for treason after the
▶ 1916 **Easter Rising** in Dublin. The same trait could be cited in defence
of Shaw's judgement of 1933 that Hitler was 'a very remarkable, very
able man', and his admiration for Stalin's regime in the Soviet Union.
But he certainly did have a tendency towards hero-worship, as befitted
someone who took most of his ideas from other people (such as Nietzsche, Ibsen and Bergson).

Shaw's image as a gadfly for the national conscience was founded
on over 50 plays, many of which were written in the garden shed at
'Shaw's Corner', his house in rural Hertfordshire. He had been an
unsuccessful novelist before he turned to criticism, and his plays were
little noticed at first. Even such a fitting piece for the 'naughty
nineties', *The Philanderer* (1894), was rejected for the stage; in the
previous year *Mrs Warren's Profession* had been banned by the Lord
Chancellor. But Shaw's savagely satirical account of social developments in his homeland, *John Bull's Other Island* (1904), was a major
success, emulated by *Pygmalion* (1913, later adapted into the musical
My Fair Lady), and, after a brief post-war lull, *Saint Joan* (1924).

In his heyday Shaw was perhaps the best-known European playwright. He was awarded the Nobel Prize for Literature in 1925 (having
spurned all domestic honours). But although many of the plays were
re-staged in the years following his death, his appeal had waned long
before the end of the twentieth century. At his best he could rival the
epigrammical style of his countryman Oscar Wilde, but he tended to
use his plays as vehicles for the latest bee in his bonnet. It would be
▶ difficult to say that he left any 'Shavian' disciples; the dramatist **John
Osborne**, who was haunted by his grandfather's prediction that he
would either become prime minister or a second Shaw, deplored his
apparent flippancy.

Despite his strong political convictions, Shaw befriended many
leading public figures regardless of their own views, and was a witty

and prolific writer of letters. While far from being conventionally attractive – to the joy of those who relished national stereotypes, he closely resembed a leprechaun – women found him irresistible. The 'philanderer's' list of admirers is still an inspiration for all ugly intellectuals; it included the daughters of Karl Marx and William Morris, as well as the actress Ellen Terry, and the Fabians Annie Besant and Edith Nesbitt. But unlike the seducer Don Juan, with whom he was strangely fixated, he respected women as well as finding them attractive. He later supported the **Suffragette movement**, though he criti- ◄
cised its tactics. Probably of all his works the accessible, polemical tract *The Intelligent Woman's Guide to Socialism and Capitalism* (1928) is the most characteristic; Shaw was a born teacher, who had the misfortune to be side-tracked by his own sense of humour.

■ Sitcoms

Abbreviated term for the situation comedy – the most popular form of comedic entertainment in the second half of the twentieth century, which is usually defined as an 'episodic series of programmes in which a well-defined cast of characters, confined in one location or set of circumstances, responds predictably to new events'. Although comedy was an established part of the **BBC** radio schedules from the ◄
1930s onwards, sitcoms, like **soap operas**, were imported from ◄
America during the 1950s, the first being *The Burns and Allen Show* (CBS/BBC, 1955–61), starring the veteran vaudeville act, George Burns and Gracie Allen as a Beverly Hills husband and wife.

The first home-grown TV sitcom was Ray Galton and Alan Simpson's *Hancock's Half Hour* (BBC radio 1954–6, BBC TV 1956–61). Centring around Anthony Aloysius Hancock, a bumptious, disgruntled daydreamer from East Sheen, it established a common feature of British sitcoms: the constraints of life in **suburbia**, a neurosis that is ◄
more pronounced in the world's first industrialised nation. A nuanced exemplar of this theme was John Esmonde and Bob Larbey's *The Good Life* (BBC1, 1975–8), set in Surbiton. It satirised the pretensions of conventional *and* alternative bourgeois lifestyles, as Tom Good quits his career as a draughtsman and, in the face of disdain from neighbours Jerry and Margo Leadbetter, struggles with wife Barbara to become self-sufficient by turning their **garden** into a farm. ◄

With a few exceptions, the funniest and most innovative shows were produced by the BBC and, as such, they testified to the reclamation of its position as the main conduit of national culture in Britain after ITV's early triumphs. Some sitcoms began life as comedy dramas, ◄
piloted on *Comedy Playhouse* (BBC1, 1961–74); like the best soaps they often starred classically-trained actors and, unlike American sitcoms,

S

they were created by one or two gifted individuals rather than a team of jobbing writers. The most influential product of the *Comedy Playhouse* was Johnny Speight's *Till Death Us Do Part* (BBC1, 1966–8; 1972–5).

Speight broke new ground by overtly discussing party politics. The
▶ show revolved around the arguments between **Conservative**-voting
▶ Cockney, Alf Garnett, and his daughter's Liverpudlian, **Labour**-voting boyfriend, Mike (played by Anthony Booth, future father-in-law of
▶ **Tony Blair**). Broadly speaking, their characters represented the Britain
▶ of **Winston Churchill** on the one hand and that of Harold Wilson on
▶ the other, with Alf raging against the **permissiveness** into which he believed the country had been led by socialism. *Till Death Us Do Part* is chiefly remembered for the fact that it aired Alf's racist views, shared by many of his 18 million viewers and discontinued for that reason. However, the show was initially criticised by conservatives like Mary Whitehouse, angry at the amount of swearing and because it satirised the mores of the wartime generation; or rather how that generation liked its mores to be remembered (rates of illegitimacy and divorce were higher in the 1940s than in the 1960s). In doing so, *Till Death Us Do Part* laid the foundation for what is seen as the golden age of British sitcom: the 1970s.

Carla Lane's *The Liver Birds* (BBC1, 1969–79), about a pair of Liverpudlian flatmates, illustrated the growing independence of British women and in particular their ability to leave home before marriage. Dick Clement and Ian La Frenais's *The Likely Lads* (BBC2/BBC1, 1964–6) and *Whatever Happened to the Likely Lads?* (BBC1, 1973–4) depicted the tensions between working-class roots and social aspirations within the friendship of two Geordies, Bob Ferris and Terry Collier. Ray Galton and Alan Simpson's *Steptoe and Son* (BBC1, 1962–5; 1970–4), set in a west London rag-and-bone business, explored the same theme within a father-and-son relationship. Eric Chappell's *Rising Damp* (Yorkshire, 1974–8), about Rupert Rigsby's seedy northern boarding house, showed how personal inadequacy and thwarted ambition can generate social prejudices. And it remains the only sitcom with a black character (Philip Smith, an African medical student) who effectively challenges the protagonist's racism instead of being a comic foil for it.

The popularity of two shows – Clement and La Frenais's prison-based *Porridge* (BBC1, 1974–7) and John Sullivan's *Only Fools and Horses* (BBC1, 1981–93; 1996–) about a south London street trader – reflected the nation's anti-authoritarian love of small-time criminals. Both shows also illustrated the gently anti-intellectual character of the British. The tensions between cynical old lag Fletcher and his well-meaning young cell-mate Godber in *Porridge* and those between the wily 'DelBoy' and his conscientious kid brother Rodney in *Only Fools* depended heavily on the older men's dismissal of the young men's

attempts to get an **education** and a career. And in each episode, ◄
Fletcher and DelBoy seem to demonstrate that street wisdom from
'the **university** of life' is the only way to triumph in a class-bound ◄
country like Britain.

Yet British sitcom is really about losers. Whether they are pathetic
or admirable, naive or canny, upper-, middle- or working-class, sitcom ◄
heroes are people who never escape their upbringing, however hard
they try. It is a comedy of confinement which is why it appeals so
much to the British. And that is one reason why the most popular
sitcom of all time is Jimmy Perry and David Croft's *Dad's Army* (BBC1,
1968–77). Based on Perry's experiences in the Home Guard during the
Second World War, it followed the attempts of a platoon of aged part- ◄
time soldiers to defend the fictional south-coast town of Warmington-
on-Sea from Nazi invasion. With characterisation of Dickensian
quality, the show explored the relationship between seven men of
different classes, ages and nationalities thrust closer together by war,
and in the platoon leader, Captain Mainwaring, Perry and Croft
created a character that became synonymous in the British mind with
ineffective pomposity. Like the real Home Guard, *Dad's Army* appealed
to the British fondness for 'muddling through' against the odds,
which made the show especially popular during the period of violent
upheaval in which it was first screened.

John Cleese and Connie Booth's *Fawlty Towers* (BBC2, 1975; 1979), set
in misanthropic Basil Fawlty's Torquay hotel, combined a conventional
sitcom scenario with the anarchic, intellectual humour of **Monty** ◄
Python from which Cleese had sprung. Among its heirs were *Absolutely
Fabulous* (BBC, 1992–2003), *The League of Gentlemen* (BBC, 1999–) and
Father Ted (Channel Four, 1995–8). Towards the end of the century wise-
cracking American sitcom regained a popularity it had not enjoyed
since *The Phil Silvers Show*, aka *Sgt Bilko* (CBS/BBC, 1957–60). *Taxi* (Para-
mount/BBC1, 1980–5), *Cheers* (Paramount/Channel 4, 1982–93), and its
spin-off *Frasier* (Paramount/Channel 4, 1994–) reinvigorated the format, as did the most popular show, *Friends* (Warner Brothers/
Channel 4, 1995–) which illustrated the less familial structure of late
twentieth-century Western society.

If what a society laughs at is an indication of its outlook, then
British sitcom testified to a people who had little time for pomposity,
pretension or prudishness. And although the genre was a vehicle for
social prejudices as often as it satirised those prejudices, it usually
functioned as a safety valve and not as a rabble-rouser. Despite
frequent flops and periodic signs of torpor, the situation comedy
remains one of the great achievements of British television, with a
cultural impact far beyond its original remit to entertain.

S

■ Soap operas

▶ Sentimental, melodramatic popular drama serials on radio and TV, centring around domestic and community life. Like **situation comedies**, the format originated in the United States during the 1930s, was exported to the UK in the 1950s and became an accepted feature of British culture. The origin of the term lies in the fact that US serials were originally sponsored by detergent companies because they were thought to be wholesome family viewing. At first nicknamed 'soaps' by radio producers, the word 'opera' was added when they appeared on TV, to denote their increasingly portentous tone. Despite storylines involving rape, murder, incest and drug addiction, they are still shown in the early evenings and are deemed by most Britons to be family viewing, attracting audiences ranging from 2 to 20 million per episode.

Commercial television, possessing as it does fewer qualms about populism, has dominated production of the genre. However, the first
▶ British soap was **BBC** radio's *The Archers* (1950–), 'an everyday story of country folk', set in the fictional Midlands village of Ambridge, which attracted 20 million listeners at the height of its popularity in the mid-1950s. The show's producer, Godfrey Baseley, had previously worked on
▶ **agricultural** programmes and his original aim was to entertain and inform farmers. But many more listeners, primarily from the middle
▶ **classes**, warmed to its cosy evocation of English rural life, in which working people were either amusing yokels like Walter Gabriel or else, like Dan Archer, earthy sages with a heart of gold. By the 1960s, the sexual exploits of the show's land-owning and professional characters had come to mirror the racy novels of Jilly Cooper (1937–) rather than the bucolic ones of H.E. Bates (1905–74). But the programme continues to reflect an enduring belief, shared by conservatives and liberals alike, that the countryside is where a true Englishman or woman *ought* to be.

▶ *The Dales* (1948–69) did the same for **suburbia** over its 5,531 episodes. Starting life on radio as *Mrs Dale's Diary* it depicted the lives of a doctor, Jim Dale, his wife and their two children, who lived in Virginia Lodge, a 16-room mansion in the imaginary London suburb of
▶ Parkwood Hill. The **Queen Mother** once said of the show, 'It's the only way of knowing what's going on in a middle-class family.' Those with a wider social circle knew that the cut-glass accents were no longer representative, and Mrs Dale's catchphrase 'I'm worried about Jim' became a gift for satirists. In 1963, the show was moved to TV and the family to a new town, Exton, where they acquired smoother accents, a social conscience and more encounters with the modern world. Listeners were particularly shocked to hear Mrs Dale's brother-in-law
▶ confess to being a **homosexual**.

It was a 23-year-old homosexual, Tony Warren, who created Britain's longest-running and most popular soap, *Coronation Street* (Granada, 1960–). Based on his experiences of Lancashire's matriarchal society, and inspired by the social realism of contemporary British cinema, the *Street* centred around three women – Annie ◄ Walker, Elsie Tanner and Ena Sharples – who lived in a predominantly working-class suburb of Manchester called Weatherfield. Beneath the chimney pots of its redbrick Victorian terraced houses, many of the country's finest character actors have played out every permutation of comedy and tragedy. The quality of the writing and acting helped to make it a national institution, with average audiences of 18 million, made up of all social classes, including intellectuals like John Betjeman who counted it his favourite TV programme. ◄ Some of its features became models for other soaps, notably the use of the local pub – the Rover's Return – as the meeting place for its ◄ diverse characters.

Emmerdale Farm (Yorkshire, 1972– ; from 1989 called just *Emmerdale*), created by Kevin Laffan and set around the village of Beckindale and its pub the Woolpack, combined the rural setting of *The Archers* with the grittiness of *Coronation Street* and became Britain's second soap until the BBC launched *EastEnders* (1985–). Created by Julia Smith and Tony Holland, this was set around Albert Square in the East London borough of Walford, its pub the Queen Vic, its market stalls and its greasy-spoon café. *EastEnders* moved the genre on. Less campy comedic than *Coronation Street* and more multi-racial, sexual and violent, its storylines dealt seriously with issues only hinted at in other soaps or ignored altogether. These included AIDS, which salt-of-the-earth, heterosexual Mark Fowler caught and fought to be accepted. By 1988 it was the most watched soap in the UK and others were forced to match its style and storylines. Asian characters appeared in the *Street* in 1990, belatedly reflecting the large Asian population of northern England; and at Christmas 1993 *Emmerdale* had a plane crashing on the village, controversially echoing the Lockerbie disaster of December 1988.

Other attempts to alter the soap format have been less successful. Phil Redmond's Liverpool-based *Brookside* (Channel 4, 1982–2003) attempted to fuse the suburban setting of *The Dales* with the storylines of modern soaps, including a memorable lesbian kiss, the first to be shown on British TV. Brookside was not a safe place to live. In the first 12 years of the series, its 6 leading families suffered 19 deaths, many of them violent. The series dispensed with the pub as a dramatic vehicle and, in a less patronising manner than Mike Leigh's play *Abigail's Party* (1977), it showed that the suburbs were increasingly populated with working- and lower-middle-class families. But it never won more than

S

5 million viewers. *Eldorado* (BBC1, 1992–3), from the same team that created *EastEnders*, reflected the nation's engagement with the Conti-
▶ nent as a result of cheap foreign **holidays**. Trailed as a tale of 'sex, sun and sangria', it portrayed an affluent British ex-pat community in Spain, filmed on location with a cast of characters that included not only local Spaniards but also Germans, French and Scandinavians.

Australian productions like *Neighbours* (Grundy/BBC1, 1986–) have been successful. But the slow death of *Brookside* and the spectacular, costly, failure of *Eldorado* perhaps demonstrate that, although the British have relished their soap operas becoming grittier and faster-paced, they don't like too much reality. *EastEnders* and the *Street* may deal with contemporary 'issues' in socially variegated settings. But the human dramas through which those issues are played out remain as sentimental as any in *The Archers*. Ultimately, the essence and appeal of the soap opera is that it displays a level of emotional intensity that is impossible to sustain in everyday life. Moreover, it displays a degree of communitarian engagement that hasn't taken place in urban, suburban or, for that matter, rural society since the unique conditions of the Second World War thrust Britons closer together. The soap, therefore, is not so much an exercise in nostalgia as a means by which the hard edges of peacetime individualism are temporarily smoothed down.

■ Social Darwinism

▶ In a 2002 **BBC** poll to decide the greatest ever Briton, the naturalist Charles Darwin (1809–82) came a very respectable fourth, ahead of any twentieth-century scientist. It was remarkable testimony to the enduring appeal of a modest Victorian scholar, who had been acutely conscious that his findings on the origin of species destroyed the literal interpretation of the Bible, which had already been weakened by textual criticisms and geological discoveries. Yet his scientific authority was also claimed in support of a range of influential and often repugnant moral and political theories. He was not entirely guiltless in this process, but it had gone far enough ten years before his death for him to reflect on the 'power of steady misrepresentation'.

In the context of non-human species Darwin argued that the variations best fitted to their environment were most likely to survive and breed in their turn. Hence 'natural selection' would continually winnow out the 'unfit'. However, when he came to apply his theory to humans, his definition of 'fitness' no longer applied to those who bred most and whose offspring survived, but rather to those regarded as 'morally fit' by the prevailing standards of his day. This presented problems, since these individuals tended to be from the upper and

professional **classes**, and to have relatively fewer **children**. Social ◄
Darwinism was a response to this dilemma, of how to preserve the
morally fittest by encouraging them to breed, and to exert an opposite
effect on the poor and the unfit.

Darwin, who held conventional Victorian views on white and male
superiority, never repudiated this extrapolation from his theory. The
tendency to confuse biology with social theory – to derive ethical values
from prejudiced notions about human nature masquerading as 'facts'
– became even more influential after his death. But it actually began
before he published *On the Origin of Species* (1859). The main culprit was
the British social commentator Herbert Spencer (1820–1903), who had
found his inspiration in the French writer Lamarck (1744–1829). In
contrast to Darwin, Lamarck had seen evolution as a creative process.
On this view (for example) the giraffe had developed a long neck in
response to its feeding requirements, while on Darwin's theory those
giraffes which had been blessed with long necks had advantages which
ensured that they were better adapted for survival.

Lamarck was more interesting to would-be social engineers, who
could use his work to argue for deliberate intervention, either for
selective breeding to turn out 'fitter' human specimens, or to improve
the species by eradicating the 'unfit'. Herbert Spencer fell into the
latter category, and thought that the starvation of 'the idle', or of
widows and orphans, was a cause for celebration; those who argued
otherwise simply did not understand the natural forces of progress.
But watching with approval while the poor starved to death was too
passive for some social Darwinists, who became full-blooded eugenicists. The fashion was by no means restricted to right-wing ideologues.
George Bernard Shaw, the **Fabian** socialist who could never resist the ◄
chance to shock his readers, wrote that 'if we desire a certain type of
civilisation and culture, we must exterminate the sort of people who
do not fit into it'. Even the philosopher **Bertrand Russell**, whose genes ◄
were impeccably liberal, had no objection to the sterilisation of the
'unfit' – a outlook which caused him inconvenience later, when the
mental health of his own homosexual son proved unequal to the
emotional tyranny of his upbringing.

For understandable reasons, the virus of genetic determinism
spread easily from intellectuals to politicians who were in a position
to act on the theories. The idea of 'the survival of the fittest' was obviously compatible with the policies of those who wanted Britain to
retain its **Empire** against increasing competition from other nations. ◄
To imperialists such as **Rudyard Kipling** the British were self-evidently ◄
'fitter' than the races they ruled. But they could no longer be sure that
they were superior to the **Germans** and the **Americans**, who after all ◄
shared their Anglo-Saxon ancestry.

In fact, an alternative reading of natural selection theory gives rise to some counter-intuitive conclusions for international relations. ▶ Particularly in the era of nuclear **war**, weak countries which claim neutrality could be better adapted for survival than their well-armed, bellicose counterparts. But this kind of thinking was too subtle for the 'Darwinists', who have always confused 'fitness' with 'strength', or with wealth, and wanted to argue that 'might is right'. Their ideas could be applied to domestic affairs, as well as the struggle between nations. Ironically, on this point the evolutionary theory, which had helped to undermine the Christian religion, was yoked together in Britain with half-remembered Protestant prejudices which asserted that worldly prosperity was readily taken as a sign of Divine favour. The rich were thus assumed to be healthier than the poor in body, mind and spirit; and the 'racial stock' was supposedly threatened by the falling birth-rate among the prosperous. After 1911, when the official ▶ statistics began to divide the **population** into arbitrary social classes, even casual observers could spot this alarming trend for themselves.

Fortunately for the British, social Darwinism could flow into more constructive channels. The right to vote had spread beyond the middle classes, and a programme of mass sterilisation of the poor was unlikely to carry universal electoral appeal. Instead, eugenicists, who included many leading geneticists and evolutionary biologists, argued for the segregation of the mentally weak to prevent their breeding, as opposed to the situation in the US and Scandinavia where sterilisation was relatively common. More seriously for policy-makers, an overextended empire required substantial armies. When many volunteers for the Boer War were found to be undernourished, the authorities ▶ were suitably perturbed. The **Liberal** government of Herbert Asquith ▶ laid the foundations of the **welfare state**, in the hope of inducing a general rise in 'fitness' levels without resorting to selective breeding. Asquith was still in office when the First World War delivered a shuddering blow against the idea that 'progress' meant 'life getting better' – another long-cherished presupposition which the Darwinists falsely assumed to have been underpinned by the theory of evolution.

Attempts to derive ethical and political proposals from biological theories should have been discredited further by the struggle against Nazi Germany, which took the abuse of racist and eugenicist ideas to new extremes. But instead of debunking social Darwinism, the course of the war merely suggested a new twist for those who believed in genetic determinism. For some, the Nazi movement proved that there was something inherently degenerate about the Germans. This idea was the more popular because it enabled Britons to overlook the extent to which their own desire to make Germany pay in full for the First World War had created a favourable environment for Hitler.

Those who despaired of humanity in general when they contemplated the atrocities commited on both sides could reflect on Darwin's revelation that humans and apes shared a common ancestor. If humans were no different from animals, **morality** is essentially bogus. Some even came to share Rousseau's view that the human ability to think made that species even more depraved than the **animals**, and this conviction helped to foster the animal rights movement.

It seems that there will always be 'determinists' of one sort or another, who hope to reduce the diversity of human experience to a single causal factor. While the social Darwinists argued that genes lay at the root of everything, Karl Marx believed that consciousness was determined by experience. The contrast is best illustrated by comparing **George Orwell**'s anti-communist *Nineteen Eighty-Four* (1949) with Aldous Huxley's harrowing portrait of genetic engineering, *Brave New World* (1934). The outcome of the **Cold War** has helped to secure a victory (of sorts) for the Darwinists. Since the mid-1970s, a new school of 'sociobiologists' and 'evolutionary psychologists' have emerged to pick up the soiled mantle of genetic determinism. Much of their work is apparently benign in intent, trying to explain (for example) why humans choose particular partners for reproduction rather than hoping to meddle in the process. Unfortunately, in a post-**Freudian** age any trespass into this field is open to serious abuse. Some sociobiologists have even claimed that healthy males are 'naturally' promiscuous, since they can reproduce almost at will throughout their life cycle. **Women**, by contrast, have to pick and choose, and to pounce at an opportune moment. Despite the different challenges facing members of both sexes, women and their partners are assumed to act in the interests of their genes. Since the sociobiologists share with Freud a dogmatic conviction that all motives to action are unconscious, those who protest that they want to have children merely because they have 'fallen in love' can be brushed aside as superficial thinkers.

In itself, the theory has reactionary implications which were quickly identified by feminists. It suggests, for example, that soldiers in an invading army who kill their male captives and rape the females are acting 'naturally'. Sociobiology also gave a kind of 'scientific' reinforcement to **Thatcherism** through its basic premise that human beings are genetically programmed to be selfish. The idea of 'the brotherhood of man', or even of treating people outside one's immediate genetic family with basic courtesy, emerges as a sort of confidence trick that we play on ourselves. Alternatively, the whole history of ethical thought has been a cunning selfish strategy, building a framework of rules which will allow gene-carriers some hope of living unmolested by rivals.

Not content with explaining the development of ethical thought, some sociobiologists modestly suggest that their theory should unite the academic disciplines of the arts and the sciences, since everything is 'really' about genes. This idea would be laughable, if the approach were not so sinister in other respects. Genetic determinism offers an answer to burning questions for social conservatives in the West, such as **homosexuality** and family breakdown. Attempts to isolate a gene which 'causes' attraction towards the same sex are promoted as a means of getting rid of the former problem; genetic modification of embryos, to produce the 'perfect' offspring, offers a plausible route to the restoration of happy extended families without the awkward preliminary of having to form any kind of emotional bond with a suitable reproductive partner. Designer children are likely to become the next 'must-have' accessory for a **consumerist** society. But when combined with new techniques of artificial insemination, and the prospect of cloning, genetic determinism has unmistakable totalitarian overtones. John Dryden's joke about Charles II, that 'wide as his command / [he] scattered his maker's image throughout the land' will soon become (if it is not already) a practical proposition for all would-be dictators, as well as ego-crazed pop 'superstars'.

The intellectual environment in Britain since the Second World War has been propitious for genetic determinists not simply because of the eclipse of Marxism. The positive ideas which used to be derived from a misreading of Darwin have also lost their relevance since the invention of the atomic bomb. The poor are no longer needed in any war between nations, so their 'fitness' is now irrelevant to questions of high state policy. This new situation assisted in the begrudging acceptance of Thatcherism, which was a return to the spirit of Herbert Spencer – even if a full-blooded programme, red in tooth and claw, was still considered to be politically hazardous. Competition was held to be the law of life, and riches were the only badge of success worth having in the absence of an empire to govern. Attacks on the welfare state focused on its perverse incentives for the poor to bring more 'unfit' babies into the world. Even with the defeat of the **Conservatives** in 1997, and the advent of 'New' **Labour**, these saloon-bar assumptions permeated into policy presentation.

The 'power of steady misrepresentation', it seems, was even greater than Darwin supposed.

■ Social Democratic Party (SDP)

The Social Democratic Party was founded in 1981, after the **Labour Party** adopted a system for electing its leader which gave the **trade unions** more influence than either MPs or constituency parties. The founder-members of the party – the so-called 'Gang of Four' – had between them held all the highest political offices bar the top job. Roy Jenkins, David Owen, Shirley Williams and William Rodgers were dismayed at the prospect that Labour would move decisively to the left in the wake of its 1979 election defeat. Although Labour's pledge to leave the **European** Community was regarded as the main policy issue ◄ which provoked the defections, the 'Gang' was at odds with current Labour thinking on a range of subjects, including nuclear disarmament and import controls.

For a few months over the winter of 1981–2, it looked as if the SDP would fulfil Jenkins's dream of 'breaking the mould of British politics'. After forming an alliance with the **Liberals**, the new party's ◄ opinion poll rating reached 50 per cent in December 1981. Over these months the Alliance overturned **Conservative** majorities in three by- ◄ elections, including Crosby and Glasgow Hillhead, which were won by Williams and Jenkins respectively. The other victory, at Croydon North-West in the south-eastern heartland of Conservatism, was clinched by Bill Pitt, a Liberal who had fought the seat unsuccessfully on three previous occasions. In 1979 he had trailed the two main parties' candidates so badly that he lost his deposit. After Croydon North-West it seemed that almost anyone could stand on behalf of the Alliance with a good chance of winning any seat.

But the high tide of SDP popularity had begun to recede, even before the event which truly transformed British politics – the **Falk-** ◄ **lands War**, which allowed the Conservatives to coast to victory in the 1983 general election. The Alliance was left to fight for second place, but although its share of the popular vote was not far behind Labour it won only 23 seats. Like the Liberals, the SDP advocated a change from the first-past-the-post electoral system to proportional representation; although their fate proved their point, the understandable fears of the other two parties made reform less than likely. At the dissolution of parliament there had been 29 SDP MPs; despite winning 3.5 million votes, the Alliance managed to hang on to only 6 of these seats. Williams and Rodgers were both defeated, along with Christopher Brocklebank-Fowler – the only MP to defect from the Conservatives.

There was another surge of support for the Alliance in 1986, and for a few months it briefly regained the lead in the **opinion polls**. But the ◄ surge was short-lived. In 1987 the Alliance again received more than 3 million votes, but it suffered a further net loss of one seat. Jenkins himself was defeated at Hillhead, leaving Owen (who had been leader since 1983) as the only founder-member still in the Commons. By this time the party was being undermined by differences of personality and outlook. While Jenkins had always been sympathetic to the Liberal Party, the ambitious Owen was determined to preserve at least

S

partial independence for the SDP. After the 1987 election the Liberals proposed a merger between the two parties. This was agreed in March 1988, but Owen refused to accept the demise of the SDP. With two parliamentary colleagues he soldiered on, but only until June 1990 when he disbanded the party. Owen himself went to the House of Lords after the 1992 general election; his two remaining followers lost the seats they fought as Independent Social Democrats.

To its partisan critics, the SDP was merely a media creation. More detached observers identified the lack of a reliable social basis of support as a reason why the experiment was doomed from the outset. The first view overlooks the extent to which the SDP satisfied an existing demand which went far beyond the media. In 1981 there were many good reasons for voters to feel attracted by a new political party with a more democratic structure than its main rivals. If anything, indeed, the media attention damaged the SDP, giving the impression that it was dominated by a handful of strong personalities.

▶ Certainly the SDP lacked a solid **class** base. But then so did its competitors, at a time when traditional allegiances were dissolving and the old social demarcations were losing their relevance. At its height in the summer of 1982 SDP membership was just over 60,000 – a remarkable achievement for a young party recruiting at a time of
▶ increasing **apathy**. True, the majority of activists were male, public-
▶ sector professionals. But the party was popular with **women**, and in 1987 almost two-thirds of voters thought that it was free from any class bias, while a greater proportion of the electorate thought the victorious Conservatives concentrated on the interests of a single class.

The real problem for the SDP was the bugbear of all 'third parties' – the idea that only Labour or the Conservatives can form a government, so that voting for anyone else can only be a form of protest. In this respect the claim of the Liberal leader David Steel in September 1981, that thanks to the Alliance his party could now 'prepare for government', was less of a gaffe than commentators liked to suggest. It was really a bold invitation to voters to examine their own presuppositions about the two-party system. It was a gamble well worth taking; after all, opinion-poll findings consistently suggested that the SDP would have performed far better had voters followed their 'real' preferences, so all that was needed was a psychological push to make them back up their ideas at the ballot box.

It was no surprise that the SDP was founded in 1981, given the polarisation of the two main parties. But if a similar 'Gang of Four' had broken away in 1991, arguably their fate would have been very different. At that time Labour was quickly shedding the policies which were widely regarded as electoral liabilities, but its leader, Neil Kinnock, had been undermined by persistent press denigration, leaving room for a fresh party of the centre-left. Meanwhile, the Conservatives, having won three successive elections despite unpopular policies, saw no reason to reform themselves – although some of its moderate MPs were now ready to defect. A centre-left party founded just before the 1992 general election could have taken enough votes from both of its rivals to force a stalemate, from which a new alignment could have emerged. Instead, it was left to **Tony Blair** to create ◄ 'New' Labour, which quickly attracted many ex-members of the SDP. ◄ Yet in his attempts to free his party from trade union dominance Blair allied himself with the business community, and despite the landslide 1997 victory he retained the broad outlines of Conservative policy. There was still room for a genuinely 'progressive' party in Britain; and at the end of the century the Liberal Democrats remained the only hope of 'breaking the mould'.

■ Sovereignty

In recent years the British public has grown well accustomed to hearing politicians arguing about 'sovereignty'. But the combatants rarely trouble themselves to define their terms. The subject can be approached from two sharply contrasting perspectives. On the first view, a sovereign power is one whose laws cannot be overridden by any other body. This at least has the virtue of simplicity, and had obvious attractions in Britain at a time when its right to govern itself (and others) was unchallenged; sovereignty was exercised by 'the Queen in Parliament', and there was an end to it. The same definition also has great value for national liberation movements, fighting against the dominance of 'alien forces'.

However, in the twentieth century this definition began to look unduly abstract, even for a supposedly 'hegemonic' power like the United States. One can argue that an individual still exercises 'sovereign' choice when a highwayman offers the alternatives of 'your money or your life'. But it makes more sense to say that the choice is 'unfree'. In respect of nations rather than individuals, the established law-making body may still be technically 'sovereign' if it is forced to take decisions in the face of (for example) a world economic slump. But if the range of choices is severely limited – particularly if it is more restricted than it would have been in the past – talk of 'unimpaired sovereignty' seems out of place.

In short, the rival definitions are (1) the *right* of a country to take its own decisions, even if there is little or no realistic choice on crucial questions; and (2) the *ability* of a country to choose from the greatest possible number of options, even if that means that decisions are taken in concert with other powers. On the first view, the 'sharing' of

S

sovereignty is impossible: either you have the decisive voice, in which case you are sovereign; or you do not, and your sovereignty has been
▶ surrendered (when applied by British politicians to the **European Union**, this argument reflects an assumption that 'our' position on key issues is bound to conflict with 'theirs'). On the second view, in a world where national boundaries are increasingly irrelevant, if a country 'pools' its sovereignty with others it can increase its real freedom of action (in the European context, this argument is deployed on the assumption that ultimately Britain and its partners will invariably reach a satisfactory compromise on all key issues). Thus, if true sovereignty means the *ability* to act with relative freedom, it can not only be shared but actually *increased* by the sharing.

Even after joining Europe, the British public had yet to decide between the rival definitions – mainly because the choice had never been presented with any clarity. That in itself spoke eloquently of the British experience over a difficult century. But in the crucial field of foreign policy the decision had been made for it long ago. During the
▶ **Suez crisis** Britain acted in secret concert with both France and Israel – an odd course of action in itself for a country which had once enjoyed unparalleled 'sovereignty' in the Middle East. But in the face of US opposition the adventure was abandoned. After this 'the Queen in Parliament' could still make laws; but in foreign policy the British could take no decisive step without American acquiescence.

This event, more than any other, undermined the old definition of sovereignty as it applied to Britain. On those terms, if a country cannot make an independent choice of its friends and enemies, it lacks what is arguably the defining feature of a 'sovereign' state. Some far-sighted
▶ politicians (notably **Winston Churchill**) had actually been moving towards the second definition even before 1945. But few aspirants for office were prepared to tell the voters that Britannia had no more power over the waves than King Canute, so the public debate proceeded on the old (increasingly surreal) terms, and looked set to do so even when the electorate was asked to decide on membership of the European single currency.

■ 'Special relationship'

The United States entered the First World War in April 1917, after repeated attacks on American shipping by German submarines. Previous provocations, such as the sinking of the civilian vessel *Lusitania* in 1915, had been overlooked; but by 1917 there was also evidence that Germany hoped to stir up trouble for the US on its own continent. In these circumstances the belated declaration of war by Woodrow Wilson was an obvious step, despite widespread and understandable distaste for joining a conflict between distant European nations. In particular, there was a strong anti-British lobby in America, and the two countries had nearly gone to war (over Venezuela) as recently as 1896. The anti-colonial spirit of the Boston Tea Party was still alive. Britain's behaviour in Ireland was a grievance of almost equal antiquity, but ill feeling among the influential community of Irish Americans had been running high after the repression which followed the **Easter Rising** of 1916. ◄

The arrival of fresh American troops was an important (if not decisive) moment in the war, and America's new authority on the world stage was demonstrated by the respectful European response (in public, at least), to President Woodrow Wilson's idealistic 'Fourteen Points' of January 1918. Four years later, the philosopher **Bertrand** ◄ **Russell**, who had been imprisoned during the war after making critical speeches about the US, referred to 'our American masters', and claimed that Britain could no longer pursue independent economic policies. This, perhaps, was slightly premature. But in their satirical history textbook *1066 and All That* (1930) W.C. Sellar and R.J. Yeatman lamented that history had come to a full stop at the end of the war, because America was now 'clearly top nation'. Its new dominance was not matched by a greater sense of responsibility on the world stage. The US Senate refused to ratify the Treaty of Versailles, and despite Wilson's advocacy the country also stayed aloof from the League of Nations designed for the peaceful resolution of international disputes.

The outbreak of the Second World War was an unpleasant reminder to Americans that European states still had the power to disrupt international trade. Yet this time round the country was far better prepared for its own role. Under the 1941 Lend-Lease Act, President Roosevelt could supply war materiel to favoured nations, instead of staying strictly neutral. Lend-Lease made a substantial impact on Britain's war effort. But if America was acting as 'the arsenal of democracy' Britain and its **Empire** were alone on the front line. Nevertheless, ◄ by the time that the arrangement was terminated at the end of the war, Britain had run up massive liabilities, and the Americans were sure to require repayment in one form or another.

In his attempts to woo the American government and people, **Winston Churchill** made much of the alleged 'special relationship' ◄ between the two nations. Although he was half-American himself, and generally created a positive impression during his transatlantic trips, Churchill was in fact an embodiment of Britain's most unattractive features in American eyes. An **aristocrat** who refused to ◄ accept the dismemberment of the Empire, he could only redeem himself to US policy-makers by delivering ambiguous speeches about post-war European unity, and showing that he had retained all his old hatred of Communism despite his alliance of necessity with the Soviet Union and 'Uncle Joe' Stalin.

When the US entered the war after the attack on Pearl Harbor in December 1941, it was not because of a sudden realisation that world domination by a barbaric fascist power would be attended with some negative consequences for the democratic ideal. The arrival of American soldiers in Britain – more than one and a half million at the peak of this amicable invasion – was an opportunity for better understanding between the two nations on many different levels (the new intimacy led to numerous marriages). Yet an undercurrent of antagonism persisted. After the D-Day landings in June 1944 one cool-headed observer, the Conservative MP Cuthbert Headlam, predicted that the American press and politicians were likely to claim most of the credit for the victory over fascism. He wrote in his diary, 'I fancy that the Americans after this war are likely to be more swollen-headed and tiresome than after the last war: they may well be more tiresome to us than the Russians.' At a different level, the contrast in the respective fortunes of Britain and America since the turn of the century was exaggerated by wartime rationing in the host country. A welcome source of chewing gum and nylon stockings to some, the virile 'GIs' could also be resented for their brash materialism. The Mass Observation survey of 1943 found that only a third of Britons approved of their saviours.

Before the end of the war a discussion document on the special relationship, drafted by hopeful British officials, was quietly shelved by the Americans. The reality of the relationship resembled that between a hard-nosed bank manager and an unreliable client; funds would be provided under certain conditions, but the goodwill would quickly evaporate if the debtor showed no signs of reforming his habits. The post-war loan negotiated by **John Maynard Keynes** was understood to be a hard bargain, and British unease at its supplicant posture can be detected in the decision to pull out of the **Marshall** plan before the pre-arranged term. At the same time Prime Minister Clement Attlee reassured British voters that the country was not just America's poodle by arguing against the use of the atomic bomb during the war in Korea. British scientists had played an essential role in the initial development of the bomb. But technical difficulties dashed any hopes that the country could regain some independence by deploying an effective device of its own. Indeed, the nuclear issue only tightened the American leash, which had already been firmly attached by Britain's membership of the North Atlantic Treaty Organisation (NATO) from 1949.

In December 1962 the former US Secretary of State, Dean

Acheson, remarked that Britain had lost an Empire but had yet to find itself a role. Whatever the truth of his statement, from his own perspective Acheson really meant that Britain had yet to plump for the role which America had assigned to it. In fact, he spoke at a time when Britain was behaving itself; its attempt to join the EEC was only vetoed by President de Gaulle in the following month (ironically the death blow to Britain's application was landed in December 1962, when the Americans agreed to supply Polaris missiles for the 'independent' British nuclear deterrent). The Americans had long believed that a federal **Europe** was the best way of stopping the ◄ superannuated nations from quarrelling among themselves, while acting as a plausible barrier against the spread of Communism. Acheson's speech came only six years after Britain's most spectacular act of recalcitrance, the **Suez** adventure, during which the US had ◄ taught Britain a lesson it was unlikely to forget. The 'bank manager' had stopped just short of sending the bailiffs to sell up his trouble-some client. In the wake of Suez the new Prime Minister, Harold Macmillan, took to comparing Britain's relationship with the US to that of the Greeks and the Romans. Sensitive Americans might have taken offence at the implication that the defence of the Free World rested on a combination of British brains and US brawn. Fortunately, J.F. Kennedy (who had family connections with Macmillan, but very little else in common) proved capable of dealing with the Cuban missile crisis of 1962 without too much assistance from the 'Greeks'.

When Harold Wilson became Prime Minister in 1964 it seemed that the 'special relationship' would finally be exposed as a myth. Not only was Wilson a supposed left-winger (who had already attracted atten-tion from the CIA), but he was also lukewarm at best on the European issue. At one time cuts in British defence spending would have been welcomed in Washington as further evidence that the imperial episode was over, at least on one side of the Atlantic. But during the **Cold War** it could only lead to further ill feeling. Wilson felt it neces- ◄ sary to offer moral support for the US intervention in Vietnam, but his efforts at mediation were not welcomed.

After an inconclusive interlude under Edward Heath (who finally secured membership of the EEC), Wilson returned to office in 1974. By this time Britain was regarded as an economic basket case. In imposing spending cuts in the mid-1970s, the International Monetary Fund (IMF) was certainly following US thinking; perhaps in some quar-ters there was an idea that it could rectify the post-war American mistake, when over-generous Marshall Aid had helped to finance the British **welfare state** which some US Republicans regarded as more ◄ than halfway to Communism.

Outwardly, at least, the situation was transformed by the election

▶ of **Margaret Thatcher** in 1979. She had already established a warm relationship with Ronald Reagan, who won the US Presidency in 1980.

▶ US misgivings over the **Falklands War** of 1982, and Mrs Thatcher's anger when the Americans invaded Grenada in the following year, seemed to amount to no more than minor tiffs. Thatcher and Reagan matched each other in their condemnation of the Soviet system, and the British Prime Minister was very popular across the Atlantic.

Yet even if the relationship was a bit more 'special' in the 1980s, true friendship rarely flourishes between unequal partners. More than any event since Suez, the American raid on Libya launched from British bases in April 1986 underlined this inequality. No other European country had co-operated, and the adventure proved to be worse than futile. Some felt that the government's acceptance of American cruise missiles at the end of 1983 had guaranteed British security. But there was at least equal justification for the claim that Britain was merely being used as a kind of glorified aircraft carrier by the dominant power.

The personal rapport of the Reagan–Thatcher era dwindled when the former was replaced by George Bush, who probably reminded the Prime Minister of the patrician Tories who had been purged from her Cabinet. The atmosphere relaxed again under John Major, whose support was genuinely valued during the Gulf War of 1990–1; but this was not sustained after Bush was replaced by Bill Clinton in 1992. The European centre of gravity in US eyes had obviously passed to the newly-unified Germany.

▶ By contrast, **Tony Blair** and Clinton seemed to be soulmates on the Reagan–Thatcher model (although in this case sexual chemistry was replaced by mutual dabbling in popular music). Clinton's intervention in the Northern Ireland peace process was a sincere attempt to help, rather than a demonstration of American hegemony which might win the President extra support from Irish Americans. But at the end of the century, when George W. Bush recaptured his father's position, the realities of power were exposed once again. Blair seemed to guess that he could only build a position of influence by lavishing praise on his ally. Whether public flattery could be followed by effective words of advice in private is open to doubt. By 2002 Blair had certainly made himself popular in America, but only at the risk of provoking serious misgivings among his own backbenchers. His apparent willingness to allow the US to use Britain in its dubious 'star wars' defensive system was a particular cause of unrest, even before he threw himself into Bush's 'war on terror' in the wake of the attacks in New York on 11 September 2001. In February 2003, with a new war looming in the Middle East, Blair was taunted on television with the label of 'Mr Vice-President'. By this time it was difficult to tell whether the British were acting as a restraining influence, or whether their continued public support was encouraging the Americans in their bellicosity. As the new war on Iraq came to an end, it was clear that Britain and the US had different agendas for the Middle East, but there was no sign that Blair's moral eloquence could deflect Bush from the unabashed pursuit of perceived self-interest.

At the beginning of the twenty-first century, the illusion of a 'special relationship' was a vital psychological prop for those who needed to think that Britain still mattered on the world stage. As such, British politicians felt that they should at least pay lip-service; understandably, some even convinced themselves that it really existed. The right to be the first leader on the telephone to the man in the White House puffed up their fragile self-esteem, and (as Macmillan and Margaret Thatcher had cleverly demonstrated) the seat of US executive power provided an effective backdrop for photo-opportunities in the build-up to British general elections. Admittedly, there were a few concrete benefits for Britain along the way, at least in theory: for example, the sharing of intelligence was helpful during the Falklands War, and probably at other times too. British policy-makers might reassure themselves that having to follow the broad outlines (if not every last detail) of US foreign policy really was preferable to international irrelevance. They clearly dreamed of being called in as an 'honest broker' from time to time, not noticing that their credibility in that role had worn very thin because of Britain's obvious dependence on its powerful 'partner'. All of this had very serious implications for British **sovereignty**. But despite the clear evidence of conflicting ◄ strategic interests over the twentieth century, almost everyone seemed to think that a surrender of sovereignty can only happen between nations which speak different languages.

■ Spin doctors

S

The favourable presentation of **government** performance seems ◄ inseparable from democratic politics and has now spread to other British institutions, such as the **monarchy** and even the **police** and ◄ hospitals. It long predates the intrusion of an electronic media. Leaving aside biblical examples, it could be claimed that the Athenian Pericles was the first spin doctor, with the Sophist school of deceitful rhetoric as the prototype of **'New' Labour**'s 'Millbank tendency'. But in ◄ so far as the activity demands clear departures from the truth, nowadays it has more obvious associations with totalitarian government. On balance, the British media have become more negative, intrusive and persistent in their political coverage. However, 'spin' is the hallmark of governments with something to hide and a fetish for concealment.

The term 'spin doctor' arose in the less secretive US context. It caught on very quickly in Britain after the emergence in 1994 of 'New' Labour, which employed several publicists with experience of recent US campaigning. In part, the popularity of the term was a testimony to 'New' Labour's apparent success in conveying positive messages while it was in opposition. The process began in 1985, when the

▶ former ITV producer Peter Mandelson became the party's Director of
▶ Communications. For the 1986 **Labour** conference, Mandelson unveiled a red rose as his party's new symbol. This was the ultimate triumph of style over substance. But with his television background Mandelson believed that an image can convey a thousand words, and the acclaim of his old media colleagues showed that their esteem for their profession matched Mandelson's lofty self-evaluation. The marriage between the party and presentation was now unbreakable. A political broadcast during the election campaign presented the human side of the leader, Neil Kinnock. It was an extremely effective and relatively honest piece of work, but media interest concentrated on the fact that it had been put together by the successful film director Hugh Hudson. Amid all the self-congratulation, it was possible to forget that Labour lost the 1987 general election – and the following contest in 1992.

Mandelson was elected as MP for Hartlepool in the 1992 election, but he remained a potent force behind the scenes. In 1994, though, a

▶ rival emerged when **Tony Blair** chose the former *Daily Mirror* journalist Alastair Campbell as his chief press officer. Consistently outspoken and abrasive, where Mandelson had been insinuating and cold depending on his mood, Campbell actually marked a return to

▶ the style of Bernard Ingham, **Margaret Thatcher**'s controversial press officer. Like Campbell, Ingham had been a hands-on journalist before becoming the servant of politicians. As a result, both men had a sensitive nose for an important story, so unlike Mandelson they tended to be reactive, instead of searching frantically for favourable images. Despite these crucial differences, everyone connected with policy (and personality) presentation was now assumed to be a master of the black arts, making Machiavelli look like a blushing choirboy.

▶ By contrast, the **Conservative** government led by John Major was incapable of selling itself or its policies. Its propaganda machine seemed old-fashioned, and for good reasons. Although the phrase was of recent vintage, 'spin' itself had a long history in Britain; one might

▶ even claim that **Churchill** had 'spun' Britain through the dark days of the Second World War. But for 'New' Labour's operatives no announcement or speech could be complete without embroidery, and MPs were constantly badgered with advice on how to stay 'on message'. The Conservatives could not compete with a party for which spin had become a way of life, not a weapon of last resort in exceptional circumstances.

When Blair's remodelled party won the 1997 general election Whitehall was subjected to an invasion of the spin doctors. Twenty-five out of 44 senior government information officers were quickly replaced, and while the Major government had been content with 32 special advisers, 'New' Labour could not cope without 60, all funded by the taxpayer. Once in place the spin doctors, with ministerial approval, explored the boundaries between favourable presentation and casual distortion. For example, the impression was often given that spending commitments were new, when in fact they had already been announced in different contexts. Unlike gnarled veterans such as Ingham and Campbell, these apparatchiks tended to have a limited understanding of the informal political rules, and made things up as they went along. A nadir was reached in September 2001, when a government functionary – funded by the taxpayer – sent out an email message suggesting that the terrorist attack on New York provided an ideal opportunity to 'bury' any bad news relating to Britain's crumbling transport infrastructure.

The inevitable exposure of these tricks increased public discontent with politicians, and with the democratic process in general. But for a government obsessed with presentation, the only answer to this malaise was to spin ever harder.

■ Suburbia

An Anglo-American phenomenon that began in the UK around the 1880s and which became synonymous with middle-class lifestyles and attitudes. Suburban development was generated by the unsanitary overcrowding of industrial towns and by a fetishisation of home-ownership that was less pronounced in the more agricultural societies of Continental Europe. Suburbanisation accelerated after the First World War, partly as a result of government building grants to local authorities but mostly through private development stimulated by cheaper building materials, low interest rates and better rail and road links.

London was the most affected. Between 1921 and 1931, the population of its inner boroughs declined by 2 per cent while that of the periphery increased by 27 per cent. Some areas, like Wembley in the north, Morden in the south, Hayes to the west and Chingford to the east, almost doubled in size. Villages were swallowed up in great 'ribbon developments'. Individual 'green belt' schemes like that placed around London in 1935, plus several tranches of nationwide town and country planning legislation, restricted but did not halt development.

461

In 1965, the entire county of Middlesex was absorbed by the Greater London Council, a process that had begun in 1888 when parts of it like Hammersmith were sliced off to help form the new county of London.

▶ The **architectural** style of suburbia deliberately mimicked what was perceived to be a national golden age of the sixteenth century. Just as American developments echoed the painted white wooden frames, shuttered windows and picket fences of the Pioneer home, so British ones echoed the black timber beams, brick walls and privet hedges of the Tudor manor house. This design – which the illustrator Osbert Lancaster (1908–86) called 'By-Pass Variegated' – reflected the desire of many people for an *ersatz* rural lifestyle. But practicality was always a stronger motive than fantasy. Suburban homes, with their fitted gardens and proximity to the countryside, placed their owners closer to the fresh air and recreational amenities that previous generations had desired but could not afford.

The main appeal of the suburban home was comfort and conven-
▶ ience. As well as **gardens**, most had their own bathrooms and indoor lavatories. The more expensive ones in the outer suburbs also came with garages, central heating and revolutionary labour-saving devices like washing machines. The electrification of Britain was a key factor in the growth of suburbia. Supply was patchy until the Electricity Supply Act of 1926 began the development of the National Grid. Domestic appliances were not only powered by it, they were also made in the light industrial factories around which most suburbs sprang up. The electrification of railway lines and, in the south-east, extensions to the London Underground, were augmented by the growth of car ownership, making it easier to travel to and from the city.

'Stake your claim at Edgware,' said a London Underground poster of the time in an echo of the American gold rush. 'It converts pleasant, undulating fields into happy homes . . . a shelter which comprises all the latest labour-saving and sanitary conveniences. We moderns ask much more before we are content than the ancients, and Edgware is designed to give us that much more.' Adverts like this captured the social aspirations that lured so many lower-middle-class families out to the suburbs. Those aspirations, and the essential modernity of suburbia, made it a focal point of debate about the future of British society. 'The place to look for the germs of the future England,' wrote
▶ **George Orwell** in 1941, 'is in the light industry areas and along the arterial roads.'

Most of his contemporaries were horrified at the prospect. Rural romantics on the left and the right deplored the fact that great tracts of the countryside were being destroyed and ancient villages turned into dormitory towns for commuters. Critics also saw the suburbs as
▶ the locus of a more atomised and philistine **consumer** society. In *The*

Suburbans (1905) one wrote that a visit would help you to understand 'the cheapness and out-of-jointedness of the times; you will comprehend the *raison d'être* of halfpenny journalism . . . why gramophones, bamboo furniture, pleasant Sunday afternoons, modern **language**, ◀ teas, golf, tennis, high school **education**, dubious fiction, shilling's ◀ worth of comic writing, picture postcards, miraculous hair restorers, prize competitions, and all other sorts of twentieth-century clap-trap have got a market and a use, and black masses of supporters'.

Such was the antipathy that by the 1930s some critics – most famously, **John Betjeman** – were openly relishing the suburbs being ◀ bombed by enemy aircraft. His friend, Osbert Lancaster, wrote, 'It is sad to reflect that so much ingenuity should have been wasted on streets and estates which will inevitably become the slums of the future . . . an eventuality that does much to reconcile one to the prospect of aerial bombardment.' After the Second World War, suburbia became the object more of satire than of detestation – its obsession with privacy and family life standing as much for sexual and social repression as it did for material consumption. Not for nothing did so many of Britain's pop stars (John Lennon among them) hail from the suburbs, their songs littered with mixed feelings about growing up there. Although most used their wealth to buy mansions in the Home Counties, they also helped to make the city fashionable once again.

Despite rising **crime** rates, poor schools and a decaying **transport** ◀ infrastructure, the inner cities began a revival during the 1960s for three reasons. First, the burgeoning creative industries were based there. Second, for all the mistakes made by town planners, the mess left by the Luftwaffe had been cleared up. Third, the city was a healthier place thanks to the Clean Air Act of 1954. Once the middle classes decided that they would rather like to live in town again, property prices shot up and millions were priced out of urban accommodation. Suburbs offered a relatively cheap alternative. A desire to escape the ethnic minorities who inhabited the poorer areas of the UK's cities contributed to the working- and lower-middle-class drift from them.

The electricity pylon, the arterial road and the suburban semi were emblems of the success and the failure of consumer society. The suburbs were comfortable and convenient but they could also be repressive and desolate places. Suburbia's inhabitants rested not only on a meridian between town and country, but also on one between society and the individual.

■ Suez crisis

In July 1956 Egypt's President Nasser nationalised the Suez Canal Company, whose main shareholder was the British government although the Canal itself had been constructed by the French in the 1860s. By agreement, British troops had been withdrawn from the role of guarding the Canal in June 1956, and Britain and America had just announced their refusal to finance the Aswan High Dam, which Nasser wanted to construct on the Nile. Nationalisation without compensation was Nasser's response. Various attempts at a compromise solution to the Canal issue came to nothing.

▶ The British **Conservative** Prime Minister, Sir Anthony Eden, had already concluded that Nasser was a Middle Eastern version of Hitler,

▶ and having made his reputation opposing **appeasement** he was determined to humiliate (and if possible depose) the Egyptian leader. He found a willing accomplice in the French; some of their citizens owned shares in the company, and they were currently fighting a desperate war in Algeria, against rebels backed by Egypt. France was a close ally of Israel, which was also delighted to find an opportunity to attack its greatest regional foe.

In accordance with a secret deal, Israel attacked Egypt at the end of October 1956. The British and French then offered to mediate – in the circumstances, a preposterous notion, which the two countries expected Nasser to refuse. When this duly occurred Anglo-French forces attacked and quickly captured Port Said. The road to Cairo seemed open to them; certainly the Canal zone was at their mercy, although the waterway itself had been blocked by the Egyptians. But on the day after the invasion Britain abruptly agreed to a ceasefire. The American President Eisenhower faced an imminent election, and a major international crisis would undermine his claim to have helped secure world peace. Britain required US support to halt a run on the pound, and the aid would not be forthcoming unless the fighting stopped. The invaders were also censured by the General Assembly of the United Nations (UN).

At home, Eden's position was initially strengthened on a wave of jingoistic sentiment. Only two ministers resigned but there were

▶ fierce clashes in **parliament**; **Labour**'s leader Hugh Gaitskell made a televised appeal to potential Conservative rebels to overthrow the Prime Minister. In fact, Eden was unfit to govern, mainly through the effects of a long-term illness and the mind-affecting drugs he was taking for his condition. He resigned in January 1957.

Suez is often seen as a major turning point in British history. More accurately, it marked the time when the majority of politicians realised that the world had already changed for ever, because of the Second World War. Although some Conservative backbenchers continued to resist reality, the crisis made membership of a supra-

▶ national **European** body more likely (although, ironically, the evidence that Britain was in the pocket of the Americans also increased the likelihood of a veto on British membership by the French, who somehow escaped most of the odium). It also helped to inspire a revival of the **Liberal Party** – or at least to keep that ailing ◄ body in existence – since it evoked a lasting hostility towards the Conservatives among some middle-class voters who would never dream of supporting Labour. Probably the subsequent rundown of British **armed forces** would not have been so rapid without Suez; and ◄ the retreat from Imperial outposts, notably Cyprus, was accelerated. The lasting effect on the general public is more doubtful. Although it exposed the '**special relationship**' as something like a bad joke, ◄ people did not seem to grasp even this obvious point. Perhaps they were genuinely confused because the military action, as opposed to the diplomacy, indicated that the British were still a force to be reckoned with.

It can be argued that Eden was merely unlucky with his timing, and that the Americans might have acquiesced if Eisenhower had not been up for re-election. But the duplicity leading up to the invasion, and the failure even to test the US reaction in advance by an oblique approach, suggests not. Significantly, Eden seems to have given little thought to his next steps if the invasion had proved successful. Nasser's ally, the Soviet Union, would have found it difficult to remain idle (instead, it seized the opportunity of crushing an uprising in Hungary). From that time on, the British were happy to play second fiddle to the US in the Middle East – as in most other world regions – as the only way of staying in the orchestra at all.

■ Suffragette movement

During the **parliamentary** debates leading up to the second Reform ◄ Act of 1867, the philosopher and **Liberal** MP John Stuart Mill moved ◄ that the word 'person' should be substituted for 'man' in a measure which greatly increased the existing franchise in Britain. The vote was lost 'amid much merriment', by 196 to 73. But much of the newspaper coverage was serious; and Mill's opponents had been forced to dredge up some desperate arguments, including the idea that **women** did not ◄ need the vote because they already influenced their husbands. Their real objection was that women were simply too irrational to exercise the vote; and, since the sexist system denied a satisfactory education for all but a handful of women at that time, Mill's opponents could feel that one injustice validated the other. Even so, the argument begged a subversive question, because at that time voters qualified by means of their property, not their ability to think sensibly; and whatever one thought of the discriminatory laws against married women, the position of wealthy spinsters and widows seemed grossly anomalous. Mill's

▶ opponents also had to tread rather carefully to avoid presenting a case which would cast doubt on the position of their female **monarch**; and propertied women did already enjoy the right to hold public office in their parishes.

Sweet reason having failed, some campaigners for women's suffrage decided on more militant tactics at the beginning of the twentieth century. In October 1903 Emmeline Pankhurst, the widow of a lawyer and well-known member of the Independent Labour Party (ILP), founded the Women's Social and Political Union (WSPU) in Manchester. In 1905 Mrs Pankhurst's daughter Christabel and other activists were jailed after disrupting a political meeting and refusing to pay fines. By June 1909 these tactics had been taken further, and the first 'suffragette' hungerstrike began. At first this seemed like a handy get-out-of-jail card, but later the authorities began to force-feed women who were only in prison because the government denied their civil rights. In 1913 the shameless government passed the 'Cat and Mouse Act', which provided for the re-arrest of women who were temporarily released to recover their health.

In February 1910 the Commons voted in favour of a limited franchise reform, by a majority of over a hundred. But the Bill made no further progress. More than a hundred women (and four men) were arrested during violent clashes outside the House in November 1910. After further procrastination by the government, windows were smashed along Whitehall, and later throughout central London. One previous victim of force-feeding, Emily Davison, was arrested before she set fire to a post box in Parliament Street. After her release Miss Davison helped to plant a bomb which partially destroyed the house

▶ near London which **Lloyd George** was building for himself, then threw herself under the King's horse on Derby Day. Unless she had foreknowledge of the jockey's riding tactics, it was a remarkably accurate (if fatal) lunge on her part; previously she had failed in the relatively simple task of plunging to her death from a prison balcony.

For the obstinate opponents of the suffragettes, such tactics merely proved their point: once women were involved in public life common sense would be swept away on a wave of oestrogen. Even some educated women accepted this idea, and echoed the chauvinist view that members of their sex were incapable of constructing a rational position. The logic of this argument implied that the only women who possessed the mental equipment necessary for voting were those who had no wish to vote. But before the outbreak of war in 1914 the reluctant Prime Minister, Asquith, signalled that the government would include women's suffrage in its next governing programme. The expe-

▶ rience of the **war** itself, with the emergence of so many women to ensure the smooth running of the 'Home Front' while the men were engaged in the most irrational of activities, persuaded even hide-bound misogynists that something ought to be done in a more general expansion of the franchise. At least MPs could make a token gesture in support of the old arguments; while men were now considered rational enough to vote at 21, the 1918 Representation of the People Act set the corresponding age for women at 30, and the property requirements were more rigorous than for men. Thus the militant suffragettes had only been partially successful, despite their subsequent renown as victorious amazons in the democratic cause. Rather, the 1918 settlement more closely matched the beliefs of the less radical National Union of Women's Suffrage Societies, led by Millicent Fawcett who wanted to retain the property qualification.

The anomalous treatment of women was not rectified until 1928. Afterwards, discrimination against women moved to other fields, not least their unequal representation in parliament. When **Margaret** ◄ **Thatcher** became the first woman Prime Minister in 1979, she was one of only 19 female MPs. It was ironic that Thatcher represented a party which was intimately connected to a male-dominated **Establishment**. ◄ Yet, as radicals discovered to their disappointment, for most of the century women were more likely to vote **Conservative** than to reward ◄ the parties which continued to support their claims to the full rights of citizenship.

S

■ Tariff reform; imperial preference

Britain's relative economic decline in the last years of the nineteenth century challenged many orthodox assumptions. In the earlier days of optimism it was easy to believe in the beneficial effects of international free trade, which would bring peoples together and allow purchasers of goods to choose the cheapest available option. Free trade
▶ thus guaranteed peace and prosperity; **government** interference, by contrast, allowed the inefficient to survive and caused friction between states.

On paper the theory seemed incontestable. In practice, though, it was a doctrine which was skewed in favour of the strong. Wherever possible the weak would hope to bend the rules, by protecting their industries through government subsidies or tariff barriers against overseas produce; and by 1900 Britain's economy had significantly
▶ weakened. The **Empire** seemed to offer the chance of stopping the rot. An imperial system of tariffs, which imposed a tax on manufactured goods from third countries – like Germany or the United States – would limit the choice of purchasers within the Empire. But in return they would have a guaranteed outlet for their own exports – food, and raw materials required by British industry – since a tariff wall would make it all but impossible for countries outside the Empire to compete with them in British markets.

For some tariff reformers the idea promised an additional bonus. German unity had begun with the creation of a customs union. The Empire might develop along the same lines, leaving Britain at the centre of a federal state on which the sun would never set. The defence of the Empire in its existing form was hugely expensive. It would be easier to bear if Britain's industrial prosperity were guaranteed, and the revenues raised from the duties paid on any goods imported from outside the customs union would also help to finance the British navy.

By the time of the 1897 Colonial Conference the idea appealed
▶ strongly to Joseph Chamberlain (1836–1914), the former **Liberal** who
▶ had been Colonial Secretary in Lord Salisbury's **Conservative** government since 1895. But Chamberlain's arguments were coolly received by the prime ministers of the eleven British dominions. They might have shared Chamberlain's view that Anglo-Saxons were 'the greatest governing race the world has ever seen . . . which neither climate nor change can degenerate', but they were beginning to assert the interests of their own, self-governing countries. Even if they liked the idea of a tariff wall to keep out the products of third countries, they wanted to retain the right to protect their own fledgling industries from competitors *within* the Empire.

Undeterred by this tepid response, Chamberlain became increasingly obsessed with the policy and in 1903 he resigned from the government to launch a nationwide crusade. But even Chamberlain's impassioned advocacy could not convince the sceptics, who pointed out that an increase in the price of crucial food imports, like North American wheat, would either reduce living standards or induce an increase in wages which would reduce the competitiveness of British industry. This ensured the opposition of many progressives, including the young **Labour Party** (although leading members of the **Fabian** ◄ **Society** were strongly sympathetic). But the main effect of Chamberlain's campaign was to split his own party, which was trounced in the 1906 general election. Even as late as 1923, when most Conservatives had accepted protectionism, it could still cause them trouble. **Stanley** ◄ **Baldwin**'s decision to call a general election on the issue resulted in the first (minority) Labour government.

The issue continued to dog the Conservatives up to 1932, when after much wrangling a watered-down system of 'Imperial Preference' was agreed at the Ottawa Conference. Instead of allowing free trade within a protected imperial market, the various countries merely agreed to accept each other's produce on preferential terms – i.e. instead of dismantling the tariffs they had erected against each other, they raised the duties on goods imported from everywhere else. In the wake of the **Great Depression**, what had always been a defensive ◄ strategy now seemed to be the only viable route to economic survival. Even this was too much for the remaining free-trade ideologues within Baldwin's National Government; but this time the chief resignations came from the government's Liberal (Sir Herbert Samuel) and Labour (Philip Snowden) contingents.

The awkward compromise was seen by the British Chancellor of the Exchequer, Joseph Chamberlain's son Neville, as no more than a first step; but it was as far as he ever got. Only the besotted British failed to recognise that the dominions now saw the 'Commonwealth', newly-formalised in the 1931 Statute of Westminster, as a one-way bet. In return for economic benefit and military support, the dominions graciously allowed the British to retain their self-esteem by maintaining their nominal allegiance to the Crown. The tariff system was still in place when Britain joined **Europe** in 1973 – a faded relic of ◄ what had once been a grandiose imperial vision.

■ Taylor, A.J.P. (1906–90)

Alan John Percival Taylor, the son of a wealthy businessman in the then-flourishing cotton trade, was born in Birkdale, Lancashire. His parents were staunch Liberals and opponents of **conscription**. When ◄

▶ the **Liberal Party** took Britain into the First World War and introduced the call-up something had to give, so despite their lack of proletarian credibility they threw themselves with equal enthusiasm into the Labour movement. Their son flirted with Communism at Oxford, but

▶ later joined the **Labour Party**. He was, though, too much of an individualist to be captured by any creed. During an interview for one academic post, Alan was accused of holding strong political views. He offered a more accurate characterisation of his outlook: 'extreme views, weakly held'.

After public schooling at a Quaker establishment, Bootham, near York, Taylor went to Oriel College, Oxford, where he took first-class honours in History. But he seems to have plumped for an academic career in the absence of an attractive alternative, having made a false start in his uncle's legal firm. After researching in the Viennese archives (where he taught himself German), Taylor was appointed to an assistant lectureship at Manchester University in 1930. He specialised in the history of nineteenth-century Europe, reflecting his enduring fascination with the diplomatic mind. His first book, *The Italian Problem in European Diplomacy, 1847–1849* (1934) was academically respectable, heavily crusted with footnotes and concentrating on a relatively narrow issue. Yet there were already signs that Taylor sought an audience outside the ivory towers. The prose was vivid, and he sprinkled the text with provocative one-liners.

Taylor's next book, *Germany's First Bid for Colonies, 1884–1885*, once again dealt with a restricted time-frame. But its publication in 1938 ensured that it would be widely discussed. An early and eloquent

▶ opponent of **appeasement**, Taylor managed to smuggle into a book on Bismarck's foreign policy a claim that Britain had unwittingly encouraged Germany's ambitions over the previous half-century, by bending over backwards to accommodate its demands. The book was unlikely to mollify Taylor's critics within his profession, who detected and deplored his tendency to play to an audience. He had already become a contributor to the *Manchester Guardian*, churning out a regular stream of book reviews and even writing leading articles from the beginning of 1938. Indulging in journalism to supplement an academic income was just about tolerable in itself, but Taylor turned a harmless hobby into an offence in the eyes of his peers by providing entertainment rather than pedantry. Even so, the suspicions were not widespread enough at this stage to obstruct his promotion, and in the same year he became a tutor at Magdalen College, Oxford.

Taylor's evident wish to return to Oxford – the Magdalen job was the third post he had applied for – added what seems an unnecessary complication to his career. He loved the north-west of England, and Manchester University was scarcely an academic backwater. But he wanted to be right at the centre of the action, rather than ending up as an overgrown fish in a medium-sized pond. No sooner had he settled into his post at Magdalen than he began making himself too big even for Oxford. In 1950 he became a regular panellist on the BBC ◀ television discussion programme, *In the News*. It was estimated that about half of the potential audience watched the show, and although at that time this figure amounted to less than 10 per cent of the British population Taylor still became one of the first TV 'celebrities'. Later, he transferred his lecturing technique to television, speaking straight to camera without notes in classic broadcasts on a variety of subjects including revolutions, wars and prime ministers. ◀

It was not that Taylor lacked professional recognition. In 1956 he was made a Fellow of the British Academy, and in the same year delivered the prestigious Ford Lectures at Oxford. Yet his choice of subject for the latter – dissidents in foreign policy – might have been less provocative had he not turned the whole series into something like an advertisement for his own rebellious streak. Speaking without notes in this forum seemed ostentatious, and his choice of title for the published lectures – *The Troublemakers* (1957) – spoke for itself. In the following year this particular 'troublemaker' became a founder-member of the Campaign for Nuclear Disarmament (CND). ◀

The timing of *The Troublemakers* proved unfortunate for Taylor. In June 1957 the Prime Minister, Harold Macmillan, snubbed him by preferring the younger, more conventional Hugh Trevor-Roper (later Lord Dacre) for Oxford's Regius Chair of Modern History. Taylor nursed this as a grievance for the rest of his life, and the controversy breached several important friendships.

As a dedicated Man of Letters, Taylor ought to have known that lasting fame owes little to official titles. In fact, he had already laid down a permanent memorial, in his sweeping diplomatic survey, *The Struggle for Mastery in Europe, 1848–1918* (1954). Despite his left-wing leanings, Taylor had little patience with Marxist historians who concentrated on 'the Common People' rather than 'Great Men'. *The Struggle for Mastery* was a superb narrative of high politics, in which Taylor did not hesitate to use short-hand terms like 'the British' or 'the Germans' when describing the decisions of a handful of decision-makers. Taylor's delight in exploring the inner motivations of the key players in diplomatic history was also displayed in his study of *Bismarck: The Man and the Statesman* (1955). Taylor had changed his mind on this subject since 1938. Far from being the bogeyman of popular British legend, Bismarck emerges as a skilful pragmatist, whose departure from office removed the best guarantee of lasting peace in Europe.

The failure to secure the Regius Chair seems to have provided Taylor with the necessary licence to attack other cherished preconceptions. Having rehabilitated Bismarck, it was a natural step for him to re-examine the Hitler problem in *The Origins of the Second World War* (1961). The book caused genuine offence among opponents of fascism. Amid the furore, few of these critics noticed that in emphasising Hitler's opportunism rather than his ideology, Taylor had switched the indictment from one individual to the whole German nation. In any case, he was hardly flattering about the Führer, quipping that, 'A racing tipster who only reached Hitler's standards of accuracy would not do well for his clients.'

While *The Origins* was a salutary counterpunch against prevailing orthodoxies, Taylor's refusal to take ideas seriously was a real weakness, which he shared with his erstwhile friend and colleague at Manchester, Lewis Namier. The same defect was apparent in *English History 1914–1945* (1965), in which Taylor also confessed that he had neglected scientific developments because he did not understand them. Even so, *English History* was one of the great books of the twentieth century. All the ingredients of the book which were designed to delight the general reader seemed deliberately calculated to offend his fellow historians, who in any case thought that any attempt to discuss events of the fairly recent past could be no better than hack journalism. Yet the brilliance of Taylor's book forced a respectful response from reviewers. Questions which had inspired dull and detailed monographs from plodding scholars were dismissed with a breezy epigram. Instead of a reverential reference to the work of others, the typical Taylor footnote was an aside which even he considered too pungent for inclusion in the main text. He over-emphasised the paradoxical, not only because he loved digging out unexpected twists in the narrative for his readers, but also because he knew these passages would pull them up and make them think for themselves.

▶ Taylor's last major book, a biography of **Lord Beaverbrook** (1971), was something of an anti-climax. Like other radicals, notably Michael Foot, Taylor fell under Beaverbrook's spell (although he insisted that his lucrative work for the *Sunday Express* began before he had even met the mercurial proprietor). The book shows that although Taylor was usually sound in his choice of heroes, his judgement was better when he worshipped them at a distance. Just before the onset of the Parkinson's disease which killed him, Taylor also wrote about another of his great heroes – himself. The result, *A Personal History* (1983), again fell below his highest standards. One of his difficulties was discussing his tangled private life. He solved part of the problem by failing to mention his second wife at all. But he could hardly avoid discussing the break-up of his first marriage after his wife became infatuated, first with one of Alan's students, the later historian and ITN newsreader Robert Kee, then with the poet Dylan Thomas. Although Taylor did find lasting happiness at the third attempt, with the Hungarian historian Eva Haraszti, his chequered marital career suggests that his detractors did have a point in thinking that Taylor made many of his troubles for himself.

■ Temple, William (1881–1944)

The first socialist Archbishop of Canterbury (1942–4), known as 'the People's Archbishop' and credited with beginning the Church of England's transformation from a politically conservative body into a liberal one. He was born in Exeter and got a head start in the ecclesiastical world by being the son of Frederick Temple, Archbishop of Canterbury (1896–1902). William was educated at Balliol College, Oxford, and ordained while a Fellow at Queen's College (1904–10). In 1910, he was appointed headmaster of the public school, Repton, and thereafter his progress through the Church was rapid. He became Rector of St James's, Piccadilly (1914), Canon of Westminster (1919), Bishop of Manchester (1921) and Archbishop of York (1929) before assuming the see of Canterbury at the height of the Second World War.

Temple shared his father's belief in social justice and the importance of mass education in the struggle to achieve it, but he took that belief a step further. While his father's closest friend was Matthew Arnold, his was R.H. Tawney, whose Christian socialism profoundly influenced the ideology of the Labour Party. Temple joined the party in 1918, and it formed the bedrock of his own attempt to marry secular and spiritual citizenship in works like *Mens creatrix* (1917), *Christus veritas* (1924) and *Nature, Man and God* (1934). Like many radical luminaries of his generation, such as Beveridge and Keynes, he was at heart more of a liberal. But with the Liberal Party in disarray, like them he knew that Labour offered the best hope for progressives. He left the party in 1925, feeling that its leaders were simply using him for their own political ends. He supported Prayer Book Reform in 1928, though, unusually for a religious leader, he was as good an administrator as he was a theologian. He was President of the Workers' Educational Association (1908–24), Chairman of COPEC (1924), a pioneering ecumenical summit held to discuss inequality, and Chairman of the Anglican Conference on Unemployment which resulted in the report *Men Without Work* (1938). In 1942 Temple provided the Labour Party with its finest theological justification, *Christianity and Social Order*. Written with the help of John Maynard Keynes, it argued that a Christian society could not be created without institutionalising equality of opportunity or without a welfare system that cared for those who were incapable of using that

T

opportunity. *Christianity and Social Order* became the best-selling theological tract ever published in Britain; it was widely accepted as the
Christian counterpart of the Beveridge Report and, as such, it formed
the religious basis of post-war social democracy. 'Human status,' he
wrote, 'ought not to depend upon the changing demands of the
economic process.'

▶ Although **Winston Churchill** received fair warning that Temple
was no Tory, he appointed him to Canterbury on the grounds of his
popularity, knowing that a charismatic Archbishop would help to
maintain public morale. Temple did not disappoint. While avoiding
the idea that God was an Englishman, he defined why the conflict
with Nazi Germany was a just war for the defence of Christian civilisation and he supported the RAF's bombing of German cities. In a
speech to the House of Lords on 23 March 1943, Temple became the
first Church leader in the world to condemn the Nazis' treatment of
▶ the **Jews**. Pope Pius XII's failure to do the same stretched Temple's
ecumenical beliefs to the limit but did not break them. In 1942, he
established the British Council of Churches and he was instrumental
in setting up the World Council of Churches, which met for the first
time in 1945. Unlike most British leaders of the time, Temple did not
▶ regard the prospect of **European Union** as a **Roman Catholic**
conspiracy. Indeed, he was a keen federalist, being one of the founding
members of Beveridge's pressure group Federal Union (1940).

Temple's premature death from a heart attack was genuinely
mourned by the public and by other religious leaders. His ecclesiastical
legacy, secured by the liberalising Primacy of Michael Ramsay (1904–88;
1961–74), was to detach Anglicanism from its traditional moorings to
▶ the **Conservative Party**, without allying it too closely with any other
party and while retaining the political benefits of being an established
state Church. In so doing he helped to maintain the Church of
England's popularity and relevance in an age of secularisation.

■ Thatcher, Margaret Hilda (b. 1925)

▶ The daughter of a grocer of **Liberal** sympathies who later became a
▶ **Conservative**-supporting alderman, Margaret Roberts was born in
Grantham in October 1925. After studying chemistry at Somerville
College, Oxford, she worked in the food industry before reading for
the Bar. But she already hoped for a career in politics, having been
active in the Oxford University Conservative Association (OUCA). She
▶ made her first attempt to enter **parliament** in the unwinnable
Dartford seat at the 1950 general election, losing again in 1951. A few
months after this second contest she married a wealthy divorced businessman, Denis Thatcher, and gave birth to twins in August 1953.

Women still found it difficult to make headway in the post-war ◀ Conservative Party, but attitudes were slowly changing and Mrs Thatcher had attracted some notice during her Dartford campaigns. In 1955 she won the seat of Finchley, in north London. She became a junior minister at Pensions and National Insurance in 1961. But at a time when the party tended to look for just one 'token woman' on its front bench she had to wait for further promotion. Only in 1967 did she take a front-bench role, as the Shadow spokesperson on Power. When the Conservatives won the 1970 general election Edward Heath made her Secretary of State for Education. She proved to be a doughty defender of the departmental budget, although she was unhappy with its encouragement of **comprehensive** education. Her most publicised ◀ action, cutting free school milk for 8- to 11-year-olds, won her the nick-name 'Thatcher the Milk Snatcher'. It was an unfair tag, because the policy had been imposed by the Treasury. By contrast, Mrs Thatcher's successful battle to save the fledgling Open University went almost unnoticed.

In March 1975 Mrs Thatcher was elected as Heath's successor, over-coming the dual handicaps of being a woman and a right-wing figure in a party which had avoided ideological leadership since the days of Andrew Bonar Law. Her victory owed much to the advice of skilful tactical advisers, but she also won credit for her courage in standing against her own party leader. Although her campaign was directly crit-ical of the Heath government, she seemed unabashed by claims that she had raised no objections while the policies were being devised and carried out. In fact, she had shown her interest in economic liberalism as an alternative to the general **Keynesian** consensus before 1970; she ◀ was certainly not a late convert to the doctrine.

Even at this stage, it was clear that Mrs Thatcher thought of her political career as something like a crusade – a battle between right and wrong, rather than a series of choices among flawed alternatives. But when Britain elected a Conservative government in 1979 most people had little grasp of her views on any subject other than race, where she had shown her sympathies with **Enoch Powell** in a televised ◀ 1978 interview. Since the **Labour** government was so unpopular, it ◀ could be argued that any Conservative leader would have won in 1979 – unless they said anything to frighten the voters. So Mrs Thatcher prudently accepted advice to tone down her views.

The coherence of **Thatcherism** has been much disputed, and the ◀ Prime Minister herself was usually more cautious than her critics imagined. But in office it soon became clear that her overall goal was to effect a redistribution of power and wealth towards the middle classes from which she had arisen, in the belief that the existing tax system both penalised hard work and created 'dependency' among

▶ those who relied on the **welfare state**. Like Lenin, she was only a pragmatist when this looked likely to serve the long-term interests of her revolution.

In 1981 Mrs Thatcher revealed her extraordinary will-power by fighting off demands for a radical change of course, in the face of clear
▶ evidence that **monetarism** was creating economic problems instead of
▶ solving them. Despite rising **unemployment** and inner-city rioting, she declared that there would be no policy 'U-turn'. Having attacked Heath for performing just such a detour, the Prime Minister rightly believed that her own survival in office was at stake. Although the
▶ outlook for the party had improved before the 1982 **Falklands War**, Mrs Thatcher's robust performance during the crisis made her invulnerable. Conservative victories followed in the general elections of 1983 and 1987, by which time the economic clouds had lifted for most people. A record of three successive wins was unprecedented in the twentieth century, but Mrs Thatcher still felt that her legacy was insecure. This mixture of triumphalism and pessimism reflected the balance of her Cabinet, which accommodated dogmatic Thatcherites, such as the combative Secretary of State for the Environment Nicholas Ridley; exemplars of an older style of conservatism who had accepted office out of a sense of duty; and (ever-increasingly) careerists who would back any winning horse until its luck ran out.

The party rebellion which removed Mrs Thatcher from office in November 1990 arose from a mixture of motives. Some MPs were
▶ worried by the Prime Minister's growing antagonism to **Europe**; others feared that they would lose their seats if the government
▶ retained its much-hated Community Charge (or **Poll Tax**). Although the parliamentary party had moved to the right in the image of its leader, there were still a number (including Heath himself) who had never pretended to be reconciled with Thatcherism. Although this faction was overjoyed by her ejection from Downing Street, it might have served their interests better had Mrs Thatcher survived to fight the next election. The Conservatives would almost certainly have lost, paving the way for a far-reaching policy reassessment which her successor, John Major, was never in a position to conduct: and the fact that Mrs Thatcher retired undefeated by the public allowed her supporters to contrast her unblemished record with that of Heath, who lost three elections out of four.

After her departure, Baroness Thatcher continued to advise (if not to haunt) her successors, urging in particular that they should deal with Britain's Continental partners in a manner that was incompat-
▶ ible with British membership of the **European Union** (EU). Only towards the end of the twentieth century did her appeal begin to wane among Conservative voters. People tended to forget the difficulties of

the early 1980s, when even well-run companies were driven to bankruptcy as a direct result of government policy; and once she had joined the House of Lords right-wingers could lament that 'Mrs Thatcher would have sorted out this problem', free from any possibility that their wishes would be visited on them. But Thatcher's supporters had criticised Heath for being a 'bad loser', and as the years passed their heroine opened herself to the same strictures. Her intervention on behalf of William Hague's campaign for the party leadership in 1997 was particularly unfortunate. Although Hague's own ideas had been shaped by Thatcherism the party needed a fresh start, and from the outset the ghost of the Baroness dogged his footsteps. Before the 2001 general election she made no secret of her opposition to multi-culturalism, at a time when party strategists were desperate to defuse the issue.

The apparent contradictions in Lady Thatcher's career are well known. Like many Thatcherites she was far more generous (and affable) among private friends than she was in public, where she tended to treat people according to their ideological leanings. A fierce ◄ defender of British **sovereignty**, in 1985 she championed the Single European Act which diluted the ability of ministers to veto the Community's decisions; a theoretical opponent of the central state, she attacked with vigour the autonomy of **local government**; an ◄ enthusiastic (if somewhat superficial) **moralist**, she condoned behav- ◄ iour among her key ministers which led to the association of her party with 'sleaze', and allegations of corrupt dealings touched even her own family. If there is a single key to understanding the legacy of her governments, it lies in her belief that something approaching the outlook (and prosperity) of Victorian Britain could be restored. Yet in a materialist, godless society, appeals to individual self-interest were always more likely to provoke an outburst of heedless consumption and shady dealing than a revival of thrift and upright conduct in business, politics or family life.

■ Thatcherism

Traditionally, members of the **Conservative Party** have eschewed ◄ ideology, claiming that their decisions have been based on a sceptical, pragmatic outlook. However, with the election as leader of **Margaret** ◄ **Thatcher** in February 1975, the party adopted a more confrontational approach towards the 'socialist' enemy. Mrs Thatcher herself felt that her party needed to fight a 'battle of ideas' with the same kind of weapons allegedly favoured by **Labour**. Some of her admirers still deny ◄ that there was any such thing as 'Thatcherism', and that she was guided by instinct rather than a rigid blueprint for government.

However, this objection seems to rest on a questionable definition of ideology, which would deny that even Lenin was an ideologue since he was capable of compromise.

Certainly Mrs Thatcher was highly ideological by previous British standards. When she became Prime Minister in 1979 she was determined to transform her country's fortunes, and in office she proved (comparatively) inflexible in her advocacy of a few key principles.

▶ **Inflation** should be controlled by **monetarist** methods; **trade union** power should be shackled by law; the state should abandon detailed supervision of the economy; direct taxation should be reduced as far as possible; and 'entrepreneurs' should be encouraged to create wealth. Vehement nationalism was another feature; ultimately for Mrs Thatcher it overrode all the others, but fortunately for her this only became apparent when she had already won three elections.

None of these ideas were new: far from it. But they represented a
▶ marked contrast with the post-war **consensus** – the general framework of ideas which had prevailed in political circles since 1945 (if not before). In combination, they are best characterised as the application of nineteenth-century liberalism in a new context. Mrs Thatcher, whose family background was a typical seedbed for this type of thinking, habitually alluded to the Victorian period as one in which Britain prospered because of its 'Thatcherite' ideals. Actually, this begged two unanswerable questions. If the ideas had been so successful, why were they ever abandoned? And Victorian prosperity had crucially been underpinned by widely shared assumptions regarding personal conduct, such as the value of thrift and self-denial. On Mrs Thatcher's own analysis these attributes had been eroded (by
▶ 'socialists' and '**permissives**') since 1945. But if they did not spring back to life after all those years of decadence, it was likely that the reintroduction of 'market principles' would merely accentuate existing trends which Thatcherites deplored.

From this perspective, arguments over the bare economic record of Thatcherism are of secondary importance. More to the point would be
▶ evidence of a moral revival, as reflected in the statistics for **crime**,
▶ failing **marriages** and personal debt, etc. One of the beauties of Thatcherism as an electoral strategy was that alarming evidence in these areas, where the Conservatives were traditionally trusted, was actually taken by many as an additional reason for re-electing the government which had made matters worse. It was only when senior
▶ Labour spokesmen (notably **Tony Blair** as Shadow Home Secretary from 1992 to 1994) began to take their arguments into Tory territory that significant numbers of voters began to view the social ideas associated with Thatcherism as little more than a series of vague aspirations, dusted down for rhetorical purposes. Thatcher's successor John

Major inadvertently lent a hand. His 'Back to Basics' initiative of 1993 suggested that after fourteen years of Conservative rule the 'basics' were badly in need of restoration. Press coverage of numerous scandals put to rest any idea that the parliamentary Conservative Party was a suitable vehicle for this task.

Some might argue that while Thatcherism has signally failed to bring 'harmony' out of 'discord' (as Mrs Thatcher herself promised in 1979) this would have been beyond the power of any government. For them, the ideology should be judged on the economic record after all. Only the most infatuated would acknowledge that there was no 'miracle' in this field (as some overheated commentators briefly claimed). Taxation was not reduced. The burden was shifted, instead, from the rich to the poor. Overall **economic growth** was respectable ◀ by post-war standards, but no better; and the lurches from bust to boom and back again provoked new levels of insecurity.

The argument that Thatcherism arrested a precipitate decline hinges on the assumption that Britain would have fallen apart without it, and this can never be proved. Perhaps the one unequivocal 'success' was that the gap between rich and poor has widened substantially; Thatcherites never made any bones about the need to reverse decades of redistribution through the tax system.

Thatcherism has certainly curbed trade union power. But even here there are problems. Satisfactory industrial relations rest on achieving an elusive balance between the rights of employers and workers. To the extent that Conservative governments after 1979 insisted on returning to the problem long after it seemed to have been solved, they risked making the unions more popular and provoking a backlash when conditions changed. More seriously, the path to reform was smoothed by mass **unemployment**. Like the growth in inequality, this could be ◀ marked down as a Thatcherite 'success', since the Prime Minister and her allies believed that previous governments had merely deferred the problem by subsidising 'artificial' jobs. Those who suffered long-term unemployment will probably refuse to accept that their plight was 'a price worth paying', as the loyal Thatcherite Chancellor Norman Lamont put it after she had gone. The threat of unemployment, rather than the 'incentives' provided by lower direct taxation, tended to make people work harder; but it did not make them any happier – or more inclined to exercise the 'Victorian value' of thrift.

Privatisation was a qualified success. The proceeds were squan- ◀ dered, but that was not an inevitable corollary of Thatcherite theory. Yet it was taken too far after Mrs Thatcher's departure, and here the theory is surely culpable. Council house sales were deservedly popular; but whether or not they helped, they certainly did not hinder the boom in house prices at the end of the 1980s. This unsustainable bubble, which burst at the expense of many families who thought that Thatcherism had been an unmixed blessing, was perhaps the clearest indication that the ideology could only operate with any degree of safety in specific cultural contexts, which Britain clearly lacked in the 1980s and 1990s.

After Mrs Thatcher's fall, Major hoped to 'consolidate', retaining those policies which had proved successful and jettisoning others. He ▶ got as far as disposing of the hated **Poll Tax** (almost a surreal application of Thatcherite theory) – but either could or would not deviate further. After this failure, Tony Blair was elected in 1997 in part because he seemed to offer hope of a quieter life. But Thatcherism had taken hold, not least because in practice it made life easier for ministers who no longer had to supervise industries which had never been ▶ intended to make a profit. Despite the **'New' Labour** government's rhetoric, privatisation continued, (direct) taxation was held down and inequality widened further. Thatcherite media barons were cultivated, ▶ and the ex-premier herself was invited to Downing Street. But **public opinion poll** evidence suggested that all governments since 1979 had been elected in spite of Thatcherism, not because of it. By 2003 British people and politicians were more estranged than ever before; and while it might have seemed rather convenient for remaining left-wingers to pin all the blame for this development on the 1980s, the thesis was worthy of detailed investigation.

■ Trade unions

Strong feelings about the trade unions were a constant feature in Britain throughout the twentieth century. For some, they were a malevolent force, at best irresponsible but more often treacherous. For others they were a romantic source of inspiration – a last bastion of solidarity in an increasingly atomised world. Yet since polling began their popularity has been remarkably constant. Even in 1979, when ▶ **Margaret Thatcher's Conservative Party** rose to power on an alleged wave of anti-union sentiment, the polling organisation Gallup found that more than half of the population agreed with the general proposition that trade unions were a 'good thing'. At the same time, the unions have never represented more than half of the working population (their nearest approach was in 1974, a year of almost constant industrial trouble, when the figure was almost 12 million). By the end of the twentieth century the proportion had dwindled to around a third (6.8 million members). The National Union of Mineworkers (NUM) had around 1 million members in its heyday; by the year 2000 it had almost disappeared. In the 1970s children would groan as their television programmes were interrupted by lengthy broadcasts from the annual conference of the Trade Union Congress (TUC). By the end of the century this event was hardly covered at all, even in the nightly news bulletins.

Throughout the twentieth century **governments** intervened to ◀ strike what they considered to be an appropriate legal balance between workers and employees. In 1901 the House of Lords over-turned an Appeal Court ruling in the case of the Taff Vale Railway Company. In defiance of the existing law, the Conservative-dominated Upper House had decided that unions could be sued by a company for losses incurred during a trade dispute. Since many of his MPs were delighted by the ruling, the Conservative Prime Minister, Arthur Balfour, refused to clarify the law. This task was fulfilled by the **Liberals** in 1906, but the controversy had already inspired many trade ◀ unionists to throw their weight behind the **Labour Party**, which they ◀ had helped to found in 1900. For the next hundred years and beyond, the unions would be an essential source of financial and electoral support for Labour, and for most of that period the union 'block vote' at the party conference was used to back the party's leaders. However, the relationship was not always comfortable; and it came under particular strain during the 1990s.

Things looked very different before the First World War, when the unions became increasingly militant and socialists could dream that they would act as a progressive force. Some were attracted by the idea of political strikes, designed to destroy both the elected government and the capitalist system. Social reforms introduced by the pre-war Liberal governments clearly owed much to fears of **class** conflict. Not ◀ until 1926 was there a well-supported but short-lived **General Strike**, ◀ involving nearly 3 million workers. Against the instincts of the Conservative Prime Minister, **Stanley Baldwin**, a new Trades Disputes ◀ and Trade Union Act was passed in the following year. It outlawed strikes called in sympathy with workers involved in other disputes.

The bitterness aroused by the events of 1926–7 lasted for many decades, particularly since they were followed so quickly by a world-wide economic depression. But after the General Strike a new breed of union leaders, such as Ernest Bevin of the Transport and General Workers (TGWU) and Walter Citrine (Electricians), applied a more pragmatic approach. Strikes would still be called in the last resort. But it was now felt that workers could gain the maximum advantage from playing employers at their own game and even speaking the same language. Before the Second World War, when the whole nation was mobilised as never before (or since), plans for a new co-operative rela-tionship between the 'two sides of industry' were already being laid on the assumption that the union leaders could be trusted, even if the rank and file remained suspect.

T

▸ Trade unionists were well represented in **Churchill**'s wartime coalition, and after Labour's landslide victory in the 1945 general election Bevin became Foreign Secretary. Apart from its worker-friendly
▸ policies on **nationalisation** and the **welfare state**, the Attlee government repealed the 1927 legislation. Although the Conservatives returned to power in 1951, their leaders had endorsed the broad
▸ outlines of the post-war **consensus**, which embraced government, employers and trade unions. It was no accident that in 1954 Gallup found 71 per cent approval for the unions.

Yet the feeling of wartime amity soon dissolved. The British resented prolonged economic austerity after all their sacrifices, and the union leaders wanted a full share of any profits. In 1957 more than 8 million working days were lost through strikes – the highest figure since the General Strike. Two years later, the satirical film *I'm All Right Jack* suggested that corruption and greed were at large (if not rampant) within the union movement. Eric Wigham's Penguin Special *What's Wrong with the Unions* (1961) reinforced the message. There was a growing feeling that the pendulum had swung too far since 1926, and that the unions now enjoyed power without responsibility. Before the war, few workers had been affluent enough to feel much discomfort when certain services were withdrawn. Now they dreamed of 'upward mobility' and were ready to down tools if this looked likely to further their aspirations. But their prosperous fellows were increasingly irritated by such inconveniences. In the new age, militancy and solidarity were becoming mutually exclusive, instead of complementary as the Marxist textbooks assumed.

The 1957–63 Conservative government, led by Harold Macmillan
▸ who had called for a **Keynesian** 'Middle Way' when he represented the industrial constituency of Stockton-on-Tees, pursued a conciliatory course. In 1961 Macmillan established the National Economic Development Council (NEDC, or 'Neddy') as a forum for discussion between government, employers and unions. Under Harold Wilson the next Labour government tried to entrench this 'corporate' approach,
▸ setting ambitious targets for **economic growth**. But the unions were not content with consultation, and although there was a slight fall in the number of stoppages it seemed that Wilson's hopes of painless prosperity were being dashed by his own allies. Opposition within his own party thwarted Barbara Castle's reform proposals, embodied in her 1968 White Paper 'In Place of Strife'.

The Conservatives returned to office in 1970 determined to rein in the unions. Even so, the 1971 Industrial Relations Act was a compromise measure. It introduced a new system of industrial courts to adjudicate on disputes, but also protected employees against unfair dismissal. Most union leaders were still prepared to work with the

Prime Minister, Edward Heath, and some even welcomed the new legislation. But more militant local officials, the 'shop stewards', had different ideas. A strike by miners and other key workers forced the government to introduce a three-day working week early in 1974. When the government called a general election on the issue of 'Who Governs Britain?' it was narrowly defeated. Wilson returned to office, and promptly repealed all the restrictive sections of the Conservative Industrial Relations Act. The new government entered into a 'social contract', which seemed to provide an answer to Heath's question: it was really the unions who ran Britain.

But the new masters had fallen a long way from their post-war peak of popularity. In 1972 a popular song ('Part of the Union', by the **folk** ◄ **music** group the Strawbs) had already underlined the impression that the unions were unreliable custodians of the national interest. Although the Labour Party had been created by the unions, it owed much of its popularity to the idea that its leaders, at least, were capable of looking beyond the selfish interests of union members, whose living standards had already risen markedly since the war. But now the unions were engaged in a futile game of leap-frog, where each new wage increase had to be surpassed by the next group. **Inflation** ◄ would have been the inevitable result, even without the crippling oil shock of 1973–4. Macmillan's strategy had failed. Union involvement in economic policy-making had not inspired them to take a more comprehensive view of Britain's needs.

Ironically, the series of strikes which brought this crazy game to an end could easily have been justified in normal circumstances. By 1978 low-paid public-sector workers had fallen further behind their more powerful 'brothers'; yet as the ultimate paymaster of all these workers the government was well placed to ensure that its pay guidelines stuck in this area, if nowhere else. In the end, the predictable beneficiary of the ensuing strikes (dubbed the '**Winter of Discontent**') was the ◄ Conservative Party. Although other factors were involved, the unions had played a decisive role in driving Labour out of power for eighteen years – and by the time that it returned to office it was led by a man who was far more sympathetic to business interests than to their employees.

In the meantime, the governments of Margaret Thatcher and John Major introduced an endless series of Employment and Trade Union Acts. Whereas the Heath government had definitely blundered in trying to do too much in one go, the Conservatives now erred by legislating too often. Although none of the measures was very radical in itself, there was a cumulative impression that the party was repeatedly kicking the unions when they were down. *Inter alia* they imposed strike ballots, outlawed the 'closed shop', and took away union immunity

from legal action during sympathetic strikes, thus revisiting the archaic arguments of the Taff Vale case. The miners' strike of 1984–5 was seen
▶ as a decisive encounter, from which the government (and the **police**) emerged triumphant. But after that year-long struggle the union movement as a whole regained popularity; by 1987 it had reached its old peak rating of 71 per cent approval. It was the familiar story of the pendulum being forced too far by a government which was widely seen to be acting out of sectional, rather than national, interests.

At the close of the century it was difficult to guess how the trade
▶ unions would fare in future. Arguably, **Tony Blair** was right to prevent the pendulum from swinging back too dramatically. But although
▶ 'New' Labour continued to receive trade union funding – almost £10 million in 2002 – Blair gave the impression of wanting things to stay much as they had been under the Conservatives. The pent-up demand for a redress of the balance may still prove dangerous. Having been on the defensive for so long, union leaders were ideally placed to appear responsible and statesmanlike. Meanwhile, politicians of all parties were generally derided. The number of unions had been greatly reduced – from more than 1,000 in 1939 to around 70 in the last decade of the twentieth century – and this held out the promise that the 'corporatist' vision could finally be realised. But from the government's point of view during the century the main problem had been that union leaders could not be sure of controlling their grass-roots activists – the 'shop stewards' who earned the greatest notoriety in the post-war period. Whether these radical figures, or their more pragmatic leaders, represented the true interest of ordinary workers in a globalised economy marked by drastic inequalities remained an open question.

■ Transport

'I have always thought that the substitution of the internal combustion engine for the horse marked a very gloomy milestone in the progress of mankind,' remarked Winston Churchill in 1954. A generation later the country was in gridlock.

The development of canals, roads and railways in the eighteenth and nineteenth centuries underpinned the Industrial Revolution which urbanised Britain and set it apart from the rest of the Continent. In the twentieth century, the quality of Britain's transport system fell behind that of the Continent and contributed indirectly to the nation's relative economic decline. Railways, the spinal cord of the system, reached a peak of size, usage and profitability in the 1920s. The size of the railway peaked at 21,000 miles of track in 1914, when railway companies employed 750,000 people. The amount of freight they carried rose from 167 million tons in 1870 to 513 million in 1912;

the number of passenger journeys rose from 337 million to 1,580 million in the same period (2,000 million including London). Inter-city journey times fell by a third on average during the century, thanks to the arrival of electric and diesel trains.

However, by the mid-1920s rising levels of car ownership had begun to undermine the profitability of the railways. The problem was unnecessarily worsened by poor logistical planning and low levels of investment. Train companies merged in order to maintain profits. In 1914 there were 100 companies, by 1923 only 4 giants existed. Still, only the Southern Railway extensively electrified its network, benefiting as it did from the economic migration from the north to the south of Britain between the wars. During the Second World War, the ◀ rationing of petrol and the mass transportation of workers, troops, plant and arms put people and goods back on the railways. But it also put a severe strain on the infrastructure of an already rusty system. In 1948, the four remaining train companies were nationalised. But whereas on the Continent networks devastated by Allied and Axis bombing were re-planned and re-built from scratch with massive state investment, in the UK track, stock and buildings had little more than their logos changed to read 'British Rail'.

The situation became critical a decade later with the advent of mass car ownership. In 1950 there were 2.26 million private vehicles in use; by 1970 the number had risen to 11.51 million, and finished the century at 26.5 million, with 73 per cent of households having access to a car, compared to 15 per cent in 1950. By 2001, 85 per cent of passenger kilometres travelled in the UK were by private car or taxi. The amount of freight carried by road also increased. The number of goods vehicles in use rose from 895,000 in 1950 to nearly 3 million in 2001. The death of the British car industry during the 1970s simply meant that roads were clogged with Datsuns, Fords and BMWs instead of Wolsey Hornets, Sunbeam-Talbots and Hillman Minxes (only the Mini maintained the character of British cars). Some of the strain was ◀ taken by the creation of motorways which made the road network about a third longer than it was in 1950 (from the opening of the M1 in 1960 to the end of the century, 3,400 kilometres were constructed). Other forms of road transport were hit by the rush to get behind one's own steering wheel. Bus and coach travel dropped by half despite the 1980 Transport Act which ended the monopoly of the National Coach Company. Cycling fell to only a sixth of its 1950 level.

Railways were the worst hit. Strikes by the National Union of Railwaymen made British Rail even more unreliable and lost it further passenger and freight business. Two strategies were employed to restore the railways' fortunes, both of which failed. The first, recommended by the Beeching Report of 1962, was to cut the network,

T

primarily the unprofitable branch lines that served rural areas. The result was a reduction of track from 18,849 miles in 1958 to 12,478 in 1968 and then to 10,350 in 1998. The number of stations fell from a peak of 8,448 in 1950 to 2,500 by the end of the century. The second

▶ strategy was to **privatise** the system, which the Major government did in 1995. The network was sold off to 20 operating companies, and another one – Railtrack – was established to maintain track and infrastructure. Despite massive government subsidies to these companies, investment targets were not met, fares rose and performance declined. The only beneficiaries were shareholders, and public patience snapped with the Hatfield rail crash of 2000. The crash, which killed four people, proved that safety had been surrendered in the pursuit of profit. The system was effectively shut down for three months while essential maintenance was carried out. Railtrack was put into receivership in 2001, then re-nationalised as Network Rail, though not before the Treasury paid shareholders off to the tune of £5 billion – thus proving that privatised utilities were one of the safest investments for City speculators.

Yet, unlike in the United States, the British railway survived. In America, cheap and safe domestic air travel was a boon for a country where the massive distances between towns could not be covered efficiently by car. In Britain, domestic air travel rose 38-fold in the postwar period. But the smallness of the UK meant that trains could still compete for inter-city traffic, especially since most of Britain's stations had been built by the Victorians in or near town centres, while airports for obvious reasons were not; so the time and cost of travelling to and from them reduced the appeal of cheap air fares. Hence, although the passenger traffic on railways fell from 19.5 million in 1950 to 10 million in 2000, the distance travelled by the remainder increased by 24 per cent.

The viability of the car also began to be questioned. Rural communities benefited from the ability to zip between farms and villages on empty roads, slowed only by the occasional tractor. But Britain's cities became ever more gridlocked, braking the wheels of commerce, filling lungs with noxious emissions and provoking road rage. By 1990, traffic in central London moved at a slower pace than it had in 1890 during the age of horse travel. The introduction of parking meters in 1957 did little to improve matters. The arrival of traffic wardens a decade later

▶ merely relieved pressure on **police** manpower while providing the British with another figure of uniformed authority against which to rail.

One solution to gridlock was the revival of electric light railways or trams. First introduced in Liverpool in 1868, like the rest of the rail network they peaked in the 1920s with 2,605 miles of track in 1924 and 4,706 million journeys in 1928. By the mid-1950s they had virtually disappeared, starved of capital by local authorities anxious to hold down rates and then closed because they interfered with car movement. It was that very reason that led to their re-introduction in Manchester, Sheffield and Croydon in the 1990s. The most effective measure of all was the one least liked by drivers: congestion charging. It cut traffic by a quarter after it was introduced in London in 2003 before being rolled out to other cities in the UK.

In some respects, the biggest factor in changing transport was not the car but the coming of cheap international air travel in the 1970s, as a result of the demand for foreign **holidays**. Outward and inbound ◄ trips from British airports rose 100-fold, from 1.5 million in 1950 to over 140 million in 2000. The architecture of airports, notably Norman Foster's Stansted Terminal (1990), proclaimed the modernity of air travel.

But the car was still king. In 1964 the Canadian thinker Marshall McLuhan wrote, 'The car has become an article of dress without which we feel uncertain, unclad and incomplete in the urban compound'. The British had become more mobile, and so in a sense more free, as a result of the transport revolution of the twentieth century. But they had also become prisoners of their tendency to see consumption as an expression of individuality rather than the fulfilment of need. The car, whether driven by the angry, the drunk or simply the tired, bereaved thousands every year. Globally, it not only damaged the environment; by accelerating the quest for oil, it also drove Britain and the West to war time and again. The car may be the Englishman's mobile castle. ◄ But it also became his private killing machine.

■ The 'Troubles'

Term used to describe the thirty-year civil war that took place in Northern Ireland between 1968 and 1998. Following the **Partition of** ◄ **Ireland** in 1920, the northern Protestant ascendancy – its power institutionalised in the Stormont parliament – discriminated against **Roman Catholics** in almost every area of civil life. Catholics had access ◄ to good **education**, thanks to a proliferation of church schools, grant- ◄ aided by Whitehall. However, access to higher education was restricted; so too was access to healthcare, **housing** and employment ◄ in both the public and private sectors (**unemployment** among ◄ Catholics was twice the level of that among Protestants). Electoral gerrymandering from parish council to parliament was also rife. The 1949 Irish External Relations Act, in which Éire left the Commonwealth and became a republic while retaining its constitutional claim to Ulster, drove a further wedge between north and south. It prompted

Westminster to pass the Northern Ireland Act of 1949 which guaranteed that the province would remain part of the UK until a majority of its people decided otherwise.

Under pressure from the British government, Prime Minister Terence O'Neill (1963-9) began to reform the province. Like most reform programmes it pleased no one. O'Neill didn't go far enough for Catholics and went too far for Protestants. In 1968, the Northern Ireland Civil Rights Association (NICRA) was formed by John Hume and Bernadette Devlin, ostensibly modelling itself on that formed by Martin Luther King to advance the rights of black Americans. NICRA's first march took place on 21 April 1968. It and subsequent marches were violently attacked by loyalist mobs who rightly saw NICRA as a nationalist ginger group. But attacks on Catholics became more indiscriminate while also more organised (old paramilitary groups like the Ulster Defence Association were reformed and new ones like the Ulster Volunteer Force set up). British troops were sent to the province on 14 August 1969 in an effort to keep order and they were initially welcomed by Catholics. Republican militants saw an opportunity to resume the armed struggle for a united Ireland which the Official ▶ IRA had abandoned after the failure of its 1958-62 campaign. Consequently, the Provisional IRA was formed by Sean MacStiofáin, Martin McGuinness and Seamus Twomey on 22 September 1969.

The war entered a new and more bloody phase between 1971 and 1976. Prime Minister O'Neill and his successor James Chichester-Clark (1969-71) resigned and were succeeded by Brian Faulkner, an equally well-meaning member of the Ulster Protestant gentry but equally incapable of containing either the revolutionary insurrection of the IRA or the reactionary forces of Unionism.

The British pursued a policy of unification by consent from 1969 onwards. That policy was motivated by three things: in the nuclear age, Northern Ireland was no longer strategically vital to the British; in addition to which the Irish Republic was no longer a threat, either in itself or as a springboard for other foreign powers to invade the UK: ▶ in 1971, it joined NATO and in 1973 it joined the **European Union** with Britain. Third, the north was no longer of any economic value to the UK. Like Scotland and Wales, its heavy industries went into decline during the 1950s and terrorist bombs finished off the province's economy. By 1980 it had become the most heavily subsidised part of the UK. British patience ran out following the failure of internment without trial of terrorist suspects in August 1971 and the intensification of sectarian violence which followed 'Bloody Sunday' on 30 January 1972 when British soldiers shot 14 men during a NICRA march in Derry City.

On 14 March 1972, the British government brought the fifty-year-old Stormont regime to an end, imposing Direct Rule on the province as a prelude to a tripartite settlement to the conflict. Talks were held at Sunningdale, Berkshire, in December 1973 between Faulkner, the Irish Taoiseach Liam Cosgrave and Edward Heath (the first such summit since 1925). The resulting agreement recommended a new 80-member assembly elected by proportional representation, a power-sharing executive and a Council of Ireland consisting of seven southern Irish and seven Northern Irish ministers to harmonise policy on transport, agriculture, power and tourism. On 23 March 1974, the Protestant Ulster Workers' Council was formed to bring down the Assembly with a general strike, which it achieved on 30 May. The Assembly was formally dissolved in March 1975. An IRA bombing campaign on mainland Britain in 1974–6 provoked a wave of anti-Irish sentiment and forced the government to negotiate secretly with the IRA. But its demands for a complete British withdrawal within three years could not be met and the violence resumed, the most spectacular case being the 1984 bombing of the Grand Hotel in Brighton, which almost killed **Margaret Thatcher** and her Cabinet.

Shaken by the event, in 1985 Thatcher signed the Anglo-Irish Agreement which gave the Republic a regular say in the affairs of the north for the first time. Ten years later the Downing Street Declaration of John Major admitted that the British government had 'no selfish or strategic interest' in the north. The IRA responded with a ceasefire and loyalist paramilitaries followed suit. However, like Callaghan and Wilson in the 1970s, Major was handicapped by his need for the votes of Ulster Unionist MPs (especially in order to get the Maastricht Treaty through parliament). Consequently, there was no further movement until **Tony Blair**'s majority government came to power. A second paramilitary ceasefire began in 1997 and the Good Friday Agreement followed in April 1998. In essence, it was a reprise of the Sunningdale deal, there being two differences: first, the Republic renounced its constitutional claim to the north in return for a cross-border Council of Ireland; and second, the IRA carried out a partial decommissioning of its weapons.

A referendum was held north and south on 22 May 1998 (the first all-island vote since the general election of 1918) that resulted in 71.1 per cent approving the deal. However, serious divisions remained. While 94 per cent of southern voters said yes, only 52 per cent of northern ones did. After 3,400 deaths, billions of pounds worth of material damage and several false dawns, power was devolved back to the province on 1 October 2000. But it remained to be seen how sincere Sinn Féin/IRA were about pursuing the re-unification of Ireland by democratic means and how sincere Unionists were about power-sharing. The Assembly was prorogued in 2002 with each side claiming that the other had failed to give peace a chance.

■ Turing, Alan Mathison (1912–54)

English mathematician whose pioneering theoretical work laid the foundations for the invention of the modern computer. Turing was
▶ born into an upper-middle-class imperial family. Like many children of his background, he was deposited in a boarding school while his parents lived abroad, in India where his father was a civil servant. While at Sherborne School in Dorset he showed a flair for mathematics and realised that he was homosexual. When Christopher Morcom, a boy with whom he had fallen in love, died of tuberculosis, Turing's religious faith was shattered and this led him to believe that all phenomena must have logical, material explanations.

▶ The **public-school** system also gave him a foretaste of the disdain for technology that was present in some quarters of the British ruling elite, an attitude that would hold back his career and, to some extent, his country's prosperity. After Turing carried out chemistry experiments which diverged from a teacher's brief, his headmaster wrote, 'He must aim at becoming educated. If he is to be solely a Scientific Specialist, he is wasting his time at a Public School.' As an undergraduate (1931–4) and then as a Fellow (1934–6), Turing found a more congenial home at
▶ King's College, Cambridge, which then played host to **John Maynard Keynes**. Soon after Keynes published the book that revolutionised world economics, *The General Theory of Employment, Interest and Money* (1936), Turing completed the defining work of modern computer science, 'On Computable Numbers', published for a small academic audience in *Proceedings of the London Mathematics Society* (1937).

Applying mathematical logic to mechanical engineering, Turing aimed to capture what the human mind does when carrying out a procedure, using what he called the 'Universal Machine'. Later known as the Turing Machine, it went far beyond both the 'analytical engine' of the Victorian mathematician Charles Babbage (1791–1871), who proposed the use of pre-punched cards to crunch numbers, and the teleprinter that used paper tape moving in one direction punching holes to convey alphanumeric messages. In the Turing Machine, a paper tape would move in both directions, reading, creating *and* erasing all kinds of data. These operations would be effected by systemic 'tables of behaviour' that would also allow different machines to speak to each other, the equivalent of a software programme today. Crucially, Turing also created a language for his machine, based on the decimal expansion of the digit 1 – the prototype of today's binary system. He saw that the key to practical computing was to discover how the infinite could be made 'calculable by finite means', thus avoiding the need to build a mechanical brain the size of the Albert Hall.

What Alan Turing did was to describe a computer before mathematical thought, still less electronic technology, had reached the point where the construction of one was possible. The prophetic nature of *On Computable Numbers* was not comparable to Leonardo's fifteenth-century sketch of a helicopter. It does, perhaps, compare to the relationship between Einstein's *General Theory of Relativity* (1916) and Robert Oppenheimer's explosion of an atom bomb at Los Alamos in July 1945, though with less destructive results, that bear more relation to the invention of steam power in the eighteenth century.

During a brief spell at Princeton (1937–9), Turing completed a PhD then returned to Britain and offered his services to the war effort. As in many areas of British life, the war galvanised the state into increasing the funding for scientific endeavour. Turing was recruited by the Government Code and Cypher School, based at Bletchley Park in Buckinghamshire. There, he played a major part in designing Colossus, a primitive electronic calculating machine that was able to decipher the codes sent to and from German U-boats in the North Atlantic, thus saving thousands of lives.

Soon after receiving an OBE for this work in 1945, he joined the National Physical Laboratory at Teddington and in March the following year he put forward detailed plans for what he now called an Automatic Computing Engine (ACE). Influenced by the work of the German mathematician Konrad Zuse and the Hungarian-born American, John von Neumann (who helped to develop the atom bomb), Turing substituted paper tape with electronic components because of the greater speed and storage capacity that they offered.

He soon discovered that the emergency spirit of the war had dissipated and found his ideas ignored or overruled amid bureaucracy and complacency. Frustrated, in 1948 he accepted an offer from Manchester University to work on a similar project, funded by Ferranti. In 1949 a Cambridge University team led by Maurice Wilkes beat them to creating the world's first fully operational stored-programme computer. But in 1951, the Ferranti Mark I became the world's first commercially available one and, in the same year, Turing was made a Fellow of the Royal Society. Despite the setting up of the National Research Development Corporation (NRDC) in 1949, the British rapidly lost ground to the Americans. The Professor of Mathematical Physics at Cambridge even advised Ferranti to get out of computing on the grounds that 'the machines were exceedingly difficult to use and could not be trusted to anyone who was not a professional mathematician'. By the time of the **Suez crisis**, the company in the best position to market the invention, the British Tabulating Machine Company (founded 1907), was being trounced by America's more aggressive, forward-looking International Business Machines

Company, IBM (1924). And by the time Bill Gates's Microsoft (1975) licensed his DOS operating system to IBM for use in personal computers in 1980, the UK was out of the race.

The British attitude to research and development did not stop Turing providing a second seminal theoretical text, 'Computing Machinery and Intelligence' (1950). Published in the journal *Mind*, it explored the potential applications of computers by asking whether they could re-create not only the biological/chemical mechanics of the human brain but intelligence itself. To test his supposition, he invented a simple 'imitation game' (now known as the Turing Test), comparing it to a party game in which a man pretends to be a woman. Turing argued that if a programmed computer could satisfy an impartial judge that it was human by answering questions using textual messages alone then it must be credited with intelligence. He also envisaged robots having sensory equipment that might enable them, for example, to 'enjoy' strawberries and cream.

Turing did not believe that artificial intelligence (A-I) could become artificial consciousness, a fear expressed in many science-fiction films, such as *Demon Seed* (1977) in which Julie Christie is raped by a computer. Turing wrote, 'The question "Can machines think?" I believe too meaningless to deserve discussion.' But he did envision a time when A-I was sophisticated enough to perform myriad social functions, while also being as accessible to the public as a Model T Ford. 'One day,' he wrote, 'ladies will take their computers for walks in parks and tell each other "My little computer said such a funny thing this morning."' In short, Turing is to Bill Gates what Einstein was to Oppenheimer. Unfortunately, unlike Oppenheimer, Turing never consistently had enough state backing to put his ideas into practice, and, unlike Gates, he lacked the commercial acumen and inclination to market his ideas and so become self-sufficient.

Unusually for his time, Turing took little trouble to hide his sexuality and it was that openness which led to his premature death. In February 1952, he went to the police to tell them he was being blackmailed over an affair with a young man from Manchester, as a result of which he was arrested and stood trial on 31 March of that year.
▶ Unlike Oscar Wilde, who denied his **homosexuality** in the dock, Turing's defence was that he saw nothing wrong with it. Unable to face prison, he accepted the Crown's alternative sentence of regular injections of the female hormone oestrogen to suppress his sex drive, as a result of which he developed breasts.

In addition, Turing's security clearance for GCHQ was withdrawn
▶ because, in a **Cold War** climate that equated deviance with treason, the government assumed him to be a security risk, though unlike many heterosexual scientists of his generation he had no Marxist

sympathies. Turing partially compensated for this by diversifying, studying among other things morphogenesis, the evolution of organic structure. But his exclusion from some of the latest computer research hampered his ability to progress with it. The pain this caused him was summed up in a rhyme he composed: 'Turing believes machines think. Turing lies with men. Therefore machines do not think.' He committed suicide at his home in Wilmslow, Cheshire, on 7 June 1954, by eating an apple laced with potassium cyanide. He may have had in mind Socrates who, on refusing prison for corrupting the youth of Athens, killed himself by drinking hemlock. A more compelling explanation is that Turing believed he had been expelled from an intellectual Eden and thus robbed of his life's purpose.

By the time he died, American mathematic and electronic research was already overtaking that of the UK. So it cannot be said with assurance that had he lived longer Britain would have led the technological revolution as it had once led the industrial one. Moreover, he might have returned to the US as part of what became known in the 1960s as 'the Brain Drain', lured like so many scientists by the better opportunities for research and development there. However, it is undeniable that his tragic death lost Britain one of its great scientific minds, and that happened as a direct consequence of homophobia. Oscar Wilde was considered *the* gay martyr because his camp, flamboyant artistry fitted more easily into ideas (shared by many homosexuals) of what being gay meant. Turing, on the other hand – a shy, geeky scientist – did not, even though he was more courageously open about his sexuality. Yet Turing's death was more costly to the nation than Wilde's. Another sparkling comedy of aristocratic manners would have embellished the canon of British/Irish drama. Another paper 'On Computable Numbers' might have ensured that the headquarters of Microsoft were built in Slough and not Seattle.

T

■ Unemployment

Men overloaded with work have supposed idleness to be happiness, not reflecting that the worst of conditions is that of a man who has nothing to do.
Voltaire

Until the 1940s statistics on British unemployment were misleading, since they reflected the number of *insured* people out of work rather than the overall tally. Before 1920, the figures were calculated by the
► trade unions. After the election of **Margaret Thatcher's Conservative government** in 1979, the accuracy of the figures became a source of political controversy. But fairly clear general trends can be identified over the century.

When the economic boom after the First World War came to an end, unemployment rose very sharply. It was around 2 per cent of the workforce in 1919, but climbed to an average 13 per cent in the following year. It stayed above 1 million for the whole interwar period. Between 1930 and 1935, indeed, it was generally above 2 million,
► reflecting the worldwide **Great Depression**. Some observers calculated that the 'real' figure was well over 3 million at its worst.

During the Second World War unemployment virtually disappeared. There was a short-lived upsurge over the million mark in the appalling winter of 1946–7, but until the early 1970s it seemed that the
► introduction of **Keynesian** government policies, indicated by the 1944 White Paper on unemployment, had conquered this social scourge at last. At its lowest, in July 1955, the figure was less than 200,000.

However, even before the oil shock of 1973–4 there were signs that the good times were coming to an end. Contrary to expectation, rela-
► tively high **inflation** was coexisting with rising unemployment. The
► fuel crisis forced the 1974–9 **Labour** governments to abandon the postwar commitment to 'full' employment, and by the late summer of 1978 the jobless figure exceeded 1.5 million. Under the Conservatives after 1979, governments consciously shifted their main commitment
► to the control of inflation, although as early as July 1980 the **opinion**
► **polls** showed that the majority of voters disagreed with this reordering of priorities. An international depression, an increase in
► the working-age population and (not least) the imposition of **monetarist** policies ensured a return of unemployment to levels last seen in the 1930s. The government repeatedly changed the basis for calculating the statistics, but from 1983 to 1987 the number out of work rarely dipped below 3 million even on its official figures. By June 1990 the economic recovery had almost brought them below 1.5 million; but as the 'boom' turned to 'bust' there was another steep rise. In January 1993 the tally was over 3 million again.

Before the end of the twentieth century the official unemployment figure was back below 1 million for the first time since 1975. There had been no return to Keynesianism, and the government no longer automatically stepped forward to rescue ailing companies for fear of politically-damaging job losses. Rather, it deployed the same carrot-and-stick strategy as its **Thatcherite** predecessors. There were limited ◄ job-creation schemes, and various measures discouraged 'benefit cheats'. The Prime Minister **Tony Blair** took to lecturing his **European** ◄ counterparts on the virtues of the flexible British labour market. Ugly management euphemisms, such as 'downsizing' to denote mass sackings, caused less offence than they should have done because the cast-offs apparently found it easy to secure new work. **'New' Labour** did ◄ show more energy in tackling the problem, with its 'New Deal' for the young and encouragement for single mothers to rejoin the workforce. But the rhetoric remained harsh, as if the government felt guilty about its help to the 'undeserving'. The Chancellor of the Exchequer, Gordon Brown, pointed out that the number of vacancies was similar to the official unemployment figure, implying that no one should be out of work at all.

Unemployment in Britain during the twentieth century took both 'structural' and 'cyclical' forms. Throughout the period the main structural problem was an over-reliance on **manufacturing** industry ◄ (and 'primary' production, such as mining and **agriculture**). Even ◄ before 1900 Britain had become uncompetitive in these sectors. According to 'Thatcherite' economic historians, the immediate post-war period saw a misguided attempt to stave off the inevitable, so that by 1979 millions of jobs existed only because politicians were frightened of memories of the 1930s. A radical restructuring of the economy was long overdue; and if Britain suffered badly for much of the 1980s, at least the proper remedy was applied all at once.

This account cannot withstand detailed examination – for example, it overlooks the policy mistakes which created an unsustainable boom sandwiched between two 'busts' of excessive severity and duration, and implies that the government had a far-sighted strategy in 1979 whereas in reality the scale of the problem shocked even the Thatcherites. But it did at least seem that under Conservative rule the underlying structural problem was greatly reduced. One result was that Britain now seemed less exposed to the other half of the problem – the cyclical movements associated with general world conditions. Yet some observers were troubled by the medium-term implications of Britain's reliance on imported goods. In 1970 a short-lived fluctuation in the country's balance of trade had been regarded as sufficiently serious to affect the result of a general election. After 1979, though, the British became accustomed to ignoring record

U

deficits. This development could provide the basis for a new structural problem, whether or not the country joins the euro.

While discussions of unemployment are invariably dominated by statistics, in this context rows of figures are more inadequate than usual. Harold Wilson's remark that for the jobless person the unemployment rate is 100 per cent was one of the wisest things he ever said. But since Britain's structural problems have tended to focus on specific geographical areas, at times unemployment really has approached 100 per cent in the older industrial areas; and even when the general picture has improved these 'pockets' of unemployment have recovered

▶ more slowly, reflecting the so-called **North–South divide**. The unemployment of the early 1990s was different in this respect, since it affected areas which had barely been touched in the previous recession. While it lasted, this changed context provoked a shift in the public mood. When the Conservative Chancellor Norman Lamont, during a Commons debate of May 1991, referred to unemployment as 'a price well worth paying' for the reduction of inflation, he damaged his reputation far more than Norman Tebbit had done a decade earlier, when he advised the unemployed to emulate the feat of his father, who had 'got on his bike and looked for work' during the 1930s.

It might have been expected that the traditional stigma attaching to unemployment would have been removed after a century in which the jobless figures so clearly reflected general economic trends rather than sudden surges in 'idleness'. Opinion polls in the late 1980s suggested that Margaret Thatcher had inadvertently fostered the view that the lack of gainful employment did not reflect any personal failings. Even those with no first-hand experience of enforced leisure could appreciate the real psychological impact, not just through the

▶ works of observers like Jack London, **J.B. Priestley** and **George Orwell**, but also through fiction, notably Walter Greenwood's *Love on the Dole* (1933). The changed climate of the late 1990s meant that the subject could be treated with insensitive flippancy in the hit film *The Full Monty* (1997), which depicted a group of slightly downcast unemployed men who transformed themselves into happy strippers.

But this did not mean that unscrupulous politicians could no longer exploit prejudice against the 'able-bodied poor'. After 1997 a series of government advertisements urged all good citizens to expose 'scroungers', who worked while claiming the dole, and people who had been encouraged to claim sickness benefit in order to massage the unemployment figures suddenly found themselves challenged to prove their disabilities. In this respect, at least, 'New' Labour was no different from its Conservative predecessor, and the effect of the propaganda was reflected in the fact that in 2002 almost half of the public thought that unemployment benefit absorbed most of the social security budget, when the real proportion was only 6 per cent. By contrast, politicians were reluctant to criticise employers who were registered abroad for tax purposes, and who 'downsized' their firms because of their own mistakes or their desire to appease shareholders.

No doubt there were some among the unemployed who accepted joblessness as a way of life – and others who abused the system. But in their different ways both of these categories were an indictment of post-war politicians who had manipulated an affluent economy in their own interests. The remainder of the unemployed – those who desperately wanted to find a suitable job, but could not do so for one good reason or another – were no better off than their counterparts had been in the 1930s. Indeed, in some respects their plight was even worse. Simply lacking a job was bad enough, but in addition after 1979 the rate of their benefits fell further behind the increasing living standards of the working population. By 2002 a single unemployed person was receiving just under £60 per week; had the amount kept pace with wage inflation the sum would have been more than £80. In a society where the worship of wealth had become a general phenomenon, and not just the fixation of a few, as it was in the 1930s, these figures neatly encapsulate the term 'social exclusion'. So it was understandable that the unemployed should lack self-esteem, trapping them in a vicious circle because they needed motivation to find jobs. And at least the worst-afflicted areas in the 1930s had some sense of community to fall back on. By contrast, the long-term unemployed of 2002 were poor, abused – and isolated.

■ Universities

It was a journalist and MP imprisoned for fraud, Horatio Bottomley (1860–1933), who in 1926 coined the phrase 'University of Life' and so encouraged his compatriots to believe that higher education was unnecessary. But the twentieth century witnessed the biggest expansion of university education in British history. Scotland had a tradition of relatively open higher education thanks to its four universities, St Andrews (founded 1410), Glasgow (1451), Aberdeen (1494) and Edinburgh (1583). In Wales, a surge of national sentiment in the late nineteenth century led to the foundation of three university colleges, federated as the University of Wales in 1893, and joined by a fourth, Swansea, in 1923. In England, Oxford (1185), Cambridge (1209), London (1836) and Durham (1837) were more socially exclusive. Several university colleges were founded in the north of England during the second half of the nineteenth century, some with money from local entrepreneurs like the pharmacist Jesse Boot (1850–1931) who helped set up Nottingham in 1881. But their students were prepared for the

U

▶ London University external examination. Moreover, although **Roman Catholics** were admitted to British universities after 1871 and four
▶ **women's** colleges were founded at Cambridge and Oxford between
▶ 1869 and 1879, it remained virtually impossible for working-class people of either sex to obtain higher education because little funding was available beyond a patchy scholarship system provided by local
▶ authorities, **trade unions** and private benefactors.

In the first half of the twentieth century, things progressed slowly. Charters were given to Birmingham (1900), Liverpool (1903), Leeds (1904) and Sheffield (1905), making them independent of London. In Ireland, the twinned colleges of Dublin (1591) and Belfast (1849) became separate universities in 1908. But only two entirely new universities were founded in Britain before the Second World War: Bristol (1909) and Reading (1926). Regular state funding to these institutions began in 1919 when the University Grants Committee (UGC) was set up.

▶ Grants to the students themselves did not come until the Butler **Education Act of 1944**, which compelled local authorities to set aside part of their budgets for that purpose. Furthermore, by providing free secondary education up to the age of 18, the Act enabled any child to win a subsidised university place if he or she wanted one and merited it. By 1956, the student population of Britain's universities had risen from 50,000 to 220,000, of whom three-quarters were in receipt of state funding. In addition, five new independent universities were created in the decade after the war: Nottingham (1948), Southampton (1952), Hull (1954), Exeter (1955) and Leicester (1957).

Upon Butler's foundations, the economist Lionel Robbins (1898–1984) constructed the edifice of mass higher education in the UK. In 1963, his eponymous report on the subject recommended a doubling of the student population in ten years. The target was achieved in seven, with 443,000 students by 1971. Twelve new universities were created in that period: 8 in England, 3 in Scotland and 1 in Northern Ireland. In addition, technical colleges were given university status, henceforward known as polytechnics. Arguably, the most important development of this period was the creation of the Open University by Harold Wilson in 1966. Based in England, run by a Scot and modelled on a Russian experiment, the OU offered correspondence courses in every conceivable subject, with lectures transmitted
▶ on BBC2. It was designed for, and successfully appealed to, adults who had entered the workforce with only basic qualifications, and women who had left it in order to raise children. The OU opened in 1971 and by the end of the century, it was admitting 100,000 students a year.

The content of university teaching also changed. In *Crisis in the University* (1948), UGC Chairman Sir Walter Moberley lamented the decline of a Christian ethos in British higher education; and in 1963

U

Lionel Robbins proclaimed the purpose of his expansion to be 'the transmission of a common culture and common standards of citizenship'. Little of either was evident when new universities like Sussex (1961) and Essex (1965) introduced social science disciplines like linguistics and sociology. This broadened the critical enquiry of the humanities and attracted more left-leaning lecturers. But, in doing so, it created a groundswell for the campus unrest of the period 1967–70 which brought the subsidised university system into disrepute among taxpayers. From the 1940s to the 1980s, the bulk of rising student numbers was made up by the middle and upper classes. Indeed, the proportion of students from poorer backgrounds actually fell between 1971 and 1981, from 29 to 20 per cent. This was partly the result of falling standards in state schools following the introduction of **comprehensive** education and partly because the cost of further ◄ education became prohibitive once again.

During the 1980s, Britain's universities underwent a second revolution. First, they were starved of cash by the **Thatcher** governments in ◄ an attempt to get them to raise more money from the business sector – a trend that privileged science and technology over the humanities. Second, the formal distinction between polytechnics and universities was abolished in the 1992 Education Act, which allowed polytechnics to rename themselves overnight. The Act enforced a quinquennial Research Assessment Exercise (RAE) in an effort to raise standards by making the level of UGC funding that an institution received dependent on the rating it was given for research and teaching. The Act also abolished student grants, replacing them with loans, as a result of which there was a drop in the number of poorer youths entering higher education. Grants were restored in Scotland by the Scottish Parliament in 1999, thus proving that **devolution** could have ◄ practical benefits. By the end of the century there were 90 universities serving a student population of 2 million. British universities had become more numerous and more accessible and they taught a wider range of subjects than before. But the proportion of the UK population in higher education still lagged behind the rest of **Europe**, and a child ◄ of a member of the 'professions' was still six times more likely to win a university place than the offspring of an unskilled worker.

Kingsley Amis (1922–95), whose novel *Lucky Jim* (1953) satirised the complacent self-serving dolour of academic life, wrote in 1960: 'The delusion that there are thousands of young people who are capable of benefiting from university training but have somehow failed to find their way there is a necessary component of the expansionist case.' 'More,' he concluded, 'will mean worse.' For all the failings of British universities, Amis was one of millions whose lives were bettered by their partial democratisation.

■ Wars

War has exercised a strange fascination over the British since 1900,
▶ reflected in its humour, its **children**'s comics and perhaps its greatest
poetry of the twentieth century. More importantly, the experience of
war played a crucial role in important social reforms. Yet although the
British continued to regard war as a token of national virility, the
conflicts of the twentieth century both reflected and accelerated
national decline.

The century began with Britain at war in South Africa, against the
Transvaal and the Orange Free State. This conflict, the Boer War, was
the last of Britain's expansionist wars, fought on flimsy pretexts. It
began in October 1899 and ended on 31 May 1902. For most of this
period the British were faced by a guerrilla army. The difficulty of
distinguishing enemy forces from peaceable farmers in such a conflict
led the colonial power to introduce concentration camps, which
caused the deaths from disease of more than 20,000 men, women and
children. In this case incompetence, rather than evil intent, was to
blame: but the episode was scarcely worthy of a great power which
prided itself on its moral standing. More than 16,000 British troops
also died from sickness – around three times as many as those killed
in action.

Eventual British victory brought little advantage, despite the rich
gold fields in the conquered territories. The war had underlined both
▶ the country's isolation within **Europe**, and the unfitness of much of
its male population for active service. Thus the main results of the war
were to give a new impetus to the search for reliable allies abroad, and
a fillip for those who wished to improve the 'condition of the people'
at home, through state intervention in education and the encouragement of the new high-technology industries which British entrepreneurs had failed to develop during the long years of Victorian
prosperity.

The First World War, which broke out in August 1914, was at least
in part the product of the new system of European alliances. Ostensibly, Britain's intervention was provoked by German violation of
Belgian neutrality, although tension had been building because of
Germany's imperial ambitions which had been checked by its late
arrival (1871) as a unified state. At first it was widely assumed that the
conflict would be over quickly, and this conviction was reflected in the
alacrity with which the early recruits signed up to die. It rapidly
degenerated into a series of bloody engagements, in which the
opposing armies launched futile attacks against lines of trenches
which extended from Switzerland to the Channel. At one time or
another there were almost 10 million combatants. Nearly a million

men were killed, either from Britain itself or its **Empire**. The self-sacri-
fice of young men from the self-governing Dominions (particularly
that of the Australians at Gallipoli), in a cause which reeked of European decadence, was a major factor in loosening the imperial ties
which British statesmen such as Joseph Chamberlain had been trying
to strengthen through **tariff reform**.

The UK civilian population was not seriously affected, although the
government introduced **conscription** (1916) and small-scale rationing
of goods (1917). For non-combatants the worst effects were felt afterwards, in an influenza epidemic spread by returning soldiers. Despite
a successul campaign by German submarines ('U-boats') against
British and allied shipping, the country never came close to starvation.
But the conflict exposed a fact only previously noticed by a handful of
careful observers – that most of Britain's industry was obsolete, and
that the prosperity of the country depended heavily on overseas
investments. Thanks to the dynamic intervention of the Ministry of
Munitions, production was modernised and greatly improved; but it
was a close-run thing. Eventually the German armies collapsed, and
an armistice was signed on 11 November 1918. Britain was left in
control of Iraq and Palestine – plentiful sources of oil and of trouble
for the future. Even before the end of the war British troops had been
sent on a new mission against Bolshevik Russia, which had signed a
separate armistice with the **Germans**; this ill-judged intervention
(furiously supported within the Cabinet by **Winston Churchill**) lasted
for just one ignominious year.

After exhaustive attempts to avoid a new conflict through **appeasement**, Britain declared war on Nazi Germany on 3 September 1939. On
paper the war seems to have been less damaging than the first; around
6 million people were engaged in the conflict, and just over a quarter
of a million servicemen were killed. But the war had a much greater
effect on non-combatants, particularly when Britain was devoid of
allies and was subjected to the **Blitz** from German bombers. This time,
full-scale rationing and conscription were introduced at an early stage.
In January 1940 restrictions were imposed on the sale of butter, bacon
and sugar; they were later extended to most necessities, with the
exception of bread and potatoes which escaped rationing until 1946
and 1947 respectively. Meat was still being rationed as late as the
summer of 1954.

Britain intervened in the Korean War (1950–3) in support of the
United Nations, but mainly because of the bellicose attitude of the
USA; it stopped its action over Egypt's nationalisation of the **Suez**
Canal (1956) in the face of US pressure. British casualties were less
than a thousand in the first operation, and 21 in the second. The next
major engagement for British forces – apart from the running sore of

W

- the 'Troubles' in Northern Ireland – represented a breach in the
- emerging pattern. The **Falklands War** of 1982 was undertaken despite initial US misgivings. The rapid British victory re-established the repu-
- tation of its **armed forces**; but the circumstances had been most unusual, and the conflict might prove to be the last independent British operation on a significant scale.

The Gulf War of 1990–1 represented a return to 'normalcy'. Although the British had leaned towards the Iraqis during the latter's earlier barbaric conflict with Iran, they fully supported the US demand that President Saddam Hussein should remove his troops after occupying Kuwait. The war itself, which began with heavy air strikes on Iraq, lasted barely six weeks. Only 24 British servicemen were killed (a number of them falling victim to what was euphemistically called 'friendly fire' from their own American allies). The British also took part in the bombing of Serbia in 1999, during the dispute over Kosovo. They took a central role in subsequent 'peace-keeping' activities. In April 2003 this pattern looked sure to be repeated after the second war against Saddam Hussein, although the ultimate consequences of this controversial action are unclear at the time of writing.

The impact of war on Britain during the twentieth century can scarcely be exaggerated. Internationally, it was reduced from a first-rank imperial power to an unhesitating ally of one of its former colonies. Although its strength was undermined by the First World War, the *coup de grâce* was delivered between 1939 and 1945. This sudden transformation was difficult for policy-makers to accept, and the general public was even more baffled. As a result, the British continued to behave as if they really mattered on the world stage, if only as a bastion of what they called 'democratic values'. Even if Britain merited that moral status – and its choice of friends across the

- world had nothing to do with **morality** – as a power of the second rank it was unlikely to derive much glory from it (as John Major was fond of saying in a different context, 'fine words butter no parsnips'). Meanwhile, a reluctance to square Britain's self-image with the reality of its status prevented a wholehearted commitment either to Europe, or to the only realistic alternative of impoverished isolation.

Domestically, the outcome of 'total war' was quite similar. Politicians were reluctant to spell out the consequences of Britain's reduced standing, so the electorate could be forgiven for wanting its cake and eating it. Thus after the Second World War it demanded high-quality public services, but proved reluctant to pay for them through taxation.

- Ironically, the expansion of the **welfare state** had been heavily influenced by the wars which made it much more difficult to finance. Originally, a better-nourished population was seen as essential for a state whose manpower resources would be stretched by trouble within the

Empire. After 1945 most politicians accepted that the public deserved comprehensive coverage against sickness, **unemployment** and old age, ◄ given the extent of its sacrifices; but in the nuclear age the whole edifice of state welfare began to look like a costly white elephant, given that Britain was unlikely to need many young people as cannon fodder in any future fight.

By the end of the century, despite numerous cost-cutting exercises, the armed forces still cost more than £20 billion per year. In 2003–4, thanks to the war on Iraq, spending was projected to rise to £26 billion. Among European nations, only France allocated a comparable sum to defence. Yet there was still no sign of a constructive public debate about the real purpose of this expenditure. It would be going too far to claim that Britain's failure to face up to facts had landed it with the worst of both worlds; but instead of making a decisive choice between guns and butter, it had ended up with margarine and bows and arrows.

■ Weather

'When two Englishmen meet,' observed Samuel Johnson in 1758, 'their first talk is of the weather.' Because the British enjoy the most temperate climate in Europe and because they are an island people, the weather remains central to their way of life and part of their daily communal discourse. The British Meteorological office was founded in 1841 by the Board of Trade; in 1861 it began issuing gale warnings to shipping and in 1879 to the general public via the press. But professional forecasting went hand in hand with broadcasting. The BBC ◄ transmitted the first Met Office weather forecast on 14 November 1922, and it became a regular feature the following year.

The first on-screen weatherman was George Cowling, a Yorkshireman who had previously tracked weather for the RAF. He made his debut on 11 January 1954 in front of a board, propped up on an easel, and on which were stuck simple weather symbols. Soon, Cowling and other forecasters like Jack Scott, Michael Fish, Ian McCaskill and Barbara Edwards (the first female, who debuted in 1974) were TV personalities. Their expertise, delivered in a down-to-earth, reassuringly homely manner, became part of the fabric of national life, despite the fact that in a predominantly urban society, weather was no longer as vital to the British as it had been when they tilled the land.

The weather could still occasionally be a matter of life and death – for example, in the heatwave of 1976 and the storms that buffeted the islands in 1952 and 1987. Famously, Michael Fish failed to predict those of 1987, when 12 people died. The event proved that nature could still steal a march on modern technology but it briefly damaged the reputation of his profession. Still, by the end of the twentieth

W

century, a total of 22 hours of weather predictions were broadcast each week. One of the most popular bulletins was Radio Four's nightly shipping forecast, listened to by millions who had never set foot in a boat. The British might grumble constantly about the weather. But the popularity of the bulletin – the religiously intoned warning of gales in home shores with area names like 'Dogger' and 'Fisher' – showed how the weather maintained a popular sense of being an island nation in an age of global travel and telecommunications.

■ Welfare state

It is commonly argued that the 'welfare state' only emerged in Britain after the Second World War. Certainly, a concentration on the later period lends spurious support to the false impression that the 'over-burdened' state of the 1970s was produced by the misguided compassion of post-war reformers, beginning with **Labour** from 1945 to 1951. But the term was coined in the 1930s (popularised by **William Temple**) and if it is taken to refer to the acceptance on **government**'s part of a responsibility to guarantee at least some provision against **William Beveridge**'s 'Five Giants' (Want, Disease, Ignorance, Squalor and Idleness), its origins can be traced much earlier.

In 1900 the social philosopher Herbert Spencer (1820–1903) complained to a friend that the **Liberal Party** was betraying its principles, extending the scope of state intervention in the name of 'popular welfare'. As a **social Darwinist**, Spencer had every reason to be dismayed at recent developments; if the state intervened on behalf of the 'unfit', the advance of the species as a whole would be endangered. Fortunately for Spencer he did not live long enough to reflect on the social reforms of the Liberal government of H.H. Asquith (1908–15). As a final indignity, in death Spencer was given a disagreeable new neighbour when Karl Marx's grave at Highgate Cemetery was moved opposite his own last resting place.

The Asquith government's legislation on pensions, and on insurance against both sickness and **unemployment**, represented important new departures even if the provision was inadequate. The programme, piecemeal as it was, represented a recognition that individuals could encounter misfortune through no fault of their own, and that in such circumstances the state should at least make a token contribution to their relief. The pre-war Liberals also introduced subsidised school meals, in the wake of the **1902 Education Act** passed by the **Conservatives**. Furthermore (*pace* Spencer), the reformers could support their measures without departing from the key premises of classical liberalism. If the individual can face starvation because of the mistakes of an employer, or the adverse workings of the market, then the liberal rhetoric of 'freedom' became a cruel deception. This was also true in the case of the worst-paid workers who remained in employment. Action was taken to protect them in **Winston** ◄ **Churchill**'s Trade Boards Act (1909), while Beveridge himself inspired the introduction of labour exchanges in the following year.

The interwar British governments were generally regarded as having 'muddled through' despite extravagant election promises made in 1918 and an economic depression which was hardly broken throughout the period. The 'means test' to check that claimants were poor enough to merit assistance, and the cuts in unemployment benefit carried through by the National Government, suggest something worse than inactivity. But the insurance scheme was extended, so that even domestic workers were covered by 1938, and the **Housing** ◄ Acts of 1933 and 1935 testified to the government's commitment to slum clearance. Legislation was also introduced to raise the school-leaving age to 15 (though this was postponed until 1947). For those in the twilight of life rather than springtime, the second **Baldwin** ◄ government had implemented Neville Chamberlain's Widows and Old Age Pension Act (1925), which reflected and fostered the trend towards earlier retirement, at 65 rather than 70. Chamberlain, rightly reviled for his policy of **appeasement** in foreign affairs during his later stint ◄ as Prime Minister, deserves far wider recognition for his creative domestic reforms, which also dismantled much of the old Poor Law machinery through his reorganisations of **local government** in 1928 ◄ and 1929.

If the 'welfare state' as such is a post-war phenomenon, this is because the reforms of the Attlee government made the existing measures more comprehensive, and introduced crucial new bodies, notably the **National Health Service** (NHS, 1948). The idea that social services ◄ should provide universal support was a key development; in theory, at least, it should have removed the old stigma attached to welfare claimants through the means test. Thus the NHS provided free health-care to all, and the Family Allowances Act of 1945 gave 5 shillings per week, directly to all mothers, for each child after the first-born. While to its opponents this welfare system epitomised the worst excesses of 'socialism', it was in fact still fully consistent with the liberal principles of the Asquith government. Labour's ministers still envisaged welfare as a safety net; employment of any kind was still regarded as the only route to fulfilling living standards and a sense of self-worth.

Coupled with an economic policy which made full employment a priority, the welfare state as it existed in 1950 promised to banish Beveridge's 'Giants'. Yet a service which managed to be both generous and universal in a capitalist economy with an ever-increasing proportion of pensioners could only be ensured by healthy **economic** ◄

W

growth. The first cracks began to appear even before the end of the Attlee government, which was forced by an elephantine US-imposed defence budget to introduce charges for spectacles and dental treatment in 1950. Since this covered only a minuscule fraction of the government's financial needs, it was obviously an attempt to undermine the founding principles of the NHS.

If some Labour politicians had begun to regret the universal nature of welfare provision, thoughtful Conservatives were soon brooding over the problem of 'dependency'. As a safety net for those in genuine need, the welfare state was perfectly acceptable to them. The difficulty would come if there was any evidence that the system was generating its own demands – in particular, if benefits were pitched at too high a level, the incentive to work might be eroded. Beveridge had included 'Idleness' among the evils which the state ought to combat. In some quarters, though, it was now felt that poorly-paid workers would like nothing more than to sit around at home; and if this enviable existence was being supported by taxpayers' money the system would have to be changed.

Until 1979 Britain was governed by politicians who had vivid (if not
► always first-hand) impressions of interwar **poverty**. But economic
► decline helped to convince **Margaret Thatcher** and her allies that the comprehensive post-war welfare state had indeed produced a 'dependency culture'. At a time when government economic policy was greatly increasing the tally of the unemployed, the Conservative government exploited the fact that universal provision had not succeeded in lifting the stigma from poverty and joblessness. Although the rhetoric of some senior Conservatives was designed to drive home the message, the average (employed) voter needed little persuading that the state should no longer be so generous.

► However, the **Thatcherites** could not hope to dismantle the welfare edifice in its entirety. After all, some of the measures helped rich and poor alike. Thus state education continued and the NHS was preserved (though new charges were introduced and old ones increased); the Thatcherites confined themselves to subsidising the private alternatives. But the link between pensions and earnings was broken, and the value of benefits for the unemployed progressively undermined. The Major government went even further, introducing in 1993 a new
► **Orwellian** 'Jobseekers' Allowance' and moving towards a 'workfare' system under which the unemployed would lose the right to refuse uncongenial jobs.

► **'New' Labour** was elected in 1997 at least in part because the Thatcherite counter-attack against the welfare state had been an incomplete success. Even though the Conservatives had won four consecutive general elections, their share of the vote declined and public opinion polls suggested that they would have been turned out ◄ in 1987 (if not sooner) had a united opposition carried sufficient conviction. But the Blair government had promised not to raise ◄ income tax to fund public services, and if anything complaints about standards in the NHS and state schools increased under 'New' Labour.

Labour's position was forced upon it, by a perception on the part of its strategists that the majority of voters would not tolerate a return to high (direct) taxation. Yet the welfare state was clearly in need of a thorough, objective rethink after so many decades, and having inherited a fairly prosperous economy Labour should have been in a position to launch such a wide-ranging inquiry without attracting adverse publicity. But the new government's popularity was based on its desire to please everyone, and a fundamental review would alienate its core support. The compromise solution was to be more generous, particularly to families with children, while emphasising that its chief objec- ◄ tive was to move people 'from welfare to work', and continuing the Tory policy of stigmatising 'welfare cheats'. To appease the right-wing press, the unprovable claim that £7 billion was embezzled from the welfare budget every year was more widely publicised than the government's real achievements.

At the end of the century it seemed that the broad outlines of Attlee's framework would be retained, despite a looming crisis over pension provision for an ageing population and unanswered questions ◄ about the real impact of 'dependency'. But the practical compassion of Asquith's ministers and the idealism of 1945 had been displaced by electoral opportunism (on Labour's part) and an equally cynical attempt to win back the favours of the affluent (by the Conservatives).

■ 'Winter of Discontent'

In September 1978 the Labour Prime Minister James Callaghan was expected to announce the date of a general election during his speech to the Trades Union Congress. But doubts over the likelihood of a clear ◄ Labour majority persuaded him to hang on. In hindsight, it looked like a disastrous misjudgement. Within a few months Britain was afflicted by a series of strikes, so severe that the period was awarded the Shakespearian tag of the 'Winter of Discontent'. For the Labour Party there ◄ was no ensuing 'glorious summer'; defeat in the 1979 general election led to 18 years of opposition.

Callaghan had hoped that the trade unions would acquiesce in a policy of wage restraint, but after several years of agreement they balked at a further instalment. The government's pay guidelines set the limit for increases at 5 per cent, but public-sector unions, in particular, felt that their living standards had been slipping for too

W

long in relation to other workers. The first serious action, though, involved lorry drivers who struck for 25 per cent in early January 1979. A separate dispute with tanker drivers exacerbated the situation. On 19 January Callaghan returned from an economic summit in Guadeloupe and stumbled into an ambush of reporters hoping for a comment on the situation. He denied that Britain was suffering from 'mounting chaos', and his innocuous remark was translated by the *Sun* newspaper into the far more memorable headline: 'Crisis? What crisis?' Other politicians had been mentioned in pop songs, but this apocryphal comment provided the progressive rock band Supertramp with the title of an entire album.

By the end of the month few could deny that there really was 'mounting chaos' in Britain. A one-day strike of public-sector workers was called for 22 January, and almost universally observed. Rubbish was left uncollected, hospitals picketed, and in one incident on Merseyside workers refused to bury the dead. All this gave an irresistible opening to the tabloid press; and although most of the disputes were quickly settled this peace could only be attained at the expense of the government's pay policy. Since Labour had gained office in the first place largely because it was felt to offer the best
▶ chance of containing **inflation** through improved industrial relations, the party's only winning card had been torn from its hands.

Amid all the sound and fury, the genuine case for better pay and
▶ conditions was barely audible. The **Conservative**-supporting **national newspapers** found it much easier to quote hardline union activists, some of whom gave the impression of caring far more for their own comforts than for the interests of their fellow citizens. In many cases, of course, the victims of the strike action were themselves members of
▶ the working **class**. In this respect, at least, those who attributed the fall of the Labour government to its failure to push through a distinctively socialist programme were hopelessly wide of the mark. The Winter of Discontent which brought down the government actually marked the triumph of material greed over solidarity, and in such circumstances a Labour Party which still retained some of its historic ideals was doomed to a lengthy period in opposition.

■ Women

The change in the legal, political, economic and social status of women is one of the most striking features of modern British history – a development which, more than any other, actually deserves the name of a revolution. At the beginning of the twentieth century women suffered from serious discrimination in every meaningful sphere of activity. Within a hundred years they enjoyed equality – on paper, at least. In terms of academic attainment, indeed, it looked as if the balance had tilted the other way. Young women consistently outperformed their male counterparts, provoking a search for explanations which gave media commentators the chance to bemoan the same 'laddish' culture which their newspapers encouraged on other pages. In 1900 it had been impossible for a woman to take a degree, although they could continue to study after the age of 18, in segregated colleges. Social commentators like Herbert Spencer solemnly warned that intellectual effort would induce hysteria, and even endanger fertility. By 1998, women provided more than half of the university population, without noticeable damage to themselves or others. Two women had even acted as Britain's most senior spies – a development reflected in recent James Bond films.

For middle-class liberal feminists in 1900, there was a general grievance which could be neatly summarised. Men had a virtual monopoly of public life, while women's influence was confined indoors. Even in the private sphere a woman was a second-class citizen, since men had a legal licence to indulge in moderate beatings and marital rape. For socialists, by contrast, the whole issue revolved around economics. Everything else followed from the fact that the men were the breadwinners; even if a working man handed over the housekeeping money on his return home, rather than spending it at the pub, his wife was still stuck with a servant's status. Actually, the average working-class wife enjoyed some advantages over her pampered bourgeois counterparts; particularly at times of hardship there could be something like 'parity of esteem' in a struggling partnership, while many affluent women were denied even the self-respect that comes from running a home, given the prevalence of domestic servants. But at least the divorce laws allowed middle-class women an escape route of last resort. Until the introduction of Legal Aid after the Second World War, and successive relaxations of matrimonial law, marriage contracts could spell a lifetime of misery for the poor.

From the socialist perspective, the Sex Disqualification (Removal) Act of 1919 was a greater blow for emancipation than the victory of the Suffragette movement. Women were now free to enter any of the professions, and to take degrees. Revisions of the property laws in 1926 and 1935 brought another step towards equality in this sphere, although it was not until Nigel Lawson's tax reforms of the late 1980s that a wife's earnings were automatically taxed separately from those of the husband. Early in the twentieth century the removal of economic discrimination was most likely to benefit women who had inherited property, but gradually they improved their chances of acquiring property for themselves. Even before the First World War most single women had been expected to work, but only as a

W

secondary contribution to the household budget before they graduated into servitude with an eligible male breadwinner. The influx of
▶ women into jobs vacated by men during the **war** – around 1.5 million of them – was largely reversed with the return of peace. But a trend had been established, and the contribution of women to the British war effort certainly helped to convince reluctant male decision-makers that something ought to be done for them. In 1931 about 10
▶ per cent of married women were working. The **Great Depression** drove many women back into their kitchens, and in 1934, when the crusty conservative Arthur Bryant published a cursory survey of seven typical English characters, he included only one representative woman because 'in discussing the character of the English housewife I am describing the character of the English woman'. But while Bryant thought (or hoped) that the impact of war had been a one-off and that most women would return to their natural tasks – 'to make some man happy, to bring children into the world . . . to civilise mankind' – the trend reasserted itself once the economy picked up. By 1951 the proportion of working married women had doubled. Forty years later more than half had a job of some sort, and by the end of the century about 44 per cent of the workforce were women.

▶ Yet grievances remained. The decline of **manufacturing** had increased opportunities for women, but the rise of the under-unionised service sector allowed other forms of discrimination. Only 55 per cent of working women had a full-time job, and even at the end of the century women were over-represented in such typical part-time occupations as clerical work (79 per cent of the workforce) and sales (70 per cent). This was one way in which the terms of Acts on Equal Pay (1970 and 1984) and Sex Discrimination (1975 and 1986) could be circumvented, despite the existence of the watchdog Equal Opportunities Commission from the mid-1970s. Another was the imposition of a 'glass ceiling', which denied women the promotions they deserved within professional occupations, where their representation rose from 8 per cent to 42 per cent over the fifty years after 1952. By 2002, the average pay differential between men and women had at least fallen from a scandalous 42 per cent in 1952. But it was still too high, at 18 per cent.

To remedy this situation, many progressives began to argue for positive discrimination, typically through a quota system. Thus the Labour Party introduced all-women shortlists for winnable constituen-
▶ cies, while **Conservative** activists persisted with their preference for young, middle-class males, affable but not too bright, blessed with an attractive wife and two well-behaved children. The emergence of the
▶ Conservative **Margaret Thatcher** as Britain's first female Prime Minister would have stunned the Marquess of Salisbury, but at least

she stuck to the rules by only inviting one member of her sex to join her in any of her various cabinets. Before women won the vote there was reason for radicals to hope that they would turn out to be a progressive force within the electorate. On certain occasions, such as during the **General Strike** of 1926, and during the 1980s in the miners' ◄ dispute and the protests against nuclear weapons at Greenham Common, women did fulfil these expectations. But some of their collective activities, such as the British Housewives' League formed in 1945 to protest against rationing, pointed the other way. The Conservatives enjoyed a lead over other parties among women which they only lost (ironically enough) during the Thatcher years.

During the second half of the twentieth century the forward march of women was helped by two key developments. The first of these was the introduction of relatively cheap electrical household appliances. Ownership of a washing machine, a vacuum cleaner and a microwave oven released a woman from hours of labour in the home. The second innovation was a reliable means of contraception under a woman's personal control. The 'Pill', available on **NHS** prescriptions by the end ◄ of the 1960s, allowed women of all classes to indulge in the pleasure of sex free from the fear of inconvenient pregnancy. The new pressure on men to 'perform' in the bedroom meant that by the end of the century impotence was taken very seriously as a health issue. Thanks to medical advances, men and women could swallow their pills simultaneously: one to induce sterility, and the other to increase the man's chances of bringing forth the elixir of life.

These crucial developments gave an ideal platform for the feminist movement, which was at its height in the 1960s. By that time formal equality was sufficiently close to make remaining disadvantages look ridiculous, and women had advanced far enough to make their protests impossible to ignore. By the end of the twentieth century it was commonly argued that Britain had entered a 'post-feminist' age, as if all the important battles had been won. Yet there had been very little attempt to negotiate new terms of co-existence in the new era of equality.

In the absence of any constructive discussion, the 'sex war' was always likely to resume, albeit on different terrain. Few commentators noticed that the ubiquity of labour-saving devices, and the ready availability of contraception, had been a liberation for *both* the sexes. Men could now freely philander, without the dread of unintended consequences; if a pregnancy resulted because a sexual partner had given false assurances about the chances of an 'accident', this subterfuge was more likely to terminate the relationship than to bring the couple together. And once the partnership had broken up, the man would discover that his vacuum cleaner and microwave oven gave him a

W

reasonable chance of survival. A bachelor's lot could be a very happy one, as the affluent had always known (provided that servants were plentiful).

For some, the chances of an independent life were exhilarating. But on balance the downside of a break-up was more likely to be felt by the woman, who was usually left pushing the pram. The insane gyrations ▸ of the **housing** market were also encouraged by the new spirit of 'liberation' which increased the number of singles looking for a home.

▸ Another result was the rising prevalence of **pornography** of all kinds, which found a ready market among isolated men. Ironically, 'post-feminists' conspired in this latter development, arguing that 'glamour' modelling and stripping in nightclubs were a means of 'empowering' women. Few of the gawping spectators saw things that way, although many men found it convenient to pretend they did. But even if the argument were true, a movement which advocated equality of respect should not have ended up with women exulting in a dominance over men which would end as soon as they lost their looks.

The burgeoning sex trade, though, was only the starkest illustration of a more general trend. The early middle-class feminists had lashed out against the idea that women were simply fragrant adornments to a man's private world. In practice, after the achievement of formal equality some crazy compulsion induced women to display their borrowed charms in public as well as in the home. Clearly, the obsession with personal appearance owed something to a residual sense – in defiance of all the evidence – that women did not truly *deserve* the economic equality they had fought for. Respect in the workplace could not be guaranteed merely by working hard and dressing smartly; there also had to be an undertone of sexual attraction to justify one's job. This message was reinforced by a plethora of women's magazines, none of which would have appealed very much to Mary Wollstonecraft and other pioneers of female education. These publications played upon the fixation with body image, and every issue had to feature the word 'sex' in bold lettering on the front cover.

There could be no answer to these new complications from within a prevailing liberal ideology which paid no attention to context and merely laid down a framework of rules for a market economy. Instead, a new literary genre emerged, explaining that men and women were from different planets. The nearest approach to a constructive discussion revolved around the question of whether or not women could (or should) 'have it all', in a life which squared the circle by including a ▸ profitable career and a secure family life, including **children**. The rational solution was that when a working couple decided to have a child, the partner whose career was less fulfilling should leave the labour market and take on the chief responsibilities in the home. Yet this option was unavailable for the single parent. And in any case, 'having it all' seemed to require privileges which had been denied to men in their heyday. Many women clearly wanted to combine economic independence with a full-time nurturing role. Technological change provided new opportunities for working from home, but for most women the dream would still require them to be in two places at one time.

In some well-publicised cases highly paid women resolved the dilemma by relinquishing their careers to bring up a family. These decisions were celebrated in right-wing **national newspapers**, whose ◄ readers secretly hoped that women would see the error of their ways and readopt the Arthur Bryant model after all. At the same time, though, such women were presented as having sacrificed something. In a **consumer** culture, to be economically inactive was to be some- ◄ thing less than a complete human being. Presumably there were still plenty of men and women who disputed this assumption, believing instead that true fulfilment can only be found in loving relationships of all kinds. But their voices were drowned out in the media hubbub, and it remains doubtful whether the headlong quest for material gain will ever pause long enough to allow constructive communication between the inhabitants of Venus and Mars.

■ Women's Institute

Britain's most successful women's organisation, popularly known as the 'WI'. Often misrepresented as a conservative affair, whose members accept a domestic role and do little except make jam and sing 'Jerusalem'. In fact, it is staunchly independent of political parties, and for much of the twentieth century it was an effective proto-feminist pressure group. The WI was founded in Canada in 1897 to improve women's grasp of domestic science; the first UK institute was founded at Anglesey in 1915 and the first county federation, in Sussex, followed in 1917. By 1925 it had a quarter of a million members, a figure that did not drop below until the end of the century.

The WI's aims, promoted through its magazine *Home and Country*, extended far beyond home and country. It campaigned successfully to improve women's healthcare, education and political rights (unlike the Mothers' Union, the WI supported female **suffrage**). It also pressed ◄ for state-funded childcare to enhance women's job opportunities and for the improvement of basic amenities like the electrification of the countryside. Affiliated to the Associated Country Women of the World, the WI had a non-imperial internationalist outlook from early on. In the 1930s, it supported the League of Nations; during the 1950s it opposed apartheid in South Africa; and throughout the century, its members raised money for a variety of Third World causes, usually through village fêtes and sponsored walks.

The WI's quaint image emerged during the Second World War. In 1938, the National Federation of Women's Institutes (NFWI) ruled that the WI could not carry out official war work because some of its members were Quakers. The stand was heavily criticised (although

▶ individual members were allowed to join the **armed forces**). Instead, the WI set up centres around the UK to make clothes and provisions for troops and civilians as far away as the Soviet Union. Many were run on co-operative lines. Jam became the popular symbol of their war effort. One WI leader wrote, 'Jam-making was constructive and non-militant . . . it accorded with the best Quaker traditions of feeding blockaded nations . . . And for the belligerent, what could be more satisfying than fiercely stirring the cauldrons of boiling jam and feeling that every pound took us one step closer towards defeating Hitler.'

▶ At national level, the WI was usually run by the liberal **aristocracy** and at local level by the professional middle classes, although its membership was always broadly based. What undermined its effec-

▶ tiveness in the post-war era was not so much **class** as location. It remained country-based, with little practical grasp of contemporary urban problems, however much it sympathised with them. In a nation

▶ where 80 per cent of the **population** were city dwellers, this was a fatal handicap. Furthermore, many of the WI's old battles were won thanks

▶ to the creation of the **welfare state, nationalised** industries and the more militant feminism that emerged during the 1960s. By then, the WI's work in Britain had come to focus on providing fellowship for women of the affluent urban families that were colonising Britain's villages at the expense of local inhabitants.

Attempts at modernisation were made, notably a charity fund-raising calendar of 1999, illustrated by naked WI members tastefully-posed next to their Agas. The Institutes also demonstrated their political independence at the AGM in Scarborough in 2000. Tradition-ally known as 'the Countrywoman's Parliament', delegates heckled

▶ **Tony Blair** when he tried to hijack the event to sell **'New' Labour**. But, however much observers enjoyed the Prime Minister's discomfort, the fact was that the Women's Institute was no longer of any political or social consequence to the majority of British people.

SUPPLEMENTARY INDEX

■

For the convenience of the reader, this selective index lists themes, people and institutions, which may be of specific interest.

Abdication crisis *see* Churchill; Edward VIII; monarchy; Queen Mother
AIDS 151, 247, 445
advertising 120; *see also* cult of celebrity; ITV
affluence 14, 60, 79, 85, 89, 117, 119, 141, 211, 222, 234, 258, 311, 353, 405, 414–15, 435–6, 497, 512, 514; *see also* Americanisation; Bond: children; class; consumerism; crime; DIY; drink; economic growth; environment; fashion; food; holidays; housing; poverty; suburbia; Thatcherism; trade unions; transport
Amis, Kingsley 139, 187, 379, 499
Arts Council 138, 145, 185, 274
Asquith, H.H. (Prime Minister 1908–16) 45, 53, 113, 117, 199, 240, 259–60, 280, 293–4, 297–8, 299, 308, 329, 367–8, 448, 466, 504
asylum seekers 254, 362–3
Attlee, Clement (Prime Minister 1945–51) 29, 51, 52, 114, 177, 280, 281, 282, 318, 331, 417, 456, 482, 506
Auden, W.H. 49, 96

Bailey, David 277, 327
Bacon, Francis 34
Balcon, Michael *see* Ealing Comedies
Balfour, Arthur (Prime Minister 1902–5) 117, 119, 173–4, 269, 481; *see also* Balfour Declaration
Beckham, David 133
Benn, Tony 386
Bevin, Ernest 53, 244, 281, 481
Birkenhead, Lord (F.E. Smith) 314
Blake, Peter 34, 43
Bloomsbury Group (and members of) 21, 32, 54, 113–14, 171, 272; *see also* cultural elitism; Keynes
Boer War (1899–1902) 73, 91, 202, 231, 329, 448, 500
BSE 7–8, 184, 190, 207
Britpop 328, 421
British Medical Association (BMA) 55, 99, 280, 365
British Nationality Act (1948) 74, 254
British National party *see* National Front, British National Party
British Union of Fascists (BUF) 87, 102, 109, 254, 270, 292, 362; *see also* Mosley
Britten, Benjamin 96, 114, 181, 290
Burgess, Guy, and Maclean, Donald 62, 185, 245
Butler, Rab 19, 33, 43, 88, 108, 134, 174, 185, 364, 417, 426, 497; *see also* Education Act (1944)
Butlin, Billy 241, 354

Caine, Sir Michael 97, 205, 322
Casement, Sir Roger 167, 245, 440
Chamberlain, Joseph 73, 91, 501; *see also* tariff reform
Chamberlain, Neville 93, 114, 117, 300, 331, 367, 423, 468, 505; *see also* appeasement
Channel 4 132, 266–7

Chaplin, Charlie 43, 96
charity 63, 133, 178, 249, 410; *see also* British Legion; Diana; disabled; Womens' Institute
Charles, Prince of Wales 24, 333, 345, 389, 424, 460; *see also* Diana
Clark, Sir Kenneth 32–3, 266, 287
Cleese, John 229, 443; *see also* Monty Python's Flying Circus
coal industry 50, 281, 311, 313, 346, 368, 369, 390, 428, 484, 495
Collins, Michael 261, 262, 265
comedy 42, 67, 69, 104, 229, 246, 255, 349; *see also* Carry on films; Ealing Comedies; Monty Python's Flying Circus; Morecambe and Wise; sitcoms
Commonwealth 11, 195, 340, 349, 397, 429, 469; *see also* British Empire; cricket; immigration and race relations; miscegenation; Muslims; National Front
Common Agricultural Policy (CAP) 7, 187
Connery, Sean 62
conservatism, social 161, 186, 221, 264, 315, 329, 353, 377, 426, 442, 450, 510, 513; *see also* crime; Denning; gambling; morality; 'permissive society'; pornography; Thatcherism
Cook, Peter 186
'Cool Britannia' 58, 328
countryside 101, 142, 242, 248, 414, 444, 514; *see also* agriculture; Elgar; folk music; Hardy; holidays; music festivals; suburbia

Dalton, Hugh 9, 73, 331
Darwin, Charles 14, 342; *see also* social Darwinism
Davidson, Randall 66, 86
decadence 3–4, 16, 19, 22–3, 28, 60, 95, 138, 141, 214, 224, 366, 405, 412, 462; *see also* Americanisation; apathy; Best; Bond; Brady and Hindley; BBC; children; consumerism; crime; cult of celebrity; drugs; Edward VIII; Freud; Krays; morality; national daily newspapers; 'permissive society'; Profumo Affair; suburbia; Thatcherism
decolonisation 146, 152, 276, 354, 362, 397; *see also* British Empire; Falklands; immigration; 'special relationship'; Suez crisis
deference (and decline of) 4, 43, 97, 165, 198, 266, 288–9; *see also* aristocracy; class; Establishment
divorce *see* marriage, divorce
Douglas-Home, Alec (Prime Minister 1963–4) 117, 119, 124, 186, 306–7, 327, 402, 434
Dowding, Hugh 40
drama 240, 246, 286, 288, 391, 404; *see also* BBC; ITV; Osborne; Shaw; soap operas
Dury, Ian 154, 354

economic decline 19, 74, 92, 98, 115, 117, 121, 146, 211, 228–9, 307, 390, 419, 433–6, 484, 488; *see also* economic growth; economic planning; Europe; Great Depression; inflation; Keynes; manufacturing; Marshall Aid; monetarism; North–South divide; Thatcher; Thatcherism; trade unions;

unemployment; 'Winter of Discontent'
Eden, Sir Anthony (Prime Minister 1955–7)
93, 117, 162, 250; see also appeasement;
Suez crisis
education 89, 157, 185, 203, 239, 247, 308,
355–6, 364, 378, 385, 409, 425, 428, 487,
500, 504, 506, 509, 512, 513; see also
Beveridge; children; class; cultural
elitism; Education Act (1902); Education
Act (1944); language; public schools;
Russell; welfare state; universities
Edward VII 178, 329, 331, 332
elections see parliament, elections
Eliot, T.S. 13, 43, 50–1, 137, 473
Elizabeth II 68, 90, 228, 238, 290, 346–7, 381,
419, 460; see also Diana; monarchy; Queen
Mother
Empire see British Empire

Farlie, Henry 183–4, 186
feminism 4, 123, 143, 155, 192, 196, 359,
398–9; see also marriage; women;
Suffragette movement; Women's Institute
Festival of Britain 236–7
First World War (1914–18) and impact of 8,
26, 28, 33, 53, 71, 86, 91–2, 181, 193, 196,
203, 213, 215, 217, 224, 231, 233, 236, 240,
241, 247–8, 256, 257, 260, 272, 277, 280,
294, 308, 311, 329, 337, 342, 347, 355, 388,
404, 411, 431, 435, 437, 440, 454, 461, 466,
469, 494, 509–12; see also Balfour Declaration; conscription; Easter Rising;
Germans; Lawrence of Arabia; Lloyd
George; wars; welfare state
Foot, Michael 46, 52, 56, 78, 194, 280, 283, 475
Frost, David 103

Gaitskell, Hugh 52, 78, 280, 282, 283, 284,
364, 464
Geldof, Bob 133
George V 37, 72, 177–8, 226, 228, 260, 277,
281, 329–31, 333, 422, 438
George VI 37, 179, 331, 355; see also Queen
Mother
Gladstone, W.E. (Prime Minister 1868–74,
1880–5, 1886, 1892–4) 146, 258, 262
Green Party see environmentalism, Green
Party
Gulf War (1990–1) 28, 499; Second Gulf War
(2003) 459, 503

Haley, William 68
Harris, Arthur 'Bomber' 61
Hayek, Friedrich von 170–1
health 183–4, 402, 500, 503, 506–7; see also
Bevan; death; drink; drugs; food;
National Health Service; population
Heath, Sir Edward (Prime Minister 1970–4) 117,
119, 188, 232, 237, 250, 255, 286, 296, 335,
391, 402, 406, 457, 475, 476, 477, 483, 488
Herbert, A.P. 315–6, 318
'heritage industry' 242–3, 350; see also holi-
days; monarchy
Hitler, Adolf 51, 114, 119, 186, 217, 277, 292,
342, 389, 417, 440, 447, 514; see also
appeasement; Battle of Britain; Blitz
Hitchcock, Alfred 96
Hollywood 8–9, 11, 109, 120, 265; see also
Americanisation; cinema
home ownership see housing, home ownership

Hussein, Saddam 30, 60, 502

imperial preference see tariff reform, imperial reference
India 39, 48, 53, 131, 160, 286, 337, 376, 401,
423, 490; see also British Empire; Kipling
individualism 49, 52, 58, 121, 152, 208, 284,
317–18, 333, 334, 425, 469, 487, 508; see
also art; consumerism; cult of celebrity;
Freud; morality; 'permissive society';
Russell; Thatcherism; trade unions
inequality see poverty, inequality
intellectuals 109–10; 113–14, 187, 225, 266,
284, 342, 388, 412, 435, 442; see also art;
cultural elitism; Fabian Society; Freud;
Keynes; MacDiarmid; Orwell; Powell;
Priestley; Russell; Shaw; social
Darwinism; Taylor
Ireland 19, 29, 39, 73, 76, 90, 112, 113, 117,
123, 127–8, 144, 181, 211, 222, 236, 237,
245, 244, 252, 256–60, 274, 291, 304, 312,
345, 383, 393, 394, 452, 456, 498; see also
Best; Easter Rising; Ireland, partition of;
Irish Republican Army; Paisley; Shaw;
'Troubles'

Jarrow March 234–5, 372–3

Kinnock, Neil 56, 88, 281, 283, 370, 452, 459
Korean War (1950–3) 10, 52, 74, 106, 236, 364,
456, 501

Larkin, Philip 344, 387
law and order 13, 56–7, 83, 115, 203, 214, 244,
255–6, 259, 269, 324, 348–9, 351, 353,
356, 361, 373; see also crime; Denning;
drink; drugs; general strike; Irish Republican Army; Krays; National Front; police;
Suffragette movement; 'Troubles'
Lawrence, D.H. 135, 387, 397, 434
Lawrence, Steven 256, 392
Lawson, Nigel 189, 336, 509
League of Nations 38, 161
Leavis, F.R. 135
Lee, Jennie 33, 50
leisure 206, 237, 396; see also Americanisation; class; consumerism; cricket; DIY;
drink; drugs; football; gambling;
gardening; holidays; Mods; music
festivals; music halls; pub
Lennon, John 131, 181, 462; see also Beatles
Lewis, Saunders 388–9
liberalism (economic and social) 84, 113, 116,
143, 161–3, 174, 186–7, 255, 308, 316, 356,
359–61, 379, 381, 464, 469, 510–1; see also
Beveridge; Church of England; consensus;
economic planning; homosexuality;
Keynes; Liberal Party; Lloyd George; monetarism; 'New' Labour; 'permissive society';
pornography; poverty; Powell; privatisation; Russell; Social Democratic Party;
Suffragette movement; tariff reform;
Temple; Thatcher; Thatcherism; welfare
state
literature 27, 82, 84, 96, 134, 271, 292, 356,
372, 496; see also Betjeman; Cookson;
cultural elitism; Hardy; Osborne; Orwell;
Priestley; Shaw; Taylor
London 140, 172, 235, 236, 254, 301, 326, 344,
367, 378, 392, 395, 414, 423, 445, 486; see
also architecture; Blitz; Krays; language;

North–South divide; suburbia
Longford, Lord 66, 400
Lords, House of 55, 61, 69, 103, 120, 145, 261, 278, 331, 335, 341, 396; see also aristocracy; parliament

McCartney, Paul 181; see also Beatles
MacColl, Ewan 201–3
Macmillan, Harold (Prime Minister 1957–63) 74, 117, 121, 141, 171, 188, 227, 238, 266, 402, 407, 436, 457, 459, 471, 482, 483; see also Profumo Affair
Maastricht Treaty (1991) 189–90
Major, John (Prime Minister 1990–97) 38, 103–4, 116, 117, 118–9, 150, 153, 189–90, 264–5, 316–7, 319, 371, 385, 394, 407, 436–7, 458, 460, 476, 478–9, 483, 486, 486, 499, 503
Mandelson, Peter 56, 57, 58, 235; see also spin doctors
'means test' 238, 505
media 37–8, 54, 57, 105, 121, 122, 126, 135–7, 139, 141, 143, 151, 212, 222, 285, 332, 342, 354, 377–8, 416, 451, 471, 480, 509; see also Beaverbrook; Betjeman; BBC; cult of celebrity; Diana; ITV; Morecambe and Wise; North–South divide; national daily newspapers; sitcoms; soap operas; spin doctors; weather
'meritocracy' 3–4, 28, 97, 125, 304, 322; see also children; class; Denning; disabled; Education Act (1902); Education Act (1944); poverty; public schools; universities; welfare state
Millennium Dome 219, 237–8
modernism see art; architecture; cultural elitism; Mods
Montagu of Beaulieu, Lord 242, 245, 350–1
Moore, Henry 32
Muggeridge, Malcolm 243, 331, 333
Mumford, Lewis 285
music see Americanisation; Beatles; Elgar; folk music; Last Night of the Proms; Mods; music festivals; music halls; Punk

National Lottery 219
'negative equity' 251
nonconformity (religious) 146, 215, 297, 381, 469; see also Education Act (1902)
North Atlantic Treaty Organisation (NATO) 27, 116, 339–40, 488; see also armed forces; sovereignty; 'special relationship'
North Sea oil 311, 373, 436
nostalgia 1, 36, 62, 93, 128, 301, 304, 322, 327, 354, 404, 452–62; see also architecture; Betjeman; British Empire; British Legion; Carry On films; Ealing Comedies; Elgar; Hardy; folk music; Last Night of the Proms; Lynn

patriotism 49, 55, 59, 96, 100, 109, 122, 143, 166, 181, 204, 234, 269, 299, 310, 377, 379, 424, 438–9; see also Battle of Britain; Blitz; Bond; Botham; British Empire; British Legion; Church of England; Churchill; Cold War; Conservative Party; cricket; devolution; Europe; Falklands; Germans; Last Night of the Proms; Lynn; Montgomery; Thatcherism
Pevsner, Nikolaus 30, 226
Pollitt, Harry 108, 109

pop and rock music 11, 64, 69, 76, 150, 154, 163, 181, 288, 304, 354, 483; see also Beatles; cult of celebrity; folk music; Mods; music festivals; Punk
protest movements 8, 10, 14, 16, 59, 87, 108–9, 134, 174, 201, 343, 379, 394, 405, 471, 499, 511; see also Campaign for Nuclear Disarmament; environmentalism; Russell; Suffragette movement

Quant, Mary 198, 200

race 55, 123, 126, 162, 211, 244, 276, 314, 340, 392, 423, 442, 445, 475; see also British Empire; food; immigration and race relations; Jews; Kipling; miscegenation; Mosley; Muslims; National Front; Powell
'Rachmanism' 249
railways 66, 171, 224, 231, 281; see also nationalisation; privatisation; suburbia; transport
rationing 53, 121, 195, 204–6, 456, 485, 501
Reith, Sir John 132, 198, 223, 287; see also BBC
religion 14, 21, 49, 55, 59, 65, 66–7, 70, 81, 111, 112, 142, 180, 185, 200, 212, 215–16, 235, 259–63, 316–17, 333, 341–3, 398, 438, 514; see also Church of England; Church of Scotland; cult of celebrity; death; Education Act (1902); Education Act (1944); Jews; morality; Muslims; Paisley; Roman Catholicism; Temple; 'Troubles'
Rolling Stones 43, 162, 351
Rothermere, Lord 37, 43; see also National Daily Newspapers
Royal Society for the Prevention of Cruelty to Animals (RSPCA) 13, 182
Rushdie, Salman 356

Salisbury, 3rd Marquess of (Prime Minister 1885–92, 1895–1902) 25, 116, 117, 230, 358, 382, 510
satire 69, 104, 186, 204, 405, 443, 482; see also establishment; Monty Python's Flying Circus
science and technological change 7, 14, 29, 32, 85, 102, 176, 196, 200, 243, 392, 395, 398, 433, 471, 511, 513; see also Americanisation; architecture; BBC; Campaign for Nuclear Disarmament; cinema; consumerism; cultural elitism; drink; economic growth; environmentalism; great exhibitions; manufacturing; Marconi Affair; Mini; nationalisation; suburbia; transport; Turing; wars
Scottish Nationalism 4, 75, 202, 210, 234, 287, 395; see also Church of Scotland; devolution; MacDiarmid; Scottish National Party
Second World War (1939–45) and impact of 9, 13, 22, 33, 46, 49, 67–8, 73, 75, 83, 87, 96, 98–9, 102, 121, 128, 132, 139, 146, 153, 155, 162, 165, 170, 179, 190–2, 193, 197, 204, 209, 221, 231, 232, 234, 238, 245, 249, 254, 257, 261, 270, 274, 281, 288, 289, 293, 306, 311, 316, 317, 331, 343, 346, 349, 350, 363–4, 373, 377, 388, 389, 395, 396, 400, 401, 405, 413, 423–5, 433, 443, 455–6, 460, 462, 472, 474, 485, 491, 494, 509, 514; see also appeasement; Battle of Britain; Beveridge; Blitz; Churchill; conscription; Education Act (1944); Germans; Lynn; Marshall Aid;

Index

nationalisation; wars; welfare state
services *see* manufacturing; services
sex 97, 143, 199, 291, 337–8, 341, 343, 351,
    359, 379, 396, 412, 426, 437–8, 441, 444,
    445, 490, 492–5, 511–14; *see also* Bond;
    children; crime; Freud; homosexuality;
    marriage; miscegenation; 'permissive
    society'; pornography; Profumo Affair
Sex Pistols 64; *see also* Punk
Sickert, Walter 30–1, 353
'sleaze', corruption 15, 303, 309, 360, 477,
    478, 497; *see also* Lloyd George; Marconi
    Affair; parliament; Profumo Affair
Snow, C.P. 134–5
socialism 55, 66, 110, 231, 308, 472, 505, 509;
    see also Bevan; Communist Party of Great
    Britain; Fabian Society; Labour Party;
    nationalisation; Orwell; Shaw
Soviet Union 27, 46, 51, 60, 66, 74, 121, 170,
    185, 189, 211, 281, 309, 319, 334, 339, 377,
    401, 407, 432, 440, 456, 458, 465, 501, 514;
    see also Campaign for Nuclear Disarma-
    ment; Cold War; Communist Party of
    Great Britain
Special Air Service (SAS) 27
Spencer, Herbert 504, 509; *see also* social
    Darwinism
Spencer, Stanley 32, 33
sport 67, 71–2, 228, 230, 256, 267, 410; *see also*
    Best; Botham; cricket; football; Matthews;
    rugby
state intervention (economic and social) 6–7,
    9, 22, 33, 35, 36, 73, 82, 86, 94–5, 102,
    115–16, 118, 145–7, 153–4, 159, 162, 181–2,
    189, 217, 218, 220–1, 237–8, 241, 281, 287,
    318, 348, 370, 373, 390, 399, 402, 411–13,
    461, 481, 488, 500, 509–12, 514; *see also*
    Bevan; Beveridge; civil service; compre-
    hensive schools; conscription; economic
    growth; economic planning; Education
    Act (1902); Education Act (1944); Fabian
    Society; food; government; housing;
    Keynes; Lloyd George; local government;
    manufacturing; monetarism; National
    Health Service; nationalisation; 'permis-
    sive society'; privatisation; tariff reform;
    Thatcherism; unemployment; welfare
    state
strikes, industrial action 29, 37, 50, 91, 348,
    365, 392, 489; *see also* Communist Party of
    Great Britain; General Strike; Labour
    Party; trade unions; 'Winter of Discon-
    tent'
suicide 4, 141, 492

supermarkets 10, 160, 203, 207–8, 268

Tawney, R.H. 102, 120, 473
taxation 8, 25, 35, 59, 82, 147–8, 169, 183, 217,
    230–2, 249–50, 274, 283, 297, 332, 334,
    401–2, 403, 407, 460, 476, 502, 506–7, 509;
    see also local government; tariff reform;
    Thatcherism
terrorism 30, 39, 45, 127, 260–2, 270, 291,
    458, 460; *see also* Irish Republican Army,
    'Troubles'
Townshend, Pete 327
town planning 139, 187, 220–1, 463; *see also*
    architecture; housing
Tynan, Kenneth 44, 166, 420

urban life 87, 89, 120, 125, 139, 140, 463, 503,
    514; *see also* architecture; Blitz; class;
    crime; Great Depression; housing; popu-
    lation; pub; soap operas; transport

Vaughan Williams, Ralph 181, 200, 290
Victoria, Queen (and Victorians) 5, 6, 72, 81,
    85, 86, 121, 124, 139, 158, 160–2, 185, 198,
    204, 225, 226, 233, 236, 275, 285, 300,
    327, 331–2, 340, 342–3, 379, 382, 388, 397,
    399, 414, 427, 430, 476, 486; *see also*
    Thatcherism

Waugh, Evelyn 26, 48, 224
Webb, Sidney and Beatrice 439; *see also*
    Fabian Society
Wells, H.G. 134, 226, 376
Welsh nationalism 4, 75, 86, 202, 234, 287,
    395, 425, 497; *see also* devolution; Plaid
    Cymru; rugby
Whitehouse, Mary 345, 386, 398, 442
Wilde, Oscar 14, 131, 214, 244–5, 275, 440,
    492, 493
Williams, Kenneth 246; *see also* Carry On Films
Wilson, Harold (Prime Minister 1964–70;
    1974–6) 52, 147, 186, 188, 218, 232, 255,
    281, 282–3, 304, 346, 364, 368, 397, 416,
    436, 457, 482, 483, 496

Young, Michael 82, 103
Young British Artists 34–5
youth culture 225, 244, 284; *see also* apathy;
    Beatles; children; crime; cult of celebrity;
    drink; drugs; fashion; Mods; music festi-
    vals; Punk; scouting

Zinoviev Letter 108, 223, 309